Quantitative Quality of Service for Grid Computing:
Applications for Heterogeneity, Large-Scale Distribution, and Dynamic Environments

Lizhe Wang
Rochester Institute of Technology, USA

Jinjun Chen
Swinburne University of Technology, Australia

Wei Jie
University of Manchester, UK

Information Science REFERENCE

INFORMATION SCIENCE REFERENCE

Hershey · New York

Director of Editorial Content:	Kristin Klinger
Senior Managing Editor:	Jamie Snavely
Managing Editor:	Jeff Ash
Assistant Managing Editor:	Carole Coulson
Typesetter:	Amanda Appicello
Cover Design:	Lisa Tosheff
Printed at:	Yurchak Printing Inc.

Published in the United States of America by
    Information Science Reference (an imprint of IGI Global)
    701 E. Chocolate Avenue, Suite 200
    Hershey PA 17033
    Tel: 717-533-8845
    Fax: 717-533-8661
    E-mail: cust@igi-global.com
    Web site: http://www.igi-global.com/reference

and in the United Kingdom by
    Information Science Reference (an imprint of IGI Global)
    3 Henrietta Street
    Covent Garden
    London WC2E 8LU
    Tel: 44 20 7240 0856
    Fax: 44 20 7379 0609
    Web site: http://www.eurospanbookstore.com

Library of Congress Cataloging-in-Publication Data

Quantitative quality of service for grid computing : applications for heterogeneity, large-scale distribution, and dynamic environments / Lizhe Wang, Jinjun Chen, and Wei Jie, editors.

    p. cm.

  Includes bibliographical references and index.
  Summary: "This book provides research into parallel & distributed computing, high performance computing, and Grid computing"--Provided by publisher.

  ISBN 978-1-60566-370-8 (hardcover) -- ISBN 978-1-60566-371-5 (ebook)
  1. Computational grids (Computer systems)--Quality control. 2. Parallel processing (Electronic computers) 3. Electronic data processing--Distributed processing. 4. High performance computing. I. Wang, Lizhe, 1974- II. Chen, Jinjun. III. Jie, Wei.

  QA76.9.C58Q935 2009
  004'.36--dc22
           2008040206

British Cataloguing in Publication Data
A Cataloguing in Publication record for this book is available from the British Library.

All work contributed to this book is new, previously-unpublished material. The views expressed in this book are those of the authors, but not necessarily of the publisher.

Table of Contents

Detailed Table of Contents

Chapter I

    Fangpeng Dong, Queen's University, Canada
    Selim G. Akl, Queen's University, Canada

This chapter introduces two approaches that can provide QoS features at the workflow scheduling algorithm level in the Grid. One approach is based on a workflow rescheduling technique, which can reallocate resources for tasks when a resource performance change is observed. The other copes with the stochastic performance change using pre-acquired probability mass functions (PMF) and produces a probability distribution of the final schedule length, which will then be used to handle the different QoS concerns of the users.

Chapter II

    Francesco Palmieri, Università degli Studi di Napoli Federico II, Italy
    Ugo Fiore, Università degli Studi di Napoli Federico II, Italy

In the past decade there has been a remarkable change from mainframe-based centralized computing to a distributed client/server approach. In the coming decade this trend is likely to continue with further shifts towards network centric collaborative computing. At the state of the art, the key technology in collaborative computing is the computational grid paradigm. Like an electrical power grid, the computational Grid will aim to provide a steady, reliable source of computing power. More precisely, the term grid is now adopted to designate a common computational and/or data processing infrastructure built on distributed resources, highly heterogeneous (in their role, computing power and architecture), interconnected by heterogeneous communication networks and communicating through some basic services realized by a middleware stratum that offers a reliable, simple, uniform and often transparent interface to its resources such that an unaware user can submit jobs to the Grid just as if he/she was facing a large virtual supercomputer, so that large computing endeavors, consisting of one or more related jobs or tasks, are then transparently distributed over the network on the available computing resources. Such a workload distribution strategy, that is, to balance the tasks on different idle computers on the underlying networks, is the most important functionality in computational Grids, usually provided at the service level of the grid software infrastructure.

Junwei Cao, Tsinghua University, China & Tsinghua National Laboratory for Information Science and Technology, China

Fan Zhang, Tsinghua University, China

Ke Xu, Tsinghua University, China

Lianchen Liu, Tsinghua University, China & Tsinghua National Laboratory for Information Science and Technology, China

Cheng Wu, Tsinghua University, China & Tsinghua National Laboratory for Information Science and Technology, China

Grid workflows are becoming a mainstream paradigm for implementing complex grid applications. In addition to existing grid enabling techniques, various grid ensuring techniques are emerging, for example workflow analysis and temporal reasoning, to probe potential pitfalls and errors and guarantee quality of services (QoS) at a design phase. A new state π calculus is proposed in this work, which not only enables flexible abstraction and management of historical grid system events, but also facilitates modeling and verification of grid workflows. Some typical patterns in grid workflows are captured and both static and dynamic formal verification issues are investigated, including structural correctness, specification satisfiability, logic satisfiability, and consistency. A grid workflow modeling and verification environment, GridPiAnalyzer, is implemented using formal modeling and verification methods proposed in this work. Performance evaluation results are included using a grid workflow for gravitational wave data analysis.

Chuliang Weng, Shanghai Jiao Tong University, China

Jian Cao, Shanghai Jiao Tong University, China

Minglu Li, Shanghai Jiao Tong University, China

In the grid context, the scheduling can be grouped into two categories: offline scheduling and online scheduling. In the offline scheduling scenario, the sequence of jobs is known in advance, scheduling is based on information about all jobs in the sequence. While, in the online scheduling scenario a job is known only after all predecessors have been scheduled, and a job is scheduled only according to information of its predecessors in the sequence. This chapter focuses on resource management issue in the grid context, and introduces the two cost-based scheduling algorithms for offline job assignment and online job assignment on the computational grid, respectively.

Based on the observation that not all participants are equally active or engaged in distributed online collaboration, CVRetrieval differentiates the notions of consistency maintenance and consistency retrieval. Here, consistency maintenance implies a protocol that periodically communicates with all participants to maintain a certain consistency level; and consistency retrieval means that passive participants explicitly request consistent views from the system when the need arises in stead of joining the expensive consistency maintenance protocol all the time. The rationale is that it is much more cost-effective to satisfy a passive participant's need on-demand. The evaluation of CVRetrieval is done in two parts. First, this chapter analyzes its scalability and the result shows that CVRetrieval can greatly reduce communication cost and hence make consistency control more scalable. Second, a prototype of CVRetrieval is deployed on the Planet-Lab test-bed and the results show that the active participants experience a short response time at expense of the passive participants that may encounter a longer response time.

Chapter VI

This chapter elaborates the quality of service (QoS) aspect of load sharing activities in a computational grid environment. Load sharing is achieved through appropriate job scheduling and resource allocation mechanisms. A computational grid usually consists of several geographically distant sites each with different amount of computing resources. Different types of grids might have different QoS requirements. In most academic or experimental grids the computing sites volunteer to join the grids and can freely decide to quit the grids at any time when they feel joining the grids bring them no benefits. Therefore, maintaining an appropriate QoS level becomes an important incentive to attract computing sites to join a grid and stay in it. This chapter explores the QoS issues in such type of academic and experimental grids. This chapter first defines QoS based performance metrics for evaluating job scheduling and resource allocation strategies. According to the QoS performance metrics appropriate grid-level load sharing strategies are developed. The developed strategies address both user-level and site-level QoS concerns. A series of simulation experiments were performed to evaluate the proposed strategies based on real and synthetic workloads.

This chapter focuses on presenting and describing an approach that allows the mapping of workflow processes to Grid provided services by not only taking into account the Quality of Service (QoS) parameters of the Grid services but also the potential business relationships of the service providers that may affect the aforementioned QoS parameters. This approach is an integral part of the QoS provisioning, since this is the only way to estimate, calculate and conclude to the mapping of workflows and the selection of the available service types and instances in order to deliver an overall quality of service across a federation of providers. The added value of this approach lays on the fact that business relationships of the service providers are also taken into account during the mapping process.

Opportunistic techniques have been widely used to create economical computation infrastructures and have demonstrated an ability to deliver heterogeneous computing resources to large batch applications; however, batch turnaround performance is generally unpredictable, negatively impacting human experience with widely shared computing resources. Scheduler prioritization schemes can effectively boost the share of the system given to particular users, but to gain a relevant benefit to user experience, whole batches must complete on a predictable schedule, not just individual jobs. Additionally, batches may contain a dependency structure that must be considered when predicting or controlling the completion time of the whole workflow; the slowest or most volatile prerequisite job determines performance. In this chapter, a probabilistic policy enforcement technique is used to protect deadline guarantees against grid resource unpredictability as well as bad estimates. Methods to allocate processors to a common workflow subcase, barrier scheduling, are also presented.

Grids can form the basis for pervasive computing due to their ability of being open, scalable and flexible to various changes (from topology changes to unpredicted failures of nodes). However, such environments are prone to failures due to their nature and need a certain level of reliability in order to provide viable and commercially exploitable solutions. This is causing a significant research activity which is focused on the topic of achieving certain levels of Quality of Service (QoS) in highly unreliable environments (such as mobile and ad hoc Grids). This study will focus on the state-of-the-art analysis of the QoS aspects in Grids and how this is achieved in terms of technological means. A small survey and related work will also presented. A more detailed analysis on the features of unreliable environments such as mobile Grids will be described. An innovative and efficient mechanism will be described, which is especially designed for such environments, in order to enhance them with the QoS attributes of reliability (fault tolerance through replication of tasks) and service differentiation to the Grid users through a simple task prioritization scheme. The results that this recent research work is presenting a re promising for the future advancement of Grid commercialization in such environments.

Fang Huang, Institute of Geo-Spatial Information Technology, University of Electronic Science and Technology of China, P.R. China

With the development of grid technology, the spatial information grid researches are also in progress. In China, the spatial information grid platform (abbreviation to SIG) not only can provide geo-spatial data services (GDS) for handling terabytes of geospatial data, but also can present processing functionality services (PFS) encapsulated from several Remote Sensing (RS) software to solve RS computing problems remotely. In particular, the spatial user can utilize some provided high-performance PFS to achieve those computing intensive tasks that lacking of the high-performance computing facility such as cluster or Condor platform. Unfortunately, the existing SIG paid litter attention to Geographic Information Science (GIS) field, as a result, the constitution of PFS related to GIS, especially the high-performance GIServices (HP-GIServices), are becoming the main issues for SIG's next research. Lacking of GIServices mainly resulted from the limitations of SIG architecture, difficulty of extracting parallel GIS functionalities modules, as well as the complexity for services implementation and encapsulation. Based on existing SIG platform, the chapter proposes the improved architecture for SIG, upon which the constituted GIS nodes can provide GIServices. Within the new architecture, some parallel GRASS GIS (Geographic Resources Analysis Support System) algorithms programs, which are built by different parallelization patterns and can run in cluster with better efficiency, are encapsulated to high-performance GIServices guiding by certain generic mode. Lastly, the QoS (quality of services) indexes are proposed to evaluate the quality of the constituted HP-GIServices in SIG. From the tentative experiments and analyses, the facts demonstrate that this approach can reach the aims.

Xiangfeng Luo, Shanghai University, P.R. China
Yu Jie, Shanghai University, P.R. China

Web Knowledge Flow provides a technique and theoretical support for the effective discovery of knowledge innovation, intelligent browsing, personalized recommendation, cooperative team work, and the semantic analysis of resources on Internet, which is a key issue of Web services and Knowledge Grid. This chapter firstly introduces some basic concepts related to Web Knowledge Flow. Next it illustrates the concepts of interactive computing, including the Web interaction model, the implementation of interactive computing and the generation of Web Knowledge Flow. Finally, the applications of Web Knowledge Flow will be given.

Guanfeng Liu, Qingdao University, China
Yongsheng Hao, Nanjing University of Information Science & Technology, China

This chapter mainly introduces some recent researches of reputation evaluation methods in Grid economy. The GRACE (Grid Architecture for Computational Economy architecture) is adopted to explain some mechanisms in the Grid economy for its clearly inner modules architecture. In addition, several new developed modules based on GRACE architecture are detailed discussed and two of them are laid morn emphasis on by us, which are the RCM (Reputation Control Module) and distributed reputation control architectures based on VOD (Virtual Organizational Domain). The inner communication and workflow of them are shown in this chapter. Furthermore, through experiments results, the authors discover the profit of Grid nodes and tasks execution success rate are all improved by adding these new modules.

Chapter XIII
Cheng Fu, Nanyang Technological University, Singapore
Bang Wang, Nanyang Technological University, Singapore

A major design challenge in wireless sensor network application development is to provide appropriate middleware service protocols to control the energy consumption according to specific application scenarios. In common application scenarios such as in monitoring or surveillance systems, it is usually necessary to extend the system monitoring area as large as possible to cover the maximal area. The two issues of power conservation and maximizing the coverage area have to be considered together with both the sensors' communication connectivity and their power management strategy. In this work, the authors proposed novel enhanced sensor scheduling protocols to address the application scenario of typical surveillance systems. The protocols take into consideration of both power conservation and coverage ratio to search for the balance between the different requirements. This chapter proposes both centralized and de-centralized sensor scheduling versions, and compared the performance of different algorithms using several metrics. The results provide evidence of the advantages of the proposed protocols compared with existing sensor scheduling protocols.

Chapter XIV
Kaijun Ren, National University of Defense Technology, China & Swinburne
University of Technology, Australia
Jinjun Chen, Swinburne University of Technology, Australia
Nong Xiao, National University of Defense Technology, China
Weimin Zhang, National University of Defense Technology, China
Junqiang Song, National University of Defense Technology, China

In scientific computing environments such as service grid environments, services are becoming basic collaboration components which can be used to construct a composition plan for scientists to resolve complex scientific problems. However, current service collaboration methods still suffer from low efficiency for automatically building composition plans because of the time-consuming ontology reasoning and incapability in effectively allocating resources to executing such plans. In this chapter, the authors present a QSQL-based collaboration method to support automatic service composition and optimized execution. With the proposed method, for a given query, abstract composition plans can be created in an automatic, semantic and efficient manner from QSQL (Quick Service Query List) which is dynamically built by previously processing semantic-related computing at service publication stage. Furthermore, concrete service execution instances can be dynamically bound to abstract service composition plans at runtime by comparing their different QoS (Quality of Service) values. Particularly, a concrete collaboration framework is proposed to support automatic service composition and execution. Totally, the proposed method will not only facilitate e-scientists quickly create composition plans from a large scale of service repository; but also make resource's sharing more flexible. The final experiment has illustrated the effectiveness of the proposed method.

Chapter XV

It will become increasingly popular that scientists in research institutes will make use of Grid computing resources for running computer simulations and managing data. Although there are some production Grids available, it is often the case that many organizations and research projects need to build their own Grids. However, building Grid infrastructure is not a trivial job as it involves sharing and managing heterogeneous computing and data resources across different organizations, and involves installing many specific software packages and various middleware. This can be quite complicated and time-consuming. Building a Grid infrastructure also requires good knowledge and understanding of distributed computing and Grid technology. Apart from building physical Grid, how to build a user infrastructure that can facilitate the use of and easy access to these physical infrastructures is also a challenging task. In this chapter, the authors summarize some hands-on experience in building an institutional Grid infrastructure. As Grid infrastructure usually involves computing Grid and data Grid, this chapter describes knowledge and experience obtained in installing Condor pools, PBS clusters, and Globus Toolkit for computing Grid, and knowledge and experience obtained in installing SRB for data Grid. The authors also proposed to use a User-Centered Design (UCD) approach to develop a user-level infrastructure to facilitate the use of Grid and to improve the usability.

Chapter XVI

The emergence of Grid technologies provide exciting new opportunities for large scale simulation over Internet, enabling collaboration and the use of distributed computing resources, while also facilitating access to geographically distributed data sets. This chapter presents HLA_Grid_RePast, a middleware platform for executing large scale collaborating RePast agent-based models on the Grid. The chapter also provides performance results and analysis on Quality of Service from a deployment of the system between the United Kingdom and Singapore.

Due to the rapidly increasing number of mobile devices connected to the Internet, a lot of research is being conducted to maximize the benefit of such integration. The main objective of Chapter XVII is to enhance the performance of the scheduling mechanism of the mobile computing environment by distributing some of the responsibilities of the access point among the available attached mobile devices. To this aim, the authors investigate a scheduling mechanism framework that comprises an algorithm that provides the mobile device with the authority to evaluate itself as a resource. The proposed mechanism is based on the "self ranking algorithm" (SRA), which provides a lifetime opportunity to reach a proper solution. This mechanism depends on an event-based programming approach to start its execution in a pervasive computing environment. Using such a mechanism will simplify the scheduling process by grouping mobile devices according to their self-ranking value and assigning tasks to these groups. Moreover, it will maximize the benefit of the mobile devices incorporated with the already existing Grid systems by using their computational power as a subordinate value to the overall power of the system. Furthermore, this chapter evaluates the performance of the investigated algorithm extensively, to show how it overcomes the connection stability problem of the mobile devices. Experimental results emphasized that the proposed SRA has a great impact in reducing the total error and link utilization compared with the traditional mechanism.

Chapter XVIII

Chen Zhou, Nanyang Technological University, Singapore
Liang-Tien Chia, Nanyang Technological University, Singapore
Bu-Sung Lee, Nanyang Technological University, Singapore

Web services' discovery mechanism is one of the most important research areas in Web services because of the dynamic nature of Web services. In practice, UDDI takes an important role in service discovery since it is an online registry standard to facilitate the discovery of business partners and services. However, QoS related information is not naturally supported in UDDI. Service requesters can only choose good performance Web services by manual test and comparison. In addition, discovery among private UDDI registries in a federation is not naturally supported. To address these problems, Chapter XVIII proposes UDDI extension (UX), an enhancement for UDDI that facilitates requesters to discover services with QoS awareness. In this system the service requester invokes and generates feedback reports, which are received and stored in local domain's UX server for future usage. By sharing these experiences from those requesters in the local domain, the UX server summarizes and predicts the service's performance. A general federated service is designed to manage the service federation. The discovery between different cooperating domains is based on this general federated service, and therefore the links between domains are maintained dynamically. The system handles the federated inquiry, predicates the QoS difference among different domains, and provides a simple view over the whole federation. Meanwhile, the UX server's inquiry interface still conforms to the UDDI specification.

Chapter XIX

Mirghani Mohamed, The George Washington University, USA
Michael Stankosky, The George Washington University, USA
Vincent Ribière, The George Washington University, USA

The purpose of Chapter XIX is to investigate the requirements of knowledge management (KM) services deployment in a Semantic Grid environment. A wide-range of literature on Grid Computing, Semantic Web, and KM have been reviewed, related, and interpreted. The benefits of the Semantic Web and the Grid Computing convergence have been enumerated and related to KM principles in a complete service model. Although the Grid Computing contributed the shared resources, most of the KM tool obstacles within the grid are to be resolved at the semantic and cultural levels more than at the physical or logical grid levels. The early results from academia show a synergy and the potentiality of leveraging knowledge at a wider scale. However, the plethora of information produced in this environment will result in a serious information overload, unless proper standardization, automated relations, syndication, and validation techniques are developed.

Chapter XX

    Yogesh L. Simmhan, Microsoft Research, USA
    Beth Plale, Indiana University, USA
    Dennis Gannon, Indiana University, USA

The increasing ability for the sciences to sense the world around us is resulting in a growing need for data-driven E-Science applications that are under the control of workflows composed of services on the Grid. The focus of this chapter is on provenance collection for these workflows that are necessary to validate the workflow and to determine quality of generated data products. The challenge addressed in Chapter XX is to record uniform and usable provenance metadata that meets the domain needs while minimizing the modification burden on the service authors and the performance overhead on the workflow engine and the services. The framework is based on generating discrete provenance activities during the lifecycle of a workflow execution that can be aggregated to form complex data and process provenance graphs that can span across workflows. The implementation uses a loosely coupled publish-subscribe architecture for propagating these activities, and the capabilities of the system satisfy the needs of detailed provenance collection. A performance evaluation of a prototype finds a minimal performance overhead (in the range of 1% for an eight-service workflow using 271 data products).

Chapter XXI

    Peter Brezany, University of Vienna, Austria
    Ivan Janciak, University of Vienna, Austria
    A Min Tjoa, Vienna University of Technology, Austria

This chapter introduces an ontology-based framework for automated construction of complex interactive data mining workflows as a means of improving productivity of Grid-enabled data exploration systems. The authors first characterize existing manual and automated workflow composition approaches and then present their solution called GridMiner Assistant (GMA), which addresses the whole life cycle of the knowledge discovery process. GMA is specified in the OWL language and is being developed around a novel data mining ontology, which is based on concepts of industry standards like the predictive model markup language, cross industry standard process for data mining, and Java data mining API. The ontology introduces basic data mining concepts like data mining elements, tasks, services, and so forth. In addition, conceptual and implementation architectures of the framework are presented and its application to an example taken from the medical domain is illustrated. The authors hope that the further research and development of this framework can lead to productivity improvements, which can have significant impact on many real-life spheres. For example, it can be a crucial factor in achievement of scientific discoveries, optimal treatment of patients, productive decision making, cutting costs, and so forth.

In this chapter, two algorithms have been presented for supporting efficient data transfer in the Grid environment. From a node's perspective, a multiple data transfer channel can be formed by selecting some other nodes as relays in data transfer. One algorithm requires the sender to be aware of the global connection information while another does not. Experimental results indicate that both algorithms can transfer data efficiently under various circumstances.

Preface

OVERVIEW

Grid computing is one of the most innovative aspects of computing techniques in the last decade. Distinguished from conventional parallel and distributed computing, Grid computing focuses on resources sharing among geographically distributed sites and the development of innovative, high performance oriented applications. Computational Grid can present users with pervasive and inexpensive access to a wide variety of resources. Qualities of services (QoS) fall into the most important research topics of Grid computing with following concerns:

- **Heterogeneity:** Computational Grid is a highly heterogeneous environment. Different computing sites may have different types of resources. Even the resources of the same type, located at different sites, may have different configurations, capacities and performance profiles. Application users may expect to meet various programming interfaces and user interfaces from different computing sites.
- **Large-scale distribution:** Computational Grid enables resource sharing among geographically distributed sites. These sites are linked in the Internet. Network communication delay may be extremely high when some communication intensive applications are running among these sites. In this scenario, network performance has an important effect on resource management.
- **Dynamic environment:** Computational Grid is a highly dynamic environment in that computing capacities may vary in time; computing resources could join or withdraw the VO (Virtual Organization) base on their own interests.

The research on QoS mainly includes the qualitative analysis method and the quantitative analysis method. The qualitative QoS characters the Grid QoS aspects such as service availability, reliability and user satisfaction. This book mainly focuses on the Quantitative QoS.

To help develop complex Grid systems and software, the layered model is built to abstract the architecture of Grid systems. Each layer provides various services for upper layers. This book studies the Grid QoS aspects in various layers:

- **Fabric layer:** The Grid fabric layer provides the basic Grid protocols that enable Grid applications to share resources, which can be, for example, computational resources, storage systems, network resources and sensors. In the fabric layer, QoS of computing, storage and network are considered (Chapter IX, chapter XV).
- **Connectivity layer:** The Connectivity layer defines the core communication and authentication protocols required for Grid-specific network transmission. The communication protocols enable the exchange of data between Fabric layer resources (Chapter II).

- **Resource layer:** The resource layer builds the communication and authentication protocols of Connectivity layer to define protocols (and APIs, SDKs) for the secured negotiation, initiation, monitoring, control, accounting and payment of sharing operations on individual resources. In this layer, the research of Grid QoS focuses on local resource management policies and algorithms, resource allocation and reservation and resource access control (Chapter V, Chapter VI, Chapter VIII, Chapter XIII, Chapter XVII, Chapter XVIII, Chapter XIX, and Chapter XXII).

- **Collective layer:** The collective layer in the architecture contains protocols and services (and APIs, SDKs) that are not associated with any specific resource but rather interactions across collections of resources. Many research efforts have been developed in this layer, such as, resource co-allocation & co-reservation, resource brokering (Chapter I, Chapter III, Chapter IV, Chapter VII, Chapter XIV, and Chapter XX).

- **Application layer:** The application layer in the Grid architecture comprises the user applications that operate within a VO environment. In this layer various Grid services provided by other layers are employed to fulfill different Grid application requirements (Chapter X, Chapter XI, Chapter XII, Chapter XVI, and Chapter XXI).

This book defines and characterizes the latest research achievement in the QoS aspects for Grid computing. This book is supposed to be a milestone to summarize recent research works on Grid QoS. It is expected to be an important reference of Grid computing for the academia, especially for the research field of parallel & distributed computing, high performance computing, and Grid computing. All chapters of this book are based on recent research work of Grid experts and researchers. Expected readers include researchers, engineers, and IT professionals who work in the fields of parallel computing, distributed computing, cluster computing, Grid computing and high-performance computing. This book could also be employed as the reference book for postgraduate students who study computer science.

ORGANIZATION OF THE BOOK

This book includes 22 chapters contributed by 55 scholars. These book chapters cover the recent advances in QoS aspects of Grid computing: Grid infrastructure, resource management, workflow organization and scheduling, service-oriented architecture, and Grid applications.

Chapter I introduces two approaches that can provide QoS features at the workflow scheduling algorithm level in the Grid. One approach is based on a workflow rescheduling technique, which can reallocate resources for tasks when a resource performance change is observed. The other copes with the stochastic performance change using pre-acquired probability mass functions (PMF) and produces a probability distribution of the final schedule length, which will then be used to handle the different QoS concerns of the users.

Chapter II makes a study on dynamic network optimization for effective QoS support in large Grid infrastructures. At the entity Grid network layer, queuing strategies and shaping can be configured to allow for a certain treatment of packets. This needs administrative access to entities and can only applied in a limited scope like a local network. More generally, at the network layer, advanced network services like MPLS, GMPLS or DiffServ can be used to acquire committed bandwidth, specific transport features or QoS for applications exchanging data. In particular, with the evolution of MPLS technology, GMPLS can become the unified control plane technology to provide reliable transportation, efficient resource utilization and end-to-end QoS in Grid infrastructures.

Grid workflows are becoming a mainstream paradigm for implementing complex Grid applications. In addition to existing Grid enabling techniques, various Grid ensuring techniques are emerging, for example workflow analysis and temporal reasoning, to probe potential pitfalls and errors and guarantee QoS at a design phase. A new state π calculus is proposed in **Chapter III**, which not only enables flexible abstraction and management of historical Grid system events, but also facilitates modeling and verification of Grid workflows. Some typical patterns in Grid workflows are captured and both static and dynamic formal verification issues are investigated, including structural correctness, specification satisfiability, logic satisfiability and consistency. A Grid workflow modeling and verification environment, GridPiAnalyzer, is implemented using formal modeling and verification methods proposed in this work. Performance evaluation results are included using a Grid workflow for gravitational wave data analysis.

In **Chapter IV**, a cost-based resource management and scheduling strategy is presented for the computational Grid, which borrows the idea from economic principles. The main idea is that the usage of heterogeneous resources such as CPU speed, memory capability, and network bandwidth is converted into a homogeneous cost based on some rule, although these resources are measured in unrelated units. According to the goal of better QoS, tasks are scheduled conveniently in the computational Grid.

Consistency control is important in replication-based Grid systems because it provides QoS guarantee. However, conventional consistency control mechanisms incur high communication overhead and are ill suited for large-scale dynamic Grid systems. In **Chapter V**, the authors propose CVRetrieval (Consistency View Retrieval) to provide quantitative scalability improvement of consistency control for large-scale, replication-based Grid systems.

Chapter VI elaborates the QoS aspect of load sharing activities in a computational Grid environment. This chapter defines QoS based performance metrics for evaluating job scheduling and resource allocation strategies. According to the QoS performance metrics appropriate Grid-level load sharing strategies are developed. The developed strategies address both user-level and site-level QoS concerns. A series of simulation experiments were performed to evaluate the proposed strategies based on real and synthetic workloads.

Chapter VII focuses on presenting and describing an approach that allows the mapping of workflow processes to Grid provided services by not only taking into account the QoS parameters of the Grid services but also the potential business relationships of the service providers, which may affect the aforementioned QoS parameters. This approach is an integral part of the QoS provisioning, since this is the only way to estimate, calculate, and conclude to the mapping of workflows and the selection of the available service types and instances in order to deliver an overall quality of service across a federation of providers. The added value of this approach lays on the fact that business relationships of the service providers are also taken into account during the mapping process.

Opportunistic techniques have been widely used to create economical computation infrastructures and have demonstrated an ability to deliver heterogeneous computing resources to large batch applications; however, batch turnaround performance is generally unpredictable, negatively impacting human experience with Grid resources. Scheduler prioritization schemes can effectively boost the share of the system given to particular users, but to gain a relevant benefit to user experience, whole batches must complete on a predictable schedule, not just individual jobs. Additionally, batches may contain a dependency structure that must be considered when predicting or controlling the completion time of the whole workflow; the slowest or most volatile prerequisite job determines performance. In **Chapter VIII**, a probabilistic policy enforcement technique is used to protect deadline guarantees against Grid resource unpredictability as well as bad estimates. Methods to allocate processors to a common workflow subcase, barrier scheduling, are also presented.

Grids can form the basis for pervasive computing due to their ability of being open, scalable and flexible to various changes (from topology changes to unpredicted failures of nodes). However, such environments are prone to failures due to their nature and need a certain level of reliability in order to provide viable and commercially exploitable solutions. This is causing a significant research activity which is focused on the topic of achieving certain levels of QoS in highly unreliable environments (such as mobile and ad hoc Grids). **Chapter IX** focuses on the state-of-the-art analysis of the QoS aspects in Grids and how this is achieved in terms of technological means.

Web knowledge flow provides a technique and theoretical support for the effective discovery of knowledge innovation, intelligent browsing, personalized recommendation, cooperative team work, and the semantic analysis of resources on Internet, which is a key issue of Web services and knowledge Grid. In **Chapter XI**, the authors introduce some basic concepts related to Web knowledge flow and illustrate the concepts of interactive computing, including the Web interaction model, the implementation of interactive computing and the generation of Web knowledge flow. In this chapter, the applications of Web knowledge flow are also given.

Chapter XII mainly introduces some recent researches of reputation evaluation methods in Grid economy. The GRACE (Grid Architecture for Computational Economy architecture) is adopted to explain some mechanisms in the Grid economy for its clearly inner modules architecture. In addition, several new developed modules based on GRACE architecture are detailed discussed and two of them are laid morn emphasis on by us, which are the RCM (Reputation Control Module) and distributed reputation control architectures based on VOD (Virtual Organizational Domain). The inner communication and workflow of them are shown in this chapter. Furthermore, through experiments results, the authors discover the profit of Grid nodes and tasks execution success rate are all improved by adding these new modules.

A major design challenge in wireless sensor network application development is to provide appropriate middleware service protocols to control the energy consumption according to specific application scenarios. In common application scenarios such as in monitoring or surveillance systems, it is usually necessary to extend the system monitoring area as large as possible to cover the maximal area. The two issues of power conservation and maximizing the coverage area have to be considered together with both the sensors' communication connectivity and their power management strategy. In **Chapter XIII**, Fu and Wang propose novel enhanced sensor scheduling protocols to address the application scenario of typical surveillance systems. The protocols take into consideration of both power conservation and coverage ratio to search for the balance between the different requirements. Chapter XIII proposes both centralized and de-centralized sensor scheduling versions, and compared the performance of different algorithms using several metrics. The results provide evidence of the advantages of the proposed protocols comparing with existing sensor scheduling protocols.

In scientific computing environments such as service Grid environments, services are becoming basic collaboration components which can be used to construct a composition plan for scientists to resolve complex scientific problems. However, current service collaboration methods still suffer from low efficiency for automatically building composition plans because of the time-consuming ontology reasoning and incapability in effectively allocating resources to executing such plans. **Chapter XIV** presents a QSQL-based collaboration method to support automatic service composition and optimized execution. With the method, for a given query, abstract composition plans can be created in an automatic, semantic and efficient manner from QSQL (Quick Service Query List) which is dynamically built by previously processing semantic-related computing at service publication stage. Furthermore, concrete service execution instances can be dynamically bound to abstract service composition plans at runtime by comparing their different QoS values.

It will become increasingly popular that scientists in research institutes will make use of Grid computing resources for running computer simulations and managing data. Although there are some production Grids available, it is often the case that many organizations and research projects need to build their own Grids. However, building Grid infrastructure is not a trivial job as it involves sharing and managing heterogeneous computing and data resources across different organizations, and involves installing many specific software packages and various middleware. This can be quite complicated and time-consuming. Building a Grid infrastructure also requires good knowledge and understanding of distributed computing and Grid technology. Apart from building physical Grid, how to build a user infrastructure that can facilitate the use of and easy access to these physical infrastructures is also a challenging task. In **Chapter XV**, Yang and Chiang summarize some hands-on experience in building an institutional Grid infrastructure.

The emergence of Grid technologies provide exciting new opportunities for large scale simulation over Internet, enabling collaboration and the use of distributed computing resources, while also facilitating access to geographically distributed data sets. **Chapter XVI** presents HLA_Grid_RePast, a middleware platform for executing large scale collaborating RePast agent-based models on the Grid. This chapter also provides the performance results and analysis on Quality of Service from a deployment of the system between the Untied Kingdom and Singapore.

Due to the rapidly increasing number of mobile devices connected to the Internet, a lot of research is being conducted to maximize the benefit of such integration. The main objective of **Chapter XVII** is to enhance the performance of the scheduling mechanism of the mobile computing environment by distributing some of the responsibilities of the access point among the available attached mobile devices. To this aim, the authors investigate a scheduling mechanism framework that comprises an algorithm that provides the mobile device with the authority to evaluate itself as a resource. The proposed mechanism is based on the "self ranking algorithm" (SRA), which provides a lifetime opportunity to reach a proper solution. This mechanism depends on an event-based programming approach to start its execution in a pervasive computing environment.

Web services' discovery mechanism is one of the most important research areas in Web services because of the dynamic nature of Web services. In practice, UDDI takes an important role in service discovery since it is an online registry standard to facilitate the discovery of business partners and services. However, QoS related information is not naturally supported in UDDI. Service requesters can only choose good performance Web services by manual test and comparison. In addition, discovery among private UDDI registries in a federation is not naturally supported. To address these problems, **Chapter XVIII** proposes UDDI extension (UX), an enhancement for UDDI that facilitates requesters to discover services with QoS awareness.

The purpose of **Chapter XIX** is to investigate the requirements of knowledge management (KM) services deployment in a Semantic Grid environment. A wide range of literature on Grid Computing, Semantic Web, and KM have been reviewed, related, and interpreted. The benefits of the Semantic Web and the Grid Computing convergence have been enumerated and related to KM principles in a complete service model in Chapter XIX.

The increasing ability for the sciences to sense the world around us is resulting in a growing need for data-driven e-science applications that are under the control of workflows composed of services on the Grid. The focus of **Chapter XX** is on provenance collection for these workflows that are necessary to validate the workflow and to determine quality of generated data products. The challenge addressed in this chapter is to record uniform and usable provenance metadata that meets the domain needs while minimizing the modification burden on the service authors and the performance overhead on the workflow engine and the services.

Chapter XXI introduces an ontology-based framework for automated construction of complex interactive data mining workflows as a means of improving productivity of Grid-enabled data exploration systems. The authors first characterize existing manual and automated workflow composition approaches and then present their solution called GridMiner Assistant (GMA), which addresses the whole life cycle of the knowledge discovery process. GMA is specified in the OWL language and is being developed around a novel data mining ontology, which is based on concepts of industry standards like the predictive model markup language, cross industry standard process for data mining, and Java data mining API. The ontology introduces basic data mining concepts like data mining elements, tasks, services, and so forth. In addition, conceptual and implementation architectures of the framework are presented and its application to an example taken from the medical domain is illustrated.

In **Chapter XXII**, two algorithms have been presented for supporting efficient data transfer in the Grid environment. From a node's perspective, a multiple data transfer channel can be formed by selecting some other nodes as relays in data transfer. One algorithm requires the sender to be aware of the global connection information while another does not. Experimental results indicate that both algorithms can transfer data efficiently under various circumstances.

Acknowledgment

Many collaborators and colleagues have contributed greatly to this comprehensive book. Without their help, the preparation of this book would be impossible. The editors would take this chance to thank all book chapter authors, who have contributed their pioneering research results to this book. We owe a debt of gratitude to the reviewers who have provided valuable comments on the book chapters. We also wish to record our sincere thanks to the Editorial Advisory Board members (in alphabetical order): Dr. Rajkumar Buyya (University of Melbourne, Australia), Dr. Gregor von Laszewski (Rochester Institute of Technology, U.S.), Dr. Kunze Marcel (Research Center Karlsruhe, Germany), Prof. Rob Procter (National Centre for e-Social Science, U.K.), Dr. Jie Tao (Research Center Karlsruhe, Germany) and Dr. Tianyi Zang (Oxford University, U.K). Special thanks are given to Ms. Christine Bufton, Ms. Rebecca Beistline, and Ms. Deborah Yahnke of IGI Global for their assistance in the book preparation.

Chapter I
Two Approaches for Workflow Scheduling with Quality of Service in the Grid

Fangpeng Dong
Queen's University, Canada

Selim G. Akl
Queen's University, Canada

ABSTRACT

Over the past decade, Grid Computing has earned its reputation by facilitating resource sharing in larger communities and providing non-trivial services. However, for Grid users, Grid resources are not usually dedicated, which results in fluctuations of available performance. This situation raises concerns about the quality of services (QoS). The meaning of QoS varies with different concerns of different users. Objective functions that drive job schedulers in the Grid may be different from each other as well. Some are system-oriented, which means they make schedules to favor system metrics such as throughput, load-balance, resource revenue and so on. To narrow the scope of the problem to be discussed in this chapter and to make the discussion substantial, the scheduling objective function considered is minimizing the total completion time of all tasks in a workflow (also known as the makespan). Correspondingly, the meaning of QoS is restricted to the ability that scheduling algorithms can shorten the makespan of a workflow in an environment where resource performance is vibrant. This chapter introduces two approaches that can provide QoS features at the workflow scheduling algorithm level in the Grid. One approach is based on a workflow rescheduling technique, which can reallocate resources for tasks when a resource performance change is observed. The other copes with the stochastic performance change using pre-acquired probability mass functions (PMF) and produces a probability distribution of the final schedule length, which will then be used to handle the different QoS concerns of the users.

INTRODUCTION

The development of Grid infrastructures, for example, Condor DAGMan (DAGMan), Grid Flow (Cao, 2003) and Pegasus (Deelman, 2004), now enables workflow to be submitted and executed on remote computational resources. To harness the non-trivial power of Grid resources, effective task scheduling approaches are necessary. Typically, there are two ways to map a set of tasks to a set of resources: dynamic scheduling and static scheduling. The dynamic approach makes a schedule at real time when a task is ready, while the static approach makes a schedule by planning in advance based on available information on resources and tasks. Because of its advantage of "planning ahead", a static scheduler can produce a schedule that overlaps communication time and computational time. Therefore, the makespan can be reduced. It can even achieve a near optimal schedule for some complex scientific workflows involving a larger number of computational tasks and data communications (Wieczorek, 2005). However, unlike dynamic scheduling, the static approach relies heavily on accurate resource and task information to make a schedule. Unfortunately, the performance of Grid resources is hard to accurately predict. The difficulty is due to the following facts. First, Grid resources are not dedicated to one particular Grid user. Resources' local management policies and competition from other users may make the performance acquired by a user fluctuate. Second, existing Grid resources may fail without a notice and new Grid resources may join the resource pool; both cases will change the available performance for users.

In order to benefit from the merits of static scheduling for complex workflows in the Grid, new performance prediction and modeling methods are introduced. The differences of the presentation of stochastic performance information (e.g., deterministic vs. non-deterministic) influence the way that scheduling algorithms can take to meet QoS requirements.

The rescheduling approach (Yu, 2007; Sakellarion, 2004) can modify an initial schedule according to the fluctuation of resource performance at the run-time. This approach needs to first make an initial schedule and in order to make such an initial schedule, the algorithm usually relies on performance prediction mechanisms (McGough, 2005) to acquire the estimated performance that the tasks will get when they are running on the resources. This predicted performance is usually given as a deterministically specific value, although this value might not be the exact performance that the application will archive at the run-time. For example, the approach that will be introduced in this chapter uses the PFAS algorithm (Dong, 2007) to get an initial schedule and the PFAS algorithm needs information on resource performance in different time slots. Fig. 1 presents an example of the fluctuation of available performance in different time slots.

Figure 1. Performance fluctuation resulted from advance reservation on a resource along time

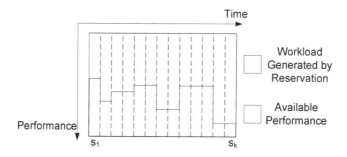

Figure 2. Performance probability mass function of a computational resource in the Grid

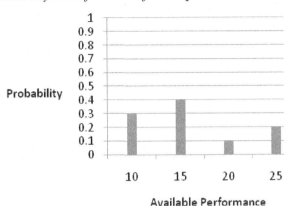

Besides the resource performance model that is based on deterministic prediction, there is an alternative way which is nondeterministic. Instead of specifying on the value of available performance, this approach tries to describe the performance by some probability functions, which can be derived from task execution records in the past (e.g., log files) (Li, 2007). Particularly, in the algorithm introduced in this chapter, we assume that the performance of a resource is a discrete random variable and its probability mass functions (PMF) can be known prior to scheduling from Grid resource information services. For example, Fig. 2 shows the PMF of the performance of a resource, which has four possible values.

Existing rescheduling algorithms rely on centralized schedulers that are independent of Grid resources. This brings two difficulties to rescheduling: (1) The scheduler should react promptly to a performance change; and (2) the cost for rescheduling puts an extra burden on the scheduler, which may have to reschedule the same workflow a number of times before the workflow is finished. The cost of most static scheduling heuristics is at $O(n^2)$, where n is the number of tasks in the workflow. Therefore the total reschedule cost can be as high as $O(k*n^2)$ where k is the number of iterations of reschedules.

To tackle these two problems, we propose a distributed rescheduling approach based on the mobile agent technology (Dong, 2007 PDCS). Because of advantages in autonomy, environmental awareness, cost-efficiency, scalability and fault-tolerance, mobile agents are used in the Grid for resource monitoring, management and discovery, service deployment, job migration and so on (Fukuda, 2003; Fukuda, 2006; Neo, 2005; Aversa, 2006). It has also been used for dynamic scheduling in the peer-to-peer system (Choi, 2005), but to our knowledge, not yet in the realm of Grid workflow scheduling and rescheduling. A mobile agent based method is feasible for workflow rescheduling in the Grid environment for the following reasons. First, it can be deployed to Grid resources easily. Therefore, it can monitor the status of the host resource more accurately and promptly. Second, as an autonomous entity, an agent carrying a computational task can reschedule and migrate itself from one resource to another in order to pursue better performance. In this way, the workload of the central scheduler can be reduced.

Regarding the probability distribution function based approach, an algorithm (Dong, 2008) that takes an input parameter as a resource selection criterion, which is a QoS requirement, is described. This algorithm is a list heuristic and consists of two phases: the task ranking phase and the task-to-resource mapping phase. In the ranking phase, tasks will be ordered according to their priorities. The rank of a task is determined by the task's computational demand, the mathematical expectation of resource performance, and the communication cost for data transfer. In the mapping phase, the scheduler will pick up unscheduled tasks in the order of their priorities and assign them to resources according to performance objective and the QoS guide.

The remainder of this chapter is organized as follows: Section 2 provides background on previous research, sections 3 and 4 describe in detail the two new approaches for workflow scheduling, and section 5 concludes this chapter and discusses future research.

BACKGROUND

Early research on job rescheduling in the Grid can be found in (Berman, 2005) and (Wu, 2004). Rescheduling is implemented in the GrADS (Berman, 2005). It introduces the concept of a performance contract, which is an agreement between users and resource providers. When a contract violation is detected, a rescheduling will be activated. In (Wu, 2004) a self-adaptive scheduling algorithm is employed to reschedule tasks on the processors showing "abnormal" performance. The algorithm uses a prediction error threshold to trigger the rescheduling process. If the estimated complete time of a Grid task is shortened after migration, the tasks will be migrated to the processor that can give it a minimum completion time according to current prediction.

Results in (Berman, 2005) and (Wu, 2004) consider only independent tasks instead of workflows. The first rescheduling algorithm for DAG (directed acyclic graph) based workflow applications was given in (Sakellarion, 2004). In order to reduce the cost of rescheduling, this algorithm only considers a selective set of tasks for rescheduling. The key idea of this selective rescheduling policy is to evaluate at the run-time the gap between the start time of a task against its estimated starting time in the static initial scheduling. Only the tasks whose gaps are larger than the the maximum allowable delay, which is the slackness of a task's scheduled start time in a workflow, will be considered for a reschedule. This algorithm avoids a dependence on an accurate prediction of resource performance, but does not consider the change of the resource pool, such as the join or leave of Grid resources. As a complement, research in (Yu, 2007) proposes an event driven adaptive rescheduling approach based on the HEFT algorithm (Topcuouglu, 2002). At the run-time, the scheduler reallocates pending tasks following the earliest-finish-time policy when it receives a performance change event from the executor. Yu et al. propose a plan switching approach in (Yu, 2006) in which a family of activity graphs is constructed and switches are triggered among members of the family when the execution of the activity graph fails. However, detailed algorithms that generate the original plan and the alternative plan according to the prediction on environment change are not discussed.

Research discussed above relies on a centralized architecture to make rescheduling. The approach presented in this chapter takes the distributed manner which is based on the agent technology. In (Negri, 2006), agents are used on behalf of Grid users to compose Grid workflows but no mobility is discussed in the paper. In (Aversa, 2006), mobile agents are used to achieve load balance in the Grid; this approach does not rely on resource performance prediction and is similar with dynamical scheduling. In (Choi, 2005), a mobile agent based adaptive scheduling mechanism is proposed for peer-to-peer systems in which mobile agents can partially take over scheduling and fault tolerance procedures from the volunteer server in order to reduce the scheduling overhead. However, this scheme still only considers independent task scheduling.

As with the stochastic performance modeling based approach, it relies heavily on the ability to model the uncertainty performance as stochastic variables. Some previous efforts have established a variety of techniques for determining the stochastic behavior of Grid resources (Li, 2007; Li 2007 CCGrid; Bermat, 2002; David 2004). Based on these efforts, research in (Shestak, 2006; Shestak, 2006 ICPP; Shestak, 2006 PDPTA; Sugavanam, 2007) investigated performance of different static resource allocation algorithms under imposed QoS constraints. However, these studies only considered independent task scheduling. In (Dogan, 2007), the authors present a genetic algorithm to optimize the makespan problem that relies on a stochastic representation of task execution times. Unlike the research in (Shestak, 2006) and (Shestak, 2006 ICPP), this paper does not consider the QoS constraint explicitly when a schedule is made.

In addition to research related to the two approaches presented in this chapter, there are certainly other ways to handle the QoS problem in workflow scheduling. In (Quan, 2007), a service-level-agreement (SLA) based workflow scheduling algorithm is proposed, which not only considers the execution time of a job but also the cost the users need to pay to resource providers. This algorithm also uses the rescheduling technique, but does not rely on stochastic performance modelling. Other research on SLA based scheduling algorithms can be found in (Zeng, 2004; Brandic, 2005).

PRELIMINARIES

Both algorithms described in this chapter assume that there is a Grid scheduler (also known as Meta-scheduler) to which a workflow will be submitted by a Grid user. The Grid scheduler can get the information on Grid resources from Grid Information Services in the format that the algorithm desires (e.g., a deterministic description of the performance as a concrete value, or a non-deterministic description as a probability mass function).

A workflow is assumed to be represented by a DAG G. An example of a DAG is presented in Fig. 3. A circular node t_i in G represents a task, where $1 \leq i \leq v$, and v is number of tasks in the workflow. The number q_i ($1 \leq i \leq v$) shown below t_i represents the computational power consumed to finish t_i. For example, in Fig. 3, $q_1 = 5$. An edge $e(i, j)$ from t_i to t_j means that t_j needs an intermediate result from t_i, so that $t_j \in succ(t_i)$, where $succ(t_i)$ is the set of all immediate successor tasks of t_i. Similarly, we have $t_j \in pred(t_i)$, where $pred(t_i)$ is the set of immediate predecessors of t_i. The weight of $e(i, j)$ provides the size of intermediate results (or communication volume, for simplicity) transferred from t_i to task t_j. For example, the communication volume from t_1 to t_2 is 1 in Fig. 3.

The targeted system consists of a group of computational resources $r_1, ..., r_n$ distributed in a Grid. The performance of r_i is denoted as p_i. Two nodes r_i and r_j can communicate with each other via a network connection $w_{i,j}$. The bandwidth of $w_{i,j}$ is denoted as $b_{i,j}$. Computational and communication costs are uniformly related with computational power and communication bandwidth respectively. Therefore, the computational cost $c_{i,j}$ of t_i on r_k and the communication cost $d_{i,j,x,y}$ for input from t_i on resource r_x to t_j on r_y can be denoted by Eq.(1) and Eq.(2), respectively.

$$c_{i,k} = \frac{q_i}{p_k} \tag{1}$$

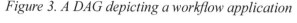

Figure 3. A DAG depicting a workflow application

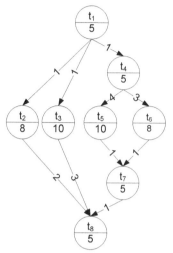

$$d_{i,j,x,y} = \frac{e(i,j)}{b_{x,y}}$$

(2)

The primary objective of both algorithms is to map tasks to proper computational resources such that the makespan of the whole workflow can be as short as possible. As an instance of list heuristics, the proposed algorithms have two phases: the task ranking phase and task-to-resource mapping phase.

In the task ranking phase, the priority of a task t_i in a given DAG is computed iteratively from the exiting node of the DAG upwards to the entrance node as Eq.(3) shows

$$rank(t_i) = avg\_c_i + \max_{t_j \in succ(t_i)} (avg\_d_{i,j} + rank(t_j))$$

(3)

Here avg_c_i is the estimation of the average execution time of task t_i, and similarly, $avg\_d_{i,j}$ is the estimate of the intermediate result transfer time from t_i to t_j. The detailed representations of avg_c_i and $avg\_d_{i,j}$ in the two algorithms are different and will be described with the corresponding algorithm. In Eq.(3), the rank of a task is computed in the bottom-up order, starting from the exit task. Initially, the rank of the exit task t_{exit} is defined as:

$$rank(t_{exit}) = avg\_c_{exit}$$

As precedence orders between tasks are considered, the start time of a task t_i on a certain resource r_x is constrained not only by the available time of r_x, but also by the ready time of intermediate results from t_i's predecessors which is then determined by the completion time of t_i's predecessors and the network transmission delay. Therefore, in general, the earliest start time (*EST*) of a task t_i on a resource r_k depends on the data ready time *DRT* and the resource ready time:

$$EST = \max(DRT, RRT) \tag{4}$$

However, the specific expression of *EST, DRT* and *RRT* will be different in the two algorithms.

THE RESCHEDULING ALGORITHM BASED ON MOBILE AGENTS

In this approach, Grid workflows are submitted to a scheduler where the initial schedule will be made by the PFAS algorithm according to predicted resource information. The scheduler also creates two types of mobile agents, the Coordinator Agent (CA) and Task Agents (TA). There is only one CA for each workflow, and for every task in the workflow there is correspondent TA, which carries the executable of that task and the related scheduling context. The scheduler dispatches the CA and TAs to Grid resources according to the initial schedule. Then the CA and TAs monitor the resource status at the run-time and work cooperatively to reschedule tasks by a distributed algorithm when necessary. By this means, the scheduler is freed from iterative rescheduling.

The Rescheduling Framework

The system framework is designed as in Fig. 4. Grid users submit their workflows to the central workflow scheduler. Based on the resource information from Grid Information Services, such as MDS, the scheduler will first generate an initial schedule by mapping every task in the workflow to a certain Grid resource. Then, it will generate a TA for each task, put context information necessary for rescheduling into the TA, and dispatch it to the resource where the task is mapped. The TA is responsible for monitoring the status of the hosting resource by referring to local resource information providers, such as Hawkeye (Hawkeye) and Ganglia (Sacerdoti, 2003), issuing a rescheduling token request if a performance change is observed and reallocates itself. For each workflow, the scheduler will also generate a CA that is responsible for rescheduling context maintenance, token management and global resource monitoring via Grid information services. Fig. 5 shows components in the TAs and CA and structures of rescheduling tokens are given in Fig. 6. The TAs and CA work with the support of agent platforms (Aversa, 2006) which facilitate message passing and agent migration in the Grid. During its lifetime, a TA could be in one of the following four states.

- **Running state:** When the task carried by the TA is running, the TA is in this state. A TA in this state will not be rescheduled. After the running state, the TA will report to the CA and terminate.
- **Pending state:** When the task a TA is carrying is in a resource's local job queue, the TA is in the pending state. In this state, the TA can receive rescheduling tokens and update its schedule context if noticed.
- **Monitoring state:** To avoid multiple token requests triggered by the same performance change event from different TAs among all pending TAs on the same resource, only the TA carrying the task with the highest rank is in the monitoring state. In this state, it monitors the local performance change and sends a rescheduling token to the CA if necessary.

Figure 4. Rescheduling components and system architecture

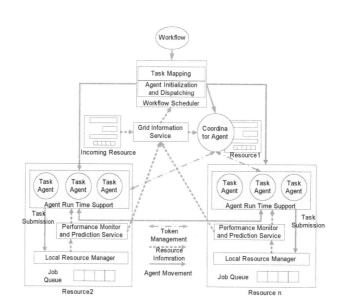

- **Rescheduling state:** The TA holding the rescheduling token is in this state and it might migrate to other resources and send schedule context update messages to its predecessor and successor TAs.

Different kinds of data flow are given in Fig. 4, and a typical scheduling and rescheduling procedure works as follows:

1. The central scheduler generates an initial schedule and initializes mobile agents.
2. A TA monitors its local resource for performance fluctuation and the CA monitors the global resource information for resources becoming available.
3. If a TA finds a performance change on its local resource, it will send a rescheduling token request to the CA. The new performance of its host resource will be included in the token request.
4. If the CA receives a token request from a TA or it finds that a new Grid resource joins the Grid and becomes available, it will generate a rescheduling token and issue the token to a selected TA according to the rescheduling algorithm.
5. When a TA receives a rescheduling token, it will reschedule its own task, migrate to a new location if necessary, and update its new location to its predecessors, successors and the CA. The token will then be passed to the next TA according to the rescheduling algorithm.
6. When the task associated with a TA completes, the TA reports the status to the CA and termi- nates.

To conduct a rescheduling successfully in a distributed manner, a TA should have the following in- formation: (1) the location of the CA; (2) the predicted performance of available resources, (3) the order

Figure 5. Functionality components of task agent and coordinator agent

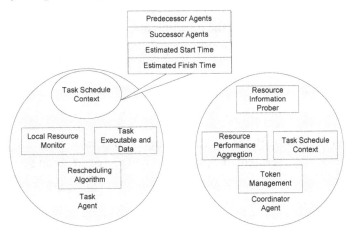

Figure 6. Structure of rescheduling token request and rescheduling token

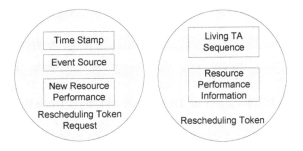

of token passing, and (4) locations of its successors and predecessors. Initially, the scheduler always assigns the CA to the same resource with the entry task, and puts this location in all the TAs' schedule context. To reduce communication overhead, the CA should not migrate unless the host resource becomes unavailable during the run time of the workflow. In this case, the CA will move to the location of the TA that has the highest task rank which is defined in the next section, and broadcast its new location to all living TAs in its task schedule context. The other job of the CA is to generate the rescheduling token. Because TAs are distributed and only have local resource information and partial schedule context, they have to rely on the information in the token to perform the rescheduling. Therefore, the rescheduling token must contain predicted resource performance information and the order in which the token should be passed among living agents. This means that, the CA needs to aggregate resource performance information obtained from global Grid Information Services and reported by TAs and compute the rank of each task. Details about ranks are introduced in the next section.

The Rescheduling Algorithm

By applying different task ranking and task-to-resource mapping policies, different rescheduling algorithms can be implemented in the framework proposed above. In this section, a distributed algorithm based on the Heterogeneous-Earliest-Finish-Time (HEFT) heuristic is described. As mentioned in Section 3, this algorithm has a task ranking phase and a task-to-resource mapping phase, and the definition of a task t_i is given by Eq.(3). However, the meaning of avg_c_i and $avg\_d_{i,j}$ needs to be clarified.

Let the average performance of all computational resources avg_p be

$$avg\_p = \frac{1}{m} \sum_{1 \le i \le m} p_i \tag{5}$$

According to Eq.(1) and Eq.(2), the average computational cost of task t_i, avg_c_i, and the average communication cost for the intermediate result from t_i to t_j, $avg\_d_{i,j}$, can be denoted as

$$avg\_c_i = \frac{q_i}{avg\_p} \tag{6}$$

$$avg\_d_{i,j} = \frac{1}{m^2} \sum_{1 \le x,y \le m} \frac{e(i,j)}{b_{x,y}} \tag{7}$$

According to the definition of *rank*, the ranking phase only needs the resource performance information, but no current scheduling context. Therefore, this phase can be easily done on the CA. After ranks are computed, the CA will order the ID of tasks into a non-incremental list, and associate each ID with the TA carrying that task. The location of TAs can be obtained from the CA's schedule context. Thus, the TA sequence in a rescheduling token is generated. The CA will then put the resource performance in the token and issue the token to the first TA in the TA list. The rescheduling algorithm conducted by the CA is given in Fig. 7.

Once a TA receives a rescheduling token, it will start to reschedule itself. In HEFT, a task is always mapped to the resource that is believed to finish the task the earliest. The earliest finish time of a task t_i on resource r_j can be denoted as:

$$EFT(t_i, r_k) = EST(t_i, r_k) + c_{i,k}. \tag{8}$$

$EST(t_i, r_k)$ is the earliest start time of t_i on r_j. As Eq.(4) shows, $EST(t_i, r_k)$ can be expressed as:

$$EST(t_i, r_k) = \max(RRT(r_k), DRT(t_i, r_k)) \tag{9}$$

$$DRT(t_i, r_k) = \max_{t_j \in pred(t_i)} (RT(t_j, r_k)) \tag{10}$$

In Eq.(9), given $t_j \in pred(t_i)$, $RRT(r_k)$ is the earliest available time of r_k, $RT(t_j, r_k)$ is the ready time of the intermediate result from t_j to t_i. Generally, $RT(t_j, r_k)$ is decided by the finish time of t_x and the communication cost to transfer the intermediate result from the resource where t_x is located to r_k. According to Eq.(3), ranks of t_i's predecessors are always greater than that of t_i. So, in the rescheduling sequence,

Figure 7. Token generation conducted by the CA

```
CA Token Generation Algorithm
Input: TokenRequest (time_stamp T, event_source S, updated_performance P)
Output: A rescheduling token K
1.   While (there is a running TA ){
2.       Wait for a TokenRequest;
3.       Update the resource information maintained using T, S and P;
4.       Update ranks of all tasks that have not started.
5.       Sort tasks in non-incremental orders and insert their locations into the a new token K;
6.       Put updated resource information into K;
7.       Issue the token to the TA with the highest tasks rank that has not started.
8.   }
```

they are rescheduled earlier than t_i. Therefore, when t_i is being rescheduled, all of its predecessors have already been rescheduled, and their new locations are known to t_i. Let RM_j denote the index of the resource to which t_j is currently mapped. Because input data transfer can only start after t_j is finished, the finish time of t_j on RM_j must be known. To get the finish time, two cases need to be considered: whether or not t_j has been completed before the current rescheduling. In the case that t_j is finished, the ready time of input data from t_j for t_i still has two sub-cases: whether or not t_i will be scheduled to the same resource as it was in the previous schedule. If it is not, the input date transfer can only start from the rescheduling time instead of the finish time of t_j, because it is still not known where the input data should go when t_j finishes. Finally, for a task t_i on resource r_k, the ready time of data from t_j as a predecessor of t_i, can be presented as:

$$RT(t_j, r_k) \mid t_j \in pred(t_i) = \begin{cases} \text{if } t_j \text{ finished} \begin{cases} RFT_j + \dfrac{e(j,i)}{b_{RM_j,k}}, \text{if } RM_j = r_k \\[2ex] clock + \dfrac{e(j,i)}{b_{RM_j,k}}, \text{otherwise} \end{cases} \\[4ex] \text{otherwise:} \quad SFT_j + \dfrac{e(j,i)}{b_{RM_j,k}} \end{cases} \tag{11}$$

In Eq.(11), RFT_j is the actual finish time of t_j if it has finished, *clock* is the wall clock time when the rescheduling is conducted, and SFT_j is the scheduled finish time of t_j if it has not been done.

In Eq.(8)~Eq.(11), all parameters can be retrieved or computed by a TA from local resource information or information given by the rescheduling token, except $RRT(r_k)$ which is determined by the status of r_k's local job queue. In HEFT, a task being scheduled can be inserted into a resource's job queue only when it does not interrupt tasks already scheduled or violate the precedence constraints. To obtain $RRT(r_k)$, the TA has to probe the resource manager of r_k. The TA rescheduling algorithm is presented in Fig. 8.

Using the DAG in Fig. 3 and the three Grid resources presented in TABLE I, we will present an example to illustrate the effect of rescheduling. In Fig. 9 (a), the initial schedule of the DAG is given, and its makespan is 8.725. At wall clock time 2, the performance of resource r_3 changes from 1 to 4, and triggers a rescheduling. The rescheduling starts from TA_5 which has the highest task rank, and then transfers to

TA_6, TA_2, TA_7, and TA_8. Because r_3 will give t_2 an earlier finish time, TA_2 migrates to r_3, as does TA_8 to r_2, and the total makespan is reduced to 8.5, therefore the QoS of the schedule is improved.

Experiment

To evaluate the effectiveness of this rescheduling approach in the Grid circumstances, simulations are performed. The new approach is compared with the centralized AHEFT algorithm which is also HEFT based. Scheduling quality measured by the scheduled length ratio (SLR) of both approaches are compared in different parameter settings. The SLR of a task graph is defined by

$$SLR = \frac{Real\,Makespan}{Estimated\,Minimum\,Critical\,Path\,Length}$$

The critical path length only includes computational cost, so that it is the lower bound of the makespan any scheduler algorithm can provide. The throughput of the central workflow schedulers of the two approaches is also compared.

In the experiments, three initial resource clusters are used. Each cluster consists of 10 processing nodes connected by a LAN, and the resource clusters are connected by a WAN. The scale of this topology matches the realistic Grid computing infrastructure of HPCVL (HPCVL) operated by the alliance of six universities in southeast Ontario. The topology and initial parameters such as processing capacity, communication cost and load of each processor are generated by GridG1.0 (Yang, 2003).

A task graph generator called Task Graph For Free (TGFF) (Dick, 1998) is used to generate DAGs submitted to the Grid. TGFF has the ability to generate a variety of graphs according to different configuration parameters, such as the average number of task nodes of each graph, the average outgoing and incoming degrees for each node in a graph, and computational and communication costs for each type of task node and edge.

Figure 8. The TA rescheduling algorithm

TA Rescheduling Algorithm:
 t_i: the task carried by the TA holding the rescheduling token;
R: resource set;
Input: Rescheduling Token K
1. *for* every resource r_k in R
2.   Compute $\max(RT(t_j, r_k))$ for every t_j as a predecessor of t_i according to Eq.(11);
3.   Probe resource r_k for $RRT(r_k)$;
4.   Compute the earliest finish time of t_i on r_j, $EFT(t_i, r_k)$ according to Eq.(8) and (9);
5.   *end of for*
6. Select the resource r that achieves $\min(EFT(t_i, r_k))$ for all k;
7. Update the new schedule context, including the new location and finish time of t_i, to the CA and t_i's successors and predecessors;
8. Remove t_i from the token passing sequence in K;
9. Pass the token to the TA at the head of the sequence in K;
10. The current TA reschedule migrates itself to r.

Table 1.

(Re)scheduling Iterate	r_1	r_2	r_3
Initial schedule	4	5	1
First Reschedule	4	5	4

	r_1	r_2	r_3
r_1	∞	1	2/3
r_2	1	∞	1
r_3	2/3	1	∞

(a) Performance of three resources in different rescheduling iterates

(b) Communication bandwidth between different resources

Figure 9. (a) Gantt chart (Morris, 1944) (makespan=8.725) of the initial schedule of DAG in Fig. 1 using the initial resource performance given by TABLE I (A) and communication cost given by TABLE I (B). (b) The result (makespan=8.5) given by rescheduling at clock time 2 when the performance of resource of r_3 is changed.

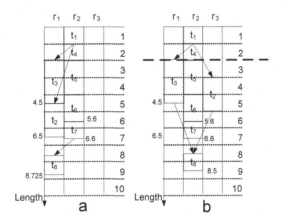

To get a comprehensive understanding of the performance of the new approach under various input DAGs and resource environments, the following parameters are considered in the experiment:

- The average number of task (*ATN*) nodes in a graph;
- The ratio of the average degree of a task node to the total number of tasks (*DTR*) in a graph (the edge density in a graph);
- The computation-to-communication ratio (*CCR*) of a task graph (the higher the *CCR* value is, the more computation intensive a job is);
- The resource performance fluctuation factor (*PFF*) which indicates the percentage by which the performance of a computational resource can decrease;
- The resource performance changing frequency (*PCR*) (a higher *PCR* causes more frequent rescheduling)

With respect to the number of nodes in a task graph, 5 different average values are applied: 20, 40, 60, 80 and 100. For each of these values, 250 graphs are generated. Fig. 10(a) illustrates the average performance of the AHEFT, the mobile agent based approach (MHEFT) and the original HEFT.

The edge density is an important character of a graph, which indicates the communication volume among tasks. To describe the edge density, the ratio of the average degree of each task node to the total number of nodes in a graph is used in our experiments. Five different settings are tested: 0.05, 0.1, 0.2, 0.3 and 0.4. For each setting, 250 different graphs are also generated as well. Fig. 10 (b) presents the simulation results.

The other parameter contributing to the characteristics of a task graph is the *CCR*. In the experiment, the ratio increases from 0.5 to 10, and for each value 250 DAGs are generated as well. The results are given in Fig. 10 (c).

To test the adaptability of the three scheduling policies to computational power fluctuation, five different values are assigned to the performance fluctuation factor: 20%, 40%, 50%, 60% and 80%. Each of these denotes the maximum allowed percentage of the full computation power drop in different time slots. Simulation results are demonstrated in Fig. 10 (d).

It can be observed from Fig. 10 that the scheduling and rescheduling quality of MHEFT matches that of the centralized AHEFT, and both MHEFT and AHEFT perform much better than the static HEFT in all four test cases. The result shows that the distributed rescheduling approach can achieve equiva-

Figure 10. (a) Average SLR with respect to different graph sizes (DRT=0.1, CCR=2, PFF=0.4 and PCR=0.06). (b) Average SLR with respect to different edge density (ATN=40, CCR=2, PFF=0.4 and PCR =0.06). (c) Average SLR with respect to different CCR (ATN=40, DRT=0.1, PFF=0.4 and PCR =0.06). (d) Average SLR with respect to different levels of performance fluctuation (ATN=40, DRT=0.1, CCR=2 and PCR=0.06).

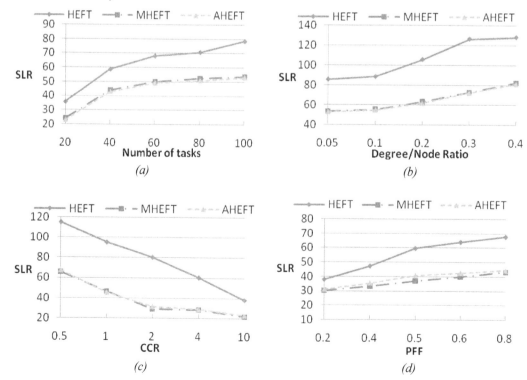

lent performance of the centralized rescheduling approach in terms of minimizing the makespan of a workflow. Further, we claim that the distributed method is also efficient for a system-centric objective, and this is supported by the following experiment on throughput of the central workflow scheduler.

The throughput of the central scheduler indicates how many workflows it can accept and schedule in a given time. If the scheduler is frequently interrupted for rescheduling, its throughput will drop. In this experiment, we let the rescheduling frequency increase from 0.02 to 0.1 and observed its impact on the throughput of different approaches. It can be found in Fig. 11 that, as the frequency increases linearly, the throughput (the throughput value on the y-axis is a value relative to the throughput of the standard HEFT algorithm) of the centralized AHEFT drops dramatically, but the MHEFT is only affected slightly, and the static HEFT is not affected at all.

Workflow graphs in the real Grid world usually have some unique characteristics. These include, for example, balanced parallel task chains, such as The Basic Local Alignment Search Tool (BLAST) (Sulakhe, 2005), periodical fork and join structures, such as Electron Micrograph Analysis (EMAN) (Ludtke, 1999). To test MHEFT more realistically, these characteristics of real Grid workflows need to be considered. In the experiments, parallel task chains that will join together at some node are generated. Fig. 12 presents an example of a balanced parallel task graph, which has four parallel chains from the entrance task to the exit task. This is quite similar to the BLAST application. If a scheduling algorithm can deal with this kind of DAG well, it will also deal well with DAGs of EMAN, because an EMAN application can be looked as a serial combination of several such DAGs.

Figure 11. The scheduler throughput with respect to different rescheduling frequencies

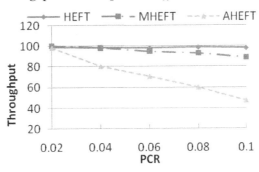

Figure 12. A sample four-way balanced parallel DAG generated by TGFF

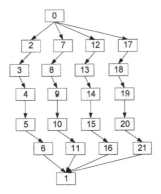

Figure 13. (a) Average SLR with respect to different graph sizes (PW=30, CCR=2, PFF=0.4 and PCR=0.06). (b) Average SLR with respect to different number of parallel task chains (ATN=600, CCR=2, PFF=0.4 and PCR=0.06). (c) Average SLR with respect to different CCR (ATN=600, PW=30, PFF=0.4 and PCR=0.06). (d) Average SLR with respect to different levels of performance fluctuation (ATN=600, PW=30, CCR=2 and PCR=0.06)

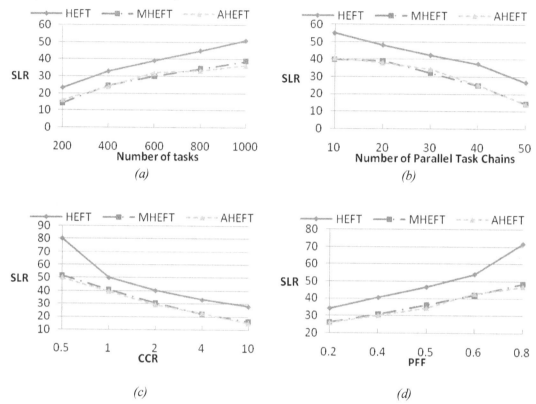

It can be observed from Fig. 13 that the SLR of the regulated DAGs is smaller than random DAGs. That is due to the balanced nature of these DAGs, which reduce the gap between "good" schedules and "bad" ones. In the realistic DAG test cases above, the scheduling quality of MHEFT is still adherent to the AHEFT and its system-centric performance outperforms its peers (Fig. 14).

THE APPROACH BASED ON STOCHASTIC PERFORMANCE MODELING

The approach introduced in this section shares the same goal of minimizing the schedule length of a workflow as a means to improve the QoS, and it is also a list heuristic having a ranking phase and a mapping phase. However, as the resource information is changed from deterministic prediction to non-deterministic formulation, the representation of parameters changes considerably.

Figure 14. The scheduler throughput with respect to different rescheduling frequencies

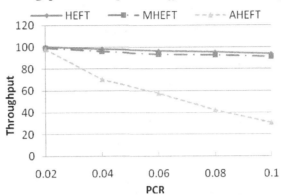

The Scheduling Algorithm

First, the available performance of both computational nodes and network connections is stochastic and follows some probability mass functions (PMF). Fig. 1 presents an example of a PMF. The PMF of the performance P_i[1] of a computational node r_i is denoted as $P_{P_i}(x)$, and the PMF of the bandwidth $B_{i,j}$ of a network connection between r_i and r_j is denoted as $P_{B_{i,j}}(x)$. It is assumed that for all $1 \leq i, j \leq n$, random variables P_i and $B_{i,j}$ are independent.

Then, the completion time $C_{i,k}$ (of task t_i on resource r_k) and the communication cost $D_{i,j,k,l}$ (for data transfer between task t_i on resource r_k and tasks t_j or resource r_l) also become two random variables that can be denoted as Eq.(12) and Eq.(13) respectively:

$$C_{i,k} = \frac{q_i}{P_k} \tag{12}$$

$$D_{i,j,k,l} = \frac{e(i,j)}{B_{k,l}} \tag{13}$$

According to Eq.(12) and Eq.(13), $C_{i,k}$ and $D_{i,j,k,l}$ are independent variables (since P_k and $B_{k,l}$ are independent), and the PMFs of $C_{i,k}$ and $D_{i,j,k,l}$, namely $P_{C_{i,k}}(x)$ and $P_{D_{i,j,k,l}}(x)$, respectively, can be easily obtained from $P_{P_i}(x)$ and $P_{B_{i,j}}(x)$.

Now, the meaning of parameters avg_c_i and $avg\_d_{i,j}$ used to compute the rank of a task in Eq.(3) also change as follows:

$$avg\_c_i = \underset{k}{Avg}(E(C_{i,k})) \tag{14}$$

$$avg\_d_{i,j} = \underset{k,l}{Avg}(E(D_{i,j,k,l})) \tag{15}$$

Here, avg_c_i is the average value of the mathematical expectation of $C_{i,k}$ (denoted as $E(C_{i,k})$) on each computational resource r_k. Similarly, $avg\_d_{i,j}$ is the average value of the mathematical expectation of $D_{i,j,k,l}$ for every network connection pair r_k and r_l to which t_i and t_j could be mapped respectively. According to Eq.(3), the rank value of a task is actually an estimate of time consumption, which is from the start time of t_i to the completion time of the whole workflow, based on the average expected performance of computational resources and network connections. Once the ranks of tasks are known, the scheduler will put the tasks in a queue in a non-ascending order (ties are broken randomly).

In the mapping phase, the scheduler will fetch unscheduled tasks from the head of the priority queue formed in the ranking phase and map it to a selected resource. Since the priorities are computed upwards, it is guaranteed that a task will always have a higher priority than all of its successors. Therefore, it will be mapped before any of its successors. This ordering eliminates the case that a successor task occupies a resource while its predecessor is waiting for that resource so that deadlocks can be avoided. For tasks that are not related with each other, this approach lets those farther from the exiting task get resource allocation earlier, which will in turn give them a greater chance of starting earlier and produce a shorter makespan.

If the resource performance is deterministic, a popular and easy way to schedule a task in a heterogeneous environment is to choose the resource that can complete that task the earliest, as do the HEFT and PFAS algorithms. However, in the scenario in this section, if only the best performance of a resource is considered, the schedule may suffer a long makespan in the real world due to the small probability of this performance being achieved. To overcome this difficulty, the mathematical expectation of the random performance can be used, as what we have done in the ranking phase. However, in a non-deterministic system, only providing an estimated mean value might not be sufficient, because the real situation might be quite different. From the users' point of view, more attentions may be given to the possibility of achieving a certain performance other than a given static mean value. Therefore, a flexible and adaptive way is to allow the user to provide a QoS requirement to guide the resource selection phase. To simplify the presentation, a binary mapping function $M(t_i, r_k)$ is defined in Eq.(16):

$$M(t_i, r_k) = \begin{cases} 1 & \text{if } t_i \text{ is mapped to } r_k \\ 0 & \text{otherwise} \end{cases} \tag{16}$$

Although the earliest start time $EST(t_i, r_k)$ of a task t_i on a resource r_k follows the same equation as Eq.(9), now $EST(t_i, r_k)$, the data ready time $DRT(t_i, r_k)$ and the resource ready time $RRT(r_k)$ are all random variables. Similarly, $DRT(t_i, r_k)$ can still be expressed by Eq.(10), but $RT(t_i, r_k)$, which is the ready time of the intermediate result from t_j to t_i, and $t_j \in pred(t_i)$ has a different representation as Eq.(17) shows:

$$RT(t_j, r_k) = CT(t_j) + D_{j,i,l,k} \mid M(t_j, r_l) = 1 \tag{17}$$

$CT(t_j)$ is the completion time of t_j, r_l is the resource to which t_j is mapped, and $D_{j,i,l,k}$ is the intermediate result transfer time from r_l to r_k.

As all tasks mapped to the same resources will be executed sequentially, the resource ready time $RRT(r_k)$ is determined by the completion time of the last task in the job queue of r_k. If t'_q be the last task in r_k's job queue currently, then $RRT(r_k)$ can be denoted as

$$RRT(r_k) = CT(t'_q) \tag{18}$$

It should be noted that t'_q is not necessarily a member of tasks in the current workflow, that is to say, t'_q may not be a predecessor of t_i. It could be any task belonging to any user sharing the same resource. The scheduler only needs to know the PMF of $CT(t'_q)$ from the resource information service.

Finally, the estimated completion time $ECT(t_i, r_k)$ of t_i on r_k is given by

$$ECT(t_i, r_k) = EST(t_i, r_k) + C_{i,k} \qquad (19)$$

To achieve a small makespan, we need to know the PMF of $ECT(t_i, r_k)$, which depends on the PMF of $CT(t_j)$, $RT(t_j)$ and $DRT(t_i, r_k)$. Since all predecessors of t_i have been scheduled by the time t_i is being scheduled, the PMF of $CT(t_j)$ is already known (see Eq.(27)), so is the PMF of $RRT(r_k)$. According to probability theory, the PMF of the sum of two independent discrete random variables is the discrete convolution of their PMF. Therefore, according to Eq.(17), the PMF of $RT(t_j, r_k)$ can be expressed as:

$$P_{RT_{j,k}}(x) = \sum_{i=0}^{x} P_{CT_j}(i) P_{D_{j,i,l,k}}(x-i) \qquad (20)$$

Now, we come to the hard part of the problem--how can the distribution of the data ready time of t_i on r_k $DRT(t_i, r_k)$ be obtained? As it is shown in Eq.(10), $DRT(t_i, r_k)$ relies on the last data transmission from t_j which is a predecessor of t_i. Ideally, $\forall t_j, t_{j'} \in pred(t_i)$, t_j and $t_{j'}$ are independent. However, this may not be the case. Even when t_j and $t_{j'}$ are not directly connected by an edge, they may still be related if they are scheduled to the same computational site or they have the same ancestors. For example, in Fig. 3, t_2 and t_3 have the same parent t_1. Although t_2 and t_3 have no precedent orders between them, their start time cannot be independent because they both are restricted by the finish time of t_1. Such correlation impedes the application of probability theories which only hold under the assumption of variable independence. As the execution time $C_{i,k}$ and data transmission time $D_{i,j,k,l}$ are independent, they can be looked at as "element" variables and we are able to get the distribution of random variables which are the sum of $C_{i,k}$ and $D_{i,j,k,l}$, just as we have done in Eq.(20). The finish time of the intermediate result transmission from t_j to t_i on r_k, $RT(t_j, r_k)$, $t_j \in pred(t_i)$ is such a "compound" random variable. However, when the maximum operation is applied to these summed-up random variables, the distribution function of $RT(t_j, r_k)$ will not be helpful because $RT(t_j, r_k)$ and $RT(t_{j'}, r_k)$ may not be independent. We have to go back to the distributions of element random variables and enumerate all different possibilities. Unfortunately, as the scheduling goes deeper into the task graph, there will be more alternative paths from the entry node to the current node and these paths will become longer. Thus, more and more element variables will be involved in the compound variables. The time complexity of enumerating all possibilities will be exponential (suppose there are N such element variables and each has η possible values, the cost will be $O(\eta^N)$). To avoid such huge time consumption, an approximation is provided.

By probability theory, the probability distribution function (also known as the *cumulative distribution function* (CDF)) of the maximum value of a set of independent variables is the product of the probability distribution functions of these variables. To avoid the exponential computational cost, this theory is applied to our circumstance, even though independence cannot be guaranteed. This approximation does not change the range of a random variable's distribution, but only affects the probabilities of different values. Let $F_{EST i,k}$, $F_{DRT i,k}$ and $F_{RRT i,k}$ be the CDF of $EST(t_i, r_k)$, $DRT(t_i, r_k)$, and $RRT(t_i, r_k)$ respectively. The following equation can be obtained according to Eq.(9):

$$F_{EST_{i,k}}(x) = F_{DRT_{i,k}}(x)F_{RRT_{i,k}}(x) \tag{21}$$

Similarly, the $F_{DRT_{i,k}}$ can be obtained from Eq.(22).

$$F_{DRT_{i,k}}(x) = F_{RT(t'_1,p_k)}(x)...F_{RT(t'_m,p_k)}(x) \,|\, t'_1,...,t'_m \in pred(t_i) \tag{22}$$

For discrete random variable X, its CDF $F(x)$ can be obtained from its PMF $P(x)$ by Eq.(23):

$$F(x) = \Pr(X \le x) = \sum_{x_i \le x} P(x_i) \tag{23}$$

On the other hand, if $F(x)$ is known, the PMF $P(x)$ can also be obtained as

$$P(x_i) = F(x_i) - F(x_{i-1}) \tag{24}$$

By Eq.(23) the CDF of $RT(t_j, r_k)$ can be acquired using the results from Eq.(20), as can the CDF of $RRT(t_i, r_k)$. The PMF of $DRT(t_i, r_k)$ can be obtained from Eq.(20), Eq.(22) and Eq.(24). Following the same procedure the PMF of $EST(t_i, r_k)$ can be obtained, which is denoted as $P_{EST_{i,k}}(x)$. According to Eq.(9), the PMF of $ECT(t_i, r_k)$ can then be expressed as:

$$P_{ECT_{i,k}}(x) = \sum_{i=0}^{x} P_{EST_{i,k}}(i)P_{C_{i,k}}(x-i) \tag{25}$$

Figure 15. An example of CDF (A) and PMF (B) of EST. Given the QoS requirement Q, the ceiling point is the left end of the first CDF interval above Q. Only ECT instances and their probabilities left to the ceiling point (shading bars in (B)) are considered when the scheduler selects a resource for the current task.

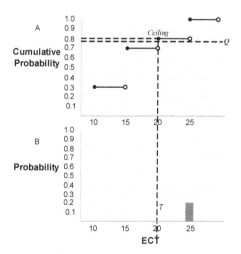

Figure 16. Pseudo code of the QoS guided workflow scheduling algorithm

---

Input: G, Q, PMF of r_i and $W_{i,j}$, $1 \leq i \leq n$.
Output: a schedule of G to $r_1, \ldots, r_n$.
1. Compute *rank* of each task in G, using Eq.(3), and order the tasks into a queue J in non-ascending order of their ranks.
2. *while* (J is not empty) *do*
3.   Pop the first task t from J;
4.   *for* every resource r
5.   Compute PMF of $RRT(r)$; //Eq.(18)
6.   *for* every $t' \in pred(t)$
7.   Compute PMF of $RT(t', r)$;//Eq.(20)
8.   *end for*
9.   Compute PMF of $DRT(t, r)$;//Using results of Line 7, Eq.(22) and (24).
10.   Compute PMF of $ECT(t, r)$; // Eq.(25)
11.   Compute $R(t, r)$, using Q and PMF of $ECT(t, r)$; //Eq.(26)
12.   *end for*
13.   Find the resource r' that $R(t, p) = \min(R(t_i, r_k))$ and insert t to the job queue of r';
14. *end of while*

Let $F_{ECTi,k}$ be the CDF of $ECT(t_i, r_k)$. $F_{ECTi,k}$ can be obtained from the PMF given in Eq.(25).

Now, given a QoS guidance Q as a percentage number, the scheduler will first find a value T in the CDF of ECT whose cumulative probability is greater than Q (Fig. 15). Let $ect(t_i, r_k)_l$ be the lth possible value of ECT and p_l be its probability, then the mathematical expectation of values to the left of T (including T itself), which is denoted as $R(t_i, r_k)$, can be denoted as Eq.(26). By this means, it will cover at least the lower Q percent set of the ECT value distribution.

$$R(t_i, r_k) = \sum_{ect(t_i, r_k)_l \leq T} p_l ect(t_i, r_k)_l \tag{26}$$

The scheduler then chooses the lowest value of all $R(t_i, r_k)$, $R(t_i, r_k)$, and maps task t_i to r_k. At this point, the PMF of $CT(t_i)$ can be known as:

$$P_{CT_i}(x) = P_{ECT_{i,k'}}(x) \tag{27}$$

When the exiting node t_v of the whole graph is scheduled, the algorithm will stop. From the PMF $P_{CTv}(x)$, we can determine the probability of different makespans of the workflow. The pseudo code of the above procedures is given in Fig. 16.

Experiment

The experiment setup is similar to that in Section 4, using the same simulation tools and having two sets of task graphs. One set is randomly generated and the other has balanced task chains. In each experiment, five groups of task graphs are used, which have 40, 80, 160, 320 and 640 tasks nodes, respectively. For simplicity, other parameters of task graphs, such as CCR, are not specified, but generated

Figure 17. Simulation result of uniform performance distribution and random generated graphs

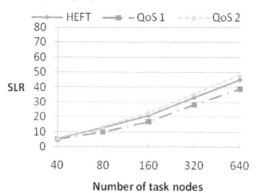

Figure 18. Simulation result of discrete normal distribution of performance and random generated graphs

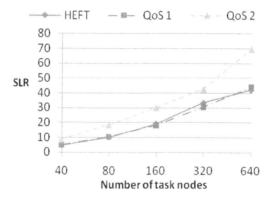

at random. To each task graph group, the HEFT algorithm and the QoS guided algorithms are applied. For the HEFT algorithm, the mathematical expectation of the resource performance is applied. For the QoS algorithm, two QoS values are applied: 80% and 50%, which are respectively denoted as QoS 1 and QoS 2 in Fig. 17~Fig. 20.

The results of experiments on randomly generated graphs are presented in Fig. 17 and Fig. 18. In Fig. 17, the resource performance follows a uniform distribution. It can be observed that the performance of all algorithms decreases as the number of tasks in a workflow increases. Due to the nature of these heuristic algorithms, the longer the critical path in a graph, the more cumulative errors they will make when computing the priorities of tasks, and the higher the probability that they will chose sub-optimal mappings.

In Fig. 17, QoS 1 achieves the best performance among the three stategies. The HEFT algorithm yields QoS 1 with a small margin and is closely followed by QoS 2 which uses 50% as the selection criterion. In Fig. 18, the HEFT and QoS 1 almost get the same results while the performance of QoS

Figure 19. Simulation result of uniform performance distribution and multi-parallel-way graphs

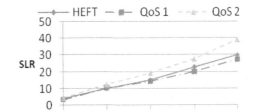

Figure 20. Simulation result of discrete normal distribution of performance and multi-parallel-way graphs

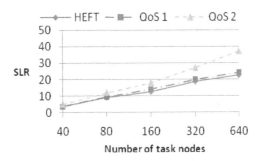

2 is significantly degraded. Filtering the 20% worst performance cases out in a uniform distribution, the expected performance can be improved noticeably, and the resources selected by these means will have a good chance (with a probability of 80%) to get a better performance than the mean value which is used by the HEFT. This explains why QoS 1 can perform better than HEFT does in Fig. 17. On the other hand, as the QoS 2 set the selection criterion as a probability of 50%, it may cut too much of the random domain and therefore suffer a higher probability of inaccurate estimate in the reality. The shortcoming of a too optimistic criterion (low QoS value) is even more obvious in Fig. 18, where the resource performance follows a normal distribution. In this kind of distribution, the mean value of a PMF happens to be the one that has the highest probability. Therefore, the HEFT algorithm can perform well in this situation.

Fig. 19 and Fig. 20 show the results of task graphs having multiple balanced parallel task chains. The three scheduling approaches present similar behaviors as they do in the previous experiments. The performance of the HEFT algorithm is still the best in the normal distribution. QoS 1 performs close to HEFT and QoS 2 suffers from its too optimistic resource selection criterion. It is worth to note that, in all cases, the SLR is shorter compared with the results in Fig. 17 and Fig. 18. This is due to the balanced structure of the task graphs, which makes the length of all paths from the starting task to the exiting task roughly identical so that the probability of sub-optimum task ranking decreases.

CONCLUSIONS AND FUTURE TRENDS

In this chapter, two approaches that can improve the quality of workflow scheduling in the Grid are introduced. Compared with other current proposals, the main contribution of the mobile-agent based approach lies in: (1) different from current centralized implementation of Grid rescheduling, this approach adopts a distributed way, which reduces the burden on the main scheduler and reacts more quickly to unpredicted resource performance fluctuation; (2) this approach produces reschedules equivalent with those made by static heuristic workflow scheduling algorithms, a feature that has not been obtained by current mobile-agent based job scheduling approaches in the Grid. According to simulation results, rescheduling is an effective way to tackle the difficulties brought by dynamic performance fluctuation in the Grid environment, without losing the merits of static scheduling. Compared with similar centralized rescheduling scheme addressing the same problem, our approach can achieve better performance at both system and application levels.

Our discussion in this chapter only considers the rescheduling of computational tasks. In fact, there are a large number of Grid applications which also have remote data access tasks. Future research should improve current approaches to include data access rescheduling. At the same time, more heuristics need to be studied, besides HEFT, on which a rescheduling algorithm can be based. The rescheduling approach in this chapter does not put constrained QoS requirement, such as the deadline of a task, into consideration, although it has the ability to shorten the makespan. Improvement can also be made to make it workable in the constrained QoS scenarios in the future.

In the stochastic performance modelling based approach, a QoS guided workflow scheduling algorithm is introduced and evaluated. The algorithm can be applied in the Grid computing scenarios, in which resource performance is not deterministically predicted, but formulated by probability functions. The contribution of this research is twofold. First, an approximation scheme to obtain the PMF of the makespan of a workflow is presented in detail. As the probabilities of different completion times are known, more sophisticated algorithms can be easily developed (although, this is not covered in this chapter). For example, if the deadline to finish a workflow is given by the user, the scheduler will be able to tell the probabilities of meeting the deadline in different schedules and then react accordingly. This is very important, as SLA is becoming a popular way for resource allocation in the Grid. Second, the proposed algorithm uses a QoS guidance to find the task-to-resource mapping, and the effects of different QoS settings in different resource performance distributions are tested. Future work may include developing new algorithms that consider SLA scenarios and testing the QoS guided method with more probability distribution functions. Although only discrete random variables are used to depict Grid resource performance in this chapter, the same approach can be extended easily to the case where continuous variables and probability distribution functions are applied. To our knowledge, static workflow scheduling on the stochastic resource performance model has just emerged and much work needs to be done. For example, new approaches may be designed to find better approximations of the distribution functions. Similarly, different task-to-resource mapping schemes can be applied and tested experimentally.

REFERENCES

Aversa, R., Martino, B., & Mazzoccal, N. (2006). MAGDA: a mobile agent based Grid architecture, *Journal of Grid Computing, 4(4)*, 395-412.

Berman, F., Casanova, H., et al. (2005). New Grid scheduling and rescheduling methods in the GrADS project. *International Journal of Parallel Programming, 33(2),* 209-229.

Bernat, G., Colin, A., & Peters, S. (2002). WCET analysis of probabilistic hard real-time systems. *Proceedings of the 23rd IEEE Real-Time Systems Symposium* (pp. 279-288). Austin, TX, U.S.A.

Brandic, I., Benkner, S., et al. (2005). QoS support for time-critical Grid workflow applications. *Proceedings of the 1st IEEE International Conference on e-Science and Grid Computing,* Melbourne, Australia.

Cao, J., Jarvis, S., et al. (2003). GridFlow: workflow management for Grid Computing. *Proceedings of the 3rd CCGrid* (pp.198-205), Tokyo, Japan.

Choi, S., Baik, M., et al. (2005). Mobile agent based adaptive scheduling mechanism in peer to peer Grid Computing. *Proceedings of International Conference on Computational Science and its Applications 2005* (pp. 936-947), Singapore.

DAGMan. http://www.cs.wisc.edu/condor/dagman/.

David, L. & Puaut, I. (2004). Static determination of probabilistic execution times. *Proceedings of the 16th Euromicro Conference on Real-Time Systems* (pp. 223-230), Sicily, Italy.

Deelman, E., Blythe, J., et al. (2004). Pegasus: mapping scientific workflows onto the Grid. *Proceddings of Grid Computing: Second European Across Grids* (pp.11-26), Cyprus.

Dick, R., Rhodes, D. & Wolf, W. (1998). TGFF: task graphs for free. *Proceedings of the 6th. International Workshop on Hardware/Software Co-design* (pp. 97-101), Seattle, WA, U.S.A.

Dogan, A., & Ozguner, F. (2004). Genetic algorithm based scheduling of meta-tasks with stochastic execution times in heterogeneous computing systems. *Cluster Computing, 7(2),* 177-190.

Dong, F. & Akl, S. (2007 PDCS) A mobile agent based workflow rescheduling approach for the Grid. *Proceedings of the Nineteenth International Conference on Parallel and Distributed Computing and Systems,* Cambridge, MA, U.S.A.

Dong, F. & Akl, S. (2007) PFAS: a resource-performance-fluctuation-aware workflow scheduling algorithm for Grid Computing. *Proceedings of the 16th Heterogeneous Computing Workshop* (*HCW*) *in conjunction with IEEE International Parallel and Distributed Computing Symposium* (*IPDPS*) *2007,* Long Beach, CA, U.S.A.

Dong, F. & Akl, S. (2008). A QoS guided workflow scheduling algorithm in the Grid. *Proceedings of the Grid Computing and Applications 2008* (pp.22-27), Las Vegas, NV, U.S.A.

Fukuda, M. & Smith, D. (2006). UWAgents: A Mobile Agent System Optimized for Grid Computing *Proceedings of the Grid Computing and Applications 2006* (pp. 107-113), Las Vegas, NV, U.S.A.

Fukuda, M. Tanaka, Y., et al. (2003). A mobile-agent-based PC Grid. *Proceedings of Autonomic Computing Workshop in conjunction with the International Symposium on High Performance Distributed Computing* (*HPDC*) *2003* (pp. 142-150), Seattle, WA, U.S.A .

Hawkeye. http://www.cs.wisc.edu/condor/hawkeye/

HPCVL. http://www.hpcvl.org/

Li, H. (2007 CCGrid). Performance evaluation in Grid Computing: a modeling and prediction perspective. *Proceedings of the 1st IEEE TCSC Doctoral Symposium in conjunction with CCGrid 2007* (pp. 869-874), Rio de Janeiro, Brazil.

Li, H., Groep, D., & Wolters, L. (2007). Mining performance data for Metascheduling decision support in the Grid. *Future Generation Computer Systems, 23(1)*, 92-99.

Ludtke, S., Baldwin, P., & Chiu. W. (1999) EMAN: semiautomated software for high resolution single-particle reconstructions. *Journal of Structural Biology, 128(1)*, 82-97.

McGough, A., Afzal, A., et al. (2005). Making the Grid predictable through reservations and performance modeling. *The Computer Journal, 48(3)*, 358–368.

Morris, P. (1994). *The Management of Projects*, Thomas Telford, p.18.

Negri, A., Poggi, A., et al. (2006). Dynamic grid tasks composition and distribution through agents. *Concurrency and Computation: Practice & Experience, 18(8)*, 875-885.

Neo, H., Lin, Q. & Liew, K. (2005). A Grid-based mobile agent collaborative virtual environment. *Proceedings of International Conference on Cyberworlds 2005* (pp. 335-339), Singapore.

Quan, D., & Altmann, J. (2007). Mapping of SLA-based workflows with light communication onto Grid resources. *Proceedings of the 4th International Conference on Grid Service Engineering and Management* (pp.135-145), Leipzig, Germany.

Sacerdoti, F., Katz, M., et al. (2003). Wide area cluster monitoring with Ganglia. *Proceedings of IEEE International Conference on Cluster Computing 2003* (pp. 289-298), Hong Kong, China.

Sakellariou, R. & Zhao, H. (2004). A low-cost rescheduling policy for efficient mapping of workflows on Grid systems. *Scientific Programming, 12(4)*, 253-262.

Shestak, V., Smith, J., Maciejewski, A. & Siegel, H. (2006 ICPP). A stochastic approach to measuring the robustness of resource allocations in distributed systems. *Proceedings of the International Conference on Parallel Processing (ICPP 2006)* (pp. 459-470). Columbus, OH, U.S.A.

Shestak, V., Smith, J., Maciejewski, A. & Siegel, H. (2006). Iterative algorithms for stochastically robust static resource allocation in periodic sensor driven clusters. *Proceedings of the 18th IASTED International Conference on Parallel and Distributed Computing and Systems* (pp. 166-174), Dallas, TX, U.S.A.

Shestak, V., Smith, J., Smith, et al. (2006 PDPTA). Greedy approaches to stochastic robust resource allocation for periodic sensor driven distributed systems. *Proceedings of the 2006 International Conference on Parallel and Distributed Processing Techniques and Applications (PDPTA)* , Las Vegas, NV, U.S.A.

Sugavanam, P., Siegel, H., et al. (2007). Robust static allocation of resources for independent tasks under makespan and dollar cost constraints. *Journal of Parallel and Distributed Computing, 67(4)*, 400-416.

Sulakhe, D., Rodriguez, A. et al. (2005). Gnare: an environment for grid-based high-throughput genome analysis. *Proceedings of IEEE International Symposium on Cluster Computing and the Grid (CCGrid)2005* (pp. 455-462), Cardiff, UK.

Topcuouglu, H., Hariri, S. & Wu, M. (2002). Performance effective and low-complexity task scheduling for heterogeneous computing. *IEEE Transactions on Parallel and Distribution Systems, 13(3)*, 260-274.

Wieczorek, M., Prodan, R. & Fahringer, T. (2005). Scheduling of scientific workflows in the Askalon Grid environment. *SIGMOD Record, 34(3):56–62.*

Wu, M., & Sun, X. (2004). *Self-adaptive task allocation and scheduling of meta-tasks in non-dedicated heterogeneous computing. International Journal of High Performance Computing and Networking, 2(1)*, 186-197.

Yang, L., Schopf, J. Foster, I. (2003). Conservative scheduling: using predicted variance to improve scheduling decisions in dynamic environments. *Proceedings of ACM/IEEE Supercomputing 2003* (pp.31-46), Phoenix, AR, U.S.A.

Yu, H., Marinescu, D., et al. (2006). Plan switching: an approach to plan execution in changing environments. *Proceedings of the 15th HCW in conjunction with IPDPS 2006,* Rhodes Island, Greece.

Yu, Z. & Shi, W. (2007). An adaptive rescheduling strategy for Grid workflow applications. *Proceedings of IEEE IPDPS 2007,* Long Beach, CA, U.S.A.

Zeng, L., Benatallah, B., et al. (2004). Chang: QoS-aware middleware for web services composition. *IEEE Transactions on Software Engineering, 30(5)*, 311-327.

ENDNOTE

[1]   As the performance is now a random variable, a capital letter is used to represent it in this section.

Chapter II
Dynamic Network Optimization for Effective QoS Support in Large Grid Infrastructures

Francesco Palmieri
Università degli Studi di Napoli Federico II, Italy

Ugo Fiore
Università degli Studi di Napoli Federico II, Italy

ABSTRACT

In the past decade there has been a remarkable change from mainframe-based centralized computing to a distributed client/server approach. In the coming decade this trend is likely to continue with further shifts towards network centric collaborative computing. At the state of the art, the key technology in collaborative computing is the computational grid paradigm. Like an electrical power grid, the computational Grid will aim to provide a steady, reliable source of computing power. More precisely, the term grid is now adopted to designate a common computational and/or data processing infrastructure built on distributed resources, highly heterogeneous (in their role, computing power and architecture), interconnected by heterogeneous communication networks and communicating through some basic services realized by a middleware stratum that offers a reliable, simple, uniform and often transparent interface to its resources such that an unaware user can submit jobs to the Grid just as if he/she was facing a large virtual supercomputer, so that large computing endeavors, consisting of one or more related jobs or tasks, are then transparently distributed over the network on the available computing resources. Such a workload distribution strategy, that is, to balance the tasks on different idle computers on the underlying networks, is the most important functionality in computational Grids, usually provided at the service level of the grid software infrastructure.

INTRODUCTION

In the past years there has been a remarkable change from mainframe-based centralized computing to a distributed client/server approach and now, this trend is likely to evolve with further shifts towards network centric collaborative computing. At the state of the art, the key technology in collaborative computing is the computational grid paradigm. Like an electrical power grid, the computational Grid will aim to provide a steady, reliable source of computing power. More precisely, the term grid is now adopted to designate a common computational and/or data processing infrastructure built on distributed resources, highly heterogeneous (in their role, computing power and architecture), interconnected by various communication networks and communicating through some basic services realized by a middleware stratum that offers a reliable, simple, uniform, and often transparent interface to its resources. An unaware user can submit jobs to the Grid just as if he/she was facing a large virtual computing cluster, so that large computing endeavors, consisting of one or more related jobs or tasks, are then transparently distributed over the network on the available computing resources. Such a workload distribution strategy, that is, to balance the tasks on different idle computers on the underlying networks, is the most important functionality in computational Grids, usually provided at the resource management services layer of the grid software infrastructure. Although much progress has been made towards grid scheduling and resource management technologies, the area that is still underdeveloped is the link between grid applications and underlying network technologies which is now the most compelling requirement to make grids truly effective. In fact, the quality and consistency of the underlying transport network services become critical success factors for the overall Grid infrastructure, since many up-to-date Grid applications are now highly network-dependent with more demanding requirements in areas such as data access or interactivity, and hence the submitted jobs can be subject to failure if the network connections between the computing and service nodes do not perform as required. More precisely, modern Grid applications require high bandwidth and quality of service (QoS) guaranteed (low latency, packet loss and jitter) end-to-end connections between Grid resources in different network domains, owned by different providers that have to cooperate in a coordinated manner in order to provide these connections on their fiber optic infrastructures. The bandwidth, delay and/or packet loss guarantees requested in a specific service class can be defined either in a deterministic or statistical way. Deterministic QoS guarantees promise an absolute end-to-end bound for every packet carried by a specific connection. On the other hand, with statistical guarantees, the end-to-end bound is accompanied with a small probability of violation. For applications that can tolerate occasional bound violations, statistical guarantees can help to reduce the resource requirement for each connection. For instance an end-to-end connection carrying sensitive traffic between a couple of Grid applications might require average bandwidth of 10Mbps, and premium service class, defined by near zero packet loss, per-packet delay smaller than 50ms, and probability of violating the delay bound smaller than 10^{-3}. Traditionally, the Grid control and management logic has been based on a partially or totally network unaware approach in which the computational resources can be chosen from different sites participating to the Grid without inspecting their connectivity characteristics, since Grid service infrastructure had no visibility of the underlying network. This may lead to a virtual cluster with proper computational power, but due to the lack of bandwidth or QoS features, the data distribution may inconsiderately use the network, leading to inefficiency. On the other side, an active network-aware approach needs a strict integration between the Grid job scheduling and resource management logic, the requesting application and the network entities that offer the connectivity services to the involved Grid nodes, to take all the scheduling and resource allocation decisions based on network related information. To achieve this we have to abstract and encapsulate the available optical network resources into manageable and dynamically provisioned grid entities in order to meet the complex demand patterns of grid applications and to optimize the overall network utilization. More precisely, we need to consider network resources as key grid resources that can be managed and controlled like any other grid resource. Hence, a new grid middleware stratum that can make optimized use of the network as a virtual coordinated resource has to be developed. Such middleware must be responsible for managing, coordinating, allocating and scheduling advance resource reservations for all the geographically available grid resources (network links, computing clusters, storage, scientific instruments, etc.) and must handle and control the establishment of optical connections with the necessary bandwidth and interface with cluster schedulers to make advance reservations. From a grid application perspective, all types of resources may be required to meet its computational needs. Specifically, application requests may be for immediate or for advance reservations. In the immediate reservations case, the application requests resources from the grid middleware for immediate use. In the advance reservation case, the requests are for a future time; i.e., there is a time period between the request arrival and the time of the resource reservation. In fact, immediate reservations can be viewed as a special case of advance reservations, with zero time periods between the request arrival and the time of the resource reservation. We believe that in a modern optical grid advance reservations are a necessity because they are the best available mechanism to guarantee the availability of resources with the required QoS. Here, advanced network control plane services like GMPLS or ASTN can be used to acquire committed bandwidth, specific transport features or Quality of Service (QoS) for applications exchanging data. In GMPLS-based optical transport networks (Mannie, 2004), the Lambda or Label Switch Paths (LSPs) mechanism may provide multi-granularity traffic/QoS engineered optical flows, with a suite of mechanisms that assign a generalized label to bundle consecutive wavelengths, such as a Waveband LSP or a Fiber LSP. Thus, based on the above architecture, the demands from application QoS embedded in advance reservation requests can be mapped to service constraints in optical transport networks, by realizing the proper end-to-end Label Switched Paths on the transport domain, triggered by the middleware layer and implemented as Grid services. Advance reservations of network resources are especially useful in environments that require reliable allocations of various resource types at different locations. Such co-allocations are necessary in order to assure that all the resources required are available at a given time. Each request has a duration and a scheduling window, i.e. the time period within which the requestor would like to make a reservation and this period becomes the lifetime of a specific LSP ensuring an end-to-end connection between the involved Grid resources. Since these LSP are dynamically created or destroyed as needed by Grid application to handle end-to-end connections between communicating tasks, the utilization of network resources needs optimization. The are many approaches in the literature to network-aware resource optimization in grid environments, involving all the techniques in the arsenal of optimization (utility based, knapsack, genetic, tabu search, simulated annealing, economic models), but even dynamic algorithms only take into account the allocation of resource to newly arriving requests, assuming that the existing allocations are fixed and cannot be modified. Requests that cannot be serviced within the scheduling window are blocked or optionally delayed and scheduled as soon as network or computing/storage resources become available. In comparison to the immediate reservations, advance reservations generally degrade resource utilization and the acceptance rate due to resource fragmentation. However, the information on future traffic, though it is not complete, since immediate requests can arrive at any moment, permits to better schedule periodic network re-optimizations, achieving the benefits deriving from almost static optimized resource re-allocation while at the same time limiting the impact on services. This can be improved by introducing some flexibility in network resource management through the re-optimization of the end-to-end connection topology by rescheduling the connection reservation requests. This can be done in two ways: either by changing the assigned LSP paths only or by changing both the path and the start time. The latter is not very desirable as it involves task relocation or at least renegotiating the time with users, and in view of this we will not be considering it in our work. While it is not generally worthwhile to consider preemption and relocation of active tasks, which should then restart from the last available checkpoint, re-routing existing LSPs can certainly an option, because users at both ends of an LSP know that they are connected but they have no knowledge of the actual routing of the LSP. This work is focused on a hybrid scenario: connections are ordinarily routed dynamically using one of the available algorithms for online routing, but occasionally the network re-optimizes existing LSPs, re-routing them in order to improve load balancing and thus the ability to efficiently accept further connections. Re-optimization should only be done when the benefits arising from it justify the risks. Furthermore, careful planning that is required in order to prevent disruption of the services carried over the provisioned connections. The new path must first be completely set up before traffic is re-routed on it, and only then the old path can be torn down, so that the impact on the service is minimized. This requires a complex search and analysis to select, among all the re-routings that result in the same improvement in the network efficiency, the one which minimizes the cost of re-routing. In addition, in an advance reservation scenario, re-optimization can be performed on different sets of connections, i.e., existing connections or pending connections. Each alternative has advantages and pitfalls. The latter is simpler because it has no impact on existing connections, but the overall benefits that can be attained are limited. The former, on the other side, can achieve substantial bandwidth savings but is far more complex. In our work we apply re-optimization to all connections.

OPTICAL TRANSPORT NETWORKS FOR HIGH PERFORMANCE GRIDS

From the earliest days of their design and development, Grids have always been based on networking services, especially those built on the Internet technologies, both for sharing computational load and distributed data access. However, high performance Grid applications are raising communication and data exchange requirements which the Internet can't meet, neither at the present nor even in the foreseeable future. In fact, traditional packet switching is a proven efficient technology for transporting burst transmission of short data packets, e.g., for remote login, consumer oriented email and web applications. It is not sufficiently adaptable to meet the challenge of large-scale data as Grid applications require. Making forwarding decisions every 1500 bytes is sufficient for emails or 10k -100k web pages. This is not the optimal mechanism if we have to cope with data size of six to nine orders larger in magnitude. For example, copying 1.5 Terabytes of data using packet switching requires making the same forwarding decision about 1 billion times, over many routers along the path. Consequently, the use of the available optical fiber and Wavelength Division Multiplexing (WDM) switching technology for large scale Grid infrastructures is now the most attractive proposition ensuring the proper QoS guarantees and huge amounts of cheap bandwidth through dedicated transparent end-to-end connections. Obviously, QoS guarantees come at a price - the involved network providers need to dedicate a portion of physical network resources (such as link capacity, buffer space and computation resources) for each connection. From network service provider's point of view, the network resources need to be utilized in the most efficient manner possible. Thus the central problem becomes the assignment of available resources to each connection needed by Grid entities so as to satisfy the following two objectives:

- The QoS guarantee for each end-to-end connection must be satisfied.
- The number of connections admitted over the long term is maximized.

The first objective is to satisfy the performance requirements for each connection. The second objective is to essentially maximize the overall network usage efficiency which in turn tries to take the most from the investment in the transport infrastructure. In this respect, WDM-based networks, according to their great success in revaluing investments in optical fiber geographical infrastructures, have been great enablers of the World Wide Web fulfilling the capacity demand generated by the ever increasing Internet traffic. In a similar way optical technologies are expected to play an important role in creating an efficient infrastructure for supporting modern data-intensive Grid applications (Foster & Kesselman, 2004). According to the WDM paradigm, the optical transmission spectrum is carved up into a number of non-overlapping wavelength bands, each supporting a single communication channel operating at whatever protocol or rate one desire (protocol and bit-rate transparency). Thus, by allowing multiple independent channels to coexist on a single fiber, we can make the most of available optical infrastructures, with the corresponding challenges being the design and development of appropriate network architectures, control plane protocols, and algorithms that should make available such connectivity resources to Grid applications. New generation WDM networks are based on automatically configurable switching nodes, often called Optical Cross-Connects (OXCs) operating transparently at the wavelength layer, to set up and tear down end-to-end lightpaths that can traverse multiple physical links and essentially create a virtual topology, available to the requiring applications, on top of the physical network topology. In order to achieve connectivity resources in terms of bandwidth and quality of service when and where Grid applications need, is necessary to perform advanced provisioning of end-to-end high performance dedicated "virtual circuits" through the network, creating the equivalent of high-occupancy-vehicle expressway lanes, implemented on properly reserved wavelengths on the available optical transport infrastructures. This introduces in alternative to the "reserved" bandwidth concept, very common on packet based networks, a new "dedicated" bandwidth paradigm together with a new Grid computing architecture, called the Optically-empowered Grid or Lambda-Grid (De Fanti et al., 2003). Lambda-Grids are Grid infrastructures that are interconnected by ultra-high-speed networks that can be directly controlled by applications through specific resource managers, often called optical *Network resource Brokers*. Typically the unit of control is a dedicated wavelength (often called a *Lambda*) traversing multiple fiber links and optical switching nodes realizing an end-to-end transmission channel or lightpath. When the network control plane provides the capability of performing advance reservation of entire new lightpaths or QoS-bound communication channels (LSPs) on already existing lightpaths, the data-intensive applications can be guaranteed to achieve certain bandwidth and quality of service in specific time slots. This can be considered the most promising mechanism to meet all the future real-time data transfer demands from Grid applications. Lightpath or LSP setup requests can be known a priori (seldom, only in case of a totally static job execution plan), or arrive unexpectedly together with each job submitted for running on the Grid, with known bandwidth demand and holding times declared according to an advance reservation policy. In presence of dynamic connection requests, each lightpath must be computed on-line at the arrival of each request based on the current network state, so when coping with this class of problems, we always need special support from control plane protocols to obtain up-to-date information about the global network layout in terms of link status and resource availability.

THE NETWORK-AWARE GRID

Network elements such as routers/switches, end devices, and physical links are essential for creating connections between end-users in any kind of distributed organization. A Grid network infrastructure is essentially an overlay network over several physical networks for connecting end systems belonging to a Virtual Organization. As such, connectivity between end systems is an essential component that glues the infrastructure together. Thus, in the modern Grid scenario, the network turns out to be a resource as important as computation and/or storage. As such, the Grid requires the same level of control towards subsets of well-defined amounts of network resources for the entire duration of a specific Grid task. A chief goal of this control is to turn the network into a virtualized resource that can be acted upon and controlled by other layers of software, realizing a service plane available to applications. Such service plane is typically concerned with path allocation, optimization, monitoring, and restoration across one or more domains. The service plane must be designed to be extensible from the ground up. It should allow adaptation of various control plane interfaces and abstract their network view, or element set, into its service portfolio. In other words, the network becomes a Grid managed resource much as computation or storage, and the service virtualization is layered upon the available optical network control plane technology in the IP/optical environment. Here, GMPLS signaling protocols such as RSVP-TE (Berger, 2003) or CR-LDP (Jamoussi et al., 2002), routing protocols such as OSPF-TE (Kompella et al., 2005), and Link Management Protocol (LMP) (Fredette & Lang, 2005), can realize the needed control plane framework. The routing computation can be based on Constrained-based Shortest Path First (CSPF) with network state information. Thus, based on this architecture, the demands from application QoS layer can be mapped to service constraints in optical transport networks through middleware QoS layer and implemented as Grid services. The Network Resource Broker (NRB), which manages network resources and supports advance reservations, is the key ingredient of the above service plane. The NRB is the unique middleware component that directly interfaces the optical network. It is responsible for path computation and wavelength assignment on the requested end-to-end lightpaths and it keeps the advance reservation link/wavelength timetable. It also monitors the network and advertises the available capabilities to the Grid by providing up-to-date status of the network resources to the grid applications through specific middleware-layer interfaces and components. The NRB performs the network resource allocation by interfacing with the specific control plane, i.e., each network domain may have a dynamic control mechanism such as GMPLS. The NRB may implement mechanisms for restoration and recovery of lightpaths in case of failures. It also can enforce policies and access control information. In a shared-lambda environment, the enforcement of policies is crucial for successful operation. Each NRB has a policy engine that gives grid administrators control over how networking resources are shared.

The signaling scheme for triggering LSP or lightpath set-up and reserving the needed bandwidth or wavelength resources along the path may be directly mutuable by the above TE-RSVP protocol. To make a reservation request, the source node needs the path and the bandwidth that it is trying to reserve. Thus, the request is sent by the source along with path information. At every hop, the involved node determines if adequate bandwidth is available in the onward link. If the available bandwidth is inadequate, the node rejects the requests and sends a response back to the source. If the bandwidth is available, it is provisionally reserved, and the request packet is forwarded on to the next hop in the path. If the request packet successfully reaches the destination, the destination acknowledges it by sending a reservation packet back along the same path. As each node in the path sees the reservation packet, it confirms the provisional reservation of bandwidth. In order to accept/reject an incoming request, every network entity must have full knowledge of the available and reserved bandwidth and wavelengths on each outgoing link. This implies that every node needs to run a distributed control-plane protocol that keeps up-to-date information about the complete network topology and available resources. The NRB discovers the network topology using control plane-level link state routing information such as OSPF-TE MIB data.

Since all the packets flowing through such LSPs o lightpath always belong, from the QoS point-of view, to a single forwarding class, there is no need to indicate the forwarding class of each packet in a specific field of the GMPLS header, because it can be directly derived from the label or wavelength information. This approach to QoS support on GMPLS is known as L-LSP (Label-Inferred LSP) based, to indicate that the service class information is inferred from the label. Stated in a more detailed way, each node that contributes to a hop into the L-LSPs, has packet scheduling logic that meets the QoS level defined by the class of service provisioned at each hop. Each node in the path examines the incoming label (or knows the incoming wavelength) and determines the QoS treatment for the encapsulated packet. Establishing an L-LSP with bandwidth reservation means that QoS and bandwidth requirements for the LSP are signaled at the LSP establishment time. Such signaled bandwidth requirements may be used at establishment time by the originating node to perform admission control depending on the reserved resources provisioned. The above LSPs with reserved resources are established using the above signaling protocols with a control-driven downstream-on-demand allocation approach, a scheme most commonly adopted in today's networks because providing more network control (all the label/lambda switching nodes belonging to the same LSP perform the label binding in an ordered manner) and better scalability in resource conservation. The TE-RSVP module first checks the link admission control module of the outgoing interface to the next hop on the path to try reserving the required bandwidth. If successful, the remaining capacity of the link is diminished by the requested bandwidth and a Label Request message is sent to the next hop in the explicit route of that LSP, which also checks its link admission control to setup a reservation and so forth until the egress node of the explicit connection route is reached. The egress node then sends a Label Mapping message back to the originating node – following the reverse explicit route path – with the label information. If the LSP setup fails due to insufficient resources along the explicit path, an error message is sent back to the originating node, and the administrator would then try another path. Once the LSP is setup, the requested bandwidth would then be available end-to-end on the explicit route for the "sum" of all aggregate traffic in all the supported classes.

THE NETWORK SERVICE INTERFACE

In our architecture the transparent on-demand advance reservation service is strictly related to basic connectivity services (like LSP set-up) that are totally hidden to the Grid application. A fundamental construct underlying many of the required attributes of the Grid interface is that of service virtualization that underpins the ability to map common service semantic behavior seamlessly onto native platform facilities. When network connection facilities are considered as resources to be managed on the Grid it becomes necessary to specify exactly what is meant for these resources, how to encapsulate them into

Grid services and how to manage these services. A Grid service is a self-contained, self described application that can be published, located and invoked over a network through properly designed interfaces. Viewing network entities as Grid Services allow us to consider the management of connections as a software transaction problem. To virtualize networks into software components, we formally divide Grid resources into two types:

1. Network Elements (NEs), e.g. switches, routers, optical cross connects, fibers or lambdas;
2. Other resources, e.g. Storage Elements or Computing Elements.

Type 2 resources are already modeled with Grid Services. We extend the same metaphor to the optical Network Elements and provide the network as a software component. The end-to-end bandwidth reservation Grid Service is constructed using these components. Such service abstracts the domain as a virtual switch device. Of special interest is the dynamic invocation interface to these different network management services and the use of the available abstraction mechanisms to publish and discover network resource characteristics. For these reasons we propose a new service oriented abstraction that, based on the existing Web Services architecture and built on the WSRF framework (Czajkowski et al., 2004), introduces a new network control layer, between the Grid customers and the network infrastructure decoupling the connection service provisioning from the underlying network infrastructure implementation. The interfaces offered by such abstraction must be compliant with the GGF's OGSA specification (Foster et al., 2002) and, in addition, conform to widely used Web Services standards (WSDL, SOAP, and XML). In the OGSA framework for Grid QoS infrastructure, network reservation services should be self-contained and modular and can be discovered, registered, monitored, instantiated, created and destroyed within a certain management framework. In such architecture, the QoS levels can be made up of three layers, i.e. the application QoS, middleware QoS, and networks QoS. The application QoS can support all kinds of Grid application and many interfaces. The middleware QoS layer can bridge the service mapping between the other two layers. It is made up of performance service, network service broker interface and policy management service. The performance service includes performance registry, monitor and adaptation service. The network service broker interface layer implement the network resource broker core functionalities including service registry, reservation and allocation manager. Finally, the policy management service is comprised of policy service, policy repository and admission control. All the services in Grid middleware layer can be realized by corresponding protocols and Web

Figure 1. The network service interface

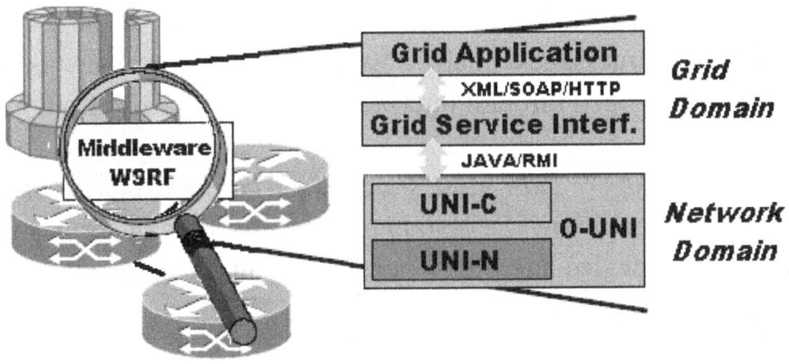

Service facilities, thus, the demands from the application layer and resource in the networks layer can be mapped correspondingly. Since this architecture is Web Services-based it can be integrated with anything based on WSRF standard. In our proposed schema we explicitly refer to the Globus Toolkit (Globus, 2004) for implementation. Communication with the top level service interface will take place via SOAP/HTTP (eventually secured by SSL) using well-defined extended WSDL interfaces. Requests and responses conform to Web Services specifications, i.e., they are SOAP messages, carried in HTTP envelopes and transported over TCP/IP connections. Access to the optical transport network control plane will be made available through an optical user-network interface (O-UNI) standardized by the Optical Internetworking Forum (OIF) (Saleh et al., 2000). The optical network services can be made available to the upper middleware layers through an O-UNI compliant programmatic interface library (i.e. Java/RMI), interfacing the client-side middleware services with the underlying routers and OXCs. A simple schematic representation of the above interface is sketched below.

The Web Service interfaces will be stateless and persistent, where data is not retained among invocations and services outlive their clients. In detail, the proposed abstractions, supporting the connectivity services concern:

- Connection Creation that allows an end-to-end transparent connection with the specific attributes to be created between a pair of Grid network access nodes
- Connection deletion that allows an existing connection to be deleted
- Connection Status Enquiry that permits the status of certain connection parameters to be queried
- Connection Modification which allows parameters of an already established connection to be modified.

Each request to the Network Resource Broker will be strongly authenticated against a Grid-wide PKI infrastructure through the GSI Generic Security Service (GSS) API (Linn, 1997) defining standard functions for verifying the identity of communicating parties, based on a Public Key Infrastructure where users authenticate to the grid using X.509 certificates.

The GRID Service Interface can announce its services by means of a Universal data base Description, Discovery and Integration (UDDI). About the specific interface implementation, the Extensible Markup Language (XML) appears to be the best candidate thanks to its representation format which can be useful to describe and transmit management information and Grid and network resources. Each network resource or node can be described by a set of XML interface elements. Every connection created will be characterized by the virtual channel or LSP tunnel (identified by the addresses engaged) that in turn is characterized by a set of attributes (Service class, Bandwidth available, and Bandwidth utilized). The ability of the Service Interface to hide the complexity of the service provisioning permits to define simple XML-based messages capable of supporting high level services. In particular we want to describe the messages exchanged through interface related to the Grid transport connection service:

- *netResourceQuery(host_src, host_dest, start_time, end_time, band, class):* is used by a Grid User or Application in order to know if a certain network resource or service is available. This method will trigger a network device interaction needed to gain a specific picture of the network resource usage between the involved nodes.

Figure 2. WSDL netResourceReservation interface

```
<message name="netResourceReservationRequest">
    <part name="hostSrc" type="xsd:string"/>
    <part name="hostDest" type="xsd:string"/>
    <part name="start_time" type="xsd:int"/>
    <part name="end_time" type="xsd:int"/>
    <part name="duration" type="xsd:int"/>
    <part name="band" type="xsd:int"/>
    <part name="class" type="xsd:string"/>
</message>

<message name="netResourceReservationResponse">
    <part name="ID" type="xsd:string"/>
</message>
```

- *netResouceReservation (host_src, host_dest, start_time, end_time, duration, band, class):* This is the main method realizing the end-to-end connections under the required bandwidth and QoS constraints. It provides a unique, overloaded interface for all the reservation services. The reservation process is asynchronous, the user ask for a service by specifying all the necessary parameters, and retrieves a specific token. After that, the re source broker synchronizes with the network control plane to create (if there are available resource) the required LSPs and activate the services.
- *netResourceReservationStatus (token):* allows the user to obtain information about the status of a Resource Reservation request, by identifying it through the token received at the reservation request time from the NRB.
- *netResourceRelease (token):* releases the unnecessary resources identified by token by removing the associated LSPs and policies.

The WSDL representation of the *netResouceReservation* interface is reported below.

The NRB supports these basic service functions within Grid middleware by relying on information models responsible for capturing structures and relationships of the involved entities. Every function is in turn mapped to a set of UNI primitives for network resource setting. Some commercial routers/OXCs are not yet provided with standard UNI but, in general, are equipped with an application programming interface (API) based on XML that routers can use to exchange information with the Network Resource Broker. Using this interface it is still possible to manage and monitor the available LSPs and relative traffic and performance parameters.

ADVANCE RESERVATION OF NETWORK RESOURCES

Modern Grid environments usually require a large number of different types of resources, e.g. computing power, storage space and QoS-guaranteed end-to-end connections, to be acquired simultaneously. To ensure the successful behavior of some data-intensive or time-critical running applications, they have to be reserved in advance, in a manner similar to the reservation of hotels, airlines, and rental cars for vacation travel. Advance reservation is a paradigm widely used in networks supporting advanced QoS features, usually achievable through the sophisticated explicit routing and traffic engineering facilities offered by the MPLS technology. Furthermore, advance reservation may now be considered an essential resource management complement in modern Grid computing environments (Chen & Vicat-Blanc Primet, 2006; Wu et al., 2005) where bandwidth resources have to be reserved for a fixed period of time in the future, usually referred to as the *bookahead* time. The time between issuing such a request and the actual start of the transmission, referred as the *reservation* time, may vary from short intervals, for example ten minutes, to relatively long time periods, e.g., weeks. Upon receiving an advance reservation request, the Grid service provider must notify the user within a certain period of time before the scheduled start of the transmission, known as the notification interval, whether it has been accepted or declined. In addition to increasing its admission chances, the strongest motivation to issue an advance instead of an immediate reservation is that it expects a reply from the network resource broker whether the reservation request can be admitted. If the network resource broker does not answer in due time or as it sees fit, the concept of planning reliability is foiled. Therefore, we employ the above notification interval concept, meaning that once a user issues a request to a resource broker, the latter must respond with an accepted or declined message within this notification interval. In case the reservation time falls short of the notification interval, this reply must be made at once.

The terms reservation and request are sometimes confused. Generally speaking, the former refers to the actual process of allocating a path within the network, while the latter term merely denotes the request for such an allocation, regardless whether it has yet been accepted. The advance reservation approach yields several benefits for the overall Grid control logic usually handled by one or more network resource brokers. On one hand, the involved network resource broker gains additional information about the future traffic pattern and can decide which connection requests to admit in order to maximize the profit from the admitted connections, on the other it has an ample scope for dealing with each individual request, e.g., it can be queued when allocating the inquired resources is temporarily impossible and the designated path on which the transmission is to be routed can be changed for any future point of time without having to put up with any rerouting costs, as long as the connection has not yet been set up. Furthermore, the decision whether to accept or to decline it can be delayed until the notification interval is reached; this time can meanwhile be used to free up resources for the request, which otherwise would need to be declined. Therefore, we can strive to not distribute the current network load more evenly but also the load requested to be allocated for any future point in time. However, a re-optimization cycle can only be performed for time spans where the demand matrix is constant; hence our goal is to put a bound on the number of changes in the demand matrix. We will refer to such a time frame with a constant demand matrix as a time slot. More precisely, the flexibility of network-aware advance resources reservation across a distributed Grid infrastructure introduces a new temporal dimension into

Figure 3. Advance reservation timing scenario

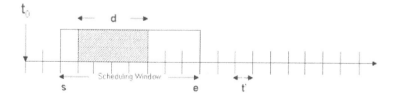

the overall resource allocation problem. In the network resource advance reservation model adapted as a reference in our work the time is slotted with a slot size equal to t' and we consider each advance reservation request R for an end-to-end connection between any two nodes as defined by the following parameters:

R = (source node, destination node, s, e, d, b)

where d is the reservation duration, and s and e are the starting and ending time of the *scheduling window* and b is the requested bandwidth. The scheduling window defines the time period within which the requesting application would like to make a resource reservation and issues a specific request to the network resource broker.

Such window must be bigger than the reservation duration d. Thus the network resource broker must check whether a path is available during interval $[s + t, s + t + d]$ where $t = 0, 1, 2, \ldots, e - s - d$. This is an online scheduling problem because the requests arrive dynamically, and for each request R the broker must compute a path and then check whether a wavelength on each link of this path can be reserved for duration d within the scheduling window $[s, e]$. The broker allocates a wavelength on each link along a path from the source to the destination nodes. If a wavelength along the path for the specified period of time is not available, another path has to be determined. In order to do this, the resource broker needs to maintain a schedule of the reservations called the reservation table. It contains all current and future reservations and is used to search for available resources for new advance reservations. This means coping with a traffic model where the setup and teardown times of the demands are known in advance. It is known as the scheduled traffic model (Kuri et al., 2003). There can be a fixed window or a flexible window with this model. The start and end times of the connection cannot be altered in the fixed window model, but with the flexible approach the start and end times can slide within a larger window. Integer linear program formulations and algorithms have been proposed to solve these problems (Kuri et al., 2003; Jaekel, 2006). In our work we will consider dynamic end-to-end connection requests that belong to a flexible scheduling window. We have developed several strategies for searching the reservation schedule to determine whether a new request R can be accepted. These strategies use a combination of different scheduling decisions and search techniques. However, our objective is to determine an "almost optimal" scheduling algorithm that minimizes the blocking probability, i.e., the probability of not scheduling a request within its window, minimizes fragmentation in the usage of each wavelength/lightpath and maximizes network utilization. We only consider flexible advance reservations as they have lower blocking probability than the fixed advance reservation model (Burchard et al., 2003; He et al. 2006). We consider two categories of advance scheduling. In the first, a connection request is blocked if it cannot be scheduled within its requested flexible window. In the second, requests are not blocked, but rather delayed and scheduled at the first available time instance, which may be outside the requested window.

MANAGING END-TO-END BANDWIDTH RESERVATION

The Network Resource Broker strives to utilize the network resources to its maximum potential by allocating available resources in an optimal fashion, whereas optimality depends on the objective function, for example admitting the maximum number of advance reservation requests, maximizing the total allocated bandwidth or maximizing the total profit gained from accepting requests. Our objective is to determine a scheduling policy capable to route each incoming advance connection reservation request dynamically while minimizing the probability that such request will be refused due to lack of available network resources and maximizing through periodic network re-optimizations the overall Grid throughput. We employ a specific routing and bandwidth reservation algorithm to allocate paths to newly arriving advance reservation requests.

Upon receiving an advance reservation request R defined as the above 6-uple, the network resource broker first of all acknowledges its receipt. Subsequently, it tries to allocate resources for the request on a per-slot-basis, by triggering a path setup from the origin to destination nodes by using an available signalling scheme. All the nodes in the path, when receive the request, run a Dijkstra-based (Lewis & Denenberg, 1991) CSPF algorithm to synchronize their view, calculate the new network topology and provisionally reserve the requested bandwidth, as follows:

- For each time slot t_i with $s \leq t_i \leq e$, the network resource broker triggers the computation of the best (or more precisely the minimum cost) path P from the originating node to the destination node with a capacity $c(P) \geq b$. For this purpose, if $N = (V,E)$ is the mathematical representation of the network, all the edges whose residual capacity is smaller than b are removed from the graph N generating an auxiliary graph $N^* = N \setminus \{e \in E \mid c(e) - x(e) < b\}$ where $c(e)$ is the capacity of the edge e and $x(e)$ is the bandwidth already allocated on e.

- The constrained Dijkstra's algorithm is run on N^* starting from the originating node, generating a shortest-path P to the destination node with a minimum capacity of b in case such a path exists. A specific additional cost factor may be associated with each edge in addition to the capacity in order to improve the best path discovery process. The most common additional edge cost is the propagation delay. However, in order to balance the load in the network we can use a link cost that is based on current and future link usage. In this case we start with all the links having a cost of 1. As lightpaths are reserved, the link cost is incremented by the number of slots reserved on that link. The cost is decreased after the request is serviced. Hence the weights only reflect the current and future utilization of the link.

- The broker repeats the above algorithm for all time slots between s and e relevant for the given request. If multiple paths $P_s \ldots P_e$ with a minimum capacity of b exist for all the time slots, the request can be allocated. In this case, the broker reserves a bandwidth of b for all time slots on the respective path computed for that slot.

- In the other case, we have encountered a slot where no path with the required bandwidth exists while iterating over the time slots. Therefore, it is momentarily impossible to accept the reservation request. The network resource broker queues the request in case the notification interval has not yet expired, otherwise the issuing user must be notified that the request had to be declined.

- If a reservation request needs to be queued, it is stored in a global repository of pending requests. Apart from this, the request is also associated with each time slot $s \leq t_i \leq e$ along with its respective state information (accepted, declined or pending). Such information will be used during the following periodic re-optimization phase. Re-optimization must also work on a time slotted basis. Clearly, time slots that have reservation requests pending for admission can benefit from re-optimization more than those for which no such requests are in the queue. However, if there are no pending requests for a slot, it still makes sense to optimize the slot since the load redistribution will still free up resources. These resources can in turn be occupied by newly arriving requests.

REOPTIMIZATION

In order to keep the connection reject ratio as low possible, efficient network flow routing algorithms have been studied extensively for immediate reservation networks (Kar, Kodialam & Lakshman, 2000). As reservation requests arrive one-by-one, the desired quick connection setup leads to an online allocation problem. This problem can be tackled with sophisticated routing algorithms which however do not scale well with the growth in network size. On the other hand, the use of simple and scalable path selection algorithms would cause routing inefficiencies within the network leading to "stranded" capacity.

Whatever the RWA algorithm that is used, the resources dedicated to serve each new connection request are computed according to the current state of the network, which is the result of the routing of the existing connections. Effective algorithms owe their performance to the fact that they aim at keeping network load as balanced as possible, which in turn means that as many routing alternatives as possible are kept open at any given time. This is necessarily the result of some estimation on the distributions of forthcoming requests. That estimation may presume that future requests will adhere to a uniform or Poisson distribution, or that future requests repeat the pattern delineated from the currently provisioned demands. However, as the network and traffic evolve, the actual distribution of requests and their sequence of appearance may substantially drift from the estimates, and the network may become unbalanced, with an uneven load distribution. As a result, routing of the existing connections becomes suboptimal, therefore creating opportunities for improvements in network efficiency.

The idea of re-optimization is by no means new in telecommunications. Carriers have been using reconfiguration over time to better manage their network assets and increase utilization on those assets, which in turn allowed them to defer investments on new infrastructure. Reconfiguration has also been used to provide better service performance, for example, by rerouting services over shortest paths if such paths become available.

In an advance reservation scenario, re-optimization can be performed on different sets of connections. One can either choose to only re-optimize existing connections, i.e. those that have been established, pending connections, i.e. existing reservations, or both. Leaving the existing connections unaffected is an attractive option, because it avoids any service disruption and eliminates the problem of re-routing active connections in a safe and efficient way. However, significantly larger improvements can be reached when re-optimization is applied to both existing and pending connections. In our time slotted re-optimizations approach, we only apply re-optimization to future connections, so that for each time slot, the re-optimization algorithms can only consider those connections whose starting time follows the time slot origin.

While the ability to reconfigure the logical connectivity is a promising feature, managing the lightwave network during the reconfiguration phase is a complex issue. Given a set of existing connections and of alternate routes for each of them, the order in which reconfigurations are carried out can have a substantial impact on the capacity that is needed in the process. The corresponding minimization problem, known as the Reconfiguration Sequencing Problem is indeed NP-hard (Xin, et al. 2006). Once that we have determined that re-optimization is beneficial, a re-optimization solution has to be found that involves minimal amount of disruption to the network, through the use of some heuristic.

In addition, the GMPLS and Optical networks "make-before-break" mechanism overcomes the challenges in terms of network services disruption due to traffic re-routing resulting from re-optimization. This involves setting up the new path (resource reservation) *before* re-routing traffic on it and only tearing down the resources on the old path *after* the service is fully established on the new path. Note

Figure 4. Re-optimization algorithm 1

Reoptimization Algorithm 1

Input: current network state for time slot t_i

Output: new network state for time slot t_i

1. begin
2.   for each request r in R_i
3.   compute a network state S where the resources used by connection r are freed
4.   find a feasible route for connection r in the state S, resulting in state S'
5.   if *goodness(S') > goodness(S)* then use S' as the current state
6.   end for
7. end

Figure 5. Re-optimization algorithm 2

Reoptimization Algorithm 2

Input: current network state for time slot t_i

Output: new network state for time slot t_i

1. begin
2.   sort all the requests in R_i in order of decreasing bandwidth
3.   for each request r
4.   find a feasible route for connection r in the state S, resulting in state S'
5.   end for
6. end

---

that the only disruption this may cause is packets arriving out of order for a small time period that it takes to switch over from one path to another.

An approach to combine dynamic online connection routing in a connection-oriented network with an offline optimization module which constantly rebalances the load in the network whenever a certain imbalance threshold is exceeded has been examined in (Bhatia, Kodialam & Lakshman, 2006). In this scenario, the network operator determines a rebalancing benefit indicating the amount of traffic that could additionally be routed if the current traffic were to be redistributed, by computing a measure of "network efficiency" before and after (a potential) re-optimization. If a threshold is exceeded, i.e. the benefits or re-optimizing the network exceeds the incurred costs of the flow rerouting, then re-optimization is performed.

The reoptimization algorithm is detailed in Figure 4, where: r is a connection request, R_i is the set of such connection requests starting in time slot t_i, S is a network state, *goodness(S)* is a measure for network quality of a network state. It should be noted that the initial state for time slot t_i is the final state from time slot t_{i-1}, and that, as detailed in the previous sections, a request can be satisfied only if suitable paths exist in all the time slots spanned by the connection lifetime.

An alternative approach, more demanding in terms of performance and impact on already routed connections but effective in diminishing request rejection is detailed in figure 5.

Algorithm 2 works by sorting the connection requests in order of decreasing bandwidth and makes no use of a ranking function. The main idea is that, once bandwidth-greedy connections are in place, the residual capacities on the network links can accommodate smaller requests, while the converse is obviously not true. This approach inherently privileges big connections over smaller ones, and as such, preference between Algorithm 2 and Algorithm 1 depends on the network provider's revenue optimization objectives.

RELATED WORK

Various projects around the world focus on building reconfigurable, dynamic, adaptable Grid infrastructures (Enlightened project; G-lambda project; Phosphorus project website; Global lambda integrated facility - glif, 2008). Advance reservation has been widely studied in several sectors of networking and applications. Zheng and Mouftah (2002) studied the design of RWA algorithms for different types of advance reservations and presented algorithms for requests having specific start time and specific duration (STSD), specific start time and unspecified duration (STUD) and Unspecified Start Time and Specified Duration (UTSD). Burchard, (2005) studied the properties of advance reservation and proposed an architecture for a bandwidth broker to improve the performance of a network based on the additional knowledge of these future reservations. The Globus Architecture for Reservation and Allocation (GARA) is a toolkit used to implement advance reservations of grid resources in Globus software (Foster, et al. 1999). Advance reservation of heterogeneous network paths in the context of Grid computing are investigated in (Curti et al, 2005), where a network resource hierarchy to integrate the path management with Grid information and authentication has also been proposed. In (Snell et al., 2000), several interesting performance issues of applying advance reservations to the meta-scheduling problem have been investigated. In (Wang et al., 2005), the authors proposed a sliding scheduled traffic model and a demand time conflict resolution algorithm to maximize resource usage in a network. In (He et al., 2006) the authors proposed a Flexible Advance Reservation Model (FARM) and described how to implement this model in the meta-scheduling problem.

CONCLUSION

In the next few years, we will almost certainly cross the "Tera" line in our high performance computing applications: Terabytes in data size, Teraflops in CPU processing, and Terabits/sec in network communication bandwidth. As a direct consequence, numerous challenges arise from supporting an adequate degree of service quality on a computing, storage and communication infrastructure with a capacity hundreds of times greater than the current one. In particular the actual Grid architectures based on traditional routed networks do not incorporate all the specialized guaranteed-QoS services and infrastructure capabilities needed by such data-intensive e-science applications, since these networks are generally designed to optimize the relatively small data flow requirements of consumer services on a common communication infrastructure, not conceived to effectively manage multiple large-scale and time-constrained data flows of several Terabytes. In addition, compared to predefined static demands, the unpredictable dynamic demands have a potential for optimization. To cope with the above problems, we propose a network-aware Grid architecture that addresses the complex integrated issues concerning the support of Quality of Service resources available at different sites and their related data transfers. The main strength in this architecture is the combination of a deterministic connection routing phase with a re-optimization phase. When an advance request for a connection with specific resource demands arrives, the network control plane computes a path with guaranteed resources so that the user can get a satisfactory response in terms of QoS. The re-optimization phase, needed when network load becomes uneven, re-organizes the connection topology by re-provisioning some connections (leaving their scheduled times unaffected), in order to achieve a better resource usage. This is a great performance improvement for Grid users who require both dynamic and deterministic scheduled data transfer services.

REFERENCES

Berger, L. (2003). Generalized Multi-Protocol Label Switching (GMPLS) Signaling Resource ReserVation Protocol-Traffic Engineering (RSVP-TE) Extensions, *IETF RFC 3473*.

Bhatia, R., Kodialam, S., & Lakshman, T. (2006). Fast network re-optimization schemes for mpls and optical networks. *Computer Networks, 50*(3), 317–331.

Burchard L.O., Heiss H.U., & De Rose C. (2003). Performance issues of bandwidth reservation for grid computing. In Proceedings of *15th Symposium on Computer Architecture and High Performance Computing.*

Burchard, L. O. (2005). Networks with advance reservations: Applications, architecture, and performance. *Journal of Network and Systems Management, 13*(4).

Chen, B. B., & Vicat-Blanc Primet, P. (2006). A flexible bandwidth reservation framework for bulk data transfers in grid networks, LIP ENS Lyon, *INRIA RESO Technical Report* - inria-00078069.

Curti, C., Ferrari, T., Gommans, L., Van Oudenaarde, S. et al. (2005). On advance reservation of heterogeneous network paths, *Future Generation Computer Systems, 21*(4), 525-538.

Czajkowski, K. et. al. (2004). From Open Grid Services Infrastructure to WS-Resource Framework: Refactoring and Evolution, Retrieved in 2008 from http://www.globus.org.

DeFanti, T., Brown, M., Leigh, J., Yu, O., He, E., Mambretti, J., Lillethun, D., & Weinberger, J. (2003). Optical Switching Middleware for the OptIPuter, *IEICE Tr. on Communications, E86-B*(8), 2263-2272.

Enlightened computing project website. (2008). Retrieved in 2008 from http://www.enlightenedcomputing.org.

Foster, I., & Kesselman, C. (2004). *The GRID2, Blueprint for a New Computing Infrastructure, 2nd Edition,* Elsevier Press.

Foster, I., Kesselman, C., Lee, C., Lindell, R., Nahrstedt, K., & Roy, A. (1999). A Distributed Resource Management Architecture that Supports Advance Reservations and Co-Allocation, Proceeding of *International Workshop on Quality of Service.*

Foster, I., Kesselman, C., Nick, J., & Tuecke, S. (2002). *The Physiology of the Grid: An Open Grid Services Architecture for Distributed Systems Integration.* Retrieved in 2008 from http://www.globus.org/research/papers/ogsa.pdf.

Fredette, A., & Lang, J. (2005). Link Management Protocol (LMP) for Dense Wavelength Division Multiplexing (DWDM) Optical Line Systems, *IETF RFC 4209.*

G-lambda project website. (2008). Retrieved in 2008 from http://www.g-Lambda.net.

Global lambda integrated facility (glif) website. (2008). Retrieved in 2008 from http://www.glif.is.

Globus Project Group. (2004). The Globus Toolkit, Retrieved in 2008 from http://www-unix.globus.org/toolkit/

He, E., Wang, X., & Leigh, J. (2006). A flexible advance reservation model for multi-domain WDM optical networks. In Proceedings of *IEEE GRIDNETS 2006*.

Jaekel, A. (2006). Lightpath scheduling and allocation under a flexible scheduled traffic model. In Proceedings of IEEE *GLOBECOM 2006*.

Jamoussi, B., et al. (2002). Constraint-Based LSP Setup Using LDP, *IETF RFC 3212*.

Jun Zheng, Z., & Mouftah, H. T. (2002). Routing and Wavelength Assignment for Advance Reservation in Wavelength-Routed WDM Optical Networks", Proceeding of *IEEE International Conference on Communications (ICC)*

Kar, S., Kodialam, M., & Lakshman, T. (2000). Minimum interference routing of bandwidth guaranteed tunnels with MPLS traffic engineering applications, *IEEE JSAC, 18*(12), 2566–2579.

Kompella, K. et al. (2005). OSPF Extensions in Support of Generalized MPLS, *IETF RFC 4203*.

Kuri, J., Puech, N., Gagnaire, M., Dotaro, E., & Douville, R. (2003). Routing and wavelength assignment of scheduled lightpath demands. *IEEE JSAC, 21*(8), 1231–1240.

Lewis, H. R., & Denenberg, L. (1991). *Data Structures and Their Algorithms*. Harper-Collins, New York.

Linn, J. (1997). Generic Security Service Application Program Interface, Version 2. *IETF RFC 2078*.

Mannie, E. (2004). Generalized multi-protocol label switching (GMPLS) architecture. *IETF RFC 3945*.

Phosphorus project website. (2008). Retrieved in 2008 from http://www.ist-phosphorus.eu.

Saleh, A., et al. (2000). Proposed Extensions to the UNI for Interfacing to a Configurable All-Optical Network, *OIF2000.278*.

Snell, Q., Clement, M., Jackson, D., & Gragory, C. (2000). The Performance Impact of Advance Reservation Meta-Scheduling, Proceeding of *IPDPS 2000 Workshop, JSSPP 2000*, Cancun, Mexico.

Wang, B., Li, T., Luo, X., Fan, Y., & Chunsheng, X. (2005). On service provisioning under a scheduled traffic model in reconfigurable WDM optical networks. Proceeding of *2nd International Conference on Broadband Networks*, 1:13 – 22.

Wu, L., Xing, J., Wu, C., & Cui, J. (2005). An adaptive advance reservation mechanism for grid computing, in PDCAT '05 Proceedings of the *Sixth International Conference on Parallel and Distributed Computing Applications and Technologies*. Washington, DC, USA: IEEE Computer Society, pp. 400–403.

Xin Y., Shayman, M., La, R., & Marcus, S. (2006). Reconfiguration of survivable MPLS/WDM networks, Proceedings of IEEE *GLOBECOM 2006*.

Chapter III
From Enabling to Ensuring Grid Workflows

Junwei Cao
Tsinghua University, China & Tsinghua National Laboratory for Information Science and Technology, China

Fan Zhang
Tsinghua University, China

Ke Xu
Tsinghua University, China

Lianchen Liu
Tsinghua University, China & Tsinghua National Laboratory for Information Science and Technology, China

Cheng Wu
Tsinghua University, China & Tsinghua National Laboratory for Information Science and Technology, China

ABSTRACT

Grid workflows are becoming a mainstream paradigm for implementing complex grid applications. In addition to existing grid enabling techniques, various grid ensuring techniques are emerging, e.g. workflow analysis and temporal reasoning, to probe potential pitfalls and errors and guarantee quality of services (QoS) at a design phase. A new state π calculus is proposed in this work, which not only enables flexible abstraction and management of historical grid system events, but also facilitates modeling and verification of grid workflows. Some typical patterns in grid workflows are captured and both static and dynamic formal verification issues are investigated, including structural correctness, specification satisfiability, logic satisfiability and consistency. A grid workflow modeling and verification environment, GridPiAnalyzer, is implemented using formal modeling and verification methods proposed in this work. Performance evaluation results are included using a grid workflow for gravitational wave data analysis.

INTRODUCTION

Grid Workflow QoS

Advance in technology has made collections of internet-connected computers a viable computational platform. Grids connecting geographically distributed resources have become a promising infrastructure for solving large problems. The definition of Grids has been redefined over time. Initially Grids were defined as an infrastructure to provide easy and inexpensive access to high-end computing (Foster, 1998). Then, it was refined in (Foster, 2001) as an infrastructure to share resources for collaborative problem solving. More recently, in (Foster, 2002) the Grid definition evolves into an infrastructure to virtualize resources and enable their use in a transparent fashion.

Grid workflows (Cao, 2003), a composition of various grid services according to prospective processes, have become a typical paradigm for problem solving in various e-Science domains (Yu, 2004), e.g. gravitational wave data analysis (Deelman, 2002). With increasing complexity of e-Science applications, how to implement reliable and trustworthy grid workflows according to specific scientific criteria is becoming a critical research issue. In addition to existing grid *enabling* techniques, e.g. job scheduling, workflow enactment and resource locating, various grid *ensuring* techniques are developed (Xu, 2006), e.g. data flow analysis and temporal reasoning.

Issues of quality of service (QoS) are of increasing importance to the success of those Grid-based applications. As defined by I. Foster in the three point checklist of the Grid (Foster, 2002), the Grid has to deliver to nontrivial qualities of service, relating for example to response time, throughput, availability, and security, and/or co-allocation of multiple resource types to meet complex user demands. This requirement is especially pronounced in experimental science applications such as the National Fusion Collaboratory (Keahey, 2004) and NEESgrid (Pearlman, 2004). Enabling such interactions on the Grid requires two related efforts: (1) the development of sophisticated resource management strategies and algorithms and (2) the development of protocols enabling structural negotiation for the use of those resources.

Most of existing research on grid workflow QoS is related to task scheduling. In the work described in (Spooner, 2005), application performance prediction is coupled with genetic algorithms for workflow management and scheduling with consideration of makespans and job deadlines. QoS guided min-min heuristic for grid task scheduling is also proposed in (He, 2003). Similar work can also be found in (Zhang, 2004) and (Brandic, 2005) for QoS aware grid workflow scheduling using performance prediction and optimization. In the grid standard organization, Global Grid Forum, a WS-Agreement model is proposed and defined in (Czajkowski, 2003). This provides an infrastructure to agreement-based application like (Keahey, K., Araki, T., et al. 2004) and (Zhang, 2004), within which QoS can be negotiated and obtained.

While all of above in common is that they show how task can be scheduled to improve efficiency of grid workflows, this work is dedicated to ensuring mechanisms on workflows as a whole. All of services in a workflow are guaranteed without redundancy and collision. Also how to make sure all services in a workflow is reachable and terminatable is another concern in this work. All these issues are modeled, verified and finally implemented using our environment, *GridPiAnalyzer*.

Grid Workflow Verification

As mentioned above, it is significant for grids to implement large scale heterogeneous resource sharing and accessing. How to ensure the correctness of design and implementation of grid workflows is a critical task. Though it is widely recognized that corporation of grid workflows are important, most of those research work are focused on grid enabling techniques, e.g. automatic execution, service binding and transaction processing. In the field of grid workflows, formal semantics, business logic verification and improving of verification performance needs to be solved. Obviously, these formal verification techniques can ensure the correctness of workflows as a whole and guarantee the fulfilling of users' demands.

These intrinsic characteristics provide several challenges to formal verification:

*   Difference in professional domains
*   Complexity of applications
*   Non-formalism semantics of grid workflows
*   Diversity in grid workflows models
*   Uniqueness of grid workflow criteria
*   Dynamicity of grid environments

IEEE defines correctness as: "……free from faults, meeting of specified requirements, and meeting of user needs and expectations" (Chen, 2006), and formal verification as: "it is mathematical verification methods to test whether those system model can meet requirements" (Clarke, 1999). Requirements here can be interpreted from two aspects. It can be restraints from the system model or business logics of users' expectations. According to definitions mentioned above, the article includes four aspects:

*   Structure verification
*   Verification of semantic restraints in grid workflows
*   Verification of users' demands
*   Consistent verification of business logics

The following problems have to be solved to verify above issues:

*   Formal theory and methods for grid workflow criteria
*   Formal semantics for existing grid workflow criteria
*   Dynamic/static verification methods
*   Implementation of a grid workflow modeling and analysis environment

Grid Workflow Modeling

Many models are introduced as grid workflows become indispensable component of grid networks. Different models have different descriptions and semantics. From different application domains, grid workflows can be categorized as follows:

*   XML-based tags, e.g. GridAnt (Amin, 2004), BPEL4WS (Andrews, 2003) and Gridbus workflows (Yu, 2004).

- Visual languages, e.g. Triana (Taylor, 2003), JOpera (Pautasso, 2006) and BPEL visual modeling.
- Customized script languages, e.g. Condor (Litzkow, 1998) DAGMan and Glue (Brown, 2007).

Different model specifications increase the complexity among various grid workflows. The integration of web and grid technologies is a clear trend since web service standards, e.g. Web Services Resource Framework (WSRF), are emerging. What's more, as BPEL4WS is gradually becoming the standard web execution language, more work is being related to the extension of BPEL4WS based on WSRF.

The motivation of our work is not to redefine a new model for grid workflows but rather try to find and propose a formal modeling and verification tool that works well with grid workflows. And hopefully the following can be achieved:

- Define critical characteristics and operations of grid workflows as well as bring out exact execution semantics of service interactions.
- Propose a uniform semantic basis as a bottom line for typical grid workflows.
- Verify grid workflows completely, automatically and effectively.

BACKGROUND

Introduction to π Calculus

π calculus (Milner, 1999) was initially introduced by Milner's work for modeling state/action hybrid systems since it is intrinsically mobile and combinable. Nowadays, this tool is efficiently used in the description of open communication systems and web/grid workflows as described in (Vander Aalst, 2005) and (Smith, 2003). The syntax of π calculus is as follows:

$$P ::= \sum_{i=1}^{n} \alpha_i . P_i \mid (new\ x)P \mid !P \mid P \mid Q \mid \phi P \mid A(y_1, ..., y_n) \mid 0$$
$$\alpha_i ::= \overline{x} < \tilde{y} > \mid x(\tilde{y}) \mid \tau$$
$$\phi ::= [x = y] \mid \phi \wedge \phi$$

The fundamental concept of π calculus is the names, which are used to express atomic interactive actions in a system. A system in π calculus evolves through the operators including *composition* '|', *choice* '+', *guard* '.', *match* '[]', *restriction* 'new' and *replication* '!'.

- An output action ($\overline{x} < \tilde{y} > .P$): This means outputting $\tilde{y}$ through $\overline{x}$ with system behaviors evolved into P. For example, in a communication system $\overline{x}$ can be considered as an output port and $\tilde{y}$ the output data.
- An input action ($x(\tilde{y}).P$): Intuitively, it means inputting $\tilde{y}$ through x with system behaviors evolved into P.
- A silent action ($\tau.P$): The system behavior evolves into P with internal actions instead of interactions with the environment.

- A composition (*P*|*Q*): Processes *P* and *Q* are independent, or synchronize with each other via an identical port.
- Choice (*P*+*Q*): Unpredictable execution of *P* or *Q*.
- March ([*x*=*y*]*P*): If *x* matches *y*, the system behavior evolves into *P*. Otherwise no actions happen.
- Restriction ((*new x*) *P*): *x* is a new name within the process *P*.
- Replication (!*P*): An infinite composition of process *P*.

Process algebras like π calculus have an explicit description of system behaviors and interactions, but state models are implicitly. For life-cycle management of system states, it is needed to enable modeling of:

- creation and destruction of states;
- access and update of states;
- association of states with system behaviors.

State π Calculus: Models and Operations

To address issues mentioned above, state π calculus is proposed in this work where a state *S* is defined as a finite set of system propositions *PROP*.

Definition 1 (system proposition). A system proposition *PROP*=(*ident*, *set*) ranged over a universe *D* is a pair, where *ident* is a unique identifier of *PROP* and *set* is the set of all valuations that make *PROP* to be true(*set*∈*D*).

Consequently, a state is $S=\{p_1, ..., p_n\}$, where p_i (*i*=1,..., *n*) is the system proposition *PROP* ranged over *D*. To enhance the capability for the states to express their relations among different components in a system, in state π calculus the identifier *ident* is defined by the following hierarchical structure: *ident::=atom | atom.ident*. Here *atom* indicates a symbolic constant value and '.' indicates a separator for the *atoms*. Consequently, a prefix/suffix relation is used to define the hierarchical structure of *ident*:

$$prefix : ident \times ident' \rightarrow ident'' \quad prefix(ident, ident') = ident'' \text{ IFF } ident = ident''.ident'$$
$$suffix : ident \times ident' \rightarrow ident'' \quad suffix(ident, ident') = ident'' \text{ IFF } ident = ident'.ident''$$

For example, a state *S*={(*AvailableSrv*, {*Srv₁*, *Srv₂*}), (*Srv₁.Status*, {*Active*}), (*Srv₂.Status*, {*Input_Pending*})} can be used to indicate that in state *S*, there are two available services *Srv₁* and *Srv₂* in the system, where *Srv₁* is running and *Srv₂* is waiting for its input. The identifier *Status* is the suffix of *Srv₁* and *Srv₂*. To complete the static semantics of states and system propositions, three functions are further defined:

- *range*: *PROP*→*set* returns the set of all constants that make *PROP* true;
- *eval*: *PROP*×*valueset*→{*true, false*} determines whether *PROP* is true for a given set of values;
- *proposition*: *S*×*ident*→{p_1, ..., p_m} returns corresponding system propositions given an identifier. Since semantics of *range* and *eval* are quite straightforward, here we focus on the implementa-

tion of *proposition*. Note that due to the hierarchical structure of identifiers *ident*, the function of *proposition* should also be able to get all system propositions identified by the prefix of an *ident*.

$$proposition(S, ident) = p \qquad \text{if } \exists p = (ident, set) \in S$$

$$proposition(S, *) = \{p_1, ..., p_k\} \qquad \text{if } \{p_1, ..., p_k\} = S$$

$$proposition(S, ident.*) = \{p_1, ..., p_m\} \qquad \text{if } \{p_1, ..., p_m\} \subset S,$$
$$\forall p \in \{p_1, ..., p_m\}, \exists\, ident' \text{ s.t. } suffix(p, ident) = ident'$$

$$proposition(S, *.ident) = \{p_1, ..., p_n\} \qquad \text{if } \{p_1, ..., p_n\} \subset S,$$
$$\forall p \in \{p_1, ..., p_n\}, \exists\, ident' \text{ s.t. } prefix(p, ident) = ident'$$

Besides static definition of system states and proposition, dynamic operational semantics of the creation, destruction and update of states based on system actions have also to be defined. Different from original π calculus, a group of state operators are introduced into the syntax of state π calculus. State π calculus aims to create dynamic association between states and actions in π calculus via state operators. Creation, destruction and update of states can thus be enabled by integrating operational semantics of original π calculus and semantics of state operators. Therefore, state π calculus reuse existing properties and analysis techniques in π calculus instead of revising the core of π calculus.

$$P \quad ::= \sum_{i=1}^{n} \alpha_i \{StateExp\}.P_i \mid (new\ x)P \mid !P \mid P \mid Q \mid \phi P \mid A(y_1, ..., y_n) \mid 0$$

$$\alpha_i \{StateExp\} ::= x < \tilde{y} > \{StateExp\} \mid x(\tilde{y})\{StateExp\} \mid \tau\{StateExp\}$$

$$\phi \quad ::= [x = y] \mid eval(Prop, valueset) \mid \phi \wedge \phi$$

$$StateExp \quad ::= (StateOp, S) \mid StateExp, StateExp$$

$$StateOp \quad ::= + \mid - \mid ++ \mid --$$

$$S \quad ::= (iden, trueset)$$

$$iden \quad ::= x \mid iden.iden$$

As shown above, in state π calculus each input/output action can be associated with multiple state expressions *StateExpr*. *StateExpr* depicts possible state operations *StateOp* that a system action can do to a state. The choice operator '?' is also support in *StateExpr*. Consequently, the expression [*Condition Expr*]*StateExpr?StateExpr* describes that when the condition *ConditionExpr* is (not) satisfied, a system action will be associated with the state expression of the former (latter) *StateExpr*. Four state operators are provided in state π calculus: state creation (+), state destruction (−), state association (++), and state removal (−−). An additional operation of state updates is also included in the state creation (+) operator. To be more intuitive, each state operator can be regarded as an association relation between states: $\Re$: *SysState×StateOp×S→SysState*. That is, a new system state is determined by the current system state (*SysState*) and the target state operation (*StateOp×S*). In state π calculus, a system state is the set of all existing states and their values in the system. Therefore, semantics of state operators are very essential to state π calculus, which define the association between system actions and states and life-cycles of system states.

Definition 2 (irrelevant states and conflict states). Two states S_1 and S_2 are *conflict* ($S_1 \Diamond S_2$) if $\exists p_1 = (ident_1, set_1) \in S_1$ and $p_2 = (ident_2, set_2) \in S_2$ s.t. $ident_1 = ident_2$. Meanwhile system propositions p_1 and p_2 are *overlapped* ($p_1 \Diamond p_2$); S_1 and S_2 are *irrelevant* ($S_1 \nabla S_2$) if they are not conflict.

Definition 3 (state preordering). For any two nonconflict states S_1 and S_2, $S_1 \prec S_2$ if $\forall p=(ident,set)\in S_1$, $\exists p'=(ident',set')\in S_2$, s.t. $ident=ident'$ and $set \subset set'$; $S_1=S_2$ if $S_1 \prec S_2$ and $S_2 \prec S_1$.

Definition 4 (well-formed states). A state S is well-formed, iff the following two conditions are satisfied: (1) $\forall p_1, p_2 \in S$, there is no $p_1 \Diamond p_2$; (2) $\forall p=(ident,set)\in S$, set is not empty.

Two propositions in a well-formed state do not conflict and each proposition in the state is not always false. Given the current system state $SysState=\{p_{11},...,p_{1n}\}$, and the state associated with the state operator $StateOp\ S=\{p_{21},...,p_{2m}\}$, formal semantics of each state operator is provided as follows, defined over well-formed states.

1. State Creation (+): Define a new state and overwrite the existing one in the current system;

$$CREATE \qquad \frac{SysState\nabla S}{+S = \{p_{11},...,p_{1n},p_{21},...,p_{2m}\}}$$

$$UPDATE \qquad \frac{SysState\Diamond S \qquad \exists p_{1i}\in SysState, p\in S \text{ s.t. } p_{1i}\Diamond p}{+S = \{p_{11},...,p_{1i-1},p,p_{1i+1},...,p_{1n},p_{21},...,p_{2m}\}}$$

2. State Destruction (−): Remove a specific state from current system states;

$$DESTROY\_VOID \qquad \frac{SysState\nabla S}{-S = \{p_{11},...,p_{1n}\}}$$

$$DESTROY \qquad \frac{SysState\Diamond S \qquad \exists p_{1i}\in SysState, p\in S \text{ s.t. } p_{1i}\Diamond p}{-S = \{p_{11},...,p_{1i-1},p_{1i+1},...,p_{1n}\}}$$

3. State Association (++): Insert a state in current system states;

$$INSERT\_VOID \qquad \frac{SysState\nabla S}{++S = \{p_{11},...,p_{1n},p_{21},...,p_{2m}\}}$$

$$INSERT \qquad \frac{SysState\Diamond S \qquad \exists p_{1i}=\in SysState, p\in S \text{ s.t. } p_{1i}\Diamond p}{++S = \{p_{11},...,p_{1i-1},p_{1i}',p_{1i+1},...,p_{1n},p_{21},...,p_{2m}\}}$$
$$range(p_{1i}') = range(p_i)\cup range(p)$$

4. State Removal (−−): Remove the specific propositions from a state in the current system states;

$REMOVE\_VOID$ $\dfrac{SysState \nabla S}{--S = \{p_{11}, ..., p_{1n}\}}$

$REMOVE\_SHALLOW$ $\dfrac{SysState \Diamond S \quad \exists p_{1i} =\in SysState, p \in S \text{ s.t. } p_{1i} \Diamond p \quad range(p_{1i}) / range(p) \neq \phi}{--S = \{p_{11}, ..., p_{1i-1}, p_{1i}', p_{1i+1}, ..., p_{1n}, p_{21}, ..., p_{2m}\} \quad range(p_{1i}') = range(p_i) / range(p)}$

$REMOVE\_DEEP$ $\dfrac{SysState \Diamond S \quad \exists p_{1i} =\in SysState, p \in S \text{ s.t. } p_{1i} \Diamond p \quad range(p_{1i}) / range(p) = \phi}{--S = \{p_{11}, ..., p_{1i-1}, p_{1i+1}, ..., p_{1n}, p_{21}, ..., p_{2m}\}}$

As previously mentioned, above semantics form a basis for implementation of the state relation $\Re$, i.e.,

$\Re : SysState \times StateOp \times S \rightarrow SysState'$

$\Re : (SysState, StateOp, S) = SysState'$

where *SysState'* is determined by the above 9 semantic rules.

2.3 State π Calculus: Extended Operational Semantics

In this section we integrate state operators with operational semantics of original π calculus, which leads to extended operational semantics for state π calculus. This interprets how system states and actions are mutually operated. Traditionally the behavior of π calculus is modeled using a standard Labeled Transition System (LTS). However, for modeling and reasoning of state/action hybrid systems, LTS should be extended to model both system actions (i.e. transition labels) and system states (i.e. state labels). Typical examples of these extensions can be found in the Labeled Kripke Structures (Chaki, 2004) and the Doubly Labeled Transition Systems (Nicola, 1995). A *State Label Transition System* (SLTS) is proposed in this work for interpreting behaviors of state π calculus.

Definition 5 (state labeled transition system). An SLTS $(S, M, \{\xrightarrow{a\{StateExpr\}} \mid a \in M\})$ consists of a set *SP* of state/process pairs, a set *M* of transition labels, and a set $\{\xrightarrow{a\{StateExpr\}}\}$ of transitions $\xrightarrow{a\{StateExpr\}} \subseteq S \times S$ where $a \in M$.

In an SLTS, a transition is represented as $(P, SysState) \xrightarrow{a\{StateExpr\}} (P', SysState')$. This means the current process and state of the system is P and *SysState*, and by executing the action a associated with the state expression of *StateExpr*, the system process evolves to P' and the system state is updated to *SysState'*. According to SLTS, a static association *transState* can be defined between the system state *SysState* and its possible modification (*StateExpr*):

$transS : SysState \times StateExpr \rightarrow SysState'$

$transS(SysState, StateExpr) = \begin{cases} \Re(SysState, Op, S) & StateExpr = (Op, S) \\ SysState & StateExpr \text{ is null} \end{cases}$

Consequently, the extended operational semantics of state π calculus is defined below based on the early transitional semantics 0 of π calculus.

$$OUT \quad \frac{}{(x<y>\{\varphi\}.P,\ \delta)\ \xrightarrow{\bar{x}<y>\{\varphi\}}\ (P, transS(\delta,\ \varphi))} \qquad INP \quad \frac{}{(x(z)\{\varphi\}.P,\ \delta)\ \xrightarrow{x(y)\{\varphi\}}\ \{y\ /\ z\}(P, transS(\delta,\ \varphi))}$$

$$TAU \quad \frac{}{(\tau\{\varphi\}.P,\ \delta)\ \xrightarrow{\tau\{\varphi\}}\ (P, transS(\delta,\varphi))} \qquad SUM-L \quad \frac{(P,\delta)\ \xrightarrow{\alpha}\ (P',\delta')}{(P+Q,\delta)\ \xrightarrow{\alpha}\ (P',\delta')}$$

$$MAT \quad \frac{(\alpha.P,\delta)\ \xrightarrow{\alpha}\ (P',\delta')}{([\phi]\alpha P,\delta)\ \xrightarrow{\alpha}\ (P',\ \delta')} \qquad \phi \text{ means } x=x \text{ or } eval(Prop, valueset)=true$$

$$PAR-L \quad \frac{(P,\delta)\ \xrightarrow{\alpha}\ (P',\delta')}{(P\mid Q,\delta)\ \xrightarrow{\alpha}\ (P'\mid Q,\delta')} \qquad bn(\alpha)\cap fn(Q)=\varnothing$$

$$COMM-L \quad \frac{(P,\delta)\ \xrightarrow{\bar{x}<y>\{\varphi\}}\ (P', transS(\delta,\varphi))\ \ (Q,\ \delta')\ \xrightarrow{x(y)\{\phi\}}\ (Q', transS(\delta',\varphi'))}{(P\mid Q,\delta'')\ \xrightarrow{\tau\{\varphi,\ \phi\}}\ (P'\mid Q', transS(transS(\delta'',\varphi),\ \varphi'))}$$

$$CLOSE-L \quad \frac{(P,\delta)\ \xrightarrow{\bar{x}<z>\{\varphi\}}\ (P', transS(\delta,\varphi))\ \ (Q,\ \delta')\ \xrightarrow{x(z)\{\phi\}}\ (Q', transS(\delta',\varphi'))}{(P\mid Q,\delta'')\ \xrightarrow{\tau\{\varphi,\ \phi\}}\ (new\ z)(P'\mid Q', transS(transS(\delta'',\varphi),\ \varphi'))} \qquad z\notin fn(Q)$$

$$RES \quad \frac{(P,\delta)\ \xrightarrow{\alpha}\ (P',\delta')}{((new\ z)P,\delta)\ \xrightarrow{\alpha}\ ((new\ z)P',\delta')} \qquad z\notin n(\alpha)$$

$$OPEN \quad \frac{(P,\delta)\ \xrightarrow{\bar{x}<z>\{\varphi\}}\ (P', transS(\delta,\varphi))}{((new\ z)P,\delta')\ \xrightarrow{\bar{x}<z>\{\varphi\}}\ (P', transS(\delta',\varphi))} \qquad z\neq x$$

$$REP-ACT \quad \frac{(P,\delta)\ \xrightarrow{\alpha}\ (P',\delta')}{(!P,\delta)\ \xrightarrow{\alpha}\ (P'\mid !P,\delta')}$$

$$REP-COMM \quad \frac{(P,\delta)\ \xrightarrow{\bar{x}<y>\{\varphi\}}\ (P', transS(\delta,\varphi))\ \ (P,\ \delta')\ \xrightarrow{x(y)\{\varphi'\}}\ (P'', transS(\delta',\varphi'))}{(!P,\delta'')\ \xrightarrow{\tau\{\varphi,\ \phi\}}\ ((P'\mid P'')\mid !P, transS(transS(\delta'',\varphi),\ \varphi'))}$$

$$REP-CLOSE \quad \frac{(P,\delta)\ \xrightarrow{\bar{x}<z>\{\varphi\}}\ (P', transS(\delta,\varphi))\ \ (P,\ \delta')\ \xrightarrow{x(z)\{\phi\}}\ (P'', transS(\delta',\varphi'))}{(!P,\delta'')\ \xrightarrow{\tau\{\varphi,\ \phi\}}\ ((new\ z)(P'\mid P'')\mid !P, transS(transS(\delta'',\varphi),\ \varphi'))} \qquad z\notin fn(P)$$

In above semantics, φ and δ are shortcut notations for *StateExpr* and *SysState* respectively; α denotes an arbitrary action in state π calculus; *fn* and *bn* are used to indicate the set of all free names and bounded names. Note that state π calculus does not tend to change the fundamental definition of Structural Congruence in π calculus, and reduction rules can also be extended similarly for state π calculus. Therefore, above operational semantics in state π calculus can be regarded as a further extension to the ones in π calculus for integrating system states with actions and management of these states.

State Bi-Simulation

Bi-simulation analysis is an important tool in process algebras to define process equivalence. In state π calculus, system states and their changes need to be further considered into the original strong (weak) bi-simulation relation in π calculus to define (observable) behavior equivalence between state/action hybrid systems. Denote $\Rightarrow^\tau$ to be a transition sequence triggered by invisible action τ. Denote $\Rightarrow^a$ and $\Rightarrow^\tau$ to be a transition sequence triggered by arbitrary action a where $a{\neq}\tau$ and $a{=}\tau$ respectively; Denote $\Rightarrow$ to be either $\Rightarrow^a$ or $\Rightarrow^\tau$ and $\Rightarrow^a$ to be the abbreviation for $\Rightarrow \xrightarrow{a} \Rightarrow$. A hybrid bi-simulation is defined below as a bi-simulation relation which considers both system states and actions.

Definition 6 (hybrid Bi-simulation). A symmetric binary relation R is a strong (weak) hybrid bi-simulation relation, iff for any $(P, SysState_P)R(Q, SysState_Q)$ and substitution σ: If $(P_\sigma, SysState_P) \xrightarrow{a} (P',$ $SysState_P')$ $(bn(a){\notin}fn(P_\sigma, Q_\sigma))$, $\exists Q'$ s.t. $(Q_\sigma, SysState_Q) \xrightarrow{a} (Q', SysState_Q'),(P', SysState_P')R(Q',$ $SysState_Q')$ and $SysState_P' = SysState_Q'$.

As an independent dimension for system description, we can also exclusively follow the lead of states to define equivalence between systems.

Definition 7 (state simulation). A symmetric binary relation R is a state simulation relation, iff $(P,$ $SysState_P)R(Q, SysState_Q)$ and any substute σ, if $(P_\sigma, SysState_P) \xrightarrow{a} (P', SysState_P')$ $(bn(a){\notin}fn(P_\sigma,$ $Q_\sigma))$, $\exists Q'$ s.t. $(Q_\sigma, SysState_Q){\Rightarrow}(Q', SysState_Q')$ and $SysState_P' \prec SysState_Q'$.

Definition 8 (state bi-simulation). A symmetric binary relation R is a state bi-simulation relation, iff R and its reverse are both state simulation relations.

FORMAL SEMANTICS OF GRID WORKFLOWS

Formalism of Services

As shown in Figure 1, each service can be *pended* for *staging in* required input data. After the service is executed (i.e. being *active*), it *stages out* the results and *cleans* any unnecessary data, or otherwise

Figure 1. Job state abstractions for grid services

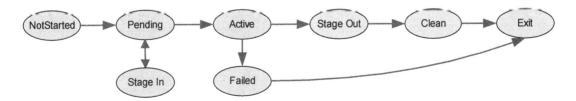

the execution of service can *fail*. Therefore, based on state π calculus the service formalism in grid workflows is as follows:

$\#STATE \quad srvactive = \{A.Status,\{Active\}\}; \quad \#STATE \quad srvstagingin = \{A.Status,\{StagingIn\}\}$

$\#STATE \quad srvpending = \{A.Status,\{Pending\}\}; \quad \#STATE \quad srvfailed = \{A.Status,\{Failed\}\}$

$\#STATE \quad srvexit = \{A.Status,\{Exit\}\}; \quad \#STATE \quad srvstagingout = \{A.Status,\{StagingOut\}\}$

$\#STATE \quad srvcleaning = \{A.Status,\{Cleaning\}\}; \quad \#STATE \quad execsrv = \{ExecutingSrv,\{A\}\};$

$ServiceA(port_1, execute, set, \overrightarrow{get_i}, succ, fail, port_2) =_{def}$

$\quad new \; ack(port_1(v:t_1)\{(+,srvpending),(++,execsrv)\}.(\prod_{i=1}^{n} StageIn_i \mid$

$\quad \underbrace{ack.....ack}_{n-1}.ack\{(+,srvactive)\}.new \; t \; f(\overline{execute} <v:t_1,t,f> \mid$

$\quad (t(res:t_3).(StageOut \mid ack.\overline{port}_2\{(+,srvexit),(--,execsrv)\} <succ>)+$

$\quad f\{(+,srvfailed)\}.\overline{port}_2\{(+,srvexit),(--,execsrv)\} <fail>))))$

$StageIn(get, ack) =_{def} get(x:t_2)\{(+,srvstagingin)\}.\overline{ack}\{(+,srvpending)\}$

$StageOut(set, ack, res) =_{def}$

$\quad new \; res \; clean(\overline{set} <res:t_3>\{(+,srvstagingout)\}.\overline{clean} \mid clean\{(+,srccleaning)\}.\overline{ack}))$

In the above formalism for a service *A*, '*#STATE*' is a reserved word for state declarations. According to the syntax of state π calculus, when no state declaration is predefined, states can also be alternatively defined in the declaration of actions. Free names *port*, *set* and *get* are channels for interaction of services and variables (their definition will be given in the next section). Since there are cases in grid systems when concurrent access to expensive resources is not desired, nested process definition is used in the formalism of *ServiceA*. The purpose is to allow the creation of a new instance of process *ServiceA* only when the old instance of *ServiceA* is finished. When multiple instance of a service is desired, the nested position of process *ServiceA* should be changed as follows:

$ServiceA(port, execute, set, get, succ, fail) =$

$\quad new \; ack(port(v)\{(+,srvpending),(++,execsrv)\}.(......\mid ServiceA)$

Formalism of Activities

Grid workflows adopt four basic activities from BPEL4WS: *Receive, Send, Invoke* and *Assign*. In BPEL4WS, data interactions between activities can be realized by sharing of variables. Consequently, activities of *Receive* and *Send* can be used to model data passing in a grid workflow and the activity of *Assign* can be used to model specific data reproduction. Their formal definitions are provided as follows:

$$Invoke(start, get, port_1, port_2, done) =_{def} \; start \; get(v:t).\overline{port_1} <v:t>.port_2(s).\overline{done}$$

$$Receive(start, port_2, set, done) =_{def}$$

$$start\{++,\{msgPort,\{port_2\}\}\}.port_2(v:t)\{--,\{msgPort,\{port_2\}\}\}.\overline{set} <v:t>.\overline{done}$$

$$Reply(start, get, port_1, done) =_{def} \; start.get(v:t).\overline{port_1} <v:t>.\overline{done}$$

$$Assign(start, get_1, set_2, done) =_{def} \; start.get_1(v:t).\overline{set_2} <v:t>.\overline{done}$$

$$Empty(start, done) =_{def} \; start.\overline{done}$$

$$Var_V =_{def} \; Var_{V0}(set, get)$$

$$Var_{V0}(set, get) =_{def} \; set(x_1:t)\{++,\{V.bSize,\{x_1\}\}\}.Var_{V1}(set, get, x_1)$$

$$Var_{V1}(set, get, x_1) =_{def} \; (set \; x_2:t_2)\{++,\{V.bSize,\{x_2\}\}\}.Var_{V2}(set, get, x_1, x_2) \; +$$

$$\overline{get} < x_1 \; t_1 > \{--,\{V.bSize,\{x_1\}\}\}.Var_{V0}(set, get)$$

......

$$Var_{Vn}(set, get, x_1, ..., x_n) =_{def} \; \overline{get} < x_n \; t_n > \{--,\{V.bSize,\{x_n\}\}\}.Var_{Vn-1}(set, get, x_1, ..., x_{n-1})$$

Here the value access and assignment in *Variable*s are realized by channels *get* and *set*. The *Variable* process implements a variable stack with arbitrary depth. In a real grid workflow, the definition of *Variable* can also be simplified as follows if its depth is 1.

$$Var_V(set, get, x) =_{def} \; \overline{get} < x \; t > .Var_V(set, get, x) +$$

$$set(y:t)\{++,\{V.CurrentVal,\{y\}\}\}.Var_V(set, get, y)$$

Moreover, all the above activities use the channel of *port* to trigger the execution of a desired service and obtain its result. Note that in BPEL4WS, 'link name', 'partner name' and 'operation name' are three elements in its activities to define the access of a service. A service in grid workflows can thus be first defined as an abstract one and later refined to an executable one by using a service mapping/selection mechanism, as described in (Németh, 2003) and (Fahringer, 2005). Therefore the *port* channel here is used to indicate both an abstract service interface (e.g. an abstract functional definition of the service), and a concrete service invocation interface (e.g. via WS-Addressing). The service mapping / selection in grid workflows is further discussed in the next section.

Service Selection

There are often scenarios when multiple candidate services are available to implement a desired abstract function. Semantics of service selection need to be formally defined. A simple way to define interaction with one of candidate services is direct composition of their corresponding state π calculus processes. For the *invocation* of 1-out-of-*n* services, the implementation is as follows:

$$ClosedInvocation - Invoke \,|\, Service_1 \,|......|\, Service_n$$

The above processes of *Invoke*, *Service*$_1$, ..., *Service*$_n$ share the same *port* channel. In this way multiple services compete for a single *Invoke* activity. The competition is resolved by a non-deterministic choice from *n* services. However, when a specific service selection strategy needs to be explicitly modeled, an addition process for service selection should be implemented:

$Selection_1(port_{sel}, port_{11}, port_{12},..., port_{n1}, port_{n2}) =_{def} \overline{port_{sel}} < port_{11}, port_{12} > .Selection_2$

......

$Selection_n(port_{sel}, port_{11}, port_{12},..., port_{n1}, port_{n2}) =_{def} \overline{port_{sel}} < port_{n1}, port_{n2} > .Selection_1$

$Selection =_{def} Selection_1 \qquad n$ is a predefined constant

$Invoke'(start, get, port_{sel}, done, fail, succ) =_{def}$

$\qquad start.get(v:t).port_{sel}(p_1, p_2).\overline{p_1} < v:t > .p_2(s).\overline{done}$

$ClosedInvocation =_{def} Invoke \mid Service_1 \mid ...... \mid Service_n \mid Selection$

The process of *Selection* stores all *port* channels for the desired abstract function. It selects these *ports* sequentially by their orders in a queue. The order of the *ports*, on the other hand, can be decided by the performance of different corresponding services such as QoS, execution time, etc. Moreover, the new invocation process *Invoke'* no longer interacts directly to a specific service by the given *port*. It queries the *Selection* process first to get what exact service it should invoke by the naming passing capability of π calculus. The interaction between *Invoke'* and the target service can thus be dynamically formed.

Formalism of Workflows

Grid workflows adopt six BPEL4WS control structures: *Sequence, While, Flow, Switch, Pick* and *Link*. The formalism of these structures is as follows.

The *Sequence* structure defines sequential relations among execution in a grid workflow:

$Sequence(fn_d(Act_1), fn_s(Act_2))$

$\qquad =_{def} Act_1 ; Act_2 =_{def} (new\ start_{Act_2})(\{start_{Act_2} / done_{Act_1}\}Act_1 \mid Act_2)$

The *While* structure defines repeat invoking of one or a group of services in a grid workflow under certain conditions:

$While(fn_{sd}(Act), start_{while}, done_{while}) =_{def} new\ start_{Act}\ done_{Act}(start_{while}.$

$\qquad ([eval(C, \{t\})](\overline{start_{Act}} \mid Act \mid done_{Act}.(\overline{start_{while}} \mid While)) + [eval(C, \{f\})]\overline{done_{while}}))$

The *Flow* structure defines synchronization of parallel execution and completion among service activities and structures in a grid workflow:

$Flow(fn_{sd}(Act_1), ..., fn_{sd}(Act_m), start_{Flow}, done_{Flow}) =_{def}$

$\qquad (new\ start_{Act_1} ... start_{Act_m}\ done_{Act_1} ... done_{Act_m}\ ack\ ack')$

$\qquad (start_{Flow}.Starter \mid Act_1 \mid ...... \mid Act_m \mid Acker \mid ack'.\overline{done_{Flow}})$

$Starter(start_{Act_1}, ..., start_{Act_m}) =_{def} \overline{start_{Act_1}} \mid ...... \mid \overline{start_{Act_m}}$

$Acker(done_{Act_1}, ..., done_{Act_m}, ack, ack') =_{def} done_{Act_1}.\overline{ack} \mid ...... \mid done_{Act_m}.\overline{ack} \mid \underbrace{ack........ack}_{m}.\overline{ack'}$

The *Switch* structure defines a conditional choice structure in a grid workflow:

$$Switch(fn_{sd}(Act_1), fn_{sd}(Act_2), start_{Switch}, done_{Switch}) =_{def} (new\ start_{Act_1}\ start_{Act_2}\ done_{Act_1}\ done_{Act_2})$$

$$(start_{Switch}.([eval(C_1, \{t\})]\overline{start_{Act_1}}\{(++, \{Branch, \{Act_1\}\})\} | Act_1 | done_{Act_1}.\overline{done_{Switch}} +$$

$$[eval(C_1, \{f\}) \wedge eval(C_2, \{t\})]\overline{start_{Act_2}}\{(++, \{Branch, \{Act_2\}\})\} | Act_2 | done_{Act_2}.\overline{done_{Switch}}))$$

The *Pick* structure defines execution selection among different services and structures in a grid workflow based on message trigger:

$$Pick(fn_{sd}(Act_1), fn_{sd}(Act_2), port_{p1}, port_{p2}, timeout, start_{Pick}, done_{Pick}) =_{def}$$
$$(new\ start_{Act_1}\ start_{Act_2}\ done_{Act_1})done_{Act_2}\ (start_{Pick}.$$
$$(port_{p1}\{++, \{msgPort_1, \{port_{p1}\}\}\}.$$
$$start_{Act_1}\{(++, \{Event, \{Act_1\}\}), (--, \{msgPort_1, \{port_{p1}\}\})\} | Act_1 | done_{Act_1}.\overline{done_{Pick}} +$$
$$port_{p2}\{++, \{msgPort_2, \{port_{p2}\}\}\}.$$
$$start_{Act_2}\{(++, \{Event, \{Act_2\}\}), (--, \{msgPort_2, \{port_{p2}\}\})\} | Act_2 | done_{Act_2}.\overline{done_{Pick}}) +$$
$$timeout\{(++, \{Event, \{Timeout\}\})\}.\overline{done_{Pick}})$$

On the other hand, the *Link* structure imposes synchronization constraints on activities in a grid workflow. Each *Link* has a source and target activity, which restricts that the target activity can only be executed after the source activity is done. Besides, when a 'death-path' is detected in a grid workflow (e.g. if a branch in a *Switch* to which the activity *A* belongs is not selected), *negative* tokens should be propagated through all outgoing *Link*s of *A* (i.e. *A* is the source activity of these *Link*s). The semantics are also known as the *Death-Path Elimination* in BPEL4WS. The formalism of *Link* is given in the following:

$$Link_i(done_{in}, neg_{in}, ack, nack) =_{def}\ EvalTransCondition_i(done_{in}, neg_{in}, ack, nack)$$

$$EvalTransCondition_i(done_{in}, neg_{in}, ack, nack) =_{def}\ done_{in}.\overline{ack} + neg_{in}.\overline{nack}\qquad i = 1, ..., n$$

$$Links(done_{in}, neg_{in}, done_{links}, deathpath) =_{def}\ (new\ ack\ nack)$$

$$(Link_1 | ... | Link_n | \underbrace{ack.(... .(ack}_{n}.\overline{done_{links}} + nack.\overline{deathpath})... + nack.\overline{deathpath}))$$

$$ActWithLinks(freeN) =_{def}\ start.(done_{links}.new\ t\ f(\overline{evaljoin} < t, f > .($$

$$t.(new\ start_{Act}\ done_{Act})(\overline{start_{Act}} | Act | done_{Act}.\overline{done}.\prod \overline{done_{out}}) +$$

$$f\{++, \{Exception, \{Act\}\}\}.\overline{throw} < joinfailure >)) + deathpath.\prod \overline{neg_{out}})$$

$$freeN = \{start, done, done_{links}, done_{out}, neg_{out}, deathpath,$$
$$evaljoin\ fault, joinfailure, fn_{sd}(Act)\}$$

In the above state π calculus process, *ActivityWithLinks* indicates the implementation of the four types of activities introduced in Section 3.2 when *Link* is considered. *ActImpl* is a shortcut notation for detailed formalism of *Receive, Send, Assign, Invoke* activities in Section 3.2. In *Activity-WithLinks*, the start of an activity is subject to completion of its previous activity (*donepreceding*) and incoming *Link*s (*donelinks*). The process then starts to evaluate execution conditions for the corresponding activity (*evalJoin*). The activity will be normally executed if all conditions are satisfied, or otherwise a *JoinFailure* exception is thrown by the *ThrowAct* process (see its implementation in the next section) and the exception is recorded into the *Exception* variable in a grid workflow. Note that in the above *Link* processes, for each received *negativein* token, it will pass the information via the *deathpath* channel such that the *negativeout* token can continue to be propagated to outgoing *Link*s of the corresponding activity.

Formalism of Handling Exceptions and Compensations

Due to the existence of dynamic interactions and long-running services in grid applications, handling of exceptions and compensations is a critical issue in grid workflows. To correctly depict this aspect of semantics in grid workflows, the *Invoke* activity needs to be further implemented as follows:

$$Invoke_S\_WithFault(start, get, port_1, port_2, done, throw, invokefailure, fail, succ) =_{def}$$

$$start.get(v:t).\overline{port_1} <v:t>.\overline{port_2}(s).($$

$$[s = fail]\tau\{(++,\{Exception,\{S\}\})\}.\overline{throw} <invokefailure> +[s = succ]\overline{done})$$

$$ThrowAct(throw, fault) =_{def} throw(failttype).\overline{fault} < failttype >$$

When the invocation of a service returns a failure *([u=fail])*, the *ThrowAct* process throws an *invoke-Failure* exception and records it into the state *Exception*. On the other hand, the *FaultHandling* process is responsible for capturing and processing the corresponding exceptions. The channel *fault* is used to receive the exception that *ThrowAct* throws out. If the received exception type can be processed by *FaultHandling* (here $type_1, ..., type_n$ can be the previously mentioned *invokefailure, joinfailure*, or other user customized exceptions), corresponding *Activity* is executed to deal with the exception (detailed implementation of *Activity* is omitted here). Otherwise *FaultHandling* sequentially invokes compensation activities to compensate the failure caused by the exception. This is defined in grid workflows as:

$$FaultHandling(\overline{faulttype}, \overline{type}, compensate, fn_s(Act_1), ..., fn_s(Act_n)) =_{def}$$

$$fault(faulttype).(new\ start_1\ ...\ start_n)$$

$$([faulttype = type_1](\overline{start_1} \mid Act_1) + ... + [faulttype = type_n](\overline{start_n} \mid Act_n) +$$

$$\sum\nolimits_{type_i \in \overline{type},\ i \neq 1..n}[faulttype = type_i](\overline{compensate}_1. ....\overline{compensate}_m))$$

m is a finite constant

$$CompensationHandler_j(compensate_j, fn_{sd}(Act_j^c)) =_{def} compensate_j.$$

$$((new\ start_j^c\ done_j^c)(\overline{start_j^c} \mid Act_j^c \mid done_j^c.CompensationHandler_j))\qquad 1 \leq j \leq m$$

Formalism of Global Termination

It is required to terminate all service activities that are being (or waiting to be) executed when certain conditions become true (e.g. abnormality in the executing). Different from the Cancellation Patterns proposed by Puhlmann (Puhlmann, 2005), it requires all activities monitor termination signals but rather withdraw the waiting for the service invoke. Meanwhile, another global termination signal is required to ensure proper termination of all activities. Formalism of global termination is described in the following:

$$Invoke(start, get, port_1, port_2, done) =_{def} start.[\phi]get(v:t).[\phi]\overline{port_1} < v:t > .[\phi]port_2(s).[\phi]\overline{done}$$

$$Receive(start, port_2, set, done) =_{def} start.[\phi]port_2(v:t).[\phi]\overline{set} < v:t > .[\phi]\overline{done}$$

$$Reply(start, get, port_1, done) =_{def} start.[\phi]get(v:t).[\phi]\overline{port_1} < v:t > .[\phi]\overline{done}$$

$$Assign(start, get_1, set_2, done) =_{def} start.[\phi]get_1(v:t).[\phi]\overline{set_2} < v:t > .[\phi]\overline{done}$$

The condition ϕ equals to *eval(Exception, {})*. Based on the semantics of state π calculus, the process behavior is *null(0)* when the condition is not satisfied. Termination of a process is easily achieved via global management of state π calculus.

FORMAL VERIFICATION OF GRID WORKFLOWS

State Labeled Transition System (SLTS)

Management of actions and behaviors with state π calculus are achieved via the state label transition system. The application of SLTS leads to complete reasoning of grid workflow behaviors in its state space.

The first critical step is the transform from state π calculus formal semantics to the corresponding SLTS. This step is used not only to complete analysis of proposition properties of grid workflows, but also to enable existing model checking techniques incorporated into the framework of state π calculus seamlessly.

In previous sections, it is mentioned that basic π calculus can be interpreted using a general label transition system. In Ferrari (Ferrari, 2003) and Pistore's (Montanari, 1995) work, it is proven that any finite π calculus process can be transformed to its equivalent general label transition system via pre-transition semantics. This is actually a transformation from a name-based to nameless formal theory. For state π calculus, although its operational semantics is also based on pre-transition semantics (see Section 2.3), additional extensions to SLTS have to be processed, e.g. creating and managing state labels when action labels are created as processes evolve. This is the dual label character of SLTS (action labels + state labels). Some critical rules of SLTS are summarized in Figure 2. Operational semantics in Figure 2 are already introduced in Section 2.3.

A complete transformation algorithm is illustrated in the flowchart of Figure 3.

Figure 2. SLTS semantic transformation rules

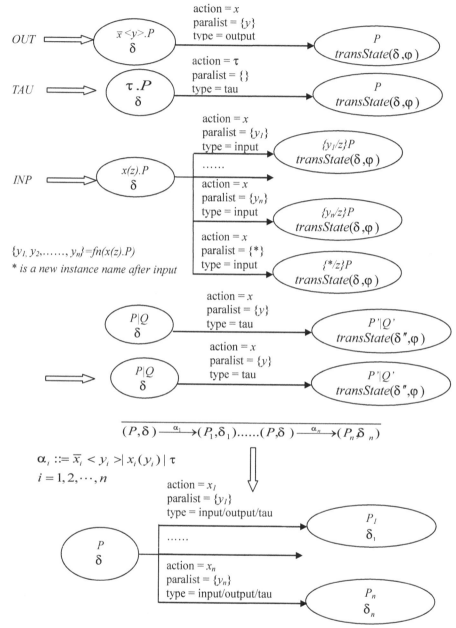

SUM-L,PAR-L,RES,OPEN,REP-ACT,REP-COMM,REP-CLOSE can be derived.

4.2 Structural Verification

Structural verification is a fundamental stage in formal verification of grid workflows. Reachability and terminatability are two aspects considered in structural verification. More specifically, given the context of a grid workflow, reachability checks whether there is some service that cannot be arrived due to restraints in the given service set; terminatability checks whether a given termination condition can be met.

Figure 3. Flowchart for SLTS transformation

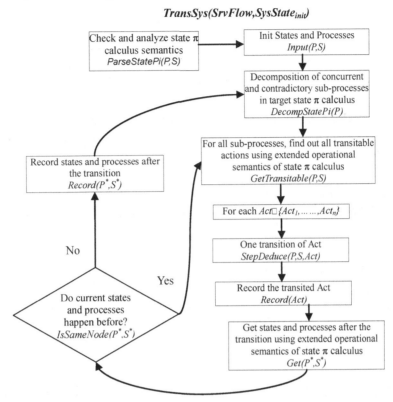

Definition 9 (execution). A tuple (α,β) is defined as an execution of state π calculus (P,S), if:

- α is an ordered finite state π calculus action sequence $\alpha=\{\pi_1\{StateExpr_1\},\ \pi_2\{StateExpr_2\},\dots,\pi_n\{StateExpr_n\}\}$;
- β is a finite state sequence $\beta=\{S_1, S_2,\dots, S_n\}$ corresponding to α;
- $(P,S)\xrightarrow{\pi_1\{StateExpr_1\}}(P_1,S_1)\xrightarrow{\pi_2\{StateExpr_2\}}(P_2,S_2)\dots\dots\xrightarrow{\pi_n\{StateExpr_n\}}(P_n,S_n)$,in which $(P_i, S_i) \neq (P_j, S_j)$, $(1\leq i\leq n,\ 1\leq j\leq n,\ i\neq j)$

Here we call P and S initial processes and states, P_n and S_n end processes and states.

Definition 10 (acceptable execution). A tuple (α,β) is an acceptable execution of state π calculus process (P,S), if:

- (α,β) is an execution of (P,S);
- There is no other execution (α',β'), where $\alpha\subset\alpha'$ and $\beta\subset\beta'$.

So here in state π calculus, an accepted execution of (P,S) is the longest transition process without looping in its corresponding SLTS.

Definition 11 (strong state assertation). For $(P,S) \vDash \lceil Sc \rceil_{(P',S')}$, $\forall(\alpha,\beta)$, which are acceptable executions of (P,S), $\forall(P,S)\to^{\alpha^*}(P^*,S^*)$, where $\alpha^*\subset\alpha$, if $P^*\equiv P'$ and $S^*\to S'$, there is $S^*\to Sc$. In this situation, the state π calculus process (P,S) satisfies a strong state assertion Sc defined on the targeting process (P',S'), $(P,S) \vDash \lceil Sc \rfloor_{(P',S')}$.

Definition 12 (weak state assertion). $\exists(\alpha,\beta)$, which are acceptable executions of (P,S), $\exists(P,S) \twoheadrightarrow^{\alpha^*}(P^*,S^*)$, where $\alpha^* \subset \alpha$, if $P^* \equiv P'$ and $S^* \rightarrow S'$, there is $S^* \rightarrow Sc$. In this situation, the state π calculus process (P,S) satisfies a weak state assertion Sc defined on the targeting process (P',S'), $(P,S) \vDash \langle Sc \rangle_{(P',S')}$.

Definition 13 (reachability). Given a state π calculus of a grid workflow $SrvFlow$ and its initial state $SysState_{init}$, a set of service $SRV=\{Srv_1,\ldots, Srv_n\}$ is reachable, if $\forall Srv \in SRV$, $(SrvFlow, SysState_{init}) \vDash \langle Srv.\ Status=Exit \rangle_{(\Phi,\ true)}$.

Definition 14 (terminability). Given a state π calculus of a grid workflow $SrvFlow$ and its initial state $SysState_{init}$, $SrvFlow$ is terminatable under termination conditions TC, if $(SrvFlow, SysState_{init}) \vDash \lceil Tc \rfloor_{(\Phi,\ true)}$.

Semantic Restraint Verification

Semantic restraint verification of grid workflows are used to ensure that the model we use is not contradictory to related restraints. Some of these restraints can be checked by its intuitive syntax (for example, in BPEL4WS *Link* structure can't form into a loop). In this work, two types of semantic restraints that cannot be directly verified from its syntax are focused, message competitive confliction and variable garbage collection.

More specifically, it's explicitly announced in BPEL4WS that any service instance shouldn't trigger two or more receiving activities to monitor one event sent from a same port to avoid message conflictions. Variable garbage collection means in the execution process of grid workflows, all temporary variables should be null at the end to ensure no extra message and data.

Definition 15 (message competitive confliction). Given a state π calculus of a grid workflow $SrvFlow$ and its initial state $SysState_{init}$, no message competitive confliction exists during its execution, if $\forall msgPort$ during transitions of $SrvFlow$, $(SrvFlow, SysState_{init}) \vDash \lceil |range(*.msgPort)|=0 \vee |range(*.msgPort)|=1 \rfloor_{(-,\ true)}$.

Definition 16 (variable garbage collection). Given a state π calculus of a grid workflow $SrvFlow$ and its initial state $SysState_{init}$, no variable garbage exists during its execution, if $\forall bSize$ during transitions of $SrvFlow$, $(SrvFlow, SysState_{init}) \vDash \lceil |range(*.bSize)|=0 \rfloor_{(\Phi,\ true)}$.

GRIDPIANALYZER

As discussed in previous sections, the correctness and reliability assurance is a critical task for QoS supports of grid workflows. More specifically, the correctness of a grid workflow refers to that it must satisfy all the desired properties and constraints from users; the reliability of a grid workflow refers to that it will loyally fulfill users' requirements without any exceptions during the execution. Based on the formal method for grid workflow QoS proposed in this work, a system implementation is introduced in this section, followed by a detailed case study.

System Implementation

Briefly speaking, model checking consists of three steps: system modeling, property specification and property verification. State π calculus is used as a formal language for modeling grid workflows in this work, and the Linear Temporal Logic (LTL) is used as the property specification language. An automatic verification prototype, namely the GridPiAnalyzer, for grid workflows models is implemented. State π calculus semantics of grid workflows are transformed in GridPiAnalyzer and verification is actually carried out using a mainstream open source engine NuSMV2 (Cimatti, 2002). Final results are also additionally encapsulated in GridPiAnalyzer. User interfaces based on the Eclipse platform are illustrated in Figure 4.

JavaCC is used in GridPiAnalyzer to check the syntax and model compiling. Correspondently, when it finished compiling, GridPiAnalyzer caches grid workflows state π calculus semantics in the meta-model included in Figure 5.

SLTS transferring, state ascertaining and formal verification are then carried out. Different output results are encapsulated in XML files. It includes criteria of grid workflow models to be tested, process logics to be tested, final results and counter examples.

A Case Study – Gravitational Wave Data Analysis

Application Background

Gravitational Waves (GW) are produced by the movement of energy in mass of dense material which fluctuate space-time structure. The analysis of unknown mass movement and formulation in the uni-

Figure 4. GridPiAnalyzer user interfaces

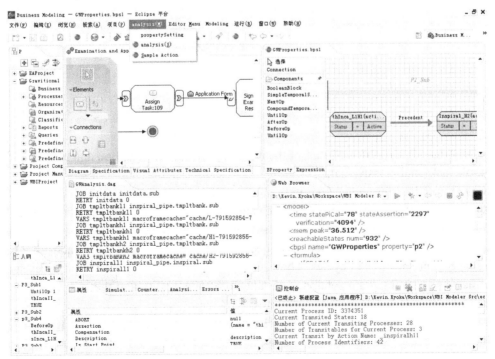

Figure 5. The meta-model of state π calculus syntax

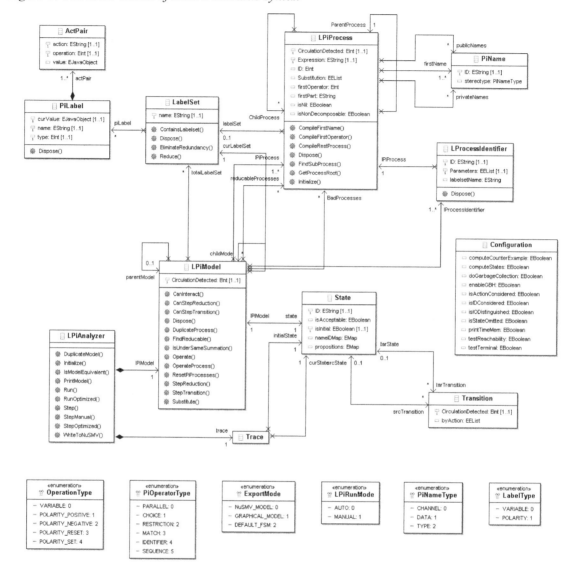

verse is stemmed from its detection. But the difficulty is that the detection and analysis of them relates to multiple tasks and massive data.

LIGO (Laser Interferometer Gravitational-Wave Observatory) includes three most sensitive GW detectors in the world, jointly built by Caltech and MIT. LIGO Scientific Collaboration (LSC) includes over 500 research scientists from over 50 institutes all over the world who are working hard on LIGO data analysis for GW detection. LIGO produces one terabyte of data per day and LIGO data analysis require large amount of CPU cycles. The LIGO data grid (Deelman, 2002) provides such a computing infrastructure to integrate petabytes of data storage capability and thousands of CPUs and enable research collaboration cross multiple institutes.

A typical example of a grid workflow for LIGO data analysis can be found in (Brown, 2007). Figure 6 includes a Condor DAGman script for inspiral GW search and its visualization.

Figure 6. An example grid workflow for GW search

```
JOB initdata initdata.sub
RETRY initdata 0
JOB tmpltbankl1 inspiral_pipe.tmpltbank.sub
RETRY tmpltbankl1 0
VARS tmpltbankl1 macroframecache="cache/L-791592854-791607098.cache" macrochannelname="L1:LSC-AS_Q" macrocalibrationcache="cache_files/
calibration.cache"
JOB tmpltbankh1 inspiral_pipe.tmpltbank.sub
RETRY tmpltbankh1 0
VARS tmpltbankh1 macroframecache="cache/H1-791592855-791607099.cache" macrochannelname="H1:LSC-AS_Q" macrocalibrationcache="cache_files/
calibration.cache"
JOB tmpltbankh2 inspiral_pipe.tmpltbank.sub
RETRY tmpltbankh2 0
VARS tmpltbankh2 macroframecache="cache/H2-791592856-791607100.cache" macrochannelname="H2:LSC-AS_Q" macrocalibrationcache="cache_files/
calibration.cache"
JOB inspirall1 inspiral_pipe.inspiral.sub
RETRY inspirall1 0
VARS inspirall1 macrocalibrationcache="cache_files/calibration.cache" macrobankfile="L1-TMPLTBANK-791592862-2048.xml" macrochannelname="L1:LSC-
AS_Q" macrochisqthreshold="20.0" macroframecache="cache/L-791592854-791607098.cache" macrosnrthreshold="7.0"
JOB trigbankh11 inspiral_pipe.trig.sub
RETRY trigbankh11 0
VARS trigbankh11 macrocalibrationcache="cache_files/calibration.cache" macrochannelname="H1:LSC-AS_Q"
JOB trigbankh12 inspiral_pipe.trig.sub
RETRY trigbankh12 0
VARS trigbankh12 macrocalibrationcache="cache_files/calibration.cache" macrochannelname="H1:LSC-AS_Q"
JOB inspiralh11 inspiral_pipe.inspiral.sub
RETRY inspiralh11 0
VARS inspiralh11 macrocalibrationcache="cache_files/calibration.cache" macrobankfile="H1-TMPLTBANK-791592863-2049.xml" macrochannelname="H1:LSC-
AS_Q" macrochisqthreshold="20.0" macroframecache="cache/FData-H1-791592855-791607099.cache" macrosnrthreshold="7.0"
JOB inspiralh12 inspiral_pipe.inspiral.sub
RETRY inspiralh12 0
VARS inspiralh12 macrocalibrationcache="cache_files/calibration.cache" macrobankfile="H1-TMPLTBANK-791592864-2050.xml" macrochannelname="H1:LSC-
AS_Q" macrochisqthreshold="20.0" macroframecache="cache/FData-H1-791592855-791607099.cache" macrosnrthreshold="7.0"
JOB sincalih1 inspiral_pipe.sinca.sub
RETRY sincalih1 0
VARS sincalih1 macroframecache="cache/L-791592854-791607098.cache, cache/H1-791592855-791607099.cache"
JOB thincalih1 inspiral_pipe.thinca.sub
RETRY thincalih1 0
VARS thincalih1 macroframecache="cache/L-791592854-791607098.cache, cache/H1-791592855-791607099.cache"
JOB trigbankh21 inspiral_pipe.trig.sub
RETRY trigbankh21 0
VARS trigbankh21 macrocalibrationcache="cache_files/calibration.cache" macrochannelname="H2:LSC-AS_Q"
JOB trigbankh22 inspiral_pipe.trig.sub
RETRY trigbankh22 0
VARS trigbankh22 macrocalibrationcache="cache_files/calibration.cache" macrochannelname="H2:LSC-AS_Q"
JOB trigbankh23 inspiral_pipe.trig.sub
RETRY trigbankh23 0
VARS trigbankh23 macrocalibrationcache="cache_files/calibration.cache" macrochannelname="H2:LSC-AS_Q"
JOB InspVeto inspiral_pipe.veto.sub
RETRY InspVeto 0
VARS InspVeto macrocalibrationcache="cache_files/calibration.cache" macrochannelname="L1:LSC-AS_Q"
JOB inspiralh21 inspiral_pipe.inspiral.sub
RETRY inspiralh21 0
VARS inspiralh21 macrocalibrationcache="cache_files/calibration.cache" macrobankfile="H2-TMPLTBANK-791592865-2051.xml" macrochannelname="H2:LSC-
AS_Q" macrochisqthreshold="20.0" macroframecache="cache/FData-H2-791592856-791607100.cache" macrosnrthreshold="7.0"
JOB inspiralh22 inspiral_pipe.inspiral.sub
RETRY inspiralh22 0
VARS inspiralh22 smacrocalibrationcache="cache_files/calibration.cache" macrobankfile="H2-TMPLTBANK-791592866-2052.xml"
macrochannelname="H2:LSC-AS_Q" macrochisqthreshold="20.0" macroframecache="cache/FData-H2-791592856-791607100.cache" macrosnrthreshold="7.0"
JOB thinca2lih1 inspiral_pipe.thinca2.sub
RETRY thinca2lih1 0
VARS thinca2lih1 macroframecache="cache/L-791592854-791607098.cache, cache/H1-791592855-791607099.cache"
JOB thinca2lih2 inspiral_pipe.thinca2.sub
RETRY thinca2lih2 0
VARS thinca2lih2 macroframecache="cache/L-791592857-791607101.cache, cache/H1-791592855-791607099.cache"
JOB returnres returnres.sub
RETRY returnres 0

PARENT initdata CHILD tmpltbankl1 tmpltbankh1 tmpltbankh2
PARENT tmpltbankl1 tmpltbankh1 tmpltbankh2 CHILD inspirall1
PARENT inspirall1 CHILD trigbankh11 trigbankh12 thincalih1
PARENT trigbankh11 CHILD inspiralh11
PARENT trigbankh12 CHILD inspiralh12
PARENT inspirall1 inspiralh11 inspiralh12 CHILD sincalih1
PARENT sincalih1 CHILD thincalih1 trigbankh21
PARENT thincalih1 CHILD trigbankh22 returnres
PARENT trigbankh21 CHILD inspiralh21
PARENT trigbankh22 CHILD inspiralh22
PARENT inspiralh21 inspiralh22 CHILD thinca2lih1
PARENT thinca2lih1 thincalih1 CHILD returnres
```

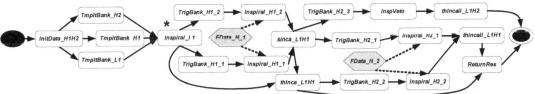

Figure 7. An example state π calculus semantics for GW data analysis workflows

$$\underline{JOB}\ Inspiral\ inspiral\_pipe.inspiral.sub\ \underline{VARS}\ VarInsp\ ...\ ...\ \ \underline{RETRY}\ Inspiral\ 0$$

$$\underline{JOB}\ sInca\ inspiral\_pipe.sinca.sub\ \underline{VARS}\ VarsInca\ ...\ ...\ \ \underline{RETRY}\ sInca\ 0$$

$$\underline{JOB}\ thInca\ inspiral\_pipe.thinca.sub\ \underline{VARS}\ VarthInca\ ...\ ...\ \ \underline{RETRY}\ thVar\ 0$$

$$\underline{PARENT}\ Inspiral\ \underline{CHILD}\ sInca\ thInca$$

$$\#STATE\ \ InitS = \{(Inspiral.status,\{NotStarted\}),$$
$$(sInca.status,\{NotStarted\}),(thInca.status,\{NotStarted\})\};$$

$$Invoke_{Inspiral}(start_{Insp}, get_{Insp}, port_{Insp1}, port_{Insp2}, done_{Insp}) =_{def}$$
$$start_{Insp}.\overline{get_{Insp}}(v).\overline{port_{Insp1}} <v>.port_{Insp2}.\overline{done_{Insp}}$$

$$Invoke_{sInca}(start_s, get_s, port_{s1}, port_{s2}, done_s) =_{def}$$
$$start_s.\overline{get_s}(v).\overline{port_{s1}} <v>.port_{s2}.\overline{done_s}$$

$$Invoke_{thInca}(start_{th}, get_{th}, port_{th1}, port_{th2}, done_{th}) =_{def}$$
$$start_{th}.\overline{get_{th}}(v).\overline{port_{th1}} <v>.port_{th2}.\overline{done_{th}}$$

$$Var_{Insp}(set_{Insp}, get_{Insp}, inspd) =_{def}\ \ \overline{get_{GWD}} <inspd> .Var_{Insp}(set_{Insp}, get_{Insp}, inspd)$$
$$+ set_{Insp}(y)\{+,\{Insp.CurrentVal,\{y\}\}\}.Var_{Insp}(set_{Insp}, get_{Insp}, y)$$

$$Var_{sInca}(set_s, get_s, sIncad) =_{def}\ \ \overline{get_s} <sIncad> .Var_{sInca}(set_s, get_s, sIncad)$$
$$+ set_s(y)\{+,\{SInca.CurrentVal,\{y\}\}\}.Var_{sInca}(set_s, get_s, y)$$

$$Var_{thInca}(set_{th}, get_{th}, thIncad) =_{def}\ \ \overline{get_{th}} <thIncad> .Var_{thInca}(set_{th}, get_{th}, thIncad)$$
$$+ set_{th}(y)\{+,\{ThInca.CurrentVal,\{y\}\}\}.Var_{thInca}(set_{th}, get_{th}, y)$$

$$SynPar(freeN) =_{def}\ \ (new\ done_{Insp}\ start_s\ start_{th})$$
$$(Invoke_{Inspiral}\ |\ Invoke_{sInca}\ |\ Invoke_{thInca}\ |\ SynParImpl)$$

$$freeN = \{start_{Insp}, get_{Insp}, port_{Insp1}, port_{Insp2}, get_s, port_{s1}, port_{s2},$$
$$get_{th}, port_{th1}, port_{th2}, done_s, done_{th}\}$$

$$SynParImpl(done_{Insp}, start_s, start_{th}) =_{def}\ \ done_{Insp}.(\overline{start_s}\ |\ \overline{start_{th}})$$

$$ServiceFlow =_{def}\ \ new\ (fn(SynPar, Var_{Insp}, Var_{sInca}, Var_{thInca}, Service_{Insp}, Service_{sInca}, Service_{thInca}))$$
$$(\tau\{+, InitS\}.(\overline{start_{Insp}}\ |\ SynPar\ |\ Var_{Insp}\ |\ Var_{sInca}\ |\ Var_{thInca}\ |$$
$$Service_{Insp}\ |\ Service_{sInca}\ |\ Service_{thInca}\ |\ done_s\ |\ done_{th}))$$

Grid Workflow Modeling

In this section, an example of state π calculus semantics for modeling GW data analysis workflows is provided in Figure 7. It is a simplified segment of the workflow described in Figure 6.

Logic Verification for Grid Workflows

The analysis of GW data involves multiple tasks and large amount of data. Because of the large scale scripts produced by LIGO data analysis tasks which in general may run from days to months, ensuring correctness and effectiveness of workflow structures and logics become critical which can be implemented using GridPiAnalyzer.

The GW detection is a complex task. To distinguish potential GW signals from noises, the whole process can be categorized into four critical logics. Model checking in state π calculus is used to verify these logics. As previously mentioned, model checking is a formal verification tool to analyze expected sequential logics be true or not in finite state system model. Structural verification and formal semantics restraints description of the four groups of LTL logics are listed below.

Logic 1 (Operations after creation of template banks): In any circumstances, once a template bank (*TmpltBank*) is created, two critical following steps: Matching with expected waves (*Inpiral*) and optimizing the matching (*TrigBank*) should be conducted to ensure effectiveness of data analysis.

1. G (*TmpltBank _ H*1.*Exit* → ((F *TrigBank _ H*1.*Exit*) ∧ (F *Inspiral   H*1.*Exit*)))
2. G (*TmpltBank _ H*2.*Exit* → ((F *TrigBank _ H*2.*Exit*) ∧ (F *Inspiral   H*2.*Exit*)))

Logic 2 (Working state restraints of interferometers): Because of different sensitivity of different interferometers, two interferometers in Handford (H1 and H2) are working simultaneously (*Init-Data_H1H2*), it is required that the process of matching with the expected wave of H2 (*Inspiral_H2*) should be suspended, until both the data in H1 and H2 pass the contingency analysis (*sInca_L1H1* and *thInca_L1H1*).

G ((*InitData _ H*1*H*2.*Active*) → ((¬ *Inspiral _ H*2.*Exit* U *sInca _ L*1*H*1.*Active*) ∧
(¬ *Inspiral   H*2.*Exit* U *thInca   L*1*H*1.*Active*)))

Logic 3 (Integrity of contingency analysis): The data collected by three interferometers have to pass all contingency analysis (*sInca, thInca and thIncall*) to minimize noise signal in final analysis. What's more, *sInca* and *thInca* should be done before *thIncall*.

((F *sInca _ L*1*H*1.*Active* ∧ (¬*thIncall _ L*1*H*1.*Exit* U *sInca _ L*1*H*1.*Active*)) ∨
(F *thInca   L*1*H*1.*Active* ∧ (¬*thIncall _ L*1*H*1.*Exit* U *thInca   L*1*H*1.*Active*)))
∧F *thIncall _ L*1*H*1.*Exit*

Logic 4 (Inevitability of contingency analysis): In any circumstance, once the process of matching with expected waves is done or template banks are created, contingency analysis should be done finally.
1. G (*Inspiral _ H*1.*Exit* → (F *thIncall   L*1*H*1.*Exit*))
2. G (*Inspiral _ H*2.*Exit* → (F *thIncall   L*1*H*1.*Exit*))
3. G (*TmpltBank _ H*1.*Exit* → (F *thIncall   L*1*H*1.*Exit*))
4. G (*TmpltBank _ H*2.*Exit* → (F *thIncall   L*1*H*1.*Exit*))

Reachability: (*SrvFlow, SysState$_{init}$*)⊨⟨*Srv.Status=Exit*⟩$_{(\Phi, true)}$, in which *Srv*∈{*initData_H1H2, tmpltBank_L1, tmplt Bank_H1, tmplt Bank_H2, Inspiral_L1, Inspiral_H1, Inspiral_H1, TrigBank_H1, TrigBank_H2, sInca_L1H1, thInca_L1H1, thIncall_L1H1, thIncall_L1H2, InspVeto, ReturnRes*};
Terminatability: (*SrvFlow, SysState$_{init}$*)⊨⌈*ReturnRes.Status=Exit*⌋$_{(\Phi, true)}$;
Message competitive conflicts: no such restraints in this case study;
Variable garbage collection: (*SrvFlow, SysState$_{init}$*)⊨⌈*range(*.bSize)*=0⌋$_{(\Phi, true)}$.

Table 1. Performance evaluation of logic verification using GridPiAnalyzer

	Time (ms)	Memory usage (MB)
Formalism of state π calculus	78	N/A
Calculating reachable states	1750	N/A
Verification of state assertation	2297	N/A
creating anti-cases	1339	N/A
Verification of Logic 1.1	2125	37.237
Verification of Logic 1.2	2688	37.412
Verification of Logic 2	4094	36.512
Verification of Logic 3	3156	37.410
Verification of Logic 4.1	2328	37.352
Verification of Logic 4.2	2500	37.389
Verification of Logic 4.3	2313	36.887
Verification of Logic 4.4	2359	37.837

In logics described above, *Inspiral_H1.Exit* is the abbreviation for *Inspiral_H1_1.Exit* $\lor$*Inspiral_H1_2.Exit*. This also applys to *Inspiral_H2.Exit, TrigBank_H1.Exit* and *TrigBank_H2.Exit*. After the transition process with SLTS mentioned above in GridPiAnalyzer, the number of reachable states in the final SLTS of above GW search's state π calculus semantics is $932(2^{9.8642})$, the total number of state proposition is 26, including 20 status variables of service activities. The total time and memory usage of the above logic formulas and specific performance is included in Table 1.

The final result shows that all services (*InitData, TmpltBank, Inspiral, sInca, thInca, TrigBank, TrigVeto, thIncall, ReturnRes*) in the LIGO GW search workflow are reachable, and under the condition *TC = "ReturnRes.Status = Exit"*, is terminatable. This means the final analysis can be completed without variable garbage. Regarding four groups of designated logic constraints mentioned above, in the LIGO GW search workflow, Logics 1, 3 and 4 can be met, though the verification result shows that there are anti-cases for Logic 2 which includes 51 state transitions. The workflow can then be further improved to avoid these anti-cases and meet requirements of Logic 2. This indicates the motivation of grid workflow verification. Since in general it will take long time and resources to execute these workflows, formal verification could be used to provide information in advance and improve grid workflow QoS.

FUTURE TRENDS

As shown in Table 1 of performance evaluation results, time and memory usage of GridPiAnalyzer is still quite high. Ongoing work is focused on performance optimization of grid workflow verification using GridPiAnalyzer. These include development of new formal methods for workflow decomposition based on standard regions. Using regional analysis, complexity of workflow verification could be dramatically decreased due to smaller numbers of states and processes in each relaxed region.

Process oriented model and semantic based Artificial Intelligence programming are two important methods in service composition. How to implement State π calculus in grid applications that require more semantic situation combined with reasoning in complex logics is another important aspect of working.

How to extend our formal verification methods from abstract and concrete workflow specification to the verification in executing codes, so different layers of models can be combined together to understand the characteristics and properties clearly is also the future work.

CONCLUSION

In this work, a new state π calculus is proposed, which facilitates modeling and verifying of grid workflows. Some typical patterns in grid workflows are captured and both static and dynamic formal verification issues are investigated, including structural correctness, specification satisfiability, logic satisfiability and consistency. A grid workflow modeling and verification environment, GridPiAnalyzer, is implemented using formal modeling and verification methods proposed in this work and validated using a grid workflow for gravitational wave data analysis. Three important future trend related closely to our work is also introduced to extend the framwork of the formalism and verification of grid workflows.

ACKNOWLEDGMENT

This work is sponsored by Ministry of Education of China under the quality engineering project for higher education "National Open Course Integrated Systems", and Ministry of Science and Technology of China under the national 863 high-tech R&D program (grant No. 2006AA10Z237). This work is carried out in collaboration with Prof. Erik Katsavounidis of LIGO (Laser Interferometer Gravitational-wave Observatory) Laboratory at Massachusetts Institute of Technology.

REFERENCES

Amin, K., von Laszewski, G., Hategan, M. et al. (2004). GridAnt: A Client-Controllable Grid Workflow System, In *Proc. 37th IEEE Annual Hawaii International Conference on System Sciences* (pp. 3293-3301). Hawaii, US.

Andrews, T., Curbera, F., & Dholakia, H., et al. (2003). Business Process Execution Language for Web Services, Version 1.1.

Brandic, I., Benkner, S., Engelbrecht, G., & Schmidt, R. (2005). QoS Support for Time-Critical Grid Workflow Applications, In *Proc. 1st IEEE Int. Conf. on e-Science and Grid Computing* (pp. 108-115). Melbourne, Australia.

Brown, D. A., Brady, P. R., et al. (2007). A Case Study on the Use of Workflow Technologies for Scientific Analysis: Gravitational Wave Data Analysis, In Taylor, I. J. (Eds.), *Workflows for e-Science: Scientific Workflows for Grids* (pp. 39-59), Springer Verlag.

Cao, J., Jarvis, S. A., Saini, S. & Nudd, G. R. (2003). GridFlow: Workflow Management for Grid Computing. In *Proc. 3rd IEEE/ACM Int. Symp. on Cluster Computing and the Grid* (pp.198-205), Tokyo, Japan,.

Chaki, S., Clarke, E. M., Ouaknine, J., et al (2004). State/Event-based Software Model Checking, In E. A. Boiten, J. Derrick, G. Smith (Eds.), *Integrated Formal Methods*, LNCS (pp. 128-147). Vol. 2999, Springer Verlag.

Chen, J., & Yang, Y. (2006). Key Research Issues in Grid Workflow Verification and Validation, In *Proc. 4th ACM Australasian Workshop on Grid Computing and e-Research* (pp. 97-104), Vol. 54.

Cimatti, A., & Clarke, E., Giunchiglia, E. et al. (2002). NuSMV2: an Open Source Tool for Symbolic Model Checking, *Computer Aided Verification*, LNCS Vol. 2404, (pp. 359-364). Springer Verlag.

Clarke, E. M., Grumberg, Jr. O., Peled, D. A. (1999). *Model Checking*. Cambridge, Mass: MIT Press.

Czajkowski, K., Dan, A., Rofrano, J., et al. (2003). Agreement-based Grid Service Management (OGSI-Agreement), *Global Grid Forum*, GRAAP-WG Author Contribution.

Deelman, E., Kesselman, C., et al. (2002). GriPhyN and LIGO, Building a Virtual Data Grid for Gravitational Wave Scientists (pp.225-234), In *Proc. 11th IEEE Int. Symp. on High Performance Distributed Computing*, Edinburgh, Scotland.

Fahringer, T., Qin, J. & Hainzer, S. (2005). "Specification of Grid Workflow Applications with AGWL: An Abstract Grid Workflow Language", In *Proc. IEEE Int. Symp. on Cluster Computing and the Grid* (pp. 676-685).

Ferrari, G. L., Gnesi, S., et al. (2003). A Model-checking Verification Environment for Mobile Processes., *ACM Transactions on Software Engineering and Methodology*, 12(4), 440-473.

Foster, I. (2002). What is the Grid? A Three Point Checklist, *GRIDToday*.

Foster, I. & Kesselman, C. (1998). *The Grid: Blueprint for a New Computing Infrastructure*, San Francisco, CA USA, Morgan Kaufmann Publishers.

Foster, I., Kesselman,C. Nick, J. M. & Tuecke, S. (2002). Grid Services for Distributed System Integration, *IEEE Computer*, 35(6), 37-46.

Foster, I., Kesselman, C. & Tuecke, S. (2001). The Anatomy of the Grid: Enabling Scalable Virtual Organizations, *International Journal of Supercomputer Applications*, 15(3), 200-222.

He, X., Sun, X., & von Laszewski, G. (2003). QoS Guided Min-Min Heuristic for Grid Task Scheduling, *Journal of Computer Science & Technology*, 18(4), 442-451.

Keahey, K., Araki, T., & Lane, P. (2004). Agreement-Based Interactions for Experimental Science, Vol. 3149. In *Proc. Euro-Par 2004 Parallel Processing* (pp. 399-408).

Keahey, K., Papka, M. E., et al. (2004). Grids for Experimental Science: the Virtual Control Room, In *Proc. 2nd IEEE Int. Workshop on Challenges of Large Applications in Distributed Environments* (pp. 4-11).

Litzkow, M., Livny, M., & Mutka, M. (1998). Condor - a Hunter of Idle Workstations, In *Proc. 8th Int. Conf. on Distributed Computing Systems* (pp. 104-111).

Milner, R. (1999). *Communicating and Mobile Systems: The Pi Calculus*, Cambridge University Press.

Montanari, U. & Pistore, M. (1995). Checking Bisimilarity for Finitary Pi-calculus, *Concurrency Theory*, LNCS Vol. 962, Springer Verlag, pp. 42-56.

Németh, Z., & Sunderam, V. (2003). Characterizing Grids Attributes, Definitions, and Formalisms, *Journal of Grid Computing*, 1(1), 9-23.

Nicola, R. D., & Vaandrager, F. (1995). Three Logics for Branching Bisimulation, *J. ACM*, 42(2), 458-487.

Pautasso, C. & Alonso G. (2006) The Jopera visual composition language. Journal of Visual Languages and Computing. 16(1-2). 119-152.

Pearlman, L., Kesselman, C., et al. (2004). Distributed Hybrid Earthquake Engineering Experiments: Experiences with a Ground-Shaking Grid Application, In *Proc. 13ᵗʰ IEEE Int. Symp. on High Performance Distributed Computing* (pp. 14-23).

Puhlmann, F. & Weske, M. (2005). Using the Pi-calculus for Formalizing Workflow Patterns, *Business Process Management*, LNCS Vol. 3649, (pp. 153-168).

Sangiorgi, D. & Walker, D. (2001). *The Pi-calculus: a Theory of Mobile Processes*, Cambridge University Press.

Smith, H. (2003), Business Process Management - the Third Wave: Business Process Modeling Language (BPML) and its Pi-calculus Foundations, *Information and Software Technology*, 45(15), 1065-1069.

Spooner, D. P., Cao, J., et al. (2005). Performance-aware Workflow Management for Grid Computing, *The Computer Journal*, Special Focus - Grid Performability, 48(3), 347-357.

Taylor, I., Shields, M., et al. (2003). Distributed P2P Computing within Triana: A Galaxy Visualization Test Case, In *Proc. 17ᵗʰ IEEE Int. Parallel & Distributed Processing Symp.*, Nice, France.

Vander Aalst, W. M. P. (2005). Pi Calculus versus Petri Nets: Let us eat 'humble pie' rather than Further Inflate the 'Pi hype', *BPTrends*, 3(5), 1-11.

Xu, K., Wang, Y. & Wu, C. (2006). Ensuring Secure and Robust Grid Applications - From a Formal Method Point of View, *Advances in Grid and Pervasive Computing*, 3947, 537-546.

Yu, J., & Buyya, R. (2004). A Novel Architecture for Realizing Grid Workflow using Tuple Spaces, In *Proc. 5ᵗʰ IEEE/ACM Int. Workshop on Grid Computing* (pp. 119-128), Pittsburgh, USA.

Yu, J. & Buyya, R. (2005). A Taxonomy of Workflow Management Systems for Grid Computing, *Journal of Grid Computing*, 3(3-4), 171-200.

Zhang, H., Keahey, K., & Allcock, W. (2004), Providing Data Transfer with QoS as Agreement-based Service, In *Proc. IEEE Int. Conf. on Services Computing* (pp. 344-353). ShangHai, China.

Zhang, S., Gu, N., & Li, S., (2004). Grid Workflow based on Dynamic Modeling and Scheduling, In *Proc. IEEE Information Technology:* Vol. 2. *Coding and Computing* (pp. 35-39).

Chapter IV
The Cost–Based Resource Management in Combination with QoS for Grid Computing

Chuliang Weng
Shanghai Jiao Tong University, China

Jian Cao
Shanghai Jiao Tong University, China

Minglu Li
Shanghai Jiao Tong University, China

ABSTRACT

In the grid context, the scheduling can be grouped into two categories: offline scheduling and online scheduling. In the offline scheduling scenario, the sequence of jobs is known in advance, scheduling is based on information about all jobs in the sequence. While, in the online scheduling scenario a job is known only after all predecessors have been scheduled, and a job is scheduled only according to information of its predecessors in the sequence. This chapter focuses on resource management issue in the grid context, and introduces the two cost-based scheduling algorithms for offline job assignment and online job assignment on the computational grid, respectively.

INTRODUCTION

As a new infrastructure for next generation computing, computational grid enables the sharing, selection, and aggregation of geographically distributed heterogeneous resources for solving large-scale problems in science, engineering and commerce (Foster, I. & Kesselman, C., 1999). Many studies have focused on providing middleware and software programming layers to facilitate grid computing. There are a number of projects such as Globus, ChinaGrid, EcoGRID that deal with a variety of problems such as resource specification, information service, resource allocation and security issues in a grid environment involving different administrative domains. However, a crucial issue for the efficient deployment of distributed applications on the grid is that of scheduling (Foster, I. & Kesselman, C. (Ed.), 1996). A computational grid consists of geographically distributed heterogeneous resources, such as CPU with different speed, and network with different bandwidth. These resources in the grid context are independent, while they are not even directly comparable because they are measured in unrelated units. This will make it difficult to choose the optimal machine from the list of available machines to which to schedule a given job. The concept of cost is adopted for the scheduling problem based on economic principles. The key of the method is to convert the total usage of different kinds of resources, such as CPU, memory and bandwidth into a homogeneous cost. According to the goal of minimizing the total cost, arrival jobs are scheduled in the computational grid. This method could facilitate the determination on scheduling, while considering variety of aspects which have influenced on the scheduling performance. However, the open issue of the cost-based scheduling strategy is how to determine the cost based on the usage factor of the variety of resources. In the grid context, the scheduling can be grouped into two categories: offline scheduling and online scheduling. In the offline scheduling scenario, the sequence of jobs is known in advance, scheduling is based on information about all jobs in the sequence. While, in the online scheduling scenario a job is known only after all predecessors have been scheduled, and a job is scheduled only according to information of its predecessors in the sequence. In this chapter, the authors focus on resource management issue in the grid context, and introduce the two cost-based scheduling algorithms for offline job assignment and online job assignment on the computational grid, respectively. Firstly, the cost-based resource management and scheduling methodology is introduced for the computational grid, which borrows the idea from economic principles. Then, a cost-based offline scheduling algorithm Qsufferage is presented for the offline scheduling mode in the grid environment. The algorithm considers the location of each task's input data, while makespan and response ratio are chosen as metrics for performance evaluation. The Qsufferage algorithm determines scheduling policy with minimizing the makespan of the whole application and minimizing the waiting time for executing as QoS for an individual task in the application. The performance of algorithm Qsufferage, Xsufferage, Sufferage, Min-min, and Max-min is tested by simulation that is based on the SimGrid Toolkit. Thirdly, a cost-based online scheduling algorithm is presented for the online scheduling mode in the grid environment. Compared to other online scheduling algorithms, the presented algorithm can provide the lower limit of performance with theoretical guarantee. For validating the effectivity of the presented algorithm, the authors compare the performance of the presented algorithm with the greedy algorithm. Experimental result shows that the presented algorithm can outperform the greedy algorithm. The work is inspired by the economic mechanism, through which the total usage of different kinds of resources, such as CPU, memory and bandwidth can be converted into a single cost. It is convenient for scheduler to assign job in the computational grid according to minimizing cost of all resources, achieving the goal of achieving the maximal performance of the grid system.

BACKGROUND

Ensuring that the variety of applications would achieve good performance in the grid environment is not a trivial task, and a number of issues make scheduling such applications challenging. Resources on the grid are typically shared so that the contention created by multiple applications results in dynamically fluctuating delays and qualities of service. Moreover, due to dynamic nature of grids, information about the whole system is typically changing with time, which further complicates scheduling. In addition, resources in a grid environment are heterogeneous and may not perform similarly for the same application. Due to these difficulties, the scheduling of applications on computational grids has been the target of considerable efforts in recent years (Casanova, H., Bartol, T.M., Stiles, J., & Berman. F., 2001; Smallen, S., Cirne, W., Frey, J., Berman, F., Wolski, R., Su, M., Kesselman, C., Young, S., & Ellisman, M., 2000; Casanova, H., Legrand, A., Zagorodnov, D., & Berman. F. , 2000; Takefusa, A., Casanova, H., Matsuoka, S., & Berman, F., 2001; Subramani, V., Kettimuthu, R., Srinivasan, S., & Sadayappan P., 2002; Heymann, E., Senar, M.A., Luque, E., & Livny, M., 2000; Ernemann, C., Hamscher, V., Schwiegelshohn, U., Yahyapour, R., & Streit, A., 2000).

There are many heuristic algorithms for offline scheduling on heterogeneous systems (Ernemann, C. et al, 2000), and attempts to extend these heuristic algorithms to the grid environment have been made, such as Min-min, Max-min, Sufferage, Xsufferage. Besides, a deadline scheduling strategy (Takefusa, A., et al, 2001) is proposed that is appropriate for the multi-client multi-server case, and augmented with "Load Correction" and "Fallback" mechanisms, which could improve the performance of the algorithm. A distributed scheduling algorithm that uses multiple simultaneous requests at different sites is presented in (Subramani, V., et al, 2002), this algorithm might be effective for scheduling when the resource information is scare and there are many redundant computers in the grid. A scheduling strategy for master–worker applications is discussed in (Heymann, E., et al, 2000), which dynamically measures the execution times of tasks and uses this information to dynamically adjust the number of worker to achieve a desirable efficiency, and minimize the impact on loss of speedup. Paper (Ernemann, C., et al, 2000) addresses the potential benefit of sharing jobs between independent sites in a grid environment, and discusses simple extensions of backfilling and host selection strategies with simulation. These heuristic algorithms are effective for scheduling in the computational grid, however most scheduling strategies have no theoretical guarantees.

Paper (Amir, Y., Awerbuch, B., Barak, A., Borgstrom, R., & Keren, A., 2000) proposes an opportunity cost approach for online scheduling, however the approach just focuses on the computing cluster environment, which is not suitable for the computational grid environment. Further, there are some resource efforts, which directly introduce the economic mechanism to resource management for grid computing. Resource allocation in this method can be decomposed into two sub-problems. One is how to determine the price of resources in accordance with the dynamic supply and need, and the other is how to allocate resources for achieving the goal of high efficient utilization of resources in response to current resource prices. At present, researches on resource management for grid computing based on economics principles include works (Wolski, R., Plank, J., Brevik, J., & Bryan T., 2001; Subramoniam, K., Maheswaran, M., & Toulouse, M., 2002; Cao, H., Xiao, N., 2002; Buyya, R., 2002): the centralized pricing method is studied in (Wolski, R., et al, 2001; Subramoniam, K., et al, 2002), and the distributed pricing method is studied in (Cao, H., et al, 2002). In GRACE (Wolski, R., et al, 2001), resource prices were given to them artificially in economic-based resource scheduling experiments, leaving no space for optimization of resources allocation (Nakai, J., 2002). Distributed pricing WALRAS algorithm is presented in (Cheng, J. & Wellman, M., 1998), and the suitable situation of this algorithm is also discussed. Distributed independent pricing methods and centralized simultaneous methods are compared in (Ygge, F., 1998). The shortcoming of this method is the pricing difficulty in the dynamic grid computing environment.

Research efforts also focus on the development of application schedulers for computational grid environments, which provide a platform for the deployment of various applications with scheduling algorithms. AppLes (Casanova, H., Obertelli, G., Berman, F., & Wolski, R., 2000) provide a methodology, application software, and software environment for deploying applications in the grid context. NetSolve (Plank, J.S., Casanova, H., Beck, M., & Dongarra, J.J., 1999) is a software environment with integration of fault-tolerance and task migration in a way that is transparent to the end user. Nimrod-G (Abramson, D., Buyya, R., & Giddy, J., 2002) is a tool for automated modeling and execution of parameter sweep applications on computational grids.

THE COST-BASED SCHEDULING METHODOLOGY

Scheduling tasks or jobs is a complicated problem in the grid environment, where the scheduler should consider the characteristic of jobs, the network topology of the grid system, the performance of computing nodes, etc. A simply and effective method is expected to facilitate the scheduling in the grid context. In this chapter, therefore we will introduce the cost-based method to achieve the goal.

In the economic activity, there are varieties of commodities with different functions, and there are many possible means to value all kinds of commodities. In practice, the price is an effective measurement to the value of one commodity, and all kinds of commodities can be exchange based on their prices. Similarly, there are varieties of computing resources such CPU, memory, network bandwidth, storage, and the measurement means of one resource is different from the other. So we can borrow the idea of economic principle, and convert the usage of different kinds of resources into the single measurement, that is the cost. Based on the concept of cost, the scheduling decision can be simply determined according to the single metric rather than considering different kinds of impact factors, and it is beneficial to resource scheduling in the grid environment with a variety of heterogeneous resources.

For example, a task will run with the memory of m MB and the CPU with c regularized seconds, and there are two machines (a and b) on which the task can execute. From the aspect of CPU's usage, the cost of the task on machine a is larger than the cost on machine b, while the cost of the task on machine

Figure 1. Cost on the two machines

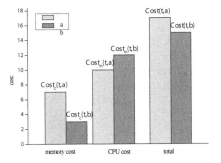

a is less than the cost on machine *b* from the aspect of memory's usage. According to the principle of minimizing the total cost, it is simply to determine on which machine the task will be assigned. Formally, this problem can be described as follows.

The cost of task *t* consists of CPU's cost $Cost_c$ and memory's cost $Cost_m$, and costs of the task executed on machine *a* and *b* can be defined:

$$Cost(t,a) = Cost_c(t,a) + Cost_m(t,a) \qquad (1)$$

$$Cost(t,b) = Cost_c(t,b) + Cost_m(t,b) \qquad (2)$$

We just compare the value of *Cost(t, a)* and *Cost(t, b)*, and could choose the machine *b* to run task *t*.

How to convert the usage of multiple kinds of resources into the single cost, is vital to the cost-based scheduling methodology. The characteristic of the task and the property of the grid system should be considered for determining the value of the cost. Sequentially the two cost-based resource scheduling strategies will be introduced in next sections respectively, which will demonstrate that the cost-based resource scheduling methodology is effective for grid computing.

COST-BASED OFFLINE ALGORITHM

In this section, we will introduce a cost-based offline scheduling (or batch scheduling) algorithm Qsufferage for the offline scheduling mode in the grid environment (Weng, C.L. & Lu, X.D., 2005). The algorithm considers the location of each task's input data, while makespan and response ratio are chosen as metrics for performance evaluation. The Qsufferage algorithm determines scheduling policy with minimizing the makespan of the whole application and minimizing the waiting time for executing as QoS for an individual task in the application.

Problem Statement

The grid environment consists of *resource domain*s that are individual and autonomous administrative domains, and contain certain number of computational hosts. A computational grid can be denoted by $RD = \{rd_1, rd_2, ..., rd_j, ...\}$, in which rd_j denotes the *j*th resource domain. In resource domain $rd_j = \{rd_{j,1}, rd_{j,2}, ..., rd_{j,k}, ..., s_j\}$, $rd_{j,k}$ denotes the *k*th host and s_j denotes a data repository in it. Hosts inside one resource domain have different relative CPU speed corresponding to heterogeneity.

Figure 2. Network topology

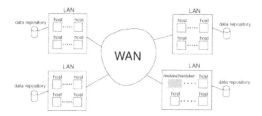

It is metascheduler that receives requirements of users in the grid environment and maps users' tasks into geographically distributed resources. There is one metascheduler in a certain resource domain that dedicates to schedule tasks of bag-of-tasks applications (illustrated in Fig. 2).

The topology of the network is shown in Fig. 2. Hosts inside the same resource domain are connected with LAN, which bandwidth is higher compared to the bandwidth of WAN through which different resource domains are connected. In addition, network bandwidth varies corresponding to realistic network. A task assigned on some host not only can access to the data repository located in the same resource domain, also can access to the remote data repositories.

For Grid applications such as massive searches (such as key breaking), MCell simulations, fractals calculations (such as Mandelbrot), tomographic reconstructions, etc., one application consists of many tasks among which existing tasks waiting to be scheduled are independent each other, do not need inter-task communication, which resembles the SPMD (Single Program Multiple Data) model. In addition, before execution tasks need an input data file, which may be shared by other tasks in the application. We call this kind of task as *Meta-task*. Based on characteristics of these kinds of applications, the Meta-task model is established as follows.

It is assumed that tasks arrive at the metascheduler according to a Poisson process. At a certain time, there is a set of tasks t_i denoted by T that waits to be scheduled to the suitable hosts in the grid environment. For each task in T, we assume an estimation of processing amount is available that can be provided by the user, computed from analytical models or historical information, or provided by facilities such as the Network Weather Service. Before execution of each task, the input data needed by the task should be retrieved from one data repository among multiply available data repositories for this task. The size of input data for each task is known in advance, and tasks do not migrate between hosts once assigned.

In addition, *response ratio* is defined as QoS for an individual task that will occur in the Qsufferage algorithm.

$$rr = \frac{the\ duration\ of\ running}{the\ completed\ time - the\ submited\ time}$$

The response ratio *rr* reflects how long the user expects to wait upon the result for an individual task, and average response ratio of all tasks in an application can measure the whole Quality of Service of the algorithm from the point of view of response time.

Figure 3. Mapping strategy

> (1) compute the time of the next mapping event: $t + \Delta t$
> (2) $T = T' +$ newly arrival tasks
> (3) retrieve the real-time information about available resources in the grid environment
> (4) evaluate $r(s_l)$, $r(rd_{j,k})$, $Tr(s_l, rd_{j,k}, t_i)$, $E(t_i, rd_{j,k})$
> (5) heuristically MAP : $T \rightarrow RD$
> (6) $T' =$ unassigned tasks in T

Mapping Strategy

In the offline mode, tasks are not mapped onto hosts immediately as they arrive; instead they are collected into a set of tasks that is examined for mapping at prescheduled times called *mapping events*. The online mode heuristic is suitable for the low arrival rate, while offline heuristics can get higher performance when the arrival rate of tasks is high because there will be a sufficient number of tasks to keep hosts busy between the mapping events, and scheduling is according to the resource requirement information of all tasks in the set.

In the offline mode batch-mode heuristic, the set of tasks waiting to be scheduled consists of newly arrival tasks and tasks that were still not mapped at earlier mapping events. At each mapping event, the mapping strategy is presented as follows:

In Fig. 3, $r(s_l)$ denotes the expected time the data repository s_l will become ready to provide service, while $r(rd_{j,k})$ denotes the expected time the host $rd_{j,k}$ will become ready to execute a task. $Tr(s_l, rd_{j,k}, t_i)$ denotes the amount of time for transferring data from s_l to $rd_{j,k}$ for execution of task t_i. The expected execution time $E(t_i, rd_{j,k})$ is defined as the amount of time taken by $rd_{j,k}$ to execute t_i when $rd_{j,k}$ has no load. t denotes the current time, and Δt denotes the mapping event interval.

Heuristic Algorithm

There are some existing heuristic algorithms: Min-min, Max-min, Sufferage, and Xsufferage, which mainly focus on the *makespan* of an application, which is the total length of the scheduling, or equivalently the time when the first task starts running subtracted from the time when the last task is completed. However, in many situations, not only minimizing the makespan of the application but also minimizing the time of each task in the application waiting for executing is the goal of scheduling. Minimizing the waiting time of each task is an important issue especially in the situation that tasks of the application have relation to their predecessors. For example, Tomography is a widely used technique to reconstruct the three-dimensional structure of an object from a series of two-dimensional projections. Minimum waiting time of each task can provide quasi-real-time feedback on the quality of the data acquisition that will affect how to generate successive tasks. Therefore, Qsufferage determines scheduling policy with minimizing the makespan of the whole application and minimizing the waiting time for executing as QoS for an individual task.

At each mapping event, the scheduling algorithm should determine how to assign tasks in T on the computational grid. For assigning one task in T (the set of tasks waiting to be assigned), Qsufferage includes three steps. The *first step* is to compute the expected completion time of each task on each host in the grid system with the data from each available data repository, which can provide input data needed by the task. $C(t_i, rd_{j,k}, s_l)$ denotes the expected completion time of task t_i on the host $rd_{j,k}$ with the data from the data repository s_l. The value of the expected completion time is determined by the earliest available time of the host, the earliest available time of the available data repository, the overhead of transferring input data from the available data repository to the host, and the execution time of the task on the host. The *second step* is to compute sufferage value suf_i of each task. For a task, one host in the jth resource domain and one corresponding data repository are determined as their index are (m_j, d_j) respectively, with which this task has the cluster-level MCT in the range of this resource domain. And for a task, $rd_{c1,m_{c1}}$ denotes the host on which this task has its minimum cluster-lever MCT with the input data from data repository $s_{d_{c1}}$, $rd_{c2,m_{c2}}$ denotes the host on which this task has its second minimum cluster-lever MCT with the input data from data repository $s_{d_{c2}}$. The sufferage value of a task is computed as the square of the response ratio of this task running on the host $rd_{c1,m_{c1}}$, multiplied by the difference between its minimum cluster-lever MCT and its second minimum cluster-lever MCT, where the square is determined through the following experiment. The *third step* is to determine the task with the maximum sufferage value, and assign this task to the corresponding host. In addition, delete this task from *T*, update the available time of the corresponding host and data repository, and decide whether to terminate this mapping event.

Experiment and Result

For performance evaluation of the Qsufferage heuristic, a series of experiments are performed, and the other four algorithms are evaluated together with the Qsufferage: Min-Min, Max-Min, Sufferage, and Xsufferage.

To run experiments, a simulator is developed based on the SimGrid toolkit. The simulated Grid consists of 5 resource domains containing 5, 6, 7, 8 and 8 hosts, and 5 data repositories that locate in each resource domain. Taking into account the characteristic of heterogeneity of hosts in a resource domain, the speed of hosts is assumed to be random and uniformly distributed among 200, 400, 600, 800, 1000 (Mflop/s). The load on each host is simulated by traces obtained from Network Weather Service measurements on actual systems. These traces contain percentum of free CPU as a function of time, and they are used in the simulation to make hosts in the experiment to behave similar to real machines. The network links are classified into LAN and WAN, the bandwidth of LAN in a resource domain is assumed to be uniformly distributed between 2.5Mbit/s and 5 Mbit/s, while the bandwidth of WAN between resource domains is assumed to be uniformly distributed between 0.4Mbit/s and 0.6Mbit/s. the LAN/WAN traffic during simulations is determined by Paxson's self-similar network traffic traces whose standard deviation is 10% of the bandwidth.

The total of tasks is 1000, and tasks arrive at the metascheduler according to a Poisson process and the average task inter-arrive time is 6 seconds. The execution time of each task uniformly distributed between 100 and 300 seconds with the average speed of CPU in the Grid. The input data needed by each task is the same size, and it can be fetched from one of two available data repository for this task, which is randomly appointed. The mapping event interval is 500 seconds.

Figure 4.(a) Makespan vs. the size of input data   *Figure 4.(b) Average response ratio vs. the size of input data*

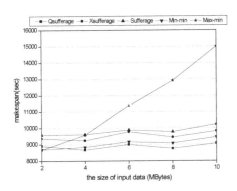
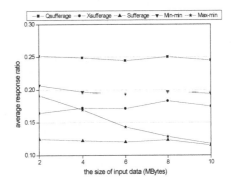

makespan is adopted as the metric for the throughput performance of algorithms and *response ratio* is adopted to measure the QoS of algorithms. *Average response ratio* is average of all tasks' response ratio in one application. With performing experiments, the performance of Qsufferage is tested compared to the other four algorithms with varying the size of input data files.

In Fig. 4a, as the size of each task's input data increases from 2 to 10 Mbytes, the makespan of the Max-min heuristic increases quickly, while the other four heuristics increase little in makespan, and the makespan of Qsufferage is the minimum. In Fig. 4b, it shows that average response ratio fluctuates while the size of input data increases. The average response ratio of Max-min decreases quickly, and the minimum of average response ratio is Sufferage's, while the maximum is Qsufferage's. Experimental results indicate that Qsufferage outperforms the other four algorithms in terms of both makespan and average response ratio.

This can be explained as follows. If the task with the maximum difference between the minimum cluster-level MCT and the second minimum cluster-level MCT is not scheduled instantly, the makespan will most likely increase quickly, this rationale has been demonstrated in Xsufferage. However it only considers one factor that affects the whole performance of execution of all tasks in one application. Besides this factor, the other factor, response ratio considered by Qsufferage concerns the performance of single task, i.e., QoS for an individual task. If each task has a maximum response ratio, it shows that each task has a minimum overhead on waiting for executing, note that it is also helpful to reduce the makespan. Response ratio reflects the QoS for an individual task, also has influence on the whole performance. So taking into account the two factors simultaneously in Qsufferage will not only contribute to increasing response ratio, but also be of benefit to reduce makespan.

COST-BASED ONLINE ALGORITHM

In this section, we will introduce a cost-based online scheduling algorithm for the online scheduling mode in the grid environment (Weng, C.L., Li, M.L., & Lu, X.D., 2006). Compared to other online scheduling algorithms, the presented algorithm can provide the lower limit of performance with theoretical guarantee.

Problem Statement

The topology of the computational grid is illustrated as Fig.5. Resources in the grid are organized as resource domains that are individual and autonomous administrative domains, which usually are in the range of Local Area Network (LAN). It is the *metascheduler* that receives the requirement of users in the grid environment and assigns users' jobs to geographically distributed resource domains, and the metascheduler is connected to resource domains by Wide Area Network (WAN). One data repository is available at the metascheduler and input data needed by users' jobs are stored in the data repository in advance.

It is assumed that the computational grid consists of m resource domains that are geographically distributed. Resource domain rd_i and the metascheduler are connected with bandwidth $r_b(rd_i)$. Compared to communication overhead of transferring job applications and input data from metascheduler to resource domains in WAN, the communication overhead in the resource domain is ignored. Host rd_{ij} in resource domain rd_i has a CPU resource of speed $r_c(rd_{ij})$, and for simplicity it is assumed that

Figure 5. Topology of the computational grid

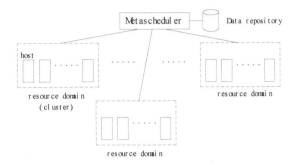

each resource domain has n computational hosts. All other resources associated with the host will be abstracted out, although the framework can be extended to handle additional resources.

There are many different factors that will influence the effective load of hosts in the grid context and the execution time of jobs running there, so the *unrelated machines* model is chosen for studying the scheduling algorithm. That is, the load of a given host added by a given job is known, but the load doesn't need to have any relationship to the load the job would add to other hosts. There are also two other relevant machine models, i.e., *identical machines* and *related machines*. In the model of *identical machines*, all of the hosts are identical so that the completion time of a unit job on a given host is determined only by the load of the host. In the model of *related machines*, the hosts are identical except that hosts' speeds differ from others so that the completion time of a unit job on a given host just depends on the load and the speed of the host.

Jobs arrive online and each job has to be immediately assigned to one of hosts in the computational grid, i.e. online scheduling. *Jobs arrive over time* is adopted as the online paradigm, i.e., the attribute of a job is known when it arrives, and each job jb_k is defined by following parameters:

- The number of CPU cycles required by the job, $n_c(jb_k)$.
- The communication amount it requires, $n_b(jb_k)$. In the following, $n_b(jb_k)$ denotes the size of input data needed by job jb_k for that usually the size of a job application can be ignored compared to the size of input data required by the job.

It is assumed that $n_c(jb_k)$ and $n_b(jb_k)$ are known upon job's arrival with the lack of knowledge of jobs arriving in the future. After assigned to a host in computational grid immediately when it arrives, a job will not be reassigned to other hosts later. The input data required by a job should be transferred to the assigned host before the execution of the job.

The scheduling goal is to minimize the *makespan* of a given job sequence by developing an appropriate method for job assignment on hosts in the computational grid.

Scheduling Algorithm

System Load

$S(rd_i, jb_k)$ denotes the set of jobs assigned in resource domain rd_i after job jb_k has been assigned on the computational grid, and $S(rd_{ij}, jb_k)$ denotes the set of jobs assigned in host rd_{ij} after job jb_k has been assigned on the computational grid. Then they satisfy the following equation:

$$S(rd_i, jb_k) = \bigcup_{j=1}^{n} S(rd_{ij}, jb_k) \tag{3}$$

The load on a given resource equals its usage divided by its capacity. Then after job jb_k was assigned, the load of the network connecting resource domain rd_i and the metascheduler is defined by:

$$l_b(rd_i, jb_k) = \sum_{jb_p \in S(rd_i, jb_k)} n_b(jb_p) / r_b(rd_i) \tag{4}$$

After job jb_k was assigned in the grid system, the CPU load of host rd_{ij} in resource domain rd_i is defined by:

$$l_c(rd_{ij}, jb_k) = \sum_{jb_p \in S(rd_{ij}, jb_k)} n_c(jb_p) / r_c(rd_{ij}) \tag{5}$$

The Cost-Based Online Scheduling Algorithm

For simplicity, we will abbreviate $l_b(rd_i, jb_k)$ as $l_b(i, k)$, and $l_c(rd_{ij}, jb_k)$ as $l_c(i, j, k)$. $l_b^o(i, k)$ and $l_c^o(i, j, k)$ are the corresponding quantities for the scheduling produced by the optimal offline algorithm, which are the counterpart of $l_b^o(i, k)$ and $l_c(i, j, k)$ produced by the online scheduling algorithm.

For normalizing the load, we introduce a positive parameter Δ, and normalize $\bar{x} = x / \Delta$ for load x.

The *marginal cost* of a job jb_k assigned to host rd_{ij} in the grid is denoted by $Cost(i, j, k)$, which consists of the marginal cost of network $Cost_b(i, k)$, the marginal cost of CPU $Cost_c(i, j, k)$, and they are defined by:

$$Cost_c(i, j, k) = \alpha^{\bar{l}_c(i,j,k-1)+\bar{n}_c(jb_k)/r_c(rd_{ij})} - \alpha^{\bar{l}_c(i,j,k-1)} \tag{6}$$

$$Cost_b(i, k) = \beta^{\bar{l}_b(i,k-1)+\bar{n}_b(jb_k)/r_b(rd_i)} - \beta^{\bar{l}_b(i,k-1)} \tag{7}$$

$$Cost(i, j, k) = Cost_c(i, j, k) + Cost_b(i, k) \tag{8}$$

Where α, β is a constant, and $\alpha > 1$, $\beta > 1$.

The *cost-based online scheduling* algorithm puts a job on the host where its resource consumption has the minimum marginal cost according to equation (8). The goal of this algorithm is to minimize the maximum of the load of hosts and networks in the grid context, and correspondingly the goal of minimizing the makespan can be attained. Given a sequence of N jobs, $jb_1, jb_2, ..., jb_N$, the *cost-based online scheduling* algorithm can be described using pseudo-code as Fig.6.

Figure 6. The cost-based online scheduling algorithm

$$
\begin{aligned}
&\text{Set } \Delta: \quad \Delta = \max_{i,j}\{l_b^o(i,N), l_c^o(i,j,N)\}; \\
&\text{while(job } jb_k \text{ arrives) } \{ \quad /* \ k = 1,2,...,N \ */ \\
&\quad Cost(i,j,k) = Cost_c(i,j,k) + Cost_b(i,k); \\
&\quad (I,J) = \arg\min_{i,j}(Cost(i,j,k)); \\
&\quad \text{Assign: } jb_k \rightarrow rd_{IJ}; \\
&\quad \text{Update: } l_b(i,k), \ l_c(i,j,k); \\
&\}
\end{aligned}
$$

Performance Analysis

For *any sequence J* of *N* jobs, $jb_1, jb_2, ..., jb_N$, the makespan of the schedule generated by online algorithm *A* is denoted by $A(J)$, and let $OPT(J)$ denote the makespan of the optimal offline algorithm for the *sequence J*. Online algorithm *A*'s competitive ratio is then

$$
c_A = \sup_J \frac{A(J)}{OPT(J)} \tag{9}
$$

Where the supremum is over any sequence *J* of jobs. In other words, online algorithm *A* is $c_A - competitive$.

Theorem 1. The *cost-based online scheduling* algorithm is $O(\log(n + 1)m) - competitive$ in the computational grid environment illustrated as Fig.5.

Experiments

In the above section, we introduce the cost-based online scheduling algorithm, and analyze the performance of this algorithm against the performance of the optimal offline algorithm in theory. In the section, we focus on testing the performance of this algorithm.

To run the experiments, a simulator also is developed based on the SimGrid toolkit. This toolkit provides basic functions for the simulation of distributed applications in the grid environment. It was built for the study of scheduling algorithms and resource management policies in the grid environment. The parameters chosen in the simulation experiment is listed as Table 1. The CPU speed of hosts in the grid is random and uniformly distributed among $[1, 10] \times 10^9$ (flops). Jobs arrive according to a Poisson Process and the input data needed by each job should be sent to the assigned host before the execution of the job. The input data of jobs and the interval of job arrivals are the average value when they are mentioned. Each experimental result is the average of values produced by 500 runs of simulation.

For testing the performance of the cost-based online algorithm, we will compare this presented algorithm with the greedy algorithm, the round-robin algorithm and the random algorithm.

Greedy algorithm also is an effective online scheduling algorithm and it can be analyzed theoretically. In the paper, the greedy algorithm can be correspondingly considered as follows: for each arrival

Table 1. Parameters used in the experiments

Grid computing environment		
m (the number of resource domains)	16	Fixed
n (the number of hosts in each resource domain)	128	Fixed
r_c (the speed of CPU) (flops)	$[1, 10] \times 10^9$	Uniform distribution
r_b (the bandwidth of network) (Mb/s)	$[10, 100]$	Uniform distribution
Job attributes		
Average interval of job arrivals (s)	2/4/6/8/10	Poisson arrivals
Total of jobs	5000	Fixed
n_c (the number of CPU cycles) (flop)	$[20, 200] \times 10^9$	Uniform distribution
n_b (average size of input data) (Mb)	20/40/60/80/100/200/400/600/800/1000	Uniform distribution
Scheduling parameters		
α (coefficient in the cost function)	1.9	Fixed
β (coefficient in the cost function)	1.9	Fixed
Simulation runs for each scenario	500	Fixed

job, the metascheduler immediately assigns the job to the host with the minimal sum of the current load of host, the current load of network connecting the metascheduler and the host, and the execution time of the job on the host.

With the *round-robin* algorithm, the arrival job is assigned to each host in each resource domain in turn. According to the *random* algorithm, the arrival job is assigned to a randomly selected host in the computational grid.

In the Fig.7 (a), the size of input data is 60Mb. As the average interval of job arrivals increase from 2 to 10 seconds, the makespan of the four algorithms increases correspondingly. For a fixed number of jobs with the same attribute except the average interval of job arrivals, the makespan naturally increases as the average interval increases, especially in the situation that the demand on CPU with regard to jobs arriving in a unit time is less than the processing capability of the grid system. And in the Fig.7 (b), the size of input data is 600Mb, and the average interval of job arrivals also increase from 2 to 10 seconds.

Fig.7 (a) and Fig.7 (b) show that the cost-based algorithm can attain less makespan than the other three algorithms. With the size of input data increases from 60Mb to 600Mb, the cost-based algorithm can perform better than the greedy algorithm. According to Fig.7, the performance of the round-robin algorithm and the random algorithm is poorer than the performance of the cost-based algorithm and the greedy algorithm, because the information of system and task is not considered into determining the assignment in the round-robin algorithm and the random algorithm.

Although the information of system and task is used to determine the scheduling in the cost-based algorithm and the greedy algorithm, the cost-based algorithm can outperform the greedy algorithm. This result can be explained as follows. The marginal cost in the cost-based algorithm is an exponential function of resource load, which benefits to determine the optimal candidate host. The merit of exponential function is that for assigning a job to the system, not only increase in resource load created by the new job but also the current resource load has influence on the marginal cost of the new job. For example, assumed two hosts' current loads are 0.2 and 0.6 respectively, and increases in two hosts'

Figure 7. Makespan vs. the interval of job arrivals

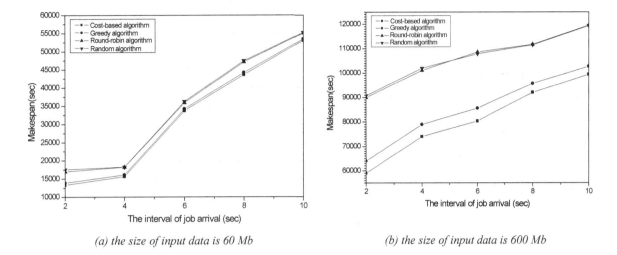

(a) the size of input data is 60 Mb   (b) the size of input data is 600 Mb

loads created by the new job both are 0.1. If the marginal cost function is linear but exponential, the marginal cost of assigning the job to two hosts is the same. However, with an exponential function, the marginal cost on the host with the heavy load will be larger than on the host with the light load, under the condition that the base of the exponential function is greater than 1. As the method of determining the cost is more effective, the performance of the cost-based algorithm is better than the performance of the greedy algorithm.

FUTURE TRENDS

In this chapter, we focus on the issue of the resource management in the grid context, and introduce the concept of cost adopted for the scheduling problem based on economic principles. Correspondingly, the two cost-based scheduling algorithms are introduced, which are suitable for the online job assignment and the offline job assignment, respectively. Experiments indicate that the cost-based resource management is an effective method.

In these presented methods, a metascheduler is expected to exist in the grid system, which is responsible for scheduling tasks on computing nodes in the grid system. This schema is suitable for the computational grid scenario, where computing nodes are connected by the high speed network, and all computational resources can be controlled and utilized by one manager computer. Generally, the scenario is that, grid resources are usually assumed to be provided by the individual organizations without considering the necessary interest of these grid participants. In other words, a grid community was considered as a utopia, where grid participants are expected that are willing to provide all kinds of computational resources selflessly.

Currently, grid technology is establishing the way out of the academic incubator and into industry environments. The economic incentive mechanism is an effective means to solve the resource sharing among multiple organizations with different interest, and some research efforts are focusing on introducing economic mechanisms such as tanonment and auction into resource management for grid computing, which usually is based on the assumption of using economic currency. However, this mode needs the specified organization to manage currency and price resources, which will become a burden and attenuate the advantage of the economic mechanism.

In the future, the economic incentive mechanism is considered as a potential method to manage all kinds of resources in the grid. However, currently, this method could not perform very well. More economic incentive methods such as auction should be studied and new incentive mechanisms should be presented, where not only the economic interest is considered but also the pricing difficulty in the dynamic grid computing environment should be avoided.

CONCLUSION

In this chapter, we pay attention to resource management in the grid environment, and introduce the cost-based scheduling strategy and algorithm for grid computing. The principle is that the total usage of different kinds of resources, such as CPU, memory and bandwidth can be converted into a single cost. It is convenient for scheduler or resource manager to assign job in the computational grid according to minimizing cost of all resources, achieving the goal of minimizing the makespan of a sequence of jobs and obtaining the better QoS.

ACKNOWLEDGMENT

This work was supported by the National Natural Science Foundation of China (No.90612018, No.90715030 and No.60503043).

REFERENCES

Abramson, D., Buyya, R., & Giddy, J. (2002). A computational economy for grid computing and its implementation in the Nimrod-G resource broker. *Future Generation Computer Systems, 18*(8), 1061-1074.

Amir, Y., Awerbuch, B., Barak, A., Borgstrom, R., & Keren, A. (2000). Opportunity cost approach for job assignment in a scalable computing cluster. *IEEE Transactions on Parallel Distributed System, 11*(7), 760-768.

Buyya, R. (2002). *Economic-based distributed resource management and scheduling for grid computing.* Ph D dissertation, Monash University, Australia.

Cao, H., & Xiao, N. (2002). A market-based approach to allocate resources for computational grids. *Computer Research and Development (Chinese), 39*(8), 913-916.

Casanova, H., Bartol, T. M., Stiles, J., & Berman. F. (2001). Distributing MCell simulations on the Grid. *Internal Journal of High Performance Computing Application, 15*(3), 243-257.

Casanova, H., Legrand, A., Zagorodnov, D., & Berman, F. (2000). Heuristics for scheduling parameter wweep applications in grid environments, in: *IEEE Proceedings of the 9th Heterogeneous Computing Workshop* (pp. 349–363). Cancun, Mexico: IEEE Computer Society.

Casanova, H., Obertelli, G., Berman, F., & Wolski, R. (2000). The AppLeS parameter sweep template: user-level middleware for the grid. *Scientific Programming, 8*(3), 111-126.

Cheng, J., & Wellman, M. (1998). The WALRAS algorithm: a convergent distributed implementation of general equilibrium outcomes. *Computational Economics, 12*(1), 1-24.

Ernemann, C., Hamscher, V., Schwiegelshohn, U., Yahyapour, R., & Streit, A. (2000). On advantages of grid computing for parallel job scheduling, in: *Proceedings of the 2nd IEEE International Symposium on Cluster Computing and the Grid* (pp. 39-46). Berlin: IEEE Computer Society.

Foster, I., & Kesselman, C. (1999). The globus project: a status report, *Future Generation Computer Systems, 15*(5-6), 607-621.

Foster, I., & Kesselman, C. (Ed.). (1996). *The grid: Blueprint for a new computing infrastructure.* Los Altos, CA: Morgan Kaufmann.

Heymann, E., Senar, M. A., Luque, E., & Livny, M. (2000). Adaptive scheduling for master-worker applications on the computational grid, in: *Proceedings of the 1st IEEE/ACM International Workshop on Grid Computing, Bangalore* (pp. 214-227). India: IEEE Computer Society.

Nakai, J. (2002). *Pricing computing resources: reading between the lines and beyond* (NAS Technical Report: NAS-01-010), NASA Ames Research Center.

Plank, J. S., Casanova, H., Beck, M., & Dongarra, J. J. (1999). Deploying fault tolerance and task migration with NetSolve. *Future Generation Computer Systems, 15*(5), 745-755.

Smallen, S., Cirne, W., Frey, J., Berman, F., Wolski, R., Su, M., Kesselman, C., Young, S., & Ellisman, M. (2000). Combining workstations and supercomputers to support grid applications: The parallel tomography experience. In: *IEEE Proceedings of the 9th Heterogeneous Computing Workshop* (pp. 241-252). Cancun, Mexico: IEEE Computer Society.

Subramani, V., Kettimuthu, R., Srinivasan, S., & Sadayappan P. (2002). Distributed job scheduling on computational grids using multiple simultaneous requests, in: *Proceedings of the 11th IEEE International Symposium on High Performance Distributed Computing* (pp. 359-367). Edinburgh, Scotland: IEEE Computer Society.

Subramoniam, K., Maheswaran, M., & Toulouse, M. (2002). Towards a micro-economic model for resource allocation in grid computing systems. In: *Proceedings of the 2002 IEEE Canadian Conference on Electrical & Computer Engineering* (pp.782-785). Canadian: IEEE Computer Society.

Takefusa, A., Casanova, H., Matsuoka, S., & Berman, F. (2001). A study of deadline scheduling for client-server systems on the computational grid, in: *Proceedings of the 10th IEEE Symposium on High Performance Distributed Computing* (pp. 406-415). San Francisco: IEEE Computer Society.

Weng, C. L., & Lu, X. D. (2005). Heuristic scheduling for bag-of-tasks applications in combination with QoS in the computational grid. *Future Generation Computer Systems, 21*(2), 271-280.

Weng, C. L., Li, M. L., & Lu, X. D. (2006). An online scheduling algorithm for assigning jobs in the computational grid. *The IEICE Transactions on Information and Systems, E89-D*(2), 597-604.

Wolski, R., Plank, J., Brevik, J., & Bryan T. (2001). Analyzing market-based resource allocation strategies for the computational grid. *The International Journal of High Performance Computing Applications, 15*(3), 258-281.

Ygge, F. (1998). *Market-oriented programming and its application to power load management.* Ph D dissertation, Department of Computer Science, Lund University, Sweden.

Chapter V
Providing Quantitative Scalability Improvement of Consistency Control for Large–Scale, Replication–Based Grid Systems

Yijun Lu
University of Nebraska-Lincoln, USA

Hong Jiang
University of Nebraska-Lincoln, USA

Ying Lu
University of Nebraska-Lincoln, USA

ABSTRACT

Consistency control is important in replication-based-Grid systems because it provides QoS guarantee. However, conventional consistency control mechanisms incur high communication overhead and are ill suited for large-scale dynamic Grid systems. In this chapter, the authors propose CVRetrieval (Consistency View Retrieval) to provide quantitative scalability improvement of consistency control for large-scale, replication-based Grid systems. Based on the observation that not all participants are equally active or engaged in distributed online collaboration, CVRetrieval differentiates the notions of consistency maintenance and consistency retrieval. Here, consistency maintenance implies a protocol that periodically communicates with all participants to maintain a certain consistency level; and consistency retrieval means that passive participants explicitly request consistent views from the system when the need arises in stead of joining the expensive consistency maintenance protocol all the time.

The rationale is that it is much more cost-effective to satisfy a passive participant's need on-demand. The evaluation of CVRetrieval is done in two parts. First, by analyzing its scalability and the result shows that CVRetrieval can greatly reduce communication cost and hence make consistency control more scalable. Second, a prototype of CVRetrieval is deployed on the Planet-Lab test-bed and the results show that the active participants experience a short response time at expense of the passive participants that may encounter a longer response time.

INTRODUCTION

A popular strategy to improve the availability of shared data in large-scale Grid systems is to replicate data on geographically dispersed nodes. In this way, participants can fetch the data from a nearby copy with improved availability and response time. After retrieving a copy to the local node, the local copy becomes a new replica of the data and can be used to serve other nodes' need. In this type of replication-based systems, it is important to guarantee the consistency among participants' copies of the same data to make collaboration meaningful. In that sense, improved consistency among participants can improve participants' perceived Quality of Service (QoS) of the application.

There are two obstacles facing the design of a highly scalable consistency control mechanism for large-scale, replication-based Grid systems. First, large-scale Grid systems have a large number of nodes that are often geographically dispersed globally. Due to the network congestions and the inability to control remote nodes, maintaining even a relaxed consistency in such systems involves formidable communication and management cost.

Second, large-scale Grid systems are often dynamic. I.e., nodes could join or leave the system at their will. With such dynamism, both the group of replicas and that of the nodes are interested in getting a replica keeps changing. Thus, any static—in the sense that the protocol fixed with certain replicas—is not suitable.

Current consistency maintenance mechanisms rely either on applying the same protocol on all participants or is based on the assumption that the replica group does not change. The former scheme is not scalable in large-scale Grid systems because it induces high communication overhead in the presence of a large number of participants (Cetintemel 2003). The dynamic nature of large-scale Grid systems means the latter scheme is not suitable as well.

In this paper, we propose a new low-overhead, hence more scalable, consistency control architecture to address this limitation, thus improving the QoS from the consistency control's point of view. This architecture is consistency retrieval. We also present the design, implementation, and evaluation of Consistent View Retrieval (CVRetrieval), a system that supports the consistency retrieval functionalities.

Consistency Retrieval *vs.* Consistency Maintenance

Consistency retrieval is in contrary to the notion of consistency maintenance. In this paper, consistency maintenance refers to the enforcement of consistency through communication among all the participants. The maintenance cost grows with the number of participants. In a truly large system, the consistency maintenance cost can be formidable.

Consistency retrieval reduces maintenance cost by reducing the number of participants that a consistency maintenance module needs to include. This approach is both doable and preferable in practice.

This is doable because not all participants in a collaboration application are equally active or engaged. In a digital white board scenario where students listen to a lecture, for example, the lecturers are more likely to issue updates while a majority of the students are observers—they monitor the white board and rarely issue updates. From a consistency maintenance point of view, the lecturers are more important than passive students. So there is really no need to consider the passive students group as far as consistency maintenance is concerned at most of the time. The rationale is that, if a participant does not have intensive updating activities, it is far more cost-effective to satisfy his or her needs on-demand. This approach is also preferable because it does not change the way most current consistency control protocol work. Thus it is easier to be adopted. In this paper, we refer to this on-demand-based consistency control mechanism as consistency retrieval.

It is noteworthy that, while it is easy to statically separate passive participants from active participants and only maintain consistency for active participants, CVRetrieval is significantly different from such an approach in two aspects. First, CVRetrieval is not merely differentiating active and passive participants once and staying with a fixed differentiation permanently. Instead, differentiation in CVRetrieval is a dynamic one, meaning that the active and passive participants are relative concepts and can change from time to time. The ability to capture this dynamics is a salient feature that sets CVRetrieval apart from any static approaches. Second, CVRetrieval assumes that passive participants do occasionally care about consistency, instead of assuming that they are not interested in the shared data[1] at all.

CVRetrieval

CVRetrieval is a system that supports the consistency retrieval functionalities. CVRetrieval is built on top of IDEA (Lu 2007b; Lu 2008), an efficient consistency maintenance protocol proposed by the authors, as the consistency maintenance module. The relationship between CVRetrieval and IDEA is illustrated in Figure 1.

The evaluation of CVRetrieval is done in two parts. First, we theoretically analyze the scalability of CVRetrieval and compare it to other consistency maintenance protocols. The results show that CVRetrieval can greatly reduce communication cost and hence make consistency control more scalable. Second, a prototype of CVRetrieval is developed and deployed on the Planet-Lab test-bed (Peterson 2003) for performance evaluation. The results show that active participants in CVRetrieval have faster

Figure 1. The relationship between CVRetrieval and IDEA

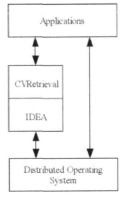

response times than in pure consistency maintenance protocols at the slight expense of passive participants that can experience longer response times depending on the system setting, although the retrieval performance is still reasonably efficient for the latter.

The rest of the paper is organized as follows. Section 2 discusses background and related work. Section 3 discussed the design issues of CVRetrieval. The design of CVRetrieval is then presented in Section 4. Section 5 analyzes the scalability improvement of CVRetrieval. Section 6 experimentally evaluates CVRetrieval based on a prototype deployed on Planet-Lab. Section 7 discusses future trends in consistency control research for large-scale Grid systems. Finally, Section 8 concludes this paper and discusses future work.

BACKGROUND

Improving the scalability of consistency control has been a major research topic in distributed collaboration applications.

Most collaboration applications nowadays originate from single-user applications. For example, MS Word was previously used by a single user to edit his or her file and is then modified to incorporate collaboration capabilities. A straightforward way to share these applications is to place a central control for consistency maintenance. In MS NetMeeting, for example, only one participant can operate on the shared object; all other participants will be blocked (Begole 1999).

To prevent blocking, which causes access delay, the granularity of sharing is often adjusted to make the sharing unit small enough to prevent blocking to some extent. However, this approach is inherently not scalable for two reasons. First, for any given system, the granularity cannot be spited indefinitely. Second, it is still a centralized system and, in the presence of an active unit, the blocking cannot be prevented and that makes it not suitable for a large-scale system with a large number of participants.

Newly developed distributed online collaboration applications use replication-based scheme to improve scalability and availability. As all the replicas have a copy of the collaboration application, inconsistency level among them hence is relaxed (Prakash 1994; Schuckmann 1996). While this scheme works well in many applications and helps distributed collaboration applications scale to large-scale distributed networks, relaxed consistency does not provide QoS guarantee.

Recently, researchers have been trying to achieve relaxed yet bounded inconsistency for distributed online collaboration applications. Yu and Vahdat defined metrics to evaluate consistency level for a wide range of applications (Yu 2000). Chang et. al. derived an algorithm to support different consistency level for different users in an online conference application (Chang 2002). Also, Local-lag and Timewarp were developed by Vogel and Mauve to eliminate short term inconsistencies and repair inconsistency, thus prevent unbounded inconsistencies (Vogel 2001). A more recent work extended Vogel and Mauve's work by considering the same problem in a larger network (Li 2004). However, these works are still use consistency maintenance for all participants, which cause high overhead for a system with a large number of participants.

CVRetrieval differs from previous work in the sense that it considers the consistency retrieval aspect, not just consistency maintenance. To the best of our knowledge, CVRetrieval is the first work to explicitly consider the retrieval aspect of consistency control in distributed online collaboration applications.

DESIGN ISSUES

CVRetrieval has two design issues. First, we need to differentiate different roles of CVRetrieval and the conventional consistency maintenance protocol. Second, we need to define a procedure for CVRetrieval to satisfy passive participants' consistency needs on demand.

The Roles of IDEA and CVRetrieval

IDEA achieves efficient consistency maintenance by detecting and resolving inconsistencies among active writers more frequently than passive participants, in which active writers are dynamically tracked by IDEA. To reduce the number of nodes maintained by IDEA, CVRetrieval only lets IDEA handle active participants who are actively updating their replicas.

Satisfying Passive Participants' Consistency Needs on Demand

Since CVRetrieval does not actively maintain consistency for passive participants who may need to access their replicas occasionally, CVRetrieval provides a way for these passive participants to access consistent objects when the need arises. From the passive participants' point of view, the only thing that they need to know is where to find a consistency object. In IDEA, any active writer can provide a consistent object. So CVRetrieval just has to inform passive writers about this active writers' information.

CVRetrieval deploys a publish-subscribe infrastructure (Banavar 1999) to publish the active writers information to the passive participants. In this way, CVRetrieval satisfies passive participants' consistency needs with an on-demand fashion. Moreover, CVRetrieval chooses publishers and subscribers in a way to capture the common interest among participants. In this way, passive participants associated with the same subscriber can help each other without fetching data from publisher all the time. As we will see in Section 6.3, exploiting common interest greatly improves the scalability of CVRetrieval.

CVRETRIEVAL DESIGN

We try to address several design issues here:

- How do participants join the system and how to map the participants to the IDEA infrastructure?
- What is the workflow of CVRetrieval?
- How does IDEA communicate with the publishers so that the publishers have the updated information of the top layer nodes (that includes all active writers) for different object?
- How to choose subscribers for observers?
- How does the publish-subscribe scheme work?

Throughout this section, we use a virtual white board application to make the discussion concrete.

A Virtual White Board Scenario

We consider a distance education scenario in which several lecturers give lectures and a group of students join the discussions by manipulating a virtual white board (logically centralized and physically distributed on each participant's site). Other students who are not part of the discussion group will passively observe the discussion by watching the virtual white board.

In this scenario, the lecturers and the students in the discussion group conduct active discussions by issuing updates on the white board. Due to the nature of discussion, not all the members in the discussion group will speak up at the same time. During the discussion, membership of the active white-board-based speaker group will change constantly, and such change is usually unpredictable because the spontaneity of an active discussion.

Participants Join the System

We assume that there is a mechanism for participants to know the ID of the white board session and the time when the session starts. In practice, this can be done by some offline method, such as through an email list.

After all the participants log in, they form a group. Each participant modifies his or her own white board and those updates will show on others' white boards.

Mapping Between Participants and the IDEA Infrastructure

As illustrated in Figure 2, we differentiate three types of participants: active writers, passive writers, and observers. They are mapped to IDEA as follows.

First, CVRetrieval differentiate observers from writers. When participants log in the white board application, they are required to indicate whether they are members of the discussion group. If yes, they are characterized as writers that are handled by IDEA; if no, they are classified as observers that are handled by CVRetrieval.

Second, IDEA differentiates active writers from inactive writers after the system starts to run using a two-layer structure. IDEA tracks active writers (by its top layer) and passive writers (by the bottom layer) based on frequency of their updating activities.

Figure 2. Three classes of participants

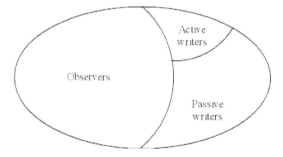

The Workflow

Figure 3 shows the workflow of the publish-subscribe mechanism as well as the retrieval process.

The basic publish mechanism is shown in Figure 3.1. In step 1, the active writers notify publisher about their presence; in step 2, a publisher notifies its subscriber about the up-to-date active-writer group; finally, in step 3, a subscriber notifies its clients (the observers) about the active-writer group.

A client can issue an on-demand retrieval request, as shown in Figure 3.2. In step 4, an observer issues a retrieve request to its subscriber. If the subscriber has a valid cache, it will return the local copy to the observer (step 7); otherwise, it requests a consistent view from one of the active writers (step 5) and, after receiving the view (step 6), it returns the copy to the observer (step 7) and caches the view locally.

An observer can also indicate his or her preference to retrieve a consistent view periodically. In this case, the observer does not need to explicitly issue a retrieval request on-demand. As shown in Figure 3.3, this process is similar to that in Figure 3.2 except that there is no step 4, and steps 5 through 7 are executed periodically.

If the subscriber is already overwhelmed by the retrieval requests or publishing, there is no point of sending more retrieval request to it, and that is where the active-writer group information received by observers in step 3 comes into play. As shown in Figure 3.4, an observer can use its knowledge of the active-writer group to contact a nearby active writer directly (step 8 and 9). As an optional step, the active writer can forward a copy to the subscriber so that the subscriber will have a fresh copy as long as it is able to handle more requests again (step 10).

Finally, the complete process is illustrated in Figure 3.5. We will discuss the key components of the process in more details in the rest of this section.

Communication Between IDEA and Publishers

In CVRetrieval, each object has a designated publisher, which is responsible for publishing the top layer nodes' information on behalf of the objects. There are two issues here: (1) how to map an object to a publisher? (2) how do publishers learn the top layer nodes' information from IDEA?

There are two ways to map an object to a publisher based on the total number of shared objects. If the number of shared objects is small in an application, such as in the white board application, the shared objects can be mapped to a single publisher. If the number of shared objects is large, such as in online gaming, certain mechanism is needed to balance multiple publishers' load. Hash-table-based scheme (choose publishers based on the hashed value of the object IDs), such as Distributed Hash Tables (DHT) (Ratnasamy 2001; Rowstron 2001; Stoica 2001), is desirable for both its load balancing and its easy lookup (subscribers can find the right publishers by simply hashing the object IDs).

The publishers learn the top layer nodes through communication with them. From the mapping procedure, the top layer nodes of an object know where their corresponding publisher is. The top layer nodes will communicate with their publisher whenever a node joins or leaves the top layer. The publisher will publish these updates to its subscribers subsequently.

However, this published information may become obsolete due to the propagation delay. For example, a subscriber could have old information (it states that A is in the top layer of object f but A is in fact no longer in the top layer anymore). We use pointers to solve this problem. In an example illustrated in Figure 4, we let A keep two pointers of its fellow members when it is in the top layer of object f (left half

Figure 3. Workflow of CVRetrieval

3.1. Basic publish mechanism   *3.2. Active retrieval for observers*   *3.3. Automatic/Periodic retrieval from observers*

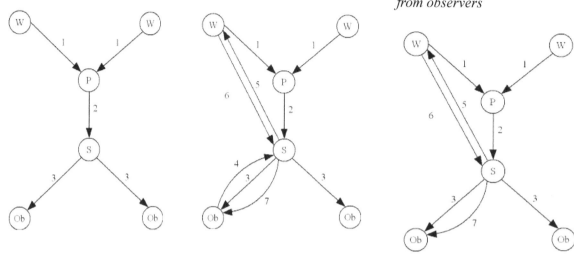

3.4. When subscribers are already overwhelmed   *3.5. The complete process*

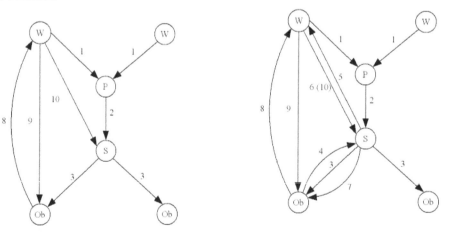

of Figure 4) and, when *A* is no longer in the top layer, it can at least forward the request to the other top layer nodes (*B* or *C* in this case, see the right half of Figure 4). Because it is very unlikely that all three nodes are leaving the top layer during the time of the propagation delay, this kind of old information will be transparent to users. In the case that this mechanism does not work, the request can always be returned back to the subscriber, who can then pull updated information from the publisher (see Section 4.7).

Choose Subscribers for Observers

While there are many ways to choose subscribers, we use ISPs (Internet Service Providers) of the observers, rather than some observers themselves, as the subscribers for two reasons. First, the ISPs are much more stable than their clients (i.e., observers) because of their status as Internet entry point. Hence, using ISPs as the subscribers makes the publish-subscribe structure (i.e. the positions of publishers and subscribers) much more stable. Second, while clients change their interests rather frequently, which—if we use clients as subscribers—causes frequent membership change for a publisher and the publisher that in turn needs to adjust its publishing scheme to reflect that change, ISPs' interests are relatively stable because their interests do not change with respect to how many and which clients are interested in an object, as long as some client is interested in that object.

When a client becomes interested in an object, it informs its ISP, which will subscribe the object's information if it hasn't done so. If the ISP has already subscribed for that object, it will just add the client into its client list and inform the client about all the future updates about that object's top layer nodes. When a client is not interested in an object anymore, it informs its ISP too. If, after this client's exit, the ISP has no client for that object, it will unsubscribe this object; otherwise, it simply deletes the client from its client list.

A subscriber has two responsibilities. First, it informs a publisher to periodically push new updates to it at a predefined rate and, when a new update arrives, immediately forwards the update to its clients. Second, when a client is in need of a consistent view immediately, the client can explicitly ask the subscriber to retrieve the view on its behalf. When a subscriber receives the retrieval request, it either returns a view from its cache (if it has one because other clients have just retrieved it before) or retrieves the view directly from the writer.

The Publish-Subscribe Scheme

As shown in Figure 3, we use a multicast tree and filters to sent information from publishers to their subscribers. In this scheme, each publisher builds a multicast tree and an interior node forwards the packets further down the tree only if there are some nodes in its subtree that have subscribed it.

In the naïve form, the publisher sends all the active writers' information down the tree structure and all the subscribers will receive that information. To improve the system's scalability and efficiency, CVRetrieval incorporates the following optimizations.

First, a publisher in CVRetrieval only sends a subset of the list of the top layer nodes to each subscriber to preserve the network bandwidth. This raises two questions: how to choose a subset for a given

Figure 4. Use pointers to handle stale information

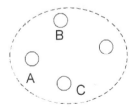 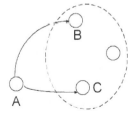

subscriber and how to disseminate different subset of top-layer node information through a multicast tree?

When choosing the subset, the publisher has several factors to consider. First, the active writers in the subset should be physically close to the subscribers so that the retrieval can be done efficiently. Second, one or two remote active writers can be included in each subset to provide redundancy because physically close machines tend to go down at the same time (for example, a power outrage). Third, the publisher needs to consider load balance so that no active writer is overwhelmed by retrieval requests.

Now we illustrate how to disseminate the different subsets via a multicast tree. First of all, the subscribers report their physical locations to the root in a bottom-up fashion and the messages are aggregated at each interior node. Second, the publisher chooses different subsets for its immediate children in the multicast tree based on these children's subtree's interests (i.e. the collective interest of the nodes in its children's subtree) and disseminate the subsets. For each interior node, it further divides the subset for its own immediate children. This process continues until the leave nodes are reached.

SCALABILITY OF CVRETRIEVAL

In this section, we compare the communication cost of the CVRetrieval with two consistency maintenance protocols—Deno and IDEA—because these two are the most similar approaches to CVRetrieval. Due to page limit, interested readers are referred to Chapter 5.3 of (Lu 2007a) for a full discussion about the rationale behind this comparison.

Deno and IDEA

Deno (Cetintemel 2003) is a peer-to-peer voting protocol in which each writer's update travels across the whole replica group to detect and resolve any inconsistency. During Deno's serialization process, further updates are allowed but their updates need to be serialized at a single point to maintain a consistency state.

IDEA is a detection-based consistency maintenance protocol for large-scale distributed systems proposed by the authors. Instead of enforcing a fixed consistency protocol beforehand, IDEA detects inconsistencies when they arise and resolve them based on the applications' ongoing need for consistency.

In this analysis, we assume that all the protocols incur the same average message size and, on average, each message travels the same distance. Hence, the differentiator of the protocols is the total number of messages incurred by each protocol.

Assumptions

In this analysis, we make the following assumptions and definitions.

1. c: the average number of simultaneous writers.
2. n: the total number of nodes in the system that join the consistency control process.
3. n_l: number of writers.
4. n_{hot}: number of active writers among the n_l writers.

5. f_1: number of updates of active writers during a given period of time t.
6. n_{pass}: number of passive writers among the n_1 writers, where $n_{hot} + n_{pass} = n_1$.
7. f_2: number of updates of passive writers during a given period of time t.
8. n_2: number of observers, where $n_2 = n - n_1$.
9. p: total number of publishers in CVRetrieval.
10. s: total number of subscribers in CVRetrieval.
11. q_1: number of publishings during a given period of time t.
12. q_2: number of retrievals during a given period of time t.
13. C_deno: total number of messages exchanged in Deno.
14. C_idea: total number of messages exchanged in IDEA.
15. C_r: number of messages exchanged in CVRetrieval.

The Analysis

In this analysis, we consider the consistency control for one single object because this simplifies the analysis and, based on the result, it is easy to extend the analysis to multiple objects.

Communication Cost of Deno

In Deno, each update travels the whole group and, when it meets another conflicting update, the update will be resolved at that time. In this analysis, each time an update reaches a node, we consider it as a new message because the node that is reached essentially regenerates the original message by relaying it. Thus, given an update, it only stops traversal when it meets another conflicting update. From the assumption 1, we know that there are c conflicting updates in the system at one time on average. For simplicity, we further assume that the updates propagate along a linear structure (without this assumption, the updating process becomes intractable). Then, on average, an update travels 1/c of the network to meet a conflicting update and stops.

Now we calculate the communication cost as follows. Because there are n nodes in the system, each update needs to travel n/c hops, which equals to n/c messages in total. In a given period of time t, there are $n_{hot}*f_1 + n_{pass}*f_2$ updates, so the total number of messages generated in a given period of time t is:

$$C\_deno = \frac{n}{c} \times (n_{hot} \times f_1 + n_{pass} \times f_2) \qquad (1)$$

Communication Cost of IDEA

In IDEA, the updates from active writers will be detected among the active writers and those from the passive writers will need to go through the whole network to be detected.

Similarly to the analysis in Deno, we assume the existence of c concurrent conflicting updates at one time. However, in the case of IDEA, the updates from active writers stay at the top layer, implying that the active writers actually see less than c concurrent updates because the updates from passive writers won't show up in the top layer at the same time. So, while passive writers still see c concurrent updates, we assume that the active writers sees only c_{hot} concurrent updates, where $c_{hot} < c$. Then an update from an active writer will generate n_{hot}/c_{hot} messages, and that from a passive writer will generate n/c messages. There are n_{hot}*f_1 updates from active writers and n_{pass}*f_2 updates from passive writers in a given period of time t.

For the communication cost associated with observers, we follow the calculation used in the Deno case and conclude that the overhead is two messages (one for request, one for reply) for each retrieval type request. Then, because we have assumed that, on average, each observer will issue q_2 requests in time t, the total communication overhead is 2*n_2*q_2.

Putting the communication cost of writers and observers together, the communication cost of IDEA is:

$$C\_idea = \frac{n_{hot}}{c_{hot}} \times n_{hot} \times f_1 + \frac{n}{c} \times n_{pass} \times f_2 + 2 \times n_2 \times q_2$$

(2)

Communication Cost of CVRetrieval

The communication cost of CVRetrieval involves three parts: (1) the detection of inconsistency among active and passive writers; (2) the cost associated with the publish-subscribe scheme, which includes the communication cost between writers and publishers, between publisher and subscriber, and between subscribers and their clients; and (3) the retrieval operation for observers.

First, CVRetrieval detects inconsistency among active writers in the same manner with that of IDEA because it depends on IDEA to maintain consistency. Thus the communication cost incurred by active writers is (n_{hot}/c)*n_{hot}*f_1. For passive writers, however, they need not to go through the whole network; instead, they only need to detect among the writers' group (with n_1 writers) that excludes the observers. Thus, the communication cost associated with the updates from passive writers is (n_1/c)*n_{pass}*f_2.

Second, for the communication cost associated with publish-subscribe scheme, we first derive the cost for one round of publish and then multiply it by the publish rate q_1 to get the total communication cost in a given period of time t. Because an active writer only notifies its publisher when it becomes an active writer and when it becomes a passive writer. Here we conservatively assume that, in one round of publish, half of the active writers are new ones (this is indeed a very extreme scenario because we essentially assume 50% of the active writers leave the group and the same number of new active writers join the group). Thus, in one round of publish, there are n_{hot} messages exchanged between writers and publishers because each old active writer or new active writer needs to inform exactly one publisher.

Then, there are s messages exchanged between publisher and subscribers because there are s subscribers in total and each needs to be informed exactly once. Finally, let's conservatively assume that all the n_2 observers will need to be informed about its subscription. Then we know that n_2 messages are exchanged in one round. Adding the three parts of cost together and then multiplying the publishing frequency, we get the total communication cost associated with the publish-subscribe scheme in time t is q_1*(n_{hot}+s+n_2).

Third, each observer will retrieve a consistent view for the object he or she is interested in, which results in n_2 retrievals. Because each retrieval consists of two messages (one request, one reply), there are 2*n_2 messages exchanged in one retrieval operation. Finally, because we assume that each observer retrieve q_2 consistent views in time t, the total number of message exchanged in t is 2*q_2*n_2.

So the total communication cost in a given period of time t, incorporating all three parts, is:

$$C\_r = \frac{n_{hot}}{c_{hot}} \times n_{hot} \times f_1 + \frac{n_1}{c} \times n_{pass} \times f_2$$
$$+ q_1 \times (n_{hot} + s + n_2)$$
$$+ 2 \times q_2 \times n_2 \tag{3}$$

Note that parameter s is related to n_2 because there are s subscribers serving the n_2 clients (recall that each observer subscribes k objects). Although there is no ground rule about how many clients a subscriber should have, it is intuitive that the number of clients should not overwhelm the subscribers. Considering that the information that is being published is rather small in quantity (it is only a list of active writers and the message is maybe only a few KBs), we believe that each subscriber should support at least up to 50 clients, which incurs less than 1MB data traffic and should not be a burden for a subscriber. Thus, in the following analysis, we use $n_2/50$ as the value for s.

Further, the value of q_1 is associated with how frequent the active writer group changes and q_2 is associated with the observers' interests. Because CVRetrieval deals with loosely coupled distributed online collaboration applications, we believe that, in a short period time of t, it is sufficient to assign a small numerical value for q_1. For q_2, we believe that it should be reasonably large so that it can satisfy observers' need of consistent view. However, q_2 cannot be too large, which implies smaller inter-retrieval time, because there is no point of issuing the second retrieval before response of the first request has arrived. Thus, we believe that it should be reasonable to make q_2 two to three times as large as q_1.

The Comparison

In this comparison, we first do an asymptotic analysis to compare the overall growth rate of Deno, IDEA, and CVRetrieval. Since the asymptotic analysis is approximate in nature, we then use a sensible setting of the parameters to calculate and compare the three protocols.

We conduct the asymptotic analysis as follows. In the equation 1 for the communication cost of Deno, n_1 and n_2 are fractions of n, so n_1 and n_2 grows as fast as n. Then, f_1 and f_2 are updates in a period of time and is not supposed to be a large number and won't grow with n, so we can safely treat them as rough constants. Hence, the cost of Deno would be $O(n^2)$.

For the analysis of the communication cost of IDEA, we follow the analysis the same way as that of Deno—n_2 have similar growth as n, f_1 and f_2 are more like constant. Then, from equation 2, the cost of IDEA is $O(n^2 + n)$, which is also $O(n^2)$. Similarly, the cost of CVRetrieval, derived from equation 3, is also $O(n^2)$.

The main message here is this, while there are differences in the communication cost among all the three protocols, the difference is not an exponential one. This makes sense because all three protocols,

Table 1. Analytical results

Sets	n	n₁	n_hot	c	c_hot	f₁	f₂	q₁	q₂	s	Deno	IDEA	CVRetrieval
1	1000	50	10	4	3	5	3	2	5	19	42500	39667	13125
2	1000	100	20	4	3	5	3	2	5	18	85000	69667	17543
3	1000	200	50	4	3	5	3	2	5	16	175000	124667	36399

to some extent, depend on intercommunication of a group of nodes, which results the $O(n^2)$ result. The real difference is how large the group is—the larger the group, the more communication cost will be incurred. From this aspect, Deno has the largest group (the whole system), IDEA has a smaller number (only for the group of active writers). CVRetrieval has the same group size as that of IDEA but has a much smaller size of passive writers, hence achieving the smallest communication cost.

We now proceed to the second step of this comparison by comparing C_deno, C_idea, and C_r by assigning real numbers to the parameters in their respective expressions. Based on the logic presented earlier, we set $s = n_2/50$ and assign 2 and 5 to q_1 and q_2, respectively. We also set c_{hot} as $3*c/4$, which is actually quite conservative and put IDEA and CVRetrieval in disadvantage considering that most updates should come from active writers. The analytical results are summarized in Table 1.

As shown in Table 1, CVRetrieval incurs much lower communication cost than pure consistency maintenance protocols in all three sets of data. This observation indicates that the majority overhead of CVRetrieval comes from the consistency maintenance of writers, which validates our hypothesis that, by separating observers from writers, the consistency control overhead can be substantially reduced.

Additionally, the overhead of CVRetrieval increases in a slower speed than those of Deno and IDEA when the number of updates increases (reflected by the number of active writers). Comparing the results of set 1 and set 3 and we can see that the overhead of CVRetrieval in set 3 is 2.8 times as large as that in set 1, while that ratio is 4.1 for Deno and 3.1 for IDEA. We believe that this is an indication that CVRetrieval scales better than the other two methods.

EXPERIMENTAL RESULTS

We have implemented a prototype of CVRetrieval on top of the Planet-Lab (Peterson 2003). We use this prototype to evaluate the performance of CVRetrieval. The metric we use is response time.

For a consistency maintenance protocol, the response time is defined as the time difference between the point when an update of an object is first committed and that when a participant receives that update (with a certain level of consistency guarantee). In the case of CVRetrieval, the response time has different definition for writers and observers. For writers, the definition of response time is the same as that in a consistency maintenance protocol. For observers in CVRetreivals, however, the response time is between the point of time when an observer issues a retrieval request for a consistent view of an object and that when it receives the view.

Experiment Setup

We emulate a white board application for evaluation purposes. The application is emulated by following its operational sequences. Further, we assume that these updates are all conflicting with one another. A writer informs its publisher when it becomes or ceases to be an active writer. The publisher then informs its subscribers (the ISPs who subscribe on behalf of their clients) periodically. Observers specify their interest and inform their subscribers about that.

In the current setting, there are ten writers among which four are active writers and the other six are passive ones. There are one publisher and four subscribers. Each subscriber serves three observers. In other words, this is a 22-nodes system, excluding publisher and subscribers. At the beginning of the experiment, each active writer issues one update every 5 seconds until the experiment ends. These updates got disseminated among active writers immediately and, once it starts to propagate to passive writers, each hop will only disseminate the updates once every 5 seconds. Each observer retrieves the consistent view every 20 seconds. The experiment runs 300 seconds.

We also implemented a Deno-like protocol for comparison. In the Deno-like protocol, we organize the 22 participants (here, we don't consider the publisher and subscribers as participants because they are only facilitating CVRetrieval) in a linear fashion in which the updates are propagated from one to the other. To make the results comparable, we assume the same updating patterns for the ten writers.

Response Time for Writers

We measure response times for active writers and that for passive writers. The experiment was run ten times and the average response time, as well as maximum and minimum values, are measured and shown in Table 2.

From the result, we can see that the response time of active writers is very small. This is because the dissemination of updates is instant among active writers. While it is usually very costly to disseminate update instantly among participants, CVRetrieval can afford to do so because, via classification, there are only a relatively small number of active writers in existence.

As shown here, the average delay for passive writers is over 10 seconds, which looks rather high. However, this is because we set a five-second delay between the dissemination of updates among passive writers. In practice, system administrators can choose a shorter delay to improve the response time for passive writers at the expense of increased bandwidth overhead.

Response Time for Observers

There are two aspects of response time for observers. First, the time that it takes for them to receive the periodically published updates. Because this part of delay primarily depends on the publishing rate, we do not measure it here. Second, the response time for an explicit retrieval operation, i.e. when the observers actively retrieve the most updated view from the subscribers, the time it takes to get the view.

The delay of explicit retrieval depends on whether the observer can find the view in its subscriber's local cache (because another observer retrieved the same view a moment ago). Intuitively, the more retrievals can be satisfied with the subscriber's cache (a higher cache hit rate), the smaller the response time is. In this experiment, we give three settings of the cache hit ratio: 50%, 66.7%, and 75%. For each setting, we run ten experiments and the results are summarized in Table 3.

The result shows that the retrieval process is indeed very efficient and this efficiency increases with cache hit rate in subscribers.

Table 2. Response time for writers

Type	Max (seconds)	Min (seconds)	Average (seconds)
active writer	1.73	1.41	1.59
passive writer	11.8	10.2	10.98

Comparison to Consistency Maintenance Protocols

We now compare the performance of CVRetrieval with a pure consistency maintenance protocol. For a pure consistency maintenance protocol, we assume that all participants are treated equal. In terms of updates dissemination, there are two types: active ones that disseminate a received update to other participants as soon as it arrives and passive ones that only periodically disseminate all the updates it received so far. Because the passive ones work similarly to the way CVRetrieva/IDEA treats passive writers, but with more participants, it is doubtless that CVRetrieval/IDEA will have a better performance. For this reason, we only experimentally compare CVRetrieval to the active ones.

The consistency maintenance protocol we considered here has all the 22 participants we used in the CVRetrieval evaluation. Because this protocol actively disseminates updates, each participant relays a received update as soon as it is received. Finally, the writers have the same updating patterns as in previous experiments. We run this experiment ten times and the results are shown in Table 4.

From this table, we can see that the response time of the pure maintenance protocol is larger than that of CVRetrieval's active writers (comparing to the data in Table 2). However, the absolute value of the response time is not that large. We suspect that is because, due to the heavy load of Planet-Lab nodes, the write operation alone needs too much time to be committed. To validate our hypothesis, we profile one run of the experiment with the pure consistency maintenance protocol and record the response time for all 21 participants (this does not include the writer who committed this update) and the result is depicted in Figure 5.

From this figure, we can clearly see that the first hop delay dominates the system's response time. With greater computing power that can minimize the cost of committing updating operations, we expect the advantage of the CVRetrieval approach to be much more obvious.

It is worth noting that most current protocols uses passive update dissemination method, with which the advantage of CVRetrieval will become more pronounced. Furthermore, the most important advantage of CVRetrieval is its saving of communication cost, especially in a system with a large number of participants, as analyzed in Section 5. We believe that the two features—efficiency and scalability—together make CVRetrieval a viable alternative to pure consistency maintenance protocols.

FUTURE TRENDS

As Grid computing becomes a key enabling technology for large-scale collaboration application, quantitatively guaranteeing its QoS will become more and more important. In terms of consistency control, advances in QoS will, based on the authors' opinion, be on two fronts: scalability and reliability.

Scalability refers to a protocol's ability to scale to a large number of geographically dispersed nodes. With the size of Internet keeping increasing, it becomes necessary for the Grid systems to maintain a meaningful consistency among different nodes while at the same time imposing very low communication overhead. Without this ability, practitioners will face a dilemma: either accept poor QoS in order to run the system in a large scale, or achieve high QoS at the expense of not cooperating with remote nodes. CVRetrieval presented in this paper is one way to improve scalability. Other alternatives are certainly possible.

Reliability refers to the robustness of a protocol. As Grid becomes an essential computing platform upon which numerous applications run, it is essentially that any key component of the Grid itself, in-

Table 3. Response time for observers

Cache hit rate	Max (seconds)	Min (seconds)	Average (seconds)
50%	0.48	0.33	0.37
66.7%	0.3	0.24	0.28
75%	0.16	0.12	0.14

Table 4. Response time of a pure consistency maintenance protocol with active update dissemination

Max (seconds)	Min (seconds)	Average (seconds)
2.45	1.77	2.07

Figure 5. Response time for different hops

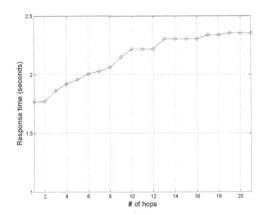

cluding consistency control, is resilient to frequent packet delay/loss and node failure. In this respect, any new consistency control protocols will need to explicitly consider packet delay/loss and node failure in the design phase. Reliability in CVRetrieval depends on the robustness of the publish/subscribe infrastructure. It is interesting to see other alternatives that can provide even stronger and low overhead reliability guarantee.

CONCLUSIONS AND FUTURE WORK

In this paper, we presented the design, analysis, implementation, and evaluation of CVRetrieval, a system that improves the scalability of consistency control in large-scale, replication-based Grid systems by separating consistency retrieval from consistency maintenance.

CVRetrieval is fully evaluated by both analysis and prototyping. The analysis result showed that, comparing to pure consistency maintenance protocols, CVRetrieval incurs significantly less communication overhead and hence improves the scalability of consistency control in general. Through prototyping on the Planet-Lab test-bed, we evaluated the response time of CVRetrieval and the results showed that CVRetrieval achieves a sensible tradeoff: it achieves shorter response times for writers at the expense of a longer response time for observers and, more importantly, improves the system's scalability as a whole.

In the future, we plan to improve the scalability and performance of CVRetrieval further through optimization. For example, we can drive active writer information towards the most needed subscribers by controlling the publishing rates along different paths. In such a scenario, the subscribers (the ISPs) will report their interests (in terms of frequency of issued requests) to the publisher, which in turn adjusts the publishing rates by publishing at a higher rate to a path that can reach subscribers that reveals higher interest than others.

REFERENCES

Banavar, G., Chandra, T., Mukherjee, B., Nagarajarao, J., Strom, R. E., & Sturman, D. C. (1999). An Efficient Multicast Protocol for Content-based Publish-Subscribe Systems, *International Conference on Distributed Computing Systems* (pp. 262-272). Washington D.C. USA.

Begole, J., Rosson, M. B., & Shaffer, C. A. (1999), Flexible Collaboration Transparency: Supporting Worker Independence in Replicated Application-Sharing Systems. *ACM Trans. On Computer-Human Interaction, 6*(2), 95-132.

Cetintemel, U., Keleher, P. J., Bhattacharjee, B., & Franklin M. J. (2003). Deno: A Decentralized, Peer-to-Peer Object-Replication System for Weakly-Connected Environments. *IEEE Transactions on Computers, 52*(7), 943-959.

Chang, T., Popsecu, G., & Codella, C. (2002). Scalable and Efficient Update Dissemination for Interactive Distributed Applications, *International Conference on Distributed Computing Systems* (pp. 143-152). Viena, Austria.

Li, F., Li, L., & Lau, R. (2004). Supporting Continuous Consistency in Multiplayer Online Games. *ACM Multimedia* (pp. 388-391). New York, New York, USA.

Lu, Y. (2007a). Improving Data Consistency Management and Overlay Multicast in Internet-scale Distributed Systems. Ph.D. Dissertation, University of Nebraska-Lincoln.

Lu, Y., Lu, Y. & Jiang, H. (2007b). IDEA: An Infrastructure of Detection-based Adaptive Consistency Control. *16th International Symposium on High Performance Distributed Computing* (pp. 223-224). Monterey, CA.

Lu, Y., Lu, Y., & Jiang, H. (2008). Adaptive Consistency Guarantees for Large-Scale Replicated Services. *2008 IEEE International Conference on Networking, Architecture and Storage,* Chongqing, China.

Peterson, L. L., Anderson, T. E., Culler, D. E., & Roscoe, T. (2003). A Blueprint for Introducing Disruptive Technology into the Internet. *Computer Communication Review. Vol. 33*(1). 59-64.

Prakash, A. & Shim, H. S. (1994). DistView: Support for Building Efficient Collaborative Applications using Replicated Objects. *ACM conference on computer supported cooperative work.* (pp. 153-164). Chapel Hill, NC.

Ratnasamy, S., Francis, P., Handley, M., Karp, R., & Shenker, S. (2001). A Content Addressable Network. *ACM SIGCOMM* (161-172). San Diego, CA.

Rowstron, A., & Druschel, P. (2001). Pastry: Scalable, distributed object location and routing for large-scale peer-to-peer systems, *IFIP/ACM International conference on distributed systems platforms (Middleware)* (pp. 329-350). Heidelberg, Germany.

Schuckmann, C., Kirchner, L., Schummer, J., & Haake, J. M. (1996). Designing Object-oriented Synchronous Groupware with COAST. *ACM conference on computer supported cooperative work* .(pp. 30-38). Cambridge, MA.

Stoica, I., Morris, R., Karger, D., Kaashoek, M. F., & Balakrishnan, H. (2001). Chord: A Scalable Peer-to-peer Lookup Service for Internet Applications. *ACM SIGCOMM.* (pp.149-160). San Deigo, CA.

Vogel, J. & Mauve, M. (2001). Consistency Control for Distributed Interactive Media. *ACM Multimedia.* (pp. 221-230). Ottawa, Canada.

Yu, H., & Vahdat, A. (2000). Design and Evaluation of a Continuous Consistency Model for Replicated Services, *4th conference on Symposium on Operating System Design & Implementation.* San Diego, California.

ENDNOTE

[1]   We use the term "share data" and "shared object" interchangeably depending on the scenarios.

Chapter VI
QoS–Based Job Scheduling and Resource Management Strategies for Grid Computing

Kuo-Chan Huang
National Taichung University, Taiwan

Po-Chi Shih
National Tsing Hua University, Taiwan

Yeh-Ching Chung
National Tsing Hua University, Taiwan

ABSTRACT

This chapter elaborates the quality of service (QoS) aspect of load sharing activities in a computational grid environment. Load sharing is achieved through appropriate job scheduling and resource allocation mechanisms. A computational grid usually consists of several geographically distant sites each with different amount of computing resources. Different types of grids might have different QoS requirements. In most academic or experimental grids the computing sites volunteer to join the grids and can freely decide to quit the grids at any time when they feel joining the grids bring them no benefits. Therefore, maintaining an appropriate QoS level becomes an important incentive to attract computing sites to join a grid and stay in it. This chapter explores the QoS issues in such type of academic and experimental grids. This chapter first defines QoS based performance metrics for evaluating job scheduling and resource allocation strategies. According to the QoS performance metrics appropriate grid-level load sharing strategies are developed. The developed strategies address both user-level and site-level QoS concerns. A series of simulation experiments were performed to evaluate the proposed strategies based on real and synthetic workloads.

INTRODUCTION

This chapter elaborates the *quality of service* (QoS) aspect of load sharing activities in a computational grid environment. Load sharing is achieved through appropriate job scheduling and resource allocation mechanisms. A computational grid usually consists of several geographically distant sites each with different amount of computing resources. Different types of grids might have different QoS requirements. In most academic or experimental grids the computing sites volunteer to join the grids and can freely decide to quit the grids at any time when they feel joining the grids bring them no benefits. Therefore, maintaining an appropriate QoS level becomes an important incentive to attract computing sites to join a grid and stay in it. This article explores the QoS issues in such type of academic and experimental grids. We first define QoS based performance metrics for evaluating job scheduling and resource allocation strategies. According to the QoS performance metrics appropriate grid-level load sharing strategies are developed. The developed strategies address both user-level and site-level QoS concerns. A series of simulation experiments were performed to evaluate the proposed strategies based on real and synthetic workloads.

BACKGROUND

Without grid computing users can only run jobs on their local site. A computational grid is an emerging platform for enabling resource sharing and coordinated computing work, which integrates resources across multiple geographically distant institutions. In most current academic and experimental grid systems, participating sites provide their resources for free with the expectation that they can benefit from the resource sharing in terms of improved job turnaround time. The improved job turnaround time is an example of QoS indicator which users care about. A grid system has to provide strong incentives concerning improved QoS for participating sites to join and stay in it. Job scheduling and resource allocation strategies fulfilling users' QoS requirements thus become a crucial research area. The QoS of a grid system can be explored at different levels. At the grid system level participating sites are concerned with the potential performance improvement of their local users' jobs once they join a grid. Therefore, fair resource sharing can be considered as the most important grid-level QoS requirement. We say the resource sharing is fair if it can bring performance improvement and the improvement is achieved in the sense that all participating sites benefit from the collaboration.

At the individual user level users concern mostly their jobs' turnaround times. Usually shorter turnaround time implies better QoS. Some research work on QoS based job scheduling associates each job with a hard completion deadline or a fixed budget which are strict QoS requirements. The deadline and budget are then taken into consideration when performing job scheduling. On the other hand, this article focuses on the academic and experimental computational grid environments where the resources are shared for free and usually the users just want their jobs to finish as soon as possible without strict deadlines associated with the jobs. Therefore, we do not discuss the issues related to the deadline and budget constraints. The improved job turnaround time is the sole concern of the user-level QoS requirement in the following studies.

Heterogeneity is another important issue in a computational grid. Many previous works (England & Weissman, 2005; Hamscher, Schwiegelshohn, Streit, & Yahyapour, 2000; Huang & Chang, 2006) have shown significant performance improvement for homogeneous grid environment. However, in the real world a computational grid usually consists of heterogeneous sites which differ at least in the computing speed. Heterogeneity puts a challenge on designing QoS-based scheduling methods. Methods developed for homogeneous grids have to be improved or even redesigned to make them effective in a heterogeneous environment. This article addresses the issues of QoS-based job scheduling and resource management in a heterogeneous computational grid.

Job scheduling for parallel computers has been subject to research for a long time. As for grid computing, previous works discussed several strategies for a grid scheduler. One approach is the modification of traditional list scheduling strategies for usage on grid (Carsten, Volker, Uwe, Ramin, & Achim, 2002; Carsten Ernemann, Hamscher, Streit, & Yahyapour, 2002a, 2002b; Hamscher et al., 2000). Some economic based methods are also being discussed (Buyya, Giddy, & Abramson, 2000; Carsten, Volker, & Ramin, 2002; Rajkumar Buyya, 2002; Yanmin et al., 2005). In this paper we explore non economic scheduling and allocation strategies with support for a heterogeneous grid environment.

England and Weissman in (England & Weissman, 2005) analyzed the costs and benefits of load sharing of parallel jobs in the computational grid. Experiments were performed for both homogeneous and heterogeneous grids. However, in their works simulations of a heterogeneous grid only captured the differences in capacities and workload characteristics. The computing speeds of nodes on different sites are assumed to be identical. In this article we deal with QoS based load sharing strategies regarding heterogeneous grids in which nodes on different sites may have different computing speeds.

For resource allocation there are several possible methods for selecting which site to allocate a job in a computational grid. Earlier simulation studies in our previous work (Huang & Chang, 2006) and in the literature (Hamscher et al., 2000) showed the best results for a selection policy called *best-fit*. In this policy a particular site is chosen on which a job will leave the least number of free processors if it is allocated to that site. However, these simulation studies are performed based on a computational grid model in which nodes on different sites all run at the same speed. In this article we explore possible QoS based site selection policies for a heterogeneous computational grid. In such a heterogeneous environment nodes on different sites may run at different speeds.

The issue of fair resource sharing has been discussed for several kinds of computing systems. In (Emmanuelle, Maria, & Aina, 2005) the authors addressed the fair resource sharing problem in peer-to-peer systems. The proposed mechanism comprises a fair differential service incentive and an algorithmic part encapsulated in a middleware layer. The works in (Ngan, Wallach, & Druschel, 2003) deal with fair sharing of storage resources through economic incentives. In (Uwe Schwiegelshohn, 2000) the authors discussed the fairness issue among different jobs running on the same parallel computer. A scheduling strategy is said to be λ-fair if all jobs submitted after job *i* cannot increase the flow time of *i* by more than a factor λ. In (Rajkumar, 1999) fair resource sharing among different parties over a specific period of time was discussed. They attempt to establish the defined resource entitlements within a sliding time window. Therefore, such policies take respect to past usage and compensate for low resource usage in an earlier time interval or punish for over-utilization. This way, over time, the entitlements of all parties utilizing a computing resource can be met. In this article we study the fairness issue as a grid-level QoS requirement in a load sharing computational grid.

In the literature (Barsanti & Sodan, 2007; John et al., 1994; Sabin, Lang, & Sadayappan, 2007; Srividya, Vijay, Rajkumar, Praveen, & Sadayappan, 2002; Sudha, Savitha, & Sadayappan, 2003; Walfredo & Francine, 2000, 2002) several strategies for scheduling moldable jobs have been introduced. Most of the previous works either assume the job execution time is a known function of the number of processors allocated to it or require users to provide estimated job execution time. In our previous work (Huang, 2006b) without the requirement of known job execution time three adaptive processor allocation policies for moldable jobs were evaluated and shown to be able to improve the overall system performance in terms of average job turnaround time. In this article adaptive processor allocation policies are evaluated for a heterogeneous computational grid.

QOS METRICS ON COMPUTATIONAL GRID

This section defines the QoS metrics which will be used for evaluating the job scheduling and resource allocation strategies in the following sections. The user-level QoS metric concerns each individual job's performance. Usually *turnaround time* is used to measure the performances of individual jobs. The turnaround time consists of two parts: *waiting time* and *execution time*. As the target execution environment is determined, the execution time of a job is fixed. The waiting time for a job is the time period when the job stays in a queue waiting for the required computing resources to become ready or available. The length of this time period depends on the workload as well as the job scheduling and resource allocation strategies used in the system. If a job is submitted for execution to the same machine for several times, its execution time would remain consistent across different executions. On the other hand, the waiting time might vary from time to time. Therefore, it is the waiting time that has direct impact on user's satisfaction with a system. However, the waiting time itself might not be an appropriate QoS indicator for individual jobs. This is because the waiting time affects user's satisfaction in ways not so straightforward. The same amount of waiting time for two jobs could lead to different levels of user's satisfaction if the jobs require unequal execution times. Ten-minute waiting time may be acceptable to a job requiring 1000 minutes of execution, but could be relatively too long for a short job running for only 5 minutes.

In our previous work (Huang, 2006a) we introduced the concept of *reasonable waiting time*. A job is said to be with a reasonable waiting time if the ratio of its waiting time to execution time is within a certain range, leading to acceptable user's satisfaction. We defined the ratio as *waiting ratio* and suggested using it as the user-level QoS metric for evaluating various job scheduling methods. Apparently

Figure 1. Different average waiting ratios with the same average waiting time

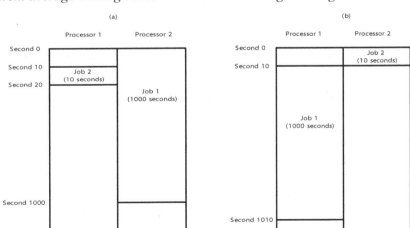

lower waiting ratio could lead to higher user's satisfaction. On a single-processor computer, if jobs' execution times are known in advance, a schedule leading to least average waiting ratio can be found through solving the minimum average waiting time problem which has long been known and can be solved optimally by the shortest-job-first greedy algorithm (Abraham, James, & Peter, 1991). On a single-processor system where jobs have to be processed sequentially, minimum average waiting time implies least average waiting ratio.

However, when running jobs on parallel computers, minimum average waiting time does not guarantee the least average waiting ratio. Figure 1 is an example describing two different scheduling decisions.

In Figure 1 jobs 1 and 2 requiring 1000 and 10 seconds of single-processor runtime, respectively, are both submitted to a parallel machine with two processors at second 0. However, only processor 2 is available at second 0 and processor 1 will become available at second 10. Cases (a) and (b) illustrate two different scheduling decisions, respectively. In case (a) job 1 is scheduled to run first. On the other hand, job 2 is scheduled to run first in case (b). Both scheduling decisions in Figure 1 lead to the same average waiting time: $(10 + 0)/2 = 5$. However, the waiting ratios for these two cases are quite different as shown in Table 1. Obviously, the waiting ratios in case (b) are much lower than those in case (a), promising in leading to a higher level of user's satisfaction. This example illustrates that conventional methods for solving the minimum waiting time problem cannot be directly applied to minimizing the average waiting ratio on parallel computers.

The above definition of waiting ratio is an appropriate user-level QoS indicator in a homogeneous grid environment. However, the waiting ratio is inappropriate in a heterogeneous computational grid. The following is an example. Since computing resources on different sites might run at different speeds in a heterogeneous grid, assume a job would take 100 seconds for execution on site A and 200 seconds for execution on site B, respectively. If on both sites, the waiting times for a specific job are the same, *e.g.* 10 seconds, the values of waiting ratio on the two sites would be 0.1 and 0.05 respectively. This result implies that the lower waiting ratio, 0.05, would lead to a higher user's satisfaction on site B. However, this can not be true because execution on site B takes a longer turnaround time, 210 seconds, than execution on site A requiring 110 seconds. Therefore, it is necessary to develop a new user-level QoS metric for heterogeneous grids. The following is such a QoS metric we propose.

$$Metric_u = \frac{WaitingTime + \left(ExecutionTime_{target} - ExecutionTime_{home}\right)}{ExecutionTime_{home}}$$

In the new metric the denominator is the required execution time if a job is executed on its home site. The numerator, in addition to the waiting time, takes into account the difference between the two execution times on the target site and the home site, respectively. Therefore, if a job is dispatched to a target site faster than its home site, it would get a lower value for this metric and indicate a higher user's

Table 1. Waiting ratios for cases in Figure 1

	Case (a)		Case (b)	
Waiting ratio	Job 1	Job 2	Job 1	Job 2
	0	1	0.01	0

satisfaction. Thus, this user-level QoS metric, like the waiting ratio, also implies that lower values lead to higher user's satisfaction. This metric can be applied to both homogeneous and heterogeneous grids. When applied to a homogeneous grid, the execution time on the target site would equal to its counter part on the home site and cancel each other out in the numerator. Then, the metric reduces to the waiting ratio definition. One thing to be noted is that this metric can produce negative values in heterogeneous grid environments when the jobs are dispatched to faster sites for execution and the reduced execution times are larger than the waiting times. However, this does not violate the principle that lower values imply higher user's satisfaction.

The site-level QoS metrics concern the fair sharing of grid resources and thus involve the comparison of performances under the grid architecture and under the original non-grid architecture, respectively. In this article, we propose two possible site-level QoS metrics as follows.

$$Metric_{s\_count} = \frac{NumberOfJobsWithL\arg erMetric_u Values}{NumberOfJobs}$$

This metric counts the ratio of jobs which attain higher values of the user-level metric after joining the grid. Therefore, lower values of this metric imply higher levels of fair resource sharing and provide stronger incentives for the participating sites to stay in the grid. The following is another site-level QoS metric. This metric summarizes the difference of the values for the user-level metric under the grid architecture and under the non-grid architecture, respectively, for all jobs. Again, lower values imply higher levels of fair resource sharing.

$$Metric_{s\_difference} = \sum_{all} \left(Metric_u ForGrid - Metric_u ForNonGrid \right)$$

COMPUTATIONAL GRID MODEL AND EXPERIMENTAL SETTING

In this section, the computational grid model is introduced on which the evaluations of the job scheduling and resource allocation strategies in this article are based. In the model, there are several independent computing sites with their own local workload and management system. The computational grid integrates the sites and shares their incoming jobs. Each participating site is a homogeneous parallel computer system. The nodes on each site run at the same speed and are linked with a fast interconnection network that does not favor any specific communication pattern (Feitelson & Rudolph, 1995). This means a parallel job can be allocated on any subset of nodes in a site. The parallel computer system uses space-sharing and run the jobs in an exclusive fashion.

The system deals with an on-line scheduling problem without any knowledge of future job submissions. The jobs under consideration are restricted to batch jobs because this job type is dominant on most parallel computer systems running scientific and engineering applications. For the sake of simplicity, in this article we assume a global grid scheduler which handles all job scheduling and resource allocation activities. The local schedulers are only responsible for starting the jobs after their allocation by the global scheduler. Theoretically a single central scheduler could be a critical limitation concerning efficiency and reliability. However, practical distributed implementations are possible, in which site-autonomy is still maintained but the resulting schedule would be the same as created by a central scheduler (C. Ernemann, Hamscher, & Yahyapour, 2004).

All computing nodes in the computational grid are assumed to be binary compatible. The grid is heterogeneous in the sense that nodes on different sites may differ in computing speed and different sites may have different numbers of nodes. When load sharing activities occur a job may be dispatched to a remote site for execution. In this case the input data for that job have to be transferred to the target site before the job execution while the output data of the job is transferred back afterwards. This network communication is neglected in our simulation studies as this latency can usually be hidden in pre- and post-fetching phases without regards to the actual job execution phase (C. Ernemann et al., 2004).

In this article we focus on the area of high throughput computing, improving system's overall throughput with appropriate load sharing strategies. Therefore, in our studies the requested number of processors for each job is bound by the total number of processors on the local site from which the job is submitted. The local site which a job is submitted from will be called the *home site* of the job henceforward in this article. We assume the ability of jobs to run in multi-site mode. That means a job can run in parallel on a node set distributed over different sites when no single site can provide enough free processors for it due to a portion of resources are occupied by some running jobs.

Our simulation studies were based on publicly downloadable workload traces ("Parallel Workloads Archive,"). We used the SDSC's SP2 workload logs[1] on ("Parallel Workloads Archive,") as the input workload in the simulations. The workload log on SDSC's SP2 contains 73496 records collected on a 128-node IBM SP2 machine at San Diego Supercomputer Center (SDSC) from May 1998 to April 2000. After excluding some problematic records based on the *completed* field ("Parallel Workloads Archive,") in the log, the simulations in this article use 56490 job records as the input workload. The detailed workload characteristics are shown in Table 2.

In the SDSC's SP2 system the jobs in this log are put into five different queues and all these queues share the same 128 processors on the system. In the following simulations this workload log will be used to model the workload on a computational grid consisting of five different sites whose workloads correspond to the jobs submitted to the five queues respectively. Table 3 shows the configuration of

Table 2. Characteristics of the workload log on SDSC's SP2

	Number of jobs	Maximum execution time (sec.)	Average execution time (sec.)	Maximum number of processors per job	Average number of processors per job
Queue 1	4053	21922	267.13	8	3
Queue 2	6795	64411	6746.27	128	16
Queue 3	26067	118561	5657.81	128	12
Queue 4	19398	64817	5935.92	128	6
Queue 5	177	42262	462.46	50	4
Total	56490				

Table 3. Configuration of the computational grid

	total	site 1	site 2	site 3	site 4	site 5
Number of processors	442	8	128	128	128	50

the computational grid under study. The number of processors on each site is determined according to the maximum number of required processors of the jobs belonged to the corresponding queue for that site.

To simulate the speed difference among participating sites we define a speed vector, speed=(sp1,sp2, sp3,sp4,sp5), to describe the relative computing speeds of all the five sites in the grid, in which the value 1 represents the computing speed resulting in the job execution time in the original workload log. We also define a load vector, load=(ld1,ld2,ld3,ld4,ld5), which is used to derive different loading levels from the original workload data by multiplying the load value ld_i to the execution times of all jobs at site *i*.

QOS GUIDED PERFORMANCE MEASUREMENT OF LOAD SHARING POLICIES IN COMPUTATIONAL GRID

This section uses the QoS metrics defined in the preceding section to evaluate various job scheduling and resource allocation strategies in a computational grid environment.

Job Scheduling Strategies

Most parallel computing systems schedule parallel batch jobs based on the variable partitioning scheme (Feitelson, 1994), meaning each job receives a partition of the parallel computer with its desired number of processors. Usually the partitions of processors are allocated to the submitted jobs based on the first-come first-serve (FCFS) policy. However, for the FCFS policy, once the number of available processors cannot meet the requirement of the first job in queue, all the jobs would be blocked until enough processors for the first job become available. This might lead to a resource-wasting problem, where the available processors is less than the need of the first job but equal to or more than the needs of one or more of the jobs behind the first one. The FCFS policy does not allow jobs to run out of the order in queue. Therefore, some jobs with enough available processors are forced to wait while the processors remain idle. This would degrade system utilization and performance (Jones & Nitzberg, 1999; Krueger, Lai, & Dixit-Radiya, 1994).

It is know that the best solutions for the problem are to use dynamic partitioning (Cathy, Raj, & John, 1993) or gang scheduling (Feitelson & Morris, 1997). However, these methods have practical limitations (Mu'alem & Feitelson, 2001). A simpler approach is to use non-FCFS policies (Feitelson, Larry, Uwe, Kenneth, & Parkson, 1997), reordering the jobs in the queue. In the following, the non-FCFS policies are further divided into two categories. The first category contains backfilling based scheduling policies (Mu'alem & Feitelson, 2001), and the second category refers to other non-FCFS job reordering policies. With backfilling policies, users are asked to provide an estimate of the runtime before job submission. This enables the scheduler to predict when jobs will terminate and when the next queued jobs will be able to run. Therefore, it is possible to identify processor/time free spaces in the schedule and jobs that can fit into these spaces. Backfilling policies support two conflicting goals. The first is to move as many jobs forward as possible in order to improve utilization and responsiveness. The second is to avoid starvation for jobs and to be able to predict when each job will run. Different versions of backfilling policies balance these goals in different ways (Mu'alem & Feitelson, 2001).

The main problem with the backfilling policies is that they require the estimates of job runtimes to be available. In this section, we use the QoS based performance metric to evaluate several non-FCFS policies (Huang & Chang, 2006) that do not require users' estimates of runtimes before job submission and need much less calculation upon making scheduling decisions than backfilling policies.

The following describes the non-FCFS scheduling policies to be evaluated in this section.

- **Backfilling.** Among the many variations of backfilling scheduling methods, the backfilling policy in this section refers to the conservative backfilling method (Mu'alem & Feitelson, 2001). In this policy, backfilling a specific job is done subject to checking that it does not delay any previous job in the queue. We choose the conservative backfilling method instead of other more aggressive versions such as EASY (Mu'alem & Feitelson, 2001) because of its advantage that it allows scheduling decisions to be made upon job submission and, thus, has the capability of predicting when each job will run and giving users guaranteed response times. This is the most important feature that distinguishes the backfilling policy from other non-FCFS policies. It is clear that there is no danger of starvation for the backfilling policy as a reservation is made for each job when it is submitted.

The following are three non-FCFS policies which do not require users' estimates of runtime before job submission and need much less calculation upon making scheduling decisions than backfilling policies. Theoretically the following three non-FCFS policies run the risk of starving the large job, which requires more processors, as small jobs continue to pass it by. However, in practice this starvation problem can be avoided by allowing only a limited number of jobs to pass a job by and then starting to reserve the processors for it anyway.

- **First available.** In this policy each job is put into the queue according to the arrival order and at each time making a scheduling decision, the scheduler scans the queue to find a job which can run with current available processors.
- **Smallest first.** In this policy, each job is put into the queue according to its requirement of processors. Jobs with smaller requirements of processors will be put before jobs with larger requirements of processors. When two jobs have identical requirement of processors their order in the queue is determined by their arrival times. At each time making a scheduling decision, the scheduler just picks up the first job in the queue. In this policy smaller jobs tend to get the requested resources earlier.
- **Largest first.** In this policy, again each job is put into the queue according to its requirement of processors. However, jobs with larger requirements of processors will be put before jobs with smaller requirements of processors. In this policy larger jobs tend to get the requested resources earlier.

The following discusses the simulation studies with the workload log on SDSC's SP2. In the original SP2 system the jobs in this log are put into five different queues, and all these queues share the same 128 processors on the system. In the following simulations, all the 56490 jobs are assumed to be submitted to the same queue on a 384-processor computing cluster. A much larger 384-processor cluster is assumed instead of 128 processors in order to be able to simulate much heavier workloads. To evaluate the effectiveness of the scheduling policies from light to heavy workloads, our studies conduct simula-

Table 4. Average Metric$_u$ values for different scheduling policies

	FCFS	First Available	Smallest First	Largest First	Backfilling
Load Factor=1.0	0.77	0.17	0.15	0.21	0.16
1.5	1.89	0.51	0.40	0.53	0.53
2.0	4.08	0.86	0.79	1.15	0.85
2.5	10.38	1.68	1.29	2.03	1.75
3.0	26.92	3.15	2.19	5.27	3.22
4.0	840.93	62.63	21.99	153.65	50.72

tions for workloads with different load factors: 1.0, 1.5, 2.0, 2.5, 3.0, 4.0. Load factor 1 represents the original workload and the workloads with the other load factor values are formed by multiplying the runtime of each job by the corresponding load factor value.

Table 4 shows the performance results for different scheduling policies under workloads with different load factor values, respectively. The results indicate that all non-FCFS policies outperform the FCFS policy and in general the *smallest first* policy is superior in terms of the QoS-based performance metric. Therefore, it is possible to provide a better quality of job scheduling service by using the less complex smallest-first policy, compared to the backfilling policy.

Resource Allocation Strategies

The scheduler on the computational grid would first try to schedule an entire parallel job onto a single site. Only when no single site can accommodate such job, the scheduler then arranges that parallel job to run across site boundaries. It is not uncommon that at the same time there are more than one site which are all be able to accommodate an entire parallel job. In that situation, although different choices of the target site make no difference to the job itself, different choices can lead to different probabilities for the succeeding jobs to confront the situation where there are no sites being able to accommodate the jobs. This in turn can affect the overall system performance. Therefore, processor allocation policies become a critical issue.

The processor allocation problem can be further divided into two parts (Huang & Chang, 2006). The first part is how to choose an appropriate site for a parallel job among several candidate sites which all can fulfill the resource requirement of that job. The second part is to select a set of sites among all the sites in the computational grid for multi-site parallel execution when there is no single site being able to accommodate a job. In the following simulations, we evaluate five different allocation methods for single-site processor allocation.

- **First-fit.** Allocate the first site found in the searching process that has enough available processors for the waiting job.
- **Best-fit.** Allocate the site with the least available processors among all the sites with enough processors for the waiting job (Carsten, Volker, Uwe et al., 2002; Hamscher et al., 2000). This method produces the least leftover processors for the selected site.
- **Worst-fit.** Allocate the site with the most available processors that can fulfill the requirement of the waiting job. This method produces the most leftover processors for the selected site which may be more likely to accommodate the next waiting job.

- **Median-fit.** Among all the sites that have enough processors for the waiting job, allocate the site with the median number of available processors.
- **Random-fit.** Randomly allocate a site among all the sites that have enough available processors for the waiting job.

In the following simulations we assume a homogeneous grid where all the five sites contain the same type of processors and interconnection networks with the same speed. However, different sites may have different number of processors. Table 5 shows the performance results of the five processor allocation methods under different load factors, using the QoS-based performance metric. In general, the *best-fit* method outperforms the other four methods. When the load factor is less than or equal to two, the performance order of these five methods from high to low is *best-fit = first-fit > median-fit > random-fit > worst-fit*. However, when the slowdown ratio is larger than or equal to four, the *random-fit* method beats the *first-fit* and the *median-fit* methods, and the performance order changes to *best-fit > random-fit > first-fit > median-fit > worst-fit*.

In the following we use the QoS-based performance metrics to evaluate the resource allocation strategies in a heterogeneous computational grid environment. Since the computing speeds at different sites in a heterogeneous grid might be different, the resource allocation procedure becomes more complicated. We first adopt a two-phase procedure (Huang, Shih, & Chung, 2007). At the first phase the grid scheduler determines a set of candidate sites among all the sites with enough free processors for a specific job under consideration by filtering out some sites according to a predefined threshold ratio of computing speed. In the filtering process, a lower bound for computing speed is first determined through multiplying the predefined threshold ratio by the computing speed of a single processor on the job's home site, and then any sites with single-processor speed slower than the lower bound are filtered out. Therefore, adjusting the threshold ratio is an effective way in controlling the outcomes of site selection. When setting the threshold ratio to 1 the grid scheduler will only allocate jobs to sites with single-processor speed equal to or faster than their home sites. On the other hand, with the threshold ratio set to zero, all sites with enough free processors are qualified candidates for a job's allocation. Raising the threshold ratio would prevent allocating a job to a site that is much slower than its home site. This could ensure a job's execution time would not be enlarged to a too large extent due to being allocated to a slow site. However, the job may consequently need to wait in the queue for a longer time period. On the other hand, lowering the threshold ratio would make it more probable for a job to get allocation quickly at the cost of extended execution time. The combined effects of shortened waiting time and extended execution time are complicated for analysis. In this section we use the QoS-based performance metrics to help explore the combined effects. At the second phase the grid scheduler adopts

Table 5. Average Metric$_u$ values for different allocation policies

Load factor	First Fit	Median Fit	Random Fit	Best Fit	Worst Fit
1	0.37	0.37	0.37	0.37	0.37
2	0.47	0.50	0.65	0.47	0.76
4	0.90	1.28	0.86	0.51	5.06
5	1.88	10.11	1.14	0.75	23.11

a site selection policy, such as the best-fit policy, to choose an appropriate site from the candidate sites for allocating the job.

Table 6 compares the performance results of two different values, 0 and 1, for the threshold in a heterogeneous grid with the speed vector (0.6, 0.7, 2.4, 9.5, 4.3). The results of all the three QoS-based performance metrics indicate that the *best-fit* site selection policy without considering the speed difference among participating sites, *i.e.* threshold = 0, may not achieve good QoS performance in a heterogeneous grid, resulting in even worse performance than the original *independent-site* architecture. On the other hand, setting an appropriate threshold value, *e.g.* threshold = 1, is promising in leading to a great QoS improvement. This illustrates that site selection becomes an important and complicated issue which largely affects the load sharing performance in a heterogeneous grid.

Most modern parallel programs are written to have the *moldable* property (Feitelson et al., 1997), meaning these parallel programs are capable of running on a range of different numbers of processors. Based on the *moldable* property, the adaptive processor allocation method (Huang, 2006b) was developed. When a job can not fit in any single site in a computational grid, the adaptive processor allocation policy would allocate a smaller number of processors than specified upon submission to a job, allowing it to fit in a single site for immediate execution. This would improve system utilization and shorten the waiting times for user jobs at the cost of possible enlarged job execution time. An important part of applying adaptive processors allocation in a heterogeneous grid environment is the site selection process regarding the calculation and comparison of computing power of different sites. A site's free computing power is defined as the number of free processors on it multiplied by the computing speed of a single processor. Similarly, the required computing power of a job is defined as the number of required processors specified upon job submission multiplied by the computing speed of a single processor on its home site. A configurable threshold parameter, *power*, with its value ranging from zero to one can be defined in the adaptive processor allocation procedure. A site will be selected to allocate the job only when the site's free computing power is equal to or larger than the job's required computing power multiplied by the predefined threshold value and it provides the largest available computing power among all sites in the grid.

Table 7 shows that the value of the *power* parameter greatly affects the performance of the adaptive processor allocation method based on the measured data of the QoS-based performance metrics. Therefore, selection of an appropriate value for the *power* parameter becomes a critical issue when applying the adaptive processor allocation method to a heterogeneous grid. According to the average $Metric_u$ data, adaptive processor allocation policies with different power values all bring QoS performance improvement. Looking at the $Metric_{s\_count}$ data, different power values lead to similar numbers of jobs which incur degraded $Metric_u$ performance. However, based on the $Metric_{s\_difference}$ data which summarize all jobs' performance changes, the power value of 0.5 is the best choice while the power value of 1 leads to the worst QoS performance.

Table 6. Performance results of allocation policies in heterogeneous grid

Performance metrics	Independent clusters	Best-fit allocation (threshold=0)	Best-fit allocation(threshold=1)
Average $Metric_u$	2.04	2.28	-0.25
$Metric_{s\_count}$	×	0.554	0.004
$Metric_{s\_difference}$	×	128861	-13993

Table 7. Performance of adaptive processor allocation in heterogeneous grid

Performance metrics	Independent clusters	Adaptive processor allocation (power=0)	Adaptive processor allocation (power=0.1)	Adaptive processor allocation (power=0.5)	Adaptive processor allocation (power=1)
Average Metric$_u$	71.029	-0.110	-0.195	-0.197	0.513
Metric$_{s\_count}$	×	0.0248	0.0255	0.0257	0.0284
Metric$_{s\_difference}$	×	-6224.19	-11037.49	-11136.66	28999.53

SCHEDULING FOR FAIR AND EFFICIENT RESOURCE SHARING

In most current grid systems, participating sites provide their resources for free with the expectation that they can benefit from load sharing. Therefore, it is important to ensure that load sharing is performed in a somehow fair manner. Fairness could be an important incentive for the participating sites to stay in the grid. However, fairness and efficiency are sometimes two conflicting goals for the grid-level resource sharing. This section uses the QoS-based performance metrics to help find an effective grid-level job scheduling strategy for balancing these two goals.

The following are three grid-level job scheduling strategies to be evaluated by the QoS-based performance metrics.

- **Ordinary sharing.** In the strategy the job at the front of the waiting queue can be allocated to any site which can accommodate it for immediate execution. If there is no site with enough available resources, the job keeps waiting in the queue. This is the simplest resource sharing strategy without any special concern of the fairness issue.

- **Local priority-based sharing.** This strategy gives each job a higher priority at its home site over remote jobs. When the grid scheduler chooses the next job from the waiting queue and finds that there exists no single site with enough free processors for this job's immediate execution, instead of simply keeping the job waiting in the queue the grid scheduler inspects the status of the job's home site to see if it is possible to make enough free processors by reclaiming a necessary amount of occupied processors from some of the running remote jobs. If so, it deletes a necessary amount of these running remote jobs to collect enough free processors and re-submits the deleted remote jobs directly to the front of the waiting queue to be re-scheduled to other sites for execution. Figure 2 describes the detailed procedure when the grid scheduler tries to schedule jobs according to this strategy.

- **Proportional sharing.** This strategy maintains a separate waiting queue for each participating site. Each waiting queue is associated with a dynamic priority value calculated by dividing the corresponding site's total computing power contribution (the number of processors multiplied by the speed factor) by the total consumption of computing power so far by the jobs dispatched from the queue. Each time a job finishes its execution, the dynamic priority value of its corresponding waiting queue is updated accordingly. The grid scheduler tries to schedule jobs from the waiting queue with the highest priority value. With the dynamic priority values, this strategy tries to ensure somehow fair resource sharing.

Figure 2. Detailed procedure of the local priority-based sharing strategy

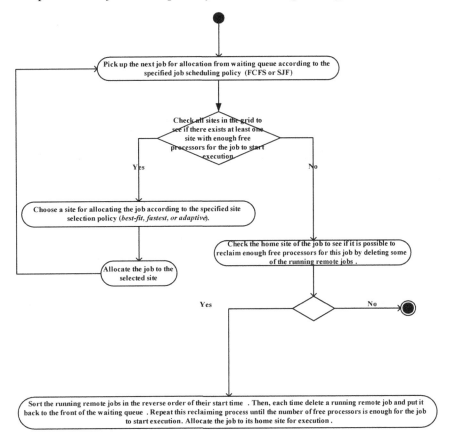

Tables 8 to 10 evaluate the above resource sharing strategies in a heterogeneous computational grid. The SJF scheduling policy and the *fastest-one* site selection policy are used in the simulations. Table 8 applies the commonly used performance metric, average turnaround time, to evaluate the strategies. The results indicate that all three resource sharing strategies outperform the non-grid architecture (independent sites) at the entire grid level. However, when looking into each individual participating site, it is found that site 5 attains a greatly degraded average turnaround time for both the ordinary sharing and the proportional sharing strategies. Therefore, the local priority-based sharing strategy seems to be the most appropriate choice since no sites' average turnaround times get degraded compared to the original non-grid architecture.

However, when applying the QoS-based Metric$_{s\_difference}$ to evaluate the strategies as shown in Table 9, a different insight is revealed. Only the ordinary sharing strategy leads to significant QoS performance improvement. Among the five participating sites four of them attain improvement and in average the entire grid benefits from the strategy. According to Table 9 site 5 seems to suffer from large performance degradation with the Metric$_{s\_difference}$ value equal to 12252. However, as we consult another QoS based performance metric, Metric$_{s\_count}$, as shown in Table 10, it is clear that only about 2.26% of the jobs belonging to site 5 incur QoS performance degradation when using the ordinary sharing

Table 8. Average turnaround times (sec.) for speed=(1,3,4,4,8) and load=(5,4,5,4,1)

	Entire grid	Site 1	Site 2	Site 3	Site 4	Site 5
Independent sites	9260	14216	10964	10199	6448	57
Ordinary sharing	4135	192	4759	4799	3881	560
Local priority-based sharing	4158	193	4803	4799	3936	57
Proportional sharing	4112	192	4595	4791	3882	560

Table 9. Metric$_{s\_difference}$ results for speed=(1,3,4,4,8) and load=(5,4,5,4,1)

	Entire grid	Site 1	Site 2	Site 3	Site 4	Site 5
Ordinary sharing	-2566	-3511	-282	-2699	-8326	12252
Local priority-based sharing	10424	95	3257	6906	166	0
Proportional sharing	20848	0	410	7853	334	12252

Table 10. Metric$_{s\_count}$ results for speed=(1,3,4,4,8) and load=(5,4,5,4,1)

	Entire grid	Site 1	Site 2	Site 3	Site 4	Site 5
Ordinary sharing	0.0252	0.0	0.0259	0.0440	0.0050	0.0226
Local priority-based sharing	0.0300	0.0007	0.0381	0.0482	0.0092	0
Proportional sharing	0.0268	0.0	0.0237	0.0478	0.0054	0.0226

strategy. This should be an acceptable ratio without much hurt to the fair sharing goal. This section thus provides a good example showing that the proposed QoS based performance metrics can help much more effectively analyze different resource sharing strategies compared to the commonly used average turnaround time.

SUMMARY

The commonly used performance-oriented metrics such as average waiting time and average turnaround time might not appropriately reveal the strengths and weaknesses of job scheduling and resource allocation strategies in some cases. Such metrics are also weak in reflecting user's satisfaction. This article proposes three QoS based performance metrics for evaluating the job scheduling and resource allocation strategies in a heterogeneous grid environment. The three metrics based on the concept of reasonable waiting time, represented by waiting ratio, can effectively reflect the user's satisfaction-related QoS performance of the evaluated strategies. We use these metrics to evaluate several job scheduling, resource allocation, and resource sharing strategies in a heterogeneous computational grid. The results illustrate that the proposed QoS based metrics are superior to the performance-oriented metrics in gaining insights into the effectiveness of the evaluated strategies.

REFERENCES

Abraham, S., James, L. P., & Peter, B. G. (1991). *Operating system concepts (3rd ed.)*: Addison-Wesley Longman Publishing Co., Inc.

Barsanti, L., & Sodan, A. (2007). Adaptive Job Scheduling Via Predictive Job Resource Allocation. In *Job Scheduling Strategies for Parallel Processing* (pp. 115-140).

Buyya, R., Giddy, J., & Abramson, D. (2000). *An Evaluation of Economy-Based Resource Trading and Scheduling on Computational Power Grids for Parameter Sweep Applications.* Paper presented at the Second Workshop on Active Middleware Services (AMS2000), Pittsburgh, USA.

Carsten, E., Volker, H., & Ramin, Y. (2002). *Economic Scheduling in Grid Computing.* Paper presented at the 8th International Workshop on Job Scheduling Strategies for Parallel Processing.

Carsten, E., Volker, H., Uwe, S., Ramin, Y., & Achim, S. (2002). *On Advantages of Grid Computing for Parallel Job Scheduling.* Paper presented at the 2nd IEEE/ACM International Symposium on Cluster Computing and the Grid.

Cathy, M., Raj, V., & John, Z. (1993). A dynamic processor allocation policy for multiprogrammed shared-memory multiprocessors. *ACM Trans. Comput. Syst., 11*(2), 146-178.

Emmanuelle, A., Maria, G., & Aina, R. (2005). *Incentives for P2P Fair Resource Sharing.* Paper presented at the Fifth IEEE International Conference on Peer-to-Peer Computing.

England, D., & Weissman, J. B. (2005). Costs and Benefits of Load Sharing in the Computational Grid. In *Job Scheduling Strategies for Parallel Processing* (pp. 160-175).

Ernemann, C., Hamscher, V., Streit, A., & Yahyapour, R. (2002a). Enhanced Algorithms for Multi-site Scheduling. In *Grid Computing — GRID 2002* (pp. 219-231).

Ernemann, C., Hamscher, V., Streit, A., & Yahyapour, R. (2002b). On Effects of Machine Configurations on Parallel Job Scheduling in Computational Grids. *Proceedings of International Conference on Architecture of Computing Systems, ARCS*, 169-179.

Ernemann, C., Hamscher, V., & Yahyapour, R. (2004). *Benefits of global grid computing for job scheduling.* Paper presented at the Fifth IEEE/ACM International Workshop on Grid Computing.

Feitelson, D. G. (1994). *A Survey of Scheduling in Multiprogrammed Parallel Systems* (Research Report No. RC 19790 (87657)): IBM T. J. Watson Research Centero.

Feitelson, D. G., & Rudolph, L. (1995). Parallel job scheduling: Issues and approaches. In *Job Scheduling Strategies for Parallel Processing* (pp. 1-18).

Feitelson, D. G., Larry, R., Uwe, S., Kenneth, C. S., & Parkson, W. (1997). *Theory and Practice in Parallel Job Scheduling.* Paper presented at the third International Workshop on Job Scheduling Strategies for Parallel Processing.

Feitelson, D. G., & Morris, A. J. (1997). *Improved Utilization and Responsiveness with Gang Scheduling.* Paper presented at the third International Workshop on Job Scheduling Strategies for Parallel Processing.

Hamscher, V., Schwiegelshohn, U., Streit, A., & Yahyapour, R. (2000). Evaluation of Job-Scheduling Strategies for Grid Computing. In *Grid Computing — GRID 2000* (pp. 191-202).

Huang, K.-C. (2006a). Minimizing Waiting Ratio for Dynamic Workload on Parallel Computers. *Parallel Processing Letters (PPL), 16*(4), 441-453.

Huang, K.-C. (2006b). *Performance Evaluation of Adaptive Processor Allocation Policies for Moldable Parallel Batch Jobs.* Paper presented at the Third Workshop on Grid Technologies and Applications.

Huang, K.-C., & Chang, H.-Y. (2006). *An Integrated Processor Allocation and Job Scheduling Approach to Workload Management on Computing Grid.* Paper presented at the 2006 International Conference on Parallel and Distributed Processing Techniques and Applications (PDPTA'06), Las Vegas, USA.

Huang, K.-C., Shih, P.-C., & Chung, Y.-C. (2007). Towards Feasible and Effective Load Sharing in a Heterogeneous Computational Grid. In *Advances in Grid and Pervasive Computing* (pp. 229-240).

John, T., Walter, L., Joel, L. W., Lisa, F., Prasoon, T., Jason, G., et al. (1994). *Scheduling parallelizable tasks to minimize average response time.* Paper presented at the sixth annual ACM symposium on Parallel algorithms and architectures.

Jones, J., & Nitzberg, B. (1999). Scheduling for Parallel Supercomputing: A Historical Perspective of Achievable Utilization. In *Job Scheduling Strategies for Parallel Processing* (pp. 1-16).

Krueger, P., Lai, T. H., & Dixit-Radiya, V. A. (1994). Job Scheduling is More Important than Processor Allocation for Hypercube Computers. *IEEE Transactions on Parallel and Distributed Systems, 05*(5), 488-497.

Mu'alem, A. W., & Feitelson, D. G. (2001). Utilization, predictability, workloads, and user runtime estimates in scheduling the IBM SP2 with backfilling. *IEEE Transactions on Parallel and Distributed Systems, 12*(6), 529-543.

Ngan, T.-W. J., Wallach, D., & Druschel, P. (2003). Enforcing Fair Sharing of Peer-to-Peer Resources. In *Peer-to-Peer Systems II* (pp. 149-159).

Parallel Workloads Archive. from http://www.cs.huji.ac.il/labs/parallel/workload/

Rajkumar, B. (1999). *High Performance Cluster Computing: Architectures and Systems*: Prentice Hall PTR.

Rajkumar Buyya, D. A. J. G. H. S. (2002). Economic models for resource management and scheduling in Grid computing. *Concurrency and Computation: Practice and Experience, 14*(13-15), 1507-1542.

Sabin, G., Lang, M., & Sadayappan, P. (2007). Moldable Parallel Job Scheduling Using Job Efficiency: An Iterative Approach. In *Job Scheduling Strategies for Parallel Processing* (pp. 94-114).

Srividya, S., Vijay, S., Rajkumar, K., Praveen, H., & Sadayappan, P. (2002). *Effective Selection of Partition Sizes for Moldable Scheduling of Parallel Jobs.* Paper presented at the 9th International Conference on High Performance Computing.

Sudha, S., Savitha, K., & Sadayappan, P. (2003). *A Robust Scheduling Strategy for Moldable Scheduling of Parallel Jobs.* Paper presented at the Fifth IEEE International Conference on Cluster Computing.

Uwe Schwiegelshohn, R. Y. (2000). Fairness in parallel job scheduling. *Journal of Scheduling, 3*(5), 297-320.

Walfredo, C., & Francine, B. (2000). *Adaptive Selection of Partition Size for Supercomputer Requests.* Paper presented at the 6th International Workshop on Job Scheduling Strategies for Parallel Processing.

Walfredo, C., & Francine, B. (2002). Using moldability to improve the performance of supercomputer jobs. *J. Parallel Distrib. Comput., 62*(10), 1571-1601.

Yanmin, Z., Jinsong, H., Yunhao, L., Ni, L. M. A. N. L. M., Chunming Hu, A. C. H., & Jinpeng Huai, A. J. H. (2005). *TruGrid: a self-sustaining trustworthy grid.* Paper presented at the First International Workshop on Mobility in Peer-to-Peer Systems.

ENDNOTE

[1]   The JOBLOG data is Copyright 2000 The Regents of the University of California All Rights Reserved.

Chapter VII
Grid Workflows with Encompassed Business Relationships:
An Approach Establishing Quality of Service Guarantees

Dimosthenis Kyriazis
National Technical University of Athens, Greece

Andreas Menychtas
National Technical University of Athens, Greece

Theodora Varvarigou
National Technical University of Athens, Greece

ABSTRACT

This chapter focuses on presenting and describing an approach that allows the mapping of workflow processes to Grid provided services by not only taking into account the quality of service (QoS) parameters of the Grid services but also the potential business relationships of the service providers that may affect the aforementioned QoS parameters. This approach is an integral part of the QoS provisioning, since this is the only way to estimate, calculate, and conclude to the mapping of workflows and the selection of the available service types and instances in order to deliver an overall quality of service across a federation of providers. The added value of this approach lays on the fact that business relationships of the service providers are also taken into account during the mapping process.

INTRODUCTION

Although initially designed to cover the computational needs of high performance applications (I. Foster, 2001; W. Leinberger, 1999), Grid technology of nowadays aims at providing the infrastructure for the general business domain. Advanced infrastructure requirements combined with innate business goal for lower costs have driven key business sectors such as multimedia, engineering, gaming, environmental science, among others towards adopting Grid solutions into their business. Furthermore, complex application workflows are emerging along with specification languages used to enable the workflow description and execution on Grid environments. The final success of this business orientation of Grid technology however will primarily depend on its real adopters; the end users whose main demand refers to the offered level of quality.

This shift from science Grids to business Grids in parallel with the replacement of simple job executions to complex workflow management (Workflow Management Coalition, 1999) and enactment in Grids resulted in advanced requirements in the field of workflow mapping with regard to QoS metrics / resources' special attributes (e.g. performance profile). Based on the fact that each workflow contains processes that can be executed from a set of service providers / instances (candidates), which are annotated with QoS information, workflow mapping refers to the mapping of the aforementioned workflow processes to Grid provided services taking into account the QoS metrics in order to provide a selection of candidates guarantying end-to-end QoS for the submitted workflow. In bibliography, it is referred as Workflow QoS Constraints and remains one of the key factors in a Grid Workflow Management System and more specific in the Workflow Design element (J. Yu, 2005).

As presented in the Background section of this chapter, there are many approaches that address the QoS issue in Grid environments while in one of our previous works (D. Kyriazis, 2007) we have presented in detail a QoS-aware workflow mapping mechanism. However, the business relationships between the service providers are not taken into consideration during the selection process. In greater detail, the service providers may have business relationships that can be Cooperating, non-Cooperating or even Antagonistic, Cheating, or Malicious. These relationships affect the workflow mapping since the QoS metrics of a service provider may change based on a selection of another provider. In many occasions, a service provider may alter his offered services' QoS values based on the selection of another service provider depending on their business relationships.

What we discuss and present later on is a modeling of the business relationships within Grid workflows and an approach that provides a metric for defining a service providers "friendliness" bases on the relationships that service provider has with other ones. Furthermore, we discuss how this metric can be reflected into the Service Level Agreements (SLAs). The aforementioned metric can be used by QoS-based selection mechanisms to take into account business relationships during the selection process and meet the user's QoS requirements.

The remainder of the chapter is structured as follows: the Background section introduces the terminology that will be used in this chapter and presents related work in the field of QoS-based workflows management in Grids. The next section, entitled "QoS-based Workflow Mapping addressing Business Relationships" introduces the concept of Business Relationships in workflows and provides a modeling approach for them while a proposal for defining a metric to characterize a service provider's friendliness, is also included. The chapter proceeds by describing the architecture of the proposed model. Finally, it concludes with a discussion on future research and potentials for the current study (in the Future Trends section) and the conclusions of the work presented in this chapter.

BACKGROUND

Managing the application workflow operations within Grid environments requires the orchestration of the distributed resources (E. Deelman, 2003). In that frame, workflow is an important factor for application composition on Grids (E. Deelman, 2004) promoting inter-organizational collaborations by integrating the teams involved in managing of different parts of a workflow. Besides, literature (E. Deelman, 2004) describes additional advantages of the workflow management such as the utilization of resources to increase throughput or reduce execution costs and the ability to build dynamic applications which orchestrate these resources.

Since workflow is a wide concept in technology, the terminology regarding workflows that is used afterwards in this chapter is defined. Workflow Management Coalition (WfMC) provides the following general definition (B. Ludäscher, 2003): "Workflow is the automation of a business process, in whole or part, during which documents, information or tasks are passed from one participant to another for action, according to a set of procedural rules".

In Grid environments, workflow can be defined as the orchestration of a set of activities to accomplish a complicated goal including application processes, business processes, and infrastructure processes (M. Bubak, 2005). Workflow is an architecturally important factor for dynamic interoperability and adaptation to different business models, which can be addressed as workflow policies, and deployment contexts.

A Workflow Model / Specification is used to define a workflow both in task and structure level. There are two types of workflows, namely Abstract and Concrete (J. Yu, 2005; D. Kyriazis, 2007) while concrete workflows are also referred to as executable workflows in some literature (D.P. Spooner, 2004). In an abstract model, the tasks are described in an abstract form without referring to specific Grid resources for task execution since it provides the ability to the users to define workflows in a flexible way, isolating execution details. Furthermore, an abstract model provides only service semantic information on how the workflow has been composed and therefore the sharing of workflow descriptions between Grid users is feasible, which is of major importance for the participants of Virtual Organizations (VOs) (W. Leinberger, 1999). Abstract workflow can be composed with systems like the one presented in (G. Bochmann, 1996).

In the concrete model, the tasks of the workflow are bound to specific resources and therefore this model provides service semantic and execution information on how the workflow has been composed both for the service instances and for the overall composition (e.g. dataflow bindings, control flow structures). In correspondence with the abstract model and the relationship to the VOs, the tasks included in a concrete model may also refer to data movement requests in order to publish newly derived data into VO (D. Kyriazis, 2007). There has to be mentioned that the service instances do not necessarily correspond to resources since within a resource more than one service instances may be available and executable.

On the following figure (Figure 1) we present the aforementioned workflow definitions.

Following the workflow models' definitions, tasks in an abstract model are portable and can be mapped onto any suitable Grid services by using suitable discovery and mapping mechanisms. A workflow mapping mechanism is an integral part of the QoS provisioning, and especially the end-to-end Quality of Service, since this is the only way to estimate, calculate and conclude to the mapping of workflows and the selection of the available service types and instances in order to deliver an overall quality of service across a federation of providers.

Figure 1. Workflow definitions (application, abstract, concrete workflow)

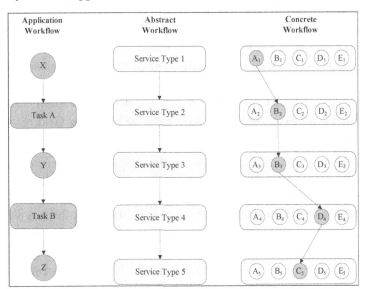

However, supporting end-to-end QoS with workflow mapping mechanisms requires the pursuit of a number of aspects that need to be addressed. Given that the current approaches handle the quality requirements efficiently, we focus our work on modeling the service providers' business relationships that affect the QoS values of the service instances. We also present how the outcome of this modeling can be included in the SLAs, from which the majority of the workflow mapping mechanism obtain the QoS values. The latter allows the rapid and straightforward integration of the proposed approach to any workflow management system.

In general, there are various approaches for QoS-based workflow management in Grid environments. In some cases, the selection process is based on the Service Level Agreement (SLA) negotiation process, as discussed in (G. Bochmann, 1996; R. J. Al-Ali, 2004; Padgett, J., 2005). The end-user's constraints and preferences are parsed to several service providers through the functionality offered by a broker (usually the SLA Management Service) for allocating the appropriate service providers. The Globus Architecture for Reservation and Allocation (GARA) (I. Foster, 1999) addresses QoS at the level of facilitating and providing basic mechanisms for QoS support, namely resource configuration, discovery, selection, and allocation. Outcomes of the research on QoS-based selection for workflows are also presented in (J. Yu, 2005; L. Guo, 2007; L.M. Khanli, 2007). The first one proposes an algorithm that minimizes cost in the time constraint while the second work presents a system that is able to meet pre-defined QoS requirements during the workflow mapping process. Authors of (L.M. Khanli, 2007) discuss a system that based on event condition action rules maps workflow processes to Grid resources taking into account QoS information. A workflow QoS specification and methods to predict, analyze and monitor QoS are presented in (Jorge Cardoso, 2002; J. Cardoso, 2002). The work is focused on the creation of QoS estimates and the QoS computation for specific metrics – time, cost, fidelity and reliability with the use of two methods: analysis and simulation. In this case, the parameters are handled one by one similar to (Jia Yu, 2005; R. Buyya, 2005) and not in a combined way while the overall estimation emerges from the individual tasks.

Authors in (T. Fahringer, 2005) present the ASKALON tool which comprises four components along with a service repository to support performance-oriented development of parallel and distributed (Grid) applications. Literatures (A. Mayer, 2003; S. McGough, 2004) discuss the ICENI environment in which a graph based language is used to annotate component behaviors and perform optimizations based on the estimated execution times and resource sharing. The gathered performance information is taken into account during the resource selection while the mapping of work onto resources through a workflow enabled scheduler (which is able to make use of performance information) is also supported. Moreover, a three-layered negotiation protocol for advance reservation of the Grid resources and a mechanism that optimizes resource utilization and QoS constraints for agreement enforcement is presented in (M. Siddiqui, 2006).

The difference between the systems presented in this section and our proposed scheme lies on the fact that while the ones presented here yield very good results for QoS-based selection, they consider as QoS parameters during the selection process either the ones published by the service providers (via SLAs) or the ones obtained from monitoring tools over the resources. However, they do not tackle an issue that may affect the selection process and refers to changes in the QoS values due to business relationships. This kind of information cannot be obtained with monitoring tools since these work during the execution of a process whilst algorithms and methods have not been published for QoS-based selection with a priori knowledge of the effects of service providers' business relationships.

QOS-BASED WORKFLOW MAPPING ADDRESSING BUSINESS RELATIONSHIPS

Following, we describe an approach for modeling the business relationships, characterizing a service provider based on these relationships and finally taking into account this information during the QoS-based selection process for Grid workflows.

Modeling Business Relationships

Firstly, one of the issues that has to be resolved is how the strategic relationships are modeled on the service provider's space. The proposed approach looks at strategic relationships from an external perspective as it focuses on how the selection of a provider affects other providers. As a result, we model each strategic relationship as a directed edge on the problem's graph from a service provider A to a service provider B. The source of the edge is the provider that stimulates the relationship and the destination is the provider that alters its service parameters in response to the selection of the source.

In the example presented on the above figure (Figure 2), service provider A triggers a change to provider's B QoS parameters and thus, we have an edge from node A to node B. In case that the selection of provider B changes the parameters of provider A we require the existence of a second edge with the opposite direction.

The above modeling is characterized "external" as it puts the stimulator instead of the actual affected node in the center of attention. On the whole service instances space, the instances that affect a great number of other instances will appear as the source of numerous vectors and as a result their total effect on other instances can be measured. The opposite approach, deriving all edges from the affected

Figure 2. A strategic relationship between two service providers

service instance, has the disadvantage of taking the focus off the influential service instances and it is not suitable for a forward-looking heuristic algorithm.

A constraint that needs to be underlined is that all business relationships should reference service providers from different workflow processes. A business relationship, either positive or negative, from a service provider to another on the same workflow process is not feasible as those two services will never be selected together on the final concrete workflow.

Measuring a Strategic Relationship's Influence

In order to design a function that characterizes a service's instance influence, we need to have a way to express the influence of a specific strategic relationship. In this section we propose a metric that rates that influence from various perspectives in an effort to express all of its aspects, relative and absolute. This metric may be applied to the QoS parameters of each service instance and as part of this study we consider as initial representative parameters the following: Cost, Execution Time and Availability. Based on that, the metric should tackle three (3) distinct influence aspects: the influence on cost, on execution time and on service availability. These metrics are all derived from the following equations.

We denote:

$$SRI_{cost/time/availability}(\text{trigger, affected, levels}) SRI_{cost/time/availability}(\text{trigger, affected, levels}) \tag{1}$$

as a metric for a *Strategic Relationship's Influence (SRI)*, where: trigger refers to the service provider that triggers a strategic relationship, affected refers to the service provider that alters its QoS parameters, and levels refers to the set of processes that we measure the influence of the relationship on.

The SRI metric consists of two addends, each one representing two distinct parts of a relationship's influence:

$$SRI(trigger, affected, levels) = $$
$$Immediate\ Influence(trigger, affected) + Future\ Influence(affected, levels) \tag{2}$$

A Strategic Relationship's Immediate Influence

The first addend that we define here is the *Immediate Influence (I.I.)*. This influence is defined as the actual advantage or disadvantage that a service provider gains by selecting the triggering provider. This Immediate Influence is measured in terms of the QoS parameters effect on the affected provider. The Immediate Influence needs not only to take account of the actual QoS parameters changes but also to express the potential of the original values.

In the above example (Figure 3), service provider A influences both service providers B and C. Since we want to measure each relationship's Immediate Influence, the first issue we need to take account of is how much node B or C alters their QoS parameters.

Moreover, a simple improvement measure is not enough as it might provide a false perception of a relationship's actual influence. In the above example, the two relationships may provide a similar amount of benefit to both providers (B and C) and thus the relationships seem equally influential. In fact, provider C may be an extremely inefficient provider and thus the influence on him is actually unimportant compared to the influence on an already efficient provider, as B may be.

From the above, we denote I.I.(trigger, affected) as the Immediate Influence of a specific strategic relationship and we have:

$$II_{\frac{cost}{time}} = \frac{Old\,Value - New\,Value}{Old\,Value}\, e^{Slope\frac{Max\,Value - Old\,Value}{Max\,Value - Min\,Value}}$$

(3)

and

$$II_{availability} = \frac{New\,Value - Old\,Value}{Old\,Value}\, e^{Slope\frac{Old\,Value - Min\,Value}{Max\,Value - Min\,Value}}$$

(4)

where: *Value* is the corresponding QoS parameter's value of the affected service provider and *Minimum* and *Maximum* values are referring to the corresponding QoS parameter inside a service process.

The first fractional factor represents the relational change in the parameter's value. The better the change the bigger the benefit from this strategic relationship. The second factor has a double role. The first one is to amplify the I.I. values of those service providers that already were close to the best of their process. The second is to express the user's interest on that specific parameter by multiplying with a slope factor that will be better clarified later on. The differentiation between cost/time and availability derives from the fact that better availability values are the largest ones, in contrast to what happens with cost and time.

The values that the I.I. metric has are positive when the service parameter is improved by the strategic relationship and negative otherwise. In case that there are no changes, the I.I. becomes zero. Additionally, the changes on critical service providers will be represented by large absolute I.I. values, either positive or negative.

Figure 3. Calculating the immediate influence of different strategic relationships

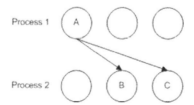

A Strategic Relationship's Future Influence

As seen in the previous section, when calculating a SRI, the first and most basic influence that we must take account of if the Immediate one. Unluckily, this influence alone is not enough to capture a relationship's effect to the whole set of processes.

The above figure adds to Figure 3 a new process with new service providers. We still want to calculate the SRI of both relationships from node A to nodes B and C. Let's assume that B and C are two identical service provider that improve their parameters in the exact same way. As a result, their I.I. values will be identical. On a second look on the whole graph, we can see that the relationship from A to C is actually better than the relationship from A to B, not because of immediate improvements but in terms of future benefit. If all of the providers in process 3 improve their QoS parameters then the SRI in the A-C relationship must be higher than the A-B one. A Strategic Relationship's Future Influence tries to capture that exact effect.

The first issue we must take into account while calculating a relationship's *Future Influence* is which future relationships we should take into account.

Figure 5 represents the same process space as Figure 4 but also adds a new relationship from provider C to provider D. The question is: when calculating the Future Influence of the relationship A-C should the relationship C-D be taken into consideration? The answer is no. The Future Influence of the A-C relationship wants to capture the further potential of a relationship, in case that the source provider is actually selected. As a consequence, the fact that the provider C can actually improve another provider on "Process 1" is actually indifferent to relationship A-C as relationship A-C requires that provider A is selected. Additionally, any relationships that service provider C has with other process levels where a selection is finalized are also discarded in the calculation as they cannot influence the selection process.

This Future Influence is not restricted to a single level. On the contrary, any of the providers in "Process 3" may have interesting influence that should be taken into consideration. Those relationships in further levels are of course of diminishing interest and their effect should be reduced gradually. Additionally, when calculating the future effects on further levels, all provider choices in processes towards them should be considered finalized. In the above example, let's assume that any of the providers in process 3 has strategic relationships with some of providers in processes 1-2 and in a new process 4. We still are counting the SRI of relationship A-C. When we will be calculating the Future Influence of providers in process 3, choices in processes 1 and 2 are considered finalized and we should only take care of those

Figure 4. A strategic relationship with future influence

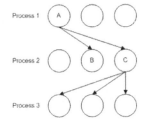

Figure 5. An indifferent relationship on future influence calculation

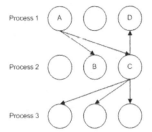

relationships from process 3 towards process 4. The above restrictions guarantee that the calculation of the Future Influence will finalize after as many iterations as the current active processes.

Another interesting issue that arises from the calculation of a strategic relationship's Future Influence is how to actually summarize a provider's Future Influence with multiple future relations. In the above example, that exact issue appears on provider C when calculating the SRI of relationship A-C. That provider has 3 strategic relationships of interest; some of which may be beneficial while other may prove harmful. Moreover, in a wider example, a small number of relationships may be very harmful while the vast majority is beneficial. If such is the case, the overall Future Influence should not be overwhelmed by the minority of harmful relationships but should reflect the fact that relationships are mostly beneficial.

Finally, one issue remains that concerns the actual weight of Future Influence compared to Immediate Influence in a strategic relationship. On the previous example, let's assume that providers B and C have equal initial QoS parameters. Moreover, the strategic relationship A-B is greatly beneficial to provider B while the relationship A-C does nothing but little changes to provider C. The problem that arises is how to compare a relationship like A-B with large Immediate Influence to a relationship like A-C with little Immediate but great Future Influence. In other words, the problem that arises is when Future Influence is important enough to actually be compared to the Immediate one. The answer to this problem derives from the observation that the more choices there are in the future processes, the harder should it be to create a, comparable to Immediate, Future Influence. On the other hand, the more affected services there are in a given set of possible relations, the more Future Influence gets important.

Denoting F.I.(affected, levels) as the Future Influence of an affected node towards a set of process levels that we are measuring it on, we have:

$$F.I.(affected, levels) =$$

$$\frac{1}{Num[remLevels]} \sum_{n \in adj(affected, remLevels)} \left(F_{balancing} \cdot SRI(affected, n, remLevels) \right) \tag{5}$$

$$F_{balancing} = \begin{cases} F_{ppositive}, & SRI(affected, n, remLevels) > 0 \\ F_{bnegative}, & SRI(affected, n, remLevels) < 0 \end{cases} \tag{6}$$

$$F_{ppositive} = \frac{Num[c = adj(affected, remLevels), SRI(affected, c, remLevels) > 0]}{Num[adj(affected, remLevels)]} \tag{7}$$

$$F_{bnegative} = \frac{Num[c = adj(affected, remLevels), SRI(affected, c, remLevels) < 0]}{Num[adj(affected, remLevels)]} \tag{8}$$

where: *remLevels* is the set (levels-level(affected)) that represents the remaining process levels that F.I. is calculated on, *Num[]* returns the current number of service providers in a given set of processes, and *adj(affected,remLevels)* is the set of adjacent to the affected node inside a set of processes.

The above equations describe the calculation of a given relationship's Future Influence. The first thing to notice is that F.I. is a recursive procedure that requires the calculation of all future relationship's SRIs. This calculation is bounded inside the affected node's relationships to process levels that have not already been visited. As the algorithm visits various levels, each one of them is considered visited and the calculation eventually finalizes.

Before adding the SRIs from affected provider's future relationships, a step of balancing the results precedes. This step uses two balancing factors, *Fbpositive*, *Fbnegative* and multiplies accordingly each positive or negative SRI. These factors represent the F.I. balance between positive and negative F.I.s and amplifies those that outvote. These factors can diminish the minority's relationships Future Influence, and thus the metric is not affected by isolated, possibly malevolent, relationships. To achieve this, *Fbalancing* is calculated as the number of each category's (negative or positive) relationships divided by the total number of relationships.

After balancing each subsequent SRI, the metric adds those results and the final outcome is divided by a new balancing factor. As described previously, this balancing factor actually represents the relation between each relationship's Immediate and Future Influences. By dividing with the half size of still existing provider choices, we decrease greatly the F.I.'s importance. This decrease is greater when we are making choices for the first processes but gets smaller as the process space is reduced. In other words, when we are making early Influence calculations we are primary interested in Immediate gains, while, when the choices diminish, Future Influence becomes more and more important. From another perspective, this division factor represents the exact number of future relationships required to surplus the Immediate Influence. Thus, better results appear when this number is equal to half the possible future relationships and that is the reason behind division by two.

Friendliness of a Service Provider

Up until now, we have created a metric that represents the true value of a business relationship. That metric that was called S.R.I. has a wide set of beneficial properties that we will take advantage of in order to create a well performing heuristic function that defines the friendliness of a service provider based on the business relationships. This heuristic function takes the focus of strategic relationships and puts it on service providers themselves. Its main goal is to utilize the properties of each provider's strategic relationships and characterize the provider according to his potential for future workflow execution benefit. This new metric that will be calculated for every service provider is called *Service Provider Friendliness (SPF)* and we will outline some of its interesting properties.

The first interesting issue that should be resolved when calculating a SPF is which strategic relationships we should take into account.

In the example in Figure 6 we want to calculate a metric that will outline which of providers A and B is more appropriate for selection in "Process 2". This metric that is called SPF should consider the SRIs of each provider's strategic relationships in order to calculate a result. In the above example let's assume that A and B provide similar QoS parameters with provider B being overall slightly better. Providers A and B influence two other providers which are identical and are influenced in the exact same manner from A and B. Additionally, provider A can be influenced from provider C. The problem here is which provider, A or B, is preferable. If we take into account the relationship C-A we can say that provider A is actually the better future choice. But if we look closer, provider B can actually give better QoS parameters now and provide equal future expansion potential. As the algorithm runs next on process level 3, no one can guarantee that provider C will make its final choice there as the SRI metric is indifferent of the triggering provider's parameters. So we cannot add value to provider A and thus, provider B should be the preferable choice on process 2. To summarize, the calculation of Service Provider Friendliness should be unaware of any strategic relationships that can influence this provider and should only take account of providers that can be influenced.

Figure 6. Calculating the SPF for service providers A and B

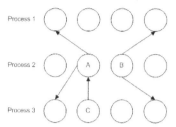

Figure 7. Handling mixed types of strategic relationships

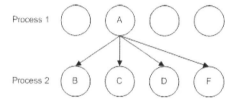

Another interesting issue that reappears on SPF as it did in SRI is how we can tackle providers with mixed type influences.

In the above figure, provider A influences all providers in process 2, with SRIs -10, 3, 3, 3 accordingly. Provider A actually has good future strategic potential, even though it can be destroyed by a single negative one. In order to minimize the minority's effect, balancing factors need to be used again that should take account of how positive and negative influences are distributed.

Considering those issues, we denote SPF as Service Provider Friendliness and we have:

$$SPF_{cost|time|availability}(provider, levels) = \frac{\sum_{level}(Affected\ Nodes \cdot \overline{SRI_{cost|time|availability}(provider) \cdot F_{balancing}})}{Num[levels]} \tag{9}$$

$$F_{balancing} = \begin{cases} F_{bpositive}, & SRI(provider) > 0 \\ F_{bnegative}, & SRI(provider) < 0 \end{cases} \tag{10}$$

$$F_{bpositive} = \frac{Num[c=adj(provider, curLevel), SRI(provider)>0]}{Num[adj(provider, curLevel)]} \tag{11}$$

$$F_{bnegative} = \frac{Num[c=adj(provider, curLevel), SRI(provider)<0]}{Num[adj(provider, curLevel)]} \tag{12}$$

where: *provider* is the service provider we are calculating the SPF for, *levels* is the set of process levels that we are calculating the SPF on, *curLevel* is the current process level from the given set of levels, *Af-*

fected Nodes is the number of adjacent to provider nodes in the current level, *Mean SRI* is the arithmetic mean of SRIs for the strategic relationships that are triggered from provider and affect other service providers only in the current level, and the *Balancing Factors* are calculated as in F.I. and they count SRI types per level.

To calculate the SPF for a service provider, each provider's strategic relationships are separated on a per process basis. For each process, we balance each relationship's SRI and we calculate the arithmetic mean of the results. In order to express that more relationships with the same mean SRI are better than less, we multiply with the actual number of the affected services per process. After we have completed the calculation for each affected process level, the final result is the average mean of the per process results.

The above metric is the heuristic function that can be used from QoS-based selection mechanisms for workflows in order to characterize each provider's future strategic potential. It should be calculated for each QoS parameter type (in this study: availability, cost and execution time). This metric includes the necessary characteristics as it takes advantage of various relationship parameters in a consistent way and it is reliable enough to avoid possible malevolent relationships between antagonistic service providers.

ARCHITECTURAL DESIGN

In this section we describe the architectural design for implementing a mechanism that takes into account the business relationships of the service providers, updates the QoS values of the service instances and includes these values into the SLAs. The latter allows any workflow mapping mechanism to utilize the outcome of this approach since it will continue obtaining the QoS information for the service instances from the SLAs. However, these SLAs will include the updated values of the QoS parameters based on the business relationships and the friendliness of a service provider (as described in the sections above).

The proposed set of components consists of the following ones (also depicted in the figure below - Figure 8):

- Workflow Enactor
- Discovery Service
- Workflow Mapping Mechanism Service
- Business Relationships Evaluator
- SLA & Business Relationships Registry.

Figure 8. Component diagram

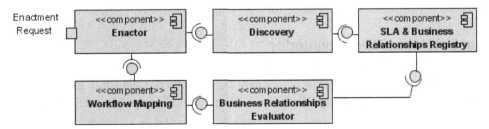

In the following sections we briefly describe the aforementioned components as well as their interfaces and interactions with the Business Relationships Evaluator component.

Enactor & Discovery

The *Enactor* component is the gateway of the overall workflow management mechanism to the Grid infrastructure through the *Enactment Request* port. The application workflow and particular QoS requirements/restrictions for the overall workflow or for specific workflow process are submitted to the *Enactor*, and the *Discovery* component, based on them, finds appropriate SLAs for each workflow process, querying the SLA Registry. The candidates and the requirements are supplied to the *Workflow Mapping* to make in order to produce the concrete workflow that is finally executed by the *Enactor*.

Workflow Mapping

The *Workflow Mapping* component is responsible the "translation" of the application workflow to the concrete one taking into account on one hand the QoS requirements and on the other hand the available resources as described in the SLA templates (SLA offers that are used in the negotiation process to sign the final SLA). The workflow mapping implementation, described in detail in (D. Kyriazis, 2007), was customized so as to exploit the business relationship parameters in the selection process. Initially this component performs a filtering of the candidates based on the QoS requirements and thereafter the updated mapping mechanism uses the "*mock*" candidates for the selection that are acquired by the *Business Relationships Evaluator* component. As "mock" we name the candidates for which the QoS values are updated based on the business relationships. However, these mock candidates are only used for the selection process and the concrete workflow definition that is returned to the Enactor. When enacting the workflow, the Enactor refers to the real SLA templates.

SLA & Business Relationships Registry

The *SLA & Business Relationships Registry* component is a dynamic repository that stores the available SLA templates from the service providers and the business relationships between them. These SLA templates are unique, and the registry keeps not only the "Unique ID" of the template but also the QoS information, such as the SLA terms, the price and the compensations. The business relationships records in the registry define relationships between service providers that affect some of the SLA parameters within a business chain as described in the previous section. Specifically, the records include the source and the destination SLA templates identifier and the particular SLA term of the destination SLA that is affected if both SLAs are used within the same workflow. The *SLA & Business Relationships Registry* implements two interfaces, one for the *Discovery* component for querying the SLA templates and one for the *Business Relationships Evaluator* for querying the business relationships.

Business Relationships Evaluator

The *Business Relationships Evaluator* component implements the algorithm for calculating the service providers' friendliness and performs the business relationships analysis to produce the mock candidates list as already described. This process is triggered by the *Workflow Mapping* component providing the

Figure 9. SLA templates

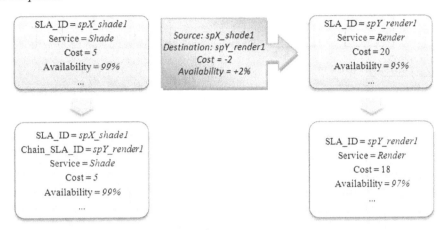

available candidates and the sequence that these will be used within the workflow. Thereafter the details the relationships are acquired by the *SLA & Business Relationships Registry* and the mock candidate list is then returned to the *Workflow Mapping*. The mock candidates have the same ID with the real ones, since they are virtual entities and consequently when the selection mechanism selects a mock candidate, in fact selects the real SLA template with the same ID and additionally defines the set of the SLAs templates (destination SLAs as described by the business relationships) the will be used in the next processes of the workflow. The following figure illustrates how the initial SLA templates are translated to the mock ones, which can be used by any workflow management process to proceed with the selection of the service providers taking into consideration possible business relationships between them.

Components Interaction

In this section we cite a Sequence Diagram (Figure 10) in order to depict the components interaction and the flow of logic within the proposed architectural approach.

Based on the components' functionality description, the following part analyzes the flow presented in Figure 10:

1. The application workflow and the QoS parameters for the overall workflow (e.g. total price, delivery deadline) and for specific processes (e.g. service availability, response time) are submitted to the *Enactor* and workflow management process is initialized.
2. The *Enactor* identifies the workflow processes and contacts the *Discovery* component find service candidates for each one of them.
3. The *Discovery* component enquires the *SLA & Business Relationships Registry* to acquire the available SLAs templates for each workflow process.
4. The *SLA & Business Relationships Registry* replies with the SLA template list.
5. A candidate list is then produced by the *Discovery* and returned to the *Enactor*.
6. In sequel, the *Enactor* submits the candidates and the user QoS parameters (requirements/restrictions) to the *Workflow Mapping* Component so as to produce the final concrete workflow.

Figure 10. Sequence diagram

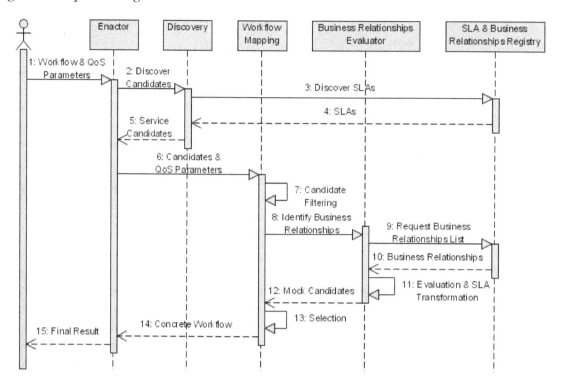

7. Initially, the *Workflow Mapping* performs an cross analysis of the QoS requirements and the candidates capabilities in order to filter the candidates and produce a candidate list for each process the is capable of addressing the user requirements and is compliant with the overall workflow restrictions (e.g. ProcessCandidateCost < TotalWorkflowCost)

8. The *Workflow Mapping* contacts the *Business Relationships Evaluator* in order to identify any business relationships between the candidates that are applicable for the specific workflow and provides the candidate list and information about the business chain that these candidates could be used within the workflow.

9. Thereafter the *Business Relationships Evaluator* requests from the *SLA & Business Relationships Registry* the relationship information for the specific service providers.

10. The *SLA & Business Relationships Registry* replies with the Business Relationships list.

11. The business relationships are analyzed by the *Business Relationships Evaluator* and a mock candidate list is produced as a result of this analysis.

12. The mock candidates for each process are forwarded to the *Workflow Mapping*.

13. Afterwards the *Workflow Mapping* component performs the selection of the service instances and maps the workflow processes to Grid provided services exploiting the business relationships through the mock candidates. The final outcome of this step is the definition of the concrete workflow.

14. The concrete workflow is made available to the *Enactor* that binds all the required resources and executes the workflow.

15. The workflow execution result is returned to the user.

FUTURE TRENDS

The advent of heterogeneous and distributed environments, such as Grid environments, made feasible the solution of computational intensive problems in a reliable and cost-effective way. In parallel, workflows with increased complexity that require specialized systems to deal with them are emerging, so as to carry out more composite and mission-critical applications. In that rationale, QoS issues need to be tackled in order to ensure that each application satisfy the corresponding user requirements.

The quality provision aspect is increasingly considered to be fundamental for enabling Grid applications to become QoS compliant. Strategic partnerships are emerging, especially between Small-Medium Enterprises (SMEs) in order to face the competition and have better chances in the market share. The aforementioned changes in the business world and the strategic relationships will also be reflected in the IT domain and the one focused on the distributed environments. In this context, Grids have to adopt mechanisms that can tackle the challenges of the business domain and serve their needs.

CONCLUSION

In this chapter we have presented an approach for modeling business / strategic relationships in Grid workflows and formulated an appropriate metric that can be used to promote the most positively influential service providers and put aside those with a negative influence during a QoS-based selection process. Our approach initially proposes a modeling of the potential business relationships between the service providers and provides a value that characterizes the service providers based on them (called "Service Providers Friendliness - SPF"). In order to allow this value to be used by any QoS-based workflow mapping mechanism, we propose a set of component along with their architectural design that creates SLAs including this information. These are called "mock" SLAs and can be used during the selection process. As soon as the concrete workflow is produced, the workflow enactor uses the "real" SLAs to proceed with the execution of it.

The added value of this approach is expected to foster the adoption of Grids in the business world since it doesn't only tackles the issue of end-to-end QoS but also takes into consideration the business / strategic relationships of the service providers. The latter allows:

* The definition of a concrete workflow that meets the user's cost constraint; which might not be feasible without considering the business relationships.
* The definition of a concrete workflow offering higher level of end-to-end QoS since the cost difference obtained due to the business relationships of the service providers may be used to select service instances with higher QoS values of other parameters (e.g. lower execution time).

Concluding, Grids have not yet adopted an effective scheme that will facilitate end-to-end QoS provisioning taking into account possible business / strategic relationships between the service providers. In that rationale, we have shown the importance of a metric that characterises the "friendliness" of a provider along with a set of components that allow the integration of it in any workflow management system. The use of this metric is expected to significantly increase the effort to address in a dynamic way the business relationships in Grid workflows.

REFERENCES

Al-Ali, R. J., Amin, K., von Laszewski, G., Rana, O. F., Walker, D. W., Hategan, M., & Zaluzec, N. J. (2004). Analysis and Provision of QoS for Distributed Grid Application., *Journal of Grid Computing*, (pp. 163-182), .

Bochmann, G., & Hafid, A. (1996). *Some Principles for Quality of Service Management*. Technical report, Universite de Montreal.

Bubak, M., Gubała, T., Kapałka, M., Malawski, M., & Rycerz, K. (2005, January). Workflow composer and service registry for grid applications. *Future Generation Computer Systems, 21*(1), 79-86.

Buyya, R., Abramson, D., & Venugopal, S. (2005, March). The Grid Economy. *Proceedings of the IEEE, 93*(3), 698-714.

Cardoso, J., Sheth, A., & Miller, J. (2002, April). Workflow Quality of Service. *Proceedings of the International Conference on Enterprise Integration and Modeling Technology and International Enterprise Modeling Conference (ICEIMT/IEMC'02)*, Kluwer Publishers.

Cardoso, J., Miller, J., Sheth, A., & Arnold, J. (2002). *Modeling Quality of Service for Workflows and Web Service Processes*. Technical Report, LSDIS Lab, Department of Computer Science University of Georgia.

Deelman, E., Blythe, J., Gil, Y., & Kesselman, C. (2003). Workflow Management in GriPhyN. *The Grid Resource Management*. TheNetherlands:. Kluwer

Deelman, E., Blythe, J., Gil, Y., Kesselman, C., Mehta, G., Patil, S., Su, M. H., Vahi, K., & Livny, M. (2004). Pegasus: Mapping Scientific Workflow onto the Grid. *Across Grids Conference 2004*, Nicosia, Cyprus.

Fahringer, T., Jugravu, A., Pllana, S., Prodan, R., Seragiotto Jr, C., & Truong, H. L. (2005). ASKALON: A tool set for cluster and Grid computing. Concurrency and Computation: Practice and Experience, *17*(2-4), 143–169.

Foster, I., Kesselman, C., Lee, C., Lindell, B., Nahrstedt, K., & Roy, A. (1999). A Distributed Resource Management Architecture that Supports Advance Reservation and Co-Allocation. *Proceedings of the International Workshop on QoS*, (pp.27-36).

Foster, I., Kesselman, C., Tuecke, S. (2001). The Anatomy of the Grid: Enabling Scalable Virtual Organizations. *International Journal Supercomputer Applications, 15*(3).

Guo, L., McGough, A. S., Akram, A., Colling, D., Martyniak, J., & Krznaric, M. (2007). QoS for Service Based Workflow on Grid. *Proceedings of UK e-Science 2007 All Hands Meeting*, Nottingham, UK.

Khanli, L. M., & Analoui, M. (2007). QoS-based Scheduling of Workflow Applications on Grids. *International Conference on Advances in Computer Science and Technology*, Phuket, Thailand.

Kyriazis, D., Tserpes, K., Menychtas, A., Litke A., & Varvarigou, T. (2007). An innovative Workflow Mapping Mechanism for Grids in the frame of Quality of Service, *Future Generation Computer Systems*.

Leinberger, W., & Kumar, V. (1999, October). Information Power Grid: The new frontier in parallel computing? *IEEE Concur., 7*(4), 75-84.

Ludäscher, B., Altintas, I., & Gupta, A. (2003). Compiling Abstract Scientific Workflows into Web Service Workflows. *15th International Conference on Scientific and Statistical Database Management*, Cambridge, Massachusetts, USA., IEEE CS Press, pp. 241-244, Los Alamitos, CA, USA., July 09-11.

Mayer, A., McGough, S., Furmento, N., Lee, W., Newhouse, S., & Darlington, J. (2003, September). *ICENI Dataflow and Workflow: Composition and Scheduling in Space and Time.* In UK e-Science All Hands Meeting, Nottingham, UK, pages 894–900., Bristol, UK: IOP Publishing Ltd.

McGough, S., Young, L., Afzal, A., Newhouse, S., & Darlington, J. (2004, September). Performance Architecture within ICENI. In *UK e-Science All Hands Meeting*, Nottingham, UK, pages 906–911. Bristol, UK: IOP Publishing Ltd Sep. 2004.

McGough, S., Young, L., Afzal, A., Newhouse, S., & Darlington, J. (2004, September). Workflow Enactment in ICENI. In UK e-Science All Hands Meeting, Nottingham, UK, pages 894–900. Bristol, UK: IOP Publishing Ltd.

Padgett, J., Djemame, K., & Dew, P. (2005). Grid-based SLA Management. *Lecture Notes in Computer Science*, (pp. 1282-1291).

Siddiqui, M., Villazon, A., & Fahringer, T. (2006). Grid capacity planning with negotiation-based advance reservation for optimized QoS. *Proceedings of the 2006 ACM/IEEE Conference on SuperComputing SC '06.*

Spooner, D. P., Cao, J., Jarvis, S. A., He, L., & Nudd, G. R. (2004). Performance-aware Workflow Management for Grid Computing. *The Computer Journal.* London, UK: Oxford University Press,

Workflow Management Coalition (1999, February). *Terminology & Glossary.* Document Number WFMC-TC-1011, Issues 3.0.

Yu, J., Buyya, R., & Khong Tham, C. (2005). *QoS-based Scheduling of Workflow Applications on Service Grids.* Technical Report, GRIDS-TR-2005-8, Grid Computing and Distributed Systems Laboratory, University of Melbourne, Australia, 2005.

Yu, J., & Buyya, R. (2005). A Taxonomy of Workflow Management Systems for Grid Computing. *Journal of Grid Computing, 3*(3-4), 171-200. Springer.

Chapter VIII
Investigating Deadline–Driven Scheduling Policy via Simulation with East

Justin M. Wozniak
University of Notre Dame, USA & Argonne National Laboratory, USA

Aaron Striegel
University of Notre Dame, USA

ABSTRACT

Opportunistic techniques have been widely used to create economical computation infrastructures and have demonstrated an ability to deliver heterogeneous computing resources to large batch applications, however, batch turnaround performance is generally unpredictable, negatively impacting human experience with widely shared computing resources. Scheduler prioritization schemes can effectively boost the share of the system given to particular users, but to gain a relevant benefit to user experience, whole batches must complete on a predictable schedule, not just individual jobs. Additionally, batches may contain a dependency structure that must be considered when predicting or controlling the completion time of the whole workflow; the slowest or most volatile prerequisite job determines performance. In this chapter, a probabilistic policy enforcement technique is used to protect deadline guarantees against grid resource unpredictability as well as bad estimates. Methods to allocate processors to a common workflow subcase, barrier scheduling, are also presented.

INTRODUCTION

Running complex applications on widely distributed resources is an unpredictable process, complicating the user experience with new systems. While opportunistic technologies and grid infrastructures dramatically increase the resources available to the application, they also increase the range and volatility of resulting behaviors. Job turnaround time, the span between the time a job is ready to run and the time results are returned, is of primary importance to users seeking larger, more powerful computing platforms, but is more difficult to measure on conglomerations of heterogeneous computation elements. The fact that users cannot easily achieve predictable turnaround results – even in the presence of increased available parallelism, and when average case performance is improved – *can cause frustration and reduce interest* in new, complex distributed computing systems.

There is a fundamental disconnect between short-term user objectives and long-term system design techniques that underlies many user frustrations with commodity computing systems. Users prefer responsive, fast turnarounds for specific workloads. Grid system designers and administrators take a long view, intending to maximize utilization, and thus the return on investment, for a given resource set, given a wider range of applications. These viewpoints translate into the various technologies available. For example, opportunistic systems (Thain, 2004) excel at improving system utilization start by locating idle resources and employing them to perform useful work. Real-time systems (Murthy, 2001), contrarily, start by admitting acceptable workloads and ensuring that the results will be returned on schedule. Ordinary workstations are a middle ground, providing a necessarily available resource that offers moderate predictability through system simplicity and isolation from external forces.

Sources of Unpredictability

We start with an examination of the underlying causes of unpredictable performance in opportunistic systems.

- **Processor heterogeneity:** Since users of opportunistic systems often employ resources owned and managed by diverse organizations, heterogeneity is an ever-present challenge. CPU heterogeneity takes two forms: "hard" heterogeneity, meaning architectural differences, and "soft" heterogeneity, meaning performance differences within a class of compatible architectures. While users can benefit from existing matchmaking techniques to select certain processors, opportunistic systems have been designed for "compute-hungry" users. These users are capable of consuming an ever-growing number of processors. Thus, they are expected to overcome hard heterogeneity obstacles by compiling for multiple architectures or using portable interpreted languages. Consequently, the impact of heterogeneous systems can be modelled by simply considering performance differences.

- **Contention:** Opportunistic systems attempt to harness the aggregate computing ability of large numbers of processors for large numbers of users. The requested workload for such a system can thus be quite variable, particularly in small scale, experimental settings. For example, in a typical university-sized Condor installation, a user may initially have access to all of the available machines, but then unexpectedly be forced to split the resources with another user.

Heterogeneous, opportunistic systems thus pose two significant performance predictability problems for users. First, performance analysis prediction for a given task on a range of potential architectures is a labor-intensive process that is not standard practice in distributed computing, nor is it appealing to potential new users of complex systems. Second, since micromanagement of job distribution is also a complex project that must take into account the contention for resources among multiple users, the actual execution site of a task in an opportunistic system is often left to the metascheduler. Consequently, while the benefits of tight runtime estimates are clear, modern systems must recognize that typical cases will rely on rough estimates given by users, and are not particularly trustworthy due to the unpredictable allocation of imperfectly understood processors.

Real-Time Computing Approaches

The difficulties experienced by users of opportunistic systems can be ameliorated in a variety of ways.

- **The deadline computing model:** In a typical single workstation or symmetric multiprocessor environment, deadlines are a natural but often unstated aspect of computing. Users are aware that jobs must be completed within a certain known time frame- when anomalous runtime performance appears, given predictable resources and low contention, they simply turn to software defect investigations. However, more complex computing systems built upon an opportunistic fabric require autonomic schedulers to maintain the expected level of predictability by managing the progress of jobs and workflows. These schedulers require an explicit user-supplied expected runtimes and deadlines with which to operate. Then, given a set of processors and contending users and jobs they can optimize system utilization to minimize unpredictability in the sense of reducing deadline misses.

- **Admission control:** Users of a deadline-aware scheduler gain the additional benefit of certain fail-fast behavior in the form of deadline rejection. For example, in a simple case in which the user provided estimate exceeds the user provided deadline, simple job rejection can force the user to reconsider the attempted workload. In the more complex case of multiple existing jobs with deadlines, if the new workload cannot be scheduled, the system can quickly inform the user that the work cannot be scheduled. However, once a job has been admitted to the system, the acceptance constitutes a guarantee that the deadline will be met. The automatic services provided by the scheduler must attempt to protect the deadline by allocating resources and managing contention as necessary.

A scheduler that implements these real-time computing concepts may be called a *deadline-driven system*. While users of such a system can be expected to be able to offer reasonable statistics and requirements in the form of estimates and deadlines, a significant *semantic shift* in job submission must be considered from both a human and a technical perspective. Real-world users are simply not used to having to provide these figures along with job submission. Thus, certain systems designers have begun to reduce the required user work in this area by building historical or analytic runtime estimators. Technically, these figures are not part of typical job submission semantics in workstation systems or opportunistic systems.

A feature that is present in typical computing systems is the concept of job priority. Processing resources are expected to be fairly distributed, possibly with the additional ability to boost performance for users considered more important by the scheduler or resource involved. However, in a deadline-driven system, the outstanding guarantees must be considered, creating a second semantic shift. Fair-share systems are thus augmented by the ability to consider and prioritize resource allocation with respect to the schedule that must be met.

Figure 1. Components of a scheduler simulator

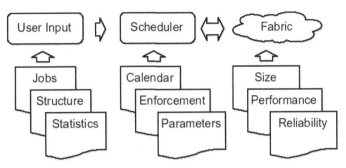

While these features are intended to improve user experience with unpredictable resource fabrics, the pervasive unreliability of the resources themselves is capable of defeating the best efforts of a deadline-aware job manager. Additionally, erroneous estimates may disrupt a feasible schedule, pushing many jobs past their deadlines. First, it must be recognized that such a system must be considered a soft real-time system, in that deadline misses that are small from a user perspective are undesirable but usually acceptable. Second, it must be recognized that bad estimates will be offered even by well-meaning users because of the difficulty predicting job runtime on complex resources, and that this should be tolerated and corrected by the system- penalizing users for rare, small errors will again damage the user experience. Consequently, the scheduler must be capable of managing the system in difficult circumstances, in a way that achieves several objectives, including good predictability, performance, and utilization.

Trade-Offs

These two computing paradigms – opportunistic and real-time computing – result in trade-offs that must be made by system designers. Increasing the predictability of opportunistic systems through real-time techniques increases the set of responsibilities given to the scheduler and poses constraints on fair-share processor allocation. Additionally, deadline guarantee strategies such as over-provisioning reduce the utilization of volunteered resources, constituting a direct ideological challenge to these systems.

Improving the predictability of user jobs on opportunistic resources requires a careful balance between these disciplines. Schedulers intended to straddle this design space must be capable of reducing the impact on the users and systems that it connects. Studying the effects of such schedulers before implementation is difficult because the required experimental testbed would need to consist of a large number of machines comparable to those used in the desired setting. Additionally, the effects of heterogeneous, unreliable hardware is difficult to mimic. Therefore, simulation is typically used as a low-cost first step in the trial of new scheduling strategies. These tests are tied to reality by the ability of the software to incorporate real-world trace data from existing computational systems. Then, new strategies may be applied to real-world workload cases to obtain predicted performance characteristics.

The remainder of this chapter is organized as follows. Section 2 describes policy questions to be investigated in the grid computing community. Next, Section 3 frames a simulation-based approach to exploring the intersection of these areas by describing a simulator framework that provides insight into the effects of novel scheduler behaviors. Then, Section 4 presents an investigation of probabilistic policy enforcement methods, and Section 5 describes barrier scheduling. Finally, Section 6 offers several concluding remarks.

INVESTIGATIONS IN SCHEDULER POLICY

East enables scheduler architects and policy makers to bridge the gap between real-time computing and grid computing- areas which traditionally have very different objectives. For example, in a hard real-time system, jobs are scheduled with respect to their worst-case computation time, and any deviation exceeding schedule limits is expected to result in termination. Therefore, some previous work has investigated how conservative schedulers must be when computing on the grid. This may be combined with heuristic methods to approximate optimal workflow task placement to pack batches onto the grid, improving performance and predictability. Our work, however, intends to satisfy the grid objective of high utilization and prevent job termination due to *relatively small* runtime fluctuations while providing a high guarantee ratio.

While a variety of grid-enabled schedulers have been proposed such as Globus GRAM (Czajkowski, 1998), GridBus (Venugopal, 2004) , GrADS (Dail, 2002), and others, quality requirements are often managed through strict business-flavored structures such as service level agreements, which have seen rapid recent entry into grid computing (Yarmolenko, 2006). The scheduler model here, however, intends to gain the functional benefit of timely computing while maintaining the benevolence of opportunistic computing by the construction of a lightweight, autonomic front-end scheduler. This component is the object of the policy study presented here.

SIMULATOR ARCHITECTURE

To approach these policy investigations, an appropriate simulator structure must be developed. Scheduler simulators must incorporate three major aspects of the problem as shown in Figure 1:

- **User input:** User input to the system takes the form of submitted jobs, estimates, and deadlines. These jobs may be presented as individual executions, batches of interdependent jobs, or as structured workflows of dependent tasks. Such workloads may be obtained through idealized models or through traces of real-world workloads that include execution information and the resulting statistics.
- **Scheduler behavior:** The simulated scheduler is the object of study and thus the heart of the simulator model. However, as the policy tester attempts to improve scheduling results, it must be possible to *plug in* new schedulers for rapid evaluation, through parameter tuning as well as algorithmic overhaul.
- **Resource fabric:** Finally, the resource fabric must also be modelled by the simulator. These models may be quite simple for initial tests, but the validity of the returned results depends on the similarity of the model to typical or specific real-world infrastructures, including the effects of heterogeneity and unreliability. Additionally, resource model inputs to the system must be correlated with any trace data used as user input to the system.

System assembly is shown in Figure 1 as vertical arrows that incorporate subcomponents into the structure. Internal simulator runtime interactions are shown as horizontal arrows that transmit time-dependent events among components. Once the three-component system has been assembled, the simulation may be executed over time by modelling the underlying events as they occur. Since most events relevant to typical experiments are discrete – such as job start and stop events or machine availability changes – discrete event simulation is a viable choice, operating at a relatively high level on relatively large entities such as whole jobs.

As an example implementation of this simulation model, a simulator called East (Wozniak, 2007) was constructed to allow the rapid construction of each of the three components by a flexible software architecture that allows subcomponents to be quickly plugged into the assembled system. The system performs a discrete time experimental evaluation of idealized or trace-based workloads.

East simulates the distributed computing case in which a deadline-aware front-end scheduler accepts client requests and services them by employing pre-existing simple batch queues. This model is proposed as an alternative to a stovepipe solution because it simplifies the construction of the new system and reduces the risk involved in the deployment of the hypothetical new metascheduler. By controlling pre-existing resources we intend to obtain any required scheduling properties. East is ultimately a first step towards the construction of the real system, and may be used to examine the hypothetical behavior of future schedulers.

CHARACTERISTICS OF SCHEDULER POLICY

In this section, we present two examples of deadline-driven scheduler policy that may be examined by simulation. The utilization trade-off is presented, a property which makes it difficult to provide services meeting multiple performance demands. Secondly, the quality of estimates is considered as policing strategies may be used to promote user behavior that enhances system characteristics.

The Utilization Trade-Off

As described in the introduction, a trade-off exists between high utilization systems and predictable, timely systems capable of delivering high guarantee ratios. Utilization is a metric that measures the effectiveness of the shared resource arrangement as negotiated by the cooperating parties. Commodity grid computing and storage systems intend to make the most of the available resources primarily by increasing their utilization. Once this is accomplished, other more advanced grid techniques are used to provide other desired qualities.

However, high utilization systems are simply *too busy* to provide the timely service that users may require in time-sensitive applications. An example of this is shown in Figure 2. In this simulated experiment, a range of workloads are presented to an admission-regulated scheduler that provides guarantees based on user-provided estimates. For each input workload, a resulting utilization and guarantee ratio may be observed from the resulting simulator output. In this case, a simple cluster of 10 homogeneous computers was presented with single job submissions, each paired with an estimate good within 50% of the actual runtime. Over-provisioning was applied at 25% above the estimated required computation time.

As shown in Figure 2, the resulting behavior forms a band of likely characteristics that decreases as the workloads degrade the quality of the guarantees available from the scheduler.

Figure 2. Guarantee ratio under increasing utilization stresses

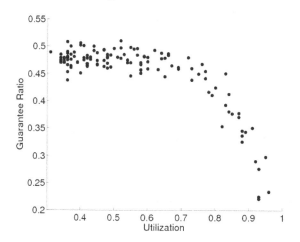

Quality of Estimates and Contention

While it is assumed that users of the opportunistic systems are generally benevolent and desire to improve the user experience for all stakeholders, the system presented thus far is easy to manipulate if estimate enforcement is not applied. Since the admission control system takes user estimates and uses them to schedule jobs with respect to deadlines, erroneous or malicious under-estimates can defeat the whole schedule, causing swaths of deadline misses and penalizing all users.

Thus, the motivation of the following experiment is to answer the following question: Given an environment of related tasks with low quality information, how strictly should policing be enforced and what effects will result on throughput and deadline guarantees? In short, when multiple users offer bad estimates, who should pay the price?

An estimate enforcer may be applied in the scheduler layer to simply terminate all user jobs that exceed their estimates, but given the known unpredictability of grid resources and the sensitivity of large interdependent batches of jobs or workflows, killing jobs that only exceed their estimate by a small amount would result in poor results even for well-intended users. Additionally, known system behavior such as simple over-provisioning may be manipulated just as easily as no enforcement, by providing careful underestimates intended to slip into a highly utilized schedule but abuse the system by intentionally overrunning the alloted time.

A probabilistic enforcer is thus applied, which embraces the unpredictability of grid resources while preventing wild unreliability due to schedule problems. This component terminates jobs that have exceeded their estimate with a probability proportional to the estimate violation. Thus, users that stay close to their estimates are likely to receive good performance, but users that attempt to manipulate the system are unlikely to receive desired results.

To demonstrate the success of this technique, two contending user groups were simulated with the East simulator. *Group A* provided job estimates centered on their true runtimes, while *Group B* provided consistent underestimates. Both groups submitted similar jobs to a heterogeneous cluster of *N* hosts.

As shown in Figure 3, both user groups are simulated as they provide estimates of varying quality (QoE). As the error in the given estimates increases, indicating more unpredictable grid conditions,

Figure 3. Schedule results for contending users

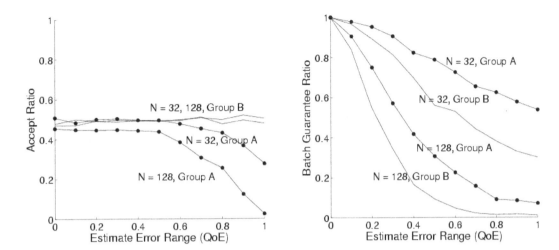

Group B is able to maintain a high acceptance ratio by simply misrepresenting expected job performance. However, a correction is applied by the enforcer, resulting in better guarantee ratios for the Group A users. This guarantee ratio advantage is maintained even in highly unpredictable settings.

The intended consequence of simulating proposed advanced scheduling and enforcement methods is to moderate the effects of the utilization trade-off. In the case of probabilistic enforcement, this is attempted by promoting good user input, resulting in better system performance as measured by multiple metrics.

BARRIER SCHEDULING

A more complex scheduling example is exemplified by barrier-dependent computations. A multiprocessor barrier operation is a programmatic step which must be passed by all processes within a barrier group at the same time. This method may used to begin a synchronized all-to-all communication or, in a Monte Carlo setting, to allow intermediate processing to interleave rounds of parallel computation. This operation may be phrased in deadline-driven terms by specifying that the deadline for a batch is the time that the fastest job hits the barrier. Executing barriers on the grid is challenging for a variety of reasons, including (1) heterogeneity of computation resources, (2) resource unreliability, and (3) the potentially high cost of job migration. For example, previous work scheduling a barrier-dependent molecular dynamics computation in an opportunistic computing system used dedicated clusters of faster processors to advance jobs that were lagging behind or encountered resource failure .

The barrier scheduling problem may be generalized for an arbitrary case in which multiple competing users schedule these workloads. In these complex, unpredictable cases, certain user jobs will lag behind their peers, resulting in potential lost utilization.

The simulated model for barrier dependent jobs in East, consists of a batch of jobs. Within each batch, all jobs must pass a certain number of barrier in a synchronized manner, thus all jobs in the batch

Figure 4. Barrier scheduling performance

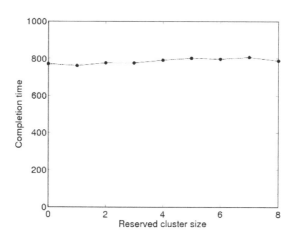

are part of the same barrier group. Jobs are further divided - as if by a checkpoint technique – into segments that may be quickly examined to determine which jobs are lagging behind.

The first technique that may be applied in such a case is for a job to block upon reaching the barrier until all other jobs in the group have reached the barrier, at which point all proceed. However, this is highly deadlock-prone: as each job reaches the barrier, the number of available processors decreases, increasing the probability of the system running out of free processors.

Assuming a small number of high performance processors are available for use, these may be isolated into a cluster reserved for jobs that lag behind in an attempt to provide timely performance near the barrier. However, this architecture removes nodes from general use, thus trading utilization for timeliness in an attempt to improve overall throughput.

This setting was modelled in East by in a homogeneous cluster of 24 hosts augmented by a high performance cluster of 8 hosts that run 4 times as fast as the normal hosts. A varying number of the high performance hosts were reserved for specialized usage.

As shown in Figure 4, however, this architectural method can fail in seemingly useful cases. In this case, batches of jobs varying in runtime by up to a factor of 10 were submitted to the cluster. Jobs that were found to be delaying a barrier transition were promoted to the reserved cluster. However, this strategy did not succeed in enhancing overall batch completion time. Any gains that were made by promoting the timeliness of lagging jobs were lost to the underutilization of the fastest hosts in the cluster. It should be noted that the model used here did not take into account job migration time, which could additionally impact scheduling strategies.

CONCLUSION

Overall, the matter of integrating concepts from grid computing and real-time computing involves trade-offs. Common real-time strategies such as reservations and overprovisioning result in low resource utilization. Grid computing performance strategies such as global job-data locality improve system throughput but do not benefit individual jobs directly or take a schedule into account; additionally, while the grid may function under partial failure and resource heterogeneity it does not protect the schedule from these effects. New methods to be developed through simulation must combine the ability to work with high-utilization average case estimates and probabilistic policies to promote schedule predictability in competitive settings.

REFERENCES

Czajkowski, K., Foster, I., Karonis, N., Kesselman, C., Martin, S., Smith, W., & Tuecke, S. (1998). A Resource Management Architecture for Metacomputing Systems. *Lecture Notes in Computer Science, 1459*, 62-82.

Dail, H., Casanova, H., & Berman, F. (2002, November). A Decoupled Scheduling Approach for the GrADS Program Development Environment. *Proc. Supercomputing*, 55.

Murphy, C., Ram, S., & Manimaran, G. (2001, April). Resource Management in Real-time Systems and Networks. USA: MIT Press.

Thain, D., Tannenbaum, T., & Livny, M. (2005). Distributed Computing in Practice: The Condor Experience. *Concurrency and Computation: Practice and Experience, 17*(2-4), 323-356.

Venugopal, S., Buyya, R., & Winton, L. (2004, October). A Grid Service Broker for Scheduling Distributed Data-Oriented Applications on Global Grids. *Proc. Workshop on Middleware in Grid Computing*, 75-80.

Woods, C. J. et. al. (2005, August). Grid Computing and Biomolecular Simulation. *Philosophical Transactions of the Royal Society A, 363*(1833), 2017-2035.

Wozniak, J. M., Jiang, Y., & Striegel, A. (2007, March). Effects of Low-Quality Computation Time Estimates in Policed Schedulers. *Proc. Annual Simulation Symposium*, 283-292.

Yarmolenko, V., & Sakellariou, R. (2006, April). An Evaluation of Heuristics for SLA Based Parallel Job Scheduling. *Proc. High Performance Grid Computing Workshop*.

Chapter IX
Achieving QoS in Highly Unreliable Grid Environments

Antonios Litke
National Technical University of Athens, Greece

ABSTRACT

Grids can form the basis for pervasive computing due to their ability of being open, scalable, and flexible to various changes (from topology changes to unpredicted failures of nodes). However, such environments are prone to failures due to their nature and need a certain level of reliability in order to provide viable and commercially exploitable solutions. This is causing nowadays a significant research activity which is focused on the topic of achieving certain levels of Quality of Service (QoS) in highly unreliable environments (such as mobile and ad hoc Grids). This study will focus on the state-of-the-art analysis of the QoS aspects in Grids and how this is achieved in terms of technological means. A small survey and related work will be also presented. A more detailed analysis on the features of unreliable environments such as mobile Grids will be described. An innovative and efficient mechanism will be described, which is especially designed for such environments, in order to enhance them with the QoS attributes of reliability (fault tolerance through replication of tasks) and service differentiation to the Grid users through a simple task prioritization scheme. The results that this recent research work is presenting are promising for the future advancement of Grid commercialization in such environments.

INTRODUCTION

Grid computing has recently migrated from traditional high performance and distributed computing to pervasive and utility computing based on the advanced capabilities of the wireless networks and the lightweight, thin devices. This has as result the emergence of a new computing paradigm which is the

Mobile Grid. Mobile Grid is a full inheritor of Grid with the additional feature of supporting mobile users and resources in a seamless, transparent, secure and efficient way. It has the ability to deploy underlying ad-hoc networks and provide a self-configuring Grid system of mobile resources (hosts and users) connected by wireless links and forming arbitrary and unpredictable topologies. However, it is also the basis and the enabling technology for pervasive and utility computing due to the ability of being open, highly heterogeneous and scalable.

This modern approach that combines thousands of parts into a large system provides generally less reliable platforms, which in combination with the long running codes results into application execution times that exceed the mean time to failure of the machines. For this reason *fault tolerance* is of vital importance in this new mobile grid paradigm since both mission-critical systems and computational intensive applications belong in the context of diverse, dependable and cross-organizational environments which is the case of the emerging mobile Grid. Mobile Grid computing is a typical example of highly unreliable computational environment and thus it is not expected to be fault free, despite the fact that individual techniques such as *fault avoidance* and *fault removal* (Lyu 1995) may additionally be applied to its resources. Therefore fault tolerance mechanisms need to be deployed to allow the Grid system to perform correctly in the presence of faults enhancing it with the appropriate reliability.

We present a fault tolerant model for task scheduling in mobile Grid systems based on the task replication concept. The basic idea is to produce and schedule in the Grid infrastructure multiple replicas of a given task. The number of replicas is calculated by the Grid middleware and is based on the failure probability of the Grid resources and the policy that is adopted for providing a specific level of fault tolerance. The adopted replication model is based on *static replication* (Nguyen-Tuong, 2000), meaning that when a replica fails it is not substituted by a new one. The introduction of task replicas causes an overhead in the *workload* that is allocated to the Grid for execution. Scheduling and resource management are important in optimizing Grid resource allocation (Ramamritham, Stankovic, & Shiah, 1990), and determining its ability to deliver the negotiated Quality of Service (QoS) to all users ("Scheduling Working Group," 2001; Wang, Ramamritham, & Stankovic, 1995). The idea in this paper is to handle the additional tasks with a resource management scheme based on the knapsack problem formulation (Pisinger, 1995), where to each task a *weight* and a *profit* for its correct execution have been assigned. By this we allow for an efficient time scheduling of the tasks and their replicas so as to maximize the utilization of the Grid resources and the profit we can gain from the successfully executed ones. Moreover a prioritization scheme for the tasks is applied in order to allow an efficient scheduling complementing the QoS attributes of the Grid.

The remaining of the paper is structured as follows. Section 2 gives a short discussion on how QoS is perceived in Grid environments and what are the issues that affect it. Section 3 presents related work in the field of the fault tolerance in Grid computing as well as in Grid scheduling and formulation as Knapsack problem. Section 4 gives an overview of the problem formulation and the notation that is followed in the paper. Section 5 provides the concept and analysis of the task replication model adopted for achieving the desired fault tolerance in the Grid infrastructure. Section 6 enhances the qualitative parameters of Grid operation by introducing a simple and efficient prioritization scheme for the task scheduling. In section 7 we present the simulation results in terms of their efficiency as well as the overall evaluation of the proposed scheme in terms of performance for profit optimization. Finally, section 8 concludes with a discussion on future research and potentials for the current study.

ACHIEVING QOS IN GRIDS

There is not a unique definition of the term QoS in Grids. However, in relevance to the networking domain, where QoS is interpreted as the ability of the network infrastructure to prioritize the data packets as the travel through the routers and switches, we explore in this study the QoS term as the ability of the grid services to enable such a prioritization scheme. Additional qualitative features can be also present, such as reliability, security, availability, overload protection, monitoring and management capabilities, deadline guarantee etc. In this study we focus on the fault tolerance feature of the proposed mechanism, which can guarantee the execution of any submitted task within a predetermined level of tolerance, increasing thus the overall reliability of the Grid system.

The mobile Grid is a dynamic system where environmental conditions are subject to unpredictable changes: system or network failures, system performance degradation, removal of machines, variations in the cost of resources, etc. This problem causes a direct impact on various functionalities of the Grid itself such as the job scheduling and fault tolerance. The Job Scheduling problem is classified as an NP-complete problem due to the fact that an algorithm has to be applied that would allocate jobs to resources in an efficient and cost effective manner, so as to minimize the resource utilization gaining the maximum profit and satisfying at the same time the user constraints (Security, Quality of Service, Fault tolerance etc). In a mobile Grid environment there are many more constraints that would make the job scheduling problem more complicated. The optimization criteria for a job scheduling mechanism should take into consideration not only the cost and the performance of each resource, but also the current availability of resources in the Gird context and their reliability in providing the specific resources for the execution of the job under the given QoS constraints. In such context job migration and re-scheduling, as well as job replication and co-scheduling are both (from different perspectives) efficient ways to guarantee the completion of the jobs according to the restrictions set by the users. Job monitoring and checkpointing (especially in the case of long running tasks) is difficult in dynamic environments. Especially job monitoring is responsible for detecting alert situations that could initiate a migration and alternatively identify if a job has been completed so as to suspend/stop/cancel the execution of the other replicas.

In order to design and develop architectures that will cover the aforementioned issues we propose in this study a mechanism that enriches OGSA-based Grids in a manner that covers the provision of QoS attributes such as prioritization of jobs and fault tolerance, especially applicable for the requirements of the Mobile Grids.

RELATED WORK

There are various approaches to make grid computing fault tolerant (Lyu 1995; Weissman, 1999; Wang et al, 1995). The basic however are the *checkpoint recovery* and the *task replication*. The former is a common method for ensuring the progress of a long-running application by taking a checkpoint, i.e., saving its state on permanent storage periodically. A checkpoint recovery is an insurance policy against failures. In the event of a failure, the application can be rolled back and restarted from its last checkpoint—thereby bounding the amount of lost work to be recomputed. Task replication is another common method that aims to provide fault tolerance in distributed environments by scheduling redundant copies of the tasks, so that to increase the probability of having at least a simple task executed. A brief overview of the options in the fault tolerant computing on the Grid can be found in Weissman, 1999. Moreover, in Hwang & Kesselman, 2001, a very interesting analysis of requirements for fault tolerance in the Grid is presented along with a failure detection service and a flexible failure handling framework.

There has been a variety of implementations that have addressed the problem of fault tolerance in Grid and distributed systems. Globus ("The Globus project," n.d.) provides a heartbeat service to monitor running processes to detect faults. The application is notified of the failure and expected to take appropriate recovery action. Legion (Nguyen-Tuong & Grimshaw, 1998; Chapin, Katramatos, Karpovich, & Grimshaw, 1999) provides mechanisms to support fault tolerance such as checkpointing. Other Grid systems like Netsolve (Casanova, Dongarra, Johnson, & Miller, 1998; Plank, Casanova, Beck, & Dongarra, 1999), Mentat (Grimshaw, Ferrari, & West, 1996) and Condor-G (Gartner , 1999) have their failure detection and failure recovery mechanisms. They provide a single user-transparent failure recovery mechanism (e.g. retrying in Netsolve and in Condor-G, replication in Mentat). FATCOP (Chen, Ferris, & Linderoth, 2001), is a parallel mixed integer program solver that works in an opportunistic computing environment provided by the Condor resource management system, using an implementation of a branch-and-bound algorithm. Peer-to-peer (P2P) systems follow also various methods for fault tolerance in their operation. An interesting overview of P2P systems is presented in Zhuge et al. (2005) and Shenker (2002).

The difference between these systems and our proposed scheme lies on the fact that the one presented here addresses the fault tolerance as a metric that is adjusted in the Grid infrastructure based on the reliability model of its resources. Moreover it applies to all Grid environments and is especially beneficial for low workload jobs in unreliable environments, such as Mobile Grids ("Access to Knowledge," n.d.; Litke, Skoutas, & Varvarigou, 2004), which consist of mobile resources (hosts and users) connected by wireless links and forming arbitrary and unpredictable topologies.

As far as it concerns scheduling in Grid, there are several systems that have been developed. The most significant attempts can be found in meta-schedulers such as Nimrod-G (Abramson, Sosic, Giddy & Hall,

1995; Abramson, Buyya, & Giddy, 2002), software execution environments such as GRaDS (Berman et al., 2001) and task brokers such as Condor-G (Frey, Tannenbaum, Foster, Livny, & Tuecke, 2002). The latter is a product of a much more complicated entity that consolidates scheduling policies which comprised specialized workload management systems. Additionally, AppLeS (Faerman et al., 2003) is a scheduling system which primarily focuses on developing scheduling agents for individual applications on production. Other interesting works on scheduling and meta-scheduling are presented in Weng & Lu (2005) and Subramani, Kettimuthu,

Srinivasan & Sadayappan (2002), where in the first one the authors present a heuristic scheduling of bag-of-tasks with QoS constraints, while the latter handles the problem of distributed job scheduling in Grids using multiple simultaneous requests. However, in coherent, integrated Grid environments (such as Globus ("The Globus project," n.d.) and Unicore (Berman et al., 2001; Frey, Tannenbaum, Foster, Livny, & Tuecke, 2002; Faerman et al., 2003) there are also scheduling and resource management techniques applicable in a more standard manner.

Finally, other studies have also addressed resource management in Grids as a Knapsack formulation problem. In Parra-Hernandez, Vanderster, & Dimopoulos (2004), the resource allocation in a Grid environment is formulated as a knapsack problem and techniques are developed and deployed so as to maintain QoS properties of a schedule and at the same time to maximize the utilization of the grid resources. This approach although presenting very interesting results does not take into account the mobility aspect of the Grid (having unreliable links) and moreover the reliability model of the Grid infrastructure so as to provide a fault tolerance threshold for the tasks that are going to be executed.

NOTATION AND PROBLEM FORMULATION

We consider a Grid infrastructure consisting of a set of N_p computational machines either fixed or mobile (like Personal Digital Assistants, Personal Computers, notebooks, workstations) which will be also mentioned as *resources* of the mobile Grid. Each resource has a *computational rate* which is denoted as $\mu_j, j \in \{1,2,...,N_P\}$, and represents the ability of this resource to perform specific operations in a given time period (for instance Million Floating Operations Per Second – MFLOPS). The aggregate computational rate of the Grid is

$$\mu_G = \sum_{j=1}^{N_P} \mu_j.$$

We also consider a set of N different tasks $T_i, i \in \{1,2,...,N\}$ which are to be assigned to the Grid for execution. We assume that the tasks are non-preemptable and non-interruptible (Leung & Merrill, 1980; Jackson & Rouskas, 2002). This means that a task cannot be broken into smaller sub-tasks or modules and it has to be executed as a whole on a single processor of a given resource. Additionally as soon as a task starts its execution on a processor, it cannot be interrupted and it occupies the whole processor until its execution completes successfully or a failure occurs. In the analysis we follow in this paper, we consider typical Grid tasks as they are met in various Grid platforms (such as Globus). These tasks can be executables together with their input files and parameters, or only executables submitted for remote execution, or only input files which are going to be processed in a remote machine. Each task T_i has an *execution time* ET_i and a *deadline* D_i. The execution time ET_i corresponds to the time interval that the execution of T_i lasts if it is executed in a processor of unitary rate $\mu = 1$. Otherwise we denote as ET_{ij} the time interval that the task T_i lasts on resource j with computational rate μ_j. The deadline D_i of the task T_i represents the latest time at which the Grid has to deliver the results to the user. It is a quantity specified by the end-user who is willing to pay for the resources that has consumed.

We introduce the concept of *workload* $w_i, i \in \{1,2,...,N\}$ which is the load of computational work that task T_i stresses on a resource for its successful execution. We have:

$$w_i = \mu_j ET_{ij} \tag{1}$$

which is measured in *computational units* (such as Million Floating point Operations – MFLO). In the special case of having a resource with unitary rate, we get $w_i = ET_i$, which represents that the workload of the task T_i when executed on unitary rate resource is equal to the execution time.

Finally, each task T_i is associated with a *profit* v_i indicating the revenue produced by the successful execution of the task. This profit is measured in *currency units* and may refer to the price the user is paying for the provided service. It may also be a more abstract notion of value incorporating revenue in other situations (for example, in a crisis management scenario, or in a workflow of orchestrated services, a task that produces results which help to handle the crisis or is critical for the sequel of the workflow may not be charged – similarly as in emergency calls - but still its execution yields a very high value due to the importance of the situation which can be translated in a virtual profit).

During a task execution on the mobile Grid, various errors might occur. These kinds of errors are commonly met in distributed systems as well as in Grid environments (Nguyen-Tuong, 2000; Weissman, 1999; Tanenbaum & van Steen, n.d.; Varvarigou & Trotter, 1998), and most often include: (i) *Crash failures*, where a server halts, but was working correctly until that moment, (ii) *Omission failures*, where server fails to respond to incoming requests and to send messages, (iii) *Timing failures*, where the server succeeds to respond but its response is beyond the specified time interval.

We define as *failure probability* Pf_i of a task T_i the probability that the task fails to be executed on the Grid. The proposed *fault tolerance* scheme in this paper is based upon the notion of replication. According to that, task *replicas* are generated by the Grid middleware and are assigned to the resources for execution. The term *replica* or *task replica* is used to denote an identical copy of the original task. By producing task replicas, the failure probability of each task can be significantly lowered; however, the number of tasks that are finally assigned to the mobile Grid increases, increasing respectively the total workload that is assigned to the Grid for execution. We assume that m_i replicas –denoted by T_{ik}, $k = 1,..., m_i$– of a task T_i are produced and are placed among other tasks and replicas going to be assigned to a processor of a mobile node by the scheduler. The number of the tasks including their replicas will be denoted as N'. Therefore

$$N' = N + \sum_{i=1}^{N} m_i .$$

Given the failure probability Pf_{ik} of each one of the m_i replicas T_{ik} of task T_i, the new failure probability Pf_i' for task T_i is:

$$Pf_i' = Pf_i \cdot \prod_{k=1}^{m_i} Pf_{ik} \tag{2}$$

The above corresponds to the probability of the event "all the replicas and the original task fail". Respectively, the *success probability* is equal to the probability of the event "the original task or at least one of its replicas executes successfully". The number of replicas issued depends on the failure probabilities of the original tasks and on the desired fault tolerance level in the Grid infrastructure. We denote as λ the desirable failure probability threshold. Thus for each task a sufficient number of replicas is created to satisfy the condition:

$$Pf_i' \le \lambda \tag{3}$$

where λ ∈ (0, 1).

In this paper we examine the failure probability of a task with respect to the mobile resource it is assigned for execution. Based on the various types of failures we assume that a task or a replica fails if the resource on which it is assigned fails during the execution time. This failure is not necessarily a processor (crash) failure, but can also be an omission (such as time omission) due to an unreliable connection. For this reason the *mean time to failure* (MTTF) is used which is the expected time that a mobile Grid resource will function before it fails for any reason. Conventionally, MTTF refers to non-repairable objects while *mean time between failure* (MTBF) refers to repairable objects. In large and complex systems such as mobile Grids, although the individual component reliabilities can be high, the overall reliability of the system can be possibly low (Reed, Lu, & Mendes, 2006), due to coupled failure modes or various extrinsic factors. The lifetime of the mobile Grid resources under discussion is assumed to start at time $t = 0$, and any events occurring at times $t < 0$ are irrelevant.

RELIABILITY THROUGH TASK REPLICATION

The model that is used is based on the *Weibull distribution* since this model effectively represents machine availability in large scale computing environments (Nurmi, Brevik, & Wolski, 2003) such as wide-area enterprises, Internet and Grids. The Weibull distribution is often used to model the time until failure of many different physical systems and for this reason it is more suitable for our study compared to other distributions like Poisson or exponential. The parameters in the distribution provide a great deal of flexibility to model systems in which the number of failures increases over time (e.g. bearing wear), decreases over time (e.g. some semiconductors), or remains constant with time (e.g. failures caused by external reasons to the system) (Montgomery & Runger, n.d.).

If X is a random variable then the *probability density function* (*pdf*)

$$f(x) = \frac{\beta}{\delta}\left(\frac{x}{\delta}\right)^{\beta-1} e^{-\left(\frac{x}{\delta}\right)^{\beta}}$$

(4)

is a Weibull distribution for $x > 0$, with *scale* parameter $\delta > 0$ and *shape* parameter $\beta > 0$. Especially for the case of $\beta = 1$ the Weibull distribution is identical to the *exponential distribution*.

The reliability function $R(x)$ of machine that follows a specific distribution is the probability that the machine does not fail in the time interval $(0, x]$ is given by:

$$R(x) = e^{-\left(\frac{x}{\delta}\right)^{\beta}}$$

(5)

A system that follows a Weibull failure law (WFL) has a *hazard function* (instantaneous failure rate function) (Meyer, 1970; Scheaffer, 1995) of the form:

$$h(x) = \rho\alpha x^{\alpha-1}$$

(6)

where α and $\rho > 0$. There are three cases according to the values of α

- If $\alpha = 1$, then the hazard rate is constant and the Weibull failure law is an Exponential Failure Law.
- If $\alpha > 1$, the hazard function increases as the system gets older. In most areas of application this is the most common case. In this case the system has memory and remembers its age.
- If $\alpha < 1$, the hazard function decreases as the system ages.

We deal with failures that occur due to the fact that we have unreliable machines in the mobile Grid infrastructure. We will omit other cases of failure caused by the network connections (such as timing failures) or failures from the application software, in order to simplify the study. However the proposed model can be enhanced so as to incorporate the failure during the submission of the task and the results in the execution time interval, and allowing an additional probability of having the failure from errors that occurred during the execution due to the application software.

Irrelevant from the scheduling algorithm (our scheme is not limited by the scheduling algorithm adopted) we assume that a task is to be scheduled on the mobile grid. In this case we assume that a task (before the replication) is to be scheduled on the mobile Grid for execution. Each resource of the mobile Grid is characterized by a reliability function and thus a hazard function. In the general case and regardless of any scheduling and resource assignment policy we assume that the task is going to start its execution on the moment t. We suppose that a mobile resource has survived until time t. The hazard function $h(t)$ is its failure rate during the short time interval $(t, t+\Delta t]$. Given that a mobile resource is still alive at time t, the probability of failure during the next Δt time units can be expressed generally as follows:

$$P(t < s < t + \Delta t \mid s > t) = P(t < s < t + \Delta t) / P(s > t) \tag{7}$$

where s represents the time of failure. For small Δt we get $h(t) = f(t)/R(t)$.

In case of having the execution time of a task on a given resource we can calculate this probability by having the following equation:

$$P(t_0 < s < t_0 + ET_{ij} \mid s > t_0) = P(t_0 < s < t_0 + ET_{ij}) / P(s > t_0) \tag{8}$$

where t_o is the time when the task T_i is assigned to the resource for execution and ET_{ij} the execution time that it lasts on the specific resources.

Sometimes and in order to estimate this probability it is necessary to know a priori the execution time of a task on a given resource or at least a good estimation. There are several ways to predict the execution time for a task/resource pair that are presented in Doulamis et al. (n.d.), He, Sun, & von Laszewski (2003) Carrington, Snavely, & Wolter (2006), Wolski, Spring, & Hayes (1999), Gong, Sun, & Waston (2002), and Gao, Rong, & Huang (2005). Some of them use the previous resource performance. For large applications or non-stable running environments, application-level prediction model are applied. Additionally, a non-linear prediction model for legacy applications with un-known source code can be used so as to allow confidentiality for commercial applications (Litke, Tserpes, & Varvarigou, 2005).

In case of having small execution times we can use the hazard rate function for the WFL, or otherwise in case of having longer execution time and in order to be more accurate, we get:

$$P(t_0 < s < t_0 + ET_{ij} \mid s > t_0) = [F(t_0 + ET_{ij}) - F(t_0)] / R(s) = g(ET_{ij}, s) \tag{9}$$

In this case the $g(\cdot, \cdot)$ function gives the conditional probability for having the failure of the resource while executing the specific task. The calculation of the number of replicas is based on the condition:

$$\prod_{k=1}^{m_i} g_{ik} \leq \lambda \tag{10}$$

where g_{ik} represents the probability of $g(\cdot;\cdot)$ for the k-th replica of task T_i denoted as T_{ik}.

In the specific case where we have the same constant hazard rate for each resource then the WFL becomes an Exponential Failure Law, which is a case identical to a normal operation of a machine (excluding the "burn in" and the "wear out" phases). In this case, for every replica T_{ik} we have $g_{ik} = g_i$ and we get:

$$g_i^{(m_i+1)} \leq \lambda \Rightarrow (m_i + 1) \cdot \log(g_i) \leq \log(\lambda) \tag{11}$$

and given that $g_i < 1 \Rightarrow \log(g_i) < 0$, we have

$$m_i \geq \frac{\log(\lambda)}{\log(g_i)} - 1 \tag{12}$$

Finally, we conclude that the minimum number of replicas required to achieve a failure probability less than or equal to the given threshold λ is:

$$m_i = \left\lceil \frac{\log(\lambda)}{\log(g_i)} - 1 \right\rceil \tag{13}$$

The Grid is considered to have a total computational rate

$$\mu_G = \sum_{j=1}^{N_P} \mu_j,$$

where $\mu_j, j \in \{1,2,...,N_P\}$ is the computational rate of each one of the N_P contributing processors of the mobile nodes. Thus, in a period of time T_{per}, the capacity of the Grid, meaning the amount of computational work the Grid can execute is:

$$C = \mu_G \cdot T_{per} \tag{14}$$

measured in the same *computational units* as the workload (e.g. MFLO).

Each task T_i submitted for execution is characterized by a workload w_i, a failure probability Pf_i based on the failure probability of the resource it is assigned for execution and a profit v_i that is achieved if its execution is completed successfully. The total workload for the system is

$$W = \sum_{i=1}^{N} w_i .$$

In order to achieve a high Grid throughput which is translated to the maximum utilization of the Grid resources and to gain the maximum profit out of it, it is necessary to decide which tasks should be executed in the given time period T_{per} so as to fulfill these requirements. We suppose that the period is selected so as to fulfill the deadline constraint for the tasks set by the users. In the case of having a Grid capacity greater than the total workload of the tasks to be submitted ($W \leq C$) then all tasks can be submitted to the Grid resources for execution. However if $W > C$ only a subset of the tasks may be selected. To optimize the profit from the task execution, a resource management mechanism is needed that will decide which tasks will be selected for execution. The objective of this mechanism is to select a subset of tasks $T' \subseteq T$, so that the total profit is maximized given that $W_{T'} \leq C$.

This problem can be formulated as an instance of the Knapsack Problem, and in particular the 0/1 Knapsack Problem (Pisinger, 1995), which is defined as follows:

"There are $N \geq 0$ items and a knapsack of capacity $C > 0$. Each item $i \in \lceil 1, N \rceil$ has a profit $v_i > 0$ and a weight $w_i > 0$. Find the selection of items ($z_i = 1$ if selected, $z_i = 0$ if not) so that

$$\sum_{i=1}^{N} z_i \cdot w_i \leq C \ and \ \sum_{i=1}^{N} z_i \cdot v_i$$

is maximized."

Our process becomes more complicated when replication mechanisms are employed. In this case, the total workload, denoted as W_R, for the system is the sum of the workload of each pending task, including their created replicas, thus

$$W_R = \sum_{i=1}^{N} (1 + m_i) \cdot w_i,$$

where m_i denotes the number of replicas created for task T_i. We will assume that the successful execution of more than one replicas of the same task does not generate additional profit. This assumption has been made since otherwise a concrete economic driven analysis for the identification of an exact price would be needed, which is out of the scope in this paper. The total profit that can be gained by successfully executing the set of the N tasks is

$$V = \sum_{i=1}^{N} v_i.$$

However the profit of the tasks inside the knapsack is

$$V_{knap} = \sum_{i=1}^{N} z_i \cdot v_i$$

while the *actual profit* can be formulated as:

$$V_{actual} = \sum_{i=1}^{N} z_i \cdot v_i \cdot \zeta_i$$

(15)

where $\zeta_i = 1$ if at least one of the copies (original or replica) of task T_i has executed successfully, otherwise $\zeta_i = 0$.

According to the pricing and charging policy adopted by the Grid system, the profit v_i of a task may be greater in case of replication, either by a fixed amount or by an amount that depends on the number of replicas created, since additional charge can be claimed for providing fault tolerance which is regarded as a QoS aspect in the provision of services. In simple words, task replication increases the probability of some tasks to be left out, resulting in profit loss, while on the other hand increases the probability of the selected tasks to execute successfully, resulting in profit gain. The decision on how to resolve this trade-off is made according to the values of the parameters involved (failure probability, workload compared to grid capacity, task profits) in each instance of the problem.

The idea behind the specific fault tolerance and resource management model is to enable various scheduling mechanisms that already exist in various Grid middleware implementations so as to enhance the overall functionality with the fault tolerance attribute through the replication and assignment of redundant task copies to different Grid resources. In simple mobile Grid environments (such as the one depicted in Fig. 1), various failures can happen resulting in deviation form the user deadlines but also to the total omission of executing the task set by the mobile user. The task replication and resource management scheme based on the knapsack formulation that is presented in this paper is residing in the Grid middleware and is responsible to replicate tasks based on the reliability function of the resources it is associated with.

As soon as a new resource is attached to the mobile Grid infrastructure (notebooks but also fixed servers), the middleware is updated so as to estimate its Weibull parameters based on the input it will

Figure 1. A simple case of a mobile grid environment indicating the framework of the task replication fault tolerance

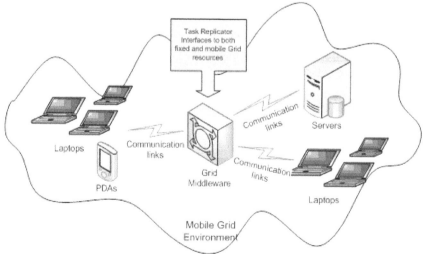

receive in the first failures (e.g. 4 failures). Having known the Weibull failure model for the given resource it is able to estimate the failure probability for the next assignments of tasks for execution, and based on each task's estimated execution time on the specific resource.

The proposed fault tolerance and resource management scheme can collaborate with various scheduling mechanisms that would (based on their own criteria) produce a time-schedule and processor assignment for the incoming tasks. Such mechanisms are derived by a much more complicated entity that consolidates scheduling policies and examples of them can be found in various scheduling systems and Grid middleware solutions such as The Globus project (n.d.), Abramson, Sosic, Giddy & Hall (1995) Berman et al. (2001), Frey, Tannenbaum, Foster, Livny, & Tuecke (2002), Faerman et al. (2003) , The Unicore Project (n.d.) and others. For each task that is assigned to a resource for execution the proposed mechanism performs a check to identify the failure probability of the resource during the task execution. If inequality (3) is not met then a new replica is produced and scheduled for execution on a new resource based on the scheduling scheme. The new failure probability of the replicated tasks based on equation (2) is then calculated and this process is repeated until the total failure probability of all replicas of the task is less than the specified threshold λ.

The adoption of the knapsack formulation has been made because it is not possible to assign all the tasks for execution to the Grid since the total workload exceeds the capacity of the Grid infrastructure. The tasks that have been left out of the knapsack will be considered for re-scheduling and submission in the next iteration of the algorithm. Postponing the execution of a task may result in some cases to a deviation from deadline. This deviation can be also handled by other mechanism such as in (Litke, Tserpes,Dolkas, & Varvarigou (2005) so as to guarantee a specific level of QoS. All versions of the Knapsack Problem belong to the family of NP-hard problems, meaning that no polynomial algorithm has been devised until now for these problems. Therefore, to find the optimal solution, an enumeration of the solution space is required. However, substantial effort may be saved by employing techniques like branch-and-bound, dynamic programming, state space relaxation and preprocessing (Pisinger, 1995). Overviews of exact solution techniques are also presented in Martello, Pisinger, & Toth (2000) and Martello & Toth (1990). Moreover, heuristics, generating feasible, and usually suboptimal, solutions within short execution times can be found in Martello & Toth (1990) and Ghosh (1997).

The performance of the algorithm depends on the nature of the data instances considered in the specific application. The data instances may be (i) *Uncorrelated*: where no correlation exists between the profit and the weight of the items. These instances are generally easier to solve, since a) the large variance among the weights makes it easier to obtain a filled knapsack and b) it is easier to eliminate numerous items a-priori by applying upper bound tests. (ii) *Weakly correlated*: In these instances there is some degree of correlation between the profit and the weight. Due to the existence of correlation it is difficult to eliminate items by upper bound tests. However the large variation in the weights makes it easier to obtain a filled knapsack, and, due to the correlation, filled solutions are generally very close to the optimal solution. (iii) *Strongly correlated*: In these instances the profit of an item is a linear function of its weight. Strongly correlated instances are the hardest case to solve, and therefore they are often used as a measure of an algorithm's ability to solve difficult problems.

In the case of tasks submitted to the Grid for execution, the degree of correlation between the weight and the value of each task depends on the adopted pricing and charging policy. In most cases it is reasonable to assume that we deal with weakly correlated data, since: (a) a higher task weight means higher consumption of grid resources and thus a higher price charged for the execution of the task and (b) the price charged for a task may also be subject to parameters other than the resource usage (e.g. in an emergency situation a heavy task may receive little or no charge, a client may be willing to pay a high price for a light task if it is of critical importance to him, etc.)

In our study, for the solution of the Knapsack problem we have considered four techniques: *Backtracking (BT), Branch and Bound (BB), Dynamic Programming (DP)* and a *heuristic greedy* algorithm *(GR)*. The first three techniques are based on a systematic examination of the list of all candidate solutions, which achieves significant run-time savings in both the worst and expected cases (Sahni, 2004). In Backtracking the solution space is first organized in a tree structure so that it can be searched easily. Then the solution space is searched in a depth-first manner, beginning at a start node, using bounding functions to avoid moving into subspaces that lead to solutions that are either infeasible or impossible to be the answer. Like Backtracking, Branch-and-Bound also organizes the solution space in a tree structure, but a breadth-first or least-cost search is performed instead. Branch-and-bound is presented in the literature as finding the optimal solution a bit sooner than Backtracking (Sahni, 2004). However, branch-and-bound algorithms have more space requirements than backtracking resulting in successful answers where memory limitations are applicable. Dynamic programming is frequently used when a recursive solution to a problem has exponential run time, due to repeated computation. The technique used is to store the results of particular calls of a method or computation that have already been computed, using a table indexed by the different argument values. In general, this technique is known as "memoization". Although this technique is very useful, it can potentially require a large amount of space because of creating arrays big enough to cover all possible argument values. Dynamic programming involves the use of a memo storing past results, but also involves changing the order of computation, bringing the memo to the fore by systematically building up and recording sub-problem results, to provide a time- and space-efficient overall solution.

As the number of tasks increases, the running time required for the total enumeration of the solution space and the selection of the optimal one can be prohibitive. A *greedy* solution strategy can be employed in these cases in order to find a "near-optimal" solution. In this approach the items are placed in the knapsack in a "one-by-one" basis and once an item has been selected it can not be removed. A greedy algorithm for an optimization problem always makes the choice that looks best at the moment and adds it to the current sub-solution. For the 0-1 Knapsack Problem, the most common criteria that can be used to select the next item to be placed into the knapsack are: (1) Profit: At each step select from the remaining items the one with the highest profit (without exceeding the total capacity of the knapsack). This approach tries to maximize the profit by choosing the most profitable items first. (2) Weight: At each step select from the remaining items the one with the least weight (provided the capacity of the knapsack is not exceeded). This approach tries to maximize the profit by putting as many items into the knapsack as possible. (3) Profit density: At each step select from the remaining items the one with the largest profit density (p/w) (provided the capacity of the knapsack is not exceeded). This approach tries to maximize the profit by choosing items with the largest profit per unit of weight (Preiss, 1999).

SIMPLE AND EFFICIENT PRIORITIZATION SCHEME

The study that follows is focusing on system behaviour in overload conditions, where the adoption of the prioritized mechanism is suitable to apply differentiated service provision for the customers.

For this reason we introduce a prioritization scheme which can be assigned the following states:

1.   **Medium or Middle:** Normal add to queue (could be renamed Normal).
2.   **Low:** Stick to back until no other jobs to process.
3.   **High:** Go to front, but behind Top priority jobs.
4.   **Top:** Go to front. Next job to be processed.

As the priority can be considered as optional there should be a default value in case it is not specified by the user-customer, which in our case is Medium or Middle. This distinction gives the opportunity to have four kinds of task priority, making the Grid middleware to perform special handling for each one of them and thus adapting the QoS. In case that the priority is set on Middle, then the tasks are served in the same order in a first-in-first-out fashion. The special handling is performed in case that Low, High or Top priorities are set. This prioritization scheme, although simple, provides enough functionality to distinguish between different classes of services. We can consider that the Top priority is applicable in special and critical events that are reserved for the control of the application that is provided in the Grid platform (involving security issues or other critical and urgent administrative operations to recover or maintain service containers). The priorities that are to be provided to the customers as classes of differentiation are High and Medium, so to have a simple distinction between them. The Low priority is foreseen for the some administrative batch procedures (i.e. for maintenance) that can be executed when the Grid system is not loaded (overnight).

Applying Little's law (Cooper, 1981), *mean number of tasks in the system = task arrival rate * mean response time of the system*, we derive:

$$L_{System} = r_{arrival} * T_{System} \tag{16}$$

where $r_{arrival}$ is the task arrival rate to the Grid system, T_{System} the demanded time for a task until it is finally executed and L_{System} the length of the system's queue.

In the general case with no prioritization all the tasks that are submitted to the mobile Grid for execution are fed in a queue with length L_q, and each new task must be added at the end waiting. The execution of each task demands a *mean time of service*. If a task is in the server then it needs an Average Residual Service Time ($_{p} * T_{Av}$) which is the waiting time of a new task before the server (computational resource) finishes the previous one, in order to be finally executed. The probability that the N_p computational resources will be busy is P_{N_p}, therefore the expected time for execution will be: $P_{N_p} * T_{Av}$. Thus:

$$T_q = L_q * T_{Server} + P_{N_p} * T_{Av} \tag{17}$$

where T_q is the mean time interval that a task is waiting in the queue and T_{Server} the mean time that it takes to the server to dispatch a task.

The utilization of the systems can be expressed by: $U_{N_p}(\rho) = r_{arrival}/r_{service}$, where $r_{service}$ is the service rate of the system. The value of ρ must be between 0 and 1, otherwise the system will be unstable meaning that the arrived tasks would be more than the ones that could be processed and hence the capacity of the system would be exceeded.

In this paper we assume that the arrival of the task into the system follows a Poisson distribution. Poisson is most commonly used to model the number of random occurrences of some events in a specified unit of time (i.e. the number of phone calls received by a telephone operator in a specific period). For a Poisson random variable X, the probability that X is some value x is given by the formula:

$$P(X = x) = \frac{r^x e^{-r}}{x!}, x = 0,1,...,$$

where r is the average number of occurrences in the specified interval. For the Poisson distribution, we have $E(X) = Var(X) = r$, which in our case equals to the arrival rate $r_{arrival}$.

Based on the prioritized task scheduling on the grid in a differentiated mode, we investigate the behavior of the system in overload conditions, but with respect to the stability of the system. Although the arrival rate is constant for all the different priorities, we examine the balance of the utilization with respect to the *different* service rates. In fact, the distinguished priorities have an impact in the different rate of service for the specific classes of tasks. This means that each priority queue will be treated in a different manner something that will result in a different waiting time for the tasks that reside in it for execution.

RESULTS

Task Replication Analysis

The proposed scheme has been implemented and evaluated through simulation results. In order to be able to guarantee a desired fault tolerance level for the mobile Grid, we have to identify the fault tolerance threshold λ. Based on experimental results and on general practices from real world applications, a satisfactory level of fault tolerance in such a distributed environment with unreliable wireless links and mobile devices (normally prone to omissions and energy limitations) has to be increased enough in order to allow a normal operation. Current practices in various Service Level Agreement contracts imply a continuous operation of the services provided by their infrastructure which is in total about 99% of the total time. As we already mentioned, it is important to identify (based on the reliability of the individual Grid resources) the number of the replicas that have to be produced and scheduled for execution. For various values of a fault tolerant threshold we obtain the number of replicas according to equation (13) as presented in the following table:

While evaluating the system through simulation results, we defined a virtual mobile Grid environment of a specific computational rate μ_G. In order to identify the instances used for the various algorithms, we defined the quantity of *capacity ratio*, which represents the ratio of the total workload of all the tasks that are to be submitted for execution to the total capacity of the Grid over the given period. The capacity ratio (CR) can be represented as: $CR = W/C$ and practically represents the relation between the demand for computational capacity of the Grid resources (expressed by the user task submissions) and the capability of the Grid infrastructure to accept and execute these tasks (practically its capacity over this given period). Although the bigger this capacity is the more tasks its can execute, there is no commercial oriented system which can undertake successfully the 100% of its user requests at the same time. It is therefore mandatory to evaluate such a resource management scheme in a manner that

Table 1. Calculation of the number of necessary replicas m_i in order to achieve the desired fault tolerance threshold λ, assuming the special case of having constant failure probability g_i for each grid resource

g_i	$\lambda = 0.01$			$\lambda = 0.05$			$\lambda = 0.10$		
	$\dfrac{\log(\lambda)}{\log(g_i)} - 1$	m_i		$\dfrac{\log(\lambda)}{\log(g_i)} - 1$	m_i		$\dfrac{\log(\lambda)}{\log(g_i)} - 1$	m_i	
0.01	0.000	0		-0.349	0		-0.500	0	
0.02	0.177	1		-0.234	0		-0.411	0	
0.03	0.313	1		-0.146	0		-0.343	0	
0.04	0.431	1		-0.069	0		-0.287	0	
0.05	0.537	1		0.000	0		-0.231	0	
0.06	0.637	1		0.065	1		-0.182	0	
0.07	0.732	1		0.127	1		-0.134	0	
0.08	0.823	1		0.186	1		-0.088	0	
0.09	0.912	1		0.244	1		-0.044	0	
0.10	1.000	1		0.301	1		0.000	0	
0.15	1.427	2		0.579	1		0.214	1	
0.20	1.861	2		0.861	1		0.431	1	
0.25	2.322	3		1.160	2		0.661	1	
0.30	2.825	3		1.488	2		0.912	1	
0.35	3.387	4		1.854	2		1.193	2	
0.40	4.026	5		2.269	3		1.513	2	
0.45	4.767	5		2.752	3		1.887	2	
0.50	5.644	6		3.322	4		2.322	3	

would make visible its operation in various load instances. Especially, in mobile Grids, which are very dynamic and subject to topological changes, it is possible to have more often peaks of computational capacity demand on given periods. For this reason the proposed model has been stressed for instances up to *CR*=33%.

As the various correlation instances tend to be "weakly" and "un-" correlated and for every case of capacity ratio we observe that BB and BT present a more or less similar curve (for reasons of simplicity we have omitted a detailed description of this experiment instance). BB appears to be more efficient in terms of time and both outperform the DP algorithm. But what explains the performance of BB (and BT) is the philosophy of the algorithms to totally exclude "branches" of no good solutions (which can be the case of weakly or uncorrelated instances where we can have cases of very heavy tasks with very small profit) and taking thus quicker decisions on which tasks to load on the Grid resources. The heuristic greedy algorithm which uses the profit density as criterion for the selection of the tasks to be put in the knapsack presents a significantly better performance in terms of response time. The drawback in this case is the fact that, since it uses a heuristic method for the filling of the knapsack, it does not necessarily conclude to the overall optimal value. We measured the deviation from the optimal value for a given instance and we received the following results presented in Table II. The difference between the *optimal values* achieved through BB, BT and DP and the heuristic *greedy solution* value for the case of having 300 tasks with a Grid capacity ratio 80%, is within specific limits which advance the usage of such an algorithm for very large amounts of tasks to be scheduled. When the profit measured in *currency units* that can be achieved as optimal value of BB, BT and DP for correlated, weakly correlated and uncorrelated instances the greedy heuristic provides a solution ranging from 99,6% to 99,9% of the optimal one. If we consider that the greedy algorithm does not have exponential behavior with respect to the input size of the problem (number of tasks), it can be an ideal solution to be used for very large scale Grid systems

Table 2. Comparison between the optimal value for the profit gained from BB algorithm (measured in currency units) and the one achieved as solution from the Greedy algorithm for 10 different inputs of 300 tasks in a Grid infrastructure with CR=80%, and for the 3 different correlation instances

Correlated Instance		Weakly correlated Instance		Uncorrelated Instance	
Optimal Value (currency units)	Greedy solution (currency units)	Optimal Value (currency units)	Greedy solution (currency units)	Optimal Value (currency units)	Greedy solution (currency units)
61111	61067	61482	61461	60498	60481
60917	60701	61203	61102	60266	60162
61052	61045	61499	61430	59373	59357
61082	61045	60699	60469	60058	60005
61026	61019	60982	60904	61843	61760
61188	60950	60024	59914	61379	61274
61119	61110	63074	63063	62693	62638
61157	60926	63159	63155	60177	60055
61076	60839	63214	63094	61578	61499
60685	60648	63932	63834	59565	59527

with many tasks submissions per time units. From the perspective of commercial exploitation, the profit gained from the greedy algorithm is less than the optimal one which can be derived by BB algorithm (for example). In case of having a small set of tasks (i.e. 50 or 100 tasks) the difference in time is very small and can be balanced with the additional profit that can be achieved with this algorithm. So, the usage of such an algorithm would be more beneficial for the Grid service provider.

A set of $N=300$ tasks have been created to be scheduled in a mobile Grid environment. The tasks follow a weakly correlated model having a profit variance between 10-100 *currency units*. We associate a failure probability for each task between specific values. This failure probability (as already described in previous sections) is derived by the failure probability model of the resource where the task is going to be executed. We have considered two different approaches. The first is to use the knapsack scheme only on the primary tasks without applying the replication mechanism while the second involves the replication procedure. The tasks have been assigned for execution on specific resources and resource failure has been applied (based on the proposed model) so as to have the realistic scenario of task failures in this context. We examined the efficiency of the system in terms of the number of succeeded tasks (which is the number of tasks that have been selected to be loaded in the knapsack and have finished successfully) and the achieved profit which is the profit associated with these tasks. Recall that we do not use any "pricing" scheme for adapting the task profit to the new weight caused by the additional workload of the replicas. For each individual case we repeat the execution 10 times so as to examine the system for having diverse task failures for the given set of tasks. The simulated results are presented in Fig.2.

We observe that the variation in profit for the case of filling the knapsack with tasks that have not been replicated is higher than the one in the case of the replicated tasks. This is due to the fact that the replicated tasks minimize the failure probability and provide a more guaranteed result based on the fault tolerance threshold of the Grid environment. We have to mention that the total achieved profit in the case of having no replicas is higher since for a given workload (weight) we receive a specific profit,

Figure 2. Simulation results of the proposed scheme. Column 1(a1-b1) shows the achieved profit of the succeeded tasks for both techniques "with replication" and "without replication". The iteration in the horizontal axis of the figures means the multiple execution of the same instance in order to examine the failure of the tasks. Column 2(a2-b2) gives the number of the succeeded tasks for both techniques. Each figure gives the instance on which it refers to in terms of fault tolerance threshold, capacity ratio and interval of the tasks failure probabilities.

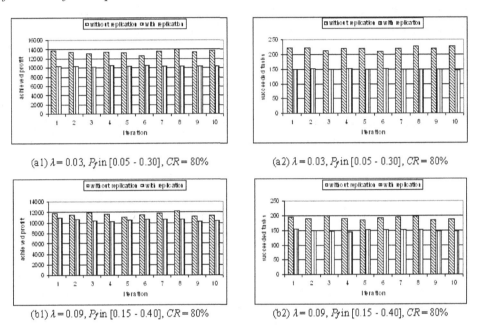

(a1) $\lambda = 0.03$, P_f in $[0.05 - 0.30]$, $CR = 80\%$

(a2) $\lambda = 0.03$, P_f in $[0.05 - 0.30]$, $CR = 80\%$

(b1) $\lambda = 0.09$, P_f in $[0.15 - 0.40]$, $CR = 80\%$

(b2) $\lambda = 0.09$, P_f in $[0.15 - 0.40]$, $CR = 80\%$

while in the case of replicas we get the same profit for multiple times of its workload. The presented results are interesting since they show the relation of the profit to the fault tolerance threshold, the reliability of the resources and the capacity ratio of the Grid. Moreover, although someone would expect that such an increase in the workload would have a significant impact on the reduction of the gained profit we see that the guarantee of having successful executions in unreliable environments is beneficial. Especially, in the case of having a desired overall reliability of 91% (λ=0.09), capacity ratio 80% and highly unreliable resources, the achieved profit in the case of replication is very close to the one in the case of not having replicas (with a minimum deviation 9%).

The non-replication case usually presents a higher profit and number of succeeded tasks than the case where we have replication. In the non-replication case, a significant number of tasks that were initially scheduled in the system fail to complete execution. These failures result in not receiving the profit that is associated to the successful execution of the concrete task. Not to mention other costs that may be applied which are related to deadline violations, Service Level Agreement (SLA) violations, etc, and which are not examined in this paper. In this way the actual profit that may be achieved could be even less. The interesting aspect of the results presented here is that in the cases of replication the number of successfully executed tasks, as well as their achieved profit, is very close to the ones initially scheduled in the system (which is being contained in the knapsack). They are also close enough to the achieved profit that we get (for the same instances) in the cases of not having replication. This means that by providing fault tolerance in highly unreliable environments with the proposed scheme we can achieve a profit which is comparable to the case of having non-replication. Moreover, by using replication we enhance the mobile Grids with reliability which allows for respecting the deadlines set by the users and guarantying QoS that satisfies the customers' requirements. The proposed replication scheme is especially suitable for cases that the successful execution of tasks is important in unreliable environments (e.g. critical situations, deadlines that have to be met, etc). In that cases the benefit from minimizing the failures overcomes the trade-off for allowing some resources to be occupied by task replicas rather than accepting more of prototype tasks in the system.

Prioritization with Replication

We examine the proposed scheme from a Grid service provider perspective who aims to commercially exploit such a fault tolerant and prioritization scheme in order to enhance with reliability and QoS attributes a mobile Grid infrastructure. The assumptions that we make for the simulation relate mainly the fact that given a specific dimension of a Grid infrastructure (number of resources, known Poisson arrival rate, workload of the tasks), what balance between the HIGH and the MID tasks would be efficient to allow in order to have a proper operation of the system. In other words, what threshold for HIGH priority jobs is the best to sell as a QoS attribute to the users who are willing to pay more for this, but at the same time not to ignore the satisfaction of the MID priority users who are left behind in this "differentiated priority" system. In such an environment tasks with TOP priority would be emergency requests (i.e. critical security events, urgent tasks for cases of disasters handling) while the LOW priority tasks would be mainly some batch procedures executed for the maintenance of the infrastructure (i.e. backups, automatic software updates, replication of large data sets). We assume that both cases belong to the jurisdiction of the Grid service provider / administrator, and thus do not target the customer base of the Grid service users. The different classes of priority that are targeted for exploitation by the Grid infrastructure administrator as commodity, are the HIGH and MID, and these and their relation will be examined in the sequel of the simulation results. A number of configurations were selected (percentage of HIGH tasks, etc) and a number of iterations was defined so that each experiment was executed multiple times to avoid variations caused by randomness. The tasks were generated with a workload according to a distribution (the Poisson distribution was selected as it is a common practice in experiments of this kind) and were assigned to queues, implemented as tables in a database. The queue sizes were directly linked to the capacity of the resources in the simulated distributed environment.

The factors that influence the mean waiting time in a queue (Mean Time in Queue – MTQ) of the tasks (whether we refer to the HIGH or MID queues) are: i) the size of the Grid (i.e. the resources that comprise it which affect the throughput of the task execution), ii) the arrival rate of the tasks, iii) the mean execution time of the task itself (which is straightly related on the workload), and iv) the ratio of HIGH and MID task priorities in the queues. In our simulation instance, given the fact that the failure probability is 5% for each Grid resource and that the desired reliability is 99%, each task will be replicated, duplicating thus the workload that is submitted to the Grid system for execution. However, this does not mean that all replicas will be executed.

In order to maintain the stability of such a system, the number of the available Grid resources must increase. Or alternatively, another admission policy must be deployed for the arriving tasks since otherwise this duplication of the workload will result in the overflow of the waiting queues. But generally, the scalability of such a system is depending on the dimensioning that will be deployed by the Grid infrastructure owner, who will deploy the necessary resources based on the arrival rate of the tasks before being replicated. This replication does not imply necessarily the duplication of the resources themselves. The algorithm applied in the middleware, foresees such conditions and handles them accordingly by deleting from the waiting queues any replicas whose copy has been successfully executed. In the respective simulation results we have use the instance of 9 Grid resources. The experiment finishes as soon as 300 tasks (regardless if they are replicas or not) have been executed. Each experiment is performed 10 times for reasons of surpassing randomness. The results are depicted in Fig. 3.

If the reliability was of different percentage (for example from 60% to 99% which is often in unreliable mobile environments) then more Grid resources would be needed for the replication. Table III gives an overview of the mean number of failed tasks for the various ratio instances and for both cases (with replication and without) for the experiments that are depicted in Fig. 3.

The uniformity in the Grid resources and the fact that they are of the same capabilities has an impact in the overall execution time and the MTQ for all the tasks. This means that when each task is submitted in the Grid, its replicas are generated and assigned to the other available resources for execution. In this way, when a task is being executed on a resource it is observed that its replicas are most likely to be executed concurrently in an other Grid resource. This would be not the case if we have a random filled queue for each resource. In the latter case, the canceling of execution for specific tasks would be more often since the finished tasks would inform the middleware to delete the remaining replicas from the queues, resulting thus in a more efficient utilization of the system.

An interesting observation is that in cases of having a HIGH priority percentage more than 80%, then the MTQ of the MID priority tasks is very large and the execution rate (the rate that the task successfully leave the Grid system) of the MID tasks is less than the arrival rate. This results in having an unstable system with high risk of having a starvation or overflow problem in the relative queues if the jobs are practically never executed or the capacity of the queue is exceeded respectively.

Figure 3. Mean time in queue for various ratios of HIGH/MID tasks priorities with task replication. The arrival of tasks is a Poisson distribution with mean value 13 sec. The execution of tasks is a Poisson distribution with mean value 66 sec.

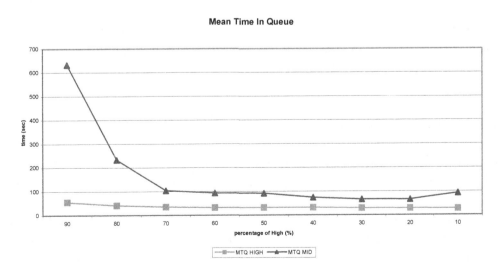

Table 3. Mean number of failed tasks for the various ratio instances and for both cases (with replication and without) referring to the experiments of Figures 4 and 6

	HIGH/MID ratio	90/10	80/20	70/30	60/40	50/50	40/60	30/70	20/80	10/90
Mean Failed Tasks	No repl.	16.6	16	16	14.7	15	15.2	14.9	16.2	14.9
	Replic.	1.6	1.7	2.2	1.5	1.5	2.5	0.5	0.5	0.5

Figure 4. Example for having two equivalent queues HIGH and MID but with no priority and replication in the tasks. The example has been taken for 150 tasks with arrival rate 13 sec (Poisson) and a size of Grid with 5 resources executing each task in 66 sec (Poisson)

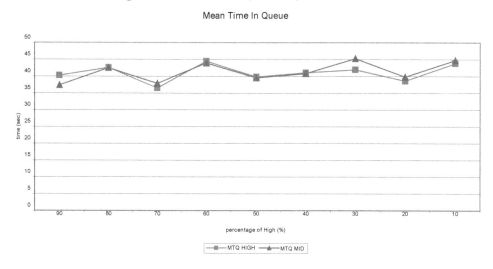

For reasons of consistency we present also the case of keeping the two different queues but with no fault tolerant and prioritization mechanisms (Fig. 4). As it can be seen, there are no behavioral class differences for the various priorities. Based on the randomness of the execution instance, the MTQ values range between two time intervals based only on attributes such as the arrival rate of the tasks, the execution time and the size of the Grid. No stability in behavior can be guaranteed, and thus no QoS properties can be applied.

CONCLUSION AND DISCUSSION (OPEN ISSUES)

In this paper we have studied a fault tolerant model for mobile Grid environments based on the task replication concept. The tasks are replicated based on their failure probability and the desired fault tolerance level. The estimation of the failure probability for a task that has been scheduled to a Grid resource for execution is based on the Weibull reliability model. Since the additional replicas produce an overhead on the workload stressed to the Grid's total computational capacity, we introduce an additional mechanism, based on the knapsack formulation, for managing the tasks and their replicas in terms of their scheduling so as to maximize the Grid resources utilization in terms of the achieved profit. For this model four different algorithms have been used (Backtracking, Branch and Bound, Dynamic programming with "memoization" and a greedy algorithm based on the optimization of profit density). The model has been implemented and evaluated for a variety of tasks with a diverse set of failure probabilities and their replicas and with various instances for correlation between the 'weight' of the tasks and the profit that their execution would result in a commercial oriented Grid. The results have indicated the efficiency of the proposed scheme for the response time, Grid resources utilization and profit maximization and are promising for future research in this topic.

An interesting aspect for future research is to deploy other algorithms for the solution of the knapsack problem (for instance stochastic dynamic programming, or other heuristics) which show better theoretical results in the literature (Martello, Pisinger, & Toth, 2000; Martello & Toth, 1990; Ghosh, 1997). Additionally, we can assume that the failure to execute a task (or at least one of its replicas) results in a cost q_i for the system. This cost may be due to the consumption of resources or the price (penalty) that has to be paid to the user due to deadline and SLA violation or the discontent caused to the client (harming the company's image), etc. It is an interesting topic to examine how in such a dynamic environment a viable economic model could be developed for estimating the cost of the replicas so that not only the 'weight' of the total task raises but also the profit that will be gained in an adjusted manner so that the total profit will be guaranteed as if the grid had only reliable resources. The idea of preserving the QoS attributes of the system, adds an important aspect to various Business Models, because of the static QoS information that can then be integrated into SLAs. This can contribute into simplifying the dynamic SLA mechanisms and in turn the dynamic workflow techniques, that are currently one of the major concerns of the Grid scientific community. Finally, a hybrid model could be designed and developed that would estimate the expected profit and decide which strategy would be ideal to follow in terms of performance and profit optimization.

ACKNOWLEDGMENT

The work has been partially supported by the AKOGRIMO Integrated Project (FP6-2003-IST-004293) (Access to Knowledge, n.d.).

REFERENCES

Abramson, D., Buyya, R., & Giddy, J. (2002). A computational economy for grid computing and its implementation in the Nimrod-G resource broker. *Future Gener. Comput. Syst., 18*(8), 1061–1074.

Abramson, D., Sosic, R., Giddy, J., & Hall, B. (1995). Nimrod: A Tool for Performing Parametised Simulations using Distributed Workstations. *In Proceedings of 4th IEEE Symposium on High Performance Distributed Computing*, Virginia, USA.

Berman, F., Chien, A., Cooper, K., Dongarra, J., Foster, I., Gannon, D., Johnsson, L., Kennedy, K., Kesselman, C., Mellor-Crummey, J., Reed, D., Torczon, L., & Wolski, R. (2001). The GrADS Project:

Software Support for High-Level Grid Application Development. *International Journal of High Performance Computing Applications, 15*(4), 327-344.

Carrington, L., Snavely, A., & Wolter, N. (2006). A performance prediction framework for scientific applications, *Future Generation Computer Systems, 22*, 336–346.

Casanova, H., Dongarra, J., Johnson C., & Miller, M. (1998). Application-Specific Tools. In I. Foster & C. Kesselman (Eds.), *The GRID: Blueprint for a New Computing Infrastructure*, (pp. 159–180).

Chapin, S. J., Katramatos, D., Karpovich, J., & Grimshaw, A. (1999). Resource management in Legion. *Future Generation Comput. Syst., 15*(5/6), 583–594.

Chen, Q., Ferris, M., & Linderoth, J. T. (2001). FATCOP 2.0: Advanced Features in an Opportunistic Mixed Integer Programming Solver. *Annals of Operations Research, 103*(2001), 17-32.

Cooper, R. B. (1981). *Introduction to Queueing Theory.* (2nd edition), (p. 347). Available at: http://www.cse.fau.edu/~bob/publications/IntroToQueueingTheory_Cooper.pdf

Doulamis, N., Doulamis, A., Panagakis, A., Dolkas, K., Varvarigou, T., & Varvarigos, E. (2005). A Combined Fuzzy -Neural Network Model for Non-Linear Prediction of 3D Rendering Workload in Grid Computing. *IEEE Trans. on Systems Man and Cybernetics, Part-B.*

Faerman, M., Figueira, S., Hayes, J., Obertelli, G., Schopf, J., Shao, G., Smallen, S., Spring, N., Su, A., & Zagorodnov, D. (2003). Adaptive Computing on the Grid Using AppLeS. *IEEE Transactions on Parallel and Distributed Systems, 14*(4), 369-382.

Frey, J., Tannenbaum, T., Foster, I., Livny, M., & Tuecke, S. (2002). Condor-G: A computation management agent for multiinstitutional grids. *Cluster Computing, 5*, 237-246.

Gao, Y., Rong, H., & Huang, J. Z. (2005). Adaptive grid job scheduling with genetic algorithms. *Future Generation Computer Systems, 21*, 151–161.

Gartner, F. C. (1999). Fundamentals of Fault-Tolerant Distributed Computing in Asynchronous Environments. *ACM Computing Surveys, 31*(1).

Ghosh, D. (1997). *Heuristics for Knapsack Problems: Comparative Survey and Sensitivity Analysis.* Fellowship Dissertation, IIM Calcutta, India.

Gong, L., Sun, X. H., & Waston, E. (2002). Performance Modeling and Prediction of Non-Dedicated Network Computing. *IEEE Trans. on Computer, 51*(9).

Grimshaw, A. S., Ferrari A., & West, E. A. (1996). *Mentat.* In G.V. Wilson & P. Lu (Eds.), *Parallel Programming Using C++* (pp. 382–427).

He, X., Sun, X., & von Laszewski, G. (2003). QoS Guided Min-Min Heuristic for Grid Task Scheduling. *Journal of Computer Science and Technology, Special Issue on Grid Computing, 18*(4).

Hwang, S., & Kesselman, C. (2003). A Flexible Framework for Fault Tolerance in the Grid. *Journal of Grid Computing, 1*, 251–272.

Jackson, L. E., & Rouskas, G. N. (2002). Deterministic Preemptive Scheduling of Real Time Tasks. *IEEE Computer, 35*(5), 72-79.

Litke, A., Skoutas, D., & Varvarigou, T. (2004). Mobile Grid Computing: Changes and Challenges of Resource Management in a Mobile Grid Environment. *Access to Knowledge through the Grid in a Mobile World Workshop*, held in conjunction with *5th Int. Conf. on Practical Aspects of Knowledge Management*, (PAKM 2004) Vienna, Austria.

Litke, A., Tserpes, K., & Varvarigou, T. (2005). Computational Workload Prediction for Grid oriented Industrial Applications: The case of 3D-image rendering. *In proceedings of Cluster Computing and Grid 2005 (CCGrid2005) 2*, 962- 969.

Litke, A., Tserpes, K., Dolkas, K., & Varvarigou, T. (2005). A Task Replication and Fair Resource Management Scheme for Fault Tolerant Grids. *Lecture Notes in Computer Science*, 3470(Advances in Grid Computing - EGC 2005), 1022–1031.

Lyu, M. R. (1995). *Software Fault Tolerance*. Chichester, UK: John Wiley & Sons.

Martello, S., Pisinger, D., & Toth, P. (2000). New trends in exact algorithms for the 0-1 knapsack problem. *European Journal of Operational Research, 123*, 325–332.

Martello, S., & Toth, P. (1990). *Knapsack Problems: Algorithms and Computer Implementations*. John Wiley & Sons.

Meyer, P. L. (1970). *Introductory Probability and Statistical Applications* (2nd ed.), Chapter 11. Addison-Wesley.

Montgomery, D. C., & Runger, G. C. (2003). *Applied Statistics and Probability for Engineers*. An Interactive e-text, 3rd edition.

Nguyen-Tuong, A., & Grimshaw, A. S. (1998). *Using Reflection to Incorporate Fault-Tolerance Techniques in Distributed Applications*. Computer Science Technical Report, University of Virginia, CS 98-34.

Nguyen-Tuong, A. (2000). *Integrating Fault-Tolerance Techniques in Grid Applications*. PhD Dissertation, University of Virginia.

Nurmi, D., Brevik, J., & Wolski R. (2003). *Modeling Machine Availability in Enterprise and Wide-area Distributed Computing Environments*. UCSB Computer Science Technical Report Number CS2003-28.

Parra-Hernandez, R., Vanderster, D., & Dimopoulos, N.J. (2004). Resource Management and Knapsack Formulations on the Grid. *In Proc. of the 5th IEEE/ACM Int. Workshop on Grid Computing*.

Pisinger, D. (1995). *Algorithms for Knapsack Problems*. Ph.D. Thesis, Dept. of Computer Science, University of Copenhagen.

Plank, J. S., Casanova, H., Beck, M., & Dongarra, J. J. (1999). Deploying fault tolerance and task migration with NetSolve. *Future Gener. Comput. Syst., 15*(5), 745–755.

Preiss, B. R. (1999). *Data Structures and Algorithms with Object-Oriented Design Patterns in C++*. John Wiley & Sons.

Ramamritham, K., Stankovic, J. A., & Shiah, P. F. (1990). Efficient Scheduling Algorithms for Real-time Multiprocessor Systems. *IEEE Trans. on Parallel and Distributed Systems, 1*(2), 184-194.

Reed, D. A., Lu, C., & Mendes, C. L. (2006). Reliability challenges in large systems. *Future Generation Computer Systems, 22*, 293–302.

Sahni, S. (2004). *Data Structures, Algorithms, and Applications in Java.* 2nd Edition, Silicon Press.

Scheaffer, R. L. (1995). *Introduction to Probability and Its Applications* (2nd ed.), Section 4.9, (Duxbury).

Subramani, V., Kettimuthu, R., Srinivasan, S., & Sadayappan, P. (2002). Distributed job scheduling on computational grids using multiple simultaneous requests. *In Proc. of the 11th IEEE International Symposium on High Performance Distributed Computing*, Edinburgh, Scotland.

Varvarigou, T., & Trotter, J. (1998). Module replication for fault-tolerant real-time distributed systems. *IEEE Transactions on Reliability, 47*(1), 8-18.

Wang, F., Ramamritham, K., & Stankovic, J. A. (1995). Determining redundancy levels for fault tolerant real-time systems. *IEEE Trans. Computers, 44*.

Weissman, J. B. (1999). *Fault Tolerant Computing on the Grid: What are My Options?* HPDC 1999.

Weng, C., & Lu, X. (2005). Heuristic scheduling for bag-of-tasks applications in combination with QoS in the computational grid. *Future Generation Computer Systems, 21*, 271–280.

Wolski, R., Spring, N., & Hayes, J. (1999). The Network Weather Service: A Distributed Resource Performance Forecasting Service for Metacomputing. *Future Generation Computer Systems, 15*, 757-768.

Chapter X
Implementation and QoS for High–Performance GIServices in Spatial Information Grid

Fang Huang

Institute of Geo-Spatial Information Technology, University of Electronic Science and Technology of China, P.R. China

ABSTRACT

With the development of grid technology, the spatial information grid researches are also in progress. In China, the spatial information grid platform (abbreviation to SIG) not only can provide geo-spatial data services (GDS) for handling terabytes of geospatial data, but also can present processing functionality services (PFS) encapsulated from several Remote Sensing (RS) software to solve RS computing problems remotely. In particular, the spatial user can utilize some provided high-performance PFS to achieve those computing intensive tasks that lacking of the high-performance computing facility such as cluster or Condor platform. Unfortunately, the existing SIG paid litter attention to Geographic Information Science (GIS) field, as a result, the constitution of PFS related to GIS, especially the high-performance GIServices (HP-GIServices), are becoming the main issues for SIG's next research. Lacking of GIServices mainly resulted from the limitations of SIG architecture, difficulty of extracting parallel GIS functionalities modules, as well as the complexity for services implementation and encapsulation. Based on existing SIG platform, this chapter proposes the improved architecture for SIG, upon which the constituted GIS nodes can provide GIServices. Within the new architecture, some parallel GRASS GIS (Geographic Resources Analysis Support System)[1] algorithms programs, which are built by different parallelization patterns and can run in cluster with better efficiency, are encapsulated to high-performance GIServices guiding by certain generic mode. Lastly, the QoS (quality of services) indexes are proposed to evaluate the quality of the constituted HP-GIServices in SIG. From the tentative experiments and analyses, the facts demonstrate that this approach can reach our aims. In all, the chapter firstly gives an overview of existing SIG platform. Facing to the problem of lacking of HP-GIServices, the improved architecture, various parallelization patterns to extract parallel GIS algorithms based on GRASS GIS are proposed. Furthermore, the encapsulation guidance and QoS for evaluating HP-GIServices are also discussed.

SIG AND THE IMPORTANCE OF HP-GISERVICES

Grid can provide resources for sharing and collaboration through different administrative domains. Those resources can include hardware, software, data, and even frameworks (Expert Group, 2004). Virtual organization (VO) is the key concept in grid applications, and is defined as a temporal or permanent set of entities, groups or organizations that provide or use those resources (Foster and Kesselman, 1998). With the development of grid, the use of grid computing is continuously increasing and is being introduced into application fields such as biocomputing, finance and image processing, as well as consolidation in more traditional areas such as high-energy physics and geosciences (Blanquer et al., 2005). In particular, spatial information research plans such as DATA GRID in Europe,[2] Earth System Grid in the US,[3] and the Spatial Information Grid of China[4] are in progress.

Generally speaking, spatial information grid is a fundamental infrastructure that can collect and share all types of geospatial information rapidly and effectively, with powerful capabilities for service on demand, geospatial data management and information processing. SIG is an innovational framework that provides end users with approaches for querying, accessing, manipulating and analyzing the information available. In addition, SIG is a distributed environment that combines resources such as geospatial data and computing, story and processing tools to supply services to geospatial applications. (Jin, J.J., 2004).

Status Quo of SIG

SIG platform, one part of the whole spatial information grid in China, is constituted by 3 types of nodes, namely, data grid services node (DGS-Node), computing grid services node (CGS-Node) and management grid services node (MGS-Node), supplied by 4 different research units that located in different areas geographically. DGS-Nodes have several types' geo-data and various formats. CGS-Nodes mainly point to the computing platform including Cluster and Condor. Upon CGS-Nodes, some software as Titan (one type of commercial software for RS image processing),[5] PIPS (one parallel RS image processing software in cluster developed by CEODE, CAS),[6] are integrated into. MGS-Node can manage different types of nodes and the main communications and controlling issues related to the whole platform.

The various types of grid nodes are constructed based on basic grid middleware, SIG CONTAINER, which is a middleware combination of several grid tools selectively that is quite suitable for using grid technology in the geospatial field. When CONTAINER is installed in different Nodes, the basic protocol between different Nodes is achieved, as well as some tools or packages for Web Services encapsulation are also provided. Additional, it not only supports several OS (Operation System) such as Windows, Linux, but also has the capability of updating and version identification etc. (Huang, Z.C. et al., 2007)

Through the CONTAINER, DGS-Nodes and CGS-Nodes can provide geo-spatial data services (GDS) and processing functionality services (PFS) respectively. The former can handle terabytes of data; the latter not only provides normal RS services (came from sequential RS algorithms), but also offers some high-performance RS services (encapsulated from parallel RS algorithms in cluster with high performance and better efficiency). (Huang, F. et al., 2008)

In all, the whole services of SIG can be classified into:

- GDS for RS. This mainly focused on querying, retrieving, accessing, and presentation of raster data;
- Normal PFS for RS. Based on those geospatial data, some RS algorithms, e.g. provided by MODIS, Titan CGS-Nodes are encapsulated into normal RS PFS in SIG;
- High-performance PFS for RS. Those PFSs, e.g. located in PIPS CGS-Node, are encapsulated from some parallel RS algorithms that have high performance and better efficiency in high performance platform. Thus, those kinds of PFS can offer high processing capability than Normal PFS for RS.
- Moreover, the MGS-Node can present some state management services (SMS) for SIG. The supplied services varied from the state of node's registry, to the state of hardware resources, such as CPU, memory and disk.

Urged Problems in SIG

However, the existing SIG paid litter attention to Geographic Information Science (GIS), as a result, the constitution of PFS related to GIS, especially the high-performance GIServices (HP-GIServices), are becoming the main issues for SIG's next development. Lacking of high-performance GIServices mainly resulted from:

- Limitations of the existing SIG architecture. The existing architecture is not suitable to extend providing GIServices flexibly, because the GIS node construction and services procedure is much more different than that of RS;
- Difficulties of extracting some parallel GIS functionalities modules utilizing common commercial GIS packages. Those modules require running in high-performance computing platform with better speedup and efficiency; and
- Lacking of some instruction or guidelines for HP-GIServices implementation and encapsulation.

Owing to those limitations, most geospatial end users cannot access the services related to GIS available through SIG. Thus, the challenges that arise are how to overcome the architecture limitation and how to implement some GIServices, especially providing some high performance processing functionality with one easy and convenient approach in SIG.

Analyzing and Our Approach

Facing to the problems mentioned above, we need to take some measures. To the limitation of architecture, we need:

- Proposing one new or improved architecture of SIG. Under the new architecture, GIS node can be more easily to add into the existed SIG platform.

Thus, the left 2 problems mentioned above are ascribed into how to construct HP-PFS for GIS. According to the experience of the construction of RS, this problem can be solved by the following steps similarly:

Step 1: It's critical to get some parallel GIS programs with high speed-up and better efficiency in Linux cluster; and
Step 2: Guiding by some encapsulation mode, those programs can be encapsulated into SIG services;

Relatively, step 1 should be paid more attention for implementation high-performance GIServices, because:

- Utilizing commercial GIS packages, we can not get some parallel programs with certain GIS algorithms according with our demands, for we can not get any source codes of them; and
- Those commercial packages mostly run in Windows, while our computing platform is Linux system. From the point of performance and convenience, it will add extra difficulties to extract source codes.

Obviously, because those factors, the subsequent step cannot work due to lacking of some parallel GIS algorithms programs produced in step 1. With carefully studies, we select one open source GIS package in Linux, GRASS GIS, as our research object, which can overcome the difficulties in step 1. After the parallel GIS functionalities are reconstructed, the next is to discuss the way to encapsulate those parallel modules to HP-GIServices.

Thus, the following sectors will concentrate on:

- Discussing the improved architecture of SIG, upon which, the principle of constructing HP-GIServices are demonstrated;
- Utilizing GRASS GIS, several paralleling realization patterns are expounded. The experiment test demonstrate that those parallel modules utilizing the mentioned patterns can achieve better speed-up can be easily reconstructed; and
- Exploring the generic encapsulation mode, invoking procedure. Moreover, in order to evaluate the quality of those constructed HP-GIServices, some issues related to QoS (quality of services) are also discussed.

IMPROVED ARCHITECTURE OF SIG

As vector, one data structure type of GIS, has different characteristics from RS, on which make the algorithms based become relative complicated. The difference makes it much difficult to extract some parallel programs from the GIS package in Linux cluster, and to wrap into GIServices, especially into the high-performance GIServices. Meanwhile, the existing architecture of SIG considered litter to these aspects, resulting out that it become difficult to provide GIServices in SIG platform directly. Thus, the overall layout of SIG need be improved when considering these factors.

Improved Architecture

Different to old architecture, the new architecture, illustrated as Fig. 1, add some special GIS nodes to it (Huang, F. et al, 2007 (a)). Thus, when considering those GIS nodes, the overall arrangement will appear 4 types of nodes in SIG:

- SIG management & controlling node (SIG MC Node);
- geo-spatial data Grid Service node (GDS Node);
- processing functionality service node (PFS Node); and
- SIG Web portal.

SIG Web portal is the only entrance of SIG. Through the authentication and authorization, the user can select the appropriate geo-spatial services.

SIG MC Node is the controlling and management centre of SIG. It not only manages all kinds of the operations as authentication and authorization, transaction controlling in SIG Web portal, but also takes responsibilities for Grid services node, comprising updating of services registry information, version management, node maintenance, state controlling, resources scheduling and services controlling.

GDS Node can publish the storied RS/GIS data with the form of services through SIG. Those services called GDS for RS and GDS for GIS, respectively. The users can share or download them through SIG Web portal.

Figure 1. Improved architecture of SIG. In the initial stage, there are only some RS nodes. In the new arrangement, some GIS nodes are added and can provide some GDS and PFS of GIS. Especially, the new architecture facilitates providing high-performance GIServices.

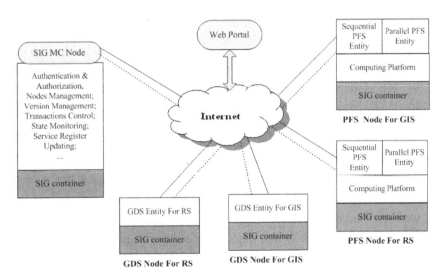

Figure 2. The scenario of providing HP-GIServices in the new SIG architecture accomplished by the collaboration of the whole nodes in SIG.

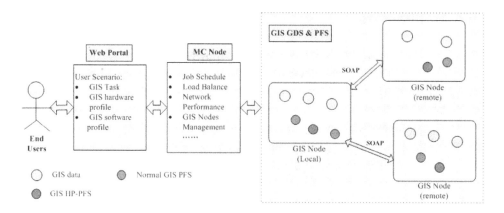

Meanwhile, PFS Node can serve PFS related to RS and GIS, respectively called PFS for RS and PFS for GIS. Among those 2 types of PFSs, they are respectively divided into normal PFS (sequential programs before encapsulation) and high-performance PFS (parallel programs in cluster before encapsulation) according to the computing environment and other factors. Thus, we can provide 4 kinds of PFSs, namely, S-PFS for RS/GIS and HP-PFS for RS/GIS.

Obviously, all those nodes are collected based on SIG CONTAINER, the fundamental part of SIG. Through CONTAINER, the different grid nodes can be easily to communicate and achieve one task collaboratively in the distributed heterogeneous environment.

Working Principle of Providing HP-GIServices in SIG

According to the architecture, the providing GIS GDS or PFS are located in local Nodes or in remote Nodes. Under this situation, the realization of GIServices, including high performance GIServices, is the collaboration result of the whole Nodes in SIG, i.e., comprising SIG MC Node and SIG Web portal. The GIServices located in different Nodes can be invoked alternately by means of Web Services among the Nodes. Scheduled by the MC Node through SIG CONTAINER, the scenario of the GIServices invoked by SIG is demonstrated in Fig. 2. When one GIS task is submitted, Web portal then will initialize the task firstly, and with the result of some profiles of hardware and software. According to the profiles, the SIG MC Node will dynamically select the appropriate GIServices from different Nodes in Registry Center of MC Node. Protected by some measures of SIG authentication and authorization, the GIServices will be complete successfully.

RECONSTRUCTION OF PARALLEL GIS MODULES BASED ON CLUSTER

From above, we know that our approach to get the parallel GIS functionalities is based on GRASS GIS with parallel computing technique. Thus, it needs some brief introduction to them firstly.

Brief Introduction to Parallel Computing

When you can not solve or want to solve a large problem faster than possible using single, commodity computer, the new technique of High Performance Computing (HPC) may help you. Many problems have been solved with HPC techniques that were impossible to solve with personal computers or individual workstations. HPC has had tremendous impact on all areas of computational science and engineering in academia, government, and industry. In general, HPC mainly divided into parallel computing, distributed computing and Grid computing.

Parallel computing is the technique that use of multiple computers or processors working together on a common task, which has the advantages of total performance and total memory. With the rapidly developing of the technologies with computer hardware and software, people can obtain and easily build the effective parallel computing environment, such as Beowulf cluster etc. According to the factor of sharing memory or disk, cluster falls into different architectures, namely, shared memory architecture, shared disk architecture, and shared nothing architecture.

Some specific tools, such as PVM (Parallel Virtual Machine),[7] especially MPI (Message Passing Interface),[8] are developed to design parallel programs. MPI is a standard library rather than a programming language. MPICH[9] is an implementation of MPI standard. The goals of MPICH are to provide an MPI implementation for important platforms, including clusters, SMPs (Symmetrical Multi-Processing), and massively parallel processors. It is also helpful for MPI implementation research and for developing newer and better parallel programming environments.

When one parallel program is built in cluster with MPI, there is still need some indexes to evaluate its performance. The important indexes are Speedup and Efficiency. Speedup indicates the execution time for the parallel algorithm, which is the ratio of T_S (the execution time for the single stream algorithm) to T_P (the execution time for the parallel) (Brawer, S., 1989):

$$Speedup = T_S / T_P \tag{1}$$

While efficiency is the ratio of Speedup to P, the number of process executing the algorithm:

$$Efficiency = Speedup / P \tag{2}$$

The closer the Efficiency to 1, the more efficient the parallel algorithm is.

Development Methods

In parallel programming, developers create a single computer program so that more than one processor can execute a program simultaneously. At runtime, the system creates a number of processes and each processor executes the program or part of the program. After they finish their works, the processes terminate.

The speedup that we achieve with parallel programming depends on the number of processors available, to extent which workloads are balanced among the processors, and the overhead for parallel computing. Therefore, in adapting an application for efficient parallel processing, we must choose the right parallel programming techniques so that the system can distribute the subtasks as evenly as possible among the processors. Data partitioning and function partitioning are the effective parallel programming technique for most applications.

When using data partitioning, programmers divide the data to be processed into portions, and then execute the same program on multiple processors. Each program in execution handles a portion of the data. Data partition best suits applications for which loops must perform the same operations on large data sets. In different loop iterations, the system performs the operations on different portions among the processes.

Function partitioning involves creating multiple unique processes and having them simultaneously perform different operations. This method is suitable for applications in which different, independent operations can be performed at the same time. (Brawer, S., 1989; Wang, F.J., 1992)

GRASS GIS

Referred to as GRASS, it is a Geographic Information System used for geospatial data management and analysis, image processing, graphics or maps production, spatial modeling, and visualization. GRASS is currently used in academic and commercial settings around the world, as well as by many governmental agencies and environmental consulting companies. It is widely used in many fields such as resource management, landuse planning, hydrology, mineral exploration, groundwater modeling, fires management etc.

GRASS GIS was originally developed at the US Construction Engineering Research Laboratories (USA-CERL) and is a full-featured GIS with a wide range of analytical, data management, and visualization capabilities. Currently GRASS GIS is a community-supported, free GIS distributed under the GNU Public License.[1]

Several Parallelization Patterns Based on Cluster

Parallel programming involves developing a single computer program in such a way that it can be executed by more than one processor simultaneously. From above, we know that data partitioning and function partitioning are effective parallel programming techniques for most applications. Taken account of the characteristics of cluster, the database and other factors of GRASS GIS, we tentatively put forward several parallel patterns for GRASS GIS. Those patterns mainly comprise multi-user data paralleling pattern (MUDPP) and GRASS GIS algorithm parallel pattern (GGAPP).

MUDPP is the method of data partitioning based on the multi-user runtime environment (MURE) and geo-database of GRASS (Huang, F. et al, 2007 (b)). In fact, MUDPP is one universal development method that can make several GRASS GIS modules paralleling with the development mode of M/S (Maser/Slave). GGAPP dedicates to summarize some general method based on several independent parallel GIS programs with function partitioning technique, which is much suitable adopting SPMD (single program multi data).

MUDPP and Its Implementation

When adopting data partition technique in GRASS directly, the problem occurs that the other nodes except the active user in cluster can not run any GRASS functions without the fundamental module support. This difference can make full use of the multi-users characteristic, here called MURE (multi-users runtime environment).

Principle of MUDPP

GRASS GIS was originally designed for the UNIX environment, and its current development is primarily Linux-based. Especially, GRASS has a file system database which is a standard subdirectory used to save geospatial data internally. A subdirectory tree, called Location, will automatically be created for each project region defined in GRASS. All project data are saved in Location. The Location can be further divided into map subdirectory called Mapsets (instantiated in Figure 3). PERMANENT is a special Mapset, which is automatically created by GRASS to store some important information about projection, resolution and extent of the project area. Other Mapsets can read the data from PERMANENT but has not the "write" permission. Each GRASS user can create one or several Mapsets in which he administers his own project data.

This database structure makes it possible to realize multi-user working environment, which several users can work with on one project at the same time in computer networks, without running the risk of changing or destroying another user's data. All the users belong to one location just as illustrated in Figure 3. For instance, there are several users (e.g. user01, user02 etc) in Location of RSGS-WK01. Thus those users can accomplish their own analysis processing with different input maps concurrently. Of course, they can read the same data at a same time. The resulting maps of any analysis are saved in the Mapset of the user's current GRASS session.

Making full use of the MURE described above, we put forward the MUDPP in cluster. In MUDPP, we establish several GRASS users both in master and slave nodes. As instantiated in Figure 4, the user0X (X=1,2, …, N, N is equal to the number of slave nodes) are located in corresponding slave node while user0 locates in master when running one analyzing functionality. Not same to MURE, those users work with the different parts of the same input map and generate processing results by invoking the same function module. When it received the processing instruction from the master user, the slave users firstly get the parts of the input map in this task (subtask), and then call the function model to process concurrently. After all slave nodes finished their own subtask, the master user will merge all the results located in different slave user as a whole output map. Of course, the output map must be

Figure 3. MURE of GRASS GIS, which utilize the database structure of GRASS GIS

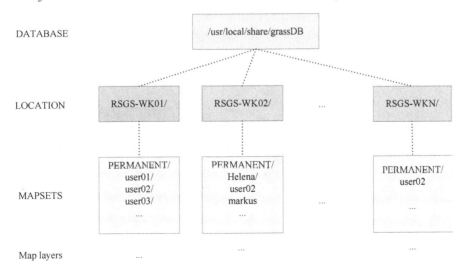

same as the processing result when the same task processed in sequential. The running mechanism of MUDPP has been instantiated in Fig. 5.

Improved Data Structure

Under MUDPP, it's much common that there will be conflict resulted from several computing nodes visit the same data. Thus, it's very important to improve the existing data structure. In order to protect the data visiting safely, we tentatively improved the data structure based on GRASS.

We also know that, raster and vector are the main data type of GRASS data (M. Neteler, 2002; 2004). Raster data are stored in the directories of cats, cell, cellhd, cell_misc, colr, fcell and hist, according to the raster data components. Namely there is, e.g., one raster data named archisites, then the file named

Figure 4. Based on MURE, MUDPP can be established in Linux cluster

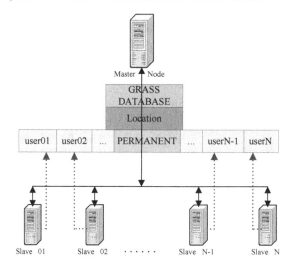

Figure 5. The running mechanism of MUDPP

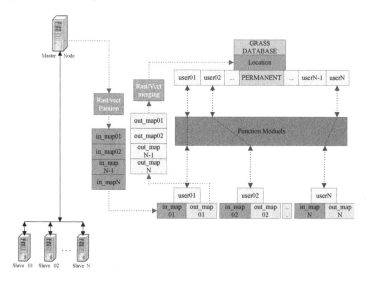

archisites will appear in the directories as cats, cell etc. However, the organization of vector data is different from raster. Mentioned to vector, it divides into 2 parts, geometry and attributes, which are stored in vector and dbf directory respectively. In directory of vector, e.g., forest is the name of one vector, there will be exist a directory called forest. In the forest directory, the corresponding file of coor, dbln, hist, sidx and topo, which are components of vector, will appear (illustrated in Fig. 6).

In Fig. 6, we add one specific directory or files, named lock, for raster and vector, respectively. For instance, one raster name archisites, and vector called forest, the corresponding locking file, archisites in lock directory, lock file in forest directory, will fulfill the responsibility. When open raster or vector, the lock tag will be changed to 1 from the default value of 0. Thus, the other Mapset can not visit the same dataset until the lock tag return to 0 after the former Mapset close the data.

Besides changing the data structure, the corresponding function as vector/raster reading/writing/closing also need to reconstruct, which has been expounded in the following pseudo codes.

```
/*According with the new parallel GIS data structure, the functions of read/write vector data have to
add the lock tag. Note: vect_read_old()_parallel()/vect-read_new()_parallel() and vect_close_parallel()
must be appear in pair.*/


// for reading use
vect_read_old()_parallel(){
        //setting the lock tag 1.
        ...
        //invoking the existing vect_read function.
        vect_read_old();
        ...
}

// for writing use
vect-read_new()_parallel(){
        //setting the lock tag 1.
        ...
        //invoking the existing vect_read function.
        vect_read_new();
        ...
```

MUDPP Generalization Model

According to MUDPP, the problems of data partition and merging in the course of input map and output map should be attached sufficient importance to. Because the GRASS has only 2 data type, raster and vector, we maybe easily realize MUDPP if we can solve the problems of partition and merging related to

Figure 6. In the left side, is the organization of GRASS database; In the right side, it is the new parallel data structure of cluster-based parallel GIS based on GRASS, which add lock file to avoid conflict when visiting one same data concurrently.

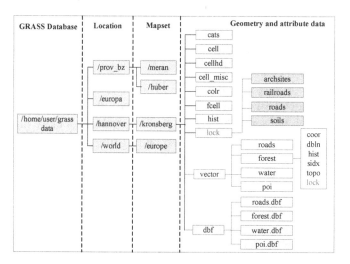

Figure 7. The general model of MUDPP and its realization mechanism

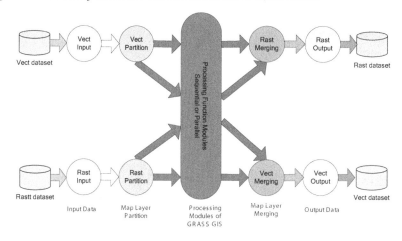

those 2 types. Sequentially, parts of the GRASS function modules can obtain high performance in cluster without changing much code. The mechanism of the generalization model is illustrated in Fig. 7.

Implementation of MUDPP

In order to accomplish MUDPP, it is requirement to establish some modules firstly, which includes 2 kinds: partitioning & merging modules, and universal module. The former can partition and stitch the input/output dataset of raster/vector. The latter can parallel several GRASS GIS functionalities with one universal program by invoking the other modules. The functionalities of those modules are listed in Table 1.

Table 1. Fundamental modules for implementing MUDPP

Module name	Functionality
RunModuelInOneUser.sh	Start GRASS GIS in one Mapset either in master or slave, thus the functionality modules can run on the active Mapset.
p.universal	The implementation of MUDPP.
p.r.in.partition	Finished the partitioning processing for raster map.
p.r.out.merge	Accomplished the merging procedure for raster map.
p.v.in.partition	Finished the partitioning processing for vector map.
p.v.out.merge	Accomplished the merging procedure for vector map.

Figure 8. Flow chart of MUDPP development. The universal module invokes the partitioning and merging modules with MPI under GRASS GIS environment

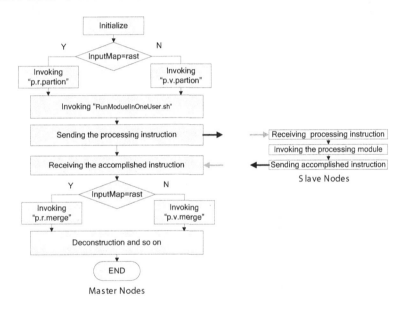

Fig. 8 illustrates the development of MUDPP, which based on the fundamental modules of GRASS GIS, and MPI.

GGAPP and Its Implementation

Through MUDPP, some parallel GRASS modules can be constructed. However, some modules or algorithms that has complicated data structure or the computing procedure requires the whole input data, e.g., shortest path (SP) algorithm, Inverse Distance Weighting (IDW) algorithm etc., are not suitable to use this pattern. To those algorithms, adopting function partition technique is the right option. Through the tentative test on some algorithms, we can get one parallel pattern for GRASS in the abstract, namely, GGAPP. GGAPP mainly focus on several independent algorithms with function partition technique, and then summaries the general parallel method that can guide the parallel algorithms implementation.

Up to now, GGAPP mainly has 2 types of methods: WCTAE/OTG (whole computing task assigned evenly/one time gathering) and EICTDE/EIG (each iteration computing task distributed evenly/ each iteration gathering). Supposing T is the sum computing task in one algorithm, and each task has N time's iterations. In each iteration, there is existing M times computing operations. And the number of the processors is P.

To the former, the whole computing task, e.g., generating contours number is T in r.contour module will be assigned to each processor in cluster, namely, the task of each node will be T/P. When each processor finished their own computing task, one node (master) will gather the results by using MPI function such as MPI_Allreduce(), MPI_Allgather(), and MPI_AllgatherV(). After that, the result will be written by master (illustrated in Fig. 9).

From above, we know that WCTAE/OTG method distribute the whole computing task before the iterations. Some algorithms or modules such as r.contour are suitable for this method.

Figure 9. Principle of WCTAE/OTG method

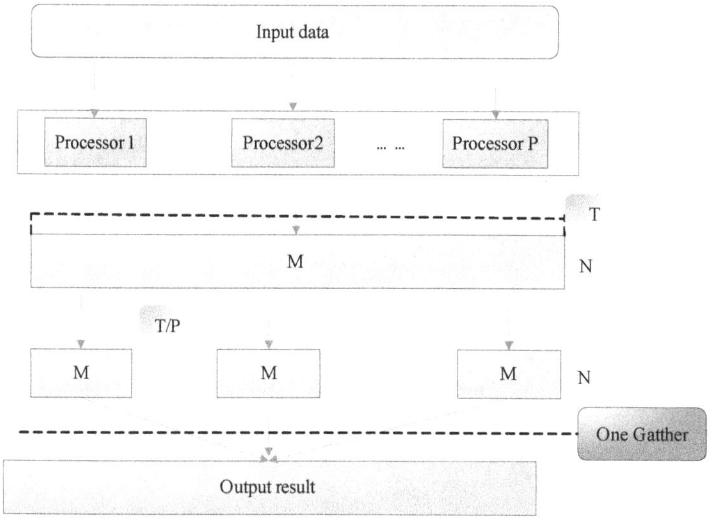

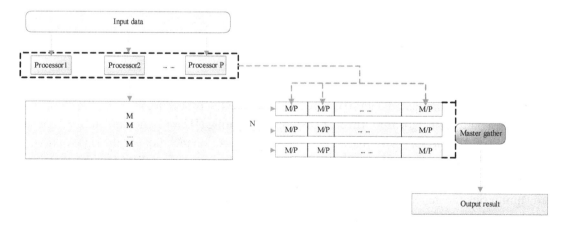

Figure 10. Principle of EICTDE/EIG method

However, EICTDE/EIG will not do so. During each iteration, the sum computing operations, e.g., you need to get one line (here, M will be column) interpolation data in r.idw2 module, will be distributed to each processor evenly. In other words, each processor will do M/P computing operations in the iteration. After the processors finished the computing, the master will gather the results from each node and then do the next iteration until the iteration is end (illustrated in Fig. 10). This method can be used in SP algorithm, IDW interpolation algorithm and so on.

GGAPP should better take account of SPMD, not M/S developing method. For instance, in the Dijkstra parallel algorithm different processor deal with different parts of the total nodes. Thus, each processor will need the whole input data and each processor will do different computing with these data. It's obvious that it should adopt SPMD method.

Experimental Results

Configuration of the Test Cluster

In order to invalidate the efficiency of those parallel modules, we established a test cluster by several independent PCs, which ascribes to shared disk architecture and the configurations are just described in Tab. 2.

Efficiency of the MUDPP

When running parallel modules reconstructed by MUDPP, the first step is starting the multi-users with shell program (instantiated in Fig. 11 a)). Figure11 b) demonstrates that several users invoke the functionality module to process.

Figure12 demonstrated the working principle and invoking procedure of MUDPP with the example of p.u.r.contour. The output map is illustrated in Fig. 12 c).

We select several modules, e.g., r.example, r.contour, r.thin, and their parallel module with MUDPP, respectively named p.u.r.example, pu.r.contour, and p.u.r.thin. Fig. 13 demonstrates their elapsed time in the test.

According to the formula (1), and (2), the speed-up and efficiency of them are illustrated in Fig. 14. We can see that the efficiency of MUDPP is acceptable with the best value of 0.612, although our test cluster is relatively sample, resulted from that there are some objective conditions, such as lacking of the specified Switch, poor performance PCs and the bad network environment.

In all, the modules under MUDPP can have acceptable speedup and efficiency than the sequential.

Table 2. Configuration of the test cluster

Node	IP	OS	Hardware	Software
C1	192.xx.xxx.175	CentOS 4.0	Intel(R) P4 3.00GHz 256M 160G	GRASS GIS 6.2.0 &
C2	192.xx.xxx.176	CentOS 4.0	Intel(R) P4 2.80GHz 512M 140G	MPICH 1.2.6 etc.
C3	192. xx.xxx.186	CentOS 4.0	Intel(R) P4 2.26GHz 512M 40G	
C4	192. xx.xxx.187	CentOS 4.0	Intel(R) P4 2.00GHz 256M 40G	

Figure 11. When running MUDPP, it needs to start multi-users first (a), and invoke the processing functionality (b)

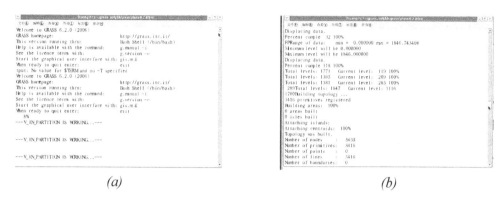

(a)   *(b)*

Figure 12. Process of r.contour running under MUDPP. a) is the whole input map, b) is the result of one user processed, and c) is the stitched outmap located in master node

(a)   *(b)*   *(c)*

Figure 13. Contrast of elapsed time with several sequential modules and their opposite parallel modules constructed with MUDPP

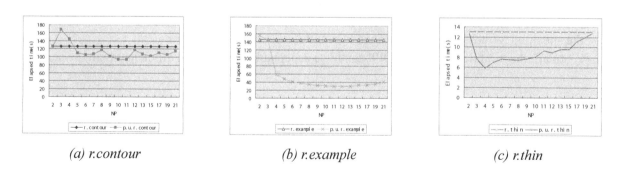

(a) r.contour   *(b) r.example*   *(c) r.thin*

Figure 14. Speed up and efficiency of the several parallel modules

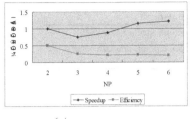 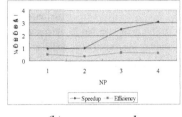 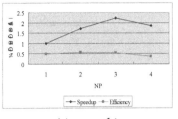

<table>
<tr><td> (a) p.u.r.contour </td><td> (b) p.u.r.example </td><td> (c) p.u.r.thin </td></tr>
</table>

Figure 15. The result of parallel IDW interpolation algorithm

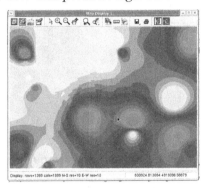

Efficiency of the GGAPP

We have reconstructed several parallel modules, such as p.a.v.net.path, p.a.r.contour, and p.a.r.idw2 etc. In order to demonstrate the efficiency of GGAPP, we only select one module, p.a.r.idw2, as the example. Figure 15 demonstrated the result of interpolation.

In the test, there are 2 group input data, group B has more interpolation points than A (illustrated in Table 3).

According to the elapsed time of the 2 group data, we can calculate their speed up and efficiency, which are illustrated in Fig. 16 and Fig. 17.

From the contrast, we know p.a.r.idw2 can obtain high speed up and better efficiency to the big size of data, which full of intensive computing operations. Moreover, from the test in several parallel modules reconstructed by GGAPP, we found that GGAPP can reach better efficiency than MUDPP.

ENCAPSULATION OF HIGH-PERFORMANCE GISERVICES

The parallel executed GRASS modules are available in cluster through these patterns. With some relevant tools, they can be wrapped into high-performance GIServices under certain encapsulation mode.

Table 3. 2 types of input data and their attributes description for the test of p.a.r.idw2

Group	Attributes of the input data
A	The file arch_sites has 25 interpolation points, and file size is almost 56k.
B	Another file named sites_cont has 3000 interpolation points and size beyond 19M.

Figure 16. Speedup contrast for the different input data in p.a.r.idw2

Figure 17. Efficiency contrast for the different input data in p.a.r.idw2

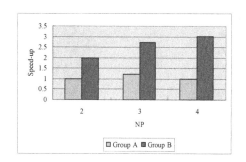

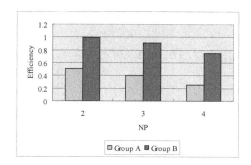

Figure 18. Generic encapsulation mode for Implementation High-performance GIServices

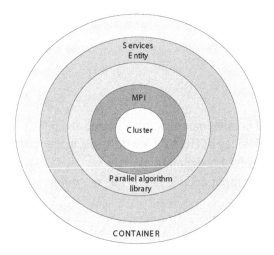

Generic Encapsulation Mode

In SIG, the platform supplied high performance GIServices are mostly concentrated on cluster. Thus, only taking cluster into account, the encapsulation model for high performance GIServices are mostly like Fig. 18. (Huang, F., 2007(a))

In the general encapsulation mode, the procedure can be divided into 5 layers. Based on the fundamental layers, layers of hardware and software, the extracted parallel algorithms formed the services entity layer. Within the SIG CONTAINER, the services entity can present corresponding GIServices.

Main Encapsulation Steps

As those parallel programs are running in Linux cluster, and still need the support of GRASS fundamental environment, all of those make its encapsulation become more different than that of RS PFS. Integrating with the existing SIG platform, 4 steps are summed up according to the generic encapsulation mode (illustrated in Fig. 19):

- **Step 1.** Extracted some executed parallel program (C programs) from GIS package. Those programs can reconstructed by the patterns mentioned above;
- **Step 2.** Those executed programs need be encapsulated to *.class* files with help of Java JNI (Java Native Interface). When the java program can be run successfully in local, it indicates the service entity is implemented successfully;
- **Step 3.** Publish the service entities (Java class files) to SIG services with Tomcat. As the result, the WSDL (Web Services Description Language) file will be produced;
- **Step 4.** The published high-performance GIServices should be registered to the SIG MC Node with corresponding tools.

Figure 19. The high-performance GIServices encapsulation mode. The details for each step are illustrated below the figure.

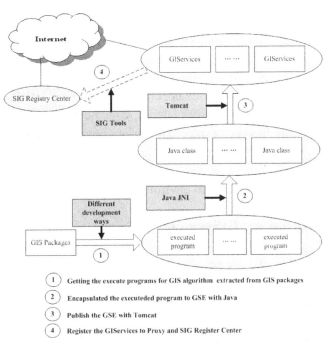

① Getting the execute programs for GIS algorithm extracted from GIS packages

② Encapsulated the executeded program to GSE with Java

③ Publish the GSE with Tomcat

④ Register the GIServices to Proxy and SIG Register Center

Figure 20. Invoking workflow of the published high-performance GIServices in SIG. Follow the figure, some explanations for the invoked steps are listed.

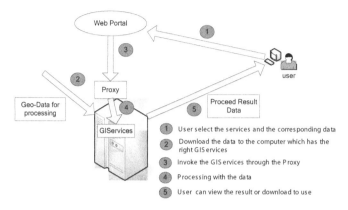

Invoking Workflow of HP-GIServies in SIG

When the published GIServices is needed, the user should select the corresponding data for processing located in SIG. After the processing accomplished, the results can be either viewed online or downloaded to the user's computer. Fig. 20 instantiates the whole work flow of the services invoked in SIG platform in detail.

QOS OF HP-GISERVICES

In the field of computer networking and other packet-switched telecommunication networks, the traffic engineering term quality of service (QoS) refers to resource reservation control mechanisms rather than the achieved service quality. Quality of service is the ability to provide different priority to different applications, users, or data flows, or to guarantee a certain level of performance to a data flow.

Two types of QoS attributes can be distinguished: quantitative and qualitative. Qualitative characteristics can refer to aspects such as service dependability and user satisfaction. Quantitative characteristics can refer to aspects such as network latency, CPU performance in terms of speed, or storage capability. Quality of Service has been explored in various contents. It is widely used in network related technologies. It is recently introduced into the field of Grid and Grid research to express service level. (Zhu, S.H., et al., 2007) Although, many scholars studied QoS of Grid, there is not exist one approach can solve all the QoS requirements in Grid environment.

QoS for High-Performance GIServices

There is also requirement to use one suitable way to validate the efficiency of the high-performance GIServices through those parallelization patterns. It seems to be the best method to contract the high-performance GIServices with the corresponding normal GIServices directly under identical conditions. In fact, the sequential GIServices may be developed based on some commercial GIS packages, which has different computing efficiency from GRASS GIS. Moreover, some uncertain factors such as the state of the network etc. may exist in the respective services procedure. Those factors must be considered to evaluate the services efficiency (SE). Thus, we propose the following formula to ascertain the services efficiency.

$$T_{GIServices} = T_{Data\_Acquision} + T_{Data\_Processing} + T_{Communication} + T_{Result\_Dowload} + T_{Others} \qquad (3)$$

Here, $T_{GIServices}$ represents the sum elapsed time of the whole services; $T_{Data\_Acquisition}$ is the consuming time of the data acquisition, by means of downloading or sharing; $T_{Data\_Processing}$ means the processing time of the program with the same datasets in one some computing platform; $T_{Communication}$ is the communication time related to network; $T_{Result\_Download}$ indicates the time for user to download the results; while the last part T_{Others} is the elapsed time for the remainder except the parts mentioned. The equation illustrates the consuming time of the GIServices in the dynamic environment, which can be used to represent the efficiency of GIServices indirectly.

When we suppose those 2 kinds of GIServices are in same conditions, namely, all of items expect $T_{Data\_Processing}$ have the identical values in (3). Therefore, the whole services efficiency depends on $T_{Data\_Processing}$, i.e., we can use it to represent the corresponding GIServices efficiency.

Example and Analyzing of SE QoS

In order to illustrate the excellent efficiency of high-performance GIServices, we select the sequential and parallel programs developed both from GRASS GIS, which can avoid the computing capability differences result from different GIS packages. Table 4 shows the value of $T_{Data\_Processing}$ in r.example and r.contour in the form of sequential and parallel respectively.

From the contrast results, we know that the values of $T_{Data\_Processing}$ have much difference. When they in the right numbers of processors (>2), the parallel modules has a better efficiency than the common modules. Therefore, we can deduce that under the same conditions, including the same dataset, network environment, computing platform and so on, the high performance GIServies has a better efficiency than that of the common GIServies, especially for the big size of data, whose processing are full of computation intensive.

Table 4. The approximate consuming time(s) of r.example and r.contour in sequential and parallel forms under different processors in the same computing platform

Module name	Number of the processes							
	1	2	4	6	8	10	12	20
r.example	158	/	/	/	/	/	/	/
p.universal/r.example	/	129	119	91	101	105	106	115
r.contour	148	/	/	/	/	/	/	/
p.universal/ r.contour	/	157	63	45	38	37	34	39

CONCLUSION AND FUTURE WORKS

Much work is still needed to explore efficient approaches to make GRASS GIS algorithms parallel in cluster except the mentioned 2 parallelization patterns. Moreover, there is also a requirement to construct more high-performance GIServices based on the new architecture with GRASS GIS. Specially, extra additional indexes need to propose to evaluate the QoS of the HP-GIServices. However, the test examples and analyses to the experimental GIServices have led to some useful conclusions:

- The new architecture is practicable for constructing GIServices;
- The parallelization patterns, especially GGAPP, are suitable for presenting some parallel GIS algorithms in cluster; As a result, the reconstructed paralleling modules have better speedup and efficiency than the opposite normal modules.and
- From the SE QoS experimental example, it demonstrated that the constructed high-performance GIServices have better quality.

ACKNOWLEDGMENT

The chapter is mainly extracted from my dissertation "Research on the Key Techniques and Application of Cluster-Based Parallel GIS", which is supported by the National High Technology Research and Development Program of China (863 Program), and under the instructions of Prof. Dingsheng Liu, and finished at the Key Laboratory, CEODE, CAS.

Especially, the background and some tentative results are based on the existed SIG platform, Guoqing Li, Jian Wang, and Wenyang Yu offered supports and suggestions. Meanwhile, Yi Zeng, Runxuan Yan etc. also present their helps in the procedure for services encapsulation. Lastly, Xicheng Tang presents excellent enlightenment to this work. Here, give the kindest regards to them.

REFERENCES

Blanquer, I., Hernández, V., Mas, F., & Segrelles, D. (2005). Medical databases and information systems—A framework based on web services and grid technologies for medical image registration. *Lecture Notes in Computer Science 3745*, 22–33.

Brawer, S. (1989). *Introduction to parallel programming*. San Diego, CA: Academic Press.

Expert Group (2004). *Next Generation Grids 2*. European Commission, Brussels, ftp://ftp.cordis.europa.eu/pub/ist/docs/ngg2_eg_final.pdf

Foster, I., & Kesselman, C. (1998). *The GRID: Blueprint for a New Computing Infrastructure*. Morgan Kaufmann Inc., San Francisco.

Huang, F., Liu, D. S., Li, G. Q., Zeng, Y., & Yan, Y. X. (2008). Study on Implementation of High-performance GIServices in Spatial Information Grid. ICCS 2008, *LNCS 5102*, 605-613.

Huang, F., Liu, D. S., Li, G. Q., Zeng, Y., Yu, W. Y., Wang, S. G., & Liu, P. (2007a). Discuss on High Performance Grid-Based GIS [in Chinese]. *Geomatics World, 4*(5), 33-39.

Huang, F., Liu, D.S., Liu, P. et al. (2007b). Research on Cluster-Based Parallel GIS with the Example of Parallelization on GRASS GIS. *GCC 2007*, 642-649.

Huang, Z. C., Li, G. Q., Du, R. et al. (2007). SIGRE — An Autonomic Spatial Information Grid Runtime Environment for Geo-Computation. APPT 2007, *LNCS 4887*, 322-329.

Jin, J. J. (2004). *The applications of grids in geosciences* [in Chinese], http://support.iap.ac.cn/bbs/viewthread.php?tid=176&extra=page%3D1.

Li, G. Q. (2005). *Report on the SIG*, Beijing, China Remote Sensing Ground Station of Chinese Academic of Science.

Neteler, M., & Miltasova, H. (2002). *Open Source GIS: A GRASS GIS Approach.* London: Kluwer Academic Publishers.

Neteler, M., & Miltasova, H. (2004). *Open Source GIS: A GRASS GIS Approach* (Section Edition), London: Kluwer Academic Publishers.

Wang, F. J. (1992). A Parallel GIS-Remote Sensing System for Environmental Modeling. *IGARSS'92*, 15-17.

Zhu, S. H., Du, Z. H., Chen, Y. N., Chai, X. D., & Li, B. H. (2007). QoS Enhancement for PDES Grid Based on Time Services Prediction. *GCC 2007*, 423-429.

ENDNOTES

[1]   http://grass.itc.it/.
[2]   http://eu-datagrid.web.cern.ch/eu-datagrid/.
[3]   http://www.earthsystemgrid.org/.
[4]   http://159.226.224.52:6140/Grid/application/index.jsp.
[5]   http://www.otitan.com/index.shtml.
[6]   http://www.ceode.ac.cn/en/.
[7]   http://www.csm.ornl.gov/pvm/.
[8]   http://www.mpi-forum.org/.
[9]   http://www-unix.mcs.anl.gov/mpi/mpich

Chapter XI
The Interactive Computing of Web Knowledge Flow:
From Web to Knowledge Web

Xiangfeng Luo
Shanghai University, P.R. China

Jie Yu
Shanghai University, P.R. China

ABSTRACT

Web Knowledge Flow provides a technique and theoretical support for the effective discovery of knowledge innovation, intelligent browsing, personalized recommendation, cooperative team work, and the semantic analysis of resources on Internet, which is a key issue of Web services and Knowledge Grid/ Web(Zhuge, 2007; Zhuge, 2005). In this chapter, first the authors introduce some basic concepts related to Web Knowledge Flow. Next they illustrate the concepts of interactive computing, including the Web interaction model, the implementation of interactive computing and the generation of Web Knowledge Flow. Finally, the applications of Web Knowledge Flow will be given.

WEB KNOWLEDGE FLOW

Concept of Web Knowledge Flow

Many efforts have been done on the knowledge flow area. Some researchers study knowledge flow based on the organization of workflow, which is about the knowledge demand of the logic relationship and the role between the tasks of workflow. It can be realized by the way of pushing (Zhao, 2001; Wolverton, 1997). Taxonomy model aims at providing an overall picture of grid workflow verification and validation

(Chen, 2007). Chen and Yang develop a novel checkpoint selection strategy that can adaptively select not only necessary but also sufficient checkpoints (Chen, 2007). Spiral model proposed by Nonaka describes the knowledge flow from epistemology to ontology. In the epistemology, knowledge flows from implicit knowledge to explicit knowledge, then from explicit knowledge to implicit knowledge. In the ontology, knowledge flows from person to group, and then from group to person (Nonaka, 1994; Nonaka, 1995). Based on Spiral model, Knowledge Flow Dynamic Model (*KFDM*) proposed by Nissen makes the knowledge flow over time explicitly. It can support a multi-dimensional representation that enables a new approach to analyze and visualize diverse knowledge flow patterns in enterprises (Nissen, 2002). Knowledge energy model proposed by Zhuge et al. takes knowledge energy as the driving cause to form an autonomous knowledge flow and explores the hidden principles (Zhuge,2005). The principles of knowledge flow engaged in cooperative cognition are explored by Dou from the perspective of learning and cognition evolution (Dou, 2006). Textual knowledge flow proposed by Luo et al. aims to provide an effective technique tool and theoretical support analysis for the discovery and cooperation of knowledge innovation, intelligent browsing, and personalized recommendation in Web services and e-Science Knowledge Grid (Zhuge, 2002). Other knowledge flow models are peer-to-peer team knowledge sharing and management based model (Luo, 2008), agent based model (Nissen, 2004), and the trust based model (Guo, 2005), etc.

Definition 1 (Web Knowledge Flow, WKF)

Web Knowledge Flow(WKF) is a sequential link between topics with rich semantics, which is activated by user's demands and changes with the demands.

Compared with other multiple types of knowledge flow (Nissen, 2002; Zhuge, 2005), WKF has some special characteristics as follows.

- WKF reflects the flow of knowledge between topics on Internet;
- WKF contains rich semantics between topics, which leads to similar WKF, associated WKF, and causal WKF etc;
- WKF is activated by user's demands, in other words, WKF is a kind of service on demands;
- WKF changes with the change of user's demands.

When a user browses topics, a WKF is a browsing path of topics recommended to the user. When some browsing paths of topics are activated at the same time, one of them should be chosen and recommended according to user's demand.

As can be seen, Web knowledge flow provides a technique and theoretical support for the effective discovery of knowledge innovation, intelligent browsing, personalized recommendation, cooperative team work, and the semantic analysis of resources on Internet, which is a key issue of Web services and Knowledge Grid.

According to different relationship between nodes in Web Knowledge Flow, WKF can be classified into Association Web Knowledge Flow (Luo, 2008) and Similarity Web Knowledge Flow (Luo, 2008).

Definition 2 (Association Web Knowledge Flow, AWKF)

Association knowledge flow is a sequential link with rich semantics between associated topics, which is activated by user's demands and changes with the demands.

Compared with other knowledge flows, *AWKF* has the following distinguished characteristics.

- *AWKF* can reflect the flow of knowledge between topics;
- *AWKF* can contain associated relation between topics;
- *AWKF* can be activated by users' demands, i.e., *AWKF* is a kind of service on-demand;
- *AWKF* can updates with users' demands.

When a certain user browses topics in the Web or an e-Science environment, *AWKF* is a browsing path of topics. When several browsing paths of topics are activated at the same time, they should be evaluated according to the user's demand and their contents, and then one of them should be chosen and recommended to the user.

Definition 3 (Similarity Web Knowledge Flow, SWKF)

Similarity knowledge flow is a sequential link whose only difference from *AWKF* is that the relationship between topics in SKF is similarity relationship.

Therefore, if the user wants to browse similar topics on the Internet, an SWKF is helpful.

We know that web resources have two features in common:

- **Various types of representation:** Web resources exist in many kinds of representation: video, audio, text, and so on. First, it is impossible that the huge amounts of web resources are represented in one form. Second, different users have different requirement, which make the variety necessary. Even for one user, he/she must have different requirements in different time;
- **Out-of-order organization statement:** Web resources are distributed in out-of-order statement, which generates some challenges to the user's web activity, such as web search. First, out-of-order statement makes resource searching cost lots of time, which affects the search quality. Secondly, out-of-order statement can not lead to high accuracy of search.

On the other hand, requirement of users is not limited to one form of media. For example, the user may want to browse the web resources whose contents meet his requirement, whatever its representation form is.

Therefore, in order to facilitate high qualified web activity it is indispensable to do the following work:

- Unify the web resources into one representation;
- Organize all the web resources in order;

These are the basis for the generation of WKF. Element Fuzzy Cognitive Map(E-FCM) is used to represent web resource, whatever it is a video, audio, or text file. Semantic Link Network(SLN) is used to organize the web resources in order by introducing certain relationship. Next sections will include the contents of these two aspects.

Representation of Web Resource

Element Fuzzy Cognitive Maps (E-FCMs) have a good capability to represent Web resource with rich semantics and can be understood by machine easily (Kardaras, 2006; Perusich, 2006). Therefore, E-FCM is proposed to represent Web resources.

Term 1 (Element Fuzzy Cognitive Map, E-FCM)

Element Fuzzy Cognitive Map (E-FCM) is a fuzzy cognitive map, whose element concepts are represented by keywords; state values of element concepts are computed by the function of its frequency, position and font size in paragraphs or a section; theme concept is represented by the implied semantics of co-occurrence keywords appearing in a topic; the relations between concepts and their weights are represented by the relations between keywords and topic as well as their weights.

Figure 1 gives an example of E-FCM generated by the algorithm in (Luo, 2008), the vector of element concepts is {Smoking, Life, Nicotinism, Breath}

The knowledge of topic is represented by E-FCMs, which reflects the keywords' relations and their weights as well as the state values of co-occurrence keywords in a topic. Semantic information of co-occurrence keywords expressed by E-FCM is richer than a set of separate keywords because E-FCM stores topic information instead of the separate keywords of topic.

According to the capability of tagging topics, concepts can be classified into three categories (Luo, 2008): general concept, functional concept and seldom concept. Different type of concept has different contribution to the computing of web knowledge flow.

Figure 1. "Smoking on the life of people" represented by E-FCM (denoted as Topic 1)

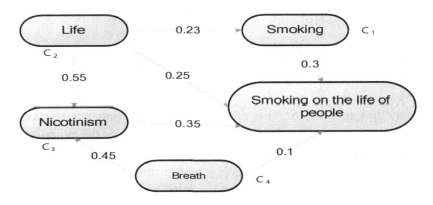

Term 2 (General Concept, GC)

General concept is an element concept of E-FCM, which is a ubiquitous element concept appearing in an E-FCMs/topics library.

General concept has low capability of tagging topics for it has general semantics in an E-FCMs/topics library. For example, in the domain of semantic Web, the keyword "semantic" has no specific function to tag topics because it is a ubiquitous concept in the topics library.

Term 3 (Functional Concept, FC)

Functional concept is an element concept of E-FCM, which has specific semantics in an E-FCMs/ topics library.

Functional concept has high capability to tag topics for it has specific semantics in a domain. For example, in the domain of semantic Web, the keyword "OWL", "WSDL" have a specific function to tag topics because these keywords have particular meanings in the presented topics library.

Term 4 (Seldom Concept, SC)

Seldom concept is an element concept of E-FCM, which has a low frequency in a domain E-FCMs /topics library.

Seldom concept has low capability to tag topics for it has a low frequency in a domain. For example, in the domain of semantic Web, the keyword "Knowledge Grid" has low frequency in the presented topics library.

The semantic value of a seldom concept is bigger than a general concept. So when calculating semantic similarity degrees between topics, the common seldom concepts will bring bigger influences on the semantic similarity degrees than the common general concepts.

Ordered Organization of Web Resources

Semantic Link Network (SLN) (Zhuge, 2007) can link not only textual topics but also multimedia topics (e.g. relation of topics between text and video). Therefore SLN is introduced to link these Web resources based on the discovery of associated/similar topics, which can guide users' intelligent browsing of topics.

Term 5 (Semantic Link Network, SLN)

A semantic link network consists of semantic nodes and semantic links (relations) between nodes. A semantic node can be a semantic community, a schema, a concept, a feature, an entity or an identity (Zhuge, 2007).

The semantic link network (*SLN*) is designed to establish semantic relationships among various resources (data, image and various documents) aiming at extending the hyperlink network World Wide Web to a semantic-rich network (Zhuge, 2007).

Herein, the semantic nodes are the topics (e.g. multimedia topics or textual topics) and the semantic relations are the associated relations in a semantic link network. The knowledge flow based on *SLN*

Figure 2. 2-layer hierarchy organization of Web resources

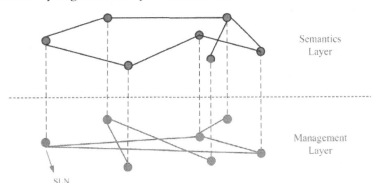

guides users to browse the cross media information* that makes the Web browsing more vivid, diversiform, and visual.

The web resources are organized in a 2-layer hierarchy way which is illustrated in Figure 2. The first layer is called semantics layer that the resources are organized by content and relationship with each other. The second layer is called management layer which is based on P2P structure (Dejan, 2002). Each node in these two layers is a SLN and represented by feature set. When a user's requirement is presented, first with semantics computing technique, the node which matches the requirement is located in semantics layer. Then mapping to management layer, the physical position this resource is got by P2P computing. Finally, similarity and association relationship computing is used to get the E-FCM which represents the specific topic and recommended to the user. After analyzing user's activities, analysis result is used in finding the node which has some relationship with user's preference. Then again, the node is mapped to management layer to get the physical position. In this way, a WKF is generated.

As can be seen, in this hierarchy structure semantics layer is used for high accuracy of web activity. Nodes on this layer are organized by semantics relationship which makes finding specific topic more accurately. Management layer is used for high efficiency of web activity. It has the special use of managing and locating resources. With P2P technique, the physical position can be got efficiently. In addition, by dividing all the web resources into several SLN, this hierarchy can deal with the great number of web resources well.

INTERACTIVE COMPUTING OF WEB KNOWLEDGE FLOW

When a user is browsing on the Internet, the topics he wants to read have some common characteristics in most cases. Maybe they all limited to one domain, or focus on one event. In other words, the topics have some relationship with each other. These topics that have the same relationship with each other are the nodes of WKF. How to find these topics according to a user's requirement is an important task. The key technique is interactive computing. It is a method which can get quantified information by analyzing user's requirement and behavior.

The key issues of generation of the WKF are the discovery of certain relations and the construction of the semantic links between topics. The discovery methods of association rules include Apriori

(Agrawal, 1993), sequential pattern mining (Agrawal, 1995); episodes mining (Mannila, 1997); space association rules mining (Koperski, 1995); ring based association rules mining (Ozden, 1998); negative association rules mining (Savasere, 1998); association rules mining between affairs (Savasere, 1998); and calendar shopping basket analysis (Lu, 1998), etc. This section will introduce how to get the nodes of WKF and generate WKF by interactive computing.

Web Interaction Model

We know that Interaction Machine (Wegaer, 1997; Wegner, 1998; Goldin, 1998) is the extension of Turing Machine (Goldin, 1999).

Term 6 (Interaction Machines, IM)

IMs extend TMs by adding dynamic input/output (read/write) actions that interact directly with an external environment (Wegner, 1998).

Interaction machines may have single or multiple input streams and synchronous or asynchronous communication, and can differ along many other dimensions, but all IMs are open systems that express dynamic external behavior beyond that computable by algorithms.

Term 7 (Interaction Histories)

Observable behavior of IMs is specified by interaction histories.

As can be seen, the process of Web exploration can be modeled by interaction machine. The prediction of the user's next behavior is not only related to the user's present behavior and the history of his/her exploration. The behavior is represented by the semantics of the topic he/she browses. To describe the user's web activity and build the web knowledge flow, Web Interaction Model is given.

Definition 4 (Web Interaction Model, WIM)

Web Interaction Model is used to build Web Knowledge Flow. It is a triad $M = (S, I, F)$, in which

- S is an enumerable set of states which describe the user's browsing state. Browsing state reflects the topics that the user have browsed and the interest that the user is interested in;
- I is an enumerable set of input states. Input state describes the user's behavior in browsing.
- $F : S \times I \rightarrow S \times O$ is a computable function which is called semantic computing of Web Knowledge Flow.

In WIM, the same input states may correspond to different output states, because of the history of browsing. With WIM, we can predict the user's interest and recommend corresponding pages to him/her.

The properties of WIM are as following:

- Dynamic binding of inputs: the input state may depend on the previous output. The user may react differently to different recommended topics which affect the input state;

- Semantics dependence: interactive computing is processing on the semantics layer of the organization of web resources. How to get the physical position of resources is the duty of management layer. In the process of computing, the semantics of topics are taken into account which makes the recommendation of topics based on content;
- History dependence: output can depend on previous history of browsing. The history of browsing is the basis for interactive computing;
- Hidden information: The user's interest is hidden and can be attained by semantics interactive computing with browsing history.

Implementation of Interactive Computing*

Semantics interactive computing is the key essential in WIM. It performs the task of semantics computing, and can be implemented by Markov Chain.

Assumption 1: Assuming that the process of user's browsing is in accord with homogeneous discrete Markov Chain. Therefore, the user's browsing process can be represented by a sequence which is composed of the web pages that he/she browsed.

This Markov Chain is represented by a triad $C = (X, P, \lambda)$, in which

- X is a discrete random variable. It is represented by an E-FCM which represents the topic user has browsed.
- P is the transition probability matrix. Each element p_{ij} of this matrix is the probability that $topic_i$ transits to $topic_j$, i.e. after a user browses $topic_i$ the probability that he/she browses $topic_j$.

$$
P = \begin{vmatrix}
p_{11} & p_{12} & p_{13} & \cdots & p_{1n} \\
p_{21} & p_{22} & p_{23} & \cdots & p_{2n} \\
& & \cdots & & \\
p_{n1} & p_{n2} & p_{n3} & \cdots & p_{nn}
\end{vmatrix},
$$

n denotes the number of the total topics.

- λ is the initial state distribution of the topics. $\lambda = (p_1, p_2, ..., p_n)$

In this Markov Chain, how to decide P is a key task. Before discussing the implementation of this model, some structures used here will be introduced.

Definition 5: History Vector, VH(t)

For each user, we use a vector $VH(t) = h_1, h_2, ..., h_n)$ to represent the history of his/her browsing history till the moment t. If the user browses the ith topic, then the corresponding element value v_i will be added by 1. The initial the value of V is $VH(t) = (0, 0, ..., 0)$.

Definition 6: Visiting State Vector, VS

Visiting State Vector $VS = (vs_1, vs_2, ..., vs_n)$ is a vector which labels the topics that has been visited. If topic$_i$ have been visited, then the vs_i should be set 1.

Definition 7: User State Vector, US(t)

User state vector $US(t) = us_1, us_2, ..., us_n)$ is a vector which indicates the user's state which is related to the content of the topics that he/she browses. When a user browses topic$_i$, the topics which are similar to topic$_i$ may also be interests for the user. Therefore, the user state $US(t)$ should be computed by the following formula:

$$us_i = \frac{\sum_{j=1}^{n} v_j \cdot sdm_{ij}}{\sqrt{\sum_{j=1}^{n} v_j^2} \cdot \sqrt{\sum_{j=1}^{n} sdm_{ij}^2}}$$

On the other hand, the next topic the user may browse is related to not only other users' browsing history, but also the semantic relationship. The topic that has association relationship with this topic might be the one the user wants to browse next time. Therefore, the association relationship between topics should be taken into account.

$$P = \alpha \cdot ADM + \beta \cdot S$$

$$s_{ij} = \frac{a_{ij}}{\sum_{j=1}^{n} a_{ij}}$$

α and β are the weight of *ADM* and *S*, and $\alpha + \beta = 1$. $A = (a)_{ij}$ denotes the number of visiting pair *i-j* in all the users' visiting history. Therefore, for each user, the user's state in the next moment *NS(t)* can be computed by the following formula:

$$VS(t) = US(t - 1) \times A$$

If all the topics have not been visited, then the element which has the biggest value In *NS(t)* will be the topic that the user will probably interested in. Obviously, the user doesn't want to visit the topic that he/she has already visited again. In this paper, an AND operation is used to filter this kind of topics by the following formula:

$$US(t)' = US(t) \text{ and } VS$$

Therefore, the biggest element in *NP(t)'* may correspond to the topic which will be the one that the user will be most interested in. And in the application, this topic can be recommended to the user.

As can be seen, in the process of semantics interactive computing, not only all the user visiting histories but also semantics relationship between topics are related to the state of topic. In other words, the content of the topics is taken into account in this paper which improves the accuracy of state description.

Generation of Web Knowledge Flow

Based on the discussion above, the main steps of construction of Web Knowledge Flow should be the following:

1. According to the user's requirement, generate its corresponding feature vector;
2. With similarity relationship, get the first node of WKF;
3. According to the user's behavior, update the history vector and visiting state vector.
4. With similarity SLN, attain the state of the user which is represented by *US(t)*;
5. With association SLN and the visiting history of all the users, attain the transition probability matrix *P*;
6. With visiting state *VS*, get the new *NS(t)'*, and take the element which has the biggest value as the next node in WKF, and update the visiting history vector by $h_i = h_i + 1$;
7. If all the value in *NS(t)'* are less than the threshold, then stop and the WKF is generated. Otherwise, go to 5).

In this way, the Web Knowledge Flow is generated. As can be seen that due to the semantics relationship including similarity and association relationship between topics are involved in the process of generation, the generated WKF can well reflect the user's interest and meet his/her requirement.

APPLICATIONS

In order to acquire many new customers and keep the existing ones, Internet-base business provides more objective information and better service. This section will show how to apply WKF to one important field, Web personalization.

With the help of user's browsing activities, interactive computing can be used to recommend some topics that the user may be interested to the user. For example, a user's browsing activities are traced, and some information are shown in table 1.

Then the corresponding history vector *HV(t)* is generated: $hv_{83}=hv_{79}=hv_{88}=hv_{228}=hv_{339}=hv_{443}=hv_{506}=hv_{542}=hv_{575}=hv_{704}=hv_{708}=hv_{913}=hv_{916}=hv_{925}=hv_{968}=1;\ hv_{847}=hv_{898}=2.$

We also generate the SLN with similarity relationship and SLN with association relationship of 1000 Web pages which belong to the field of environment. The corresponding SLN are shown in figure 3 and figure 4, respectively.

Then the corresponding WKF which is composed of five nodes(shown in figure 5) is generated. From the user's browsing history, we can see that the user interested in the topics about climate change. And the nodes of generated WKF are also focus on this topic. Therefore, WKF can well grasp the user's interest and recommend corresponding pages to him/her. In addition, it can be seen that the nodes in

Table 1. Records of browsing activity

Topic	Times of Browsing
Asia will bear brunt of climate change-linked deaths WHO	1
Aussies Kyoto should have been ratified	1
Australia, New Zealand to cooperate on climate change	1
Canada blasted by own environmental watchdog	1
Environmentalist pleads not guilty in OR	1
EU to adopt climate fight plan despite differences	1
FACTBOX What is the Kyoto Protocol	1
France's Besson plans film focusing on environment	1
Hewlett Foundation plans climate change grants	1
House bill lets California restrict car emissions	1
Nations seek compromise in climate change talks	1
Minorities the forgotten victims of climate change	2
Lawyers say considering court challenge to Korea	2
Nature and man jointly cook Arctic	1
New Australian PM seals Kyoto ratification at climate meet	1
Obama, Clinton top McCain on environment votes report	1
At E.U. summit, climate change billed as major security risk	1

Figure 3. SLN with similarity relationship

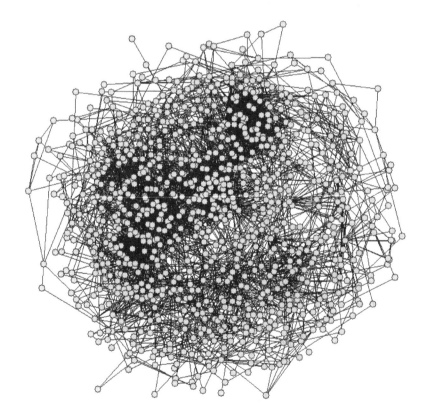

Figure 4. SLN with association relationship

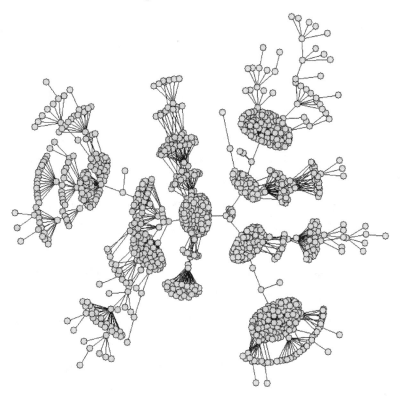

Figure 5. Generated WKF

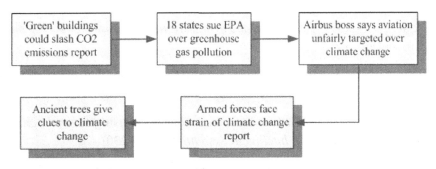

WKF are dispersed in SLN with similarity and SLN with association relationship. It accords with the dynamics features of WKF. With this generated WKF, the user can get his/her interested topics and doesn't need to search them by himself/herself on the Internet.

REFERENCES

Agrawal, R., & Srikant, R. (1995). Mining sequential Patterns. *Proceedings of the 11th International Conference on Data Engineering* (pp. 3-14). IEEE Computer Society Press.

Agrawal, R., Imielinski, T., & Swami, A. (1993). Mining association rules between sets of items in large databases. *In Proceedings of the 1993 ACM SIGMOD International Conference on Management of Data* (pp. 207-216). ACM Press.

Ashok S., Omiecinski, E., & Shamkant, N. (1998). Mining for Strong Negative Associations in a Large Database of Customer Transactions. *In Proceedings of the 14th International Conference on Data Engineering* (pp. 494-502). IEEE Computer Society Press.

Chen, J., & Yang, Y. (2007). Adaptive Selection of Necessary and Sufficient Checkpoints for Dynamic Verification of Temporal Constraints in Grid Workflow Systems. *ACM Transactions on Autonomous and Adaptive Systems*, *2*(2), Article No. 6.

Chen, J., & Yang, Y. (2008). A Taxonomy of Grid Workflow Verification and Validation. *Concurrency and Computation: Practice and Experience, 20*(4), 347-360.

Dejan M. S., Kalogeraki, V., & Lukose, R. (2002). *Peer-to-Peer Computing* (Tech. Rep. HPL-2002-57). HP Lab.

Dou, W., Chen, G., Cheung, S. C., & Cai, S. (2006). Cooperative Cognition and Its Implementation under Web Environment. *Proceedings of the Second International Conference on Semantics, Knowledge and Grid* (pp. 46). Washington, DC: IEEE Computer Society.

Goldin, D., & Wegner, P. (1998). *Persistence as a form of interaction* (Tech Rep: CS-98-07). Brown University.

Goldin, D., & Wegner, P. (1999). *Behavior and expressiveness of persistent Turing machines* (Tech Rep: CS-99-14). Brown University.

Guo, W. Shi, X., Cao, L., & Yang, K. (2005). Trust in Knowledge Flow Networks. *Proceedings of International Conference on Semantics, Knowledge and Grid* (pp. 405 -412).

Kardaras, D., & Karakostas, B. (2006). E-Service adaptation using fuzzy cognitive maps. *The 3rd International IEEE Conference on Intelligent Systems* (pp. 227-230).

Koperski, K., & Han, J. (1995). Discovery of Spatial Association Rules in Geographic Information Databases. *Proceedings of the 4th International Symposium on Large Spatial Databases* (pp. 47-66), Springer Publisher.

Lu, H., Han, J., & Feng, L. (1998). Stock movement prediction and n-dimensional inter-transaction association rules. *Proceedings of the 3rd ACM-SIGMOD Workshop on Research Issues on Data Mining and Knowledge Discovery* (pp. 121-127). ACM Press.

Luo, X., & Fang, N. (2008). Semantic Representation of Scientific Documents for the e-Science Knowledge Grid. *Concurrency and Computation: Practice and Experience, 20*(7), 839-862.

Luo, X., & Hu, Q. (2008). Similar Knowledge Flow based Intelligent Browsing of Topics. *In Proceedings of 3rd International Workshop on Workflow Management and Application in Grid Environments.*

Luo, X., Hu, Q., & Xu, W. (2008). Discovery of Textual Knowledge Flow based on the Management of Knowledge Maps. *Concurrency and Computation: Practice and Experience* (pp. 1791-1806).

Luo, X., Xu, Z., & Yu, J. (2008). Discovery of Associated Topics for the Intelligent Browsing. *The First IEEE International Conference on Ubi-media Computing* (pp. 119-125). Digital Object Identifier: 10.1109/UMEDIA.2008.4570876.

Mannila, H., Toivonen, H., & Verkamo, A. I. (1997). Discovery of Frequent Episodes in Event Sequences. *Data Mining and Knowledge Discovery, 1*(3), 259-289.

Nissen, M. E. (2002). An Extended Model of Knowledge Flow Dynamics. *Communications of the Association for Information Systems, 8,* 251-266.

Nissen, M. E., & Levitt, R. E. (2004). Agent-Based Modeling of Knowledge Flows: Illustration from the Domain of Information Systems Design. *Proceedings of the 37th Hawaii International Conference on System Sciences.*

Nonaka, I. (1994). A Dynamic Theory of Organizational Knowledge Creation. *Organization Science, 5*(1), 14-37.

Nonaka, I., & Takeouchi, H. (1995). *The Knowledge Creating Company.* NY: Oxford University Press.

Ozden, B., & Ramaswamy S., & Silberschatz, A. (1998). Cyclic Association Rules. *In Proceedings of the 14th International Conference on Data Engineering* (pp. 412-421). IEEE Computer Society Press.

Perusich, K., & Mcneese, M. D. (2006). Using Fuzzy Cognitive Maps for Knowledge Management in a Conflict Environment. *IEEE Transactions on Systems, Man and Cybernetics, Part C: Applications and Reviews, 36*(6), 810-821.

Ramaswamy, S., Mahajan, S., & Silberschatz, A. (1998). On the Discovery of Interesting Patterns in Association Rules. *Proceedings of the 24th International Conference on Very Large Databases* (pp. 368-379). Morgan Kaufmann.

Wegaer, P. (1998). Interactive foundations of computing. *Theoretical Computer Science, 192*(2), 315-351.

Wegner, P. (1997). Why interaction is more powerful than algorithms. *Communications of the ACM, 40*(5), 80-91.

Wolverton, M. (1997). Exploiting enterprise models for the automatic distribution of corporate information. *In Proceedings of the 6th International Conference on Information and Knowledge Management* (pp. 341-347). New York: ACM Press.

Zhao, J., Kumar, A., & Stohr, E. A. (2001). Workflow-Centric information distribution through email. *Journal of Management Information Systems, 17*(3), 45-72.

Zhuge, H. (2002). A Knowledge flow model for peer-to-peer team knowledge sharing and management. *Expert Systems with Applications, 23*(1), 23-30.

Zhuge, H. (2005). Semantic Grid: Scientific Issues, Infrastructure, and Methodology. *Communications of the ACM, 48*(4), 117-119.

Zhuge, H. (2007). Autonomous semantic link network model for the Knowledge Grid. *Concurrency and Computation: Practice and Experience, 7*(19), 1065-1085.

Zhuge, H., Guo, W., Li, X., & Ding, L. (2005). Knowledge Energy in Knowledge Flow Networks. *Proceedings of the First International Conference on Semantics, Knowledge and Grid* (pp. 3). Washington, DC: IEEE Computer Society.

Chapter XII
Reputation Evaluation Framework Based on QoS in Grid Economy Environments

Guanfeng Liu
Qingdao University, China

Yongsheng Hao
Nanjing University of Information Science & Technology, China

ABSTRACT

This chapter mainly introduces some recent researches of reputation evaluation methods in Grid economy. The GRACE (Grid Architecture for Computational Economy architecture) is adopted to explain some mechanisms in the Grid economy for its clearly inner modules architecture. In addition, several new developed modules based on GRACE architecture are detailed discussed and two of them are laid morn emphasis on by us, which are the RCM (Reputation Control Module) and distributed reputation control architectures based on VOD (Virtual Organizational Domain). The inner communication and workflow of them are shown in this chapter. Furthermore, through experiments results, the authors discover the profit of Grid nodes and tasks execution success rate are all improved by adding these new modules.

INTRODUCTION

The Grid computing technology has developed rapidly in recent years (I.Foster, 1998). The fields it covered are becoming more and more extensive. Therefore many more new research directions appeared, for example Grid economy. It combines different economy models with Grid computing and schedules resources by economic elements in the Grid environment. Many governments and enterprises around the world have implemented the Grid economy projects. One famous project is the program of UK e-Science (S.Newhouse, 2001). It is laid down and implemented by UK's Core Program. This project uses economic models to schedule resources in UK e-Science center and sets up the GESA (Grid Economy Service Architecture) according to it. G-Commerce (R.Wolski, 2000) project mainly compare the different functions and effects between the Commodity model and auction model in the Grid economy. To schedule resources reasonably, Rajkumar Buyya proposes a GRACE (Grid Architecture for Computational Economy, R.Buyya, 2000) architecture and develops a resource dispatching management tool, Nimrod-G, based on market models. This architecture is improved constantly and the Grid economy is becoming more practical.

At the meanwhile, the security issue of Grid is getting increasingly important, especially after the combination of Grid computing and economy architectures. The user and services provided by resources in Grid environments are dynamic. Therefore, the malicious nodes may exist in Grid systems. It will significantly affect the Quality of Service (QOS) requirements of users, even lead to the economic loss of users in the Grid economic environment.

Therefore in the Grid economy environment, it is significant to build a resource scheduling framework which could block access of malicious nodes and ensure the safety of the resource providers and resource consumers. Former methods usually consider the safety of transactions. Lots of trust models and reputation calculation methods are developed during the process of the reputation research. However few of these models are used in the Grid economy and most of them are lack of consideration about the influence of economy on Grid computing. For example, some of the models use the soft incentive way (M.Feldman, 2004; Y.Kwok, 2005; K.Ranganathan, 2003). The nodes that share more resources with others could accumulate higher value of reputation. Therefore they can have the authority to access other resources. While, if some nodes want to obtain profit by providing resources, this soft incentive way will not suitable in this situation. In the other researches that adopt hard incentive methods (B.Chun, 2004; M.Feldman, 2005; P.Golle, 2001) nodes provide its resources to obtain the virtual money, and then this virtual money is used to bid for other resources. This method also has weakness. The amount of virtual money could not be the evaluating standard of trust, thus it still cannot satisfy the trust requirement of Grid economy. Additionally, the function of economic elements in the reputation control always is neglected. They are also could not adapt to the dynamic extension of nodes in Grid environments.

This motivated us to design the distributed reputation architecture which could extend through multi-VOD in the Grid economy. In this chapter, we propose the architecture which is based on Virtual Organizational Domains (VOD) and propose reputation evaluation methods which span these domains. The inner structure and this framework are also detailed discussed here. At last, through the simulating experiments, it can be proved that this architecture could block the assessment of malicious nodes effectively and improve the efficient and stability of nodes in Grid economy environments.

BACKGROUND

Different approach, policy and architecture are developed in reputation management. In Peer-to-Peer system, there are some reputation control models, like The EigenTrust system for P2P networks (S.D.Kamvar, 2003). This system form directly trust relation and recommendation trust vector through the interaction of nodes, then it performs the iterative operation on recommendation trust vector, so that this vector tend to a fixed value. This value is the reputation of nodes. However, this model hasn't taken the punishment factors and time factors into consideration. Damiani (2002) adopts distributed polling algorithm to share the trust information. However this system still has disadvantages because of the randomicity of polling and the huge expense of the system. Gupta (2003) calculates the reputation by using reputation computation agents. He adopts debit-credit reputation computation and credit-only reputation computation. The dynamic trust metric (Junsheng.C, 2006) adopts a method named forget factor to punish malicious peer. TrustMe (A.Singh, 2003) is a secure and anonymous underlying protocol for trust management in Peer-to-Peer.

Many reputation models have been applied into Grid computing. For example, Grid Secure Electronic Transaction (gSET) (Weishaupl.T, 2006) establishes trust and privacy between entities in a Grid environment by adapting the concept of Secure Electronic Transactions (SET). In the Grid economy, the model, which based on the auction policy also consider about the security factor (Bubendorfer.K, 2006). It can detect malicious nodes and guarantee the smooth implementation of the auction. Farag Azzedin (2002) presents a formal definition of behavior trust and reputation and discusses a type of behavior trust management architecture. However these researches are only focus on the security of transaction and not consider about the economy factor in Grid computing

The reputation factor of nodes also is considered by some payment systems in Grid computing. Such as Grid bank (Barmouta.A, 2003) that is a payment middleware of GRACE, DGAS (A.Guarise, 2003) that is used in Europe data Grid project, GSAX (J.Magowan, 2003) that is an accounting architecture of IBM in Grid environments. They use the strategy that the users with good reputation have priority to use resources and pay for it after using resources, and the account of malicious nodes will be blocked or deleted. However this strategy only provides services for accounting but not for resource selection.

REPUTATION DEFINITION

Different people have different definitions for what is the reputation. B.Alunkal (2003) gives the definition of reputation is the value we attribute to a specific entity, including agents, services, and persons in the Grid, based on the trust exhibited by it in the past. F.Azzedin (2002) defines the reputation of an entity is an expectation of its behavior based on other entities' observations or information about the entity's past behavior with a specific context at a given time. Alfarez Abdul-Rahman (2000) defines the reputation is an expectation about an agent's behavior based on information about or observations of its past behavior.

The definition of reputation that we will use in this chapter is as follows:

The reputation of an entity is an evaluation of its behavior in a certain time. The evaluation is managed by third party and varying with the change of entity's behavior.

That is to say, the reputation evaluation of entities in the Grid should meet three requirements as follows,

- Considering the recent behaviors. In most cases, the recent behaviors of an entity can illustrate the entity's situation clearly and show the reputation of the entity truly.
- Reflecting the entities past behaviors correctly. Although entities recent activities embody the reputation better, the contributions of entities in the past should not be ruled out.

- The reputation is decreased as the increase of time. It embodies the rule that the recent activities of entities do more contributions to reputation.

REPUTATION EVALUATION MODEL

Ian Foster (2002) proposed a Grid resource management method which adopts VOD. This method either maintains the original resource management form, or achieves the resource share. Therefore in our scenario, we divide reputation into inner-VOD nodes reputation and inter-VOD nodes reputation according to the VOD unit. Nodes in the Grid economy environment are divided into Grid Service Provider (GSP) and Grid Service Consumer (GSC). The two types of nodes have different goals and scheduling strategies. So we will divide every node in VOD into GSP reputation and GSC reputation according to the different rolls that they play in the Grid.

The Reputation of Different VOD

The reputation between VOD is asymmetrical. From B's view the reputation of Domain A is not equal to the reputation of Domain B from A's view. As indicated in the figure 1, from Domain B's part, Domain A's reputation is 0.75. While from Domain A's part, Domain B's reputation is 0.55(value of reputation is set between 0 and 1, 1 represents the best reputation, 0 represents the worst reputation).

If Grid nodes in VOD_B provide a service for Grid nodes in VOD_A or pay service fee for using services from nodes in VOD_A according to contracts, it means that nodes in VOD_B satisfy SLA (Service Level Agreement is a formal contract between service provider and user). Then domain A makes a task successful record for domain B represented with S_{AB}. If VOD B doesn't provide services according to contracts, domain A makes a task failed record represented with F_{AB}. Similarly we use S_{BA} and F_{BA} to represent the successful and failed record made by domain B for Domain A. In numbers of transactions, a record series exists among VOA. We use E^i_{AB} to represent the task record made by Domain A after the Ith transaction between nodes in domain A and Domain B. S^i_{AB} represents the task is successful in the Ith time, F^i_{AB} represents the task is failed. We give definitions as follows for calculating VOD reputation.

Definition 1: DR (A, B, Z) represents the reputation of VOD_B to VOD_A within $Grid_z$. A and B are VOD ID. Z is a Grid ID.

Figure 1. Reputation to different VOD

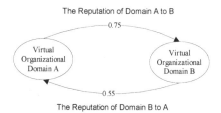

The Reputation of Domain A to B
0.75
Virtual Organizational Domain A
Virtual Organizational Domain B
0.55
The Reputation of Domain B to A

Definition 2: $\sum_i E^i_{AB}$ represents the total amount of the entire records made by VOD A. $\sum_i S^i_{AB}$ represents the total amount of all the trade successful record.

Definition 3: tim_B is the time from VOD_B enrolled in $Grid_z$. TIM_z is the time from creating $Grid_z$.

Then we show the calculation model,

$$DR(A,B,Z) = \alpha_1 \cdot (\frac{\sum_i S^i_{AB}}{\sum_i E^i_{AB}})^{\mu_1} + \beta_1 \cdot \frac{tim_B}{TIM_z} \quad i = 1,2,3,\cdots (1). \quad 0 \le \alpha_1 \pounds \ \beta_1 \le 1 \ \text{AND} \ \alpha_1 + \beta_1 = 1$$

$\alpha_1 \pounds \ \beta_1$ represent the weight of different parts. μ_1 is an influence factor of success rate. If the node of VOD_B has not implemented according to the SLA, which means VOD_B breaks contracts, then $\mu_1 > 1$ or else $\mu_1 = 1$. It can make VOD_B hard to build up a good reputation and decline the reputation rapidly when breaking contracts. The time of VOD_B existing in the Grid also has a significant influence on the reputation of it. The value of DR (A, B, Z) is between 0 and 1.The larger number of DR (A, B, Z) means the higher value of reputation of VOD_B.

The Reputation of Nodes in VOD

Different VOD have different reputation evaluation methods of nodes in it. This incarnates the autonomy of VOD and flexibility of this framework. The reputation of nodes in one VOD inherits the reputation of this VOD.

GSP Reputation

Definitions firstly are given as follows,

Definition 4: SP (A,Y,Z) represents the reputation of GSP_Y within VOD_A. A is a VOD ID, Y is a GSP ID and Z is a Grid ID.

Definition 5: S_rate_Y represents the rate the number of resources provided by GSP_Y according to contracts to the number of all resources provided by GSP_Y.

Definition 6: S_profit_Y is the total profit of selling resources provided by GSP_Y. SUM_z is the total profit of selling resources in $Grid_z$.

The reputation calculation model of GSP within the same VOD is shown as follows,

$$SP(A,Y,Z) = \alpha_2 \cdot (S\_rate_Y)^{\mu_1} + \beta_2 \cdot \frac{S\_profit_Y}{SUM_z} + \chi_2 \cdot \frac{tim_Y}{tim_A}$$
$$i = 1,2,3,\cdots (2). \quad 0 \le \alpha_2 \pounds \ \beta_2 \neg \chi_2 \le 1 \ \text{AND} \ \alpha_2 + \beta_2 + \chi_2 = 1$$

α_2£ β_2¬ χ_2 represent the weight of different parts. μ_2 has the same meaning of μ_1. If GSP wants to get a high value of reputation, it should have a high profit by trading in the history. Because the more money that GSP has earned the more impossible for GSP to cheat. So we take the profit of one GSP as an influence factor into account in this model. The duration of GSP existing in VOD has similar function with the duration of VOD existing in Grid.

If GSP provides services for the nodes in other VOD, then the reputation calculation model of GSP is as following,

$$SP(A,Y,Z)=\alpha_2 \cdot (S\_rate_Y)^{\mu 1}+\beta_2 \cdot \frac{S\_profit_Y}{SUM_Z}+\chi_2 \cdot \frac{tim_Y}{tim_A}+\delta_2 \cdot DR$$

$$i=1,2,3,\cdots(3).\ \ 0\le\alpha_2\text{£ }\beta_2\text{¬}\chi_2\ \ \delta_2\le 1\ \ AND\ \ \alpha_2+\beta_2+\chi_2+\delta_2=1$$

$\delta_2 \cdot DR$ represents the influence of VOD reputation on nodes in the VOD.

GSC Reputation

Similar with GSP reputation, we define several variables in the GSC reputation calculation model.

Definition 7: SC (A,Y,Z) represents the reputation of GSC_Y within $Grid_Z$. Y is the GSC ID and Z is the Grid ID.

Definition 8: C_rate_Y represents the ratio that the number of tasks provided by GSC_Y according to contracts to the number of all tasks provided by GSC_Y.

Definition 9: C_pay_Y is the total fee that GSC_Y pays for its tasks. SUM_Z is the total amount money of transaction between GSC_Y and other GSP in $Grid_Z$.

If GSC requests services provided by nodes in VOD in which it exists□then reputation calculation model of GSC is as following,

$$SC(A,Y,Z)=\alpha_3 \cdot (C\_rate_Y)^{\mu 3}+\beta_3 \cdot \frac{C\_pay_Y}{SUM_z}\ \ i=1,2,3,\cdots(4).\ 0\le\alpha_3,\beta_3\le 1\ AND\ \alpha_3+\beta_3=1$$

Similarly if GSC request services provide by nodes in other VOD, the reputation of GSC has to add the influence factor of $\chi_3 \cdot DR$.

The value of C_pay_Y reflects the economic strength of GSC_Y. The higher value of C_pay_Y means GSC_Y has the better financial condition. So GSC is not likely to break the contract when it has a higher value of C_pay. Other parameters and factors have the same explanation as above formula two.

ARCHITECTURE AND WORKFLOW

RCM Inner Architecture and Workflow

In order to guarantee an objective reputation evaluation, RCM is independent and managed by third-party. The inner architecture of RCM is shown in the figure 2. It consists of information collection manager, reputation calculation manager, and reputation storage unit, reputation reporter.

Functions of Different Parts

- *Information collection manager.* The information collection manager is responsible for collecting information from middleware, such as Grid Bank, Grid Market Director and Information Server. The information includes the number of resources provided by GSP, the total money of trade between GSP and GSC. And whether the entity breaks the contract.
- *Reputation calculation manager.* The Reputation calculation manager uses the reputation calculation model to calculate the reputation of GSC and GSP according to the information that is sent by information collection manager.
- *Reputation storage unit.* Reputation storage unit stores the reputation information of GSC and GSP. It uses a tree structure to store reputation information. In the tree structure storage, the root node represents the Grid and the leaf nodes stand for the GSC and GSP reputation in VOD.
- *Reputation reporter.* Reputation reporter is responsible for report the reputation. The reputation can be published in public server or transmit to entities which inquire the reputation.

New GRACE Architecture and Workflow

The GRACE proposed by Buyya has clearly inner modules architecture and most of functions of Grid economy can be implemented well in this model (R.Buyya, 2005). Following we will give the new GRACE architecture added RCM module and detailed discuss the main functions of GRACE modules.

Figure 2. Inner architecture of RCM

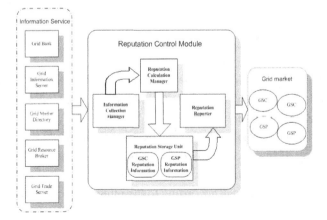

Figure 3. The new GRACE architecture with RCM

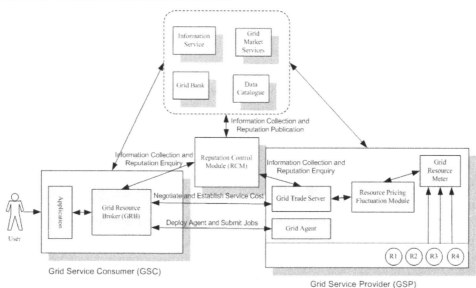

New GRACE Architecture

As shown in the GRACE new architecture in the figure 3, the core modules of GRACE include GSC (Grid Service Consumers), GRB (Grid Resource Broker) and GSP (Grid Service Providers).

- Grid resource meter. Grid resource meter gathers Resource Usage Records (RUR, http://www.gridforum.org). Grid resource meter optionally performs usage check with Grid Agent.
- Grid resource broker. The Grid Resource Broker (GRB) acts as a mediator between the user and grid resources using middleware services. It is responsible for resource selection, biding of software, data, and hardware resources, initiate computations, adapt to the changes in grid resources and present the grid to the user as a single, unified resource.
- Grid trade server. Grid Trade Server (GTS) is responsible to communicate with Grid Trade Manager (GTM). GTS is a resource owner agent that negotiates with resources consumers and providers access to resources.

Workflow of the New GRACE Architecture

We call the first step is system initialization. Resources are enrolled in Grid Resource Meter (GRM) through RUR. This information also is sent to Grid Market Directory, and information server. The initial reputation of these nodes is added into RCM.

The second step is the negotiation between GRB and Grid Trade Server (GTS). In this process, GSC inquires the reputation of resources provided by GSC from RCM. At the same time, GSP also inquires the reputation of tasks provided by GSC. After the negotiation, GSP and GSC decide whether they can choose each other to execute the task according to the integrated conditions, such as reputation, deadline and the price of the resource.

At last, GSC connects to Grid Bank for payment. We let GSC pay the fee of using resources after execute tasks (Barmouta.A, 2003). If GSC not pays the money in accordance with the agreement, GSC will break the contract. Subsequently, the information of payment is sent to RCM. GRB and GTS upload the information of negotiation and execution to RCM. If the service provided by GSP cannot achieve the Quality of Service that has promised in the SLA, we deem the GSP breaks the contract. After execution, the system completes the feedback of execution information and RCM updates the reputation of GSC and GSP according to the reputation calculation model that we have proposed. Then GSP publishes its resources list to Grid market directory through GRM.

DISTRIBUTED REPUTATION ARCHITECTURE

In order to guarantee an objective reputation evaluation, the reputation servers are independent and managed by third-party. The reputation control architecture is shown in the figure 4. It consists of several VOD and remote servers.

Local Servers

A local reputation server and a local information server constitute local servers in every VOD. The different functions of each part are discussed as follows,

- *Local reputation server.* The server controls the reputation of the VOD in which it exists and the nodes within this VOD according to the local information server. It will also upload the reputation information to the remote reputation server during the spare time of Grid.
- *Local information server.* It is responsible to requests the information of VOD in which it exists from remote information server. The nodes information in this VOD are also recorded and provided to reputation server by local information server.

Figure 4. Distributed reputation control architecture

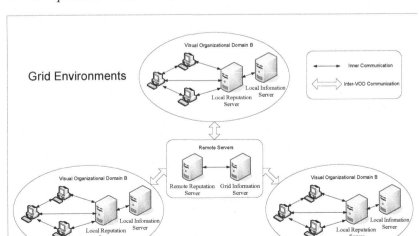

Remote Server

When nodes coming from different VOD make trade with each other, users need to inquire remote reputation server to obtain the reputation. One remote server includes remote reputation servers and Grid information servers. We also introduce the functions of them.

- *Remote reputation server.* It records an evaluation series of different VOD and Calculates VOD reputation according to the information provided by Grid information server. The VOD reputation matrix and reputation table of all nodes in the Grid are also stored in it.
- *Grid information server.* It Stores the information of every VOD and the situation of trades among notes in the Grid. This information must include the number of resources provided by GSP, the total money of transaction between GSP and GSC and so on.

SIMULATION EXPERIMENTS AND RESULTS

Simulation Details

We set three VOD in the Grid environment. Every VOD has two GSP and two GSC. The initial value 0.5 is give to VOD reputation. A random number between 0.3 and 0.5 is assigned to the node's reputation as its initial value.

To simplify the experiment, only the computing resource is taken into consideration. We use Million Instructions Per Second (MIPS) to stand for processing capability. Every GSP provides a series of computing resource and every GSC provides a series of tasks. We set the time-consuming of communication between nodes and local reputation servers is 50ms and 80ms between nodes and remote reputation servers in once resource scheduling.

We can find the detailed settings values of GSP and GSC nodes in the table 1. What's more, the tasks information is given in the table 2. Two strategies of resource scheduling are adopted in experiments. One is using Cost Optimization (R.Buyya, 2005) algorithm without reputation control. The other is us-

Table 1. Setting values of GSP and GSC

MIPS Rating	500	1000	1500	2000	2500
Price($G)	6	12	18	24	30
Deadline(sec)	70	60	50	40	30

Table 2. Ten tasks

Task ID	T1	T2	T3	T4	T5	T6	T7	T8	T9	T10
Payment(G$)	(3-5)	(4-6)	(12-16)	(15-17)	(16-20)	(16-18)	(17-25)	(18-28)	(24-30)	(24-35)
Deadline(sec)	65	60	35	32	28	27	18	17	13	14

Figure 5. Success rate of tasks execution without reputation control

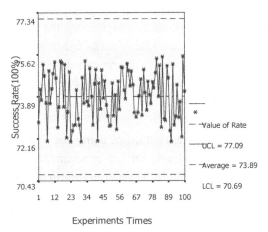

Figure 6. Success rate of tasks execution with reputation control

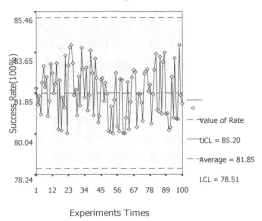

Figure 7. Time-consuming of communication

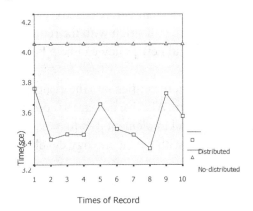

ing deviation test method in Cost Optimization. In this method, GSP could trade with GSC only when the absolute value of the difference between the reputation of GSP and GSC is less than a fixed value U. In this chapter, we set this fixed value U=0.2. To stimulate the real situation better, 10 % malicious nodes is set in the Grid system. The success rate of tasks execution is calculated every 5 minutes and the overall cost of communication among nodes are recorded every 50 times resource scheduling.

Simulation Results and Analysis

Figure 5 shows the success rate of task execution of using the Cost Optimization algorithm without reputation control. The horizontal axis stands for the experiments times and the vertical axis stands for the success rate. As indicate in the figure 5. The maximum success rate of them is 75.62%—the minimum rate is 72.16%—the average is 73.89%.

Figure 6 uses the distributed reputation control architecture. As illustrated in the figure, the average success rate of resource scheduling is 81.85%. From the experiments we can see that reputation framework prevent the damage of malicious nodes on Grid system efficiently. It can improve the system reliability and success rate of tasks.

Figure 7 shows the different values of communication time among nodes in Grid system adopted different reputation control architectures. Every spot in the figure represents the sum time-consuming of communication in 50 resource scheduling periods. We record 10 times data. As the finger shows, if the distributed reputation control architecture is not used in the Grid system, even ignoring the network delay and mistakes caused by increasing of communication, the time-consuming of communication is also much more than it in the Grid system which combines distributed reputation control architecture. Therefore, the distributed reputation architecture based on VOD could save the cost of communications and improve the efficiency of the Grid system.

CONCLUSION AND FUTURE WORK

In this chapter, we propose a reputation evaluation framework which is suitable in the economic-based Grid computing environment and design a new module RCM to extend the GRACE architecture. Then we propose a distributed reputation control architecture based on RCM for resource selection in the new GRACE architecture. It combines resource selection with the reputation of nodes. Through simulating experiments, we prove the new model and new policy can help both GSP and GSC to maximize their benefits.

In the following step, we will bring more entities into the evaluation scope, such as Grid bank, Grid resources directory, and other middleware. Also we prepare to construct a reputation evaluation system that spans more than one Grid system and implement it in to a real Grid environment. It is believe that the Grid economy has a broad prospect with the technology development.

REFERENCES

Abdul-Rahman, A., & Hailes, S. (2000). Supporting trust in virtual communities. *International Conference on System Sciences*, Hawaii.

Alunkal, B., Valjkovic, I., & Laszewski, G. V. (2003). Reputation-Based Grid Resource Selection. *Proceedings of the Workshop on Adaptive Grid Middleware,* New Orleans LA, USA.

Azzedin, F., & Maheswaran, M. (2002). Evolving and Managing Trust in Grid Computing Systems. *Proceedings of the IEEE Canadian Conference on Electrical and Computer Engineering,* Canada.

Barmouta, A., & Buyya, R. (2003). GridBank: A Grid Accounting Services Architecture (GASA) Distributed Systems Sharing and Integration. *Proceedings of the 17th Annual International Parallel and Distributed Processing Symposium, IEEE Computer Society Press* (pp.245-252), USA.

Bubendorfer, K., & Thomson, W. (2006). Resource Management Using Untrusted Auctioneers in a Grid Economy, *Proceedings of the Second IEEE International Conference on e-Science and Grid Computing* (pp.74-81), Netherlands.

Buyya, R., Abramson, D., & Giddy, J. (2000). An Economy Driven Resource Management Architecture for Global Computational Power Grids. *Proceedings of the 2000 International Conference on Parallel and Distributed Processing Techniques and Applications* (pp.517-525), Las Vegas, USA.

Buyya, R., Abramson, D., & Venugopal, S. (2005). *The Grid Economy.* Proceedings of the IEEE (pp.698-714), PA: IEEE Press.

Chun, B., Ng, J., & Parkes, D. (2004). *Computational resource exchanges for distributed resource allocation.* Technical Report, Harvard University.

Damiani, D., Vimercati, D., & Paraboschi, S. (2002). A Reputation-Based Approach for Choosing Reliable Resources in Peer-to-Peer Networks. *Proceedings of the 9th ACM Conference on Computer and Communications Security* (pp.207-216), Washington, USA.

Feldman, M., Lai, K., & Stoica, I. (2004). Robust incentive techniques for peer-to-peer networks. *Proceedings of the 5th ACM Conference on Electronic Commerce,* New York, USA.

Feldman, M., Lai, K., & Zhan, L. (2005). A price-anticipating resource allocation mechanism for distributed shared clusters. *Proceedings of the 6th ACM conference on Electronic Commerce* (pp.127-136), New York.

Foster, I., Kesselman, C., & Tuecke, S. (1998). *The Grid: Blueprint of a New Computing Infrastructure.* Morgan Kaufmann Publishers.

Foster, I., Kesselman, C., & Tuecke, S. (2002). *The Physiology of the Grid: An Open Grid Service Architecture for Distributed System Integration, Global Grid Forum.*

Global Grid Forum, RUR-Resource Usage Record Working Group, from http://www.gridforum.org.

Golle, P., Brown, K. L., & Mironov, I. (2001). Incentives for sharing in Peer-to-Peer network, *Proceedings of the 3rd ACM Conference on Electronic Commerce* (pp.264-267), New York.

Guarise, A. (2003). Data grid accounting system architecture, *(Tech. Rep. No. 1 on Data Grid),* Italy.

Gupta, M., Judge, P., & Ammar, M. (2003). A Reputation System for Peer-to-Peer Networks. *Proceedings of the 13th International Workshop on Network and Operating Systems Support for Digital Audio and Video* (pp.144-152), USA.

Junsheng, C., Huaimin, W., & Yin, G. (2006). A Dynamic Trust Metric for P2P System. *Proceedings of the 5th International Conference of Grid and Cooperative Computing Workshops* (pp.117-120), Changsha, China.

Kamvar, S. D., Schlosser, M. T., & Garcia-Molina, H. (2003). The EigenTrust Algorithm for Reputation Management in Peer-to-Peer Networks. *Proceedings of the 12th International Conference on World Wide Web* (pp.640-651), New York, USA.

Kwok, Y., Song, S., & Hwang, K. (2005). Selfish grid computing: Game-Theoretic modeling and NAS performance results. *Proceedings of the Cluster Computing and Grid* (pp.1143-1150), Washington.

Magowan, J. (2003). Extreme blue grid accounting project (Grid service accounting extensions–GSAX). *GGF Resource Usage Service Working Group.*

Newhouse, S., & Darlington, J. (2001). *Trading Grid Services within the UK E-Science.* London e-Science Center, Imperial College London, London, UK.

Ranganathan, K., Ripeanu, M., & Sarin, A. (2003). To share or not to share: An analysis of incentives to contribute in collaborative file sharing environments. *Proceedings of the Workshop on Economics of Peer-to-Peer Systems*, USA.

Singh, A., & Liu, L. (2003). TrustMe: Anonymous Management of Trust Relationships in Decentralized P2P Systems. *Third International Conference on Peer-to-Peer Computing* (pp.142-149), Sweden.

Weishaupl, T., Witzany, C., & Schikuta, E. (2006). gSET: Trust management and secure accounting for business in the Grid. *Proceedings of the Sixth IEEE International Symposium on Cluster Computing and the Grid* (pp.349-356), Singapore.

Wolski, R., Plank, J. S., & Brevik, J. (2000). *G-Commerce: Market formulations controlling resource allocation on the computational Grid*, University of Tennessee Technical Report.

Chapter XIII
Distributed Scheduling Protocols for Energy Efficient Large–Scale Wireless Sensor Networks

Cheng Fu
Nanyang Technological University, Singapore

Bang Wang
Nanyang Technological University, Singapore

ABSTRACT

A major design challenge in wireless sensor network application development is to provide appropriate middleware service protocols to control the energy consumption according to specific application scenarios. In common application scenarios such as in monitoring or surveillance systems, it is usually necessary to extend the system monitoring area as large as possible to cover the maximal area. The two issues of power conservation and maximizing the coverage area have to be considered together with both the sensors' communication connectivity and their power management strategy. In this chapter, the authors proposed novel enhanced sensor scheduling protocols to address the application scenario of typical surveillance systems. Their protocols take into consideration of both power conservation and coverage ratio to search for the balance between the different requirements. They proposed both centralized and de-centralized sensor scheduling versions, and compared the performance of different algorithms using several metrics. The results provide evidence of the advantages of our proposed protocols comparing with existing sensor scheduling protocols.

INTRODUCTION

The rapid advancements in wireless sensor networks (WSNs) have been made possible by recent developments in wireless communication technologies, embedded systems, and sensor devices. Nowadays, commercial WSN platforms are widely available, and the sensor nodes are tiny in size, low cost, and power efficient. These small sensor nodes are capable of sensing the environment, storing and processing the collected sensor data, and interacting and collaborating with each other within the network. WSNs have very important applications where the continuous data collection and information processing are required. Some typical applications include surveillance systems, environment monitoring and healthcare monitoring as in (Akyildiz, 2002; Huang, H., 2005).

In many application scenarios, the deployment environment of a wireless sensor network may be hazardous or difficult to access. For example, a seismic monitoring system may be deployed on a volcano. The growing size of the sensor network also makes it costly and impractical to manually replace or recharge the battery of each sensor nodes. The sensor network deployments in some applications may contain hundreds of sensor nodes. In these cases, the power supply for the sensor nodes becomes a serious problem that needs to be addressed during the system design. *How to prolong the life time of the WSN system?* A straight forward solution is to limit the number of sensor nodes which are assigned duties and thus consume their battery power, while keeping the rest of the nodes inactive. By intelligently distributing the power consumption among all of the deployed sensor nodes, the system can significantly extend its lifetime and be robust to unexpected sensor node failures.

However, a major design challenge for energy-efficient surveillance sensor network is to provide the optimal coverage for the monitoring area meanwhile considering the energy conservation issue. This coverage ratio is one of the main performance metrics to evaluate the quality of service for the system. The coverage problem cannot be solved alone without the consideration of sensor scheduling strategy. It is heavily dependent on the coverage model and locations of the deployed sensor nodes. Sensor coverage model can be considered as a metric for the quality of service of each sensor's sensing function, and it is subject to a wide range of interpretations due to a large variety of sensors and applications. On the other hand, network coverage can be considered as a collective measure of the quality of service provided by sensor nodes at different geographical locations.

In the literature, the coverage problem in WSNs has been formulated in various ways with different assumptions and objectives (Cardei, 2004; Cardei, 2006; Huang, C.F., 2005a; Huang, C.F., 2005b). The sensor coverage model may need to take into consideration of specific signal processing techniques for individual sensor node as well as cooperative signal processing techniques for multiple sensor nodes. In the design stage, one may want to know at least how many sensor nodes are needed such that the entire sensor field is covered. During the deployment stage, sensor nodes may be deterministically placed into the sensor field or simply randomly scattered. Also mobile sensor nodes may move to more preferable locations after the initial deployment. During the operation stage, one may want to schedule different sensor nodes to work collaboratively in order to prolong the network life time while still preserving network coverage. Other network performance metrics such as energy consumption and network connectivity may need to be integrated with the coverage problem in the context of WSNs.

In this chapter, we propose novel enhanced sensor scheduling protocols designed for the implementation of large-scale sensor networks for surveillance applications. The paper is organized as follows. In Section 2, we briefly review the related work in sensor scheduling and coverage control. Section 3 presents the system model, assumptions and some definitions. The centralized and de-centralized scheduling protocols' designs are presented in Sections 4 and 5 respectively. Section 6 focuses on the performance evaluation of the designed protocols, followed by a brief discussion in Section 7. Finally, we conclude in Section 8.

RELATED WORK AND DESIGN CONSIDERATIONS

Wireless sensor network consists of large number of sensor nodes. A sensor node which is specifically designed for executing certain sensing task, such as collecting environmental status sample data and sensing specified occurred events, is in general with small size, light weight and limited battery energy. A sensor node normally has very short lifetime if it is running with full power status without any duty scheduling management.

Although a single sensor may only have limited sensing, processing and communication capabilities, a large number of geographically distributed sensors can form networks and collaborate to achieve high performance for most applications in a large field of interests. Due to different application requirements, the subject to be covered by a WSN can be the whole field of interests or only some particular discrete points.

Sensors may be deterministic placed or randomly scattered into a sensor field. In random sensor deployment, the number of scattered sensors is in general larger than the optimal one to compensate for the lack of exact positioning. Roughly speaking, a sensor can be in one of the following three states: transmit and receive state, sensing and processing state, and sleep state. Although different types of sensors may have different energy consumption models, the most energy consumption state in general is the transmit and receive state and the least one is the sleep state. Since replacing sensor battery is not feasible in many applications, it is desirable to schedule sensors' states to save battery energy. Besides the sensing task, it is required in many applications that sensors can deliver their sensed data to a sink for further processing.

In this section, we review and explain our design choices based on the consideration of several aspects in WSNs: coverage types, deployment methods, activity scheduling, network connectivity and sensor heterogeneity.

According to Cardei (2006), the coverage types in WSNs can be classified into three types, namely area coverage (Cardei, 2002; Slijepcevic, 2001; Tian, 2002; Ye, 2002), points/targets coverage (Cardei, 2005; Chakrabarty, 2002; Lin, 2005) and barrier coverage (Huang, H., 2005; Meguerdichian, 2001). The most considered coverage type is the area coverage which addresses how a sensor field is covered. Discrete points/targets coverage addressing the coverage of a set of discrete targets with known locations has been researched. Complete coverage is an important performance metric for area and point coverage. Barrier coverage is different from the area and point coverage in that the subjects to be covered are not known before sensor deployment.

Deterministic sensor deployment is to place sensors to desired locations such that certain objectives can be achieved such as minimum number of sensors deployed. When the network size is large and the deployment field is remote and hostile, random sensor deployment is mostly often used. In a randomly deployed sensor network, critical sensor density is an important performance metric indicating at least how many sensors per unit area is required for complete area coverage.

As mentioned above, the scattered sensors may be more than required in a randomly deployed sensor network in which the area covered by one sensor may also be covered by other sensors. Such sensors are considered to be redundant and can be temporarily transited into the energy saving sleep state without sacrificing the coverage requirement. Many distributed algorithms (Tian, 2002; Ye, 2002; Zhang, 2005) and centralized algorithms (Cardei, 2002; Slijepcevic, 2001; Yan, 2003) have been proposed for scheduling sensor activity based on different assumptions and objectives. In distributed algorithms, the decision process is decentralized and in many cases localized in each individual sensor by using information only from a few neighboring sensors. In centralized algorithms, a central controller makes all decisions and distributes the results to sensors.

In WSNs, two sensors are directly connected if they are within each other's radio transmission range and two sensors can also be connected by multi-hop transmissions with some other sensors serving as relays. Complete connectivity ensures that the sensed data of any sensor can be transmitted to all other sensors in the sensor field as well to the sink possibly via multi-hop transmissions. The transceiver unit is in general independent of the sensing unit in a sensor and the sensing range and the communication range of a sensor can be with different distance. In Zhang (2005), the result has shown that a complete coverage of a monitoring area implies connectivity of the network if the communication range is more than twice the sensing range.

In WSNs, the deployed sensors may have different sensing, processing and communication capabilities, i.e., sensors are heterogeneous. For example, some sensors are resource rich nodes in that they have more power supply and/or equipped with better sensing, processing and communication units. However, deploying with homogeneous sensor nodes can help to reduce the hardware cost, system complexity and maintenance efforts.

SYSTEM MODEL AND DEFINITIONS

We consider a large scale wireless sensor network which consists thousands and hundreds of sensor nodes. The sensor nodes are randomly deployed in an open field and connect into a network. The purpose of the deployed sensor network is to capture the desired event/target as quickly as possible when it appears within the area. In order the achieve the goal, the middleware service needs to control the sensor nodes scheduling by assigning some of the sensor nodes the on-duty role while turning off the power of the rest sensor nodes to avoid wasting precious battery energy.

The design of the sensor scheduling protocols can be either centralized so that all deployed sensor nodes are running on the order from the control centre, or distributed so that each sensor node is running on its own decision. In our design approach, we consider that each sensor node has two power statuses, called ACTIVE and SLEEP modes. Understandably the ACTIVE mode is the full functional mode of a sensor node, in which the sensor node executes the tasks of wireless communication, collecting the sensor data and performing other necessary functions. In SLEEP mode, the sensor node shuts down all of its energy-consuming components such as the communication module and sensing module. However, it still needs to be awaken on pre-defined schedule.

The system module is based on the assumptions presented below and applies to all of the discussions accordingly:

1. We assume that all of the sensor nodes are identical which results in the same sensing ability with the same sensing range.

2.   We assume that the sensing range (sr) and the communication range (cr) of each sensor node follow the requirement:

$$cr > 2 \times sr \tag{1}$$

3.   We assume that a sensor node is able to capture any desired event/target appeared within its sensing range when its sensor module is powered on.
4.   We assume that the network is an ideal network in which the transmission of every message is guaranteed and error free.
5.   We also assume that each sensor node has full knowledge of its own location coordinate.

The following definitions are given to facilitate the discussion of the protocols' design in the followed sections.

Definition 1 (Private Sensing Area). *The private sensing area of a sensor node S(i) is defined as the disk area with the sensing range S(i)->sr in which any appeared target will be captured.*

Definition 2 (Monitoring Area). *The monitoring area of the designed sensor network system is defined as the combination of the private sensing area of each individual sensor node which is in ACTIVE status.*

Definition 3 (Sensor Node Coverage). *A sensor node S(i) is said to be covered by another sensor node S(j) iff*

- $S(j) \rightarrow mode = ACTIVE$ and
- $S(j) \rightarrow sr > Distance (i \leftrightarrow j).$

Definition 4 (Coverage Rate). *The overall monitoring system coverage rate is defined as the size of the monitoring area defined in Definition 2 against the size of the entire sensor deployed field.*

Based on the described system model, a relatively small number of the total deployed sensor nodes are assigned to keep in ACTIVE status while all of the rest sensor nodes will be turned into SLEEP status. Each single sleeping node should be covered by at least one active sensor node. Meanwhile, none of the active sensor nodes is covered by any other active sensor node. The monitoring area defined in Definition 2 does not necessarily equal to the whole deploying area due to the random deployment method.

CENTRALIZED SENSOR SCHEDULING PROTOCOL

We first exam the centralized approach for the scheduling of the sensor nodes' activities. The centralized version of the sensor scheduling protocol is running on two different operation processes. Considering a large scale densely deployed wireless sensor network with the sensor nodes' set *S(n)* of *n* nodes, in order to determine the individual sensor node's power status, a central node, so called the initiator, needs to collect the necessary information from all the sensor nodes inside the network. The crucial information to support the running of the protocol includes the location information and the battery energy level of each sensor node.

The Approach

The central initiator disseminates the management request into the network, and collects the responses from all sensor nodes. We call this operation process of *Information Collection*. In this process, the central initiator must consistently query each sensor node in the system till the response has been received. Any non-response sensor node will be considered as failure.

The second operation process is called the *Role Assignment*. In this process, the initiator node makes the decision on assigning the new power status for each sensor node in *S(n)* based on the information collected in the previous operation process. The decision will be disseminated into the network and be executed by individual sensor node.

The key point in the *Role Assignment* process is how to decide a sensor node's new power status based on the combination of its location information and battery energy level. In our approach, we define a parameter *M*, the *Merit*, to indicate the impact of setting the power status of a sensor node to be active. The idea is to select those sensor nodes that can cover more other sensor nodes with more energy remaining in its own battery to stand in the higher chance of being active. The relations between the battery energy level and the number of covered neighbors can be represented in different models which is not the major concern of our discussion. We adopt a simple equation as given below to facilitate our discussion on the scheduling protocol.

For a sensor node *S(i)*, the *M(i)* is calculated by

$$M_{(i)} = \alpha \cdot P + \beta \cdot N \tag{2}$$

where *P* is the battery energy level indicated by the percentage of remained energy comparing with the full energy level. *N* is the number of neighboring sensor nodes which are located within *S(i)*'s private sensing area as defined in Definition 3. The empirical coefficients α and β are determined by the experiments and should be varied due to different situations, such as the deployment density and environmental effects.

Once the central initiator has obtained all the necessary information, including the location of each sensor node and its remaining battery energy level indicator, it sorts the full list of all sensor nodes. A brief description of the decision process for the initiator node is presented in Algorithm 1.

Step forward, an advanced approach is to using the sum of the *Merit* in all of the covered neighbor nodes as the new parameter for each sensor node for comparison. We define the new parameter $\overline{M}$, the *Covered Merit*. It is calculated by

$$\overline{M}_{(i)} = M_{(i)} + \sum M_{(j)} \tag{3}$$

where $M_{(j)}$ represents the set of all sensor nodes within *S(i)*'s private sensing area.

Algorithm 1. Direct approach for role assignment in centralized sensor scheduling

Require: $S(i) \in S(n)$, $i \le n$

1. Sort the set $S(n)$ by the order of $M_{(i)}$ from the highest to the lowest.
2. Assign $S(0) \rightarrow mode = ACTIVE$.
3. Search
for $S(i) \in S(n)$, $j \le n$ do
  if $S(j) \rightarrow sr > Distance(0 \leftrightarrow j)$ then
    Assign $S(j) \rightarrow mode = SLEEP$,
    Remove $S(0)$ and $S(j)$ from the set $S(n)$.
  end if
end for
4. Repeat steps 1 - 3.

Algorithm 2. Advanced approach for role assignment in centralized sensor scheduling

Require: $S(i) \in S(n)$, $i \le n$

1. Sort the set $S(n)$ by the order of $\overline{M}_{(i)}$ from the highest to the lowest.
2. Assign $S(0) \rightarrow mode = ACTIVE$.
3. Search
for $S(j) \in S(n)$, $j \le n$ do
  if $S(j) \rightarrow sr > Distance(0 \leftrightarrow j)$ then
    Assign $S(j) \rightarrow mode = SLEEP$,
    Remove $S(0)$ and $S(j)$ from the set $S(n)$.
  end if
end for
4. Repeat steps 1 - 3.

Now the central initiator sorts its sensor nodes list based on the *Covered Merit* and gives the priority to the sensor nodes with the highest *Covered Merit* value. Algorithm 2 presents the details of decision making process for the central initiative node.

Theorem 1 shows that the new sensor scheduling protocol satisfies the sufficient condition of providing full coverage to all of the deployed sensor nodes.

Theorem 1. *For the complete set S(n) for a wireless sensor network fulfilling the assumptions presented in Section 3, the combination of the private sensing area of all ACTIVE sensor nodes is sufficient to cover all of the deployed sensor nodes.*

Proof: *According to Step 3 in both Algorithms 1 and 2, a sensor node S(i) will be and only be de-listed from the set S(n) when it has been assigned an ACTIVE role or has been covered by an ACTIVE sensor node. An un-covered sensor node results an un-empty set S(n) and consequently the Steps 1-3 in Algorithm 1 or 2 will be executed till all sensor nodes have been covered.*

Both of the ACTIVE and SLEEP modes of the sensor nodes are not and should not be permanently assigned. Any un-expected sensor node failure or any changes on the network topology can cause un-optimal result for the designed sensor scheduling protocol. Over running of the ACTIVE sensor nodes' battery is sure not an option and may quickly cause the damage to the completion of the sensor network. The initiative sensor node periodically invokes the sensor scheduling protocol based on an empirical time interval Δ. By doing so, the roles of ACTIVE and SLEEP status can be rotated among all the participated sensor nodes and evenly consumed the battery energy of each sensor node.

DE-CENTRALIZED SENSOR SCHEDULING PROTOCOL

The centralized sensor scheduling protocol presented in the previous section requires a central sensor node acting as the initiator, and to invoke the protocol on a preset regular time interval. This becomes a weak point of the protocol as all of other similar centralized approach, which are vulnerable to the central node failure and have the limitation of computational and communication capabilities of the node. A de-centralized version of our previous approach is presented in this section to eliminate the un-wanted shortcomings caused by the centralized approach.

In the de-centralized approach, a non-specified sensor node $S(i)$ initiates the execution of the sensor scheduling protocol, it broadcasts sensor management request to all of its neighboring sensor nodes, denoted by the set $S(n)$. For any node within the private sensing range of $S(i)$, it starts an individual *Information Collection* process. The process includes $S(i)$ itself.

Theorem 2 shows that only the sensor nodes within $S(i)$'s communication range are required to participate in this process.

Theorem 2. *For any sensor node S(i), its scheduling decision process is determined only based on the collected information from the sensor nodes in the set S(n), in which each sensor node S(j) ∈ S(n) fulfils the requirement Distance (i ↔ j) < S(i) → cr.*

Proof: *According to Equation 2, for any sensor node S(i), its Merit M(i) is calculated from the information collected from S(i)'s neighbor set S(n) in which each sensor nodes S(j) ∈ S(n) fulfils Distance (i ↔ j) < S(i) → sr.*

Similarly, S(j) only needs to communicate with its neighbor nodes within $S(j) \to sr$, which is equal to $S(i) \to sr$. Therefore, only the sensor nodes within distance $2 \times sr$ are involved in the process. It approves the theorem based on Equation 1 in which $2 \times sr < cr$.

Similar to the centralized version of the sensor scheduling protocol, there are two choices for the decision making of selecting the ACTIVE role of the sensor nodes. In the direct approach, all the participated sensor nodes calculate their own *Merit* according to Equation 2. The sensor node $S(j)$ with the highest *Merit* value will claim its role to be ACTIVE and all those un-assigned sensor nodes within $S(j) \to sr$ will turn into SLEEP. For the sensor nodes belonging to $S(n)$ but outside $S(j) \to sr$, they will either go back to the role of SLEEP if they are covered by any other ACTIVE node or compete with other un-assigned node in $S(j)$ for the ACTIVE role. The description of the direct approach is given in Algorithm 3.

Algorithm 3. Direct approach for role assignment in de-centralized sensor scheduling

Require: $S(i) \in S(n)$, $i \leq n$

1. $S(i)$ broadcast management request to the set $S(n)$.

2. Repeat

for $S(j) \in S(n)$, $j \leq n$ do

  if $S(i) \rightarrow sr > Distance(i \leftrightarrow j)$ then

     a. Initiate Information Collection process,

     b. Update its neighbors' information and calculate $M_{(j)}$,

     c. broadcast the result $M_{(j)}$

  end if

end for

3. Search

for $S(j) \in S(n)$, $j \leq n$ do

  if $M_{(i)} > M_{(j)}$ then

    Assign $S(i) \rightarrow mode = ACTIVE$

  else

    Assign $S(i) \rightarrow mode = SLEEP$

  end if

end for

Algorithm 4. Advanced approach for role assignment in de-centralized sensor scheduling

Require: $S(i) \in S(n)$, $i \leq n$

1. $S(i)$ broadcast management request to the set $S(n)$.

2. Repeat

for $S(j) \in S(n)$, $j \leq n$ do

  if $S(i) \rightarrow sr > Distance(i \leftrightarrow j)$ then

     a. Initiate Information Collection process,

     b. Update its neighbors' information and calculate $\overline{M}_{(j)}$,

     c. broadcast the result $\overline{M}_{(j)}$

  end if

end for

3. Search

for $S(j) \in S(n)$, $j \leq n$ do

  if $\overline{M}_{(i)} > \overline{M}_{(j)}$ then

    Assign $S(i) \rightarrow mode = ACTIVE$

  else

    Assign $S(i) \rightarrow mode = SLEEP$

  end if

end for

Instead, in the advanced approach, the comparable parameter is changed to the *Covered Merit*, and the sensor nodes execute the similar process as in the direct approach. The process is also shown in Algorithm 4.

PERFORMANCE EVALUATION

We have simulated the proposed sensor scheduling protocols using recently developed WISDOM simulation platform (Lim, 2008) and evaluated the protocols performance with other well-known protocols in different aspects. The setting of simulation parameters is given in Table 1. In the simulation, all sensor nodes are randomly deployed in the monitoring area. We are focusing on two important comparison parameters: the average coverage ratio and the number of active sensor nodes that requires to achieve the average coverage ratio. We use a grid structure with grid unit length 0.5m to calculate coverage ratio. Such grid points are called *pixels* here after for convention. The coverage ratio is the number of covered pixels divided by the number of all pixels.

DSSP and DSSP+

We first evaluate the De-centralized Sensor Scheduling Protocol (DSSP) in both direct approach and advanced approach (DSSP+) according to the discussion in Section 5. Meanwhile, we have also implemented the simple Random Independent Sleeping (RIS) scheme (Gui, 2004; Kumar, 2004) and another well-known protocol PEAS (Ye, 2002). The two protocols are both designed as distributed sensor management schemes for the coverage problem. They both do not need the information of the sensor nodes' location coordinates.

In order the compare the performance of different protocols, the simulation has been executed for ten rounds. In each individual simulation round, the sensor nodes have been randomly deployed with a new set of random seeds. The round length is set to 1000 ticks for our simulations. The results of RIS are averaged from the samples collected every 100 ticks. While for other three protocols, the results are taken as from the point of 1000 tick. The coverage algorithm module in WISDOM has been switched among the four algorithms. Figures 1 and 2 present the simulation results of the percentage in coverage rate and the number of active sensor nodes accordingly in each round of test.

When comparing the percentages in coverage rate, both DSSP and DSSP+ have consistent performances which are much better than the performance of RIS. However, their performances are competitive when compared with PEAS which is a slightly better. All of them can reach the average coverage ratio around 90% under various random deployments. In each round of test, the DSSP+ which considering the *Covered Merit* instead of the *Merit* only achieves higher coverage ratio than DSSP.

Table 1. Simulation parameters setting

Parameters	Values
Number of sensor nodes	204
Monitoring area	200×150 square meters
Sensing range	40 meters
Battery energy	1000 units

Both of the two algorithms DSSP and DSSP+ require much less number of active sensor nodes comparing with RIS and PEAS, while the numbers are between 50 - 60. The numbers for PEAS is always between 60 - 70 while the average number for RIS is consistently around 72 against the total deployment number of 204.

Coefficients' Effects

When we consider the effects of the two coefficients for calculating the *Merit* in Equation 2, the simulations results are given in Figures 3 and 4 for the percentage in coverage rate and the number of active sensor nodes respectively. In ten rounds of testing, we simulate different coefficients' setting for DSSP.

Figure 1. Percentage in coverage rate

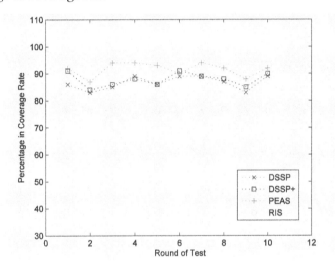

Figure 2. Number of active nodes

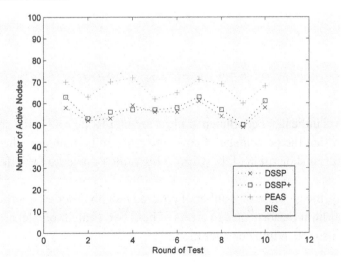

Figure 3. Percentage in coverage rate

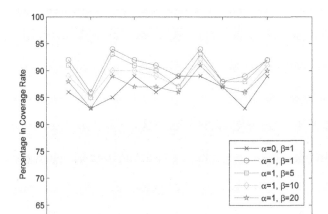

Figure 4. Number of active nodes

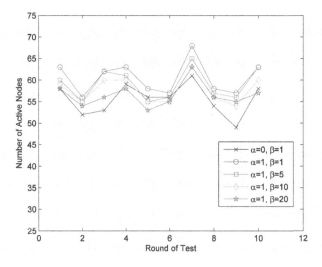

The energy level indicator's coefficient α plays an interesting role in the sensor scheduling protocol. Both figures show that the percentage of coverage rate can be increase when the battery energy level has been taken into consideration of the *Merit*. This is the same case for reducing the number of active sensor nodes.

Controversially, the increase of number of covered neighbor nodes' coefficient β does have negative impact on the algorithm performance in terms of both two evaluation metrics when the battery energy level indicator is also taken into consideration.

Figure 5. Percentage in coverage rate

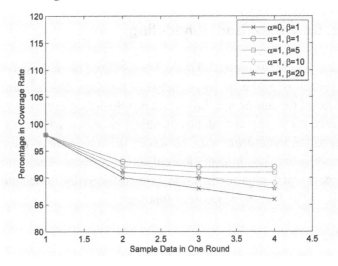

Figure 6. Number of active nodes

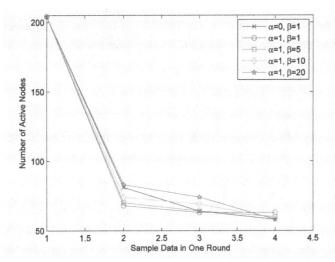

Figures 5 and 6 also provide the examination results of DSSP performance in one round running with different coefficients' setting. A single round running is defined as the ending by the time when the number of active sensor nodes reaches the bottom in the first time. The sample data is picked up at fixed points in the single round simulation.

DISCUSSIONS

Centralized vs. De-centralized Scheduling

In previous discussion, we have presented the solutions based on both two design methods. In general, de-centralized approach is robust to sensor network topology changes and unexpected sensor node failure. The initiation of the sensor scheduling and re-scheduling process can be started from any place of the network. Hence the system can adaptively adjust its sensor scheduling strategy timely to provide maximal coverage to the monitoring area. However, the downside of the de-centralized approach is mainly concentrated on its slow information collection process. The centralized approach provides faster decision process which requires only one round information collection. It provides an alternative choice for medium size and clustered network topology.

Merit Calculation

We have introduced in previous discussion the parameter *Merit* as well as *Covered Merit*. The role assignment process in the sensor scheduling protocol is based on the calculation of the parameter's value on each sensor nodes. We have adopted Equation 2 for the evaluation of the designed sensor scheduling algorithm. However, more research effort on discovering the relation between the battery energy level and the number of neighboring sensor nodes may bring further improvements on the performance of the sensor scheduling protocols to prolong the system lifetime and to increase the coverage ration.

CONCLUSION

To design robust, energy-efficient large-scale sensor networks for surveillance systems with long operation time, it is necessary to develop a good sensor scheduling and management protocol while addressing the sensing coverage problem at the same time.

In this chapter, we have proposed two versions of novel design approaches of enhanced sensor scheduling protocols. We have discussed both the centralized and the de-centralized versions. We have also taken direct and advanced approaches for each scheduling protocol with the consideration of energy efficiency issue. The algorithm is especially designed for the random sensor deployment scenario. We have implemented and evaluated the proposed protocols using the WISDOM simulation platform, and compared it with two other coverage control protocols. The results show that our proposed sensor scheduling protocols outperforms existing similar protocols in terms of both the percentage in coverage rate and the number of active sensor nodes.

REFERENCES

Akyildiz, I. F., Su, W., Sankarasubramaniam, Y., & Cayirci, E. (2002). Wireless sensor networks: A survey. *Computer Networks, 38*(4), 393–422.

Cardei, M., MacCallum, D., Cheng, X., Min, M., Jia, X., Li, D., & Du, D. Z. (2002). Wireless sensor networks with energy efficient organization. *Journal of Interconnection Networks, 3*(3-4), 213–229.

Cardei, M., Thai, M., Li, Y., & Wu, W. (2005). Energy-efficient target coverage in wireless sensor networks. *Proc. of the 24th IEEE INFOCOM,* 1976–1984.

Cardei, M., & Wu, J. (2004). Coverage in wireless sensor networks. *Handbook of Sensor Networks.*

Cardei, M., & Wu, J. (2006). Energy-efficient coverage problems in wireless ad-hoc sensor networks. *Computer Communications, 29*(4), 413–420.

Chakrabarty, K., Iyengar, S. S., Qi, H., & Cho, E. (2002). Grid coverage for surveillance and target location in distributed sensor networks. *IEEE Transactions on Computers, 51*(12), 1448–1453.

Gui, C., & Mohapatra, P. (2004). Power conservation and quality of surveillance in target tracking sensor networks. *Proc. of the 10th Intl. Conf. on Mobile Computing and Networking,* 129–143.

Huang, C. F., & Tseng, Y. C. (2005). A survey of solutions to the coverage problems in wireless sensor networks. *Journal of Internet Technology, 6*(1), 1–8.

Huang, C. F., & Tseng, Y. C. (2005). The coverage problem in a wireless sensor network. *Mobile Networks and Applications, 10*(4), 519–528.

Huang, G. T. (2003). Casting the wireless sensor net. *Technology Review, 106*(6), 50–56.

Huang, H., Richa, A. W., & Segal, M. (2005). Dynamic coverage in ad-hoc sensor networks. *Mobile Networks and Applications, 10,* 9–18.

Kumar, S., Lai, T., & Balogh, J. (2004). On k-coverage in a mostly sleeping sensor network. *Proc. of the 10th Intl. Conf. on Mobile Computing and Networking,* (pp. 144–158).

Lim, H. B., Wang, B., Fu, C., Phull, A., & Ma, D. (2008). WISDOM: simulation framework for middleware services in wireless sensor networks. *Proc. the 5th IEEE Consumer Communications and Networking Conference.*

Lin, F. Y. S., & Chiu, P. L. (2005). Energy-efficient sensor network design subject to complete coverage and discrimination constraints. *Proc. of the 2nd IEEE Intl. Conf. on Sensor and Ad Hoc Communications and Networks, 2,* 586–593.

Meguerdichian, S., Koushanfar, F., Potkonjak, M., & Srivastava, M. B. (2001). Coverage problems in wireless ad-hoc sensor networks. *Proc. of the 20th IEEE INFOCOM, 3.*

Slijepcevic, S., & Potkonjak, M. (2001). Power efficient organization of wireless sensor networks. *Proc. of IEEE Intl. Conf. on Communications, 2.*

Tian, D., & Georganas, N. D. (2002). A coverage-preserving node scheduling scheme for large wireless sensor networks. *Proc. of the 1st ACM Intl. Workshop on Wireless Sensor Networks and Applications,* (pp. 32–41).

Yan, T., He, T., & Stankovic, J. A. (2003). Differentiated surveillance for sensor networks. *Proc. of the 1st Intl. Conf. on Embedded Networked Sensor Systems,* (pp. 51–62).

Ye, F., Zhong, G., Lu, S., & Zhang, L. (2002). PEAS: a robust energy conserving protocol for long-lived sensor networks. *Proc. the 10th IEEE Intl. Conf. on Network Protocols,* (pp. 200–201).

Zhang, H. H., & Hou, J. C. (2005) Maintaining sensing coverage and connectivity in large sensor networks. *Wireless Ad Hoc and Sensor Networks, 1*(1-2), 89–123.

Chapter XIV
A QSQL–Based Service Collaboration Method for Automatic Service Composition, and Optimized Execution

Kaijun Ren
National University of Defense Technology, China & Swinburne University of Technology, Australia

Jinjun Chen
Swinburne University of Technology, Australia

Nong Xiao
National University of Defense Technology, China

Weimin Zhang
National University of Defense Technology, China

Junqiang Song
National University of Defense Technology, China

ABSTRACT

In scientific computing environments such as service grid environments, services are becoming basic collaboration components which can be used to construct a composition plan for scientists to resolve complex scientific problems. However, current service collaboration methods still suffer from low efficiency for automatically building composition plans because of the time-consuming ontology reasoning and incapability in effectively allocating resources to executing such plans. In this chapter, the authors present a QSQL-based collaboration method to support automatic service composition and optimized execution. With this method, for a given query, abstract composition plans can be created in an automatic, semantic, and efficient manner from QSQL (Quick Service Query List) which is dynamically built by previously processing semantic-related computing at service publication stage. Furthermore, concrete service execution instances can be dynamically bound to abstract service composition plans at runtime by comparing their different QoS(Quality of Service) values. Particularly, a concrete collaboration framework is proposed to support automatic service composition and execution. Totally, the authors' proposed method will not only facilitate e-scientists quickly create composition plans from a large scale of service repository; but also make resource's sharing more flexible. The final experiment has illustrated the effectiveness of their proposed method.

INTRODUCTION

In high performance computing field such as climate, biology, we often need to integrate resources across distributed, heterogeneous, and autonomous systems to enable e-scientists to solve complex scientific problems in collaborative way. Currently, service oriented grid computing platforms are becoming their problem-resolving environments where a service is a basic collaboration component. In such service grid environments, scientists can not only construct composition plans by selecting different services from large service repositories, but also submit their composition plans to grid computing platforms for executing them. Recently, many methods have been proposed aiming at enhancing the automation in constructing a composition plan and simultaneously improving the comprehensive utility of allocating resources to execute such plans. However, most existing collaboration methods still face the following solid problems. On one side, they still remain at low efficiency stage for automatically building a composition plan because of the involved ontology reasoning and manual processing. For example, semantic service composition methods that take semantics of services into account to automatically solve the discovery and composition problem, have been a recent active research field[Keita Fujii et al., 2005, Danny Gagne et al., September 2006, Ulrich Küster et al., May 2007, Brahim Medjahed et al., 2005, Katia Sycara et al., 2003]. However, they mostly rely on taking direct ontology reasoning style which is generally time-consuming to lead to a low efficiency. For instance, the paper[Matthias Klusch et al., May 2006] provided a hybrid match method based on the direct reasoning for OWL-S[David Martin et al., 2004] described services. The provided examples contain 582 services, 29 query requests, the average response time for each query is about 8 seconds when being simulated in the computer with 2.4G cpu, 1024M memory. Therefore, if there is no single service satisfying the requests, a composition plan by constructing multiple services has to be generated, thus the response time will be much longer. On the other side, when executing a composition plan in a service grid platform, the flexibility of scheduling resources to execute single service has not been well addressed. For example, the traditional meteorological application programs are often bundled with specific hardware resources or platform, which means that these programs are only to be able to be executed in those grid nodes in which concrete meteorological application programs have been deployed previously. As such, even if other grid nodes are free, the user-selected meteorological application service can only be responded and processed by those grid nodes. As a result, grid resources cannot be shared and collaborated efficiently and flexibly.

For the aforementioned issues, in this chapter, we present a QSQL-based collaboration method to support automatic service composition and optimized execution. With this method, QSQL where the important reasoning relationships among ontology concepts and the published service information have been recorded in specially-designed data structures can make sure the quick query response during service discovery. Based on QSQL, service composition can be reached in an automatic, semantic and efficient manner. Particularly, when executing a composition plan, concrete service execution instances which can implement single service interface in different grid nodes can be dynamically bound to each individual abstract service in a composition plan at runtime by comparing their different QoS(Quality of Service) values. Particularly, a concrete collaboration framework is proposed to support automatic behavior for service composition and execution. Totally, our proposed method will not only facilitate e-scientists quickly create composition plans from a large scale of service repository; but also make resource's sharing more flexible. Finally, the experiment has been conducted to demonstrate that our proposed method is not only feasible, but more efficient and applicable.

The remainder of this chapter is structured as follows. Section 2 presents the background. Section 3 gives QSQL-based collaboration framework. Section 4 presents QSQL-based service planning method. Section 5 presents QoS-based service instance selection technique for optimized execution. Section 6 gives the simulation and evaluation. Section 7 gives the future trend and the final section gives the conclusions.

BACKGROUND

Grid computing has been considered as an infrastructure able to provide distributed and heterogeneous resources in order to deliver computational power to resource demanding applications in a transparent way[Ian Foster et al., 2003]. Built on pervasive internet standards, Grids allow organizations to share computing and information resources across department and organizational boundaries in a secure and highly efficient manner. Grids support the sharing, interconnection and use of diverse resources, integrated in the framework of a dynamic computing system. Currently, Grid computing is turning into a service oriented computing environment. Under this situation, traditional Grid components including the access of hardware, legacy applications can be encapsulated as services besides newly-developed service resources. As such, for resolving a complex scientific problem, scientists can link different services together to organize a composition plan and execute them on service grid computing platform. Hence, service has been an important factor for dynamic application composition on Grid environments which can promote the collaboration across and within organizations.

In Grid environments, service composition can be defined as the orchestration of a set of services to accomplish a complicated goal including application processes, business processes, and infrastructure processes. There are two types of service composition models, namely abstract and concrete[Dimosthenis Kyriazis et al., 2007]. While concrete composition models are also referred to as executable composition models. In an abstract model, the involved services are described in an abstract form without referring to specific Grid resources for execution in that it provides the ability to the users to define a composition plan in a flexible way, isolating execution details. Furthermore, an abstract model provides only service semantic information on how the composition plan has been composed. Recently, many methods have been proposed to automatically build composition plans. [Dmytro Zhovtobryukh, 2007]Proposes a goal-driven service composition approach based on a Petri nets modeling technique. With this method, goals are recursively decomposed to be sub-goals until they become executable elementary goals. Because Petri net is a suitable tool for formal analysis and verification of correctness, this approach is of some significance. However, the author didn't give the efficiency comparison of goal decomposition. In actuality, goal decomposition may be time-consuming tasks because of similar complex AI searching. Many research efforts regard the service composition problems as AI planning problems, where a planner is used to determine the combination of actions[Incheon Paik et al., October 2007, Evren Sirin et al., 2004]. With this approach, an explicit goal definition needs to be provided. However, such explicit goal is usually not available. Therefore, most of these approaches are restricted to sequential compositions. Additionally, performance issue can also present another problem when applying sophisticated AI algorithms for automated plan generation. Some composition approaches are based on formal models such as process algebra[Gwen Salaün et al., July 2004], Finite-State Machine[Daniela Berardi et al., December 2003]. The above formal composition methods are very useful to check the existence of a composition and return a composition plan if one exists. However, they fail to automatically find most of such existing composition plans and rank them. In dynamic network environments, alternate execution plans are very important when exceptions occur. Semantics have been proposed as a key to increasing automation in applying Web services and managing Web processes within and across enterprises, and the World Wide Web Consortium (W3C) has recently finished an important standard--Semantic Annotations for WSDL and XML Schema (SAWSDL) for Semantic Web services(SWSs)[Jacek Kopecky et al., 2007]. Currently, there are many existing semantic service composition approaches[Ragone A. et al., 2007, Ulrich Küster, Birgitta Königries, May 2007, Srividya Kona et al., July 2007] and semantic composition projects such as METEOR-S[Rohit Aggarwal et al., September 2004], IRS[Liliana Cabral et al., November 2006], SHOP2[Evren Sirin, Bijan Parsia, 2004]. However, these methods still either stay in a semi-automated state, or in low efficiency of producing a composition plan due to a direct reasoning style. In this chapter, we will give a QSQL-based composition planning method to automatically, semantically, efficiently build a composition plan which can overcome the low efficiency problem brought by the traditional method.

In the concrete model, concrete service execution instance which have been previously deployed in different grid nodes to implement abstract service interfaces are selected to execute the function of each abstract single service in a composition plan. At this phase, different execution instances deployed in different grid nodes may execute the same function, but different QoS. Currently, how to effectively coordinate individual QoS constraints for single service to achieve the best overall QoS benefits without violating end-to-end QoS constraint requirements has been a critical issue. With an increasing number of abstract services in a service composition, the possibility of execution path by selecting different service execution nodes for each abstract service blows up exponentially. Therefore, service selection problem for service composition is a computational-hard problem, which can be regarded as a Multiple choice Multiple dimension Knapsack Problem (MMKP) that has been proved np-hard[Danilo Ardagna et al., 2007, Xiaohui Gu et al., 2006, Tao Yu et al., 2007]. Recently, a lot of approaches such as graph-based techniques[John Gekas et al., October 2005, Jin Xiao et al., 2005], runtime adaptation-based techniques[Girish Chafle et al., September 2006, John Harney et al., September 2007, Swaroop Kalasapur et al., 2007, Kunal Verma et al., September 2006], Service Level Agreement(SLA), negotiation and auction based techniques[Vu L.H. et al., October 2005, Shamimabi Paurobally et al., 2007, Jun Yan et al., 2007, L. Zhang et al., November 2004], user-driven techniques[Yi Sun et al., 2007], Integer Linear Programming (ILP) based techniques[Liangzhao Zeng et al., 2004] have been proposed to resolve overall QoS constraints for optimizing execution path in a service composition. No matter what the merits and the importance current existing methods have, they rely on directly judging constraint conditions to detect multiple paths for picking out a critical execution path, which easily produces a high-time complexity and even an unsatisfactory result in comparison to the best path. As such, the issue on resolving overall QoS constraints to achieve an optimal execution path has not yet been well addressed.

In this chapter, we discuss a QSQL-based service collaboration method including a QSQL-based abstract service composition strategy to automatically build a composition plan and a comprehensive QoS-based service execution instance selecting technique to construct an optimized execution path to execute a composition plan on geographically distributed Grid computing platform.

QSQL-BASED COLLABORATION FRAMEWORK

Figure 1 shows our proposed overall collaboration framework. With this framework, when service providers advertise their services, the produced wsdl documents will be recorded in a virtual service center. Especially, these wsdl documents will be departed into two parts. One part represents service functional description mainly including inputs/outputs and operations; and the other part represents concrete service instances which mainly includes non-function properties. Service functional description will be annotated by semantic information such as adding ontology concepts to their inputs/outputs parameters by semi-automatic methods[Jacek Kopecky, Tomas Vitvar, 2007] (as shown in the middle of Figure 1). Further, these semantic-annotated services will be published to QSQL by service publication algorithm for forming a quick service index list. The upper right part of Figure 1 shows the dynamically built QSQL (we will discuss this in Section 4.1). The upper left part of Figure 1 is the registration center of grid service instances which implement abstract service interfaces. The main aim of this center is to make grid resource's collaboration more flexible. First, in grid environments, when service providers advertise their services, these services will probably be deployed in many grid nodes. Thus, the function of an abstract service can be executed in multiple grid nodes. Therefore, we need an efficient method to decide which grid node will be more suitable to execute an abstract service. For this aim, in our methods, we developed and designed grid service instance center which offers important information for dynamically binding concrete service execution instances to abstract service model. The basic working procedures are as follows. First, all gird nodes, where concrete service implementations of some abstract service models in virtual service center have been deployed in advance, should be registered to this center. Second, the execution conditions of service instances such as precondition and effects should be simultaneously advertised to this center. Third, some non-functional properties(QoS values) of services such as cost, time should also be bounded to this center with corresponding service instances. Finally, the dynamic information of grid nodes including the state of CPU/MEMORY, running processes, job queue needs to be updated periodically. Normally, users care more about whether their needs can be quickly met rather than which grid nodes will respond to their requests. Therefore, ideal grid systems should be transparent for users, and our collaboration approach is exactly an embodiment of such requirements. First of all, as shown in the right-hand bottom of Figure 1, e-scientists or users can quickly and intelligently find a single service or more abstract services as a combination to form an abstract composition plan by our provided service composition algorithm from QSQL. Second, the concrete QoS-based service execution instance selection strategy will dynamically determine which grid nodes to execute the corresponding service instances by judging the global information such as QoS information, user-demanded constraints and other information. The left bottom of Figure 1 shows the ideas. Consequently, our QSQL-based solution results in an effective sharing and collaboration of

Figure 1. QSQL-based collaboration framework

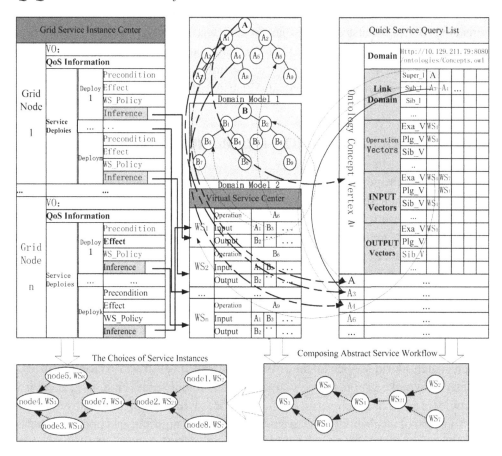

grid resources and services. In the following sections, we will give a detail about the automatic building of abstract service composition plans and their optimized execution.

QSQL-BASED SERVICE COMPOSITION

Overview of QSQL

In order to address the low discovery efficiency brought by the traditional semantic service discovery algorithm based on the direct reasoning manner, we have proposed a pre-reasoning based service discovery method in [Kaijun Ren et al., December 2007]where a preliminary quick service query list (QSQL) has been built to support single service discovery. Then, basing on this work, we have successfully presented an efficient composition algorithm in[Kaijun Ren et al., July 2008] to automatically construct composition plans to meet user's requirements. In order to clearly understand our previous built QSQL, here we give a brief introduction. Generally, when a service provider publish a service to a registration center such as UDDI for facilitating the invocation by other services or applications, an interface description document such as WSDL should be offered on the web. To better support service searching and matching than the keyword-based style, such service description documents should be annotated by semantically-meaningful concepts such as OWL ontologies[Abhijit Patil et al., May 2004]. As a result, based on these semantically-annotated documents, semantic discovery and composition engines by using OWL/RDF reasoners can intelligently search suitable services or combine multiple services to match user requests. However, current such methods are inefficient because ontology reasoning is time-consuming. To overcome the low efficiency problem, we have designed and built QSQL in [Kaijun Ren, Junqiang Song, December 2007] to make a large scale of ontology reasoning processed in advance when a semantically-annotated service is published. Specifically, QSQL can depend on specially-designed data structures to record the important reasoning relationships and the published service information. Such data structures primarily include two parts. One part is the domain of link, and the other part is the domain of data. The purpose of link domain is to avoid repeated reasoning when service models to be published possibly have the same mapped ontology concepts that have already existed in QSQL. The other part is the domain of data, which is primarily used to record service information in corresponding INPUT/OUTPUT data vectors such as Exact_vector—Plugin_vector—Sib_vector—Grapar_vector—Grachd_vector according to their corresponding semantic relationships. Table 1 gives the formal definition of all INPUT/OUTPUT vectors in the domain of data for ontology concepts.

Let us take a concrete example to explain the process of building QSQL. Assume there are some web service models which need to be published to QSQL in Table 2. Particularly, we ignore the semantic annotation processes and directly map the parameters of service inputs/outputs to the best ontology concepts. Some semantic relationships between ontology concepts of the corresponding domains are as follows.

- $USprice \supseteq USdollar$ $datetime \supseteq somedatetime$
- $somedatetime \supseteq givendatetime$ $cityid \equiv citycode$
- $areacode \supseteq cityid$ $location \supseteq cityname$

Table 1. The definition of input/output data vectors for ontology concept in QSQL

Notes: A_i :an ontology concept; $WS_i(I_v, O_v)$: an abstract service model; I_v : the collection of input parameters of WS_i ; O_v : the collection of output parameters of WS_i ; UID: Unique Identification of WS_i	
A_i·Input·Exact_vector	If $\exists C_j \in I_v$, s.t. $A_i \xleftarrow{has-equalclass} C_j$, or $C_j \xrightarrow{has-subclass} A_i$,then WS_i·UID $\in A_i$·Input·Exact_vector
A_i·Input·Plugin_vector	If $\exists C_j \in I_v$, s.t. $C_j \xrightarrow{has-superclass} A_i$, then WS_i·UID $\in A_i$·Input·Plugin_vector
A_i·Input·Sib_vector	If $\exists C_j \in I_v$, s.t. $A_i \xleftarrow{has-sibling} C_j$, then WS_i·UID $\in A_i$·Input·Sib_vector
A_i·Input·Grapar_vector	If $\exists C_j \in I_v$ s.t. $A_i \xrightarrow{has-grandparent} C_j$, then WS_i·UID $\in A_i$·Input·Grapar_vector
A_i·Input·Grachd_vector	If $\exists C_j \in I_v$, s.t. $A_i \xrightarrow{has-grandchild} C_j$, then WS_i·UID $\in A_i$·Input·Grachd_vector
A_i·Output·Exact_vector	If $\exists C_j \in O_v$, s.t. $A_i \xleftarrow{has-equalclass} C_j$, or $A_i \xrightarrow{has-subclass} C_j$, then WS_i·UID $\in A_i$·Output·Exact_vector
A_i·Output·Plugin_vector	If $\exists C_j \in O_v$, s.t. $A_i \xrightarrow{has-superclass} C_j$,then WS_i·UID $\in A_i$·Output·Plugin_vector
A_i·Output·Sib_vector	If $\exists C_j \in O_v$, s.t. $A_i \xrightarrow{has-sibling} C_j$, then WS_i·UID $\in A_i$·Output·Sib_vector
A_i·Output·Grapar_vector	If $\exists C_j \in O_v$, s.t. $A_i \xrightarrow{has-grandchild} C_j$, then WS_i·UID $\in A_i$·Output·Grapar_vector
A_i·Output·Grachd_vector	If $\exists C_j \in O_v$, s.t. $A_i \xrightarrow{has-grandparent} C_j$, then WS_i·UID $\in A_i$·Output·Grachd_vector

According to the introduced service publication algorithm in[Kaijun Ren, Junqiang Song, December 2007], part publication records in QSQL for services of Table 2 are given in Table 3.

For example, when publishing ws5(getregioncode(input(location),output(areacode)), *areacode* is an output parameter of ws5, the publication algorithm first inserts ontology concept *areacode* into QSQL, then adds unique ID of ws5 to its Output•Exact_vector domain(NO 13 of table 3, o.exact means Output•Exact_vector, similar for other abbreviations); further the algorithm depends on ontology reasoning to find out all other related ontology classes such as equivalent, super, sub classes etc. for *areacode*; then respectively adds ID of ws5 to their corresponding output vectors. For instance, in the above semantic relationships, due to *areacode* ⊇ *cityid*, *cityid* ≡ *citycode*, the algorithm inserts ontology concepts *cityid* and *citycode* into QSQL, and adds ID of ws5 to their Output•Plugin_vector domains(NO 6, 9 of Table 3). Repeatedly, the publication algorithm processes each parameter of ws5. As such, all ontology concepts which have semantic relationships with WS5 could be found and inserted into QSQL to record the information of ws5 in corresponding input/output vectors by publication algorithm.

Therefore, QSQL can make sure that a large number of ontology reasoning can be processed at service publication stage. Further, based on QSQL, an planning algorithm offered by us in [Kaijun Ren,

Table 2. Abstract web service models

ID	Operation	Input1	Input2	Input3	Output1
ws1	UStoRMB	USprice	givenDatetime		RMBPrice
ws2	getStockPrice	cityID	someDatetime	stockID	USdollar
ws3	citytoCode	cityname			citycode
ws4	getStockid	stock-name			stockid
ws5	getRegioncode	location			areacode

Table 3. Part records of QSQL for services in Table 2

id	ontology	domain	i.exact	i.plugin	i.sib	i.grapar	i.grachd	o.exact	o.plugin	...
1	rmbprice	...						ws1		
2	USprice	...	ws1					ws2		
3	givendatetime	...	ws1,ws2							
4	USdollar	...						ws2		
5	somedatetime	...	ws2	ws1						
6	cityid	...	ws2					ws3	ws5	
7	cityname	...	ws3,ws5							
8	stockid	...	ws2					ws4		
9	citycode	...	ws2					ws3	ws5	
	location	...	ws5	ws3						
	stockname	...	ws4							
	datetime	...		ws2	ws1					
	areacode	...						ws5		

Xiao Liu, July 2008] can quickly construct composition plans to meet a given user query without much ontology reasoning and user interventions. We have proved the high efficiency brought by our QSQL-based composition methods. More details are presented in [Kaijun Ren, Xiao Liu, July 2008].

Creating Abstract Composition Plan from QSQL

Algorithm 1 shows the main idea to search composition plans from QSQL to meet the user's query. Our designed composition algorithm was mainly taken in a target-based and backward way. For a given user's query, the algorithm first forms the extended input set IC^r for user's inputs by making use of racer reasoning (step 1). These extended input set includes the implied subclasses, super classes, equivalent classes, etc. In the next step, all the specified outputs in a query are pushed into the stack to be searching sub goals (step 2). Then the algorithm pops each sub goal from the stack (step 3). For each sub goal, the algorithm checks if the input set IC^r semantically contains the sub goal (step 4). If it is true for $IC^r \supseteq subgoal$, it means the sub goal can be matched directly by the user's inputs, and the weighted arc between some of query's inputs and sub goal should be a part of a successful searching path. Therefore, the algorithm inserts the path ($I_v^r(i)$, *subgoal*, *matchingweight*) to the composition plan (step 6). Then the algorithm begins to pop and match the next sub goal (step 7) from the stack. However, if IC^r doesn't semantically contain *subgoal*, it means this *subgoal* can't be met by the user's inputs. Hence the algorithm begins to search QSQL and retrieve the related service models to meet *subgoal* (step 9). For this step, because all published service models have been semantically recorded in output vectors V_x^o, x=1,2,3,4,5 (defined in Table 3) of each ontology concept in QSQL, the algorithm can easily retrieve all service models to match *subgoal* by finding it's corresponding ontology concept from QSQL. If $\forall x$, $subgoal.V_x^o$ is null, it means this *subgoal* is unreachable; further all related paths with this sub goal should be deleted from the composition plans (step 11). Contrarily, for any V_x^o, if they are not null, all service models ws_i which belong to $subgoal.V_x^o$ (x=1,2,3,4,5) can sequentially match the sub goal, so the algorithm adds the path (WS_i, *subgoal*, x) to the composition path with the weight value x(step 14). Notably, x simultaneously represents the meaning of the matching degree according to the definition of Table 4. For example, if $WS_i(I_v^s, O_v^s).UID \in subgoal.V_5^o$, then ($WS_i$, *subgoal*, 5) shows ws_i meets *subgoal* with the matching degree EXACT. Now back to the algorithm, if $\forall i, j, x$, $WS_i(I_v^s, O_v^s).UID \in subgoal.V_x^o$, $WS_j(I_v^s, O_v^s).UID \in subgoal.V_x^o$, then the relationship between ws_i and ws_j is $WS_i \otimes WS_j$, which means they can be the alternate path to meet this *subgoal* (step 15). In particular, for each $WS_i(I_v^s, O_v^s).UID \in subgoal.V_x^o$, the inputs I_v^s needs to be concurrently met by either user inputs, or the outputs of other service models so that ws_i can be successfully executed to meet *subgoal*. Therefore,

Table 4. The definition of symbols in algorithm

$WSR(I_v^r, O_v^r)$: user's query	$WS_i(I_v^s, O_v^s)$:service models
I_v^r :specified inputs by	I_v^s :inputs of service model
O_v^r :specified outputs	O_v^s :outputs of service
V_1^o : Output•Exact_vector	V_1^I : Input•Exact_vector
V_2^o : Output•Plugin_vector	V_2^I : Input•Plugin_vector
V_3^o : Output•Sib_vector	V_3^I : Input•Sib_vector
V_4^o : Output•Grapar_vector	V_4^I : Input•Grapar_vector
V_5^o : Output•Grachd_vector	V_5^I : Input•Grachd_vector

Algorithm 1. Find AllProcessPlans

```
Inputs:  WSR($I_v^r, O_v^r$), QSQL;
Outputs: composition plans

1   For $I_v^r$, $IC^r \leftarrow extendingInputsource( I_v^r )$ ;
       //Forming extended input source $IC^r$ of $I_v^r$ by racer reasoning
2   push( $O_v^r$ ) ;
       //For each output o , $o \in O_v^r$ , pushing o to stack so that o will be a search goal
3   subgoal $\leftarrow$ pop() ;
       //Retrieving a subgoal from target stack;
4   relation.Judging($IC^r$, subgoal) ;
       //Judging the semantic relations if $IC^r \supseteq subgoal$
5       Case 1(true): $IC^r \supseteq subgoal$
6       addpath( $I_v^r$ (i), subgoal, matchingweight) ;
           /*Subgoal has been founded, adding path from one input of $I_v^r$
           to subgoal, inserting the matching weight value on this path*/
7       GO TO 3  ; //Poping next subgoal;
        EndCase 1
8       Case 2(false): $IC^r \not\supseteq subgoal$
9       $V_x^o \leftarrow retrieveAllO\_vectorsfromQSQL(subgoal)$, x = 1, 2, 3, 4, 5 ;
           //Retrieving all output vectors $V_x^o$ of subgoal from QSQL
10      If $\forall x$, subgoal.$V_x^o = \emptyset$  Then
11          deleteLocalPath(subgoal) ;
               /* It is impossibile for subgoal to be arrived. Deleting the paths which are
               related with subgoal*/
12          GO TO 3 ;
13      Else For  $\forall i, j, x, WS_i ( I_v^r, O_v^r ).UID \in V_x^o, WS_j ( I_v^s, O_v^s ).UID \in V_x^o$  Do
14              insertSequenceOperatorPath($WS_i$, subgoal, $\succ$, x ) ;
                   // $WS_i$ can match subgoal with matching degree x
15              insertChoiceOperatorPath($WS_i, WS_j, \otimes$) ;
                   //Because of meeting the same subgoal , existing relationship $WS_i \otimes WS_j$
16              push( $I_v^s$ );
                   /*For  $WS_i ( I_v^s, O_v^s ).UID \in I_v^s$ ,making $I_v^s$ become subgoals,
                   pushing $I_v^s$ to stack*/
17              insertParallelismOperatorPath($WS_i, I_v^s, \oplus$ ) ;
                   /*For inputs $I_v^s$ of $WS_i$ ,they need to be meeted simultaneously to
                   execute $WS_i$  */
18          EndFor
        EndElse
        EndCase 2
19  Repeat 3 and 17 until stack is null
```

the inputs I_v^s of ws_i should be pushed into the stack to be next searching goals (step 16). Considering the concurrent, these new sub goals should be added to the path of composition plans in parallelism order (step 17). Similarly, all sub goals should be popped from the stack and processed by step 3 to 17 until the stack is null. When the stack is null, either all composition plans in QSQL will be generated, or there is no such plans to meet the user's query. Because the algorithm has taken the extended and weighted Petri net model, all final composition plans can be represented by Petri nets.

According to algorithm 1, for a given query, composition plans can be reached in an automatic, semantic, and efficient manner from QSQL.

QOS-BASED SERVICE INSTANCE SELECTION STRATEGY FOR OPTIMIZED EXECUTION

Using Local Optimization Policy to Building Initial Execution Path

Assuming a composition plan consists of n abstract services denoted as $ws_i(i = 1,2,...,n)$, and each ws_i has l_i candidate service providers; for each ws_i, c_{ij} denotes the *jth* service provider. $q_{ijr}(r = 1, 2,...m)$ denotes QoS value of c_{ij} on the *rth* QoS attribute where m denotes the total QoS attributes. Thus, considering all QoS values of candidate service providers for each ws_i, $(q_{ijr}, 1 \leq j \leq l_i, 1 \leq r \leq m)$ leads to the following quality matrix Q_i where each row corresponds to a c_{ij} while each column corresponds to a quality dimension.

$$Q_i = \begin{bmatrix} q_{i11} & q_{i12} & \cdots & q_{i1m} \\ q_{i21} & q_{i22} & \cdots & q_{i2m} \\ \cdots & \cdots & \cdots & \cdots \\ q_{il_i1} & q_{il_i2} & \cdots & q_{il_im} \end{bmatrix} \tag{1}$$

Generally, different c_{ij} with different QoS values means different benefits to a user. Thus, for a given composition request with end-to-end QoS constraints, a suitable c_{ij} for each ws_i should be selected for constructing an execution path to achieve the best overall QoS benefits without violating such constraints. However, with an increasing number of services in a service composition, the possibility blows up exponentially. Therefore, service selection problem for service composition is a computational-hard problem and which can be regarded as a Multiple choice Multiple dimension Knapsack Problem (MMKP) that has been proved np-hard [Danilo Ardagna and Barbara Pernici, 2007, Xiaohui Gu and Klara Nahrstedt, 2006, Tao Yu, Yue Zhang, 2007].

In our methods, we take the local optimization policy to select the locally best c_{ij} for matching each ws_i. For this policy, the basic steps are described as follows. Due to different metric of different QoS attributes in the above-mentioned quality matrix Q_i, normalization should be applied to uniform all different metric so that the ranking of c_{ij} will not be biased by any QoS attribute with a large value. We use the following equations (2) and (3) which use their averages to normalize Q_i.

$$q_{ijr}' = q_{ijr} \Big/ \left(\frac{1}{l_i} \sum_{j=1}^{l_i} q_{ijr} \right) \tag{2}$$

$$q_{ijr}' = \left(\frac{1}{l_i} \sum_{j=1}^{l_i} q_{ijr} \right) \Big/ q_{ijr} \tag{3}$$

Especially, in the normalization phase, there are two directions called positive and negative direction in quality dimensions. Positive quality dimension means the higher the value, the higher the quality and negative quality dimension means the higher the value, the lower the quality. For positive quality dimension, we use (2), and for negative, we use (3). After the normalization of Q_i, it can be transformed into another matrix $Q_i' = q_{ijr}', 1 \leq j \leq l_i, 1 \leq r \leq m$). To rank all candidates c_{ij} for each ws_i, supposing ws_r, $r = 1, 2, ..., m$ to be the weights for each QoS attribute ($\sum_{r=1}^{m} ws_r = 1$), we can rank all the candidate c_{ij} by the following score formula (4).

$$Score(c_{ij}) = \sum_{r=1}^{m} q'_{ijr} w_r,$$ (4)

As such, c_{ij} with the highest score can be selected to best map ws_i. Further, for all ws_i included in a service composition, the corresponding c_{ij} with the highest score can be selected to construct an initial execution path.

However, the initial execution path by local optimization policy, does not guarantee all end-to-end QoS constraints. Therefore, we need to calculate the global QoS values on the selected path for checking what constraints have been broken.

Global QoS Computing and Violation Checking

The global QoS computing model is to aggregate QoS values on each quality dimension on the execution path. The literatures in [Danilo Ardagna and Barbara Pernici, 2007, Jorge Cardoso et al., 2004, Michael C. Jaeger et al., September 2004, Tao Yu, Yue Zhang, 2007, Liangzhao Zeng, Boualem Benatallah, 2004]have offered some concrete methods to aggregate QoS values on a service composition execution path. Normally, a service composition path includes sequential structure (Figure 2(a) where service ws_2 will not be executed until service ws_1 is finished), parallel structure (Figure 2(b) where ws_2 and ws_3 are executed concurrently), choice or conditional branch(Figure 2(c) where ws_2 and ws_3 are executed alternatively, i.e., either one service is executed or another, but not both), loop structure(Figure 2(d) where ws_1 is repeated multiple times until some end conditions are satisfied). Particularly, loop structure can be treated as sequential structure by unfolding the cycles[Jorge Cardoso, Amit Sheth, 2004].

Thus, for different structures, different strategies can be applied to aggregate QoS values. Further, global QoS values can be achieved. Here we take QoS attributes such as execution cost, execution time, reputation as examples to demonstrate the computing process. Table 5 shows several global QoS computing formulas where p denotes a composition execution path which has n abstract services, each with $l_i(i=1,2,...n)$ candidate service providers; $\sum_{j=1}^{l_i} x_{ij} = 1$ guarantees that one service provider c_{ij} of all candidates for ws_i is selected to offer the corresponding function. From Table 2, the total execution price on path p equals to the sum of individual price of c_{ij}. Differently, the execution time is the maximum time among all possible sub paths where each parallel or conditional branch can be treated as independent sequential flow [Danilo Ardagna and Barbara Pernici, 2007]. Additionally, the overall reputation, reliability and availability are defined by the multiplication of the individual reputation of c_{ij}. More details about other QoS attributes such as data quality, compensation rate have been respectively presented in [Danilo Ardagna and Barbara Pernici, 2007, Jorge Cardoso, Amit Sheth, 2004, Michael C. Jaeger,

Figure 2. Composition structures

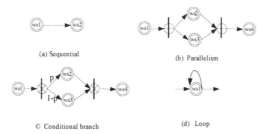

(a) Sequential

(b) Parallelism

© Conditional branch

(d) Loop

Gregor Rojec-Goldmann, September 2004, Tao Yu, Yue Zhang, 2007, Liangzhao Zeng, Boualem Benatallah, 2004].

When a user submits a request, QoS requirements can be expressed as end-to-end composition QoS constraints. As mentioned in Section 2, the initial execution path by local optimization policy is unnecessarily required one to meet such QoS constraints. Therefore, for each user' constraint, we need to execute a constraint checking. We use the following equation groups (5)-(12) to check end-to-end QoS constraints. The left sides of these equations mean the global QoS values on the corresponding quality criteria as demonstrated in Table 5 for the selected execution path *p*. The right sides are the corresponding quality constraints expressed by a user. According to these constraint checking models, all occurred violations can be detected. Particularly, the following equation groups should be extensible and flexible to be adapted to the concrete application scenario. For example, the following equations (5), (6) and (7) can be applied to check if the constraints violate when a user has some QoS requirements on the concrete execution price, time, and reputation.

$$q_{pri}^{total}(p) \leq price_{user},$$ (5)

$$q_{tim}^{total}(p) \leq time_{user},$$ (6)

Table 5.Global QoS computing model

Execution price	$q_{pri}^{total}(p) = \sum_{i=1}^{n} \sum_{j=1}^{l_i} q_{pri}(c_{ij}) x_{ij}, \sum_{j=1}^{l_i} {}_{ij} = 1, x_{ij} \in \{0,1\}$
Execution time	$q_{tim}^{total}(p) = \underset{sp_m \in p}{Max} \sum_{c_{ij} \in sp_m} q_{tim}(c_{ij})$
Reputation	$q_{rep}^{total}(p) = \prod_{i=1}^{n} (\sum_{j=1}^{l_i} q_{rep}(c_{ij}) x_{ij})$
Reliability	$q_{rel}^{total}(p) = \prod_{i=1}^{n} (\sum_{j=1}^{l_i} q_{rel}(c_{ij}) x_{ij})$
Availability	$q_{ava}^{total}(p) = \prod_{i=1}^{n} (\sum_{j=1}^{l_i} q_{ava}(c_{ij}) x_{ij})$
Data quality	$q_{daq}^{total}(p) = \underset{i}{min}(\sum_{j=1}^{l_i} {}_{daq}(c_{ij}) x_{ij})$
Compensation rate	$q_{cop}^{total}(p) = \sum_{i=1}^{n} (\sum_{j=1}^{l_i} (q_{cop}(c_{ij}) q_{pri}(c_{ij}) x_{ij})) / q_{pri}^{total}(p)$
Penalty rate	$q_{pen}^{total}(p) = \sum_{i=1}^{n} (\sum_{j=1}^{l_i} (q_{pen}(c_{ij}) q_{pri}(c_{ij}) x_{ij})) / q_{pri}^{total}(p)$

$$q_{rep}^{total}(p) \geq reputation_{user},\tag{7}$$

$$q_{cop}^{total}(p) \geq compensationrate_{user},\tag{8}$$

$$q_{ava}^{total}(p) \geq availability_{user},\tag{9}$$

$$q_{daq}^{total}(p) \geq data-quality_{user},\tag{10}$$

$$q_{rel}^{total}(p) \geq reliability_{user},\tag{11}$$

$$q_{pen}^{total}(p) \leq penalty-rate_{user},\tag{12}$$

Constraint Violation Corrections

Composition Execution Path for Weighted Graph Model

An abstract composition plan can be converted into a weighted service provider graph according to following rules[Tao Yu, Yue Zhang, 2007]:

- Candidate service providers for each abstract service ws_i are nodes in the graph;
- If a link exists from ws_i to ws_j in the composition plan, then from each service provider for ws_i to each service provider for ws_j, there's a link;
- Add a virtual source node I and sink node O. I is connected to all nodes without incoming links and O is connected to all nodes without outgoing links.
- Add the corresponding rank scores of each service provider to their incoming links. The incoming link of sink node O is set to zero;

Figure 3. Composition weighted-graph model

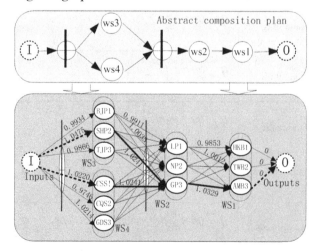

- All execution relationships such as sequential, parallel order between nodes which are controlled by composition structures are kept in the graph.

Figure 4 shows the weighted composition graph for the aforementioned stock query example by above rules. To evaluate each execution path in a weighted composition graph, we give a total score to evaluate the performance for each execution path. For a composite service that has n abstract services, each with l_i ($i=1,2,...n$) candidate service providers, the total score function is defined as follows:

$$F^k = \sum_{i=1}^{n}\sum_{j=1}^{l_i} score(c_{ij}^k) \, x_{ij} \, , \ \ \sum_{j=1}^{l_i} x_{ij} = 1 \, , \ \ \{x_{ij} \in 0,1\} \tag{13}$$

where, F^k denotes the total scores of the kth selected execution path; $\sum_{j=1}^{l_i} x_{ij} = 1$ guarantees that one of service providers is selected to offer the function for each abstract service; c_{ij}^k denotes such selected service provider, and the definition of $score(c_{ij}^k)$ is the same to equation 4 of Section 2. Thus, F^k equals to the sum of all scores of individual score on the kth selected execution path. Thus, the higher the score of F^k is, the better performance the kth selected execution path has.

According to the equation 13, the total scores of the initial execution path by local optimization policy is the sum of the highest scores of all candidate service providers for each abstract service. Hence, the path by local optimization policy will be the best path without considering user end-to-end QoS composition requirements in the weighted graph model. Thus, if we can make a small adjustment along this best path by replacing some service execution instances to exactly correct all occurred constraint violations, the modified execution path will be a good choice for a user to be close to the optimal one. In the following sections, we use a Reverse Order-based algorithm to correct all occurred constraint violations.

Constraint Violation Correction

Figure 4 gives the key procedures for correcting global QoS constraint violations. At the beginning, the algorithm uses the local optimization policy to produce an initial execution path called **LOIEPath** for a user-requested composition plan (step 1). Then **LOIEPath** can be temporarily regarded as an initial value for a global optimal execution path variable called **GOIEPath**. After the initialization of **GOI-EPath**, the algorithm begins to correct all occurred constraint violations. First, the global QoS values on all quality dimensions need to be respectively calculated according to the global QoS computing formulas introduced in Section 5.2(step 3). Then the algorithm checks all constraint violations according to user's end-to-end QoS requirements and all occurred QoS constraint violations can be reached (step 4). Particularly, these constraint violations are ranked by user's preferences. The purpose on doing this is to guarantee that comparably important constraint violations can be corrected in a high priority and the later violation correction cannot breach the previously-corrected constraints. In the next steps, the algorithm begins to process concrete constraint corrections. At first, the algorithm calculates the violation space on each violated QoS constraint attribute, and the space equals to the global QoS value subtracting user-required constraint value (step 7). For example, a user hopes that he can get all services with the price of only 100 dollars. But the global execution fee for the selected execution path is 120 dollars, so the violation space is [0, 20]. Then the algorithm ranks critical nodes which have significant influence on the corresponding constraint violation. For example, with respect to the price violation, the algorithm can rank all nodes in **GOIEPath** according to their individual price. The higher the price is, the more important influence the node has (step 10). For each critical node, step 11 to 19 gradually lower the viola-

Figure 4. The violation correcting operations

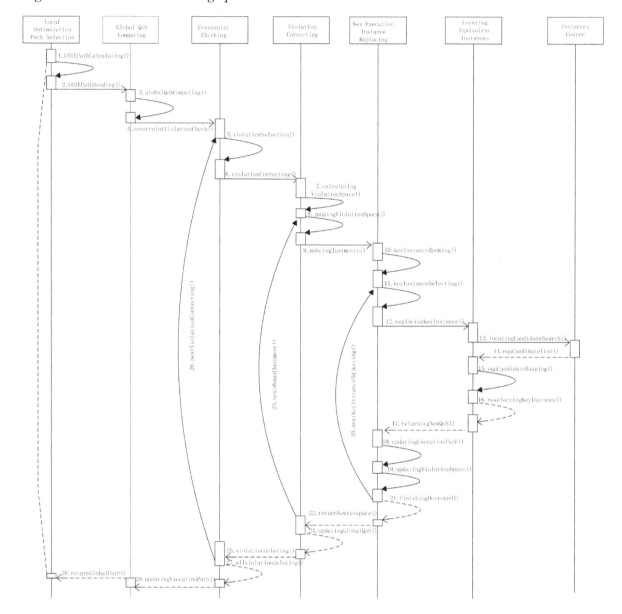

tion space by selecting a more suitable service provider. Specifically, in step 18, for each critical node, there is an associated service provider. Then, the algorithm relocates all other functionally-equivalent service nodes (step 13). In step 15, all candidates are ranked by the aforementioned score equation 4. In step 16, the service node with the highest ranking among all candidates whose corresponding values are less than the original one, is selected to replace the original critical node without violating other previously-corrected quality constraint which has a higher priority. In step 19, the violation space is updated by the new selected QoS value and transmitted to next critical nodes for further decreasing (step 20). Then, the global execution path is modified by the reselected service provider (step 18). Steps

8 to 23 are repeatedly executed until the violation is removed. When a constraint violation is deleted, the global QoS values for other quality attributes should be recalculated on the new execution path for judging the possible existence of constraint violations (step 24). Steps 5 to 26 are repeatedly executed until all constraint violations are deleted. Finally, an updated and optimized path can be returned to meet overall end-to-end composition requirements (step 29).

SIMULATION AND EVALUATION

Simulation Environment

An experiment was performed on our real-world grid workflow management system called SwinDew-G[Jinjun Chen et al., May 2008, Jun Yan et al., 2006, Yun Yang et al., December 2007]. Based on SwinDeW-G, we have designed and developed several related modules to implement our collaboration framework. The overall process flow is shown in Figure 5. Firstly, *QSQL Process Composer Module* can quickly and automatically construct an abstract process plan which consists of abstract services at build-time for a given user query [Kaijun Ren, Xiao Liu, July 2008]. Secondly, for each included abstract service, *Local QoS Computing Module* will rank all candidate service providers. Thirdly, *Local Optimal Selection Module* can select the best service providers for single service to construct an initial execution path. Then, *Global QoS Computing Module* can calculate the aggregated QoS values such as time and price on this path. In addition, *Global Constraint Checking Module* will judge what violations occur. Furthermore, *Violation Correction Module* will employ the proposed algorithm to correct each occurred violation. Finally, an optimized execution path can be rebuilt for scheduling on the SwinDeW-G distributed platform to meet all end-to-end QoS composition requirements.

Environment Results

Test case generation: As a basis, we have published 3500 services to form QSQL. Additionally, candidate service providers are produced as a random value [3, 10] for being associated with corresponding abstract services. Particularly, 5 concrete QoS attributes such as price, time, and reliability, which are randomly generated with a uniform distribution between [1,100], are assigned with each service provider. We totally have produced 30 composition queries.

Composition time: Figure 6(A) shows the execution time for each query by using two different composition methods to build abstract composition plans. As shown in Figure 6(A), the following distinctions can be easily achieved. On one hand, the average execution time (11544ms) of each query by direct reasoning-based composition methods is higher than the time by QSQL-based composition method (2297ms). On the other hand, the fluctuation of each query by direct reasoning is obvious. For the first distinction, the reason is that the direct reasoning-based composition methods need to involve much ontology reasoning when creating the process flow to meet the user's query. By comparison, because the large number of ontology reasoning has been processed previously in QSQL, our algorithm can offer a quick response for each query. For the second distinction, different queries contained different numbers of ontology reasoning by direct reasoning-based methods, which directly caused to the fluctuation of composition time. While in our composition algorithm, ontology reasoning only

Figure 5. Overall process flow

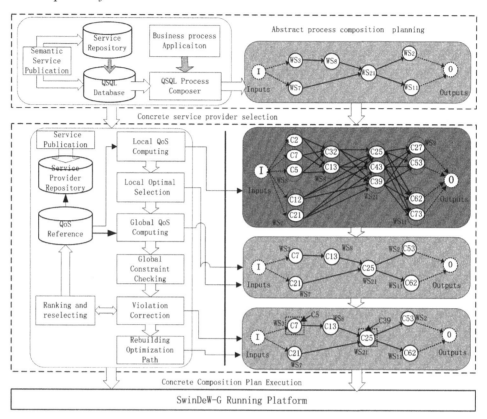

Figure 6. Experiment results

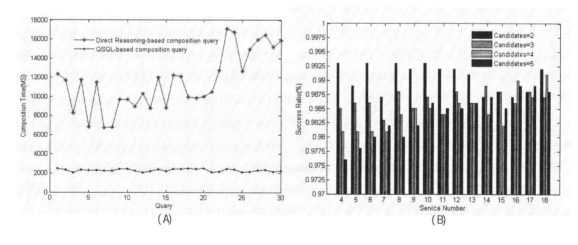

happened in the beginning when forming the extended user's input collection, thus the composition time is relatively stable.

Success ratio: To demonstrate how well our proposed QoS constraint correction methods are, we give the comparison of the success ratio, which is measured by considering the ratio of the total scores of the generated path and the total scores of the best path according to the total score equation 13. Figure 6(B) shows the average success ratio trend for 15 queries including 4 to 18 service number with 3 QoS constraints. First, we can see that the least success ratio is around 97.6%. Additionally, with the increasing number of candidate service providers from 2 to 5, the success ratio decrease slightly. Dramatically, with the increasing service number, the success ratio tends to be increasing trend.

FUTURE TRENDS

Currently, Cloud computing is becoming a new popular topic. Consumers of cloud computing purchase services such as computing capacity on-demand and are not generally concerned with the underlying technologies used to achieve the increase in server capability. The applications of cloud/utility computing models are expanding rapidly as connectivity costs fall, and as computing hardware becomes more efficient at operating at scale. As a result, the services that can be delivered from the cloud have expanded past web applications to include storage, raw computing, or access to any number of specialized services. In future, bringing the power of Service-Oriented Architecture (SOA) and Cloud Computing together to deliver business and practical value to emerging software applications, hardware, and business process provisioning services over the Internet are becoming a future trend. The leading companies are moving their data and services to the internet. Therefore, with the economic incentive, in future, QoS-based service selection are still important challenges in developing a unified service development environment for Cloud Computing as well as creating a scalable, reusable, and configurable service provisioning platform.

CONCLUSION

In this chapter, we have presented a QSQL-based service collaboration framework to support automatic service composition and optimized execution. Specially, with QSQL (Quick Service Query List), the large number of ontology reasoning is processed at service publication stage which enables the quick query response in service discovery or composition. We also have presented a concrete QoS-based service execution instance selecting strategy to build an optimized execution path for achieving overall QoS composition requirements. Our methods can enable grid resource and service sharing to be more flexible. The final simulation has demonstrated the effectiveness of our proposed method.

REFERENCES

Aggarwal, R., Verma, K., Miller, J., & Milnor, W. (September 2004). Constraint Driven Web Service Composition in METEOR-S. *In the proceeding of 2004 IEEE International Conference on Services Computing.* Shanghai,China: IEEE computer society.

Berardi, D., Calvanese, D., De Giacomo, G., Lenzerini, M., & Mecella, M. (December 2003). Automatic Composition of E-services That Export Their Behavior. *In the proceeding of the 1st international conference on service-oriented computing.* Trento,Italy: Springer.

Cabral, L., Domingue, J., Galizia, S., Gugliotta, A., Tanasescu, V., Pedrinaci, C., & Norton, B. (November 2006). IRS-III: A Broker for Semantic Web Services Based Applications. *In the proceeding of the 5th International Semantic Web Conference.* Athens,USA: LNCS.

Cardoso, J., Sheth, A., Miller, J., Arnold, J., & Kochut, K. (2004). Quality of service for workflows and web service processes. *Journal of Web Semantics, 1*(3), 281-308.

Chafle, G., Dasgupta, K., Kumar, A., Mittal, S., & Srivastava, B. (September 2006). Adaptation in Web Service Composition and Execution. *In the proceeding of IEEE 2006 International Conference on Web Services.* Chicago, USA: IEEE Press.

Chen, J., & Yang, Y. (May 2008). Temporal Dependency based Checkpoint Selection for Dynamic Verification of Fixed-time Constraints in Grid Workflow Systems. *In the proceeding of the 30th International Conference on Software Engineering (ICSE2008).* Leipzig, Germany.

Ardagna, D., & Pernici, B. (2007). Adaptive Service Composition in Flexible Processes. *IEEE Transaction on Software Engineering, 33*(6), 369-383.

Foster, I., & Kesselman, C. (2003). *The Grid 2: Blueprint for a New Computing Infrastructure:* Morgan Kaufmann Published.

Fujii, K., & Suda, T. (2005). Semantics-Based Dynamic Service Composition. *IEEE Journal on Selected Areas in Communications, 23*(12), 2361-2372.

Gagne, D., Sabbouh, M., Bennett, S., & Powers, S. (September 2006). Using Data Semantics to Enable Automatic Composition of Web Services. *In the proceeding of 2006 IEEE International Conference on Services Computing.* Chicago,USA: IEEE computer society.

Gu, X., & Nahrstedt, K. (2006). On Composing Stream Applications in Peer-to-Peer Environments. *IEEE Transactions on Parallel and Distributed Systems, 17*(8), 824-837.

Harney, J., & Doshi, P. (September 2007). Adaptive Web Processes Using Value of Changed Information. *In the proceeding of the 5th International Conference on Service-Oriented Computing.* Vienna,Austria: LNCS.

Jaeger, M. C., Rojec-Goldmann, G., & Uhl, G. M. (September 2004). QoS Aggregation for Web Service Composition using Workflow Patterns. *In the proceeding of the 8th IEEE International Enterprise Distributed Object Computing Conference.* California, USA: IEEE computer society.

Gekas, J., & Fasli, M. (October 2005). Automatic Web Service Composition Based on Graph Network Analysis Metrics. *In the proceeding of the 5th International Conference on ontologies,Databases and Applications of Semantics.* Agia Napa,Cyprus: Springer.

Kalasapur, S., Kumar, M., & Shirazi, B. A.(2007). Dynamic Service Composition in Pervasive Computing. *IEEE Transaction on Parallel and Distributed Systems, 18*(7), 907-918.

Klusch, M., Fries, B., Khalid, M., & Sycara, K. (May 2006). Automated Semantic Web Service Discovery with OWLS-MX. *In the proceeding of the 5th International Joint Conference on Autonomous Agents and Multiagent Systems.* Hakodate, Japan: ACM.

Kona, S., Bansal, A., & Gupta, G. (July 2007). Automatic Composition of Semantic Web Services. *In the proceeding of 2007 IEEE International Conference on Web Services.* Salt Lake City, USA: IEEE computer society.

Kopecky, J., Vitvar, T., Bournez, C., & Farrell, J. (2007). SAWSDL: Semantic Annotations for WSDL and XML Schema. *IEEE Internet Computing, 11*(6), 60-67.

Küster, U., Königries, B., Stern, M., & Klein, M. (May 2007). DIANE: An Integrated Approach to Automated Service Discovery, Matchmaking and Composition. *In the proceeding of the 16th International World Wide Web Conference.* Banff, Alberta, Canada: ACM Press.

Kyriazis, D., Tserpes, K., Menychtas, A., Litke, A., & Varvarigou, T. (2007). An innovative workflow mapping mechanism for Grids in the frame of Quality of Service. *Future Generation Computer Systems, In Press, Corrected Proof, Available online 27 July 2007.*

Martin, D., Burstein, M., & Hobbs, J. (2004). OWL-S: Semantic Markup for Web Services. Retrieved from: http://www.w3.org/Submission/OWL-S/. Accessed on Jul 5, 2008.

Medjahed, B., & Bouguettaya, A. (2005). A Multilevel Composability Model for Semantic Web Services. *IEEE Transactions on Knowledge and Data Engineering, 17(7)*, 954-968.

Paik, I., & Maruyama, D. (October 2007). Automatic Web Services Composition Using Combining HTN and CSP. *In the proceeding of the Seventh International Conference on Computer and Information Technology.* Fukushima, Japan: IEEE computer society.

Patil, A., Oundhakar, S., Sheth, A., & Verma, K. (May 2004). METEOR-S Web Service Annotation Framework. *In the proceeding of the 13th International World Wide Web Conference.* New York, USA: ACM Press.

Paurobally, D., Tamma, V., & Wooldrdige, M. (2007). A Framework for Web Service Negotiation. *ACM Transactions on Autonomous and Adaptive Systems, 2(4)*, 14, 1-14:23.

Racer reasoner. Retrieved on Jun 12, 2008. From: http://www.racer-systems.com/index.phtml.

Ragone A., Di Noia, T., Di Sciascio, E., Donini, F. M., Colucci, S., & Colasuonno, F. (2007). Fully automated Web services discovery and composition through concept covering and concept abduction. *International Journal of Web Services Research, 4*(3), 85-112.

Ren, K., Song, J., Chen, J., Xiao, N., & Liu, C. (December 2007). A Pre-reasoning based Method for Service Discovery and Service Instance Selection in Service Grid Environments. *In the proceeding of the 2nd IEEE Asia-Pacific Service Computing Conference.* Tsukuba Science City, Japan: IEEE Press.

Ren, K., Liu, X., Chen, J., Xiao, N., Song, J., & Zhang, W. (July 2008). A QSQL-based Efficient Planning Algorithm for Fully-automated Service Composition in Dynamic Service Environments. *In the proceeding of 2008 IEEE International Conference on Services Computing(SCC 2008).* Honolulu, Hawaii, USA: IEEE Press.

Sala, G. U., Bordeaux, L., & Schaerf, M. (July 2004). Describing and Reasoning on Web Services using Process Algebra. *In the proceeding of 2004 IEEE International Conference on Web Services.* San Diego, USA: IEEE computer society.

Sirin, E., Parsia, B., Wu, D., Hendler, J., & Nau, D. (2004). HTN planning for Web Service composition using SHOP2. *Journal of Web Semantics, 1*(4), 377-396.

Sun, Y., He, S., & Leu, J. Y. (2007). Syndicating Web Services: A QoS and user-driven approach. *Decision Support Systems 43 (2007) 243–255, 43*(1), 243-255.

Sycara, K., Paolucci, M., Ankolekar, A., & Srinivasan, N. (2003). Automated discovery, interaction and composition of Semantic Web services. *Journal of Web Semantics, 1*(1), 27-46.

Verma, K., Doshi, P., Gomadam, K., Miller, J., & Sheth, A. (September 2006). Optimal Adaptation in Web Processes with Coordination Constraints. *In the proceeding of IEEE 2006 International Conference on Web Services.* Chicago, USA.

Vu, L. H., Hauswirth, M., & Aberer, K. (October 2005). QoS-based service selection and ranking with trust and reputation management. *In the proceeding of the International Conference on Cooperative Information Systems.* Agia Napa, Cyprus.

Xiao, J., & Boutaba, R. (2005). QoS-Aware Service Composition and Adaptation in Autonomic Communication. *IEEE Journal on Selected Areas in Communications, 23*(12), 2344-2360.

Yan, J., Kowalczyk, R., Lin, J., Chhetri, M. B., Goh, S. K., & Zhang, J. Y. (2007). Autonomous service level agreement negotiation for service composition provision. *Future Generation Computer Systems-the International Journal of Grid Computing Theory Methods and Applications, 23*(6), 748-759.

Yan, J., Yang, Y., & Raikundalia, G. K. (2006). SwinDeW-a p2p-based decentralized workflow management system *IEEE Transactions on Systems, Man, and Cybernetics—Part A: Systems and Humans, 36*(5), 922-935.

Yang, Y., Liu, K., Chen, J., Lignier, J., & Jin, H. (December 2007). Peer-to-Peer Based Grid Workflow Runtime Environment of SwinDeW-G. *In the proceeding of the 3rd International Conference on e-science and Grid Computing.* Bangalore,India: IEEE Computer Society

Yu, T., Zhang, Y., & Lin, K. J. (2007). Efficient Algorithms for Web Services Selection with End-to-End QoS Constraints. *ACM Transactions on the Web, 1*(1), *6, Publication date: May 2007., 1(1)*, 6:1-6:26.

Zeng, L., Benatallah, B., Ngu, A. H. H., Dumas, M., Kalagnanam, J., & Chang, H. (2004). QoS-Aware Middleware for Web Services Composition. *IEEE Transaction on Software Engineering, 30*(5), 311-327.

Zhang, L., & Ardagna, D. (November 2004). SLA-Based Profit Optimization in Autonomic Computing Systems. *In the proceeding of the 2nd International Conference on Service Oriented Computing.* New York, USA.

Zhovtobryukh, D. (2007). A Petri Net-based Approach for Automated Goal-Driven Web Service Composition. *Simulation, 83*(1), 33-63.

Chapter XV
Hands–On Experience in Building Institutional Grid Infrastructure

Xiaoyu Yang
University of Cambridge, UK

Gen-Tao Chiang
University of Cambridge, UK

ABSTRACT

It will become increasingly popular that scientists in research institutes will make use of Grid computing resources for running computer simulations and managing data. Although there are some production Grids available, it is often the case that many organizations and research projects need to build their own Grids. However, building Grid infrastructure is not a trivial job as it involves sharing and managing heterogeneous computing and data resources across different organizations, and involves installing many specific software packages and various middleware. This can be quite complicated and time-consuming. Building a Grid infrastructure also requires good knowledge and understanding of distributed computing, parallel computing and Grid technologies. Apart from building physical Grid, how to build a user infrastructure that can facilitate the use of and easy access to these physical infrastructures is also a challenging task. In this chapter, the authors summarize some hands-on experience in building an institutional Grid infrastructure. They describe knowledge and experience obtained in the installations of Condor pools, PBS clusters, Globus Toolkit, and SRB (Storage Resource Broker) for computing Grid and data Grid. The authors also propose to use a User-Centered Design (UCD) approach to develop a Grid user infrastructure which can facilitate the use of the Grid to improve the usability.

INTRODUCTION

"Grid computing is an infrastructure that enables flexible, secure, coordinated resource sharing among dynamic collections of individuals, institutions and resources" (Foster, 2001). However, this description still does not give a concrete definition to Grid and people use the term "Grid" with different meanings.

For instance, the most widely used "Grid" refers to computing Grids. This type of Grid refers to the sharing of computer resources, such as High Performance Computing (HPC), High Throughput Computing (HTC), or Condor-like desktop Grids, over the Internet. It aims ultimately to turn the global network of computers into one vast resource of computing power. LHC Computing Grid (LCG), now called Enabling Grid for e-Science (EGEE) (http://www.eu-egee.org), is a typical computing Grid project. It integrates more than 60,000 processors all over the world for processing petabytes of data generated by the Large Hadron Collider (LHC) at CERN (Lamanna, 2004).

The second interpretation of "Grid" is a data Grid. This type of Grid aims to allow data discovery and data sharing easily between collaborators. One example is the NERC Data Grid (NDG) (http://ndg.badc.rl.ac.uk). It creates a data Grid through which data from several NERC projects is accessible. Another example is the Biomedical Informatics Research Network (BIRN) (http://www.nbirn.net/). It is a biomedical science collaboration project within the USA. It consists of several projects on neuron-imaging of human neurological disorders and associated animal models.

The third interpretation of "Grid" is a collaborative Grid. This type of Grid tries to improve the communication between collaborators by using multiple participants video conferencing system and related applications. The Access Grid (AG) is an example. It provides such video conferencing along with other tools for sharing applications and data within a Virtual Organization (VO). A VO is a group of individuals or institutions who share the computing and other resources of a "Grid" for a common goal (Clery, 2006).

However, none of these single interpretations reflects the whole picture of the "Grid". An ideal Grid infrastructure should provide the functions of the most important parts from three types of Grids: Computing Grids, Data Grids, and Collaborative Grids. Since there are several collaborative tools and they are relatively easy in terms of deployment, this chapter will focus on building up computing and data Grid.

It will become increasingly popular that scientists in research institutes will make use of Grid computing resources for running computer simulations and managing data, this involves building a Grid infrastructure. Although there are some existing production Grids, such as National Grid Services (NGS) (http://www.grid-support.org) in UK, EGEE in EU, or Open Science Grid (OSG) (http://www.opensciencegrid.org) in the USA, it is still often the case that many organizations and research projects need to build their own Grids due to various reasons. For example, there are some security and data policy issues which do not allow either computing or data resources to be shared with others, that a test Grid environment is required for testing configurations and running applications before migrating to productions sites, or building research project-specific Grid, etc. Apart from the physical Grid, a user-level infrastructure to facilitate the use of physical Grid also needs to be built.

In this chapter, we summarize some hands-on experience in building small-scale Grid infrastructure. As Grid infrastructure usually involves computing Grid and data Grid, we describe knowledge and experience obtained in installing Condor pools, PBS clusters, Globus Toolkit and SRB. We also introduce some job submission tools, and Grid monitoring and management tools. Furthermore, tools and technologies which can be employed in User-Centered Design (UCD) approach to develop a user-level infrastructure to facilitate the use of Grid are reviewed, and a case study is discussed.

BUILDING COMPUTING GRID

Serial Job and Parallel Job

There are different use cases for using Grids. Ideally, the Grid is good for embarrassingly parallelization which means that each job does not have to communicate between processors and each job is independent to others. A typical use case is parameter sweep or time series analysis. However, there are still many cases that applications require communication between processors due to the nature of the model or the legacy code, for example, the program was written with MPI (http://www.mpi-forum.org/) and it would be time-consuming to take them out. Thus, a computing Grid should include both High Performance Computing resources which support running MPI or parallel jobs and High Throughput Computing resources which is suitable for running a number of serial jobs.

The computing Grid described in this chapter includes a Condor pool (http://www.cs.wisc.edu/condor/) and a small PBS cluster (TORQUE, 2008). Each of them should provide a Globus (http://www.globus.org) gatekeeper as an interface for those users outside the institutional administration domain to access the resources. More details will be described in the following sections. Conceptually, people can submit jobs from anywhere across the Internet to this computing Grid, as long as they can be authenticated with valid X509 certificates. A resource broker can also be implemented as a workload management and job submission system, through which users can submit jobs to the Grids without worrying about Globus, Condor, or PBS commands.

Condor

Condor Overview

Condor is a workload management system for computation-intensive jobs developed at the University of Wisconsin. Condor differs from traditional batch scheduling systems in that it does not require the underlying resources to be dedicated. Like PBS or other queuing systems, Condor provides a job queuing mechanism, scheduling policy, priority scheme, resource monitoring, and resource management. Users submit their serial or parallel jobs to Condor, Condor places them into a queue, chooses when and where to run the jobs based upon a policy, monitors their progress, and ultimately informs the user upon completion. Condor's architecture allows it to succeed in areas where traditional scheduling systems fail, such as managing heterogeneous computing resources (Thain et al., 2005).

The whole Condor system has different services and each of them plays a different role. One of the most important services is the central manager. A group of machines that share the same central manager is called a pool, and pools can be connected by a process called "flocking". Condor will match jobs (*matchmaking*) to suited machines in a pool according to job requirements and community, resource owner and workload distribution policies and may vacate or migrate jobs when a machine is required. The central manager is like a resource broker for the entire pool, tracking where the jobs run and finding which resources are available. Most importantly, when a job is submitted, it determines which machine will run that job. Every machine in a pool must be able to talk to the central manager. The mechanism of a Condor can be described in Figure 1. Users can submit jobs from a submit machine to the central manager, which will find available resources within the pool and pass the jobs to the execution machine(s).

Figure 1. A graphical representation of Condor pool architecture (Condor manual, 2008)

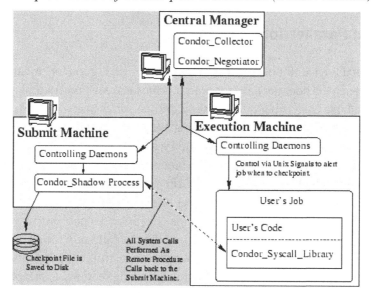

This service-based architecture of Condor can enable many of these services to be adapted for different uses and purposes, represented by different *Universes*, or Condor run-time environments. The *standard* universe provides the entire set of Condor functionality such as checkpointing and migration to programs re-linked with a special Condor library. The *Vanilla* universe provides fewer features but suited to a wider range of programs. Condor also supports specialized universes for *Java*, *PVM* (parallel applications), and *MPI* applications, as well as interaction with Grid resources managed by an array of Grid middleware technology (e.g. Globus Toolkit, Unicore).

An important characteristic of Condor for the matchmaking capabilities is the use of Class Advertisements (*ClassAds*). Matchmaking is a symmetric process where job and machine requirements, and ranks, are considered. A *ClassAd* is a set of uniquely named expressions which use a schema-free semi-structured model. *ClassAds* enable mappings between attributes and expressions to be specified and evaluated with respect to another *ClassAd*. A *ClassAd* in Condor will either express a job's characteristics, requirements and preferences (e.g. memory, OS, etc.), or describe the characteristics of a computing resource and any requirements or preferences upon the jobs.

Condor provides a very flexible mechanism. We can modify condor configuration files to determine which service to be run on which machine. For example, we can configure to allow both *central manager* and *submit machine* to run on the same machine. If this is the case, this machine will run most Condor core daemons, such as *condor_master* for managing other daemons, *condor_collector* for collecting all the information about the condor pool, *condor_negotiator* for all the match-making within the condor system, *condor_schedd* for representing resource requests to the condor pool. A submit machine also needs to run *condor_schedd*. All working nodes need to run two daemons: *condor_master* and *condor_startd*. *Condor_startd* is required for execution machines (Condor manual, 2008).

Installation of Condor

There are some preparation jobs before installing Condor. Firstly, we need to decide which machine will be used for running Condor *central manager*. Usually, this machine should be a dedicated server machine. Secondly, we need to decide whether we are to use dedicated submit machine(s), or to allow all the Condor executable nodes to submit jobs. This is one of the advantages of using Condor that we do not need to logon to a dedicated submit machine to submit jobs. Thirdly, we need to decide whether this Condor pool use NFS or AFS as sharing file system, and whether this pool will support Java. Lastly, we need to decide whether root or other Unix user will be the Condor administrator. It is recommended to create a Unix/Linux user called "condor" as a Condor administrator, who owns Condor related files.

We are now ready to start the Condor installation. Condor installation files can be downloaded from Condor website. After Condor file is untared, we will see two Perl scripts (i.e. *condor_configure* and *condor_install*) and several directories such as bin, etc, example, lib, libexec, and man, etc. *Condor_configure* and *condor_install* are the same program which can be used for installation. Although *condor_configure* is easier in terms of the installation process, *condor_install* is more likely to be used due to its interactive installation procedure. For more comprehensive installation procedures, we can refer to Condor online manual.

There are several Condor configuration files. The global Condor configuration file *condor_config* is shared by all machines in the pool. Condor has also got a local configuration file which is used for configuring the local machine. The configuration parameters within *condor_configu.local* file can override settings in global configuration file. For instance, we can set DAEMON_LIST = MASTER, COLLECTOR, NEGOTIATOR in the *condor_config.local* file to decide which daemons are running in this machine. In this case, the machine will be running as a *central manager* which requires master, collector and negotiator daemons.

Condor daemons can be started by running *condor_master* which will spawn other daemons defined in DAEMON_LIST. We can simply use ps –aux |grep condor to see whether Condor daemons are running correctly, as shown in Figure 2.

After repeating the same procedure for other work nodes, we can use *condor_status* to check which machines have successfully joined the pool.

We can now run a simple job to test the functionality of the pool. Assume we are going to run a simple script hostname.sh (which simply outputs the hostname of the machine) on a working node of the Condor pool, we need to define a basic Condor job description file (shown in Figure 4.), We can set Requirement=Machine=="the hostname" to test whether the job can be submitted and executed on a specific work node. The flag "Requirement" can define the user or job requirements such as the architecture of the machine, memory size, or even a specific executable machine. The job can be sub-

Figure 2. An example of process running on Central Manager

```
condor   21285  0.0  0.1   7136  2580  ?        Ss   May22   0:20 condor_master
condor   21345  0.0  0.1   7920  3736  ?        Ss   May22   0:27 condor_collector -f
condor   21361  0.0  0.1   7708  3704  ?        Ss   May22   0:13 condor_negotiator -f
```

Figure 3. An example shows the status of executable nodes within a pool

```
Name         OpSys      Arch   State      Activity   LoadAv Mem   ActvtyTime

vm1@badger1-- LINUX      INTEL  Claimed    Busy       1.080  2000  0+01:40:06

vm2@badger1-- LINUX      INTEL  Claimed    Busy       1.090  2000  0+01:16:09

vm2@badger8-- LINUX      INTEL  Claimed    Busy       1.000  2000  0+00:04:04

vm1@badger9-- LINUX      INTEL  Claimed    Busy       0.350  2000  0+00:02:50

vm2@badger9-- LINUX      INTEL  Claimed    Busy       1.000  2000  0+19:55:10

vm1@donkey--n WINNT51    INTEL  Unclaimed  Idle       0.040  1022  0+03:30:49

...............................................

              Total Owner Claimed Unclaimed Matched Preempting Backfill

       INTEL/LINUX    20    0      18        2       0          0         0

     INTEL/WINNT51     1    0       0        1       0          0         0

            Total    21    0      18        3       0          0         0
```

Figure 4. Condor job description file

```
Universe = vanilla

Executable  = hostname.sh

should_transfer_files = YES

when_to_transfer_output = ON_EXIT_OR_EVICT

Requirements = Machine == "condor-test1.xxx.xx.xx"

Log = test.1.log

output = test.1.out

error = test.1.err

Queue
```

mitted by using the condor_submit command. The queuing status can be checked by using condor_q, and status of the entire pool can be checked by using condor_status. In this example, if the job has been successfully executed on the request working node, the output file 'test.1.out' will then record the hostname of the machine where the job was executed.

We have now set up a functional Condor pool. In practice, there will be many different problems which can cause the pool to not function properly. It is recommended to join the official Condor mailing list where further information and community assistance can be obtained.

CamGrid: A University of Cambridge Computational Grid

CamGrid is a project in University of Cambridge which aims to build a university-wide Grid based on Condor. It was conceived by many departments and institutions within the university who decided to federate their computational facilities. Those resources could be desktops or dedicated machines, which may or may not be behind firewalls (Calleja et al., 2004).

In order to make this Condor pool work as part of CamGrid resources and be able to "flock" to other department Condor pools, campus wide IPs have to be arranged and routed. In CamGrid, each participating machine is given an IP address assigned by Cambridge eScience Centre (CeSC). This IP address is routable only within the Cambridge University Data Network (CUDN). A machine may have several IP addresses, but Condor is forced to use the CUDN one during operation by setting the parameter NETWORK_INTERFACE in the *condor_config* file. Each host is assigned a CamGrid hostname in domain Grid.private.cam.ac.uk, which the university DNS servers recognize (Calleja et al., 2004). Moreover, FLOCK_TO and FLOCK_FROM in the *condor_config* file has to be modified to reflect which pools are accepted to run the jobs.

In order to ensure that machines within a pool can talk to each other, and central managers can communicate with other central managers within the campus, several firewall ports need to be opened. Condor uses port 9618, for the Collector on the Central Manager. It also uses a number of dynamically chosen transient ports, and it is possible to restrict the range of these dynamically chosen ports. However, one thing needs to be noted that, if Globus is built on top of the Condor, this port range will then limits the Globus port range.

PBS Cluster

PBS Overview

Portable Batch System (PBS) was originally developed for NASA in the early to mid-1990s. PBS is a job scheduler that allocates network resources to batch jobs. It can schedule jobs to be executed on networked, multi-platform UNIX environments.

PBS has several versions. OpenPBS is the original open source version. PBS Pro is an enterprise-level professional version maintained and sold commercially by Altair Engineering. Terascale Open-Source Resource and QUEue Manager (TORQUE) is an open source work of OpenPBS maintained by Cluster Resources, Inc. TORQUE also incorporates many scalability, fault tolerance, and feature extension patches provided by NCSA, and other HPC centers (TORQUE, 2008).

Unlike Condor, PBS is often used for managing homogeneous resources and it has better support for running parallel jobs using the Message Passing Interface (MPI) toolkit. Although Condor also supports running MPI jobs, we tend to use PBS cluster for this purpose, as using Condor in heterogeneous environment usually causes huge latency and is not ideal for parallel jobs. This chapter uses the TORQUE version of OpenPBS along with its default job scheduler.

A PBS cluster is basically a master-slave architecture. The main function of the master machine or so called head node is to allocate jobs to other salve machines or work nodes. Work nodes simply run the jobs which are assigned by the head node. The most important part of a cluster is the communication between the master and slave machines.

Installation of PBS

The cluster usually refers to an architecture which has a submit machine (i.e. head node) along with many other working nodes. However, several Linux services have to be deployed in advance in order to run a cluster properly.

Since a cluster requires master and slave machines talking to each other and running several sensitive daemons, it is better to setup a cluster in a private network. Thus, a master node usually needs two network cards, one for public IP and one for internal private IP. The master node also requires a relative big hard disk or even mounts a disk array.

In addition to physical requirements, master node needs to run some Linux services or some tools need to be installed, which include: (i) A Network Address Translation (NAT) server which can enable the private network to access the public internet resources. (ii) RSHD (Remote Shell Daemons) which allows the execution of shell commands as another user, and on another computer across a computer network. Alternatively, we can use SSH. (iii) Network Information Services (NIS) which can let the master and slave machines share same account and password information. (v) Network File System (NFS) is used to let the whole cluster to share the same file system. (vi) MPICH is a toolkit that implements the Message Passing Interface (MPI) standard and allows many processors to communicate with each other. MPICH consists of mpirun command and compiling tools such as *mpicc* and *mpif90* for compiling MPI programs written in C/C++ or Fortran. Slave machines usually require RSH or SSH client, NIS client, and NFS client to be installed.

More detail about the configuration of those Linux services can be found in many Linux administration books or from Web. About configuration of MPICH, we can modify the machines.LINUX file to add the hostname or IP addresses regarding work nodes. If all the configuration and setting are correct, we should be able to run an MPI test job by using the *mpirun* command and *mpich* test program on head node, see a screenshot in Figure 5.

The system can now support running parallel jobs. However, a local batching system (TORQUE) is required to be installed in order to allocate jobs to the work nodes. We need to download the TORQUE distribution file, extract and build the distribution on the machine that will act as the "TORQUE server", the head node running *pbs_server* daemon. A quick start guide of TORQUE can be found at ("TORQUATE Quick Start", n.d.). After the installation of TORQUE server, we can then run *torque-package-server-linux-i686.sh* to configure it. The TORQUE is usually installed at */var/spool/torque*. We can modify */var/spool/torque/server_priv/nodes* file to add the host name of compute nodes. For slave machines, we can follow the same installation procedure but run different script to configure

Figure 5. A screenshot of running MPI program

```
./mpirun -np 2 cpi

Process 0 on cluster1.private.cam.ac.uk

Process 1 on cluster2.private.cam.ac.uk

pi is approximately 3.1416009869231254, Error is 0.0000083333333323

wall clock time = 0.000253
```

compute nodes. The compute nodes run *pbs_mom* daemon. We also need to modify */var/spool/torque/ mom_priv/config* to configure compute nodes. This file basically tells the PBS client which machine is the head node. Since we are using NFS, we have to use *$usecp* parameter to specify how to map to a user's home directory.

The head node needs to run a scheduler daemon, The scheduler interacts with *pbs_server* to make decisions on resource usage and allocate nodes to jobs. TORQUE has a default scheduler, *pbs_sched*, which is very basic and can just provide poor utilization of cluster's resources. In many cases, we can use other advanced scheduler like *Maui* or *Moab* workload manager.

In order to use PBS cluster, we also need to install client commands (e.g. qsub, qstat) at local machines to submit jobs to *pbs_server*, which will then informs the scheduler to obtain instructions to run the job with the node list.

The PBS can be started by simply typing *pbs_server* and *pbs_mom* at head node and computer nodes. There are several commands available to test whether the PBS is installed successfully. For example, we can use *pbsnodes −a* to check the status of all the compute nodes within the cluster. Alternatively, we can use *qsub* to submit the job and use *qstat* to check the queuing status.

Globus

Overview

The concept of the "computing Grid" can be thought as a virtual super computer across the public network. It consists of multiple heterogeneous resources (e.g. clusters, condor pools) and allows users from different organizations to use them (e.g. run jobs on other's clusters or condor pools). However, treating multiple resources across the network domain as a virtual computer is hard and there will be some issues such as security, computing resources allocation, system monitoring, networking, and data management, which need to be addressed.

Globus Toolkit (http://www.globus.org/toolkit/) is developed to deal with those issues. Globus is the most well known Grid middleware, and is developed by the *Globus Alliance*. It is a realization of Open Grid Services Architecture (OGSA) proposed by the Global Grid Forum (GGF). OGSA describes an architecture for a service-oriented Grid computing environment. Services that the OGSA defines include resource monitoring and discovery service, a job submission infrastructure, a security infrastructure, and data management services, etc.

The Globus Toolkit 4 (GT4) also includes a complete implementation of the WSRF specification (http://www.globus.org/wsrf/), which specifies how to develop a stateful Web services. In WSRF, Web Service and associated state are treated as separate entities. WSRF uses an entity called *resource* to store all the state information. A stateful Web service can then be realized by instructing the Web service to use a particular resource. A paring of Web Service with associated resource is called WS-Resource. The address of WS-Resource is called endpoint reference which can be presented by *WS-addressing*. Major specifications comprised in WSRF include: *WS-ResourceProperties, WS-ResourceLifetime, WS-ServiceGroup, WS-BaseFaults*, etc. Related specifications include *WS-Notification* and *WS-Addressing*.

Some services provided by Globus Toolkit are briefly introduced as follows:

1. *Grid Security Infrastructure (GSI).* GSI is used for security checking. It uses certificates for identity checking instead of traditional username and password. A certificate uses a digital signature to

Figure 6. pbsnodes –a shows the status of all working nodes of the cluster

```
pbsnodes -a
cluster1
    state = free
    np = 1
    properties = all
    ntype = cluster
    status = opsys=linux,uname=Linux iguana 2.6.9-67.0.1.EL #1 Wed Dec 19 15:20:48
CST 2007 i686,sessions=4174 4354 4363 4370 4404 4408 4410 4417 12571 13380 13766
13974,nsessions=12,nusers=2,idletime=84134,totmem=4103344kb,availmem=3741840
kb,physmem=1034940kb,ncpus=1,loadave=0.00,netload=1151846112,state=free,jobs
=? 0,rectime=1211635572
cluster2
    state = down
    np = 1
    properties = all
    ntype = cluster
```

bind together a public key with identity information such as the name of a person, organization, email, and so forth. The certificate can be used to verify that a public key belongs to an individual. A certificate needs to be issued by Certification Authority (CA). CA is an entity which issues digital certificates for use by other parties. Clobus Toolkit provides a software tool *simpleCA* for certificate management. Since GSI is very sensitive to time setting, Network Time Protocol (NTP) should be configured for synchronization.

2. *GridFTP.* GridFTP is used for data transfer. It extends the standard FTP protocol for data transfer. Specific features of GridFTP includes support of the Grid Security Infrastructure (GSI) and Kerberos authentication, parallel file transfer, partial file transfer, etc.

3. *Monitoring and Discovery System (MDS) for information services.* The information regarding the Grid resources or running jobs can be gathered by using MDS. In Globus Toolkit 4 MDS uses standard interfaces defined within the Web Services Resource Framework (WSRF) and WS-Notification specifications.

4. *Grid Resource Allocation Management (GRAM), also known as gatekeeper.* GRAM is the most important service provided by Globus, which enables users to locate, submit, monitor and cancel remote jobs on Grid-based compute resources. GRAM can figure out how to convert a request for resources into commands that local computers can understand. However, GRAM itself does not provide the job scheduler functions. In fact, it provides a single interface for different job scheduler such as PBS, Condor, or LSF. The GT4 release includes the Pre WS GRAM (i.e. GRAM 2) and WS GRAM (i.e. GRAM 4) which contains a WSRF implementation.

Installation of Globus

The installation of Globus requires some prerequisite software to be installed such as Globus installer, J2SDK, Apache Ant, and Perl, etc. The full list of prerequisites can be found in Globus administration guide.

The installation of Globus usually refers to installing Globus at cluster or Condor pool end (e.g. at PBS head node or Condor Central Manager). We assume the WS GRAM will be installed. Before installation, a Unix user "globus" has to be created and a directory owned by the user "globus" need also be created for installing packages. This directory usually is /usr/local/globus. Untar the Globus installer *gt4.0.1-all-source-installer.tar.gz* and run the "*configure*" with prefix pointing to the Globus installation directory defined previously. We also need to define which job scheduler should be used.

Figure 7. A command line for configuring Globus installation and enabling WSGRAM condor installation

```
./configure --prefix=/usr/local/globus-4.0.2 --enable-wsgram-condor
```

Figure 8. A start-stop script for launching WS-GRAM

```
#! /bin/sh
set -e
export GLOBUS_LOCATION=/usr/local/globus
export JAVA_HOME=/usr/java/j2sdk1.4.2_10/
export ANT_HOME=/usr/share/ant
export GLOBUS_OPTIONS="-Xms256M -Xmx512M"
. $GLOBUS_LOCATION/etc/globus-user-env.sh
cd $GLOBUS_LOCATION
case "$1" in
    start)
        $GLOBUS_LOCATION/sbin/globus-start-container-detached -p 8443
        ;;
    stop)
        $GLOBUS_LOCATION/sbin/globus-stop-container-detached
        ;;
    *)
        echo "Usage: globus {start|stop}" >&2
        exit 1
        ;;
esac
```

If the Globus is to be installed on the Condor central manager, *--enable-wsgram-condor* should be used (see Figure 7). If it is to be installed on the PBS head node, *--enable-wsgram-pbs* should be used. Globus will then compile and install the job manager which is a Perl scrip on Condor central manager machine or PBS head node.

We also need to add environmental variables $JAVA_HOME and $ANT_HOME in the /etc/profile in addition to the $PATH. Now we should be able to run the *make* and *make install* to install the Globus.

Next step is to setup a local CA or using existing CA (e.g. UK e-Science CA). The procedures of setting up CA can refer to the *simpleCA* part in Globus installation guide. If we know which CA is going to be used, the CA certificates along with singing policy can be put in */etc/grid-security/certificates*. The host certificate (*hostcert.pem*) and host key (*hostkey.pem*) can be put under */etc/grid-security*.

We can create a start-stop script as shown in Figure 8 to start Globus web services container.

If to use Pre WS GRAM (GRAM 2), we can create services description file under xinit.d (shown in Figure 9), and then add associated service name and port number to */etc/services*.

Finally we need to create a Grid-mapfile under */etc/grid-security*. This file has a list of Distinguished Names (DN) and serves as an access control list for GSI enabled services. The file also maps each DN to a local user account (see Figure 10).

Since our Condor pool does not use a share file system, the Globus job manager can not handle this situation well. Thus, the Condor job manager file located at *$GLOBUS_LOCATION/lib/perl/Globus/GRAM/condor.pm* has to be modified to realize the file sharing. The following two lines have to be added, as shown in Figure 11.

The Globus GRAM server has now been installed and configured. In order to test it, we can either run some Globus client commands on the machine where the GRAM server is just installed or use some Globus client tools written by third parties to connect to the GRAM server. For example, we can use a client tool, namely, GSI-SSH developed by NGS to connect to the Globus GRAM server and run some Grid services (http://grid.ncsa.uiuc.edu/ssh/). Make sure to import the CA certificate, user certificate, and userkey before using it.

Globus itself also provides several GRAM client commands which can be used to test whether the GRAM is working or not. Assume the users' certificates (i.e. usercert.pem and userkey.pem) have been

Figure 9. A xinit.d script for Pre WS GRAM gatekeeper service

```
service gsigatekeeper

{

socket_type = stream

protocol = tcp

wait = no

user = root

env = LD_LIBRARY_PATH=/usr/local/globus/lib

server = /usr/local/globus/sbin/globus-gatekeeper

server_args = -conf /usr/local/globus/etc/globus-gatekeeper.conf

disable = no

}
```

Figure 10. A screenshot of Grid mapfile

```
"/C=UK/O=eScience/OU=Cambridge/L=UCS/CN=gen-tao" gtniees
"/O=NERC/OU=NIEeS/OU=niees.group.cam.ac.uk/CN=Gen-Tao" gtniees
"/C=UK/O=eScience/OU=Cambridge/L=UCS/CN=andrew" andrew
"/C=UK/O=eScience/OU=GENIE/CN=test01" test01
```

Figure 11. Two lines added to condor.pm for file sharing

```
print SCRIPT_FILE "should_transfer_files = IF_NEEDED\n";
print SCRIPT_FILE "WhenToTransferOutput = ON_EXIT\n\n";
```

Figure 12. globus-job-run example

```
globus-job-run cete.niees.group.cam.ac.uk/jobmanager-condor /bin/hostname
pip-escience
```

located in $HOME/.globus, we have to run *Grid-proxy-init* to initiate a proxy before running these commands. The *globus-job-run* is an online interface to job submission, featuring staging of data and executables using a Global Access to Secondary Storage (GASS) server. The example use of *globus-job-run* is shown in Figure 12.

If we like to stage the executable files, -s can be used. *Test.sh* is the shell scrip executing /bin/hostname in this case (shown in Figure 13).

The *globus-job-submit* is a batch interface to the GRAM server. It immediately returns a contact string that we can use to query the status of the job. This is very similar to *globus-job-run*.

The contact string is functionally opaque and looks like as follows (Figure 14)

This contact string can be used to query the job status by using *globus-job-status,* as shown in Figure 15.

Once the job is done, the output can be collected using *globus-job-get-output*

If those commands can be successfully run and return correct results, this means that the GRAM has been successfully installed. More information regarding the installation and test of GridFTP, MDS, and other Globus services can refer to the official Globus website.

The commands shown above are for Pre WS GRAM (GRAM 2). It is very similar to test WS GRAM using command *globusrun-ws*. An example use of WS GRAM (GRAM 4) is shown in Figure 16.

Job Submission Tool

We can build several PBS clusters and Condor pools on top the Globus GRAM. Although Globus GRAM has provided a single interface and users do not have to remember all the commands of local batching system, how to find appropriate resources is still an issue. Currently there are some solutions available. For example, LCG or gLite uses a concept called Resources Broker, which can query the information

Figure 13. globus-job-run with executable file staging

```
globus-job-run cete.niees.group.cam.ac.uk/jobmanager-condor -s Test.sh
```

Figure 14. globus-job-submit command

```
globus-job-submit cete.niees.group.cam.ac.uk/jobmanager-condor /bin/hostname
https://cete.niees.group.cam.ac.uk:32863/3669/1144673079/
```

Figure 15. Querying job status using contact string

```
globus-job-status https://cete.niees.group.cam.ac.uk:32863/3669/1144673079/
PENDING
globus-job-status https://cete.niees.group.cam.ac.uk:32863/3669/1144673079/
DONE
```

Figure 16. Using globusrun-ws for WS-GRAM

```
globusrun-ws -submit -Ft Condor -s -so output2.txt -c /bin/hostname
Delegating user credentials...Done.
Submitting job...Done.
Job ID: uuid:ce1cc8d8-c310-11da-90c0-0013204b41d4
Termination time: 04/04/2006 12:53 GMT
Current job state: Pending
Current job state: Active
Current job state: CleanUp-Hold
Current job state: CleanUp
Current job state: Done
Destroying job...Done.
Cleaning up any delegated credentials...Done.
```

published by computing element, storage element and allocate appropriate resources to the jobs. The latest version of Globus includes a GridWay for meta-scheduling which provides a higher level interface for job submission. The eMinerals (http://www.eminerlas.org) project has developed some tools such as RMCS for job submission, meta-scheduling, and load balancing. OMII (http://www.omii.ac.uk) has developed a Web service, namely, GridSam (http://gridsam.sourceforge.net) for job submission and monitoring.

MCS and RMCS

My_condor_submit (MCS) is a tool developed by the eMinerals project to allow simplified job submission to remote Grid resources with built-in meta-scheduling and load balancing, data management and metadata management functionality. The meta-scheduling is implemented within MCS itself while the job submission is handled by Condor-G (Allowing Condor to Globus) and the metadata capture and storage are handled by RCommands respectively (Bruin et al., 2006). The RCommands framework consists of a back-end metadata database, a set of client tools, and an application server that maps the web services calls to SQL calls (Dove et al., 2007). Data management is handled using the SRB (Storage Resource Broker) (http://www.sdsc.edu/srb/) (More about SRB can be found in a later section). Scommands are SRB client command line tools for manipulating data for SRB.

The process of submitting a job is handled in three stages. Firstly, data are downloaded to the computing resources. Secondly, the job is executed. Finally, data are uploaded back from the compute resource to the data Grid which is SRB. This workflow is managed using Condor DAGman, which is a simple workflow management system. Using DAGman means that MCS does not need to directly manage the workflow itself (Bruin et al., 2006).

MCS uses a job description file, which is an extension over a standard Condor submission script. This job description file allows simple Condor job description in addition to directives controlling aspects of data and metadata storage using SRB and AgentX (Couch et al., 2005) which uses ontology for extracting information, commands arguments.

MCS can submit jobs to a Grid with data management using SRB. Integrating with SRB has a major advantage. It bypasses some of the IO problems associated with retrieving files (Bruin et al., 2006). Using Condor or GridFTP alone, it is not possible to retrieve the outputs without knowing the output file names in advance, however with SRB this problem can be solved just by simply using asterisk "*" to retrieve all the output data.

MCS requires the installation of Globus and Condor, and the installation SRB SCommands on the local machine. However, those tools are either too heavy or relatively hard to deploy. Remote MCS (RMCS) is a web services wrapping of MCS, with a set of tools to submit, monitor and manage jobs. RMCS built on top of the MCS can make running Grid jobs extremely easy. Users do not have to worry about firewall and Grid middleware issues (Dove et al., 2007).

The user's certificate needs to be uploaded to a MyProxy server, which is used to manage certificates and private keys. We can choose either the myproxy tools which come from Globus or STFC MyProxy Upload Tool (http://tiber.dl.ac.uk:8080/myproxy/). RMCS client can be installed on any desktop machine and using port 8443 talking to RMCS server. Unfortunately, deploying RMCS server is complicated and has no proper documentation at this moment.

GridSam

GridSam is another job submission and monitoring tool, which is funded by UK OMII (Open Middleware Infrastructure Institute). The aim of GridSam is to provide a Web service for submitting and monitoring jobs managed by a variety of Distributed Resource Managers (e.g. PBS, Condor). The installation of GridSam requires the OMII server to be installed. One of main benefits of using GridSam is that the job can be described using Job Submission Description language (JSDL) (http://www.gridforum.

org/documents/gfd.56.pdf), which is an extensible XML specification from the Open Grid Forum for the description of simple tasks to non-interactive computer execution systems.

Grid Monitoring and Management Tools

Grid monitoring is a popular research topic, and monitoring resources across different network domains is also a challenge task. There are several Grid monitoring tools available.

Ganglia (http://ganglia.info/) is a scalable distributed monitoring system for clusters and Grids. It is based on a hierarchical design targeting federations of clusters. It relies on a multicast-based listening/announcement protocol to monitor state within clusters. A set of operating system-dependent parameters is gathered from the */proc* file system by Ganglia (Massie, 2004). If the standard matrices could not meet the requirements, gmetric tool can be used to extend the measuring parameters. A screenshot of Web-based monitoring is shown in Figure 17.

Figure 17. The web interface for monitoring the network and cluster usage of the computing Grid infrastructure

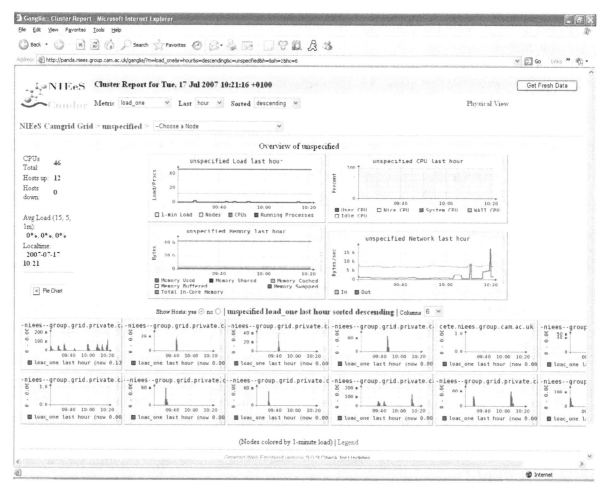

In addition to Ganglia, Nagios (http://www.nagious.org) is another great monitoring tool, which provides the monitoring of more environmental information such as monitoring temperature and the network services. If the temperature goes too high or any service goes down, it can send email or instant message to the mobile phone.

There are several cluster management tools such as LCFGng (http://edg-wp2.web.cern.ch/edg-wp2/LCFGng/index.html) developed by University of Edinburgh, ROCK (http://www.rocksclusters.org) cluster management tools developed by SDSC, and QUATTOR (http://quattor.web.cern.ch/quattor/) developed by CERN. However, most of them either require a steep learning curve or are tied to a specific Linux distribution.

For an institutional Grid environment, the most important function needed in terms of management is simply to enable command line operations to be performed on all nodes. We can use this function to deploy/update new software without typing and logging into different machines every time. C3tools, which is part of the cluster management tool called OSCAR (Luethkea et al., 2003), can be chosen for this purpose.

C3tools provide several useful commands for cluster management, such as *cexec* for executing a given command string on each node of a cluster, *cget* for specifying a file from each node of a cluster and places it into the specified target directory, *cpush* for pushing files from the local machine to the nodes of the cluster, *ckill* for killing a specified process on each node (Luethkea et al., 2003).

BUILDING DATA GRID USING SRB

We can use data Grid to access geographically distributed data. A data Grid can be used to control the sharing and management of those distributed data. The Storage Resource Broker (SRB) (http://www.sdsc.edu/srb/) developed by San Diego Supercomputer Center (SDSC) has been chosen as the data Grid for this infrastructure. SRB is the most mature data Grid project and have better support than other data Grid solutions.

SRB provides access to distributed data from any network-accessible point. From the viewpoint of the user, the SRB gives a virtual file system, with access to data based on data attributes and logical names rather than on physical location or real names. The physical location is seen as a file characteristic only. One of the features of the SRB is that it allows users to easily replicate data across different physical file systems in order to provide an additional level of file protection (Baru et al., 1998).

The results generated from the computing Grid can be put into the SRB directly. Files are actually stored in multiple "vaults" where the Metadata CATalogue (MCAT) server can extract files on demand. MCAT is used for mapping the location of logical and physical files ("MCAT installation", 2006). All these information are stored in the backend database. For a large and heavily loaded SRB, it is better to use a commercial database (e.g. Oracle). For an institutional infrastructure which is relatively small, we can use Postgresql (http://www.postgresql.org). According to the MCAT installation guide, Postgresql works fine for light to moderate data loads. It is also relatively easy to install via SRB *install.pl* script.

The installation of SRB is relatively trivial. SDSC provides a good installation Perl script called *install.pl*. There are only few parameters have to be modified in the script. $POSTGRES_FILE and $ODBC_FILE are used to defined the filename of the postgresql tar file. Others such as SRB administrator's name $YOUR_ADMIN_NAME, SRB zone name $YOUR_ZONE, and resource name $RE-

SOURCE_NAME. The architecture of SRB can be thought as a Condor pool. Each SRB zone has a metadata server (MCAT), and each zone could have multiple resources or vaults.

There are several ways to access data within the SRB. MySRB is a Web-based browser and search interface. InQ is a GUI client but only for MS Windows. Scommand is a command line tool for both MS Windows, and Linux. Scommands is quite useful. Although it is also usable in the Mac OSX environment, we encountered issues due to the Mac's case insensitivity, for example, it is impossible to distinguish *scp* (secure ssh copy) and *Scp*, the SRB copy command.

USING GRID

An example of using the Grid is given in this section. Assume we are going to run a simulation over the Grid and then harvest the data. The simulation output is a KML (Keyhole Markup Language) which can be visualized in Google Earth. We have also developed a FORTRAN library for generating KML files directly from the simulations within Grid environment (Chiang et al., 2006, 2007). The full workflow diagram is shown in Figure 18. First, the user has to use his/her user certificate to generate a credential proxy and upload this proxy to proxy server. This part of work can be done by using STFC My_Proxy_Upload tool (http://tiber.dl.ac.uk:8080/myproxy/) or Globus MyProxy tools. Then, all other Grid services such as RMCS server, computing Grid resources, SRB, and metadata server can retrieve credentials from proxy server. Users can then upload their input files and application to the SRB data Grid and then submit jobs via RMCS.

The RMCS server will find the most suitable computing resource automatically or follow the user's preferred machine list. Then it will submit jobs through MCS, Condor-G, Globus, and Condor, and copy all required input files and application to the computing node.

Computing nodes retrieve the proxy credential and make sure that this user has privileges to run jobs on those resources. If so, the jobs are executed on those resources.

When the jobs are finished, the output KML file will be uploaded back to the SRB and metadata will be put in the metadata server. Users can define which output information is put in metadata by the AgentX commands for the RMCS. AgentX is a tool which uses the ontology and the mapping in order to locate information of interest and enables the extraction of information from XML files using a series of logical queries (Couch et al., 2005).

Users can then go to SRB using any SRB client tools such as InQ, Scommands, or web based SRB clients. One can just simply click the output KML files and visualize the outputs in Google Earth directly from his/her desktop.

Basically, using RMCS, users do not have to worry about the underlying Grid technologies such as Globus, Condor, and MCS. User just needs to simply write a MCS job description file, submit job(s), and the results will be returned automatically once job completed.

This job description file shown in Figure 19 contains the information about the location of the application executable file in the SRB (PathToExe), preferred running machine list (preferredMachineList), SRB arguments, Rcommands arguments, and AgentX arguments. Rcommands is command line tool used to manage the metadata.

This job description file is similar to Condor job description file but more arguments are added for Rcommands and AgentX. RdatasetId is an argument of Rcommands. A dataset is a group of files associated with one aspect of the study. For example, in a study of sea surface temperatures, it might be

Figure 18. The workflow and data life cycle of this case study. Environmental scientists can create grid proxy and using proxy server to store the credential for several grid services. SRB is used for archiving data and computing grid for running jobs. Metadata server is used to store the metadata. Finally using Google Earth to visualize the outputs generated from grid. ©2008 Xiaoyu Yang. Used with permission.

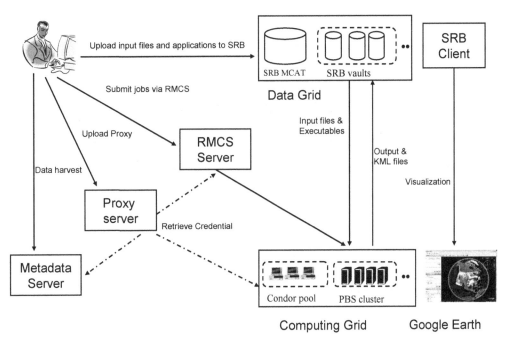

one season or one region. getEnvMetadata is asking Rcommands/AgentX to extract the environmental metadata information. AgentX arguments are a series of AgentX commands used for extracting properties (model outputs) from an xml file. For example, those AgentX commands will extract the value from the last entity of variable *src_cusp*, *src_lat*, *src_lon*, *src_dep*, and *max_magnitude*. Those information are the longitude, latitude, the depth of the hypocenter, and maximum magnitude of the earthquake.

BUILDING GRID USER INFRASTRUCTURE

The previous section "Using Grid" has shown that running a simulation over the Grid typically involves the following steps: (i) creating the simulation input files, (ii) copying input files and simulation code to remote computational resources, (iii) logging into the resource and submitting the simulation job, (iv) waiting for the job to finish, and once the job finishes copying back the simulation output files to the local machines, (v) harvesting the data or metadata after the simulation.

This approach works successfully but it does have disadvantages for end users: Firstly the approach involves a lot of human interactions. Secondly in order to submit job(s) to remote resources, some Grid software has to be installed (e.g. Globus) in a local machine, or log into a machine where such Grid

Figure 19. A RMCS job description file

```
PathToExe            = /home/gtniees.eminerals/hypoDD/

preferredMachineList = grid-compute.oesc.ox.ac.uk

GlobusRSL = (arguments=hypoDD.inp)

jobType = performance

# Force overwriting when uploading / downloading files

SForce       = true

# If not metascheduling then need the following:

Sdir         = /home/gtniees.eminerals/hypoDD/

Sget         = *

# Specify where to store metadata

#RStudyId     = 1914

RDatasetID    = 495

#RDatasetName  = "dataset of hypoDD metadata test"

Sput         = hypoDD.kml

Rdesc        = "This is a test for hypoDD with metadata"

# Specify metadata to get from files with Agent-x (Tied to the previous Sdir)

GetEnvMetadata = true

AgentXDefault  = hypoDD.kml

AgentX         =
src_cusp,hypoDD.kml:PropertyList[$].Property[title='src_cusp'].value

AgentX         =
src_lat,hypoDD.kml:PropertyList[$].Property[title='src_lat'].value

AgentX         =
src_lon,hypoDD.kml:PropertyList[$].Property[title='src_lon'].value

AgentX         =
src_dep,hypoDD.kml:PropertyList[$].Property[title='src_dep'].value

AgentX          = max_magnitude, hypoDD.kml:Property[title='max_magnitude']
Queue
```

software has been installed. Thirdly, it will be ideal if we can have an integrated environment where these operations can be carried out. In order to accommodate these requirements to improve the usability, we have proposed to employ User-Centered Design approach to develop a Grid user infrastructure which can facilitate users to use Grid computing resources without having to understand Grid and direct control or interactions to Grid. UCD is a design approach which grounds the process in information about the people who will use the product, and the processes focus on users through the planning, design and development of a product ("User Centered Design", n.d.).

Technologies which can be employed in UCD approach to build a user-level infrastructure for the use of Grid are discussed, and a case study of developing such a user-level infrastructure is introduced.

Portal

Web Portals are web based applications that commonly provide personalization, single sign on, content aggregation from different sources and hosts the presentation layer of information systems. They are designed to integrate distributed applications, different numbers and types of middleware and hardware to provide services from a number of different sources. Grid portal is "a web based application server enhanced with necessary software to communicate to Grid services and resources" (http://www.gridsphere.org). It provides access to Grid technologies through sharable and reusable components for web-based access to domain-specific applications. Grid portal is built upon the familiar Web Portal model, such as Yahoo or Amazon, to deliver the benefits of Grid computing to virtual communities of users, providing a single access point to Grid services and resources.

According to the way of building portals, Grid portals can be classified into non portlet-based and portlet based (Yang et al. 2006). Many early Grid portals or early version of existing Grid portals are non-portlet based, for example, Astrophysics Simulation Collaboratory (ASC) portal (Allen et al.,2001), UNICORE (Romberg,1999), etc. These Grid portals can provide a uniform access to the Grid resources. Usually these portals were built based on typical 3-tier web architecture: (i) Web browser, (ii) application server/Web server which can handle HTTP request from the client browser, and (iii) back-end resources that include computing resources, databases, etc.

Portlet-based portal have become one of the most exciting areas for portal server platform in recent years (Novotny, 2004). A portlet is a Web component that generates fragments – pieces of markup (e.g. HTML, XML) adhering to certain specifications. Fragments are aggregated to form a complete web page. Portlet-based portal is based on component-based development, and portlets in the portal are engineered independently from each other. A portlet is an individual class that processes the user request and returns the content for display within a portal. It is contained in portlet container, which is part of portal and instantiates and executes the portlet classes.

Developing portlet-based portals can bring many benefits to both end-users and developers, which now gets more recognition (Kelly et al., 2005). This can be reflected through evolution of some Grid portal projects. For example, although ASC portal (Allen et al., 2001) did provide functionalities for astrophysics community to remotely compile and execute applications, it was difficult to maintain when the underlying supporting infrastructure evolved. Eventually the ASC portal was retired and its functionality moved into the Cactus portal developed by adopting GridSphere. Another example is the GridPort portal (http://gridport.net). The early GridPort was implemented in Perl and made use of HotPage (Boisseau et al., 2000) technology for providing access to Grid access. Now the GridPort adopts GridSphere.

One of the main advantages of using portelt-based portal is that there are two standards for portlet development, namely, JSR-168/JSR-286[1] and WSRP (Web Service for Remote Portlets) (http://docs.oasis-open.org/wsrp/v2/). JSR-168 establishes a standard API for creating portlets (Linewood et al., 2004), while WSRP is a standard for Web portals to access and display portlets on a remote server. JSR-168 and WSRP work at different levels. JSR-168 specifies the interfaces for local portlets whilst WSRP specifies the interfaces for accessing portlets across portal frameworks. Using standard portlets can ensure they can plug-and-play in any standard-compliant portlet containers (e.g. WebSphere Portal, GridSphere).

Workflow

According to Workflow Management Coalition (WfMC) (http://wfmc.org), an international organization for workflow vendors, users and research, the workflow can be defined as "the automation of a business process, in whole or parts, where documents, information or tasks are passed from one participant to another to be processed, according to a set of procedural rules". This definition can be extended to scientific workflow, which is a set of components and relations between them used to define a complex process from simple building blocks. Relations may be in the form of data links, transferring information from the output of one component to the input of another, or in the form of control links which state some conditions on the execution of a component (Oinn et al, 2006). The component is a reusable building block which performs some well defined function within a process, and may consume information and may produce output to provide information and knowledge. These components can be implemented as web services and hosted by computing resources where external users can access.

Two approaches to compose the workflow have been identified: (i) job-based approach, and (ii) service-based approach (Glatard et al., 2005; Yu et al., 2005). In the job-based approach, the workflow manager is responsible for the actual processing of data by programs on physical resources. As this approach is much closed to the Grid infrastructure, it allows the optimization of submission rate, the dispatch rate and scheduling rate, etc. (Glatard et al., 2005; Singh et al., 2005). For example, Condor DAGMan (http://www.bo.infn.it/calcolo/condor/dagman/) is a workflow manager which adopts this job-based approach where a child node will not start until its parents have successfully completed. In the service-based approach the workflow manager is responsible for the transmission of the data to remote services and for the collection of the results. The workflow manager is just aware the interface of the programs and does not access the actual binary files. Jobs are submitted to the Grid by the services. The WSDL is used to describe the services. In service-oriented approach, the workflow description stipulates that a particular output of a program is linked to a particular input of another. Hence, the iteration of such workflows on a number of input data sets is straightforward and does not require any rewriting of the workflow (Glatard et al., 2005). In job-based approach, data dependencies between programs are not explicitly described. Iterating a single workflow on many datasets requires writing specific jobs. The service-based approach is more independent from the infrastructure than the job-based one. Services themselves are responsible for the submission of jobs but in job-based approach it is the workflow manager to submit jobs to the Grid.

AJAX

AJAX is a combination of techniques such as JavaScript, DOM, XML, and HTML/DHTML, etc., which allows a Web browser to update parts of a Web page asynchronously by communicating with a Web server using JavaScript through an *XMLHttpRequest* component. It is particularly useful in portal as portal page refresh is an expensive action as one portlet refresh can result in other portlets refreshing at the same time. AJAX can improve the user experience and make Web pages feel more responsive by exchanging small amounts of data with the server behind the scenes, so that the entire Web page does not have to be reloaded each time the user makes a request. This is meant to increase the Web page's interactivity, speed, and usability.

Case Study

The case study briefly discusses how portal, workflow and AJAX technologies are employed to build a user-level infrastructure for running quantum mechanical simulation over Grid for material properties in a UK government funded MaterialsGrid project. MaterialsGrid (http://www.materialsgrid.org) aims to create a pilot dynamic database of materials properties based on quantum mechanical simulations run within Grid computing environments within eScience. This involves developing a user infrastructure which can facilitate the scientists to the use of the Grid.

The IBM WebSphere Portal framework has been employed for building the Grid portal, and the AJAX technology has been adopted for portlets (Figure 20 and 22). The portal integrates functionalities for material property query, creation of simulation input files in various approach (e.g. by uploading existing files, by user providing data, by using CML dictionary), access to WebDav-based file system, visualising the cell structure using Jmol (http://jmol.sourceforge.net/), enacting the workflows and monitoring the workflows.

In order to automate the whole simulation run process without human interaction, a workflow system, namely Pipeline Pilot (http://accelrys.com/products/scitegic/) has been used. Pipeline Pilot uses

Figure 20. A screenshot of portal in the case study, where it provides an intergrated environment for running quantum mechanical simulatio over Grids. The Task-driven Job Submission portlet integrates the operations for setting-up, submitting, managing and tracking of Grid-enabled simulation jobs, and data harvesting without direct user control. The data query portlet employs AJAX technology for material properties query.

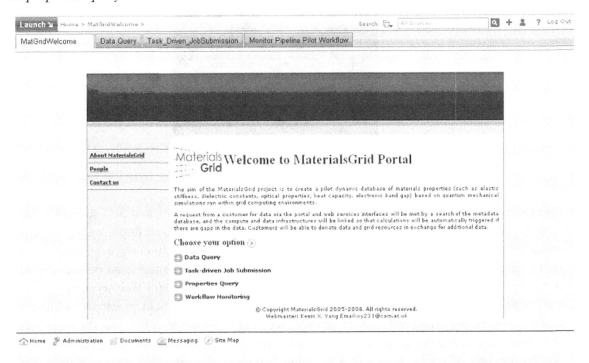

Figure 21. A job submission sub-workflow which integrates Metascheduling Web service, Create Output File List Web service and JobSubmisison Web service. This sub-workflow can be reused many times in a whole workflow.

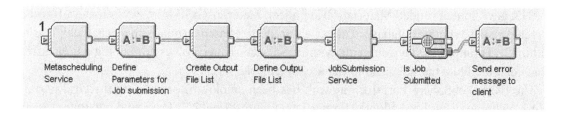

Figure 22. The portal integrates the functionality of viewing material cell structure in Jmol. AJAX technology is used to capture user input and send them to the server-side. End users do not need to click Submit button, which takes user to the next page breaking the consistency of cell information input, and it is not user-friendly for viewing the cell structure due to cell information input and cell structure visualization being at different pages.

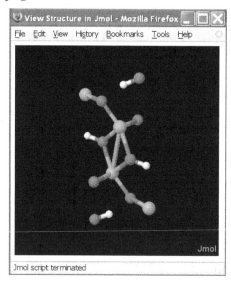

data pipelining technology which "wraps" computational components and data sources in code and provides powerful scripting capabilities to enable the construction of workflows. It adopts client-server architecture, whereas the client side provides a GUI-based interface to construct workflows, and the server-side acts as a workflow engine. It is a lightweight workflow management system and well supports the modelling of service-oriented workflow by integrating standard Web services.

The SOA approach is employed in the creation of our workflows. SOA promotes building systems or workflows from distinct and autonomous Web services. By using SOA to create the service-oriented workflow, the autonomous business logic or legacy scientific code can be presented as a service, hence the development and maintenance of a workflow can be simplified. Each service is described using

WSDL and the workflow manager just needs to know the interface and does not care about the specific implementation. The service-oriented workflow decouples the specific implementation of Web service from whole workflow. For example, we can change the operation of any service to correct bugs or improve performance and that has no impact on the workflow structure. A job submission sub-workflow is shown in Figure 21.

Once the workflow is enacted, the next important step is to monitor its status via the portal. The Pipeline Pilot does provide an administrative application to monitor the status of workflow, and one possible solution is to integrate the access to administrative application into the portal by using the Portal's "single sign on" mechanism. However, the main disadvantage of the approach is that it is difficult to do any customized monitoring of workflow (e.g. monitoring Grid job status). In order to monitor the workflow and Grid job status, a portlet which can monitor the status of both workflow and Grid jobs has been developed.

The user-level infrastructure developed was tested by submitting a CASTEP quantum mechanical simulation job to the available Grid resources to calculate the properties of a material in MaterialsGrid project. CASTEP is an application which uses the density functional theory to calculate the atomistic structure and physical properties of material and molecules (Segall et al., 2002).

DISCUSSIONS / CONCLUSIONS

The interpretation of "Grid" varies. As mentioned in the chapter, most people refer "Grid" as a computing grid. Today, as the technology of computing Grid is getting mature, users can submit jobs using a submit tool or a portal to the backend computing resources with an automatic matching making mechanism. However, how to access the data and extract the information after computation becomes the main issue. We are thinking that the "Grid" should be a system through which users can access all computing and data resources with a single-sign-on and uniform interface.

In order to build such a system, simply setting up a computing Grid is not enough. In order to facilitate the use of Grid, some e-Science tools or a user infrastructure have to be developed. How to develop those tools or an infrastructure is not the main aim of this chapter. The chapter aims to provide an initial guide on how to build a core Grid infrastructure, based on which we can improve the system gradually.

There is no universal Grid infrastructure which is suitable for all communities, as requirements of building Grid can be quite different depending on the purpose or the scale of an institution. For example, a small laboratory which does not have a dedicated cluster can use the computing resources from other community. Condor itself is good enough, but it does not require a security checking and advanced data management technology. A large-scale research institute who has labs and researchers from different fields may need more security control for their jobs and data. In this situation, more advanced security control or data Grid solution with VO management may be required. In fact, many local batching systems such as Condor are constantly evolving. They can provide functionalities which used to be provided by Grid middleware (e.g. Globus toolkit). Thus, a complicated Grid system comprising many layers of middleware may be substituted by an individual batching system (e.g. Condor) in future.

In the past 5 years building the physical Grid infrastructure has been the challenge and currently there are many production Grids available ranging from campus Grid such as CamGrid, OxGrid to European EGEE Gird, UK National Grid Service, etc. Many of these Grids have been opened or partially opened to researchers in academia and industry, and provide them with access to major computing resources and data storage resources independent of their geographic location (e.g. EGEE Grid, NGS). It is now more important than ever to build user infrastructures that can facilitate the use of and easy access to these physical infrastructures. Advantages of developing a user infrastructure for the use of Grid are obvious. For example, in order to run a simulation over Grid, all users need is just a standard Web browser and they do not have to understand Grid.

The advantages of using SOA have been demonstrated in the service-oriented workflow. For example, the implementation of some services (e.g. job submission / monitoring service) can be upgraded during the whole development process but these changes and updates have no impact on the whole workflow and portal system. The SOA and WSDL interfaces effectively decouple the workflow creation and service implementation. Although the job submission / monitoring service is currently using RMCS as job submission tool in the case study, it could also use other job submission tool (e.g. GridSam) with no impact on the rest of the system.

ACKNOWLEDGMENT

The authors would like to acknowledge the support and contributions from NIEeS (The National Institute for Environmental eScience), and UK government DTI/TSB funded MaterialsGrid project.

REFERENCES

Allen, G., Daues, G., Foster, I., et al. (2001). The Astrophysics Simulation Collaboratory Portal: A science Portal Enabling Community Software Development. *Proceedings of the 10ᵗʰ IEEE International Symposium on High performance Distributed Computing* 2001.

Baru, C., Moore, R., Rajasekar, A., & Wan, M. (1998). The SDSC Storage Resource Broker. *IBM Toronto Centre for Advanced Studies Conference (CASCON'98)* (pp.1-12), Toronto, Canada.

Boisseau, J., Mock, S., & Thomas, M. (2000). Development of Web toolkits for computational science portals: The NPACI HotPage. *Porceeding of the 9ᵗʰ IEEE international Symposium on high performance distributed computing.*

Bruin, R. et al. (2006). Job submission to Grid computing environment. *UK e-Science All Hands Meeting* (pp. 754-761), Nottingham, UK..

Calleja, M., Beckles, M., Keegan, M., Hayes, M., Parker, A., & Dove, M. (2004). CamGrid: Experiences in constructing a university-wide, Condor-based, Grid at the University of Cambridge. *UK e-Science All Hands Meeting.* Nottingham, UK. (pp. 173-178).

Clery, D. (2006). Can Grid Computing Help Us Work Together. *Science, 303,* 433-434.

Chiang, G.-T., Dove, M., Ballard, S., Bostater, C., & Frame, I. (2006). A Grid Enabled Monte Carlo Hyperspectral Synthetic Image Remote Sensing Model (GRID-MCHSIM) for Coastal Water Quality Algorithm. *Remote Sensing of the Ocean, Sea Ice, and Large Water Regions, 6360,* 636009-1. Stockholm, Sweden: SPIE.

Chiang, G.-T., White, T., & Dove, M. (2007). Driving Google Earth from Fortran. *UK e-Science All Hands Meeting* 2007. Nottingham, UK. (pp. 236-243).

Condor Manual (2008). http://www.cs.wisc.edu/condor/manual/v6.8/3_1Introduction.html.

Couch, P. et al. (2005). Towards data integration for computational chemistry. *UK e-Science All Hands Meeting,* Nottingham, UK.

Dove, M. et al. (2007). *Usable Grid infrastructures: practical experiences from the eMinerals project. UK e-Science All Hands Meeting.* Nottingham, UK. (pp. 48-55).

Foster, I., Kesselman, C., & Tuecke, S (2001). The Anatomy of the Grid: Enabling Scalable Virtual Organization. *The International Journal of Supercomputer Applications, 15*(3),200-222.

Glatard, T., Montagnat, J., & Pennec, X. (2005). *An optimized workflow enactor for data-intensive Grid applications.* Research Report I3S, number I3S/RR-2005-32-, Sophia Antipolis, France.

Kelley, I., Russell,M., Novotny, J. et al. (2005). The Cactus portal. *APAC'05.*

Lamanna, L. (2004). The LHC computing Grid project at CERN. Nuclear Instruments and Methods in Physics Research Section A: Accelerators, Spectrometers, Detectorsand Associated Equipment. In *the IXth International Workshop on Advanced Computing and Analysis Techniques in Physics Research, 534,* 1-6.

Linewood, J., & Minter, D. (2004). *Building Portals with the Java Portlet API.* Apress, USA.

Luethkea, B., Scotta, S., & Naughtona, T. (2003). OSCAR Cluster Administration with C3. *The 17th Annual International Symposium on High Performance Computing Systems and Applications (HPCS2003).* Sherbrooke, Quebec, Canada. (pp. 1-7).

Massie, M., Chun, B., & Culler, D. (2004). The ganglia distributed monitoring system: design, implementation, and experienc*e. Parallel Computing, 30*(7), 817-840.

MCAT installation guide (2006). http://www.sdsc.edu/srb/index.php/MCAT_Install.

User Centered Design Approach (n.d.). Retrieved 2008 from   http://www.usabilityprofessionals.org/usability_resources/about_usability/what_is_ucd.html

Novotny, J. (2004). Developing Grid portlets using the GridSphere portal framework. *IBM developerworks..*

Oinn, T., Greenwood, M. et al. (2006). Taverna: Lessons in creating a workflow environment for life sciences. *Concurrency and Computation: Practice and Experience, 18*(20), 1067-1100.

Romberg, M. (1999). The UNICORE architecture: seamless access to distributed resources. *Proceedings of the 8th IEEE International Symposium on High performance Distributed Computing.*

Segall, M. D., Lindan, P. J. D., Probert, M. J., et al. (2002). First-principles simulation: ideas, illustrations and the CASTEP code. *J. Phys. Condensed Matter, 14,* 211.

Singh, G., Kesselman, K., & Deelman, E. (2005). Optimizing of Grid-based workflow execution. In *HPDC'05.*

Thain, D., Tannenbaum, T., & Livny, M. (2005). Distributed Computing in Practice: The Condor Experience. *Concurrency - Practice and Experience, 17*(2-4), 323-356.

TORQUE (2008). http://www.clusterresources.com/pages/products/torque-resource-manager.php

TORQUE Quick Start (n.d.). Retrieved 2008 from http://clusterresources.com/torquedocs21/torquequick-start.shtml.

Yang, X., Dove, M., Hayes, M., Calleja, M., He, L., & Murray-Rust, P. (2006). Survey of tools and technologies for Grid-enabled portals. *UK e-Science All Hands on conference*, UK.

Yu, J., & Buyya, R. (2005). *A taxonomy of workflow management system for Grid computing.* Tech. rep., Grid and distributed Systems Laboratory, University of Melbourne.

ENDNOTE

[1]   JSR 286 is an extension of JSR-168. In this paper, the JSR-168 is used for the standard portlet.

Chapter XVI
A Grid Aware Large–Scale Agent–Based Simulation System

Dan Chen
Yanshan University, China

ABSTRACT

The emergence of Grid technologies provide exciting new opportunities for large scale simulation over Internet, enabling collaboration and the use of distributed computing resources, while also facilitating access to geographically distributed data sets. This chapter presents HLA_Grid_RePast, a middleware platform for executing large scale collaborating RePast agent-based models on the Grid. The chapter also provides performance results and analysis on Quality of Service from a deployment of the system between UK and Singapore.

INTRODUCTION

The last decade has witnessed an explosion of interest in distributed modelling and simulation techniques, not only for speeding up simulations but also as a strategic technology for linking simulation components of various types (e.g., discrete or continuous, numerical or discrete event, etc.) at multiple locations to create a common virtual environment (e.g., battlefields, virtual factories and supply chains, agent-based systems, games etc). The culmination of this activity, which originated in military applications where battle scenarios were formed by connecting geographically distributed simulators via protocols such as DIS (DIS Steering Committee, 1994), has been the advent of the High Level Architecture (HLA), a framework for simulator interoperability (Dahmann, 1998). The HLA for modelling and simulation was developed as an IEEE standard to facilitate interoperability among simulations and promote reuse of simulation models. Using the HLA and the associated executable middleware, namely Run Time Infrastructure (RTI), a large-scale simulation can be constructed by linking together a number of simulation components (or federates) distributed geographically into an overall simulation (or federation).

Such simulation systems often require huge computing resources and the data sets required by the simulation may also be geographically distributed. For example, in a supply chain simulation involving different companies, the most up-to-date data will be in the individual companies. Furthermore, the development of such complex simulation applications usually requires collaborative effort from researchers with different domain knowledge and expertise, possibly at different locations. A typical example is simulations of systems biology, which are extremely challenging in requiring the modelling of many complex phenomena at multiple spatial and temporal scales (Lees, 2007).

In order to support collaborative model development and to cater for the increasing complexity of such systems, it is necessary to harness distributed resources over the Internet. The emergence of Grid technologies provides an unrivalled opportunity for large-scale distributed simulation. While HLA enables the construction of large-scale distributed simulations using existing and possibly distributed simulation components, Grid technologies enable collaboration and provide mechanisms for the management of distributed computing resources where the simulation is being executed, while also facilitating access to geographically distributed data sets.

In the last few years, there has been an increasing interest in taking advantage of Grid technologies to execute HLA simulations over the Internet. Contributing to this global effort, this chapter presents *HLA_Grid_RePast*, a prototype platform for executing large-scale agent-based distributed simulations on a Grid.

HLA_Grid_RePast integrates two different middleware systems. At the bottom end, lies *HLA_Grid*, which has been developed as a middleware to support HLA simulations on the Grid (Xie, 2005); at the top sits *HLA_RePast*, which can support the execution of multiple interacting instances of *RePast* agent-based models within the HLA (Minson, 2004). The RePast system (Collier, 2007) is a Java-based toolkit for the development of lightweight agents and agent models. It has become a popular and influential toolkit, providing the development platform for several large multi-agent simulation experiments, particularly in the field of social phenomena. RePast has been assessed by (Railsback, 2006; Tobias, 2004) as the most effective development platform currently available for large-scale simulations of social phenomena. HLA_Grid_RePast allows large scale RePast simulation systems to benefit from the advantages of both HLA and Grid technologies.

The rest of this chapter is organized as follows: Section 2 summarises related work. Section 3 introduces HLA and provides a short summary of the two existing constituent systems, namely HLA_Grid and HLA_RePast. Section 4 presents the architecture of HLA_Grid_RePast and outlines the steps required for the deployment and execution of HLA_Grid_RePast systems on the Grid. Section 5 presents a quantitative performance evaluation of the system. Section 6 discusses future research directions based on this study. Finally, section 7 concludes this chapter and provides some ideas to further improve the system's performance.

RELATED WORK

Recent years have witnessed an increasing interest in taking advantage of Grid technologies to execute distributed simulations over the Internet. This section outlines some representative work along this research direction.

An influential initiative in this area is the Extensible Modelling & Simulation Framework (XMSF, http://www.movesinstitute.org/xmsf/xmsf.html). XMSF makes use of Web-based technologies, applied within an extensible framework, that enables a new generation of modelling and simulation applications to emerge, develop and interoperate. One of its important initiatives is to develop a web enabled RTI (Morse, 2003; Morse, 2004; Pullen, 2005). Within the XMSF framework, multiple federates reside as web services on a WAN and the federation's FOM is mapped to an XML tagset, allowing interoperation with other distributed applications supported by web services. The federates communicate using the Simple Object Access Protocol (SOAP) and the Blocks Extensible Exchange Protocol (BEEP).

Based on the concepts of XMSF, Xu and Peng (2006) developed a Service Oriented EXtensible Modeling and Simulation Supporting Environment Architecture (SO-XMSSEA) Their SO-XMSSEA encapsulates HLA federates, federations and simulation supporting software as "simulation services" and present them on Internet through the support of GT4.

Wytzisk et al. proposed (2003) a solution that brings HLA and the Open GIS Consortium (OGC) standard together. The system provides external initialisation of federations, controlled start up and termination of federates, interactions with running federates, and access of simulation results by external processes.

Fitzgibbons et al. (2004) presented IDSim, a distributed simulation framework based upon Open Grid Services Infrastructure (Tuecke, 2007). IDSim exploits Globus's Grid service data elements as simulation states to allow both pull and push modes of access. It was designed to ease the integration and deployment of tasks through inheritance.

Another related work is the framework for HLA-based Interactive Simulations on the Grid designed by Rycerz et al. (Rycerz, 2005). The framework includes discovery, and information indexing services and a single HLA Speaking service to manage multiple federates. Their work focuses on using Grid services to manage simulation federates, basically the migration of federates. However, reusability of legacy federates is unlikely to be supported by this framework.

Finally, another body of related work has looked at the execution of conventional, non-HLA distributed simulations on the Grid, for example (Iskra, 2003; Iskra, 2005).

THE CONSTITUENT MIDDLEWARE LAYERS

HLA_Grid_RePast glues together two different systems, HLA_Grid and HLA_RePast to enable the distributed execution of a RePast federation on the Grid. After a short introduction to the basic concepts of HLA and RTI, this section provides a summary of these two constituent systems of HLA_Grid_RePast. For a more detailed description of the two systems the reader is referred to (Jie, 2002; Xie, 2005; Zong, 2004) and (Minson, 2004) respectively.

High Level Architecture and Runtime Infrastructure

The HLA defines a software architecture for modelling and simulation. The HLA is designed to provide reuse and interoperability of simulation components. The simulation components are referred to as federates. A simulation federation can be created to achieve some specific objective by combining simulation federates. The HLA supports component-based simulation development in this way (Dahmann, 1998). The HLA federation is a collection of federates (observers, live participants, simulators, etc.) interacting with each other for a common purpose, for example wargaming. These federates interact with each other with the support of the RTI and the use of a common Federation Object Model (FOM). In the formal definition, the HLA standard comprises four main components: HLA Rules, Object Model Template (OMT), Interface Specification (IEEE 1516, 2000) and Federation Development and Execution Process (FEDEP) (IEEE 1516.3, 2003). The HLA rules define the principles of HLA in terms of responsibilities that federates and federations must uphold. Each federation has a FOM, which is a common object model for the data exchanged between federates in a federation. The OMT defines the metamodel for all FOMs (Kuhl, 1999). The HLA Interface Specification identifies the RTI services available to each federate and the functions each federate must provide to the federation. The FEDEP mainly defines a process framework for federation developers including the necessary activities to build HLA federations.

The HLA is an architecture defining the rules and interface, whereas the RTI is the software conforming to the HLA standard, which is used to support a federation execution. Figure[1] 1 gives an overview of an HLA federation and the RTI (Kuhl, 1999). The RTI provides a set of services to the federates for data interchange and synchronization in a coordinated fashion. The RTI services are provided to each federate through its Local RTI Component (LRC) (DMSO, 2002). The RTI can be viewed as a distributed operating system providing services to support interoperable simulations executing in distributed computing environments (Fujimoto, 2007). A total of six service categories are defined in the specification, namely Federation Management, Declaration Management, Object Management, Ownership Management, Data Distribution Management and Time Management (DMSO, 2002).

The RTI services are available as a library (C++ or Java) to the federate developers. Within the RTI library, the class *RTIAmbassador* (DMSO, 2002) bundles the services provided by the RTI. A federate may invoke operations on the interface to request a service (federate-initiated service) from the RTI. The *FederateAmbassador* (DMSO, 2002) is a pure virtual class that identifies the "callback" functions each federate is obliged to provide (RTI-initiated) service. The federate developers need to implement the FederateAmbassador. The callback functions provide a mechanism for the RTI to invoke operations and communicate back to the federate.

The HLA_Grid System

HLA_Grid is an infrastructure designed to extend the HLA to the Grid. In particular, it focuses on improving the interoperability and composability of HLA-compliant simulation components. The infrastructure is illustrated in figure 2.

Figure 1. Architecture of HLA based distributed simulations

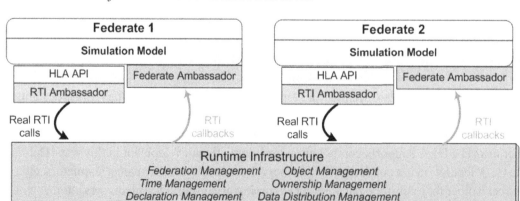

HLA_Grid achieves interoperability between simulation federates using a Federate-Proxy-RTI architecture evolved from the Decoupled Federated Architecture proposed in (Chen, 2008B). In the context of HLA_Grid, an individual federate consists of a simulation model (namely the client from the user's perspective) and a proxy which acts on behalf of the client's federate code to communicate with the proxies of other clients through the underlying real RTI. Proxies are executed over remote Grid resources. The "compound" federate executives interact with each other through a Grid-enabled HLA library, which provides the standard HLA API to the simulation model while translating the interactions into Grid service invocations.

HLA_Grid includes additional Grid services to support functions such as the creation of the RTI and the discovery of federations. The infrastructure hides the heterogeneity of the simulators, execution platforms, and how the simulators communicate with the RTI. The HLA_Grid implementation has been developed in Java using the Globus Toolkit version 3 (GT3).

The HLA_RePast System

HLA_RePast is a middleware layer which enables the execution of a federation of multiple interacting instances of RePast models within the HLA as depicted in figure 3. RePast provides an inter-dependent collection of tools and structures, which are generally useful for the simulation of agents, and a sequential discrete event simulation kernel for the execution of the model. The main task of HLA_RePast is to detect the occurrence of events in the RePast model and communicate them to the underlying RTI in a consistent, reliable and transparent manner. To achieve this, HLA_RePast provides mechanisms for mapping RePast state-transitions to RTI events (via the *PublicObject* scheme described in section 4.1), for conflict resolution and for integrating the RePast scheduling system with the RTI (as depicted in figure 4).

HLA_RePast is a promising infrastructure for developing complex agent-based models. For example, it can be used to realise a distributed and extensible architecture for modelling virtual crowd

Figure 2. Architecture of HLA_Grid based distributed simulation

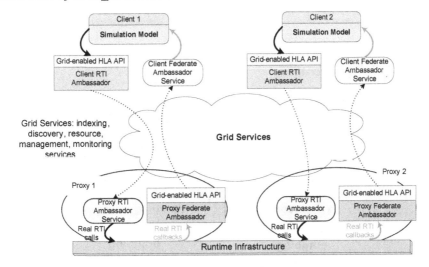

(Low, 2007). It also suits for modelling of bacterial populations, i.e., using distributed agent models t o characterise cell populations.

THE HLA_GRID_REPAST MIDDLEWARE SYSTEM

A conceptual view of HLA_Grid_RePast is provided in figure 5. HLA_Grid_RePast uses the DMSO RTI NG 1.3 (DMSO, 2002) as the underlying RTI software.

Architecture of HLA_Grid_RePast Simulation Federate

Each federate executive upon HLA_Grid_RePast consists of two major parts, one on the client side and another on the proxy side, which usually run on different machines. The client side includes the

Figure 3. The HLA_RePast model-executive interface (a single HLA_RePast federate)

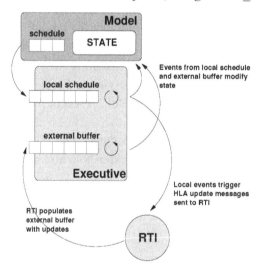

Figure 4. An HLA_RePast federation

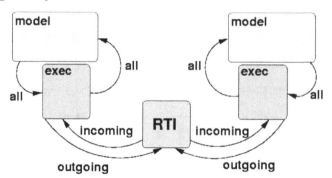

following modules: the RePast agent-based simulation model, the HLA_RePast middleware, the *Client RTI Ambassador* and the *Client Federate Ambassador Service* from HLA_Grid. These components usually run on a local machine from the simulation model's perspective.

On the proxy side, there are the *Proxy RTI Ambassador Service* and the *Proxy Federate Ambassador* which interact with the real RTI hosted by a remote machine. Both the *Proxy RTI Ambassador Service* and the *Client Federate Ambassador Service* are implemented as Grid services on different sides, shown as the round rectangle boxes in figure 5. The modules on both sides are coupled together to form a single compound federate executive.

Before the simulation starts, the Proxy RTI Ambassador Services should have been started and each federate is associated with a Proxy RTI Ambassador Service. The identity of each federate's Proxy RTI Ambassador Service will be passed to the corresponding Client RTI Ambassador. When the simulation starts, the Client Federate Ambassador Service of each federate will be initialised and registered with the corresponding Proxy RTI Ambassador Service.

During the simulation execution, the underlying HLA_RePast middleware translates the state changes (events) occurred in the simulation model into the corresponding RTI service calls. Then the RTI calls are passed to the Client RTI Ambassador, and the latter convert these RTI calls once again into Grid service invocations to access the remote Proxy RTI Ambassador Service at the proxy side.

Finally, the Proxy RTI Ambassador Service will interact with the real RTI by executing the real RTI calls with respect to the client side. The return values of a RTI call will be sent back in the form of the Grid service call's return value, while the runtime exceptions will be sent back by means of Apache Axis faults.

On the other hand, callbacks (DMSO, 2002) from the RTI to a federate are translated into invocations of the Client Federate Ambassador Service by the Proxy Federate Ambassador. The Client Federate Ambassador Service is responsible for conveying these callbacks to the HLA_RePast middleware, and the latter should then convert the federate calls into RePast events and put them into the event scheduler (see figure 4).

Figure 5. Structure of HLA_Grid_RePast

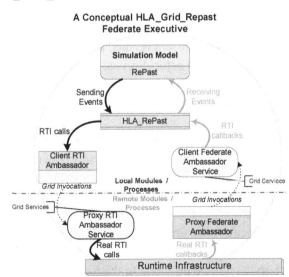

Object Encoding

A number of issues had to be addressed to be addressed to integrate HLA_Grid and HLA_RePast into HLA_Grid_RePast. One of these issues is Object Encoding, which is required by the SOAP protocol. The object encoding scheme of HLA_RePast has been modified to cooperate with HLA Grid. HLA_RePast uses a *PublicObject* scheme to translate Java expressions into HLA function calls (Minson, 2004). Java objects in the *PublicObject* scheme may be transferred between federates during simulation execution. In HLA_RePast, the Java objects are encoded into Java Byte arrays. However, Java Byte arrays cannot be used directly within HLA Grid, which, like other grid services, uses SOAP as the communication protocol between clients and servers. SOAP is based on XML which does not support binary data. The problem can be solved by modifying HLA Grid to support either the SOAP With Attachments (SwA) proposal (Barton, 2000) or the WS-Attachments proposal (Nielsen, 2007). Such an approach would require modifications to the GT3 and would affect the interoperability of HLA_Grid_RePast. Instead of modifying GT3, HLA_Grid_RePast employs an alternative object encoding scheme for Java objects as follows:

- First, the Java object is encoded into a Java byte array as in HLA_RePast.
- Then, the base64 encoding scheme (from the Apache project) is used to encode the Java byte array into a Java String Object.
- Finally, a Java Byte array is generated from the Java String and passed to HLA_Grid for encapsulation in a SOAP message.

Deployment and Execution of HLA_Grid_RePast Systems

Within the current implementation of the HLA_Grid_RePast system, two Grid service "factories" (Sotomayor, 2007) need to be deployed prior to executing a distributed agent-based simulation on the Grid; these are *ClientFactoryService* (CFS) and *ProxyFactoryService* (PFS). The two factories should be started by the system administrator and persist throughout the simulation. The ClientFactoryService is located at the client side (see figure 5) and supports the RePast simulation model and the instantiation of the Client Federate Ambassador Service. Similarly, the ProxyFactoryService resides in the proxy side and is responsible for creating the Proxy RTI Ambassador Service. The ClientFactoryService can only be accessed by the authorised simulation users verified through GT3's built-in Certification Authorization (Sotomayor, 2007), while the ProxyFactoryService is user transparent and merely responds to the authorised clients to eventually generate services for the RePast models.

Figure 6 illustrates the procedure of initiating an HLA_Grid_RePast system. First, the simulation user simply needs to request the preselected ClientFactoryService (For example, http://pdcc.ntu.edu. sg/ogsa/services/hlagrid/client/ClientFactoryService) and pass the information of the target RePast model. Once this step is successfully accomplished, the subsequent steps will continue automatically and transparently to the user. For the second step, the CFS instantiates an instance of Client Federate Ambassador Service and invokes the designated RePast model. The RePast model then requests the pre-specified remote ProxyFactoryService (For example, http://escience.bham.ac.uk/ogsa/services/hla-grid/proxy/ProxyFactoryService). After granting the RePast model's request, the PFS instantiates an instance of Proxy RTI Ambassador Service and starts the corresponding proxy process. Finally, the Proxy RTI Ambassador Service will be provided to the RePast model and the Client Federate Ambassador Service to the remote proxy. From here onwards, these processes and services collaborate with each other to execute an HLA_Grid_RePast federate executive to allow this RePast model interoperate with its peer RePast models in the distributed simulation.

The HLA_Grid_RePast has the additional advantage over HLA_RePast of dealing with network security issues. To execute two federates and an RTIExec process (similar to the scenario in figure 10) using HLA_RePast together with RTI NG 1.3, there should be one machine at one site (e.g., Singapore) and another two at another site (e.g., Birmingham, UK). The machine in Singapore has to communicate with both remote machines in Birmingham, which demands the setting of two new firewall rules in Singapore. The more federates added, the more firewall rules should be applied. In contrast, when using HLA_Grid_RePast, the machine in Singapore only needs to communicate with the machine running the HLA_Grid proxy service in Birmingham, therefore only one firewall rule is needed even if more federates are involved.

EXPERIMENTS AND EVALUATIONS

To evaluate the robustness and the performance of the system, a number of experiments have been conducted in both a LAN environment and a WAN environment between UK and Singapore.

Figure 6. Execution of HLA_Grid_RePast based simulation

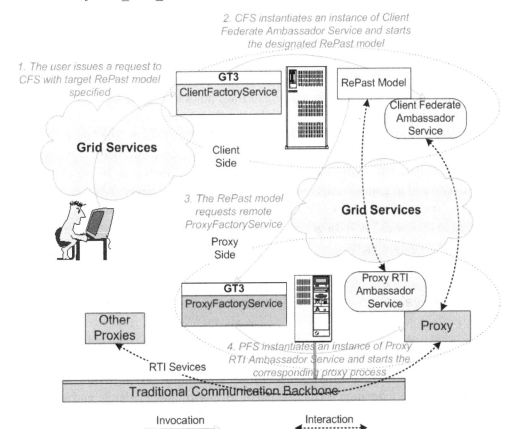

The LAN environment is a Grid-enabled PC cluster consisting of one master node and 54 worker nodes (see http://www.ep.ph.bham.ac.uk/cluster). Each node has 2G bytes of memory and two Intel Xeon 3GHz processors while connectivity is provided by a Gigabit Ethernet Switch. The RTI NG 1.3 with Java bindings is used in the experiments.

Communication Overhead

In order to investigate the communication overhead incurred by the underlying HLA_Grid infrastructures and establish a base line for future experiments, the Java based latency benchmark from DMSO's RTI package has been built and tested under LAN and WAN environments. The benchmark measures the performance of the system in terms of the latency (RTT) of federate communications, as follows: one federate sends an attribute update, and upon receiving this update, the other federate sends it back to the sending federate. The elapsed time of this communication is calculated using the real time taken at the sending and reflecting federates.

The results obtained are shown in table 1. The latency benchmark over LAN shows that HLA_Grid incurs about twice (~19 Milliseconds) the overhead of the pure HLA in a cluster. This is mainly due to the use of GT3 communication backbone, the encoding/decoding of parameters/result etc. In the case of WAN environment, such communication using GT3 becomes very costly. Comparing the latencies of HLA_Grid over WAN and LAN, the extra over head of the former case is ~50 times more than that (~19 Milliseconds) of the latter case. It can also be observed that the latency of HLA_Grid (~935 Milliseconds) is ~7 times more than that of the pure HLA case under WAN environment.

Performance of HLA_Grid_RePast in a LAN Environment

As a case study for the evaluation of HLA_Grid_RePast, we have developed a RePast federation using *Tileworld* (Pollack, 1990) as a test case. Tileworld is a well established testbed for agent-based systems. It includes a grid-like environment consisting of tiles, holes and obstacles, and agents whose goal is to score as many points as possible by pushing tiles to fill in the holes (figure 7). Whenever a hole is filled, the agent who dropped the last tile will be given a score as the initial depth of the hole. The environment is dynamic: tiles, holes and obstacles appear and disappear at rates controlled by the simulation developer. Tileworld has been used to study commitment strategies (i.e., when an agent should abandon its current goal and replan) and in comparisons of reactive and deliberative agent architectures (Pollack, 1990).

For HLA_Grid_RePast, a Tileworld simulation originally developed for HLA_RePast has been used, as described in (Minson, 2004). In general, an agent-based federation can be constructed by one environment federate containing the tiles, holes and obstacles of the model and one or more agent federates. The complexity of the simulated system increases considerably with the number of agents.

Performance Evaluation in a LAN Environment using a Single Agent Federate

Experiments have been carried out in a LAN environment with one agent federate simulating different numbers of agents. The performance of HLA_Grid_RePast and HLA_RePast is compared to evaluate the overhead introduced by the different layers of the middleware (HLA_Grid and HLA_Grid_RePast). In this case, the entire federation is constructed by an environment federate and a single agent federate hosting all agents. The number of agents varies from 1 to 512.

Table 1. Results of latency benchmarks over LAN and WAN

	LAN	WAN
Pure HLA	9.79 MilliSecs	122.26 MilliSecs
HLA_Grid	18. 49 MilliSecs	934.83 MilliSecs

Figure 7. An example of a simple Tileworld

⟨A⟩ :agent   T :tile   (H) :hole

For HLA_RePast, the two RePast federates run on two separate nodes. For HLA_Grid_RePast, two more nodes are required to host the respective HLA_Grid proxies which serve the two RePast models. In all experiments, the RTIExec is running on a separate node. The experimental results obtained are reported in figure 8.

It can be observed that when the number of agents is small (less than 32 in our experiments), HLA_ Grid_RePast exhibits a significantly higher overhead compared to HLA_RePast. As the number of agents increases further, the computation load rather than communication load becomes the determining factor. Hence, the total execution time for HLA_Grid_RePast approximates that of HLA_RePast.

Performance Evaluation in a LAN Environment using Multiple Agent Federates

This series of experiments focuses on speed-up and aims to compare the performance of HLA_RePast and HLA_Grid_RePast systems (HLA_Grid_RePast(R) adopted) in a LAN environment by evenly distributing 512 agents in multiple federates (1 to 8). Encapsulating a large number of agents in a single federate often impose a heavy computational load to the host machine. Distributing agents to multiple agent federates running on multiple hosts aims to lessen the computation load of each host. Obviously, as the number of agent federates increases, the computational load of each federate becomes lighter while resulting in higher overall communication amongst the distributed federates.

Figure 9 gives the execution times of HLA_RePast and HLA_Grid_RePast with different numbers of agent federates. The execution times of both HLA_Grid_RePast and HLA_RePast based simulations decrease with the number of agent federates. However, as the computational load in each federate decreases, the communication overhead becomes more and more significant. HLA_Grid_RePast yields a speedup pattern similar to HLA_RePast with the extra overhead increasing slightly. In HLA_Grid_RePast, each federate requires one node for the federate itself and one for the proxy services (see figure 10). Such extra complexity contributes to the increment of additional communication cost crossing Grid.

Performance in a WAN Environment

Experiments for evaluating the performance of HLA_RePast and HLA_Grid_RePast have also been conducted in a WAN environment (over Internet). In these experiments, the RTIExec and the environment federate are in Birmingham while the agent federate is in Singapore, as illustrated in figure 10. Two HLA_Grid proxy services are also hosted in Birmingham for the environment and agent federates respectively.

Similarly to the first set of experiments in the LAN environment, only one agent federate is used with the number of agents ranging from 1 to 1024. The results for a WAN environment are depicted in Figure 11.

Comparing figures 8 and 11, it can be observed that simulations take much longer to finish in the WAN environment. This is not surprising, as the bandwidth is much smaller and the communication latency much higher in the WAN environment. As shown in figure 10, the most noticeable difference is that HLA_Grid_RePast performs much worse than HLA_RePast in the WAN environment. Nevertheless, when the number of agents becomes larger, the total execution time with HLA_Grid_RePast tends to be closer to that with HLA_RePast. Figure 12 highlights the extra overhead of HLA_Grid_RePast against HLA_RePast.

At the beginning, the total execution time with HLA_Grid_RePast is ~32.6 times more than that with HLA_RePast. This difference diminishes rapidly with the number of agents (or in other words with the complexity of the simulation) becoming ~4.2 with 1024 agents. As the same computation loads

Figure 8. Execution times of HLA_Grid_RePast and HLA_RePast based simulations using a single Agent Federate

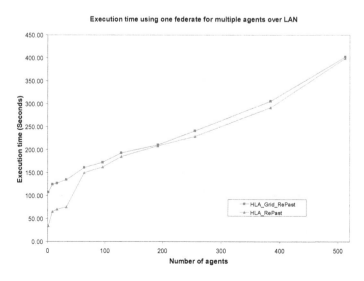

Figure 9. Execution times of HLA_Grid_RePast and HLA_RePast based simulations using multiple agent federates (512 agents)

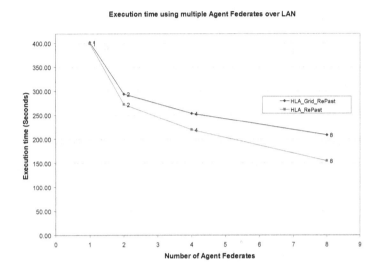

Figure 10. Configuration for HLA_Grid_RePast in a WAN Environment

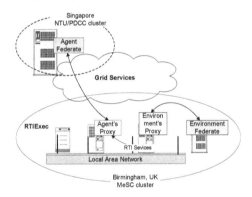

(for the equal number of agents) apply in both environments, the difference in execution times between HLA_Grid_RePast and HLA_RePast can be attributed to the communication overhead, which is much higher in HLA_Grid_RePast (see table 1).

Analysis and Further Optimisation

From the experiments presented in previous sections, clearly in a WAN environment HLA_Grid_RePast incurs much higher overhead than HLA_RePast does. As there is no difference between the RePast models used for the two systems, the extra overhead of the former is attributed to the communication load. In order to identify the cause of the performance gap, additional measurements have been taken from the experiments in terms of number/types of RTI calls, which determine a federate's communication pattern, and the underlying networking traffic. In the WAN environment, each RTI call from the agent federate has to be conveyed over Grid to the proxy to be executed. This means that the more RTI calls, the more costly Grid-crossing communication will take place. RTI calls can be classified into normal RTI Ambassador calls (normal calls) and RTI Ambassador ticks (ticks) (DMSO, 2002).

In the above experiments, the RTI related execution of an agent federate has 100 iterations, and each iteration can be illustrated as follows:

1. **Callbacks** Processing callbacks delivered by the RTI
2. **Normal RTIAmbassador calls** Generate attribute updates of RTI object instances
3. **Time Advancement** Issue time advancement request from the RTI then keep issuing ticks until the request granted

The network packages (TCP) generated between clients and proxies under WAN and LAN environments have been monitored. The performance degradation of HLA_Grid_RePast over the Internet is mainly due to a large number of RTI related messages to be delivered which then demand establishing excessive TCP connections.

Under the current GT3-based implementation, using a middleware layer may provide a solution to the problem by reducing the number of messages over Grid including both the normal RTI calls and the ticks. For instance, in each iteration, we can aggregate the attribute updates of object instances into a "combo message" at the client side. After the combo message is transmitted over the Grid, the proxy can decompose it and execute multiple attribute updates accordingly. With regard to the ticks, immediately after a federate requesting time advancement, its proxy can keep ticking and block for time advancement granted instead of issuing tick one by one driven by the remote federate. In this way, the number

Figure 11. Execution times of HLA_Grid_RePast and HLA_RePast based simulations with a single Agent Federate over WAN

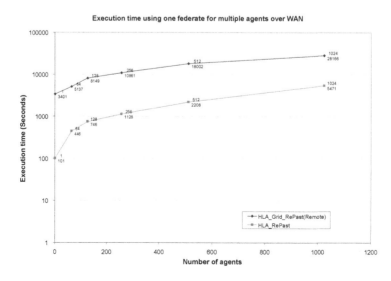

Figure 12. Ratio of the extra overhead incurred by HLA_Grid_RePast against HLA_RePast over WAN

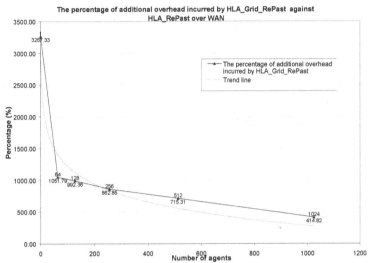

Figure 13. Execution time of HLA_Grid_RePast_Msg_Aggr and HLA_RePast based simulations with a single Agent Federate over WAN

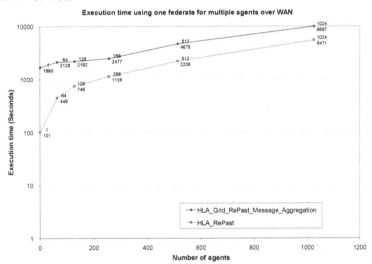

of Grid messages can be significantly reduced. For the example given above, ideally there will be only 100 combo messages and 100 tick messages to be delivered over the Grid. Iskra et al had successfully employed a similar message aggregation approach on the wide-area links to improve the performance of their Time Warp kernel on the Grid (Iskra, 2005).

The experiments described in section 5.3 have been repeated using the HLA_Grid_RePast enabled with the message aggregation method (*HLA_Grid_RePast_Msg_Aggr*). Figure 13 presents the execution times of HLA_Grid_RePast_Msg_Aggr against HLA_RePast, and figure 14 highlights the extra overhead of HLA_Grid_RePast_Msg_Aggr.

Comparing the results presented in figure 11 and in figure 13, we can observe that message aggregation has dramatically reduced the communication overhead incurred by HLA_Grid_RePast. The total execution time of HLA_Grid_RePast_Msg_Aggr is now ~15.7 times more than that with HLA_RePast at the beginning, and this ratio of extra overhead diminishes rapidly with the number of agents. It becomes less than ~1.81 times the overhead of HLA_RePast with 1024 agents. These results indicate that the overhead brought by higher payload in each combo message can be overcompensated by lessening TCP connections, therefore significant performance improvement has been achieved.

Discussion on Quality of Services

To guarantee Quality of Service (QoS) in a Grid aware system is both important and challenging. The metrics of QoS in Grid computing have been identified as latency, throughput and availability (Menasce, 2004). In order to evaluate the QoS of HLA_Grid_RePast system totally from the user's perspective, we define the three metrics only at application level as follows:

1. **Latency** The communication overhead incurred by the HLA_Grid infrastructures
2. **Throughput** The number of RTI invocations (exclusive of ticks) executed per second
3. **Availability** Fraction of time the Grid-enabled RTI services is available for use

With respect to the above definitions, table 2 presents the results on QoS evaluation of HLA_Grid_RePast (including the system enabled with message aggregation).

Since latency only concerns the delivery of each single message, HLA_Grid_RePast and HLA_Grid_RePast_Msg_Aggr incur the same latency (see table 1). The Proxy RTI Ambassador Service and the Client Federate Ambassador Service have been intended for servicing a RePast model and its proxy only. Therefore, HLA_Grid_RePast exhibits a 100% availability of service, and it makes no difference

Figure 14. Ratio of the extra overhead incurred by HLA_Grid_RePast_Msg_Aggr against HLA_RePast over WAN

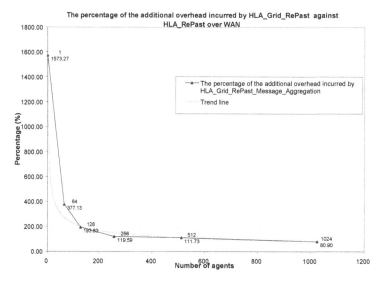

whether message aggregation is enabled. In contrast, message aggregation approach dramatically improves the throughput of HLA_Grid_RePast by about 2.6 times (from ~1.5/Second to ~5.4/Second).

Furthermore, the latest Globus Toolkit 4.1.1 (GT4.1.1) supports persistent TCP/IP connections. We have timed a Grid invocation using GT4.1.1 over the WAN environment (see figure 12) between Birmingham and Singapore. The elapsed time for an invocation is ~250 Milliseconds, while that using GT3 is ~920 Milliseconds. This feature envisions a radical solution to significant improvement of the QoS of HLA_Grid_RePast, in terms of both latency and throughput.

FUTURE TRENDS

Federate developers often already have a set of federates situating over their intranet, thus it is desirable for users to access a whole federation through Grid services to further exploit computational resources and maximize the reusability of legacy federates. Further, due to the existing firewall rules of most administrative domains, it is often the case that only few nodes of an administrative domain are accessible to the external users of HLA-based simulations. For example, the HLA_Grid_RePast experiments over WAN can only exploit the master node of the high performance cluster at Birmingham, while the other worker nodes are inaccessible to Singapore side and vice versa.

A future direction of the work can be the investigation of mechanisms to present entire HLA_Grid_RePast federations as Grid services to facilitate the interoperability of HLA_Grid_RePast with different federations for the construction of extra-large and complex agent-based simulations. The federation community technology (Chen, 2003) sounds a natural candidate to facilitate solutions to these problems. In this context, synchronization in networked federations will be a particularly important and challenging issue to be addressed.

The XMSF framework has demonstrated the advantages of Service Oriented Architectures (SoA) for distributed simulations. In the longer term we will also endeavour to enable SoA for Simulation and Grid-enabled Federation Community. The simple integration of the Grid middleware and the HLA/RTI cannot fully exploit benefits such as loose coupling, heterogeneity, and transportation protocol independence that would be provided by an SoA.

CONCLUSION

The emergence of Grid technologies provides exciting new opportunities for large scale distributed simulation. This chapter has presented HLA_Grid_RePast, which has been successfully established a middleware platform for the execution of collaborating RePast on the Grid. The system presents RePast models as services and facilitates the flexible construction and execution of large scale agent federations over the Grid. It has successfully supported reusability and user transparency, providing a relatively simple workflow for deployment and usage.

The experimental results show that communication costs are crucial for the performance of such simulations. However the additional overhead introduced in the system as a result of communication steadily becomes less significant as the complexity of the simulation models increases, suggesting that the deployment of the Grid can indeed offer performance gains for large scale computation bound simulations.

Table 2. Evaluation of quality of services on HLA_Grid_RePast

	Latency	Throughput	Availability
HLA_Grid_RePast	935 Milliseconds	1.5/Second	100%
HLA_Grid_RePast_Msg_Aggr	935 Milliseconds	5.4/Second	100%

Future work will seek to further improve the performance of the system using alternative application containers, such as the Apache Tomcat, as well as to migrate HLA_Grid_RePast from GT3 to Globus Toolkit 4.1.1 (GT4). Further minimisation of the communication overhead over WAN can be envisioned with the persistent TCP/IP connections supported by GT4.1.1.

ACKNOWLEDGMENT

The work was undertaken as part of "DS-Grid: Large Scale Agent-based Simulation on the Grid", an e-Science Project (No. GR/S82862/01) led by Dr. Georgios K. Theodoropoulos, at the University of Birmingham (UoB) in the UK. DS-Grid is a collaborative project between UoB and the Nanyang Technological University in Singapore.

REFERENCES

Barton, J., Thatte, S., & Nielsen, H. F. (2000). SOAP Messages with Attachments, W3C Note. Retrieved November 07, 2007, from http://www.w3.org/TR/2000/NOTE-SOAP-attachments-20001211

Base Object Model. (January). Retrieved November 07, 2007, from http://www.boms.info/

Cai, W., Yuan, Z., Low, M. Y. H., & Turner, S. J. (2005). Federate migration in HLA based simulation. *Future Generation Computer Systems*, *21*(1), 87-95.

Chen, D., Li, B. S., Cai, W., & Turner, S. J. (2003). Design and Development of a Cluster Gateway for Cluster-based HLA Distributed Virtual Simulation Environments. *36th Annual Simulation Symposium (IEEE Computer Society)* (pp. 193-200). USA: The Printing House.

Chen, D., Theodoropoulos, G. K., Turner, S. J., Cai, W., Minson, R., & Zhang, Y. (2008). Large Scale Agent-based Simulation on the Grid. *Future Generation Computer Systems*, *24*(7), 658-671.

Chen, D., Turner, S. J., Cai, W., & Xiong, M. (2008). A Decoupled Federate Architecture for High Level Architecture-based Distributed Simulation. *Journal of Parallel and Distributed Computing*, *68*(11).

Collier, N. (2007). RePast: An Extensible Framework for Agent Simulation, Retrieved January 08, 2007, from http://www.econ.iastate.edu/tesfatsi/RepastTutorial.Collier.pdf

Dahmann, J. S., Kuhl, F., & Weatherly, R. (1998). Standards for simulation: As simple as possible but not simpler: The High Level Architecture for simulation. *Simulation: Transactions of the Society for Modeling and Simulation International*, *71*(6), 378-387.

DIS Steering Committee. (1994). *The DIS Vision, A Map to the Future of Distributed Simulation* (Tech. Rep. No. IST-SP-94-01). Orlando, Florida, USA: Institute for Simulation and Training.

DMSO. (2002). *RTI 1.3 Next generation programmer's guide version 5*. Alexandria, VA, USA: DMSO/ DoD.

Fitzgibbons, J. B., Fujimoto, R., Fellig, D., Kleban, D., & Scholand, A. J. (2004). IDSim: An Extensible Framework for Interoperable Distributed Simulation. In B. Werner (Ed.), *The Proceedings of the IEEE International Conference on Web Services (ICWS2004)*(pp. 532-539). USA: The Printing House.

Fujimoto, R. (2007). DoD High Level Architecture. Retrieved November 07, 2007, from http://www. cc.gatech.edu/computing/pads/tech-highperf.html

IEEE 1516. (2000). *IEEE Standard for High Level Architecture*. 3 Park Avenue, New York, NY 10016-5997, USA: The Institute of Electrical and Electronics Engineers, Inc.

IEEE1516.3. (2003). *IEEE Recommended Practice for High Level Architecture (HLA) Federation Development and Execution Process (FEDEP)*. 3 Park Avenue, New York, NY 10016-5997, USA: The Institute of Electrical and Electronics Engineers, Inc.

Iskra, K., Albada, G., & Sloot, P. (2003). Time Warp Cancellations Optimisations on High Latency Networks. In S. J. Turner and S. J. E. Taylor (Ed.), *The Proceedings of the 7th IEEE International Symposium on Distributed Simulation and Real-Time Applications (DS-RT'03)* (pp. 128-137). USA: The Printing House.

Iskra, K., Albada, G., & Sloot, P. (2005). Towards Grid-Aware Time Warp. *Simulation: Transactions of The Society for Modeling and Simulation International, 81*(4), 293-306.

Jie, W., Zang, T., Lei, Z., Cai, W., Turner, S. J. & Wang, L. (2002). Constructing an OGSA-Based Grid Computing Platform. In H. P. Lee and K. Kumar (Ed.), *Recent Advances in Computational Science & Engineering: International Conference on Scientific and Engineering Computation (IC-SEC 2002)* (pp. 738-741). UK: Imperial College Press.

Kuhl, F., Weatherly, R., & Dahmann, J. (1999). *Creating Computer Simulation Systems: An Introduction to HLA*. Upper Saddle River, New Jersey, USA: Prentice Hall.

Lees, M., Logan, B., Oguara, T., & Theodoropoulos, G. K. (2003, June). *Simulating Agent-Based Systems with HLA: The case of SIM AGENT - Part II*. Presented at the European Simulation Interoperability Workshop 2003, Stockholm, Sweden.

Lees, M., Logan, B., & Kings, J. (2007, June). *HLA Simulation of Agent-Based Bacterial Models*. Presented at the European Simulation Interoperability Workshop 2007, Genoa, Italy.

Minson, R., & Theodoropoulos, G. K., (2004, June). *Distributing RePast Agent-Based Simulations with HLA*. Presented at the European Simulation Interoperability Workshop 2004, Edinburgh, Scotland.

Low, M., Yoke, H., Cai, W., & Zhou, S. (2007, June). A Federated Agent-Based Crowd Simulation Architecture. In *The Proceedings of the 2007 European Conference on Modelling and Simulation* (pp. 188-194).

Menasce, D., & Casalicchio, E. (2004). Quality of Service Aspects and Metrics in Grid Computing. In *The Proceedings of the 2004 Computer Measurement Group Conference* (pp. 521-532).

Morse, K. L., Drake, D., & Brunton, R. P. Z. (2003, June). *Web Enabling an RTI - An XMSF Profile*. Presented at the European Simulation Interoperability Workshop 2003, Stockholm, Sweden.

Morse, K. L., Drake, D., & Brunton, R. P. Z. (2004). Web Enabling HLA Compliant Simulations to Support Network Centric Applications. In *The Proceedings of the 2004 Command and Control Research and Technology Symposium* (no. 172).

Nielsen, H. F., Christensen, E., & Farrell, J., (2007) Specification: WS-Attachments. Retrieved November 07, 2007, from http://www-106.ibm.com/developerworks/webservices/library/ws-attach.html

Overstreet, C. M., Nance, R. E., & Balci, O. (2002). Issues in Enhancing Model Reuse. In *The Proceedings of the First International Conference on Grand Challenges for Modeling and Simulation*.

Petty, M. D., Weisel, E. W., & Mielka, R. R. (2003). A Formal Approach to Composability. In *The Proceedings of the 2003 Interservice Industry Training, Simulation and Education Conference* (pp. 1763-1772).

Pollack, M. E., & Ringuette, M. (1990). Introducing the Tileworld: Experimentally Evaluating Agent Architectures. In *The Proceedings of the 8th National Conference on Artificial Intelligence* (pp. 183-189).

Pollack, M. E., Joslin, D., Nunes, A., Ur, S., & Ephrati, E., (1994). *Experimental investigation of an agent commitment strategy* (Tech. Rep. No. TR 94-31). Pittsburgh, PA 15260: University of Pittsburgh.

Pullen, J. M., Brunton, R., Brutzman, D., Drake, D., Hieb, M., Morse, K., & Tolk, A. (2005). Using Web Services to Integrate Heterogeneous Simulations in a Grid Environment. *Future Generation Computer Systems, 21*(1), 97-106.

Railsback, S. F., Lytinen, S. L., & Jackson, S. K. (2006). Agent-Based Simulation Platforms: Review and Development Recommendations. *Simulation: Transactions of the Society for Modeling and Simulation International, 82*(9), 609-623.

Rycerz, K., Bubak, M. T., Malawski, M., & Sloot, P. (2005). A Framework for HLA-Based Interactive Simulations on the Grid. *Simulation: Transactions of the Society for Modeling and Simulation International, 81*(1), 67-76.

Sotomayor, B. (2007). The Globus Toolkit 3 Programmer's Tutorial. Retrieved January 08, 2007, from http://gdp.globus.org/gt3-tutorial/singlehtml/progtutorial_0.4.3.html

Splunter, S., Wijngaards, N. J. E., Brazier, F. M. T., & Richards, D. (2004). Automated Component-Based Configuration: Promises and Fallacies. In *The Proceedings of the Adaptive Agents and Multi-Agent Systems workshop at the AISB 2004 Symposium* (pp. 130-135).

Theodoropoulos, G. K., Zhang, Y., Chen, D., Minson, R., Turner, S. J., Cai, W., Yong, X., & Logan, B. (2006, May). *Large Scale Distributed Simulation on the Grid*. Paper presented at the Sixth IEEE International Symposium on Cluster Computing and the Grid Workshops, Singapore.

Tobias, R., & Hofmann, C. (2004). Evaluation of Free Java Libraries for Social-Scientific Agent-Based Simulation. *Journal of Artificial Societies and Social Simulation*, 7(1), Retrieved January 08, 2004, from http://jasss.soc.surrey.ac.uk/7/1/6.html .

Tuecke, S., Czajkowski, K., Foster, I., Rey, J., Steve, F., & Carl, G. (2007). Grid service specification. Retrieved January 08, 2007, from http://www.globus.org/research/papers/gsspec.pdf

Wytzisk, A., Simonis, I., & Raape, U. (2003). *Integration of HLA Simulation Models Into a Standized Web Service World*. Presented at the European Simulation Interoperability Workshop 2003, Stockholm, Sweden.

Xu, L., & Peng, X. (2006, May). *SSB: A Grid-based Infrastructure for HLA Systems*. Paper presented at the Sixth IEEE International Symposium on Cluster Computing and the Grid Workshops, Singapore.

Xie, Y., Teo, Y. M., Cai, W., & Turner, S. J. (2005). Service Provisioning for HLA based Distributed Simulation on the Grid. In D. M. Nicol and S. J. Turner (Ed.), *The Proceedings of the Nineteenth ACM/IEEE/SCS Workshop on Principles of Advanced and Distributed Simulation (PADS 2005)* (pp. 282-291). USA: The Printing House.

Zhang, Y., Theodoropoulos, G. K., Minson, R., Turner, S. J., Cai, W., Yong, X., & Logan, B. (2005, July). *Grid-aware Large Scale Distributed Simulation of Agent-based Systems*. Presented at the European Simulator Interoperability Workshop 2005, Toulouse, France.

Zhu, S., Du, Z., & Chai, X. (2006, May). *GDSA: A Grid-based Distributed Simulation Architecture*. Paper presented at the Sixth IEEE International Symposium on Cluster Computing and the Grid Workshops, Singapore.

Zong, W., Wang, Y., Cai, W. & Turner, S. J. (2004). Grid Services and Service Discovery for HLA-based Distributed Simulations. In S. J. Turner, D. J. Roberts, and L. F. Wilson (Ed.), *The Proceedings of the 8th IEEE International Symposium on Distributed Simulation and Real Time Applications (DSRT 2004)* (pp. 116-124). USA: The Printing House.

Chapter XVII
E–Portfolio to Promote the Virtual Learning Group Communities on the Grid

Guy Gouardères
Laboratoire LIUPPA – Université de Pau et des Pays de l'Adour, France

Emilie Conté
Laboratoire LIUPPA – Université de Pau et des Pays de l'Adour, France

ABSTRACT

In Vocational and Educational Training (VET), new trends are toward social learning and, more precisely, toward informal learning. In such settings, this article introduces a process — the e-Qualification — to manage informal learning on the ELeGI "Learning Grid Infrastructure." It argues that this process must occur in a social context, such as virtual communities. On the one hand, it describes their necessary characteristics and proprieties that lead to the creation of a new kind of virtual community: the Virtual Learning Grid Community (VLGC). On the other hand, e-Qualification cannot occur without the help of a kind of user's profile, called e-portfolio. Moreover, the e-portfolio is also a process, used to manage the Virtual Learning Grid Communities. The e-Qualification and Virtual Learning Grid Communities' management will probably rely on the cooperation of different distributed, autonomous, goal-oriented entities, called Mobile Peer-to-Peer (P2P) Agents. Furthermore, we hope that implementing these services will decrease the lack of informal learning treatment on the grid and will become the basis for new services on the Learning Grid.

INTRODUCTION

The continuous development of new technologies has brought new perspectives for more advanced and enhanced learning services. One example is the emergence of Grid computing.

According to Foster (2003, p. 1):

Grid computing has emerged as an important new field, distinguished from conventional distributed computing by its focus on large-scale resource sharing, innovative applications and, in some cases, high-performance orientation. ... The "Grid problem," which we define as flexible, secure, coordinated resource sharing among dynamic collections of individuals, institutions, and resources — what we refer to as virtual organizations.

The Globus Alliance, which is a community of organizations and individuals developing fundamental technologies behind the Grid, has defined the Open Grid Services Architecture (OGSA). This is a service-oriented architecture for the Grid Model of a computing system and is the current standard for the Grid middlewares and services.

The Semantic Grid is an extension of the current Grid, in which information and services are given well-defined meaning, better enabling computers and people to work in cooperation.

According to De Roure (2003, p. 2):

[T]he Semantic Grid is characterised as an open system in which users, software, components and computational resources (all owned by different stakeholders) come and go on a continual basis.

According to Allison, Ruddle, and Michaelson (2002, p. 102):

From the perspective of good educational practice an online collaborative learning environment should provide certain features for learners, like group-work support, interactive, engaging, responsive, real-world input, student-centred, anytime/ anywhere.

Those pedagogical goals imply a radical change of the technical requirements and bring forward a new design for the semantic Grid, in which "social learning" will be of paramount importance.

In such settings, the European Learning Grid Infrastructure (ELeGI project - contract IST-002205, 6th Framework Programme for RTD) has the ambitious goal to develop software technologies for effective human learning (Dimitrakos & Ritrovato, 2004). ELeGI has chosen a synergic approach, sometimes called "human centered design," to replace the classical, applicative approach to learning. In this approach, learning occurs as a side effect of interactions, conversations and enhanced presence in dynamic virtual communities. Two kinds of learning are pointed out: formal learning vs. informal learning. According to Allison, Cerri, Ritrovato, Gaeta, and Gaeta (2005), informal learning groups are ad hoc temporary clusters of students within a single work session. Informal learning groups can be initiated, for example, by asking students to spend 2 minutes discussing a question or problem posed by the teacher. In this case, some students gather to solve the question or problem. In this way, the informal learning groups form with the only purpose to solve the posed problematic situation, and their life expectancy is limited to the work session. In VET, informal learning refers to what the user learns during the debriefings in groups.

Nowadays, there is a real lack of tools able to manage informal learning. Our major research objective is to define a process able to point out what the learner has acquired through an informal way and to guide the learner according to this new information. This process is called e-Qualification and cannot occur without introducing new suitable tools, which are the e-portfolio and VLGC.

In the context of the learning Grid, the e-Qualification process becomes mandatory to qualify users and the provided services.

E-Qualification cannot occur without using the peer-to-peer communication mode. According to Schollmeier (2001, p. 101):

[A] distributed network architecture may be called a Peer-to-Peer (P-to-P, P2P) Network, if the participants share a part of their own hardware resources (processing power, storage capacity, network link capacity, printers,). These shared resources are necessary to provide the Service and content offered by the network (e.g. file sharing or shared workspaces for collaboration). They are accessible by other peers directly, without passing intermediary entities. The participants of such a network are thus resource (Service and content) providers as well as resource (Service and content) requestors (Servant-concept).

Our purpose in this article is to argue that these new tools are mandatory to perform the e-Qualification process and so to manage informal learning. Note that our activities are specific to VET, where informal learning has a real importance in the learning process.

Agents possess attractive features, including autonomy, proactiveness, intelligence; social ability and mentalist characterization can be used to build advanced distributed systems. So, the Multi-Agents System suits the best to the Grid and we will detail their use.

This article is structured in five sections. The first details the context in which e-Qualification occurs. The two following sections deal with VLGCs and e-portfolio. Then, we focus on the agents' work. We end by an application of the e-Qualification process to the use case Aero user-friendly SIMulation based dIstant Learning (ASIMIL), which is a training flight simulator.

CONTEXT

In the ELeGI learning vision, the learner is an active actor in the learning process, and his knowledge construction occurs through conversations, collaboration and direct experience in a social context. Informal learning can only occur in social cases (Eisenstadt & Komzak, 2005). So, virtual communities are the best place to support discussions, "informal learning." Virtual communities are social aggregations that emerge from the Internet when enough people carry on these public discussions long enough, with sufficient human feeling, to form webs of personal relationships in cyberspace (Rheingold, 1993).

We will take into consideration students who are working into virtual communities. Qualification is the passage from a knowledge state to another one, which occurs before assessment. E-Qualification is a mandatory process to continuously evaluate users during their learning process.

We define e-Qualification as a three-step process that (1) identifies the new knowledge, skills, and so forth (learned by formal and informal ways); (2) updates the learner's "profile;" and (3) places him or her into the virtual community that best suits its previous needs and upgraded skills. Note that in a learning process, each user has a profile to store personal information, skills, knowledge, evolution, and so forth. Moreover, the e-Qualification process must continuously occur to be more efficient: A user who is always in a suitable virtual community learns faster that a user who "waits" an important change in his profile to be oriented toward the suitable virtual community. So, e-Qualification is also a process that continuously identifies and qualifies the users' improvements.

The e-Qualification guiding principle is:

- Each user has a profile and must belong to at least a virtual community. (There is always a kind of "basic virtual community" in which every user is authorized to belong to.)
- Each user is continuously qualified: The process identifies new skills and knowledge before, after and during exercises.
- When the virtual community is not well suited to the user's profile, the process looks for a new one and integrates the user into it.

Of course, users are not the sole actors of this process: A user cannot continuously update his or her profile, check whether he or she matches with the virtual community or argue to enter another virtual community. This is the agents' work. Therefore, a Multi-Agents System is implemented to carry out e-Qualification and manage virtual communities.

Regarding the previous statements, the user's profile is a major tool that allows the user to integrate (or not) a community. Agents use this to perform e-Qualification and manage virtual communities. It is no more just a profile. It is a real tool for working, the user workspace, which must be accessible and understood by the agents. We call it the e-portfolio, which is described later and must not be mixed up with the general terms "portfolio" or "e-portfolio."

Having introduced the context of e-Qualification, we can now focus on the heart of the article's topic: the creation of specific virtual communities on the Grid and the e-portfolio, two mandatory tools for managing informal learning.

VIRTUAL LEARNING GRID COMMUNITY

ELeGI project has defined its own definition of Virtual Learning Community (VLC). First, we deal with the ELeGi project's beliefs and choices for VLC. Then we explain why this definition does not suit e-Qualification. Therefore, we introduce the VLGC.

VLC

According to Garber (2004, p. 2):

To be a learning community, participants must be committed to the learning process, and responsive to the contributions of other participants through "reciprocity" based on trust between the community members.

According to Schwier (2004, p. 1):

A virtual learning community is a particular type of virtual learning environment. Virtual learning environments happen when the process of learning takes place outside the boundaries of face-to-face contact, typically online. But environments are not necessarily communities. For a community to emerge, a learning environment must allow learners to engage each other intentionally and collectively in the transaction or transformation of knowledge.

The following refers to the ELeGI project's choices for VLGC.
VLC are designed to allow collaborative learning.

The term "collaborative learning" refers to an instruction method in which learners at various performance levels work together in small groups toward a common goal. The collaborative learning is a teaching strategy in which "both teachers and learners are active participants in the learning process; knowledge is not something that is delivered to students in this process, but something that emerges from active dialogue among those who seek to understand and apply concepts and techniques. ... The collaborative learning is also a democratic process, in which all the participants are equal and are treated like that, playing a role that is valued by everyone of them." (Burgstahler & Swift, 1996)

The ELeGi project treats the two kinds of learning: informal vs. formal. "An informal group is characterized by a specific task related to a single work session, on the contrary the formal group typologies are specific for task with longer duration. For this reason the informal groups can be constituted by a limited number of persons of same class that develop in the same moment, the same task. This group is only limited to the single session and it dissolves when the session finishes.

So is not necessary to define a specific structure within the group, they can be generated in random way and it is enough the presence of tutor, who support and facilitate the collaborative learning." Regarding this last quotation, it is clear that ELeGI project's VLCs are only designed for formal learning.

VLGC

As quoted before, collaborative learning is a democratic process in which all participants are equal and treated so. But in ELeGI project's definition, a VLC contains several types of members, such as visitor, reader, member, learner and technical chief administrator. It is not convenient for pure informal learning, because users have to ask permission to freely discuss. Therefore, our VLC cannot have an administrator, and the different members must not be categorized; they are just members.

Making reference to VET, informal debriefing groups are some "groups of qualification": Each trainee qualifies his or her work according to the discussions had with others and the prerequisite in his or her e-portfolio. These groups are more than VLCs; they are groups in which each member has the same 'rights'; there is no longer any distinction between trainees, instructors or tutors.

So the ELeGI Project's VLC definition cannot be efficient to make informal collaborative learning. This process does not allow centralization (e.g., even if a "virtual KapelMeister" acting as Super Peer will do it — Airlines' pilots don't accept). That explains why we must use the peer-to-peer communication mode, which is decentralized.

Training centers do not work like schools. Informal and formal training is done alternately with real-life practice. And so, informal learning cannot be seen as a limited period. It is "life-long" training.

Moreover, VLC are designed for formal learning. They are built to answer to precept objectives (e.g., succeed in exercise 1). We cannot define these objectives in the context of informal learning.

Finally, we opt to define the VLGC adapted to informal learning and, more precisely, to informal learning in VET. A VLGC can be defined as a VLC in which all members are equal (implemented on a peer-to-peer way) and which have some global objectives and continuously evolve.

The User Representation

Each user has at least one representative agent, and its behavior (past, present and future), knowledge, skills and goals are stored in an e-portfolio.

More than a storage tool, the e-portfolio is a real process that is not only used during the "regular learning process." It is made up of a personal part and a shared one. The sharing notion is really important: If the user learns by speaking with other users, he or she also learns by looking at their e-portfolio.

The agents must be able to communicate together and understand an e-portfolio. Regarding the ubiquity of the Grid, we must use a common "architecture" to allow communication between agents (that may be implemented in different languages).

One piece of the solution is the use of ontology, which consists of a set of concepts and relationships that describes an area of interest. "The role of an ontology is considered as a set of logical axioms designed to account for the intended meaning of a vocabulary" (Guarino, 1998, p. 2).

Let us assume a global ontology that contains all the existing concepts (for a given area) and is understood by all agents. A personal e-portfolio contains a "functional ontology," which is a view of this global ontology and depends on the user's category (a mechanic does not have the same fontional ontology as a pilot, but their two functional ontologies are built according to the global one).

In informal learning, the notion of personalization is very important, so the e-portfolio's ontology is made up of two kinds of ontology: a user modeling ontology and a goal driven one. The user modeling ontology contains the skills, knowledge, personal information, results, and so forth, and really depends on the user (because the architecture of the ontology depends on the user's category). The goal driven ontology contains all the user's objectives and the process to attain them.

Membership to a VLGC

Remember that the members of a VLGC must target some common goals. These goals are more important than the personal ones. The achievement of group objectives must not be a hindrance to reach their personal objectives. A major principle is that each member has the same rights, and all decisions are made according the group's thinking and the group's objectives.

A VLGC is represented at two levels. The first level is a high one: Users are grouped and work together (learning activity). On the second one are the representative agents managing VLGCs.

The multitude of activities the learner can simultaneously perform implies that we have to give each learner the possibility to belong to several VLGCs. But we distinguish "strong" membership vs. a "weak" one. A user cannot "strongly" belong to several VLGCs. He or she "strongly" belongs to one VLGC, and "weakly" belongs to other VLGCs (if he or she needs it).

To belong to a VLGC, the user must share some common knowledge, abilities, needs and goals with the VLGC's members. This common information defines the signature of the e-portfolio. (Note that we can extract several signatures from an e-portfolio).

So, the signature is an extract of e-portfolio that depends on the VLGC the user belongs to. It is a service provided by the e-portfolio and stored in each user's e-portfolio. More precisely, each member's signature has the same "shared ontology" but, of course, the content is personalized (e.g., it is impossible that every member succeeded in a same exercise with the same note). A basic level has to be defined, too.

The signature of a VLGC determines in part who is or is not allowed to integrate the community.

We define the VLGC signature as:

- The intersection of the members' ontology architecture (so a student cannot integrate a mechanics' VLGC, because he does not have the same ontology architecture).
- Some common objectives and minimum level and skills the user already has (we consider here the content of the ontology).

So, an e-portfolio contains a functional ontology and provides several signatures also stored into it.

It is an essential service for e-Qualification, because it is the basic tool for agents to manage VLGC.

The VLGC's Life Cycle

The VLGC life cycle comprises four phases: creation, operation, evolution, and dissolution.

Creation

At the creation of a learning/training domain, there must exist at least one community: the beginning VLGC, which contains all the learners. Regarding the P2P communication model, a sole administrator cannot create a VLGC; it must emerge from the decision of a whole group. Each VLGC is a real entity and has a signature, which is regularly updated.

The creation of a new VLGC occurs when a user wants to reach a particular goal but is refused by all the VLGCs. Then, if another user accepts to work with him, they can decide to form a new VLGC. The VLGC's signature is established according to the needs and abilities of the two members.

As soon as the VLGC is created, its signature will change according to either the content of new members' e-portfolios or to the evolution of the objectives of the VLGC's members.

Operation

There are three possible operations in a VLGC:

- Integration of a new member
- Work, communication
- Exit of a member

Integration of a member is based on the use of signature. It results from a communication between agents. The representative agent of the learner who wants to integrate the community communicates with one member agent. This agent will give the learner the signature's ontology. Here, we can see the real utility of the ontology: The learner agent knows what it has to extract from the e-portfolio to try an overlay. Then, the agent tries it. If the overlay succeeds (with a predefined tolerance), the two agents will discuss the different conditions to enter this community. As soon as the learner has integrated the community, the agent who has authorized this entrance informs the VLGC. This step is called "notification" (or "sonnet").

A member has to quit a community when his or her signature does not match anymore with the VLGC's. The member's agent has to inform the other members (sonnet).

As soon as the VLGC's signature is updated, the whole VLGC is informed. Each member agent has to regularly check if its signature matches with the VLGC's. Some rules must be fixed to be sure that every member is always right on mark in the community. We impose that a comparison between the member agents' signatures occurs when:

- A change of the VLGC's signature occurs.
- The user has performed an exercise and has made progress (change of level). The contrary works, too: If the user's level has decreased, he can be fired.
- The user has no more common goals with the group (then the user must quit the VLGC).
- The user has a new objective that cannot be reached within this VLGC. The user can search for a new one (with a new signature) and decide whether to leave this one. Do not forget that every user can belong to several VLGCs.

Evolution

The major difficulty is to determine if some members have to quit the VLGC or if the VLGC has to evolve. This situation can occur in two cases:

- When a sonnet indicates that a new member has integrated the VLGC. Agents discuss what this member can bring to the VLGC and choose whether they update the signature (adding, for example, new objectives).
- When a member has progressed and if that user's signature does not match anymore with the VLGC's. The member can suppose that he or she is not the only one who has evolved and contact the other agents to speak about new skills and knowledge. Then, if a great part of the VLGC has the same new skills, members can vote and decide to update the VLGC's signature.

Dissolution

A VLGC disappears when it contains only one member (or none). This last member must move to another VLGC.

E-Portfolio

A short definition of e-portfolio was given earlier to detail the VLGC management. Remember what our e-portfolio is composed of:

- A functional ontology that contains the knowledge, skills, personal data, exercises, results, goals, and so forth of the learner. This ontology is made up of a user modeling ontology and a goal driven one. Note that the functional ontology infers from a global ontology, which is known and understood by all agents.
- Some signatures, which are extracts of the e-portfolio's ontology and allow the user to belong to one or several VLGC.

We will now study the dynamicity of our e-portfolio. But first, we describe some generalities about portfolios.

The key concept of a virtual community usually involves the notion of shared knowledge, goals and intentions that function as a common binding to team members. This can be achieved by a new design for the former portfolio or electronic portfolio. The e-portfolio is a way of learning as a social activity, and it is a tool for developing one's own knowledge and competencies and a kind of virtual representation of oneself. The student's ability to learn as well as his ability to share his knowledge with others and his ability to get feedback from others are also encountered.

The e-portfolio is not just a tool, but a service that helps the student to learn into a VLGC.

An e-portfolio is a repository of data and process (*e*lectronically stored) that facilitates reflective and critical thinking and may be used for collaboration or (self-) assessment and reflection by individuals and groups.

The My.Step.Stanford project (Vanides, 2002) develops special purpose softwares which provide a secure environment and structured as "ubiquitous, portable, electronic knowledge databases that are private, personalized and shareable, and are easily accessible via the Web." An electronic portfolio uses electronic or digital technologies that enable the portfolio developer to collect and organize portfolio artifacts in a variety of media: text, audio and graphic files, video clips, HTML files, hypermedia presentations and digitized photos.

The "Learning Grid" paradigm and the associate ELeGI infrastructure throw the user into a Web learning workspace and a pervasive virtual learning world on the semantic grid (Allison, Ruddle, & Michaelson, 2002).

The current my.Step prototype offers the following features (Vanides & Morgret, 2002):

1. Ease of access both on campus and off campus.
2. Privacy is by default.
3. The data can be organized and cross-referenced according to multiple categories.
4. Supports the sharing of learning artifacts with other members of the Learning Careers community.
5. As the content grows, a summary of the contents ("what's new") will give an overview of the E-Folio at a glance.
6. Different forms of storage media, including audio files, digital pictures, video and text, in one virtual space.
7. The most recent entries are kept in a prominent location.
8. Supports reflective activities.

Components can include a wide range of information: personal information, education history, recognition (awards and certificates), reflective comments, coursework (assignment, projects), instructor comments, previous employer comments, goals, plans, personal values and interests, presentations, papers, personal activities (volunteer work), professional development; and artifacts included shall have a purpose (demonstrating a skill, an attribute and learning acquired from experience).

The introduction of virtual communities for social learning (i.e., informal learning in VET) needs very collaborative tools that add an additional dimension to electronic portfolios. Allowing learners to interact with instructors, other learners and mentors provides a more open social learning, based on virtual communities of practice (Zhang & Tanniru, 2005) designed by their proper class of portfolio.

This model is both individual and shared. It is shared because of the collaboration with other members into the VLGC. And, at the same time, the e-portfolio reveals the user's abilities and skills by performing e-Qualification and so comparing him with other users.

Some have suggested that this virtual competency group concept can be replaced by a concept of "lifetime personal Web page" (Cohn & Hibbitts, 2004, p. 8):

The virtual structure could consist of multiple cells with flexible entrance points. It would allow connections between internal cells, as well as seamless connections to external entities (Web based courses, mentors, peer reviewers, libraries, and so forth).

Our e-portfolio offers the following features:

- The e-portfolio is viewed as a real-time process based on ontologies and managed by mobile P2P agents. It is the main tool for both the formal and informal learning and the e-Qualification process.
- Learners are introduced to formal learning sessions in VET (virtual lab, simulators) by the briefing stage. During this briefing, instructors teach their know-how to trainees.
- Agents update e-portfolios when learners are completing their course work and assignments.
- Both the e-portfolio and teams of agents are used for e-assessment of learning objectives and pedagogical issues, and for updating the learner assignment to a new group of competence (VLGC). Instructor feedback can also be integrated back into the e-portfolio by the agent and treated as an artifact.
- E-qualification continuously occurs, so e-portfolios are continuously used and evaluated.
- Learners continuously advise in VLGC, evaluating their effective use of e-portfolios (this is a meta-cognitive evaluation of portfolio use).

Dialogs, debates and discussions into VLGC are supported by mobile P2P agents to maintain the correct assignment of a user into his suited group.

Next we detail the mobile P2P agents' work.

THE P2P AGENTS

According to Ferber (1999, p. 9):

An agent can be a physical or virtual entity that can act, perceive its environment (in a partial way) and communicate with others, is autonomous and has skills to achieve its goals and tendencies. It is in a multi-agent system (MAS) that contains an environment, objects and agents (the agents being the only ones to act), relations between all the entities, a set of operations that can be performed by the entities and the changes of the universe in time and due to these actions.

Agents communicate in a P2P mode to work in a decentralized way.

Usually, in a closed environment, some internal solutions are used to allow agents to work in a P2P mode depending on the MAS they are working on. But in our case, a programmer could not use his or

Figure 1. Requirements for agents

Requirement type	Description of the requirement
	Requirement for allowing agents to search in a P2P manner.
Functional	Creating and sending a research request.
Functional	Receiving an answer of the research request sent.
Non Functional	Using the information found in the answer.
	Being able to send requests and receive messages even behind a firewall and in a
Non Functional	secure private network.
	Requirement for agents to create and join VLGC
Functional	Creating a Virtual Community (VLGC).
Functional	Joining a VLGC.
Non Functional	Adding a security access mechanisms for created VLGC
Non Functional	Being able to join secure VLGC
	Requirement for agents to advertise their knowledge and services
Functional	Advertising capabilities, services and other information
Functional	Understanding
Non Functional	Being able to hide some private information, services ...
	Requirement for agents to communicate with other peers
Functional	Communicating with other peers (Agents or not).
Non Functional	Being able to communicate in "One to One" mode.
Non Functional	Being able to communicate in "One to Many" mode.

her own solution (allowing agents to operate in a peer behavior), because we have no guarantee it will work with other programmers' solutions. So, we face two problems: (1) we could not impose a common P2P mechanism for all the agents in our project, and (2) we could not allow agents to use their own P2P mechanisms.

We propose to separate the two aspects (Agents and P2P) and use a high-level conceptual model for the P2P behavior that shall be adopted by all the agents of our project. Our conceptual model is a set of conditions that shall be satisfied by agents in order to become PeerAgents (an agent that behaves in a P2P mode). Each agent could implement these requirements at a low level with any programming language. Separating the two parts (agents, P2P) provides more flexibility and offers a work with a high level of abstraction that can be used on a large scale.

We distinguish two types of requirements. The first contains functional ones, including creating and sending a request message. The second type contains what we call "non-functional requirements," including the way to use results found in the answers, and the possibility for agents to use the research tool even when they are in private networks. Let us enumerate all the requirements that must be satisfied by P2P agents to work in an open environment as the GRID (Gouardères, Mansour, Yatchou, & Nkambo, 2005).

APPLICATION

The E-Qualification Process

E-Qualification is a way to determine the transition from a state of knowledge to another state of knowledge. This process allows every learner to be "right on the mark" in his VLGC. The goal is to "qualify" the level and needs of a learner and to replace him or her into the good community.

E-Qualification can occur in two cases:

- A student has made a specific error. The agent will assist the user to find a community that can help.
- A student wants to learn something specific.

In the two cases, the integration of a trainee into a community results from communication between agents.

- **Step 1:** The user's representative agent broadcasts the trainee's signature to the whole communities (into the area of the training distributed software). It is not the current signature; it is a kind of "pre-signature" that indicates what kind of VLGC it searches.
- **Step 2:** If a peer strongly guesses that this signature could match with his or her community's one, the peer will try to establish a conversation with him or her. To communicate, they have to use the same ontology. So, the peer who wants to enter in communication with the candidate must send the candidate the ontology of his VLGC's signature. The candidate's representative peer extracts a new signature (according to the ontology received. This is the "real signature"). Then, when the conversation has been established, they will make an "overlay" of their two corresponding signatures, called "the mirror effect." If the overlay is quite good, the trainee can integrate the community of the second one, but this cannot occur without a prerequisite negotiation. Note that the trainee can communicate with several peers and choose the best overlay.
- **Step 3:** During this step, the two peers are discussing conditions for the trainee to integrate the community. If they come up to a trust, the student is accepted into this community.
- **Step 4:** An alarm indicating that someone has entered the community (gap bridged successfully between two P2P communities) is sent.

E-Qualification in ASIMIL

Let us consider the ASIMIL project (N° IST-1999-11286. FP5, http://www.cordis.lu/ist/projects) as our test bed for e-Qualification.

ASIMIL, a networked, distributed-simulator training system is currently a Web-based application. First, we will present the current version to reveal its shortcomings. Then we will focus on the new version, which integrates the e-Qualification process.

Description of ASIMIL

The experimental framework for the ASIMIL training system is made up of five main components:

- **A simulator:** Allows the trainee to perform exercises in "almost real" conditions.
- **A Procedures Follow-up Component (PFC):** Provides the text of the procedures (kind of "to-do list").
- **The MAS:** Helps the trainee and provides a suited evaluation of the session (with messages and advice at the end of the session). This MAS architecture is called Actor Specification for Intelligent Tutoring Systems (ASITS) (Gouardères, Minko, & Richard, 2000) and is directly adapted from

Figure 2. E-portfolio's ontology

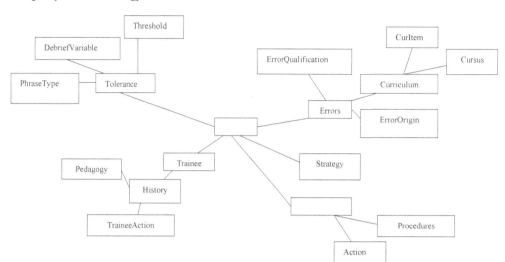

Figure 3. Signature

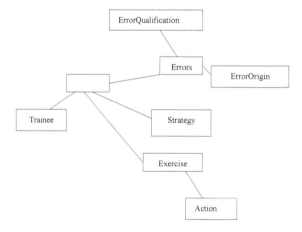

ACTORS (Frasson et al., 1996) by including a cognitive architecture based on ACT-R/PM that specifies the role of the cognitive resources in the high-level cognitive tasks and adopts proposals exchanged at the time of a conversation.

- **Virtual reality:** Improves the trainee's sensations.
- **Online assistance:** Connects the trainee to the instructor (on the Web).

Each training session contains three phases: briefing, simulation and debriefing. Of course, each learner has a profile, updated according to its performances. This profile is divided into six categories: Trainee, Strategy, History, Curriculum, Exercise, Errors and Tolerance. This profile is stored in a database. This trainee table contains trainee personal data: name, date of birth, address, and so forth, but also information on courses the trainee recorded (flight or maintenance); frequency of using system by trainee; and information on pedagogical strategy to adopt (free or guided mode), focusing on number, gravity and frequency of errors.

Errors are classified into three categories — knowledge, ergonomics and psychology — according to their origins to offer the best management possible.

The use of this method is based on the analysis of the user's history. This does not occur during the debriefing, but in real time (to stop the trainee when he or she makes too dangerous an error, etc.) The MAS ensures immediate and delayed feedback on the trainee's actions. There is some real work in tracking. Agents have to constantly look for errors. There are six kinds of agents:

- An interface agent, used as a bridge between the MAS and the other components of ASIMIL.
- An error detector agent, who detects errors made by the trainee.
- Some error evaluator agents, who make a quantitative evaluation of the trainee's errors.
- A pedagogical agent, who realizes a qualitative evaluation of the trainee's errors, formulates the teaching's intervention and stores the obtained trace in the curriculum agent's memory.

Figure 4. Illustration of in-text example

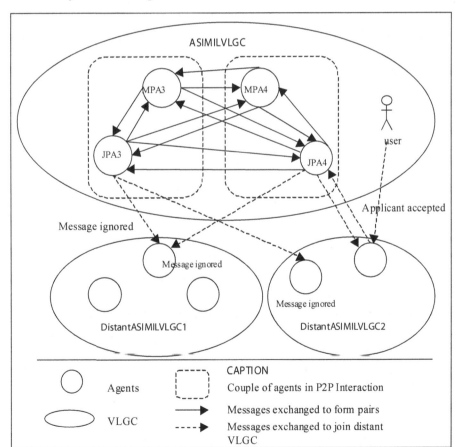

- A curriculum agent, who stores all the messages (to use again during the debriefing) and manages the trainee's profile.

Most important is the pedagogical agent, because it is the one that "finds the solutions." It helps the trainee and instructor. Its diagnostic depends on the training session in progress and the trainee's history. It is also based on evaluation results provided by the error detector agent and error evaluator agents.

E-Qualification Services in ASIMIL: The EleGI Version

The scenario is as follows: After receiving some instructions during the briefing, the trainee performs the exercise/simulation. At the end of this simulation, his or her e-portfolio is updated according to the formal results, which may lead to a change of VLGC. Then, debriefing occurs (in group, so in VLGC), which is the informal part of the learning process. Agents monitor everything. Whether the trainee has acquired some new skills or not can be checked only by participation in a new test. If the test is successful, it means that the trainee has learned in an informal way. The e-portfolio is updated, and that is what we call "the informal learning treatment."

The e-portfolio's ontology has been constructed from the user's profile and is shown in Figure 2.

The signature is an extract of the e-portfolio's ontology as represented in Figure 3.

The Signature's Extraction

We will now demonstrate an example of how the first signature (the one that will be broadcast to find an adapted community) is extracted. Consider first the current version. During the simulation, some errors are detected by the detector agents and sent to the evaluator agent (e.g., the ergonomical agent). It measures the gravity of the error and updates the error history. If the same error occurs thrice, that agent sends a message to the pedagogical agent, who makes a decision (stop the simulation/do nothing/send an alert message).

At the end of the simulation, the profile is updated according to the results.

In the ELeGI version, the pedagogical agent shares his or her work with some P2P agents. We can imagine that the ergonomical agent updates a kind of new signature simultaneously with the error history. So, at the end of the simulation, the P2P agents only need to compare the new signature with the old one and make a decision (beginning of e-Qualification).

Example of Peer-to-Peer Review

Here, we will try to explain how agents will identify the origin of a detected error without the help of a centralized service or agent. We will take the example of a distributed environment working with VLGC and P2P agents, where an error has occurred, and we will explain the agents' (peer) reaction.

In this distributed environment, there are four agents from different platforms: two from the Madkit platform (Madkit 4.0) and two from the JADE Platform (JADE 3.2). We call the two Madkit agents MadkitPeerAgent1 and 2 (MPA1, MPA2) and the JADE agents JadePeerAgent3 and 4 (JPA3, JPA4).

The first time the four agents are launched, they implement some services required for any peer using the JXTA Platform (Project JXTA, 2003). Then, they can adopt a peer behavior (i.e., communicate using a P2P mode).

The four agents join a VLGC of students that we call AsimilVLGC in this example. Note that the first launched agent does not find the VLGC and so create it. After a certain time, several agents of the ASIMIL simulator have joined the VLGC.

Assume now that a user makes the error *Error1*, which is detected by the four agents.

Agents MPA1 and JPA3 propose the *Error1*'s reason and broadcast it. Agents MPA2 and JPA4 propose *Error2*'s and broadcast it, too.

An agent who receives the message and who has not proposed anything is not concerned by this message and ignores it.

MPA1 receives three messages. It ignores the message coming from MPA2 and JPA4, because each of their "reasons" does not match MPA1's proposition. But JPA3's reason matches, so the agent decides to form a pair with JPA3.

In the same way, MPA2 and JPA4 form a pair. The two pairs will modify locally a copy of the user's e-porfolio with the proposed solution for this context. With this modification, they will try to find a VLGC with a signature that matches the user's (according to the error and pair proposition). Randomly, one of the two peers of each pair will broadcast a message to the known distant VLGCs (called DistantAsimil VLGC1 and 2). In the distant VLGCs, one PeerAgent will receive the message sent by the pairs, compare the user's signature with the VLGC's, and decide whether to accept the integration of the user in the VLGC.

At the end, the user joins the DistantASimilVLGC1, as shown in Figure 4.

Note: It is important that several agents (at least two, like MPA1 and JPA3) agree about the origin of the user's error. It shows that the solution is "reliable." If we do not process to this P2P review before searching a VLGC, it is possible that each agent searches a VLGC and the user is placed in several VLGC to solve a sole error. Note that in our example, agents are grouped in pairs, but three, four or more agents can propose the same "reason" and group to search for a VLGC for the user.

CONCLUSION

This article has presented a set of core technologies ready to be applied for a new generation of learning services, exemplified by the e-Qualification Grid learning services. The e-portfolio associated with mobile P2P agents on the Grid is the most suitable method and technique to handle VLGC. On the one hand, the e-portfolio requires a referential structure, the ontology, to contain the user's data and progress. On the other hand, tracking and monitoring the users in open learning situations (i.e., informal learning) must make maximum use of pervasive signatures extracted and maintained by agents by performing ubiquitous P2P reviews among VLGC.

To sum, in this article, we have proposed to maintain and merge new technologies on the Grid to promote:

- Collaboration in the VLGC as a basis for e-Qualification, which augments existing evaluation and certification in collaborative environments.
- The prominent role of e-portfolio equipped with ontology, to exchange structure and, with mobile P2P agents, to promote enhanced process tracking for reflections and agreements on user performances in collective learning sessions supported by the VLGCs.
- Omnipresence of P2P agents,who manage e-Qualification and VLGCs.

Finally, both the innovative process e-portfolio and the new concept of virtual organization, which is the VLGC, allow the e-Qualification process as a Grid learning service to support continuous assessment of informal learning sessions on the Grid.

ACKNOWLEDGMENT

Work partially supported by the European Community under the Information Society Technologies (IST) programme of the 6th Framework Programme for RTD - project ELeGI, contract IST-002205. This document does not represent the opinion of the European Community, and the European Community is not responsible for any use that might be made of data appearing there in.

REFERENCES

Allison, C., Cerri, S.A., Ritrovato, P., Gaeta, A., & Gaeta, M. (2005). Services, semantics, and standards: Elements of a learning Grid infrastructure. *Applied Artificial Intelligence, 19*(9-10), 861-879

Allison, C., Ruddle, A., & Michaelson, A. (2002, September 16). Systems support for collaborative learning. In *Proceedings of the 1st LEGE-WG International Workshop on Educational Models for GRID Based Services*, Lausanne, Switzerland.

Burgstahler, S., & Swift, C. (1996). *Enhanced learning through electronic communities: A research review.* Retreived February from http://164.116.18.39/research_report.html

Cohn, E.R., & Hibbitts, B.J. (2004). *Beyond the electronic portfolio: A lifetime personal Web space.* Retrieved December 10, from http://www.educause.edu/apps/eq/eqm04/eqm0441.asp

De Roure D., Jennings, N.R., & Shadbolt, N.R. (2003). The Semantic Grid: A future e-Science infrastructure. In F. Berman, G. Fox, & A.J.G. Hey (Eds.), *Grid computing: Making the global infrastructure reality.* John Wiley & Sons.

Dimitrakos, T., & Ritrovato, P. (2004, April 27-28). Progressing with a European learning Grid. In *Proceedings of the 4th International LeGE-WG Workshop — Towards a European Learning Grid Infrastructure*, Stuttgart, Germany.

Eisenstadt, M., & Komzak, J. (2005). *Peer conversations for e-learning in the Grid.* The Open University, UK: Knowledge Media Institute; and Université Montpellier II, France: Stefano A. Cerri.

Ferber, J. (1999). *Multi-agent system: An introduction to distributed artificial intelligence.* Harlow: Addison Wesley Longman.

Foster, I., Kesselman, K., & Tuecke, S. (2003). The anatomy of the Grid: Enabling scalable virtual organizations. *CCGRID 2001*, 6-7.

Frasson, C., Mengelle, T., Aimeur, E., & Gouardères, G. (1996). An actor-based architecture for intelligent tutoring systems. In *Proceedings of the 3rd International Conference on Intelligent Tutoring Systems (ITS'96), Lecture Notes in Computer Science 1086*, Montreal, Canada (pp. 57-65). Springer.

Garber, D. (2004). Growing virtual communities. *International Review of Research in Open and Distance Learning, 3*(4).

Gouardères, G., Mansour., S., Nkambou, R., & Yatchou, R. (2005). The Grid-E-Card: Architecture to share collective intelligence on the Grid. *Applied Artificial Intelligence, 199*(10), 1043-1073.

Gouardères, G., Minko, A., & Richard, L. (2000). Simulation and multi-agent environment for aircraft maintenance learning. In *Actes du Congrès 9th International Conference on Artificial Intelligence: Methodology, Systems, Applications, Lecture Notes in Artificial Intelligence 1904*, Varna, Bulgaria (pp. 152-166). Springer.

Guarino, N. (1998). Formal ontology and information systems. In N. Guarino (Ed.), *Formal Ontology in Information Systems. Proceedings of the 1st International Conference*, Trento, Italy. Retrieved from http://www.ladseb.pd.cnr.it/infor/Ontology/Papers/FOIS98.pdf

JADE (Java Agent DEvelopment Framework) version 3.2. (n.d.).

Project JXTA, v2.0. (2003). *JavaTMProgrammers guide*. Sun Microsystems. Retrieved from http://www.jxta.org

Rheingold, H. (1993). *The virtual community: Homesteading at the electronic frontier*. Addison-Wesley.

Schollmeier, R. (2001, August). A definition of peer-to-peer networking for the classification of peer-to-peer architectures and applications. In IEEE (Ed.), *2001 International Conference on Peer-to-Peer Computing (P2P2001)*. Linko ping Universität: Department of Computer and Information Science.

Schwier, R.A. (2004). Virtual learning communities. In G. Anglin (Ed.), *Critical issues in instructional technology*. Portsmouth: Teacher Ideas Press.

The MadKit project (release 4.1). (2005). Retrieved from http://www.madkit.org/

Vanides, J. (2002). *A personalized, Web-based learning electronic ePortfolio workspace* (White Paper). Retrieved from http://ldt.stanford.edu/~jvanides/eportfolio/STEP-eportfolio-workspace.pdf

Vanides, J., & Morgret, K. (2002). *STEP ePortfolio workspace: Supporting pre-service teachers with electronic portfolio creation, reflection and online collaboration*. Retrieved from http://ldt.stanford.edu/~keri/project/mySTEPstanford.doc

Zhang, Y., & Tanniru, M. (2005, January 3-6). An agent-based approach to study virtual learning communities. In *Proceedings of the 38th Annual Hawaii International Conference on System Sciences (HICSS'05) — Track 1*, Big Island, Hawaii.

This work was previously published in the International Journal of Information Technology and Web Engineering, edited by D. Rine & G. Alkhatib, Volume 1, Issue 2, pp. 25-42, copyright 2006 by IGI Publishing, formerly known as Idea Group Publishing (an imprint of IGI Global).

Chapter XVIII
QoS–Aware Web Services Discovery with Federated Support for UDDI

Chen Zhou
Nanyang Technological University, Singapore

Liang-Tien Chia
Nanyang Technological University, Singapore

Bu-Sung Lee
Nanyang Technological University, Singapore

ABSTRACT

Web services' discovery mechanism is one of the most important research areas in Web services because of the dynamic nature of Web services. In practice, UDDI takes an important role in service discovery since it is an online registry standard to facilitate the discovery of business partners and services. However, QoS related information is not naturally supported in UDDI. Service requesters can only choose good performance Web services by manual test and comparison. In addition, discovery among private UDDI registries in a federation is not naturally supported. To address these problems, we propose UDDI extension (UX), an enhancement for UDDI that facilitates requesters to discover services with QoS awareness. In this system the service requester invokes and generates feedback reports, which are received and stored in local domain's UX server for future usage. By sharing these experiences from those requesters in the local domain, the UX server summarizes and predicts the service's performance. A general federated service is designed to manage the service federation. The discovery between dif-

ferent cooperating domains is based on this general federated service, and therefore the links between domains are maintained dynamically. The system handles the federated inquiry, predicates the QoS difference among different domains, and provides a simple view over the whole federation. Meanwhile, the UX server's inquiry interface still conforms to the UDDI specification.

INTRODUCTION

With the industry's efforts on promoting the used Web services, a huge number of Web services are being developed and made available on the Web. Organizations now wish to offer electronic services worldwide and this creates several technical problems. First, being able to discover what services are available. Second, being able to determine which services match your specification. Third, being able to control which services are advertised to whom, and when. Fourth, being able to assess previous and current service usage for future selection.

There are three major roles in the Web services architecture: the service provider, the service requester and the service registry. The service provider is the business entity that provides software applications as Web services. The service requester is the entity who has a need that can be fulfilled by an available Web Service. The service registry is a searchable repository of Web services descriptions where service providers publish their Web services and service requesters locate Web services and obtain binding information to invoke the services. UDDI (Bellwood et al., 2002) stands for universal description, discovery and integration. It is a public specification that defines a service registry to publish information regarding the Web services and to make this information available to potential clients.

As more and more services appear on the Web, service requesters are presented with a group of service offers providing similar services. Different service offers may have different qualities of service. This will require sophisticated patterns of negotiation. For example, the trade-offs between quality and cost or invocation of another trade service determining the QoS of various service offers. Current UDDI registries are neither accountable nor responsible for the QOS descriptions in service offers.

Some extension can be made for UDDI to register the service's QoS description. However, even with the QoS descriptions registered on UDDI through extension, the QoS description may still be a bad prediction of the service's real performance. This is mainly caused by the following reasons. Firstly, the published description could use false information just to attract potential clients. Through the development of trust mechanism and digital signatures, this problem may be solved. Secondly, the false prediction inherits from the architectural aspect of UDDI system. The most distinctive architectures of UDDI registry system contain centralized architecture and semicentralized model (the cloud model). Single public UDDI is a centralized architecture model. To this model, UDDI is a central point which mediates service publishing/discovering in the framework. All services are registered on it and can be accessed by all those potential requesters. Different service requesters have quite different connection conditions and routing paths. This difference leads to the requester's different experiences of service QoS even when the service's server side processing condition is not changed at all. The unique service QoS description in the central UDDI is therefore not a good prediction for requester's reference. To the semi-centralized model (the cloud model), where there's more than one UDDI registries, replication technology will be used to ensure consistent content in different registries. Service provider is required to publish the service descriptions to any one of the cloud nodes. After the replica, service requesters can discover the service from any one of the cloud nodes. Through replication, the service requester can choose the most suitable cloud node and this improves the inquiry speed. However, when the services continue to emerge and the cloud continues to grow, the total amount of service description in each registry increases quickly and will affect the registry's scalability. Furthermore, the replication may still suffer from the incorrect QoS description that occurs in the centralized model. Replication of the QoS description will still remain a problem, as the correct prediction is not possible since the requester's network condition is very likely to be different from the replicated registry.

The solution being proposed in this chapter is called UDDI extension (UX) (Zhou et al., 2003). The main motivation for this work is the need to provide QoS-awareness in UDDI and service discovery between enterprise domains. It assesses previous and current service usage for future service selection. With analysis of the network model, the condition of service requester's connection is recorded by the server to enable better predictions in a future service's request. Instead of the QoS description published by service provider, QoS feedbacks made by a service requesters are used to generate summaries for invoked services. These summaries are then used to predict the services' future performance. The extended inquiry interface in UX is the counterpart of inquiry interface in UDDI and it conforms to the UDDI specification. A general federated service is designed so that server nodes can be administratively federated across network boundaries. Based on this federated service, lookup interface is provided on a UX server that facilitates the discovery between different registries and the exchange of service QoS summaries.

The chapter is organized as follows. The section, "Related Work" introduces the related work in this field. In "Network Model and Design Choices" we present the network model and design choices used in our system. The next section describes the system's components, their communications and the measured QoS metrics. In the following section, general federated service's design is presented and UX's federated discovery is discussed. The next section studies the system's implementation. The final section of this chapter presents our conclusions and directions of future work.

RELATED WORK

The UDDI specification (Bellwood et al., 2002) provides no QoS related inquiry in the discovery interface. Service requesters cannot filter the unqualified service nor can they get and compare between different services without testing them first. To solve this problem, some work has been done to enhance the UDDI registry's inquiry/publish interface to embed the QoS information in the message. For example, UDDIe project (Shaikhali et al., 2003) is targeted mainly towards the QoS-supported interface enhancement for UDDI. UDDIe extends the UDDI registry to support searching on attributes of a service and develops the find method to enable queries for UDDI with numerical and logical (AND/OR) ranges. QoS management support is provided through the definition of QoS attributes in the extended UDDI API. The QoS information is provided on publishing, and the publisher can provide arbitrary QoS attributes with selected lease for a service. If such information can be trusted, the UDDIe provides the lifetime control and QoS-supported discovery for UDDI.

Compared with UDDIe project, our system does not modify the standard UDDI interface and the client- side software can transparently plug on to our system. Although the UDDIe incorporate the arbitrary QoS attributes, the definition of the attributes is by the service provider when publishing the service. On the contrary, our system continuously collects the feedback reports so that the QoS information summarized is closer to the service's real performance. The service provider does not need to worry about the selection and publishing of proper QoS attributes in UDDI. When the service provider and service requester are located in different network domains, our system understands the difference of their connection conditions. The prediction of the service performance is therefore more precise than centralized model.

WS-policy (Box et al. 2002) provides a flexible and extensible grammar for expressing the capabilities, requirements, and general characteristics of entities in an XML Web services-based system. Together, with the WS-policy attachment (Box, Curbera, et al., 2002), policy expressions can be associated with WSDL type definitions and UDDI entities. QoS characteristics assertions may be defined in subsequent specifications and reasoned about in a consistent manner. This provides an alternative solution to the QoS-supported discovery in UDDI registry.

As discussed earlier in a centralized model or a cloud model based on replica, even if the UDDI registry is enhanced with QoS-supported discovery, it cannot provide a precise prediction for the real service performance because the performance is influenced by the service requesters' different connection conditions.

In addition to the centralized model and the cloud model, a decentralized P2P network provides another option for the service discovery. Paolucci et al. (2003) propose a pure P2P service discovery network and show how to perform matching capability between Web services on the Gnutella network. This approach avoids a single point of failure and there is no danger of a bottleneck effect. Ping/pong process is used to discover other server nodes. It is more appropriate in dynamic environments.

Our federation approach sits between the pure P2P mechanism and the static configuration. P2P systems are more appropriate in dynamic environments such as ubiquitous computing. Serious security threats may exist in pure P2P for enterprise domain's usage. Static configuration does not provide good fault tolerance and needs a bit of management work. It is suitable in static environments where information is persistent. For enterprise domains, the cross-domain connections are less dynamic than P2P networks but still need enough mechanisms for easy link managements. The proposed federation service suits this well. It has good load distribution and tolerance for network or node failures. The topology is stable and with knowledge about the global federation, each node can be reached and no service discovery information will be missed during the search.

Zhang (2002) points out that the next generation Web services discovery mechanism should meet following requirements: Using standard interface, simplifying the developer's work, hiding the complexity of UDDI search client and WSIL (Brittenham, 2001) search client, performing result aggregation from one or multiple sources, and acting as an advanced search portal on the application server. According to these requirements, BE4WS (Zhang et al., 2003) provides higher level APIs to take advantage of UDDI4J or other clients, such as the WS-inspection search tool, to define a script-based search request, aggregate search results, and explore multiple UDDI registries concurrently. The aggregation includes, but is not limited to, intersection, union, and script-based logic operation for the resulting responses from multiple sources.

In addition, Web services relationships language (WSRL) (Zhang et al., 2002) describes the relationships about the Web services rather than the requests. UDDI specification lacks the definitions and descriptions of the generic relationships among business entities, business services and operations. In WSRL, Web services relationships are defined at different levels: Business-business relationship (BBR), business-service relationship (BSR), service-service relationship (SSR), business-operation relationship (BOR), service-operation relationship (SOR), operation-operation relationship (OOR). Through the capturing of these relationships, WSRL provides better support for composing and executing dynamic business processes integration. Since it is based on UDDI, QoS related service discovery is still not supported.

WS-QoS (Tian et al., 2004) defines the XML schema for Web services to describe their services' high and low level QoS properties. The assistant framework is designed for the language specification to assist the service selection and publish. High-level QoS requirement can be mapped to the actual QoS-enabled transport layer through its proxy. It uses ontology style XML schema to define custom metrics. Two levels of metrics, the service performance level metrics, and the transport level metrics are defined in their system. However, the connection's QoS condition is not considered in their system yet, hence the discovery among different enterprise domains would lead to imprecise.

Our UX system uses the federated enhancement to provide federated registries' service inquiry and result aggregation. Standard interface is used in system and the service requester's work is simplified. In each enterprise domain, the UX system can be viewed as an advanced UDDI portal on application server. Compared with BE4WS, BE4WS provides one additional abstract layer for the client-side software to hide the complexity of UDDI search client. We keep the availability of current client side software and add one abstract layer for UDDI server to achieve the federated discovery and QoS-awareness. BE4WS does not mention the registries' link management problem. General federated service is presented in our system to achieve the dynamic link management for federation. Our approach does not support the advanced aggregation operations such as intersection and script-based logic operation presented in BE4WS. Private UDDI registries enhanced with WSRL can be used to specify confidential preference information about services. Complicated relationships among services, among business entities, and among service types can be encapsulated to enable dynamic e-business integration. Our approach uses the defined QoS metrics and service requester's customization to get the preference information about services. No explicit relationship information is currently used in our system.

NETWORK MODEL AND DESIGN CHOICES

In this section, we discuss the underlying network model and some design choices used in our UX architecture.

Network Model

In our system, the network model is abstracted into domains. Each domain has relatively high bandwidth, low latency, and uncongested connections. The properties of connections between different domains are unknown. Different interdomain connections may have quite different qualities. (See Figure 2).

In our system, these domains mainly stand for organizations such as enterprises, universities, and so forth. These organizations federate with each other by contracts. A local UDDI registry works in each domain for a Web service's discovery and it will maintain a registry of the local domain's services.

Design Choices

Our architecture incorporates five important design choices that offer value-added services over standard UDDI:

Figure 1. Network model

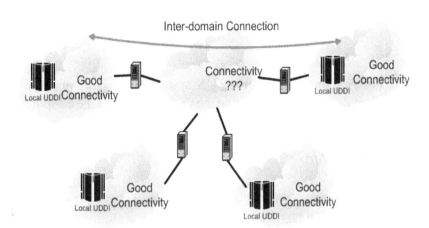

First, the architecture is aware of the provider service's QoS. The QoS reports of services are sent back and shared to predict the services' performance. We rely on service level measurements such as response time or reliability to help requesters make decisions. Many network level measurement system exists in which they use metrics such as routing metrics, link bandwidths, geographic locality, etc., to predict the relative performance of different hosts. Unfortunately, these metrics often do not correlate with service level performance. Servers' conditions, such as load, popularity, and so forth, may also affect the service's performance.

Second, the measurement results are shared (Stemm et al., 2000). Requesters explicitly share the QoS reports they made by sending them to the local UX server. By sharing the measurements, the requesters do not need to make manual test invocations. Hence, network resource is saved and server load is reduced. The decision to share measurements is followed directly from the network model. Two requesters in the same domain are likely to observe similar service performance because of similar connection condition. Measurements made in other domains may not be utilized directly because of the unknown interdomain connection properties. The way to process the cross-domain measurements is proposed in the section "Federated Support for UX Servers."

Third, customization is available in the discovery procedure (Davis et al., 2001). Different requesters may have different QoS preferences for discovery. For example, some requesters may prefer good service response time, while others prefer low cost. In order to help the requesters in locating the best fit services, the system allows the requesters to describe their preference in their profiles and then generates the result according to their preference. The requester can setup their profile on the server for customization.

Fourth, the extended inquiry interface conforms to the UDDI specification. The requesters can even use their original discovery software to make queries. In the federated discovery, the interface remains the same because the discovery is performed by the local UX server on behalf of the requester. If the requester wants to use some advanced features such as customization and authorization, client software needs to specify the user's identity in the discovery process for the server to get the user's profile. This feature is already supported in the UDDI4J package.

Lastly, additional policies are recommended to manage behavior of the UDDI registry. For example, *hop_count* is used to control the depth of the query's propagation in the UDDI federation. Some other policies such as cache's *living_time* are also designed to control the behavior of a registry.

UX System

In this section we describe the components of UX system architecture and how they communicate with each other. We also describe how we define the QoS metrics and the customization process in our system.

Components of UX System

Figure 2 shows a diagram of the components of UX system. It is comprised of service requester, UX server, test host, and local UDDI registry.

Service Requester

The service requester queries the UX server to find the matching services, chooses one, invokes the service and measures the performance of the service. During the measurement it creates QoS reports to record the performance data and sends them back in batches to the UX server. In the current system, we defined a set of the general QoS metrics that requesters are interested in, which will be described in the section "UX Server." To facilitate automatic QoS reports, a client side QoS reporter is provided. The reporter works as a SOAP intermediator and no code modification is needed from the requester

Figure 2. Components of the UX system

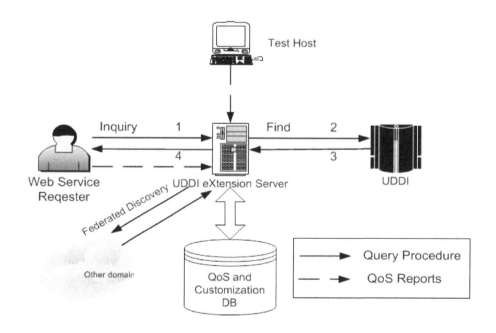

side. The reporter may cause potential security problems. Firstly, to the service requester, the unknown reporter may eavesdrop or modify the SOAP content for certain purpose. This risk can be minimized through open source and checksum verification to the reporter. Secondly, to a UX server, a malicious reporter may send false QoS reports back to UX server to fake the service performance. This may be solved by digital signature technologies and allowing only those trusted reporters to feedback. However, the security problem is not the major concern of this chapter and we will not discuss this anymore. If the measurement does not need requester's participation, it can be moved from client side to one special site in the local domain for easier control. Currently the reporter measures those synchronized request-response Web services and most Web services do belong to this category.

Local UDDI Registry

The local UDDI registry is a standard UDDI registry that records the local domain's services descriptions. Local service providers are required to publish their service descriptions to local UDDI registry, not the external ones. To ensure generic support, the local UDDI is connected to the UX server as a backend registry using SOAP (Box et al., 2000) connections. During processing of the requests, the UX server acts as a client to query the local UDDI registry for local information.

Test Host

In practice, it may sometimes be difficult to predict a service's performance because the system lacks the latest service QoS reports. The test host is designed to generate current service QoS reports only for locally registered services. It tests the service with random or predefined parameters to gain service reports. The test interval is carefully selected so that the test host will not create obvious overhead to the network and its QoS reports only occupy a small portion of the total reports. The system manager has the option to configure the interval manually.

UX Server

The UX server plays an important role in the system. When the UX server receives an inquiry from the requester, it searches the local UDDI for related results. If the number of items in the result is insufficient, the federated discovery is started to find more related items. The discovery of services across domains will be discussed later. After collecting all these results, the UX server filters and merges these results. If the inquiry is service related, the server sorts the service results according to the QoS summaries and then sends the results back to the requester. The UX server also receives the requester's QoS reports, stores them in a database, and processes them to generate the QoS summary, which is used in the sort procedure.

QoS Metrics

QoS covers a whole range of technologies that match the needs of service requesters with those of service providers based on the available resources. The major requirements for supporting QoS in Web services are like performance, reliability, security, and so forth (Mani et al., 2002). Each Web service may have different QoS metrics to evaluate and describe its QoS. In our current system, we aimed at general

Web services from an end-user's view. Based on the previous experience, we have constructed the QoS metrics that include system-centric category. Currently the QoS metrics measured in our system contain response time, cost and reliability (Cardoso et al., 2002). The type of QoS metrics is extensible in our system and it is not limited in the feedback interface. To utilize the extended metrics, the processing logic for the new metric should be defined for summarization.

Response time metric is defined as the total time needed by the service requester to invoke the service. We measure the response time from the time the requester initiates the invocation to the time the requester received the last byte of the response. This is a service level measurement and the response time can be divided into server execution time, queuing delay and the network transportation time.

Cost represents the cost associated with the execution of the service. It is necessary to estimate the guarantee that financial plans are followed. The cost in the QoS report is gained by the volunteer requester's input. If no feedback is made on this metric, the QoS report is sent back with this metric labeled unknown. The cost can be broken into major components, which include the service execution cost and network transportation cost.

Reliability corresponds to the likelihood that the service will perform when the user demands it and it is a function of the failure rate. Each service has two distinct terminating states: One indicates that a Web service has failed or aborted; the other indicates that it is successful or committed. By appropriately designed redundancy, one can build highly reliable systems from less reliable components. We use the stable reliability model proposed by (Nelson, 1973), for which the reliability of a Web service is $R(t) = 1 - failure\ rate$. Each QoS report records the terminating state of the service, which will be summarized on UX server to generate the reliability.

The UX server generates a summary of the reports for each service regularly. It calculates the response times, terminating state and cost in each received QoS report to a summary which contains response time, reliability, cost, timestamp and report number. This summary is used to sort the query result. The service's performance may depend on the service's input and the variance of the performance may be obvious. Using only the summarized value is not a perfect reflection of the service's performance. (Cardoso et al., 2002) uses min, max, avg value and the probability distribution function to describe a service's performance information. Currently we utilize only the summarized mean value to describe the service QoS. The establishment of better QoS metrics model is out of this chapter's scope and it is part of our future work.

To the summarization phase, we design and compare three types of functions to generate the summary from report fields:

1. **Average function:** $f = \sum_{i=1}^{n} r_i / n$, where r_i is the ith received QoS report's field value during the interval of two summarizations, and n is the total reports number during the interval.

2. **Low-pass filter function:** $f_i = \alpha * f_{i-1} + (1-\alpha) * r_i$ (Richard, 1994), where α is a smoothing factor, r_i stands for the ith sorted record's field value during the interval of two summarizations, and f_i stands for the calculated field value when processing the ith report. Value f_0 is initialed by the last summary's field value. To apply this function, QoS reports in the interval are first sorted by timestamp and then processed sequentially on these reports. This method helps the summary to include all the history measurement information. If α is set as 0.8, 80% of each new calculated f_i is from the previous value and 20% is from the report's value.

3. **Median function:** median value of the related field during the interval of two summarizations is selected.

In the local test, we set up two Web services with the same service function for comparison. The only difference between these two services is their processing speed: One is much faster than the other. The test is conducted on the university's LAN with a node/server pair. During each service invocation, we collected the response time and end state information. The cost is chosen to be zero. More than 400 service invocation data is collected and the experiment lasts for about 10 hours. From the experiment we find that the response time is highly converged at its summarized value, and about 80% of invocations for the faster version of the service are within 20% away from the summarized response time value. This shows that using summarized value to predict the service is reasonable for major invocation instances. To compare with three summarization functions (*average, median,* and *low-pass filter* function), we draw the diagram of the percentage deviation of Web services invocations from the summary of response time using the summarization function respectively (see Figure 3).

The weighted average of the deviation, where the deviation is percentage away from the summarized value to the invocation value and the weight is the corresponding invocations' occupied percentage, shows the mean deviation from the summarized value to the record values. The summarized function has better estimation of the record values if the mean deviation of the function is lower. By comparison

Table 1. Mean deviation of summary functions for fast add

Function Name	Mean Deviation (%)
Average Function	19.03
Median Function	17.38
Low-pass Filter Function with $\alpha = 0.8$	15.10

Figure 3. Percentage deviation of Web services invocations (fast add) from the summary of response time

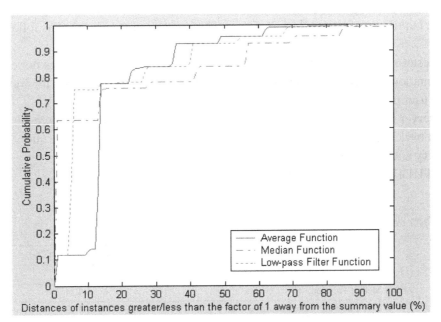

of three functions' mean deviations, we find that the *low-pass filter* function f_i has the minimum deviation (see Table 1). Furthermore, if α is chosen as 0.6960, f_i will reach the minimum value of 12.64. Therefore, the *low-pass filter* function f_i is chosen as the summary function in UX server.

Another remote test is made on the Xmethods' listed stock service (http://www.swanandmokashi. com/HomePage/WebServices/StockQuotes.asmx). During each service invocation, we collect the response time and end state information. More than 900 service invocations' data are collected and the test lasts for 24 hours. From the percentage deviation of Web services invocations from the summary (see Figure 4), we can see the response time is converged to the summarized function. More than 90% of the service invocations are within 10% away from the summarized value. The summarized value in remote test is much larger than the local test. However, the result in remote test converges better than the local test. The service's response time is divided into the server's execution time and the network transportation time. In the LAN, the network transportation time is neglectable so that the server's execution time is the major factor in the response time. Therefore the server's performance in the local LAN's test tends to be more noticeable. In the remote Web service's test, a substantial part of the response time is due to the network transportation time. The absolute network transportation time is also much higher in the public test compared with the local test and with a small server execution time. The variance in the remote test is therefore relatively small and from the test we can see that the perceived response time in remote test converges better. For the comparison of three summary functions, the *low-pass filter* function with $\alpha=0.8$ still gets the best results (see Table 2).

Communication between Components

All communications between the components of our system use SOAP (Box et al., 2000) messages for easy extensibility and adoption. There are mainly two kinds of messages in the system, the QoS report messages and the inquiry messages.

QoS report messages are sent in batch to keep the network overhead reasonable. After the report messages are received by the UX server, they are stored in a local database for processing at a later stage.

The system uses a 'pull' approach to discover the services. Requester can find the related services by sending inquiry messages to the UX server. The processing step is listed as follows (see Figure 5):

1. Requester sends the UDDI inquiry to the UX server. If the inquiry does not contain an identify information, default QoS weights are used for customization. Otherwise the weights are extracted from user profile database.
2. UX server first checks its local cache to see if the cache can provide the result. If so, it sends the result back to the requester and ends the process. Otherwise, it sends the query to the local UDDI registry and goes to step 3.
3. Local UDDI registry processes the inquiry and then returns the result.

Table 2. Mean deviation of summary functions for stock

Function Name	Mean Deviation (%)
Average Function	11.57
Median Function	4.24
Low-pass Filter Function with $\alpha = 0.8$	4.12

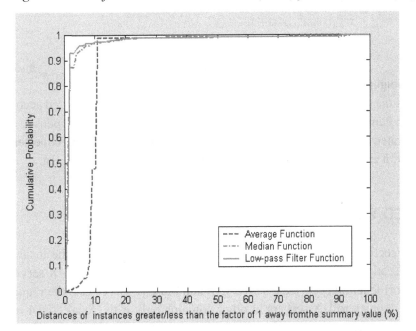

4. The UX server checks the record number in the result. If the number is less than the requester's intended number, it starts the federated discovery to get additional results and then merges the results (this will be described in the "Federated Support for UX Servers" section). If the inquiry is service related, UX server will sort the result according to QoS summary and requester's preference. Otherwise the UX server returns the result directly. The format of the returned result conforms to UDDI specification.

Customization

Service requesters may have different preference on the service's QoS metrics. By customization of his user-profile (currently we provide a Web interface to help requesters in setting up their profile), the requester can set different weights on different metrics. The requester puts his identify in the inquiry and the server extracts his profile information from the database. If weights information is unavailable, default value is used (e.g., each weight is set to 1).

If the inquiry is service related, the UX server generates the service score list according to the QoS summary and the weights. This contains two steps: Normalization of the QoS summary and score calculation.

In the normalization phase, each metric field is mapped to a value between 0 and 1 and higher normalized value means better score. Therefore, an inverse function $S_x = 1/(x+1)$ is chosen for cost and response time metrics. x is the field value and S_x is the normalized value. Reliability value has already been in the range of 0 to 1 so that its value is kept.

In score calculation phase, the service score is calculated by weighted average function:

$$score = \frac{W\cos t \times S\cos t + W resptime \times S resptime + W reliability \times S reliability}{W\cos t + W resptime + W reliability},$$

where S_{cost}, $S_{resptime}$, and $S_{reliability}$ are normalized summary scores; w_{cost}, $w_{resptime}$ and $w_{reliability}$ stand for the customized weights respectively.

The higher the score is the better the service's quality. The result is sorted according to this score list so that the top item has the highest score. If some metric field's value happens to be unknown, random value is generated so that the service has a chance to be invoked by the requester. When the requester gets the result, it can easily choose among the several top services in the list.

FEDERATED SUPPORT FOR UX SERVERS

The previous section detailed the components of the architecture and the local interactions between them. In this section, we focus on how UX server interacts with other UX servers across domains in order to support federated service discovery. When the UX server gets the requester's inquiry, it will propagate the inquiry to UX servers in other domains only if the local UDDI registry does not have enough services to form the result set.

Using the federated discovery requires the system to be able to scale and support a potentially huge number of requesters and services while adapting the underlying domains' changes (e.g., due to network partitions and node failure). This requires a proper link management and query propagation model.

In addition to the underlying model, a lookup interface between UX servers is extended to support the federated discovery. A general interface of a UX server is presented in Figure 5. The interfaces contain the UX server's extended inquiry interface, lookup interface, the original UDDI publish interface and the Admin interface. The extended inquiry interface provides the QoS-aware Web services discovery over the original UDDI and local domain's service requesters query through the local UX server. Lookup interface is designed to support federated discovery between UX servers. The original UDDI publish interface is kept for service provider to publish their business services. Extended admin interface manages the domain links and policies.

The input to the lookup interface is a string of XML (as shown in Figure 6) that describes the federated query information for other domain's UX servers' process. It contains mainly query ID, hop number, original sender, last sender and query content. The response from other domain's UX server is also a string of XML that describes the query result and related QoS summary if the query is service related. It contains mainly query ID, sender, query response and QoS summary.

Link Management and Query Propagation

In the network, different domains' links can be manually or statically established amongst individual UX server nodes. Examples of static establishment include the CORBA Trading Service, ODP Trader (ITU, 1994), DNS systems (M. P., 1987) and LDAP directory services (Wahl et al., 1997). However, works has been done in which domain links are managed dynamically. CSG (Belaid, et al., 1998) models B2B peering contracts and the policies would define the associations between how companies can use each other registries. Links are established according to these contracts and policies and they can then be managed dynamically.

Figure 5. System's interface

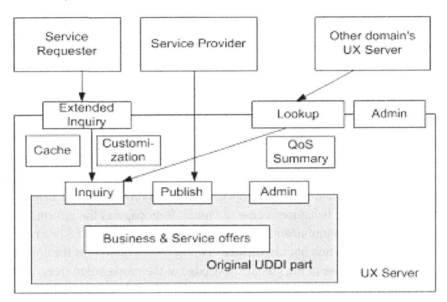

Figure 6. Federated server's propagation interface

```
public class DederatedmEssageHeadData {
  public String version; // the CSG version.
  public String messageType; // the message type "UXLookup",
"VersionUpdate", "SendbackSinceLowerVersion"
  public String queryID;
  public String originalSender, // correspond to the node Identifier
  public String lastSender;
  public PropagationCondition pCondition;
}
  public void multicast)GraphNode bypassNode, ArrayList theNodes, String head,
String content);
  public void alternativeBehavior(GraphNode failedNode, GraphNode preFailedNode,
String head, String content);
}
```

CSG Model (Balad et al., 1998)

The aim of the cooperating server graph model (CSG) is to optimize and dynamically manage links between cooperating servers over a wide area network. Based on CSG model, we extend it into the Web services arena. A general federated service has been designed and cooperated into our UDDI extension system as the message propagation layer.

CSG approach uses a minimum-weight spanning tree to optimize links between UX servers automatically. The shortest path trees are not chosen to avoid generation of star trees. The weight is defined by a distance function to represent the communication cost between the couple of nodes (e.g., the inquiry latency, the hop number, etc.). Prim (1957) algorithm is used to calculate the minimum-weight tree. In our general federated service design, each node in CSG is called a federated server (FS).

The CSG model and propagation tree have to adapt dynamically to the change of cooperating servers and the underlying network topology. In order to be more efficient for the graph's management and reduce the control overhead, different events are treated accordingly. The dynamic administration of CSG takes three levels of events into account:

1. **Alternative behavior in case of failure:** Once a federated server (FS) detects a failure of its neighbor nodes (i.e., when it cannot propagate information to one of its neighbors in the tree), the FS uses the alternative behavior in case of failure. It propagates the information, on behalf of the failed neighbor (the communication failure may come from a failed FS or a network failure), to the neighbors of the failed neighbor in the tree. This behavior maintains the continuity of the service and it is feasible because of the global knowledge of the propagation tree.

2. **Local reconfigurations:** The local reconfigurations level is used to take into account FS's long time failure, FS's long time failure recovery, as well as FS's addition and removal. Long time failure can be decided according to predefined failure time threshold. Instead of the propagation of a new CSG version, the local reconfiguration updates the local propagation tree and enables the CSG's minor change at a lower cost. A local reconfiguration is possible if and only if each node, after the reconfiguration, knows its own neighbors and the neighbors of its neighbors in the effective propagation tree. A node cannot participate in two local reconfigurations simultaneously. As a result the reconfiguration progress is made atomic. After accepting a local reconfiguration, a node buffers incoming requests so as to retransmit them at the end of the reconfiguration process.

3. **Global change of the CSG version:** A version change federated server, chosen dynamically in the federation, triggers the version change of the CSG. Each FS sends its local long time reconfigurations to the version change server, which includes the long time failures, long time distance changes, addition and removal of the nodes. Then the version change server triggers a new CSG version when the degradation rate of the propagation tree (the sum of the weights of the degraded tree divides that of the minimum spanning tree which is still in use) goes past a given threshold. The new version is then propagated to all the domains' FSs, via the propagation tree. Two nodes (sender and receiver) have to agree on a version before they can communicate through CSG. If the receiver has an older version, the request is buffered on the receiver until its version is updated. On the other hand, if the sender has an older version, it will send the request back to the source node, which in turn will reinitiate the propagation after updating its CSG version.

This model can tolerate a great number of failures. All the CSG updates are made dynamically, and the number of CSG version changes is greatly reduced by dividing the failures into different levels of events.

Federated Service Design

The federated service takes the Web services layer approach instead of network layer approach to achieve the extensibility and easy adoption. There are two basic communication semantics in the federation service: The local tree modifications and the propagation of messages. When the local tree modification happens, the local tree modification has to be made coherently on a group of neighbor servers one and two steps away from the center coordinator of the modification. This modification should guarantee that either all these neighbor server nodes make the modification or none of them does. A service node cannot participate in two local tree modifications simultaneously. In short, the behavior of modification is kept consistent and atomic.

Different from the local tree modification, the query propagation does not need to guarantee the atomicity or the message's ordering. Each federated server in the propagation's chain becomes a coordinator when it receives the information to propagate. It has to forward the information to all its neighbors in the propagation tree, except for the one from which information was forwarded. If one neighbor does not acknowledge, the propagation should still go on and the coordinator triggers the alternative behavior in case of the neighbor's failure.

According to the two different communication semantics, we divide the federated service design into two service groups: The LocalChangeGroup and the PropagationGroup. The LocalChangeGroup provides the atomic and consistent invocation for the local tree modification. The PropagationGroup offers the propagation invocation for the normal messages. The message order and the atomic of this invocation are not ensured.

The local reconfiguration procedure is showed in Figure 7. To ensure the atomic modification semantic, the LocalChangeGroup is told to multicast the save method to the neighbors of the UX server and the neighbors of its neighbor. A boolean result is returned to indicate whether the LocalChangeService is ready to process the modification. If all neighboring LocalChangeServices are ready, the commit method is invoked on all the neighboring LocalChangeServices which in turn invoke their add/remove method to modify the local graph. Otherwise, the abort method is invoked and the multicast method returns to indicate the failure of the local reconfiguration. The interface definition is shown in Figure 8. All the successful local reconfiguration information is sent to ChangingVersionFederatedServer, which controls the CSG version. It triggers a new CSG version if the degradation rate of the propagation tree (the sum of weights of the degraded tree divides by that of the minimum spanning tree which is still in use) goes past a given threshold.

The federated service can be applied to a wide range of Web services. For example, better efficiency can be supported through federating similar services together and serving the service requesters from nearer and faster servers; robustness can be increased through reconfiguration of the federation and skipping of those failure nodes; performance can be enhanced if each service finishes different portion of the target and works together for the final result. In our UDDI eXtension system, we build our special UXFederatedServer class through the generalization of FederatedServer, add "UXLookup" message type for federation propagation and define special handling logic for "UXLookup" message by providing a federatedLookup method. Additional propagation condition can also be extended in federatedLookup method to control the propagation logic. This design achieves the separation of the CSG model and UDDI lookup logic. The FederatedServer manages the message propagation and failure control, while the UXFederatedServer deals with the special UDDI lookup logic for service discovery. Therefore, complexity reduction and code reuse is achieved.

Query Propagation

When the original UX server finds its local UDDI registry does not have enough results, it begins to propagate queries (Czwerwinski, 1999). To reduce unnecessary delays in response, the propagated servers respond to the original UX server directly. Currently the propagation condition contains hop_count and intended_number. See Section 0 for their detailed descripton. The hop_count is decreased by one when the inquiry is delivered one step further along the CSG. If the hop_count reaches 0, the inquiry is not delivered further. Otherwise the system uses federatedLookup interface in UXFederatedServer to propagate the query along the CSG links. intended_number is used by the original UX server to check whether the local UDDI registry returns enough results. Each UX server is responsible for its local registered services so that they are included in the response. If the query is service related, the related services' QoS summaries are also included. When the original UX server receives the results from an external UX server, it accumulates the result number and checks it with the intended_number. The result collection ends when the result number reaches the intended_number or the timeout set according to the hop_number is reached. After the collection, it merges these results into a single result set for the service requester. If the query is service related, the result set is sorted according to the QoS summaries. The received QoS summaries are first mapped and then utilized in the sort phase. The sort procedure is similar to the local discovery mode. See the "QoS Similarity Domains" section for details of the received QoS mapping processing.

Because of the CSG model's global knowledge of the propagation tree, the cyclic dependencies can be avoided. However, the ordering of the propagated message is not guaranteed. To choose among the different returned results and then merge them according to the original query we use query identity to

Figure 7. Federated service's local tree modification

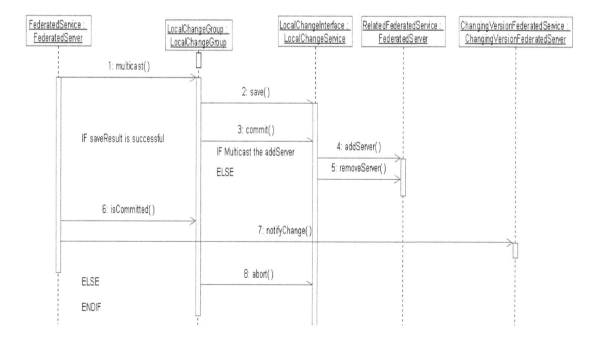

Figure 8. Federated server's local tree change interface

```
public class LocalChangeAdminMessageData {
  public String adminType; // addServer or removeServer
  public String nodeIdentity;
  public EdgeDetail[] edgesDetail;
}
public class LocalChangeGroup{
  public synchronized boolean multicast(String messageContent);
  public boolean isCommitted(String messageID);
  ...
}
public class LocalChangeService
{
  public synchronized boolean save(String messageID, String messageContent);
  public void commit(String messageID);
  public void abort(String messageID);
}
```

distinguish different results. In order for this to work, the UX server must remember the query identities of all recent federated query operations that it has performed. When a federated query is received, the UX server checks this history and then processes the results.

QoS Similarity Domains

The similarity of QoS between two domains is a measure of the differences between the same service's performances by requesters in different domains. There may be several possible ways to determine whether some other domain is QoS-similar. First, it may be manually defined by the system administrator. Second, it may be learned dynamically. The periodical test for sample public benchmark services in each domain or the analysis of the QoS summaries' differences between domains are possible ways for dynamic learning.

We take the dynamic learning approach to decide the QoS similarity by analyzing the QoS summaries. Notice that the local domain's feedback QoS reports contain two parts. The first part records the QoS of services that is registered in local domain while the second part records the QoS of services that is registered in other domain. In federated discovery, the first part is exported by the UX server while the second part is not exported because the service is not in the local domain. This part is used to measure two domains' QoS similarity. When some other domain's service QoS summary is returned in federated discovery, this service's QoS summary information in the second part of local domain's QoS summaries is located and the difference between these two summaries is judged. If the average relative difference between these domains is below a predefined threshold (e.g., 20%), these two domains are deemed as QoS similar domains. The QoS summary returned from such domains is used directly. Otherwise, two domains are not QoS similarity domains and the differences are recorded. The QoS similarity measurement is taken on regular basis to update the similarity information so that the server's performance is not influenced significantly.

If two domains are not QoS similarity domains, according to the network model, the dissimilation of service performance between two domains is mainly caused by the network connection between two domains. Therefore the correct prediction of another domain's service summary can be achieved through the translation on received summaries according to the recorded differences. To achieve better efficiency, we divide the QoS metrics into two parts: First part is the stable metrics whose change is neglectable from different domains' views (stable metrics). Second part is the changeable metrics that may change greatly from different domain's view (changeable metrics). In our selected metrics, we choose the cost and reliability as the stable metrics, while the response time as the changeable metrics. To correct these changeable metrics between domains, a simple linear function is used to change the metric response time's value (i.e., to add the average difference directly to the received QoS summary as the predicted summary). The server then uses this predicted summary to sort the result.

Discovery Policies

hop_count policy is used to control the depth of the query's propagation. When query is propagated one step further, the value of *hop_count* is decreased by one and when the *hop_count* reaches zero, the query is not propagated any more. The *hop_count* can be set statically or described in the user's profile. It makes a tradeoff between response time and total result number.

intended_number policy describes how many result items the requester intends to get. When it is specified in the inquiry, the UX server will start the federated discovery unless enough inquiry result has been found. If it is not specified in the inquiry message, local-only discovery is assumed. The *intended_number* is extracted from the UDDI inquiry's max row attribute and it is not changed during propagation.

To expedite the discovery procedure and improve the system's scalability, especially for federated discovery, each UX server stores a least-recently-used (LRU) result cache. Each cached item contains the inquiry, result, and the service summary if the inquiry is service related. Cache on the UX server only serves the local domain's requesters. Cache's *living_time* policy is set to define the cache entry's maximum living time.

System Implementation

We have implemented a prototype of the UX system. The system uses Apache Axis (Axis Development Team, 2002), UDDI4J and WSIF (Apache Software Foundation, 2003) as the basic components. The IBM UDDI registry software is used as the local registry. The UX server is mainly implemented on the Axis platform. Because the service and tModel list is returned in ID forms, a mapping between the ID and the service's location is generated by the test host and stored in the database for UX server's usage.

On the requester side, a test tool designed as a SOAP intermediator is used to facilitate the service QoS measurement and feedback. The service's access point is extracted and stored by parsing the envelope of the SOAP message. After the response message is returned from the service provider, the service's response time and the end status are decided. The cost of the service invocation is provided by requesters or left blank as unspecified. If a service invocation reaches timeout, its end status is deemed as failure and the response time is set to be unspecified.

When the service requester sends the inquiries to the UX server, the UX server extracts the intended number from the inquiry message, gets the requester's identity and preference from user profile database (default customization options will be assumed if the requester's identity is not specified or no customization information for the user is available), and then checks the local UDDI registry first. If the inquiry is service related (currently we support the find_service function's inquiry in our system. Other inquiry functions such as find_business, get_bindingDetail, get_serviceDetail, etc., will not be modified in our system), QoS summary information is retrieve from the QoS database. Then the results will be sorted according to these summarizations. If the number of returned results from local UDDI registry, compared with the intended_number, is sufficient then the results are sent back to the service requester immediately. Otherwise, the federated service discovery procedure is triggered. PropagationGroup handles the message multicast and other domain's UX server will return the results directly back to the original UX server. The cache can fasten the procedure and improve the performance. Figure 9 shows the UML sequence diagram for service discovery in UX server.

The UML class diagram of the FederatedServer is available in Figure 10. The FederatedServer uses a composite design pattern to compose the LocalChangeGroup and the PropagationGroup. It is itself a generalization of GraphNode for graph so that each FederatedServer can be easily combined into the federation graph. The FederatedServer controls the addition and removal of service nodes, encapsulates the propagation interface and accepts the requester messages from special services.

Take a stock service inquiry as an example: Service requester "Steve" has already setup his customization profile on the UX Server to specify that his preferences on response time, reliability, and cost as 2, 1, 1 respectively. He uses UDDI4J as the inquiry tool and specifies his user name and password in the configuration file. When he sends find_service inquiry to the UX server with name = "stock" and intended_number = 10, the UX server checks the cache and finds that there's no such inquiry recently. Then UX server looks for the local UDDI registry and gets six services in the returned result. According to the serviceInfos, the QoS summary for these six services is extracted. Because the result number is less than the intended_number, federated discovery is initiated. No hop_number is specified in the customization profile so that the original UX server sets the hop_number as the maximum hop_number 5 in the current CSG. The original UX server sets the timeout as 5*10 seconds (each hop waits for 10 seconds which is set by the administrator) and begins the collection of returned results. The first neighboring UX server gets the federated lookup inquiry, reduces the hop_number by 1, propagates the lookup inquiry, queries its local UDDI registry and returns five serviceInfos together with the QoS summarizations. The original UX server received this service list and finds that the total discovered services of 11 is already larger than the intended_number so the original UX server stops the collection. Additional returned results from other UX servers are not collected to improve the inquiry speed. The original UX server starts the mapping and merging of the QoS summaries. Merged results and QoS summaries are stored in the cache and then sorted according to Steve's preference. Finally the services result list is returned back to Steve.

To the CSG model's management, if the size of the CSG is N, then the size of the adjacent matrix is N^2, and the size of propagation edges is N-1. On the ChangingVersionFederatedServer, prim algorithm's computation complexity is $O(N^2)$ and the space complexity is $O(N^2)$ to store the adjacent Matrix. On each UX server, only propagation edges are stored and the space complexity is $O(N)$. The neighbor of each UX server is pre-computed so that the computational complexity is constant. To each UX server's inquiry processing, if the all returned results' number for one inquiry is S, then the complexity for merging the received result is $O(S)$, and the sorting computational complexity is $O(S \log(S))$. Therefore, the total computational complexity for UX server's query processing is within $O(S \log(S))$ and S is normally small. The performance will likely be affected by the propagation delay between UX servers and this can be reduced by the cache (see "Discovery Possibilites" section).

Compared with UDDI registries, we see that the top results returned from UX system perform as well as, if not better than, the top ones in UDDI registries. Meanwhile, the requester does not need to inquiry each private UDDI to gain enough services and compare the performance differences between services. Therefore, this saves efforts and portion of network resource as well. However, we do not recommend requesters to always choose only the top service from the result to avoid collision.

Federated experiment is performed to check the system's network overhead for service discovery. During the federated experiment, we setup four UX server nodes in our test environment to form the UX federation. On each server we run the UX server in the Tomcat servlet container with Axis deployed. These server nodes' network topology is shown in Figure 11. Nodes A, C, and D join the federation through node B. Node D receives the inquiry in its domain. If the local inquiry does not provide enough services for the requester, the federation discovery is triggered by node D. By this experiment, we try to check out the percentage of federation inquiries among the total inquires received by node D, and the network overhead for these nodes caused by the federated discovery. Since the network has good connections within the local domain, we are more interested in the network overhead among cross domain connections. The cache mechanism is disabled in this experiment to gain a precise result.

During the experiment, the inquiries in node D's domain are randomly generated with two alphabet letters. It issues a series of inquires, by which we record the network usage across the domain links. The

Figure 9. Sequence diagram of service discovery in UX system

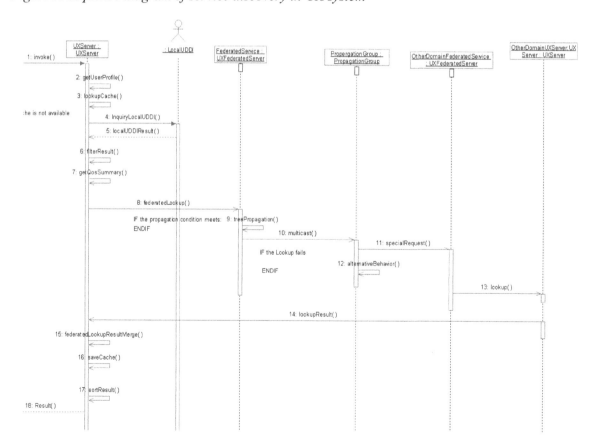

Figure 10. FederatedServer's class diagram

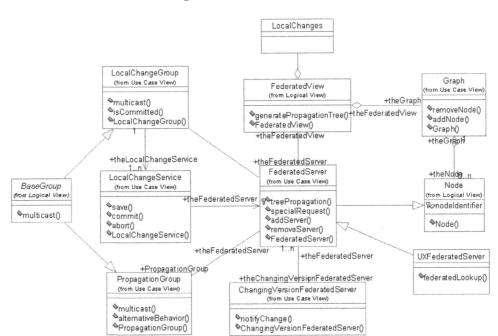

Figure 11. UX federation experiment setup

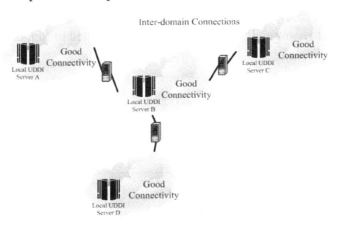

hop number is set to be 2 so that all nodes in the federation can receive the inquiry. When the federated discovery is performed, the inquiry is delivered to node B, C, and D through the propagation tree. The experiment shows that the percentage of federated discovery in all of the inquiries is about 43%. Figure 12 shows the network overhead of each cross domain network link for the inquiry. The X axis is the index of the invocation, and the Y axis is the average bandwidth overhead on each cross domain connection caused by this federation query. The zero points in the figure means that the federation discovery is not executed in this inquiry. From the figure we can see that the average network overhead for each inquiry is about 1.5 KB on each cross domain network link. This overhead is less than a normal Web page's size, which is affordable for the normal discovery in most industries. The cache mechanism can be turned on to avoid the duplicated invocations across enterprise domains. Since the requesters in enterprise domain are often interested in some common services, the network's overhead can be reduced even more by the cache mechanism.

CONCLUSION AND FUTURE WORK

In this chapter we have presented a set of challenges for Web services discovery when a large amount of Web services become available on the Internet. A number of similar Web services are also emerging on the Internet and they are competing to offer better services. Mechanisms are required to efficiently discover and compare such services and to cooperate among registries.

Our work is tightly related to the Web services discovery standards, QoS's prediction and the federated servers' management. We present a UX architecture that is QoS-aware and facilitates the federated discovery for Web services. We describe the network model and design choices that we have made during the implementation of our architecture and feedbacks from service requesters are used to predict the service's performance. Customization is also provided for the service requesters to describe their preferences for discovery.

A general federated service is designed according to the CSG model. It maintains the links among federated servers and deals with the message propagation. It can tolerate a great amount of node failures so that the global version change is reduced considerably. Based on the CSG model, UX server supports federated discovery across domains. The method to process different domain's difference based on QoS summaries as well as some additional policies are incorporated to support the system.

Figure 12. The network overhead of UX federation experiment

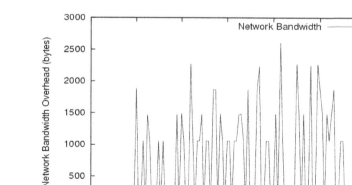

Compared with the original UDDI system, our system is aware of the basic service performance information with relatively small overhead from the feedback. The federated discovery helps the system to perform the discovery in the wider areas and estimate the QoS difference between domains dynamically. The replication consistency in a normal UDDI is a problem that is absent in our system as federated discovery is possible for UX servers. However, some drawbacks exist within UX system. The inquiry speed is slowed down during federated discovery because of the inquiry propagation. This is partially alleviated by implementing the cache at each UX server. The service requester's feedback is a potential security hole and needs certain security mechanism to overcome this.

The UX architecture presented in this chapter may be extended in the following ways. First, is to incorporate the semantic service descriptions in the registry so that the service capabilities are available in the matching procedure and precise matching can be supported. The current keyword matching cannot provide precise and flexible matching result. Second, is to design several template QoS metric classes for different kinds of Web services. These classes will provide better granularity for brokers to predict the service's performance. Measurement code reuse can be achieved according to the metric classes. The metrics can also provide more detailed information such as the variance, distribution, etc.

REFERENCES

Apache Software Foundation. (2003). *WSIF: Web services invocation framework, Version 2.0.* Retrieved from http://ws.apache.org/wsif/

Axis Development Team. (2002). *Apache Axis, Version 1.0.* Retrieved http://ws.apache.org/axis/

Belaid, D., Provenzano, N., & Taconet, C. (1998). Dynamic management of CORBA trader federation. In *Proceedings of the 4th USENIX Conference on Object-Orented Technologies and Systems (COOTS).*

Bellwood, T., et al. (2002). *UDDI API specification, Version 2.* Retrieved from http://uddi.org/pubs/ProgrammersAPI-V2.04-Published-20020719.htm

Box, D., et al. (2000). *Simple object access protocol (SOAP), Version 1.1.* Retrieved from http://www.w3.org/TR/SOAP/

Box, D., et al. (2002). *Web services policy framework (WS-policy), Version 1.* Retrieved from http://www.verisign.com/wss/WS-Policy.pdf

Box, D., Curbera, F., et al. (2002). *Web services policy attachment (WS-PolicyAttachment)* (Version 1). Retrieved from http://www.verisign.com/wss/WS-PolicyAttachment.pdf

Brittenham, P. (2001). *Web services inspection language specification (WSIL).* Retrieved from http://www.ibm.com/developerworks/webservices/library/ws-wsilspec.html

Cardoso, J., Sheth, A., & Kochut, K. (2002). *Implementing QoS management for workflow systems.* Retrieved from http://lsdis.cs.uga.edu/lib/download/CSK02-QoS-implementation-TR.pdf

Christensen, E., Curbera, F., Meredith, G., & Weerawarana, S.(2001). *Web services description language (WSDL), Version 1.1.* Retrieved from http://www.w3.org/TR/wsdl

Czerwinski, S. E., Zhao, B. Y., Hodes, T. D., Joseph, A. D., & Katz, R. H. (1999). An architecture for a secure service discovery service. In *Proceedings of Mobicom '99.*

Davis, J. S., Bisdikian, C., Jerome, W. F., & D. M. Sow. (2001). *Emerging research opportunities in service discovery.* Presented at the New York Metro-Area Networking Workshop.

ITU. (1994). *ODP trading function* (ITU/ISO Committee draft standard, ISO 13235/ITU.TS Rec.9tr).

Mani, A., & Nagarajan, A.(2002). *Understanding quality of service for Web services.* Retrieved from http://www-106.ibm.com/developerworks/library/ws-quality.html

M. P. (1987). *Domain names: Implementation and specification* (STD 13, RFC 1035).

Tian M., Gramm, A., Ritter, H., and Schiller, J. (2004). Efficient selection and monitoring of QoS-aware Web services with the WS-QoS framework. In *Proceedings of the International Conference on Web Intelligence (WI '04).*

Nelson, E. C. (1973). *A statistical basis for software reliability assessment* (TRW systems report).

Paolucci, M., Sycara, K., Nishimura, T., & Srinivasan, N. (2003). Using DAML-S for p2p discovery. In *Proceedings of the International Conference on Web Services (ICWS '03).*

Prim, R. C. (1957). Shortest connection networks and some generalizations. *Bell Syst. Techno. J., 36.*

Richard S. W. (1994). *TCP/IP Illustrated.* Addison Wesley Longman, Inc.

Stemm, M., Katz, R., & Seshan S.(2000). A network measurement architecture for adaptive applications. In *Proceedings of INFOCOM 2000* (pp. 285-294).

Shaikhali, A., Rana, O. F., Al-Ali, R. J., & Walker, D. W. (2003). UDDIe: An extended registry for Web services. In *Proceedings of the Symposium on Applications and the Internet Workshops (SAINT '03 Workshops).*

Xu, D., Nahrstedt, K., & Wichadakul, D. (2001). *QoS-aware discovery of wide-area distributed services.* Presented at CCGrid 2001.

Wahl, M., Howes, T., & Kille, S. (1997). *LDAPv3 protocol* (RFC 2251). Retrieved from http://www. ietf.org/rfc/rfc2251.txt

Zhang, L.-J., Chao, T., Chang, H., & Chung, J.-Y. (2003). XML-based advanced UDDI search mechanism for B2B integration. *Electronic Commerce Research Journal, 3*, 25-42.

Zhang, L.-J. (2002). Next generation Web services discovery. *Web Services Journal.*

Zhang, L.-J., Chang, H., & Chao, T. (2002, June). Web services relationships binding for dynamic e-business integration. In *Proceedings of the International Conference on Internet Computing (IC '02)* (pp. 561-567).

Zhou, C., Chia, L. T., Silverajan, B., & Lee, B. S. (2003). UX: An architecture providing QoS-aware and federated support for UDDI. In *Proceedings of the International Conference on Web Services (ICWS '03).*

This work was previously published in Modern Technologies in Web Services Research, edited by L. Zhang, pp. 187-216, copyright 2007 by CyberTech Publishing (an imprint of IGI Global).

Chapter XIX
The Key Requirements for Deploying Knowledge Management Services in a Semantic Grid Environment

Mirghani Mohamed
The George Washington University, USA

Michael Stankosky
The George Washington University, USA

Vincent Ribière
The George Washington University, USA

ABSTRACT

The purpose of this article is to investigate the requirements of knowledge management (KM) services deployment in a Semantic Grid environment. A wide range of literature on Grid Computing, Semantic Web, and KM have been reviewed, related, and interpreted. The benefits of the Semantic Web and the Grid Computing convergence have been enumerated and related to KM principles in a complete service model. Although the Grid Computing contributed the shared resources, most of the KM tool obstacles within the grid are to be resolved at the semantic and cultural levels more than at the physical or logical grid levels. The early results from academia show a synergy and the potentiality of leveraging knowledge at a wider scale. However, the plethora of information produced in this environment will result in a serious information overload, unless proper standardization, automated relations, syndication, and validation techniques are developed.

INTRODUCTION

Grid Computing is a significant reform in enterprise computing and is expected to bring unprecedented benefits on leveraging of knowledge management (KM) processes and procedures. The very fundamental objective of grid physical network is to speed information flow through improved processing, storage, discovery, retrieval, acquisition, and sharing within expansive colossal social networks. Grid Computing synchronizes computer resource sharing and effective deployment, which helps in faster assimilation, representation, and propagation of knowledge. Grid Computing has shown a notable success, however, it is restricted to collaboration amongst scientists and researchers in mainly what is known as the e-Science community. Accordingly, the early implementation of Grid Computing put an emphasis on computational capability and pattern recognition, but there is very little achieved in the area of business, including enterprise ecosystem relations and federated databases for sharing knowledge. As a result, the relationship between Grid Computing concepts and KM principles is still not clear. For instance, it is not obvious how Grid Computing can amalgamate collaborative machine semantics with human cognitive activities. The clarification of such a complex relationship may qualify this intergalactic network to minimize difficulties in transferring tacit knowledge across communities for creating authentic business values.

GRID COMPUTING

In historical progression, computer networks were designed to emulate social networks over time. The mainframe, then client/server, and presently the Grid Computing represent this developmental succession. Cabbly (2004) reports that "IBM defines Grid Computing as a standards based application/resource sharing architecture that makes it possible for heterogeneous systems and applications to share computing and storage resources transparently." Unlike traditional client-server architecture, Grid Computing activates dormant microprocessing power to perform parallel processes and utilize massive storage facilities around the globe. However, constructing such a network as its predecessor client/server is not trouble free. De Roure, Baker, Jennings, and Shadbolt (2003) report that the traditional client-server model can be a performance bottleneck and a single point of failure, but is still prevalent because decentralization brings its own challenges.

To mitigate the risk of global operations catastrophes during climax computing demand periods, the grid offers better performance load balancing and fault tolerance through failover on a massive scale. The main benefits of Grid Computing for many companies will be the ability to integrate systems and dynamically allocate resources, management of risk, and improvement of their Return On Investment (ROI) through maximizing the performance/cost ratio. All these will result in solving problems in less time and with less cost and through using the same computing machinery, but with more power added.

SEMANTIC WEB

Berners-Lee, Hendler, and Lassila (2001) state that the Semantic Web is not a separate Web, but an extension of the current one, in which information is given well-defined meaning, better enabling computers, and people to work in cooperation. Daconta, Obrst, and Smith (2003) report that Tim Berners-Lee has a two-part vision for the future of the Web. The first part is to make the Web a more collaborative medium. The second part is to make the Web understandable, and thus can be processed by machines. Semantic Web Services using XML protocols is an example of implementing this vision. Web Services are defined by Daconta et al. (2003) as software applications that can be discovered, described, and accessed based on XML and standard Web protocols over intranets, extranets, and the Internet.

XML is a specification for coding markup language that is suitable for building data models. It is an application and platform independent and it is both human and machine-readable language. XML upgraded the Internet to the level of machine-to-machine communication instead of human to machine communication, which is offered by HTML. Adams (2001) stated that XML is an important step towards offering efficient resource discovery on the Web, although it does not completely solve the problem. XML facilitates increased access to and description of the content contained within documents. The technology separates the intellectual content of a text from its surrounding structure, meaning that information can be converted into a uniform structure. This capability is used to improve search and index criteria for content management; however, XML itself is nothing more than a collection of tags on how information is structured for storage and search. In contrast to HTML, XML does not contribute to how information is presented. The capability of presenting a mixture of document formats in an interoperable environment through the public grid (open grid architecture) is imperative since different organizations, even those sharing the same domain, have different ways of styling, classifying, and interfacing their contents. This multiplicity makes it extremely complicated to present documents across the grid.

XML adds meaning to the document sharing only when all parties understand that the tag references or ontology is adding the meaning. This better fits into the specific domain classification that narrows the epistemological spectrum, hence, the community concept is very critical to the success of such effort. In reference to information overload, Geldof (2004) reports that one of the main obstacles is that most information on the Web is made for human interpretation and is not evident for agents browsing the Web. The Semantic Web is an effort to improve the current Web by making Web resources "machine-understandable," because the current Web resources do not respect machine-understandable semantics.

SEMANTIC GRID EVOLUTION

The recent convergence of Grid Computing and semantic Web in the Semantic Grid forms a promising platform for data-information-knowledge continuum representation. De Roure, Jennings, Nicholas, and Shadbolt (2005) define the Semantic Grid as an extension of the current Grid in which information and services are given well-defined meaning, better enabling computers, and people to work in cooperation. Originally, Grid Computing added the sharing of resources, while the semantic Web added the sharing of information and knowledge. This convergence is enhanced by the XML revolution which itself came as a natural result of the advances in computing power. XML needs huge processing power because it is a text-based rather than binary-based language (interpreted rather than compiled). In fact, the conversion happened in a broader scale as Friedman (2005) states that the world is flat because sometime in the late 1990s a whole set of technologies and political events converged—including the fall of the Berlin Wall, the rise of the Internet, the diffusion of the Windows operating system, the creation of a global fiber-optic network, and the creation of interoperable software applications, which made it very easy for people all over the world to work together—leveling the playing field. It created a global platform that allowed more people to plug and play, collaborate and compete, and share knowledge and share work than anything we have ever seen in the history of the world.

Semantic Web and grid network objectives are inextricably interrelated, and the Semantic Grid is the resultant synergetic effect of the two. The larger the grid, the more synergetic effects will result as Robert Metcalfe posits that, "the value of a communications network is proportional to the square of the size of the network (n²)" (Downes et al., 2000). Another advantage of such a network is its capability of ensuring high standards for business continuity through zero downtime of the network. Daconta et al. (2003) state that the marriage of Grid Computing and Web services may bring stability in a dynamic environment. When a Web Service shuts down, the network grid should be able to route a request to a substitute Web Service. Web Services do not offer Graphical User Interface (GUI), but could use a distributed number of machines to talk to each other and share processing power. This is where the coordination of machine-to-machine at the application level comes into play.

Most of the mature Semantic Grid initiatives are deployed for e-Science purposes, such as myGrid, CoreGRID, and CoAKTinG. MyGrid is a collaborative e-Science project between U.K. universities. The CoreGRID Network of Excellence (NoE) aims at progressing research knowledge on the grids, while CoAKTinG project acts as a gird portal. In addition, there are many promising projects from the Global Grid Forum (GGF) concerning the Open Grid Services Architecture WG (OGSA-WG).

Recently, some semantic grid projects have emerged addressing areas in the industry and services such as ARGUGRID, InteliGrid, SIMDAT, and The Biomedical Informatics Research Network (BIRN). The ARGUGRID project adopts InforSense® integrative analytics technology to develop collaborative service oriented computing using argumentation technology. InteliGrid provides the interoperability and integration of complex industry infrastructure. SIMDAT grid is used for team collaboration for federated industrial product development. And the BIRN is used for sharing clinical research and complex diagnosis between medical communities in a widely distributed geographical area.

KM Requirements Model

KM solution requirements are not inherently parts of the Grid Computing architecture, but all are added value in utilizing these networked resources to leverage knowledge for competitive advantage. Unsurprisingly, the mechanisms for these requirements exist in the market today, but not specifically deployed at the grid level. Luckily, most of the grid applications are designed with information sharing in mind; this will also qualify, with minor modifications, the existing grid applications for KM deployments.

Fox (2005) states that given the enormous multiplication of the quantity of content now available in the digital world, the need to connect ideas via commonly understood

Semantic Grid Computing presents unprecedented opportunities for the KM discipline to thrive. This contribution is expected to be in the areas of the information volume and the speed of knowledge processing and distribution. Daconta et al. (2003) define the semantic network as a structure for the expression of semantics, or a node-and-link representation of knowledge constructs and their relationships. In addition, distributed Web Services can create collaborating large groups that can solve problems on a massive scale. Consequently, Semantic Grid can assist in promoting system thinking because of the increased amount of information through sharing of information patterns and relationships on a wider range. Furthermore, the context switch that results from the provision of completely different knowledge within Grid Computing may lead to paradigm shifts and innovations. This can be attributed to the speedy and easy access of disparate knowledge ecosystems. In his fifth discipline conceptual

Table 1. Examples of KM major services and the possible associated mechanisms in semantic grid environment

Services	Description	Possible Mechanisms
Content Management	This service includes subservices such as library services,[1] rendition management,[2] Workflow,[3] and so forth.	Distribution and Discovery – soft agents Syndication and storage – metadata Locking, Federated databases, Storage Request Broker (SRB)
Integrated Search	Specific domain shared terabytes of pooled storages including coopetivite sharing contribution at SAN levels. Standard taxonomy, domain ontology, and Namespace[4] can be used for vocabulary standardization in RDF. An example is the domain best practices services across the participating grids.	Search engines based on natural languages and semantic relations. Description logic languages of Web services such as OWL, DAML+OIL, Knowledge Interchange Format (KIF), RDF, XQuery, GridFTP. Other knowledge specific mechanisms such as Hierarchical Distributed Dynamic Indexing (HDDI), Knowledge Query Language (KQL), and Unstructured Query Language (UQL).
Knowledge Assurance	This consists of information security and other KM procedures that assure the knowledge, such as intellectual right protection, and so forth.	Data security, Topic Maps, WS-security, WS-SecureConversation, WS-Trust and WS-Federation. Self-certifying File System (SFS)[5]
Collaboration	Remote collaboration for specific domains sharing computing resources including federated databases. For cognitive workflow grid, applications must deal with the cognosphere between metadata and ontology. Virtual Communities of Practice.	Web services orchestration[6]. The CoAKTinG (Collaborative Advanced Knowledge Technologies in the Grid)[7]
Expertise Locator	Profile fetching in a common registry for expertise in the specified area.	Expertise space, Personalization, LDAPs, NDSs, and so forth.

Figure 1. Knowledge services strata for transformation of e-science grid computing into e-commerce semantic grid

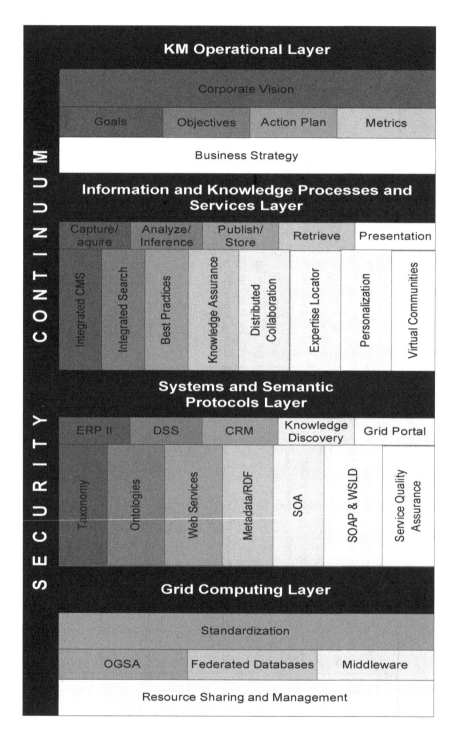

framework, Senge (1990) states that system thinking is needed more than ever because we are becoming overwhelmed by complexity. Perhaps for the first time in history, humankind has the capacity to create far more information than anyone can absorb, to foster far greater interdependency than anyone can manage, and to accelerate change faster than anyone's ability to keep pace.

There are many outstanding mechanisms and protocols of the Semantic Grid that contribute and are expected to revolutionize the way we carry out knowledge activities across geographies and domains. Table 1 shows KM main services and mechanisms that are required in Semantic Grid environment. Figure 1 depicts the model, which consists of strata of elements that satisfy the requirements of KM services within the grid environment. Each layer contributes a package of services for knowledge management.

First Layer: Grid Computing

The lowest layer consists of the major components in the Grid Computing architecture that will assist upper levels in providing needed KM services.

- **Open grid services architecture (OGSA):** Defined by Global Grid Forum (GGF) as the merger of Grid Computing and Web Service standards (Foster, Kesselman, Nick & Tuecke, 2002). OGSA adopted most of XML protocols to provide service oriented grid standards and contributed to the convergence of the Semantic Grid. The integrative nature of OGSA made the database federation possible. Foster, Kishimoto, Savva, Berry, Djaoui, Grimshaw et al. (2005) report that OGSA data services allow the creation of virtual data resources that incorporates data from multiple data sources that are created and maintained separately. When a client queries the virtual resource, the query is compiled into subqueries and operations that extract the appropriate information from the underlying federated resources and return it in the appropriate format.
- **Federated database:** A monolithic database that coalesces domains with the same subject matter from different communities. Raman, Crone, Haas, Malaika, Mukai, Wolfson et al. (2003) state that the federated DBMS provides two kinds of virtualizations to users.
  - ○ Heterogeneity transparency, via the masking of the data formats at each source, the hardware and software they run on, how data are accessed at each source, and even about how the data stored in these sources are modeled and managed.
  - ○ Distribution transparency, via the masking of the distributed nature of the sources and the network communication needed to access them.

Accessing the member databases is not the problem. However, leveraging the databases for the improvement of the query results is the crux of the issue. Hence, the success of federated databases depends on the standardization of the metadata in each of the contributing databases. The architecture of federated database involves the middleware.

- **Middleware:** Provides the main grid functionality for knowledge discovery in a seamlessly agile virtual organization. Middleware collects information from all configuration items. It consolidates these data and publishes them to increase their visibility for interfacing purposes. Middleware resembles the knowledge broker in real life; with the exception that it coordinates all the available resources used by one instance into one virtual machine. This will achieve interoperability and add meaning to information through Semantic Web Services

- **Resource sharing and standardization:** for configuration management across the Semantic Grid is critical for consolidating and distributing information from all participating domains.

Second Layer: Systems and Semantic Protocols

The second layer consists of the most popular systems and protocols that contribute to the delivery of KM services within the Grid environment. The second layer provides various capabilities of semantic services considered necessary for KM to excel in the grid environment. This layer is divided into two sub-layers.

- **Systems** sublayer: Consists of enterprise systems such as the next generation of ERP II which constitutes a major shift towards KM (Mohamed, 2002), Decision Support Systems (DSS), Customer Relationship Management (CRM), Knowledge Discovery including data warehousing, data mining, and the Grid Portal. Grid Portal allows users to access and manipulate resource information obtained and stored on remote federated databases (De Roure et al., 2003). This portal can also be personalized which makes the grid portals the appropriate access points for grid high performance resources.
- **Protocols** sub-layer: This sublayer consists of important protocols that transform the Grid Computing environment to the semantic grid where knowledge can be transformed as it transfers through the Grid nodes. This layer is critical to the success of KM in the Grid and it consists of the following elements:
  - **Taxonomy:** The taxonomy results in mapping information into predefined classes, and contains basic intrinsic child-parent relations. Classification itself is subjective and has neither standards nor specifications. It depends on how individuals understand and relate information about objects. Accordingly, each organization or unit may have its own classification hierarchy and use its own vocabulary. Hence, for each organization to be able to exchange information with other organizations, it must understand their classification scheme(s). In many environments this may be impractical and is extremely difficult even in domains within one organization, let alone multiple geographically separated organizations in a grid environment. XML schema can be used as a source of standardization within the domain; the XML schema is defined by W3C (2001b) as "XML Schemas express shared vocabularies and allow machines to carry out rules made by people. They provide a means for defining the structure, content, and semantics of XML documents." In addition, the problem of unstandardized classification can be addressed through Document Type Definition (DTD), which is an ontology-driven searching criterion that offers high degree of domain-specific semantic terms and knowable concepts.
  - **Ontology:** Ontology is a set of shared concepts and relationships commonly conceptualized and interpreted within a domain. In other words, ontology assists in developing the general conceptualization of the content. In a Semantic Grid environment, this will simplify retrieval, improve search precision, and promote synthesis of knowledge. Semantic search depends on the concept of the search and not only on the keywords or tags. As stated by Daconta et al.

(2003), semantic mapping (cognitive mapping) is particularly important in grid environment and that semantic mapping is a critical issue for information technologies considering the use of multiple knowledge sources. The magnitude of ontology hermeneutical power depends on how close it expresses the tacit knowledge. In fact, ontology offers search capabilities that are based on meanings and relationships more than static keywords. The value of ontology is expressed by Daconta et al. (2003) through their explanation of the concept of machine-interpretable ontology, as the semantics of the model is interpretable by the machine; in other words, the computer and its software can interact with the semantic model directly without direct human involvement. In the future, this will move the machines up to human level instead of the opposite, as is the norm in the current binary technology.

- **Web Services:** make sharing of data, processes, and business logic available for use. KM requirements for the Semantic Grid can be represented within the sphere of grid services and Semantic Web Services. W3C (2002) defines Web Services as a software application whose interfaces and binding are capable of being defined, described, and discovered by XML artifacts and supports direct interactions with other software applications using XML based messages via Internet-based protocols.

- **Metadata and RDF:** XML is used in encoding metadata and it offers semantic dimensions for document descriptive parameters. In Grid Computing, Atkinson, Dialani, Guy, Narang, Paton, Pearson et al. (2003) found that metadata are essential to the development of Grid services because they enables data operations to be abstracted to a sufficient degree that services can be created and made reusable. This facility makes it possible to access and manipulate data content without knowing where it is physically located, or how it is structured. Resource Description Framework (RDF) can be deployed in Semantic Grid environments to form rich semantic interrelations in metadata. This will offer more meaning to the document and increase the possibility of its sharing. Due to the semantic relations and unified vocabulary, both RDF and metadata may work toward just-in-time content processing at a global scale

- **SOA:** Service-oriented architecture (SOA) is vital in the realm of Semantic Grid because there is a high need for reusability of services, agents, and objects. Although SOA already played a significant role in Semantic Grid, the service-oriented knowledge architecture that assists in deploying the concepts of KM at the industrial level is not yet mature. This can be attributed to the architecture of the Semantic grid not being materialized for enabling virtual organization and virtual communities. Nevertheless, a comprehensive framework based on semantic Web protocols and new Grid Computing techniques may be adopted in the near future. SOA was originally designed for a client/server environment, but its architecture and functionality makes it suitable for Grid Computing. Nitais and Schulte (2003) state that SOA differs from the general client/server model in its definitive emphasis on loose coupling between software components, and in its use of a separately standing interface. The fundamental intent of SOA is the nonintrusive reuse of software services in a new runtime context. Valdes (2004) reports that when adopting SOA architecture, the frequency of data transfer will greatly increase because communication that formerly occurred inside a machine boundary will cross machine and LAN/WAN boundaries. The volume of data transfer will increase because Web Services protocols are text-based rather than binary and encoded in XML, which is more verbose than other text-based formats by up to a factor of 10.

      ○   **SOAP & WSDL:** The Simple Object Access Protocol (SOAP) and Web Service Description Language (WSDL) formed principal protocols on which Web Services are built. WSDL is descriptive language that offers information about the services, their location, role, and interface. SOAP provides a simple mechanism for exchanging structured and typed information between peers in a decentralized, distributed environment using XML (W3C, 2000). SOAP acts as an envelop that contains XML messages which travel via HTTP between Web services. WSDL is an XML format for describing network services as a set of endpoints operating on messages containing either document-oriented or procedure-oriented information (W3C, 2001a). The two protocols can be employed in application to application communication that is metadata and ontology can be accessed through WSDL.

      ○   **Service quality assurance:** In the current client/server architecture, both information and machines are under utilized. Semantic Web and its associated interoperability is one-step toward machines that gain experience and intelligently uses it to furnish seamless integration. In the grid environment, for interoperability and inter-enterprise communication that is Business-to-Business (B2B), companies must publish themselves into UDDI registry, describe their interfaces in WSDL, and enable its applications with SOAP. Therefore, it is imperative to make middleware available for KM services that perform knowledge synthesis and targeted dissemination.

Third Layer: Information and Knowledge Services

The third layer provides the platform for the knowledge continuum which includes the transformation of data to information and finally to knowledge. The transformation of knowledge in this layer can be represented in Figure 2, which depicts the relationship between social and physical networks spaces and the status of the "cognosphere" at each knowledge functional unit. Yolles (2000) refers to this sort of creation as a coalesce process, which converts information to knowledge through some form of distillation which occurs through the renewal of patterns of meaning that constitutes knowledge. The demand for knowledge is the driving force for its extraction from information. As stated by Lang (2001), the shift from information to knowledge means that the awareness of the value of knowledge in most firms is exceeding their ability to extract it from the goods and services in which it is embedded, and to create new knowledge. Skyttner (1998) concludes that pure information, like pure knowledge, signifies nothing at all; it is the context in which it is employed that gives it existence and value. Information becomes knowledge only when we decide to put it into use. Without this transformation, stored information is nothing more than physical or electronic signs.

    The transformation from data to information to knowledge involves the addition of context. Abowd and Dey (1999) define context as any information that can be used to characterize the situation of an entity. A system is context-aware; if it uses context to provide relevant information and/or services to the user, relevancy depends on the user's task. Schilit and Theimer (1994) describe context as location, identities of nearby people and objects, and changes to those objects. Hull, Neaves, and Bedford-Roberts (1997) considered context to be aspects of the current situation in a certain environment. The importance of context is not only limited to the differentiation between data, information, and knowledge, but it also contributes to the decision-making process, problem solving techniques, and sharing of tacit knowledge. Data-information-knowledge continuum contextual range is expressed by Davenport and

Figure 2. The role of physical and social networks in knowledge transformation through the continuum

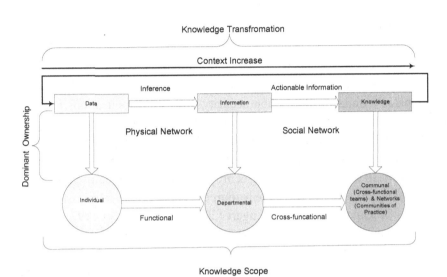

Prusak (1998) as information is "data transformed by the value-adding processes of contextualization, categorization, calculation, correction and condensation."

This layer consists of two prominent sublayers:

- **KM processes** sub-layer: The main theme of this layer in the Semantic Grid is to determine the best way to develop a knowledge life cycle that captures, coalesces, synthesizes, and disseminates domestic and exotic knowledge within Semantic Grid environment.
- **Services** sublayer: The prominent KM services and their associate tools and mechanisms for fulfilling KM processes sublayer are depicted in Table 1.

Fourth Layer: KM Operational

The fourth layer is where the KM within the Semantic Gird shows the business benefits and offers the competitive advantage. The adoption of service-oriented grid architecture in business may significantly shift the market from competition to coopetition, cooperation and competition at the same time, where proprietary knowledge dissemination occurs at a larger scale. Firms within the same domain can cooperate regardless of their geographical location. This will allow KM initiatives effects to extend beyond the enterprise boundaries. However, for this objective to be satisfied, the organization must possess a learning organization vision that is a link between intellectual capital and business strategy. In such organization, learning is the principal driver for business goals and objectives. The hosting of KM initiatives within Semantic Grid will encourage various forms of networking among employees; hence, it may propel the organization towards fulfilling its objectives through implanting knowledge culture within its environment.

The Security Continuum

Network and computer security sublayer covered the first three layers, while the security measures for the fourth layer depends on other human activities such as proper sharing, business trust, intellectual property rights, patents, and so forth. Without security-aware KM applications, knowledge in the Grid can be subjected to considerable compromises including theft and unauthorized changes. At the Grid level, Foster et al. (2005) argued that obtaining application programs and deploying them into a Grid system may require authentication and authorization. Also sharing of resources by users requires some kind of isolation mechanism. In addition, standard, secure mechanisms are required, which can be deployed to protect Grid systems while supporting safe resource sharing across administrative domains.

Meder, Welch, Chicago, Tuecke, and Engert (2004) report that in 1997, the Globus Project introduced the Grid Security Infrastructure (GSI), an implementation of a security mechanism for Grid Computing that uses the Generic Security Services Application Program Interface (GSSAPI) standard between hosts and clients. This implementation uses public key protocols for use in programming Grid applications. On the other hand, Moore and Merzky (2003) suggested the use of the GSI to authenticate users to the logical name space, and to authenticate servers to other servers within the federated server architecture. In general, the Grid security architecture are compiled (Globus, 2006) into security tools that are concerned with establishing the identity of users or services (authentication), protecting communications, and determining who is allowed to perform what actions (authorization), as well as with supporting functions such as managing user credentials and maintaining group membership information. Furthermore, domain security can be handled through authentication transparency. Moore and Merzky (2003) define authentication transparency as the ability to create a single sign-on environment for authenticating use of resources in multiple administrative domains.

It is not the intention of this article to advocate any specific security practice or protocol be deployed for any specific KM application in the Semantic Grid environment. There are miscellanea of security technologies that can be employed in such distributed environment such as Self-certifying File System (SFS), GridFTP security, Semantic Grid Security protocols, and so forth. Allcock, Bester, Bresnahan, Meder, Plaszczak, and Tuecke (2003) report that GridFTP was designed with security in mind from the start and was, in fact, the driving force that started this effort. The Semantic Grid security protocols include WS-security, WS-SecureConversation, WS-Trust and WS-Federation. WS-Security plays a major role in sharing knowledge. Atkinson et al. (2003) conclud that WS-Security describes enhancements to SOAP messaging to provide quality protection through message integrity, message confidentiality, and single message authentication. These mechanisms can be used to accommodate a wide variety of security models and encryption technologies.

Argonne, Gannon, Fujitsu, and Von Reich (2004) argue that in an open and flexible Grid Service Architecture environment, resources will over time be used for multiple content titles. Therefore, trust has to be built on the side of the content providers that such a dynamic environment will not interfere with the goal of consistent user experience. Proper isolation between content offerings also has to be ensured. This level of isolation has to be ensured by the security of the infrastructure.

At the KM operational layer, security measures depend on human activities and relations. Sharing knowledge across time and space is the essence of KM systems. Furthermore, knowledge does not obey the law of diminishing returns, that is, the more sharing of knowledge the higher likelihood that there would be more return from that knowledge and the more insight developed into it. However, when there is a need for knowledge protection, the more people that are aware of that knowledge the more vulnerable the asset would be. It is obvious that there is a conflict of interest between knowledge sharing and the knowledge assurance or information security. Knowledge can be considered a relationship, and sharing is a natural outcome of interpersonal relationships, formal and informal networks. The degree of sharing is determined by intermingling of organization, social, political, and economical factors.

The authors believe that there is a wide range of grey area between sharing and not sharing, which entails the categorization of sharing within the grid open environment into categories such as:

- **Domestic Sharing:** Knowledge for internal use of the firm only that is closed-loop. This knowledge category should not be stored in any of the Grid nodes.
- **Supportive Sharing:** Knowledge sharing within the business value network which is limited by the in-house and other partners usage such as suppliers and customers.
- **Domain Sharing:** Knowledge is shared within certain areas with standardized vocabulary, concepts, and relations, such as a scientific group collaborating in a single field. In business this can also be represented by communities of practice, communities of interest, and so forth, but collaboration in one particular field is critical here.
- **Collaborative Sharing:** Sharing for mutual benefi, such as sharing with strategic partners and the business communities at large.
- **Coopetitive:** Sharing of knowledge with other companies that compete and cooperate. There is no room for absolute competitive intelligence in the grid. However, key competitive data may not be disclosed, that is, developing a decision support system based on competitive intelligence, which can be limited to domestic sharing.

GAPS AND CHALLENGES

Most KM tool obstacles within the grid are to be resolved at the semantic and cultural levels, more than at the physical or logical grid levels. In general, challenges facing the new KM itself are related to organizations as social constructs; knowledge embedded in human behavior and knowledge production activities resulted in serious problems such as information overload, knowledge irrelevancy, knowledge leakage, and vulnerability. The seriousness of loosing knowledge is mainly attributed to its true value being compromised. This value results from the additions of proprietary contextual strata during the process of knowledge production from data. By extension, this intense context augmentation makes knowledge a super set of information and that makes the loss of knowledge more serious than the loss of information. In the business world, this knowledge value is protected through competitive intelligence practices and patents.

With the current plethora of information in the network, without developing new standards for narrowing down the search results, the grid will lead to information overload. Information explosion is one of the challenges that face the grid, where there is a movement of voluminous data and documents at global levels. There will be a high need not only for search capabilities, but also for methods of developing patterns, syndication, and validation.

Other Semantic Grid most difficult obstacles to overcome are:

- Standardization of domain specific metadata across the globe using standards such as Resource Description Framework (RDF) in federated databases.
- Replacing competition with coopetition in the market, and the mobilization of knowledge from the academia to the industry.
- Resolve the conflict between global collaboration vs. intellectual property rights and international patents.

THE FUTURE VISION

Looking at Figure 2, we may find a clear distinction between the role and capabilities of the physical network and the human network. This distinction is becoming more blurred by the introduction of the semantics into the equation. The convergence between the machine and the human thinking will be reflected in better extraction of knowledge from information, which may minimize information overload through better controlled transformations using "gridified" semantics and ontology. In fact, we are on the verge of a dynamic, adaptive convergence model for semantic Web and Grid Computing. And there is a need for machine learning algorithms, in which not only human can think and work collaboratively, but computers must follow suit as well.

THE BOTTOM LINE

To bridge the research-practice gap and to enhance productivity for better competitive advantage, organizations must move fast into this arena with their knowledge and information needs. The authors call for Semantic Grid standardization initiatives to consider the conceptual framework and requirements of KM in their efforts. Due to the exponential increase in the amount of information, Grid Computing will put the world on the verge of information danger, unless dealt with at the knowledge levels. On the other hand, data storage capabilities increased at the same rate; but this is not the solution because it results in more information overload and massive amount of data with no apparent progress in knowledge extraction mechanisms.

REFERENCES

Abowd, G. D., & Dey, A. K. (1999). *Towards a better understanding of context and context-awareness* (No. GIT-GVU-99-22). Atlanta, GA: Georgia Institute of Technology, College of Computing.

Allcock, W., Bester, J., Bresnahan, J., Meder, S., Plaszczak, P., & Tuecke, S. (2003). *GridFTP: Protocol extensions to FTP for the grid*. Lemont, IL: Global Grid Forum.

Argonne, I. F., Gannon, D., Fujitsu, H. K., & Von Reich , J. J. (2004). *Open grid services architecture use cases* (No. GFD-I.029). Lemont, IL: Global Grid Forum.

Atkinson, M., Dialani, V., Guy, L., Narang, I., Paton, N. W., Pearson, et al. (2003). *Grid database access and integration: Requirements and functionalities* (No. GFD-I.13). Lemont, IL: GLobal Grid Forum.

Berners-Lee, T., Hendler, J., & Lassila, O. (2001). The semantic Web: A new form of Web content that is meaningful to computers will unleash a revolution of new possibilities. Retrieved February 10, 2007, from *http://www.scientificamerican.com/*

Cabbly, J. (2004). The grid report. Retrieved February 10, 2007, from *http://www.1.ibm.com/grid/pdf/ Clabby_Grid_Report_2004_Edition.pdf*

Daconta, M., Obrst, L., & Smith, K. (2003). *The semantic Web: A guide to the future of XML, Web services and knowledge management.* Indianapolis: Wiley.

Davenport, T. H., & Prusak, L. (1998). *Working knowledge: How organizations manage what they know.* Boston: Harvard Business School Press.

De Roure, D., Baker, M., Jennings, N., & Shadbolt, N. (2003). *The evolution of the grid in grid computing: Making the global infrastructure a reality.* West Sussex, UK: Wiley.

De Roure, D., Jennings Nicholas, R., & Shadbolt, N. (2005). The semantic grid: Past, present, and future. *Proceedings of the IEEE, 93*(3).

Foster, I., Kesselman, C., Nick, J., & Tuecke, S. (2002). *The physiology of the grid: An open grid services architecture for distributed systems integration.* Lemont, IL: Global Grid Forum.

Foster, I., Kishimoto, H., Savva, A., Berry, D., Djaoui, A., Grimshaw, A., et al. (2005). *Open grid services architecture V.1.0* (No. GFD-I.030). Lemont, IL: Global Grid Forum.

Fox, R. (2005). Cataloging our information architecture. *International Digital Library Prespectives, 21*(1), 23-29.

Friedman, T. L. (2005). *The world is flat: A brief history of the twenty first century.* Farrar, Straus and Giroux.

Geldof, M. (2004). *The semantic grid: Will semantic Web and grid go hand in hand?* European Commission, DG Information Society.

Globus. (2006). GT 4.0: Security. Retrieved February 10, 2007, from *http://www.globus.org/toolkit/ docs/4.0/security/*

Hull, R., Neaves, P., & Bedford-Roberts, J. T. (1997). *Towards situated computing.* Paper presented at the 1st International Symposium on Wearable Computers, Cambridge, Massachusetts.

Lang, J. C. (2001). Managerial concerns in knowledge management. *Journal of Knowledge Management, 5*(1), 43-59.

Meder, S., Welch, V., Chicago, V., Tuecke, S., & Engert, D. (2004). *GSS-API extensions* (No. GFD-E.024). Lemont, IL: Global Grid Forum.

Mohamed, M. (2002). Points of the triangle. *Intelligent Enterprise, 5*(14), 32-37.

Moore, R. W., & Merzky, A. (2003). *Persistent archive concepts* (No. GFD-I.026). Lemont, IL: Global Grid Forum.

Nitais, V. Y., & Schulte, W. R. (2003). Introduction to service-oriented architecture. Gartner:

Research SPA-19-5971. Retrieved February 10, 2007, from *http://www.gartner.com*

Raman, V., Crone, C., Haas, L., Malaika, S., Mukai, T., Wolfson, D., et al. (2003). *Services for data access and data processing on grids* (No. GFD-I.14). Lemont, IL: Global Grid Forum.

Schilit, B., & Theimer, M. (1994). Disseminating active map information to mobile hosts.

IEEE Network, 8(5), 22-32.

Senge, P. M. (1990). *The fifth discipline: The art and practice of the learning organization.* New York: Doubleday/Currency.

Skyttner, L. (1998). Information theory: A psychological study in old and new concepts. *Kybernetes, 27*(3), 284-311.

Valdes, R. (2004). New application architectures will impact networks. Gartner: Research TU-21-7470. Retrieved February 10, 2007, from *http://www.gartner.com*

W3C. (2000). Simple object access protocol (SOAP) 1.1. Retrieved February 10, 2007, from *http://www. w3.org/TR/2000/NOTE-SOAP-20000508/#_Toc478383486*

W3C. (2001a). Web services description language (WSDL) 1.1. Retrieved February 10, 2007, from *http://www.w3.org/TR/wsdl*

W3C. (2001b). XML schema. Retrieved February 10, 2007, from *http://www.w3.org/XML/Schema*

W3C. (2002). Web services description requirements. Retrieved February 10, 2007, from *http://www. w3.org/TR/ws-desc-reqs/#definitions*

Yolles, M. (2000). Organisations, complexity, and viable knowledge management. *Kybernetes: The International Journal of Systems & Cybernetics, 29*(9), 1202-1222.

ENDNOTES

[1]   Check in/out of documents.
[2]   Create the document in different format.
[3]   Document authoring, review, approval, publishing, and distribution processes.
[4]   XML Namespaces, which is used for standardizing and avoidance of the conflict in the content tagging and naming of elements and attributes of XML. This will facilitate the work of metadata across the domain in the grid environment. In addition, the structure of the metadata itself and the description for each of the services necessitate the use of KM terminology for improved search, discovery, and selection performance.

5   SFS is a global network file system with decentralized control where documents can be shared with anyone anywhere.

6   Communication between different Web services.

7   The CoAKTinG project objective is to develop integrated collaborative spaces in the Grid. It consists of tools such as presence notification, instant messaging, group memory and meetings. These applications are still limited to e-Science domain.

This work was previously published in the International Journal of Knowledge Management, edited by M. Jennex, Volume 3, Issue 3, pp. 104-118, copyright 2007 by IGI Publishing, formerly known as Idea Group Publishing (an imprint of IGI Global).

Chapter XX
Karma2:
Provenance Management for Data–Driven Workflows[1]

Yogesh L. Simmhan
Microsoft Research, USA

Beth Plale
Indiana University, USA

Dennis Gannon
Indiana University, USA

ABSTRACT

The increasing ability for the sciences to sense the world around us is resulting in a growing need for data-driven e-Science applications that are under the control of workflows composed of services on the Grid. The focus of our work is on provenance collection for these workflows that are necessary to validate the workflow and to determine quality of generated data products. The challenge we address is to record uniform and usable provenance metadata that meets the domain needs while minimizing the modification burden on the service authors and the performance overhead on the workflow engine and the services. The framework is based on generating discrete provenance activities during the lifecycle of a workflow execution that can be aggregated to form complex data and process provenance graphs that can span across workflows. The implementation uses a loosely coupled publish-subscribe architecture for propagating these activities, and the capabilities of the system satisfy the needs of detailed provenance collection. A performance evaluation of a prototype finds a minimal performance overhead (in the range of 1% for an eight-service workflow using 271 data products).

INTRODUCTION

The need to access and share large-scale computational and data resources to support dynamic computational science and agile enterprises is driving the growth of Grids (Foster, Kesselman, Nick & Tuecke, 2002). In the realm of e-Science, *science gateways* are archetypes for accessing, managing, and sharing virtualized resources to solve large collaboratory challenges (Catlett, 2002; Gannon et al., 2005). Science gateways are built as a *service-oriented architecture* with Grid resources virtualized as services. These resources—including physical resources such as sensors, computational clusters, and mass storage devices, and software resources such as scientific tasks and models—are available as services that provide an abstraction to access the resources through well-defined interfaces.

A significant constituent of applications that make use of the science gateways is *data-driven applications* (Simmhan, Pallickara, Vijayakumar & Plale, 2006a). The proliferation of wireless networking and inexpensive sensor technology is allowing the sciences an increasing ability to sense the world around us (West, 2005). This is specifically resulting in a growing need for data-driven applications; that is, applications that can be computation-intense and are usually either dataflow applications in which data flows from one process to another, or demand-driven in which computations are triggered in response to events occurring in the world around us. Data-driven scientific experiments are designed as workflows composed of services on the Grid, and data flow from one service to another, being transformed, filtered, fused, and used in complex models. These workflows capture the invocation logic for the scientific investigation and may be composed of hundreds of services connected as complex graphs. Data-driven workflow executions also see the participation of thousands of data products that reach terabytes in size. At this scale of processing, users need the ability to automatically track the execution of their experiments and the multitude of data products created and consumed by the services in the workflow. Provenance collection and management, also called process mining, workflow tracing, or lineage collection, is a new line of research on the execution of workflows, and the derivation and usage trail of data products that are involved in the workflows (Bose & Frew, 2005; Moreau & Ludascher, 2007; Simmhan, Plale & Gannon, 2005).

Provenance collected about the tasks of a workflow describes the workflow's service invocations during its execution (Simmhan et al., 2005). This helps track service and resource usage patterns, and forms metadata for service and workflow discovery. In data-driven applications, however, it is provenance about the data that is central to understanding and recreating earlier runs. In *data-driven workflows*, data products are first-class parameters to services that consume and transform the input data to generate derived data products. These derived data products are ingested by other services in the same or a different workflow, forming a data derivation and data usage trail. *Data provenance* provides this derivation history of data that includes information about services and input data that contributed to the creation of a data product. This kind of information is extremely valuable, not only for diagnosing problems and understanding performance of a particular workflow run, but also to determine the origin and quality of a particular piece of derived information (Goble, 2002; Simmhan, Plale & Gannon, 2006b).

Current methods of collecting provenance are from workflow engine logs (IBM, 2005) or by instrumenting the services (Bose & Frew, 2004; Zhao, Wroe, Goble, Stevens, Quan & Greenwood, 2004). In the former case, the logs from the workflow engine are at the message level and insufficient for deciphering provenance about the data products, while instrumenting services introduce a burden on the service author to modify their service to generate provenance metadata. They also tend to be specific to the workflow framework and are not interoperable with heterogeneous workflow models that are likely to be present in a Grid environment. Work is also emerging on more general information models for provenance collection (Moreau & Ludascher, 2007).

The challenge we address in our work is to record uniform and usable provenance metadata independent of the workflow or service framework used, while minimizing the modification burden on the service authors and the performance overhead on the workflow engine and the services. The Karma provenance framework we describe collects two forms of provenance: *process provenance*, also known as workflow trace (Simmhan et al., 2005), which is metadata describing the workflow's execution and associated service invocations; and *data provenance,* which provides complementary metadata about the derivation history of the data product, including services used and input data sources transformed to generate it. These forms of provenance allow scientists to monitor workflow progress at runtime (Gannon et al., 2005) and, post-execution, mine the provenance to locate sources of errors, determine data quality (Simmhan et al., 2006b), and validate the results through repetition or simulated replay of the workflow execution (Szomszor & Moreau, 2003). It also assists resource providers to review resource usage for purposes of auditing (Greenwood et al., 2003) and provisioning (Churches et al., 2006).

This article details the Karma provenance framework for collecting and managing provenance for data-driven workflows. The current Karma system, which we describe in this article, builds upon previous exploratory work we undertook on provenance management; hence the allusion to the present Karma version 2, or Karma2. The remainder of the article is organized as follows. In Section 2, we motivate the need for provenance collection with an example from mesoscale meteorology, which is an exemplar domain for data-driven applications. In Section 3, we define a generalized data-driven workflow model for which the provenance is collected. In section 4, we discuss provenance activities that occur during the lifetime of the workflow that go toward building provenance. Section 5 describes the provenance model of Karma and the various forms of provenance that are available. Section 6 grounds the provenance model in an implementation of the framework that we discuss. Section 7 presents details on performance evaluation of provenance collection and querying. Related work appears in Section 8 and future work in Section 9.

MOTIVATION

Scientific workflows (Yu & Buyya, 2005) often use a *service-oriented architecture* to solve advanced scientific problems in a Grid environment (Gannon et al., 2005). Workflows are composed from services that provide a well-defined functionality with open interfaces to access them. Workflows model the interactions between the services as directed graphs whose edges represent dependencies and dataflows, and incorporate decision-making logic for runtime selection of execution paths (BEA, 2003). There are different models for workflow execution. Orchestration can be done by a central workflow engine that interprets the workflow document and invokes the services according to the dependencies, ensuring dataflow between connected services. Execution may also be handled in a distributed manner by the services themselves.

In the Linked Environments for Atmospheric Discovery (LEAD) (Droegemeier et al., 2005) project, regional-scale numerical weather forecasting is done using dynamically adaptive workflows, as shown in Figure 1, that run end-to-end forecast models. These computationally intense workflows may be launched on demand in response to a severe weather event and may ingest new data products at any point during execution directly from real-time observational sources. The model data products generated by

Figure 1. Sample LEAD weather forecasting workflow

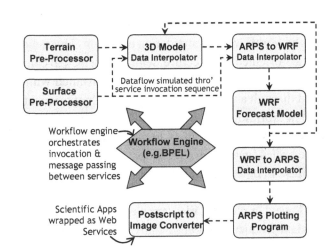

the services may be reused in the same or in a different workflow, forming a data processing pipeline (Liu, Franklin, Garlick & Abdulla, 2005; Ludäscher et al., 2006). The *dynamic* nature of the workflows means that the workflow execution path is not static and can change at runtime due to external events, while *adaptability* implies the ability to bind to an appropriate and available service instance at the time of workflow execution.

A typical meteorological experiment shown in Figure 1 is a weather prediction workflow using the Weather Research and Forecasting (WRF) Model. Pre-processing, interpolation, post-processing, and visualization are done by the Advanced Regional Prediction System (ARPS) Model. The workflow is composed using the Business Process Execution Language (BPEL) and orchestrated by a central BPEL engine (Slominski, 2006). The workflow can be broadly divided into pre-processing and grid interpolation stage (Services 1–4, Figure 1, starting with Surface Pre-Processor and moving clockwise), numerical weather prediction stage (Service 5), and post-processing and visualization stage (Services 6–8). Each of these services produces and consumes between 4 and 100 data products in the form of files, transparently referenced through URIs (Plale, 2005). This workflow applied to data from Hurricane Katrina's landfall on the Gulf Coast in 2005 is used for the performance evaluation in Section 7. More complex workflows with high degrees of parallelism and complex conditional logic are also seen in LEAD when running ensemble simulations (Droegemeier et al., 2005).

Provenance is collected from such workflows in order to verify that a simulation run was successful and to validate its results. This may be through visual inspection of the provenance graphs or through automated processes. This is important, given the dynamic and adaptive nature of the workflows, to determine what really happened. Data provenance also helps to keep track of data products used by and generated from the experiments and discover them for reuse at a later time. This can even avoid running the workflow if an identical run made by another user has generated the required output data and the workflow is deterministic. Data quality models have been developed to mine historic provenance information for patterns of service execution that can assist in making quality predictions about data products generated by services as a function of their input data and parameters (Simmhan et al., 2006b).

WORKFLOW MODEL

An abstract workflow model, for which provenance is collected, is necessary to ensure that the provenance model is independent of the workflow implementation or design. This generalized data-driven workflow model is based on a service-oriented architecture, with four principal components: *workflows, services, service clients,* and *data products* that are produced and consumed within the workflow. Services are black-box tasks accessed through a well-defined interface. They frequently are, but not limited to Web services by the model. The workflow is a *directed graph* of services, with the services forming nodes in the graph and its edges constituting dataflow between services or applications wrapped by the service. The graph can have cycles such as iterative loops. Workflows themselves are considered services, allowing them to participate in other workflows. This allows for a hierarchical pattern of constructing workflows by reusing existing workflows and services.

Data products, often logical or physical files, are passed as inputs to and generated as outputs from a service invocation. The data products are identified by a globally unique ID in the request and response messages, and they are said to be *consumed* by that service invocation if used as input, while those newly created by that invocation are said to be *produced* by it. Every service invocation in a data-driven workflow consumes or produces data products, and these form their own dataflow graph, which is captured as part of the provenance.

Paradigms for Workflow Execution and Service Invocation

There are several invocation paradigms for running workflows (Yu & Buyya, 2005). In a *centralized model,* such as used by BPEL, a central workflow engine that has the workflow dependency logic invokes the services in the workflow in succession, passing messages between the services and acting as their client. As a variation, the control could be distributed, with different engines being aware of a portion of the workflow graph (e.g., one engine for each workflow in a nested workflow) and acting as clients at different times of the workflow lifecycle. In a *component model* (Armstrong et al., 1999; OMG, 2006), each service in the workflow would be aware of the subsequent service(s) "connected" to it and invoke the next service(s) once its invocation completes, thus acting as a client to the next service(s).

An invocation of a service by a client, be it a workflow engine, another service, or just a stand-alone client, can either be *synchronous* or *asynchronous.* In the former, the invocation request message is sent to the service and the client blocks until the response message, which may be a successful result or a fault, is returned by the service. In the latter, a request by the client returns an acknowledgement message synchronously (if the request was received successfully; otherwise, an exception), while the actual response from for the invocation arrives at a later time (i.e., in the form of a callback to the client).

All these paradigms are possible in the generalized workflow model we consider, and hence, the provenance model we describe is compatible to these, too. In the interest of space, we restrict our examples in this article to a *centralized workflow engine* that acts as an *asynchronous client* to the services, which we have found is a common use case.

Resource Naming and Unique IDs

One fundamental requirement of provenance is the ability to uniquely identify the data products whose provenance is being described, as well as the services that use or generate these data products. This is driven by the fact that the service and the data products are distributed across organizational and geographical boundaries, and also by the fact that the provenance needs to be preserved for a period longer than the lifetime of the services or the workflows themselves. All resources that participate on our workflow model, including running or completed workflow instances, service instances, and data products, are assigned a globally unique identifier (GUID). These are referred to as *Workflow ID*, *Service ID*, and *Data Product ID*, respectively. It is possible to transparently map from these logical IDs to the actual physical resources, which may be an endpoint reference or a data URL, through a naming service. Use of such logical handles to resources instead of physical addresses makes the provenance independent of the data product representation since they are identified by just an ID, which could equally well point to a remote file, a database tuple, or a virtual collection. The format of the GUID does not matter as long as its uniqueness is guaranteed. Another identifier that is assigned to services in the context of a composed workflow is the *Workflow Node ID*. This ID is distinct for every service (node) in an abstract workflow. It differs from the Service ID in that late binding of workflows allows them to use different service instances for the same node when invoked in different iterations.

PROVENANCE ACTIVITIES

Provenance is collected during the lifecycle of the generalized workflow model in the form of discrete activities that are expressed using an *activity* object. These activity objects are generated by the services and clients that participate in the workflow during a service invocation, and are distributed over *time*, *space*, *depth*, and *type of operation*. Some of these activities define the boundaries of the invocation, while others describe the operation being performed. These provenance activity objects sufficiently describe the workflow execution and the dataflow to enable reconstruction of the workflow and data provenance graph exclusively from this runtime information without requiring access to the original workflow graph that was composed.

Activity Dimensions

The workflow model executes as a series of invocations over time that results in devolvement of control to different depths in the workflow execution, and within each invocation context, operations defined in the service implementation are performed. Activity objects can be distributed over several dimensions in the activity space, and certain attributes present in the activity object will help place the activity at the exact point in this space. This allows the activities to identify the invocation state and the operations that take place as part of the invocation unambiguously.

Starting with a client that initiates the workflow, control passes to the services in the workflow, and deeper still into nested workflows that these services may represent. The dimension of *depth* gives the distance of a service invocation from the root of the workflow graph, and holds for all activities generated by that service invocation. The depth comes out through the parent-child relationship between the workflow and the invoked service that is part of that workflow. The activity object contains the globally unique *Workflow ID* for the workflow that this service invocation is part of as well as the *Service ID* for the service. If this service invoked is itself another child workflow, the service invocations it performs would contain the Workflow ID of the child workflow as well as the service IDs of services invoked. These Workflow ID–Service ID pairs make it possible to determine the depth of an invocation in the workflow graph in a recursive manner.

Activities take place as discrete events ordered over time, and the logical time forms an additional dimension to distinguish between activities. A *logical timestamp* attribute present in the activity helps with temporal ordering of the activities, in addition to causal ordering that may be implicit. For example, during an invocation, the invocation started activity would have to appear before the invocation finished activity, and hence can be implicitly ordered, while activities that described several data products being generated by the invocation may have appeared in any order unless explicitly sequenced using a logical timestamp. Logical time is also necessary to order across service invocations, if there is no causality between them in the form of a dataflow from one to another. While a dataflow between all services is the norm in data-driven workflows, we presuppose a globally synchronized logical time to support non-dataflow workflows too.

The services and clients are distributed in *space*, and the workflow execution takes places across different services. The ability to identify the service instance through a globally unique ID helps distinguish between instances in space. Finally, the various *operations* that take place as part of the invocation, including dataflow operations that produce or consume a data product, are a separate dimension of the activity object. Depending on the type of operation, there may be additional attributes to fully describe them.

Activity Types

Bounding activities describe the interaction between two entities: the client invoking a service and the service being invoked. These activities are generated at the boundaries of the invocation, when an invocation request or response is being exchanged between the service and the client. For each request and response message, three activities are generated: two by the initiator of the message before and after sending it, and one by the receiver of the message upon receiving it. In the case of an invocation request message from the client to service, this includes the InvokingService activity before sending the request message to the service and the ServiceInvoked activity after the request message has been sent to the service. The service generates one ServiceInvoked activity upon receiving the request message. Similarly for the response sent by the service to the client, three activities are generated as shown in Table 1.

The activity objects that are generated contain several attributes that describe the activity's dimensions and uniquely identify the entities that participate in the interaction. The state of the client and service entities at the time of invocation is given by a set of attributes collectively referred to as the *entity ID*, which is a complex key consisting of {*Service ID*, *Workflow ID*, *Workflow Node ID*, *Logical Timestamp*}. The entity ID for a service requires the Service ID. If this service invocation is part of a workflow run, the entity ID additionally has the Workflow ID of that workflow, the Workflow Node ID of this service in that workflow, and logical timestamp of this invocation. If the client were itself another service, then it would have a similar entity ID that reflects its own state when initiating the invocation. Otherwise, the client would just identify itself through the Service ID attribute. Having both the client and service entity IDs present in the bounding activities serves two purposes: (1) it allows the client and service to present their individual views of the invocation information so that any conflicting views can be detected; and (2) in the absence of activities generated by either the client or the service, it provides the minimum, although one-sided, information required to reconstruct the invocation chain.

Operation activities describe the tasks that take place within a service invocation and occur between the bounding activities. The operations that take place depend on the type of service. However, for a data-driven workflow, two operations that are guaranteed to take place and are of interest to prov-

Table 1. List of provenance activities, the source of the activity, and the attributes present in each. The activities are listed in the order in which they are typically generated. Attributes that are underlined are required. Those in italics are complex attributes composed of those in curly braces. A '+' after an attribute represents an array, while a choice is denoted by a '|'.

Activity	Generated By	Attributes NOTE: Timestamp, Description, and Annotation are common to all activities
ServiceInitialized	Service	Service ID, is Workflow
ServiceTerminated	Service	Service ID
InvokingService	Client	*Client Entity ID* {Service ID, Workflow ID, Workflow Node ID, Logical Timestamp}, *Service Entity ID* {Service ID, Workflow ID, Workflow Node ID, Logical Timestamp}, Request Message
ServiceInvoked	Service	*Service Entity ID* {Service ID, Workflow ID, Workflow Node ID, Logical Timestamp}, *Client Entity ID* {Service ID, Workflow ID, Workflow Node ID, Logical Timestamp}, Request Message
InvokingService [Succeeded | Failed]	Client	*Client Entity ID* {Service ID, Workflow ID, Workflow Node ID, Logical Timestamp}, *Service Entity ID* {Service ID, Workflow ID, Workflow Node ID, Logical Timestamp}, [— | Failure Trace]
DataTransfer	Service	*Service Entity ID* {Service ID, Workflow ID, Workflow Node ID, Logical Timestamp}, Data ID, Source URL, Target URL, Size, Duration
Computation	Service	*Service Entity ID* {Service ID, Workflow ID, Workflow Node ID, Logical Timestamp}, Application, Duration
DataProduced	Service	*Service Entity ID* {Service ID, Workflow ID, Workflow Node ID, Logical Timestamp}, *Data Product*+ {Data ID, URL+, Size, Timestamp}
DataConsumed	Service	*Service Entity ID* {Service ID, Workflow ID, Workflow Node ID, Logical Timestamp}, *Data Product*+ {Data ID, URL+, Size, Timestamp}
SendingResponse	Service	*Service Entity ID* {Service ID, Workflow ID, Workflow Node ID, Logical Timestamp}, *Client Entity ID* {Service ID, Workflow ID, Workflow Node ID, Logical Timestamp}, Response Message {Result | Fault}
ReceivedResponse	Client	*Client Entity ID* {Service ID, Workflow ID, Workflow Node ID, Logical Timestamp}, *Service Entity ID* {Service ID, Workflow ID, Workflow Node ID, Logical Timestamp}, Response Message {Result | Fault}
SendingResponse [Succeeded | Failed]	Service	*Service Entity ID* {Service ID, Workflow ID, Workflow Node ID, Logical Timestamp}, *Client Entity ID* {Service ID, Workflow ID, Workflow Node ID, Logical Timestamp}, [— | Failure Trace]

enance are the consumption and production of data products. When a service uses a data product in an invocation, the service is said to have consumed the data product, and it generates a DataConsumed activity. When a service creates a new data product during the course of an invocation, it generates a DataProduced activity. These consumed and produced data products may or may not have been passed as parameters in the request or response messages sent to/from the service. Other than the entity ID of the service and client, these activities contain the Data Product ID of the data that were produced or consumed as attribute. In addition to these *dataflow* operations, two other operations that usually take place in scientific workflows are data transfer and computation. We define these two additional activities given the nature of the e-Science project for which Karma was designed. The operation activities and their attributes are listed in Table 1.

Example

The set of activities generated by a service invocation or a workflow changes with the pattern of execution. For example, a service could be invoked synchronously or asynchronously, and a workflow can be invoked by a workflow engine or enact as components in a dataflow. We present two examples of service and workflow execution with corresponding provenance activities generated for them plotted as a sequence diagram.

Figure 2(a) shows a client invoking a service, passing data product D1 as input and receiving D2 as output. This invocation can take place synchronously or asynchronously, and the sequence diagram for each of these styles of execution is shown in Figure 2(b) and 2(c), respectively. The diagrams show the transfer of control from the client to the service at different points in the invocation over *time*, shown in the Y Axis. The activities produced at each state are marked with a red circle, and the type of activity is in the left column. The center column shows the distribution of the client and service entities over *space* and their *depth*. Since this case has just two levels of depth—the client and the service—the depth shown on the top X axis moves from the solid line to the dotted line. The spatial location of the entity, shown on the lower X axis, varies with each unique entity. The vertical lines in the right column represent various *operations* the service performs during its invocation.

In the synchronous invocation shown in Figure 2(b), once the service is started and generates the ServiceInitialized activity, the client invokes the service. The client generates an InvokeService activity and then calls the service, and control passes to the service. The service generates the ServiceInvoked activity and starts the execution. This involves transferring the input data D1 (DataTransfer), using the data product (DataConsumed) in a computation or application (Computation), producing the output data product D2 (DataProduced), and staging the output to a remote location (DataTransfer). When the service operations are complete, the service generates the SendingResponse activity before returning control and the result to the client. The client, upon receipt of the response, generates the ReceivedResponse activity. The service can then terminate at a later point in time after generating the ServiceTerminate activity.

The asynchronous call shown in Figure 2(c) is similar but has two variations. After receiving the asynchronous request, the client does not block and receives control in parallel to the service execution (as shown by the dotted arrow). When the request has been sent successfully by the client, it generates the InvokingServiceSucceeded activity. Likewise, after the service returns the response to the client, it gets back control in parallel to the client and generates a SendingResponseSuccess activity. This three-phase protocol is necessary in order to track the fact that the invocation cycle was successful, since either of the sending request or receiving response steps could potentially fail.

A more complex scenario is shown in Figure 3(a), where a nested workflow executes. Workflow WF1 consists of two services—S1 and WF2—where service WF2 is another workflow. WF2, in turn, comprises two services—S2 and S3—that are connected. All the services take in one data product as input and generate another data product as output, which is used by the subsequent service. The sequence diagram in Figure 3(b) shows an asynchronous execution of the workflow when orchestrated by a separate workflow engine for each workflow. Before the workflow executes, services (including the workflows) are initialized, generating ServiceInitialized activities. A client (not shown in the figure) initiates the workflow and control passed to the workflow (engine) WF1. The sequence diagram starts from this stage. The workflow WF1 starts executing by invoking the first service in the workflow, S1, with input parameter data product D1. Since WF1 acts as the client to S1, it generates InvokingService and InvokingServiceSuccess activities before and after calling S1. Service S1 generates ServiceInvoked activity

Figure 2a. Client invoking a service, passing data product D1 as input and receiving D2 as output

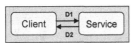

Figure 2b. Sequence diagram of a synchronous invocation of Figure 2a

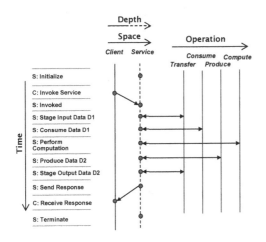

Figure 2c. Sequence diagram of an asynchronous invocation of Figure 2a

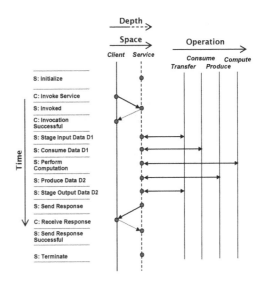

after being invoked by WF1. The service performs operations such as consuming and producing data products (DataConsumed and DataProduced), computation and file transfers (not shown). When execution completes, S1 asynchronously returns the response message to the workflow WF1, in the process generating SendingResponse and SendingResponseSuccess activities. WF1 receives the response for the invocation and generates the ReceivedResponse activity.

WF1 then invokes service WF2, which is next in the workflow sequence. Although WF2 is actually a workflow, WF1 interacts with it just as with any other service, generating the same activities as a service client; namely, InvokingService, InvokingServiceSuccess, and ReceivedResponse. WF2, upon receiving the invocation, executes the workflow as if it received an invocation from a client, and proceeds to invoke services S2 and S3. These generate the usual activities as seen before. When these services return, the final response from S3 is returned by workflow WF2 to workflow WF1, its client. Workflow WF1 then continues to completion.

PROVENANCE MODEL

The provenance model describes the structure of the provenance metadata exposed by Karma (Simmhan, Plale & Gannon, 2007). It is an aggregation of the various facets portrayed by the provenance activi-

Figure 3a. Nested workflow. The root workflow WF1 contains two services—S1 and WF2—where the latter is another workflow that is nested. WF2, in turn, has two services—S2 and S3. All services and workflows produce and consume one data product each.

Figure 3b. Sequence diagram for nested workflow in Figure 3a

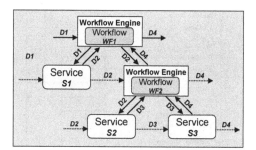

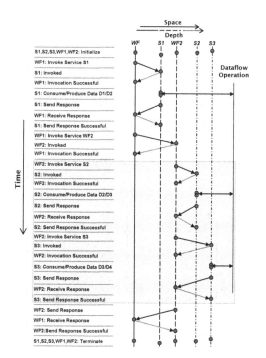

ties, and this information model forms the basis for querying over and exporting of provenance. The model describes two primary types of provenance: one centered on service invocations, called *process provenance*; and the other relating to data usage and generation, termed *data provenance*. These two concepts are complementary in that process provenance describes service invocations and makes a reference to the input and output data products to the invocation, while data provenance describes the data product and makes references to services that use it and the invocation that created it. They provide two different views over the global provenance information available from the activities.

Process Provenance

Process provenance describes the execution of a single process, which translates to an invocation of a service instance by a client. The process provenance information model, shown in Figure 4, identifies the service that was invoked and the client that invoked the service using the entity IDs described in the activities. These comprise the relevant attributes from Service ID, the Workflow ID, Workflow Node ID, and the Logical Timestamp of the service and the client at the time of invocation. It also contains attributes such as the actual timestamp of the invocation, the status of the invocation, and optionally, the messages that were exchanged by the entities. The process provenance also references the data products that were used by the invocation and that the invocation created. The data products are identified by their unique data product ID along with optional attributes describing the location of the data and the timestamp of their generation or use. When this model is seen against the activities listed in Table 1 and the database model that will be described (Figure 10), it is apparent that the activities act as building blocks for constructing the provenance model.

While process provenance describes a single service invocation, the complete workflow run is captured by the *workflow trace* shown in Figure 5. The workflow trace is a coarser degree of abstraction of the provenance and includes zero or more records of process provenance relating to service invocations that were part of the workflow execution. In addition to the service invocation steps, workflow traces can also recursively refer to other workflow traces in the case of hierarchically composed workflows. The depth of recursion is configurable, allowing an arbitrary level of granularity at which process provenance can be viewed.

Data Provenance

Data provenance describes the derivation path of a data product as the service invocation that created the data product and the inputs to the invocation. Figure 6 shows the data provenance model where the data is identified by the unique data product ID and produced by an invocation. The invocation comprises a service entity being invoked by a client entity using zero or more data products as inputs to the data. The invocation attributes are similar to those for the process provenance record seen earlier; likewise the attributes for the data products.

Data provenance is, by default, the immediate data derivation history—the service invocation that directly created this data. A recursive form of data provenance, analogous to the workflow trace, is the deep or *recursive data provenance* (Cohen-Boulakia, Cohen & Davidson, 2007) shown in Figure 7. Deep data provenance recursively tracks the data provenance for the inputs to the invocation up to an arbitrary depth. This can be used to build the complete historical record of the ancestral data and invocations that caused this data to be derived.

Data provenance looks back in time on the derivation chain. A similar model can be constructed when moving forward in time and tracking the usage of a data product in various invocations. The *data usage* model, shown in Figure 8, describes the service invocations that use a certain data product as their input. The invocations are described by the service invoked and its client, while the data are identified by the data product ID and optional locations and timestamp of when it was used.

Figure 4. Process provenance model

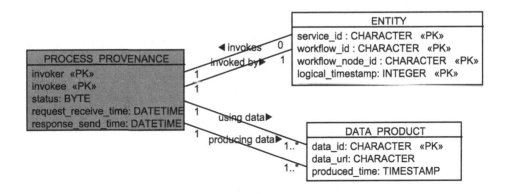

Figure 5. Workflow trace model

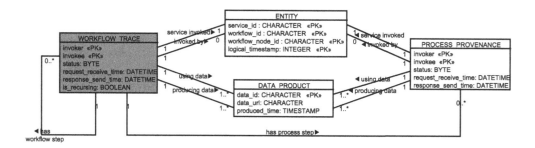

The various forms of process and data provenance are graph structures. The workflow trace consists of service invocation nodes and data product edges, with the process provenance records forming an edge-node-edge subgraph. Similarly, the data provenance and data usage have data products as nodes and service invocations as edges.

IMPLEMENTATION

The *Karma framework* implementation in the above provenance model consists of a focal Web service to collect provenance activities and query over the provenance model, client libraries to generate the provenance activities, and graphical interfaces to visualize the provenance graphs and monitor workflow execution (Figure 9). Provenance activities are modeled as XML documents whose schema maps to activity attributes. The clients and services participating in a service or workflow execution can use the provided *workflow tracking* client library to generate the provenance activity documents shown in Table 1. The Java library maintains the state information for the service or client during the invocation and fills in the relevant entity ID fields for all activities once they are initially specified. It provides a simple API, akin to logging tools, for clients and services to populate the activity attributes for the bounding and operation activities. When the services being executed are Web services, Karma also provides a SOAP library that can encode the entity ID information of the client and service in the SOAP header of the request and response messages, to allow transparent exchange of client and service state information that each need in order to fill in the activities they produce. This allows existing Web services to generate provenance activities without having to change the WSDL definition for the Web service.

The provenance service provides a Web service interface for services and clients in the workflow in order to submit the provenance activities they generate. In addition to a synchronous submission of the activities, the implementation also allows an asynchronous publishing of activities as notifications that the provenance service subscribes to. The provenance service shreds the XML provenance activities and stores them in a relational database. This then can be queried through the Web service API that provides methods to retrieve each of the five provenance models described earlier through their IDs.

Publishing Activities as Notifications

A *Publish-Subscribe* (or Pub-Sub) notification protocol is a unidirectional, asynchronous communication between publishers and consumers that communicates by means of "channels" or "topics." Consumers,

Figure 6. Data provenance model

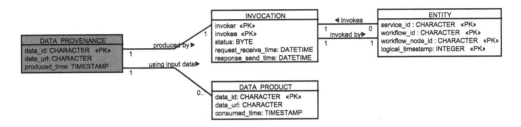

Figure 7. Recursive data provenance model

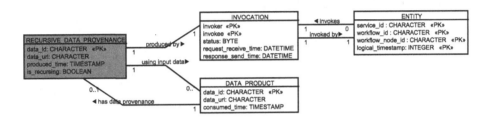

Figure 8. Data usage model

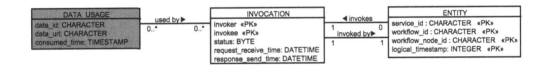

decoupled in space from the publisher, receive events by subscribing to one or more topics (Eugster, Felber, Guerraoui & Kermarrec, 2003).

A notification protocol is a good choice for publishing provenance activities from the workflows, services, and clients, since provenance gathering can be done without perturbing the publishers and can be collected independent of the provenance service location. *Time decoupling* (Eugster et al., 2003), whereby the listeners need not be active when the notification is published, puts less stringent requirements on the availability of the provenance service. Archival or message-box facilities present in many notification brokers remove the onus from workflow components in ensuring reliable delivery of activity messages. Since provenance is more often used for mining and analysis post workflow execution than for runtime monitoring of the workflow, users are tolerant to delayed receipt of activities at the provenance service. Pub-sub is a mature field with several open-source and commercial implementations, and many open standards such as JMS and WS-Eventing (Box et al., 2004), which aid interoperability when collecting provenance across different domains, as is common in Grid systems.

A representative notification service is *WS-Messenger* (Huang, Slominski, Herath & Gannon, 2006), which uses a topic-based, publish-subscribe system based on the WS-Eventing standard (Box et al.,

Figure 9. Interaction between karma provenance service and workflow

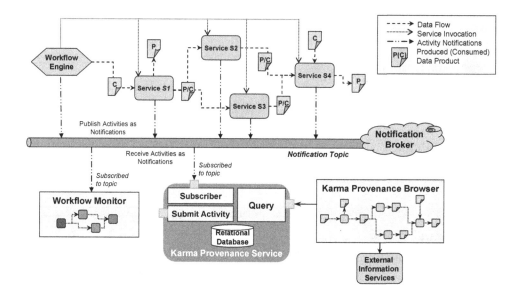

2004). WS-Messenger contains four main components relevant to Karma: the *notification publisher*, the *notification consumer*, the *notification broker*, and the *message box*. The notification publisher generates notifications that are published to a topic at the notification broker. The broker, a Web service, provides a topic-based subscription interface and routes notifications published to a certain topic to the registered listeners. Notifications consumers are Web services that subscribe with the broker for notifications and receive them via a standard Web service interface they implement. For listeners that lie behind a firewall or that would like to have notifications buffered for them, a message box service can act as a proxy and subscribe to the broker on the listener's behalf. The listeners periodically retrieve the notification from the message box, which provides a means to persist the notification for reliable delivery.

For each workflow execution, a unique notification topic is created with the notification broker. All components in the workflow and its clients use the same broker and topic to publish their notifications. This allows listeners interested in only notifications from a certain workflow execution, such as a workflow monitor, to listen to just that topic. The broker allows wildcard or "*" subscriptions, and the provenance service uses this feature to subscribe to all provenance activity notifications that are generated from all workflows that use that broker.

Database Model

The Karma provenance service uses a relational database to store the activities it receives for a workflow execution as notifications or directly submitted through the Web service API. The database schema is shown in Figure 10 (Simmhan et al., 2007). As XML activities arrive, the provenance service extracts the relevant attributes from them and creates or updates the tables in the database. The tables closely resemble the provenance data model with entities described in the *entity table* and the *invocation table* referencing client and service entity pairs along with the state of the invocation. Data products present in

Figure 10. Relational Database model for storing provenance (Simmhan, 2007)

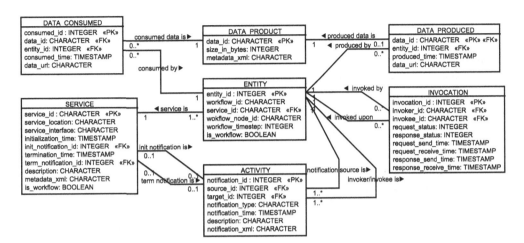

the *data product table* are consumed and produced by the invocations as captured by the *data produced* and *consumed tables* that relate the two. A separate *service table* is present to record information about the service instances, such as their initialization and termination times, and possibly their WSDL in the case of Web services. An additional *activity table* keeps a log of all activities that were used to populate the tables. This forms a provenance or audit trail about the provenance itself in case the provenance needs to be verified in the future. It should also be noted that provenance is immutable and is only appended to over time as new activities take place (e.g., when a service invocation changes from an invoked state to invocation complete state). Once all activities relating to an invocation have been received, its process provenance and the data provenance for data products created by the invocation are static.

Mapping the provenance model to a relational database helps to keep the implementation compatible with a different representation of the activities or of the provenance graphs. Any other transport mechanism or metadata representation besides XML can be used to gather the activities, as long as all attributes for each activity are present. These will require simple conversions from the activity's format to the database/provenance model. Similarly, the provenance graphs can be exported in formats other than the present XML schema, as may be required by visualization applications (Brandes, Eiglsperger, Herman, Himsolt & Marshall, 2002). Efforts are emerging to standardize provenance representation (Moreau & Ludascher, 2007); our approach allows us to interoperate with any future provenance standard that follows the broad principles of provenance being recorded as a causal graph. The availability of mature relational databases also allows for an efficient implementation of the provenance service, which gives superior performance for activity updates and provenance queries as is further described in the following section.

Provenance Queries

The Karma provenance service provides APIs to query over the provenance model and returns the various provenance graphs using an XML representation. The XML schema for each of the five types of provenance graphs maps to the information model for each provenance graph, as shown in Figures 4–8. The query API has a method for each of the five provenance graphs; namely, process provenance, workflow trace, data provenance, recursive data provenance, and data usage. In order to retrieve the process provenance or workflow trace, the entity ID (i.e., the set of Service ID, Workflow ID, Workflow Node ID, Logical Timestamp) of the client invoking the service or workflow, along with the entity ID of the service or workflow being invoked, is passed as parameter. In the case of workflow trace, an additional parameter is specified on how deep the workflow trace should recurse in case the workflow contains nested workflows. The methods return the process provenance and workflow trace graphs as XML documents. The immediate and deep data provenance and data usage methods take a data product ID as input parameter. The recursive data provenance also takes the depth into which the ancestral provenance needs to be recursed. The immediate data provenance is equivalent to invoking the recursive data provenance with the recursion factor set to 0. These return the data provenance and usage graphs as XML documents. These basic query APIs can be used as building blocks to construct and perform more complex queries, as was shown in our entry at the First Provenance Workshop (Moreau & Ludascher, 2007).

In Karma, the provenance graph is constructed natively in the service, unlike other provenance collection approaches that require external means for doing so (Groth, Luck & Moreau, 2004). The algorithm for constructing the provenance graphs from a series of provenance activities is similar to an algorithm used to construct a graph, given the set of node-edge pairs that comprise the graph. For example, in the case of process provenance, the *entity table* is looked up for the client and the service entity IDs that correspond to the provided Service ID, Workflow ID, Workflow Node ID, and Logical Timestamp for the client and the service. From these two entity IDs, the invocation in the *invocation table* is identified. The invocation ID also leads to the data produced and consumed by that invocation, available through the *data produced* and *consumed tables*. Further details about the data products are retrieved from the *data product table*, while further information about the service is present in the *service table*. These fields are sufficient to populate the process provenance model in the result. In the case of workflow trace, this step is repeated for all service invocations whose Workflow IDs match the workflow. In the case of data provenance or data usage, the procedure is similar, but the starting point is the *data produced* or *consumed tables* instead of the *entity table*. The immutability property of provenance also can be used to cache the results of building the provenance graph and reuse it, provided additional activities have not been appended to the provenance document since its construction.

Provenance Dissemination

The *Karma* provenance service's query interface can be invoked by any Web service client in order to retrieve data and workflow provenance in XML. The *Karma Provenance Browser* is a graphical tool that uses the provenance service API to integrate provenance metadata with additional metadata on the services, workflows, and data products available from external information catalogs such as service registries or metadata catalogs found in the LEAD Project (Simmhan et al., 2006a). Provenance acts as a glue to relate the services with the data products but does not include complete metadata describing the service or the data product. The browser can retrieve and visualize the provenance graph for, say, a given Workflow ID, and users can select services and data products within that workflow and retrieve metadata about them from the external catalogs. The browser also allows seamless navigation from a workflow graph to a data provenance graph or data usage graph for data products in that workflow, allowing users to jump across provenances from different workflow executions or view the graph from data or service perspectives.

The XBaya workflow monitor GUI (Shirasuna & Gannon, 2006) is another tool that allows users with access to the original workflow document to monitor the progress of the workflow execution by listening to the provenance activities sent as notifications. The monitor supports BPEL workflows and also acts as a workflow composer interface. So users can compose a workflow visually using XBaya, launch the workflow, and later use the same workflow graph to monitor it within XBaya at runtime. The workflow monitor subscribes to the notification topic for that workflow and updates the status of the different components in the composed workflow graph as it receives the provenance activity. Since activities are directly delivered as notifications to the monitor by the notification broker, this obviates the need to access the provenance service for the workflow status and makes the monitoring more realtime. We are additionally exploring the use of workflow provenance available from the provenance service to perform visual replays of the workflow execution in the workflow monitor GUI.

PERFORMANCE EVALUATION

Provenance collection incurs a cost. We quantify the overhead using the sample weather forecasting workflow given in Section 2, a workflow that exemplifies the data-driven applications in LEAD. More detailed experiments on the provenance system, both for collecting provenance as well as to query the provenance records, have been performed and are available through a separate publication (Simmhan, Plale, Gannon & Marru, 2006c). The workflow of Section 2 performs weather prediction for a 183x163 spatial domain with 53 vertical levels and 9-km grid spacing around the center at 28.5°N and −87.0°E. The experiment is initialized with observational data at 1200 Hours UTC on August 28, 2005, and simulates the weather for the next 37 hours, tracking Hurricane Katrina's landfall on the Gulf Coast. The output of the simulation model is analyzed and visualized by generating animations.

The eight services in the workflow are invoked sequentially to collect execution times for each application invocation. The service's execution time includes staging times for input and output files, the wall clock time of the computation, and the provenance overhead. The first four preprocessing and interpolation applications, and the last two postprocessing and visualization applications are executed on a Linux workstation with dual-Xeon 3 GHz processors, 2GB memory, and a Gbps Ethernet network. The WRF forecasting model and WRF2ARPS postprocessor are executed using 32 and 8 processors, respectively, on an Itanium2 1.3GHz Linux cluster with 6GB memory linked by Myrinet network and connected to a 10GB external network. The WS-Messenger notification broker runs on a Solaris workstation with dual-Sparc 1.2GHz processor, 4GB memory, and a 1Gbps Ethernet network. The *Karma* provenance service runs on a Windows XP workstation with P4 2GHz processor, 1.5GB memory, and 100Mbps Ethernet.

The bar graph in Figure 11 shows the cumulative time taken by the services in the workflow, with and without generating provenance notifications. As seen from the bars on the far right, the time taken for the entire workflow to finish is 2,834 secs when the services generate provenance notifications, and 2,809 secs when they do not. This translates to a total overhead of about 0.8% of execution time for the forecasting workflow, which is a very small overhead. Currently, the overhead percentage depends upon the number of activities generated in each script. Since the number of bounding activities for a service invocation is constant, the number of activities generated is closely tied to the number of operation activities; in particular, the number of data produced, and consumed activities are generated since those are liable to number higher. We have initial results from batching data –produced and –consumed

Figure 11. (a) [Bar Graph, Left Y Axis] Cumulative execution time, with and without provenance, for applications in workflow; (b) [Line Graph, Right Y Axis] Provenance overhead for individual applications in workflow. Σ(script provenance overhead) = 26s ≅ (total time w/ provenance – total time w/o provenance)=25s

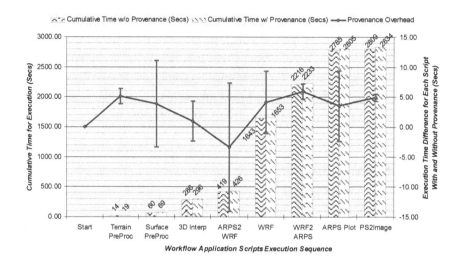

activities in the XML activity representation that circumvent this problem to achieve near constant time overhead. Each of the applications produces and consumes between 11 and 61 files each, ranging in size from 55MB to 3.5GB, for a total of 147 files consumed and 124 files produced. This corresponds to a total of 271 dataflow activities, the small number of bounding activities from the workflow, and services. These figures are typical of data-driven scientific workflows in the meteorology domain, and the provenance overhead is bound to be similarly small.

The line graph on the right Y axis in Figure 11 shows the additional time taken by each application due to publishing provenance notifications. The vertical lines mark the standard error of the mean time at each data point due to variations in the measurement caused by I/O wait times and system processes. Ignoring data points with large standard errors, we see that the overhead time for each application is in the range of 1 to 6 seconds. This is quite low, considering the normal execution time for LEAD applications is between 10s of seconds to several hours.

A separate and more detailed study (Simmhan et al., 2006c) has shown comparable results. A simulated ensemble workflow with nine services, which included a four-way parallel service invocation that iterated 10 times, has an overhead of about 70 seconds for collecting the provenance activities. That workflow has 63 service invocations and involved 2,400 data products; a real execution of the workflow would have taken several hours to complete. Hence, the relative overhead of provenance collection is minor. Those tests also show that the provenance system scaled with the number of parallel workflows, taking linear or sublinear time as the number of simultaneous workflows increase. The response time for querying provenance was equally low in that study, taking less than one second for querying individual provenance graphs and showing linear increase in query response time as the query selectivity or the number of parallel clients increases.

RELATED WORK

A synthesis of requirements for an effective and usable provenance system for scientific workflows should, in broad terms, require it to (1) provide an open and interoperable interface to collect provenance, (2) track workflow and data provenance within a virtual organization independent of workflow models and data formats, and (3) minimize performance overheads and modifications required of workflow components. While systems and techniques to collect provenance in scientific workflows exist, they fall short of these needs. Workflow environments such as the Virtual Data Grid (Foster, Vöckler, Wilde & Zhao, 2003), myGrid (Zhao et al., 2004), and GridDB (Liu et al., 2005) provide the capability to record provenance but are tightly integrated with their workflow execution environment and do not provide interoperable means for collecting and using provenance. Earth System Sciences Workbench (ESSW) (Bose & Frew, 2004) collects lineage as simple parent-child links between services and files, but recording provenance is tightly coupled to its lineage database, and lack of support for logical data products hinders tracking data across the virtual organization. Provenance Aware Service Oriented Architecture (PASOA) (Groth et al., 2004; Groth, Miles, Fang, Wong, Zauner & Moreau, 2005) defines an open protocol for recording provenance through a set of messages exchanged between service invocation actors and a provenance server. While recording the in-wire service requests and responses allows PASOA to track workflow provenance in a nonrepudiable manner, users have to extend the provided schema in order to track data products used in the invocations, and native support to build provenance graphs is absent. Workflow tracing tools such as IBM Data Collector (IBM, 2005) log request-response messages for Web service calls that can be can be correlated and visualized, but this is limited to workflow provenance and not data provenance. Distributed logging tools like Net Logger (Gunter, Tierney, Jackson, Lee & Stoufer, 2002) that provide generic logging support for distributed applications lack the higher level abstractions necessary for a service-oriented architecture. Instrumentation and performance analysis systems like svPablo (de Rose & Reed, 1999) and AutoPilot (Ribler, Vetter, Simitci & Reed, 1998) are oriented toward realtime monitoring of distributed applications in order to tune application performance and optimize resource allocation, but they do not help with holistic tracking of the dataflow and workflow execution.

Surveys on provenance systems include a metamodel for a systems architecture for lineage retrieval (Bose & Frew, 2005), present a taxonomy of approaches taken toward building provenance systems (Simmhan et al., 2005), and exemplify use cases for a provenance system in biology (Miles, Groth, Branco & Moreau, 2005). Several workshops on this topic (Bose, Foster & Moreau, 2006; Moreau & Foster, 2006), including a recent provenance challenge workshop (Moreau & Ludascher, 2007), have shown an active interest emerging in this field in the e-Science domain.

CONCLUSION AND FUTURE WORK

In this article, we have identified challenges involved in collecting provenance—both data and workflow provenance—for data-driven applications. The Karma provenance framework we propose provides a generic solution for collecting provenance for heterogeneous workflow environments and independent of the workflow orchestration model or service invocation style. Indeed, it is not specific to Web service-based workflows alone, and we have examples of it being used by workflows composed of Jython scripts. The activity model is compatible with a publish-subscribe paradigm that provides a ubiquitous means for interoperable collection of provenance; we leverage this to implement provenance collection with low perturbation. Use of the WS–Eventing standard allows the choice of the most suitable pub-sub implementation for the domain. In addition, users also have the capability to directly submit provenance activities without the requirement to publish them as notifications. The user involvement is limited to instrumenting the workflow components to generate the provenance notifications. This is similar to logging information that workflows usually generate for debugging, and the libraries we provide alleviate the burden on the service providers. We also have toolkits to automatically create services from an XML description of an application that already comes instrumented to collect provenance, completely doing away with user overhead (Kandaswamy, Fang, Huang, Shirasuna, Marru & Gannon, 2006). This toolkit is widely used in the LEAD project. Our evaluation of the framework implementation also shows that provenance collection can be done with minimal performance overhead on the workflow, on the order of 1% of the execution time for 271 files used. More comprehensive tests support these numbers and provide equally favorable performance figures for querying for provenance (Simmhan et al., 2006c).

The framework described here is the basis for our ongoing research in the use of provenance to automatically determine data product quality based on user-guided metrics and through collaborative feedback on the products and services participating in the data provenance (Simmhan et al., 2006b). Long-running workflows increase the probability of incomplete provenance. Using this information effectively is an area under investigation, as is handling missing activities and undelivered notifications, possibly using WS-Reliable Messaging (Pallickara, Fox, Yildiz, Pallickara, Patel & Yemme, 2005). Also of interest are data products that appear in collections that are themselves data products. Provenance for the collection data products and for individual data products within them needs to be tracked without breaking the transparency offered by uniform naming. Provenance collected over time serves as a promising resource for mining and detecting patterns that can assist in anything from workflow completion tools to automated resource scheduling.

ACKNOWLEDGMENT

This work is supported in part by NSF cooperative agreement ATM-0331480 and NSF grant EIA-0202048. The authors would like to thank the members of the LEAD project for their active support in this work; in particular, Marcus Christie, Yi Huang, Suresh Marru, Srinath Perera, Satoshi Shirasuna, and Aleksander Slominski.

REFERENCES

Armstrong, R., et al. (1999). Toward a common component architecture for high-performance scientific computing. *HPDC*.

BEA Systems, IBM Corporation, Microsoft Corporation, SAP AG, & Siebel Systems (2003). Business process execution language for Web services (BPEL 1.1). *Technical Report*.

Bose, R., & Frew, J. (2004). Composing lineage metadata with XML for custom satellite-derived data products. *SSDBM*.

Bose, R., & Frew, J. (2005). Lineage retrieval for scientific data processing: A survey. *ACM Computing Surveys, 37,* 1–28.

Bose, R., Foster, I., & Moreau. L. (2006). Report on the international provenance and annotation workshop. *SIGMOD Record, 35*(3), 51–53.

Box, D., et al. (2004). Web services eventing (WS-eventing). *Technical Report.*

Brandes, U., Eiglsperger, M., Herman, I., Himsolt, M., & Marshall, M.S. (2002). GraphML progress report: Structural layer proposal. *LNCS, 2265,* 501–512.

Catlett, C. (2002). The TeraGrid: A primer. Retrieved from www.teragrid.org

Churches, D., et al. (2006). Programming scientific and distributed workflow with Triana Services. *Concurrency and Computation: Practice and Experience, 18*(10), 1021–1037.

Cohen-Boulakia, S., Cohen, S., & Davidson, S. (2007). Addressing the provenance challenge using zoom. *Concurrency and Control: Practice and Experience.*

de Rose, L.A., & Reed, D.A. (1999). SvPablo: A multi-language architecture-independent performance analysis system. *ICPP.*

Droegemeier, K.K., et al. (2005). Service-oriented environments for dynamically interacting with mesoscale weather. *Computing in Science and Engineering, 7*(6), 12–29.

Eugster, P.T., Felber, P.A., Guerraoui, R., & Kermarrec, A.M. (2003). The many faces of publish/subscribe. *ACM Computing Surveys, 35,* 114–131.

Foster, I., Kesselman, C., Nick, J., & Tuecke S. (2002). The physiology of the grid: An open grid services architecture for distributed systems integration. *Global Grid Forum.*

Foster, I.T., Vöckler, J., Wilde, M., & Zhao, Y. (2003). The virtual data grid: A new model and architecture for data-intensive collaboration. *CIDR.*

Gannon, D., et al. (2005). Service oriented architectures for science gateways on grid systems. *ICSOC.*

Goble, C. (2002). Position statement: Musings on provenance, workflow and (semantic Web) annotations for bioinformatics. *Workshop on Data Derivation and Provenance.*

Greenwood, M., et al. (2003). Provenance of e-science experiments—experience from Bioinformatics. *UK OST e-Science 2nd AHM.*

Groth, P., Luck, M., & Moreau, L. (2004). A protocol for recording provenance in service-oriented grids. *OPODIS.*

Groth, P., Miles, S., Fang, W., Wong, S.C., Zauner, K.-P., & Moreau, L. (2005). Recording and using provenance in a protein compressibility experiment. *HPDC.*

Gunter, D., Tierney, B., Jackson, K., Lee, J., & Stoufer, M. (2002). Dynamic monitoring of high-performance distributed applications. *HPDC.*

Huang, Y., Slominski, A., Herath, C., & Gannon, D. (2006). WS-Messenger: A Web services based messaging system for service-oriented grid computing. *CCGrid*.

IBM (2005). Web services data collector. Retrieved from www.alphaworks.ibm.com/tech/wsdatacollector

Kandaswamy, G., Fang, L., Huang, Y., Shirasuna, S., Marru, S., & Gannon, D. (2006). Building Web services for scientific grid applications. *IBM Journal of Research and Development, 50*(2/3), 249–260.

Liu, D.T., Franklin, M.J., Garlick, J., & Abdulla, G.M. (2005). Scaling up data-centric middleware on a cluster computer. *Technical Report, Lawrence Livermore National Laboratory.*

Ludäscher, B., et al. (2006). Scientific workflow management and the Kepler system. *Concurrency and Computation: Practice and Experience, 18*(10), 1039–1065.

Miles, S., Groth, P., Branco, M., & Moreau, L. (2005). The requirements of recording and using provenance in e-science experiments. *Technical Report, Electronics and Computer Science, University of Southampton.*

Moreau, L., & Foster, I. (2006). *Provenance and annotation of data.* Proceedings of the International Provenance and Annotation Workshop, *LNCS* 4145.

Moreau, L., & Ludascher, B. (2007). The first provenance challenge. *Concurrency and Control: Practice and Experience.*

OMG (2006). CORBA component model v4.0. *Technical Report, OMG.*

Pallickara, S., Fox, G., Yildiz, B., Pallickara, S.L., Patel, S., & Yemme, D. (2005). On the costs for reliable messaging in Web/grid service environments. *e-Science.*

Plale, B. (2005). Resource requirements study for LEAD storage repository. *Technical Report 001, Linked Environments for Atmospheric Discovery.*

Ribler, R.L., Vetter, J.S., Simitci, H., & Reed, D.A. (1998). Autopilot: Adaptive control of distributed applications. *HPDC.*

Shirasuna, S., & Gannon, D. (2006). XBaya: A graphical workflow composer for the Web services architecture. *Technical Report 004, Linked Environments for Atmospheric Discovery.*

Simmhan, Y., Plale, B., & Gannon, D. (2005). A survey of data provenance in e-science. *SIGMOD Record, 34*(3), 31–36.

Simmhan, Y.L., Pallickara, S.L., Vijayakumar, N.N., & Plale, B. (2006a). *Data management in dynamic environment-driven computational science.* Proceedings of the IFIP Working Conference on Grid-Based Problem Solving Environments (WoCo9).

Simmhan, Y.L., Plale, B., & Gannon, D. (2006b). *Towards a quality model for effective data selection in collaboratories.* Proceedings of the IEEE Workflow and Data Flow for Scientific Applications (SciFlow) Workshop.

Simmhan, Y.L., Plale, B., & Gannon, D. (2007). Query capabilities of the Karma provenance framework. *Concurrency and Control: Practice and Experience.*

Simmhan, Y.L., Plale, B., Gannon, D., & Marru, S. (2006c). Performance evaluation of the Karma provenance framework for scientific workflows. *IPAW* and *LNCS* 4145.

Slominski, A. (2006). Adapting BPEL to scientific workflows. *Workflows for e-Science.*

Szomszor, M., & Moreau, L. (2003). Recording and reasoning over data provenance in Web and grid services. *ODBASE.*

West, K. (2005). Scoping out the planet. *Scientific American.*

Yu, J., & Buyya, R. (2005). A taxonomy of scientific workflow systems for grid computing. *SIGMOD Record, 34*(3), 44–49.

Zhao, J., Wroe, C., Goble, C.A., Stevens, R., Quan, D., & Greenwood, R.M. (2004). Using semantic Web technologies for representing e-science provenance. *ISWC.*

ENDNOTE

[1]   Based on work done at Indiana Univesity, USA.

This work was previously published in the International Journal of Web Services Research, edited by L. Zhang, Volume 5, Issue 2, pp. 1-22, copyright 2008 by IGI Publishing, formerly known as Idea Group Publishing (an imprint of IGI Global).

Chapter XXI
Ontology–Based Construction of Grid Data Mining Workflows

Peter Brezany
University of Vienna, Austria

Ivan Janciak
University of Vienna, Austria

A Min Tjoa
Vienna University of Technology, Austria

ABSTRACT

This chapter introduces an ontology-based framework for automated construction of complex interactive data mining workflows as a means of improving productivity of Grid-enabled data exploration systems. The authors first characterize existing manual and automated workflow composition approaches and then present their solution called GridMiner Assistant (GMA), which addresses the whole life cycle of the knowledge discovery process. GMA is specified in the OWL language and is being developed around a novel data mining ontology, which is based on concepts of industry standards like the predictive model markup language, cross industry standard process for data mining, and Java data mining API. The ontology introduces basic data mining concepts like data mining elements, tasks, services, and so forth. In addition, conceptual and implementation architectures of the framework are presented and its application to an example taken from the medical domain is illustrated. The authors hope that the further research and development of this framework can lead to productivity improvements, which can have significant impact on many real-life spheres. For example, it can be a crucial factor in achievement of scientific discoveries, optimal treatment of patients, productive decision making, cutting costs, and so forth.

INTRODUCTION

Grid computing is emerging as a key enabling infrastructure for a wide range of disciplines in science and engineering. Some of the hot topics in current Grid research include the issues associated with data mining and other analytical processes performed on large-scale data repositories integrated into the Grid. These processes are not implemented as monolithic codes. Instead, the standalone processing phases, implemented as Grid services, are combined to process data and extract knowledge patterns in various ways. They can now be viewed as complex workflows, which are highly interactive and may involve several subprocesses, such as data cleaning, data integration, data selection, modeling (applying a data mining algorithm), and postprocessing the mining results (e.g., visualization). The targeted workflows are often large, both in terms of the number of tasks in a given workflow and in terms of the total execution time. There are many possible choices concerning each process's functionality and parameters as well as the ways a process is combined into the workflow but only some combinations are valid. Moreover, users need to discover Grid resources and analytical services manually and schedule these services directly on the Grid resources essentially composing detailed workflow descriptions by hand. At present, only such a "low-productivity" working model is available to the users of the first generation data mining Grids, like **GridMiner** (Brezany et al., 2004) (a system developed by our research group), DiscoveryNet (Sairafi et al., 2003), and so forth. Productivity improvements can have significant impact on many real-life spheres, for example, it can be a crucial factor in achievement of scientific discoveries, optimal treatment of patients, productive decision making, cutting costs, and so forth. There is a stringent need for automatic or semiautomatic support for constructing valid and efficient data mining workflows on the Grid, and this (long-term) goal is associated with many research challenges.

The objective of this chapter is to present an ontology-based workflow construction framework reflecting the whole life cycle of the knowledge discovery process and explain the scientific rationale behind its design. We first introduce possible workflow composition approaches — we consider two main classes: (1) manual composition used by the current Grid data mining systems, for example, the GridMiner system, and (2) automated composition, which is addressed by our research and presented in this chapter. Then we relate these approaches to the work of others. The kernel part presents the whole framework built-up around a data mining ontology developed by us. This ontology is based on concepts reflecting the terms of several standards, namely, the predictive model markup language, cross industry process for data mining, and Java data mining API. The ontology is specified by means of OWL-S, a Web ontology language for services, and uses some concepts from Weka, a popular open source data mining toolkit. Further, conceptual and implementation architectures of the framework are discussed and illustrated by an application example taken from a medical domain. Based on the analysis of future and emerging trends and associated challenges, we discuss some future research directions followed by brief conclusions.

BACKGROUND

In the context of modern service-oriented Grid architectures, the data mining workflow can be seen as a collection of Grid services that are processed on distributed resources in a well-defined order to accomplish a larger and sophisticated data exploration goal. At the highest level, functions of Grid workflow management systems could be characterized into build-time functions and run-time functions. The build-time functions are concerned with defining and modeling workflow tasks and their dependencies while the run-time functions are concerned with managing the workflow execution and interactions with Grid resources for processing workflow applications. Users interact with workflow modeling tools to generate a workflow specification, which is submitted for execution to a run-time service called workflow enactment service, or *workflow engine*. Many languages, mostly based on XML, were defined for workflow description, like XLANG (Thatte, 2001), WSFL (Leymann, 2001), DSCL (Kickinger et al., 2003) and BPML (Arkin, 2002). Eventually the WSBPEL (Arkin et al., 2005) and BPEL4WS (BEA et al., 2003) specifications emerged as the de facto standard.

In our research, we consider two main workflow composition models: *manual* (implemented in the fully functional GridMiner prototype (Kickinger et al., 2003)) and *automated* (addressed in this chapter), as illustrated in Figure 1. Within manual composition, the user constructs the target workflow specification graphically in the workflow editor by means of the advanced graphical user interface. The graphical form is converted into a *workflow description* document, which is passed to the workflow engine. Based on the workflow description, the engine sequentially or in parallel calls the appropriate analytical services (database access, preprocessing, OLAP, classification, clustering, etc.). During the workflow execution, the user only has the ability to stop, inspect, resume, or cancel the execution. As a result, the user has limited abilities to interact with the workflow and influence the execution process. A similar approach was implemented in the DiscoveryNet (Sairafi et al., 2003) workflow management system.

The automated composition is based on an intensive support of five involved components: *workflow composer, resources monitoring, workflow engine, knowledge base,* and *reasoner*.

Figure 1. Workflow composition approaches

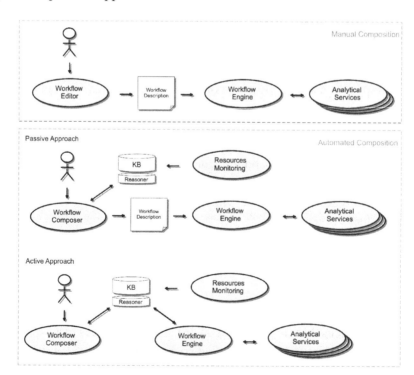

Workflow composer: Is a specialized tool, which interacts with a user during the workflow composition process. This chapter describes its functionality in detail.

Resources monitoring: Its main purpose is obtaining information concerning the utilization of system resources. Varieties of different systems exist for monitoring and managing distributed Grid-based resources and applications. For example, the monitoring and discovery system (MDS) is the information services component of the Globus Toolkit (Globus Alliance, 2005), which provides information about available resources on the Grid and their status. Moreover, MDS facilitates the discovery and characterization of resources and monitors services and computations. The information provided by resource monitoring can be continuously updated in the knowledge base (KB) to reflect the current status of the Grid resources.

Workflow engine: Is a runtime execution environment that performs the coordination of services as specified in the workflow description expressed in terms of a workflow language. The workflow engine is able to invoke and orchestrate the services and acts as their client, that is, listen to the notification messages, deliver outputs, and so forth.

Knowledge base (KB) and **reasoner:** A set of ontologies can be used for the specification of the KB structure, which is built-up using a set of instances of ontology classes and rules. The reasoner applies deductive reasoning about the stored knowledge in a logically consistent manner; it assures consistency of the ontology and answers given queries.

Due to different roles and behaviors of the presented components, we distinguish two modes of automated workflow composition: *passive* and *active*.

Passive Workflow Construction

The passive approach is based on the assumption that the *workflow composer* is able to compose a reasoning-based complete workflow description involving all possible scenarios of the workflow engine behavior and reflecting the status of the involved Grid resources and task parameters provided by the user at the workflow composition time. Although the KB is continuously modified by the user's entries and by information retrieved from the resource monitoring services, the composition of involved services is not updated during the workflow execution. Therefore, the composition does not reflect the 'state of the world,' which can be dynamically changed during the execution. It means that the workflow engine does not interact with the inference engine to reason about knowledge in the KB. Thus, the behavior of the engine (the decisions it takes) is steered by fixed condition statements as specified in the workflow document.

The essential tasks leading to a final outcome of the passive workflow composition approach can be summarized as follows:

1. The workflow composer constructs a complete workflow description based on the information collected in KB and presents it to the workflow engine in an appropriate workflow language.
2. The workflow engine executes each subsequent composition step as presented in the workflow description, which includes all possible scenarios of the engine behavior.

Active Workflow Construction

The active approach assumes a kind of intelligent behavior by the workflow engine supported by an inference engine and the related KB. Workflow composition is done in the same way as in the passive approach, but its usability is more efficient because it reflects a 'state of the world.' It means that the outputs and effects of the executed services are propagated to the KB together with changes of the involved Grid resources. Considering these changes, the workflow engine dynamically makes decisions about next execution steps. In this approach, no workflow document is needed because the workflow engine instructs itself using an inference engine which queries and updates the KB. The KB is queried each time the workflow engine needs information to invoke a consequent service, for example, it decides which concrete service should be executed, discovers the values of its input parameters in the KB, and so forth. The workflow engine also updates the KB when there is a new result returned from an analytical service that can be reused as input for the other services.

The essential tasks leading to a final outcome in active workflow composition approach can be summarized as follows:

1. The workflow composer constructs an abstract workflow description based on the information collected in the KB and propagates the workflow description back into the KB. The abstract workflow is not a detailed description of the particular steps in the workflow execution but instead a kind of path that leads to the demanded outcome.
2. The workflow engine executes each subsequent composition step as a result of its interaction with the KB reflecting its actual state. The workflow engine autonomously constructs directives for each service execution and adapts its behavior during the execution.

Related Work

A main focus of our work presented in this chapter is on the above mentioned passive approach of the automated workflow composition. This research was partially motivated by (Bernstein et al., 2001). They developed an intelligent discovery assistant (IDA), which provides users (data miners) with (1) systematic enumerations of valid data mining processes according to the constraints imposed by the users' inputs, the data, and/or the data mining ontology in order that important and potentially fruitful options are not overlooked, and (2) effective rankings of these valid processes by different criteria (e.g., speed and accuracy) to facilitate the choice of data mining processes to execute. The IDA performs a search of the space of processes defined by the ontology. Hence, no standard language for ontology specification and appropriate reasoning mechanisms are used in their approach. Further, they do not consider any state-of-the-art workflow management framework and language.

Substantial work has already been done on automated composition of Web services using Semantic Web technologies. For example, Majithia et al., (2004) present a framework to facilitate automated service composition in service-oriented architectures (Tsalgatidou & Pilioura, 2002) using Semantic Web technologies. The main objective of the framework is to support the discovery, selection, and composition of semantically-described heterogeneous Web services. The framework supports mechanisms to allow users to elaborate workflows of two levels of granularity: abstract and concrete workflows. Abstract workflows specify the workflow without referring to any specific service implementation. Hence, services (and data sources) are referred to by their logical names. A concrete workflow specifies the actual names and network locations of the services participating in the workflow. These two level workflow granularities are also considered in our approach, as shown in an application example.

Challenges associated with Grid workflow planning based on artificial intelligence concepts and with generation of abstract and concrete workflows are addressed by (Deelman et al., 2003). However, they do not consider any service-oriented architecture. Workflow representation and enactment are also investigated by the NextGrid Project (NextGrid Project, 2006). They proposed the OWL-WS (OWL for workflow and services) (Beco et al., 2006) ontology definition language. The myGrid project has developed the Taverna Workbench (Oinn et al., 2004) for the composition and execution of workflows for the life sciences community. The assisted composition approach of Sirin (Sirin et al., 2004) uses the richness of Semantic Web service descriptions and information from the compositional context to filter matching services and help select appropriate services.

UNDERLYING STANDARDS AND TECHNOLOGIES

CRoss Industry Standard Process for Data Mining

Cross industry standard process for data mining (CRISP-DM) (Chapman et al., 1999) is a data mining process model that describes commonly used approaches that expert data miners use to tackle problems of organizing phases in data mining projects. CRISP-DM does not describe a particular data mining technique; rather it focuses on the process of a data mining projects' life cycle. The CRISP-DM data mining methodology is described in terms of a hierarchical process model consisting of sets of tasks organized at four levels of abstraction: phase, generic task, specialized task, and process instance. At the top level, the life cycle of a data mining project is organized into six phases as depicted in Figure 2.

The sequence of the phases is not strict. Moving back and forth between different phases is always required. It depends on the outcome of each phase, which one, or which particular task of a phase has to be performed next. In this chapter, we focus our attention on the three phases of data mining projects' life cycle, namely: data understanding, data preparation, and modeling.

Data understanding: This phase starts with an initial data collection and proceeds with analytic activities in order to get familiar with the data, to identify data quality problems, to discover first insights into the data, or to detect interesting subsets to form hypotheses for hidden information.

Data preparation: This phase covers all activities to construct the final data set from the initial raw data. Data preparation tasks are likely to be performed multiple times and not in any prescribed order. The tasks include table, record, and attribute selection as well as transforming and cleaning data for the modeling phase.

Modeling: In this phase, various modeling techniques are selected and applied, and their parameters are calibrated to optimal values. Typically, there are several techniques for the same data mining problem type. Some techniques have specific requirements on the form of the data. Therefore, stepping back to the data preparation phase is often required.

Figure 2. Phases of CRISP-DM reference model (Chapman et al., 1999)

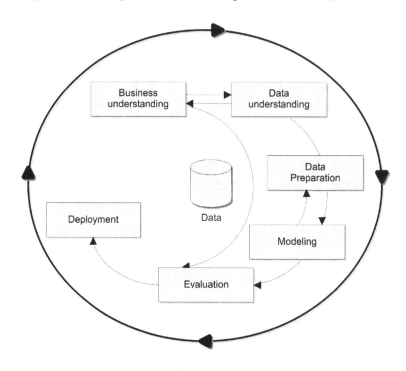

The presented phases can be delimitated into a set of tasks defined by their outputs as presented in Table 1.

Predictive Model Markup Language

Predictive model markup language (PMML) (Data Mining Group, 2004) is an XML-based language that provides a way for applications to define statistical and data mining models and to share these models between PMML compliant applications. More precisely, the language's goal is to encapsulate a model in application and in a system independent fashion so that its producer and consumer can easily use it. Furthermore, the language can describe some of the operations required for cleaning and transforming input data prior to modeling. Since PMML version 3.1 is an XML based standard, its specification comes in the form of an XML schema that defines language primitives as follows:

- **Data dictionary:** It defines fields that are the inputs for models and specifies their types and value ranges. These definitions are assumed to be independent of specific data mining models. The values of a categorical field can be organized in a hierarchy as defined by the taxonomy element, and numeric fields can be specified by their intervals.
- **Mining schema:** The mining schema is a subset of fields as defined in the data dictionary. Each model contains one mining schema that lists fields as used in that model. The main purpose of the mining schema is to list fields, which a user has to provide in order to apply the model.

Table 1. Generic tasks and outputs of the CRISP-DM reference model

Data Understanding	Data Preparation	Modeling
Collect Initial Data • Initial Data Collection Report	**Data Set** • Data Set Description	**Select Modeling Techniques** • Modeling Techniques • Modeling Assumption
Describe Data • Data Description Report	**Select Data** • Rationale for Inclusion/ Exclusion	**Generate Text Design** • Text Design
Explore Data • Data Exploration Report	**Clean Data** • Data Cleaning Report	**Build Model** • Parameter Settings • Models • Model Description
Verify Data Quality • Data Quality Report	**Construct Data** • Derived Attributes • Generated Records	**Assess Model** • Model Assessment • Revised Parameter Settings
	Integrate Data • Merged Data	
	Format Data • Reformatted Data	

- **Transformations:** It contains descriptions of derived mining fields using the following transformations: normalization—mapping continuous or discrete values to numbers; discretization—mapping continuous values to discrete values; value mapping—mapping discrete values to discrete values; aggregation—summarizing or collecting groups of values, for example, compute averages; and functions—derive a value by applying a function to one or more parameters.
- **Model statistics:** It stores basic uni-variate statistics about the numerical attributes used in the model such as minimum, maximum, mean, standard deviation, median, and so forth.
- **Data mining model:** It contains specification of the actual parameters defining the statistical and data mining models. The latest PMML version addresses the following classes of models: association rules, decision trees, center-based clustering, distribution-based clustering, regression, general regression, neural networks, naive bayes, sequences, text, ruleset, and support vector machine.

The models presented in PMML can be additionally defined by a set of extensions that can increase the overall complexity of a mining model as follows:

- **Built-in functions:** PMML supports functions that can be used to perform preprocessing steps on the input data. A number of predefined built-in functions for simple arithmetic operations like sum, difference, product, division, square root, logarithm, and so forth, for numeric input fields, as well as functions for string handling such as trimming blanks or choosing substrings are provided.
- **Model composition:** Using simple models as transformations offers the possibility to combine multiple conventional models into a single new one by using individual models as building blocks. This can result in models being used in sequence, where the result of each model is the input to the next one. This approach, called 'model sequencing,' is not only useful for building more complex models but can also be applied to data preparation. Another approach, 'model selection,' is used when the result of a model can be used to select which model should be applied next.
- **Output:** It describes a set of result values that can be computed by the model. In particular, the output fields specify names, types and rules for selecting specific result features. The output section

in the model specifies default names for columns in an output table that might be different from names used locally in the model. Furthermore, they describe how to compute the corresponding values.

- **Model verification:** A verification model provides a mechanism for attaching a sample data set with sample results so that a PMML consumer can verify that a model has been implemented correctly. This will make model exchange much more transparent for users and inform them in advance in case compatibility problems arise.

Weka Toolkit

Weka (Witten & Eibe, 2005) is a collection of machine learning algorithms, especially classifications, for data mining tasks. Moreover, Weka contains tools for data preprocessing, regression, clustering, association rules, and visualization. It is also well-suited for developing new machine learning schemes. The Weka's API is organized in a hierarchical structure, and the algorithms are delimitated by their relevancy to the classes of data mining tasks as presented in Figure 3.

Java Data Mining Application Programming Interface

The Java data mining API (JDM) (Hornick et al., 2003) proposes a pure Java API for developing data mining applications. The idea is to have a common API for data mining that can be used by clients without users being aware or affected by the actual vendor implementations for data mining. A key JDM API benefit is that it abstracts out the physical components, tasks, and even algorithms of a data mining system into Java classes. It gives a very good basis for defining concrete data mining algorithms and describing their parameters and results. JDM does not define a large number of algorithms, but provides mechanisms to add new ones, which helps in fine tuning the existing algorithms. Various data mining functions and techniques like statistical classification and association, regression analysis, data clustering, and attribute importance are covered by this standard.

Web Ontology Language for Services

Web ontology language for services (OWL-S) (Martin et al., 2004) consists of several interrelated OWL ontologies that provide a set of well defined terms for use in service applications. OWL-S leverages the rich expressive power of OWL together with its well-defined semantics to provide richer descriptions of Web services that include process preconditions and effects. This enables the encoding of service side-effects that are often important for automated selection and composition of Web services. OWL-S also provides means for the description of nonfunctional service constraints that are useful for automated Web service discovery or partnership bindings. OWL-S uses OWL to define a set of classes and their properties specific to the description of Web services. The class *Service* is at the top of this ontology (see Figure 4), which provides three essential types of knowledge about a service represented as classes: *ServiceProfile*, *ServiceGrounding* and *ServiceModel*.

- The *ServiceProfile* describes "what the service does." The profile provides information about a service that can be used in the process of service discovery to determine whether the service meets one's needs.

Figure 3. Taxonomy of algorithms as presented in Weka API

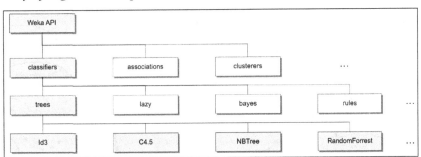

- The *ServiceModel* informs "how to use the service." In more detail, the model gives information about the service itself and describes how to perform a specific task composed by subtasks involving certain conditions.
- The *ServiceGrounding* specifies the service-specific details of how to access the service, for example communication protocols, message formats, port numbers, and so forth. It is a kind of mapping from abstract activity description to its concrete implementation.

As we deal with the services composition, the aspects of *ServiceModel* and its main class *process*, including subclasses *AtomicProcess*, *Simple Process*, and *Composite Process* and their properties are discussed here in more detail.

Atomic process: The atomic process specifies an action provided by the Web service that expects one message as an input and returns one message in response. It means that the atomic processes are directly invokable and have no other subprocesses to be executed in order to produce a result. By definition, for each atomic process there must be grounding provided, which is associated with a concrete service implementation.

Simple process: The simple process gives a higher abstraction level of the activity execution. It is not associated with groundings and is not directly invokable, but like the atomic process, it is conceived of having a single step execution.

Composite process: Web services composition is a task of combining and linking Web services to create new processes in order to add value to the collection of services. In other words, it means that composition of several services can be viewed as one composite process with its defined inputs and outputs.

Moreover, OWL-S enables inclusion of some expressions to represent logical formulas in Semantic Web rule language (SWRL) (Horrocks et al., 2004). SWRL is a rule language that combines OWL with the rule markup language providing a rule language compatible with OWL. SWRL includes a high-level abstract syntax for Horn-like rules in OWL-DL and OWL-Lite, which are sublanguages of OWL. SWRL expressions may be used in OWL-S preconditions, process control conditions (such as if-then-else), and in effects expressions.

Figure 4. Selected classes and their relations in OWL-S ontology (Martin et al., 2004)

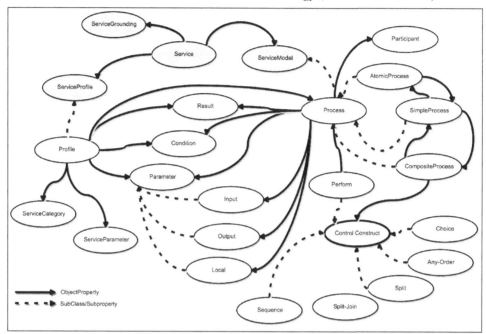

GRIDMINER ASSISTANT

Design Concepts

To achieve the goals presented in the Introduction section, we have designed a specialized tool—**Grid-Miner Assistant** (GMA)—that fulfils the role of the workflow composer shown in Figure 1. It is implemented as a Web application able to navigate a user in the phases of the knowledge discovery process (KDD) and construct a workflow consisting of a set of cooperating services aiming to realize concrete data mining objectives. The main goal of the GMA is to assist the user in the workflow composition process. The GMA provides support in choosing particular objectives of the knowledge discovery process and manage the entire process by which properties of data mining tasks are specified and results are presented. It can accurately select appropriate tasks and provide a detailed combination of services that can work together to create a complex workflow based on the selected outcome and its preferences. The GMA dynamically modifies the tasks composition depending on the entered values, defined process preconditions and effects, and existing description of services available in the KB. For this purpose we have designed a **data mining ontology** (DMO), which takes advantage of an explicit ontology of data mining techniques and standards (as presented in the above sections) using the OWL-S concepts to describe an abstract Semantic Web service for data mining and its main operations.

The service named **abstract data mining service** (ADMS) simplifies the architecture of the DMO as the realization of the OWL-S service with a detailed description of its *profile* and *model*. To clearly present the process of workflow composition using operations of the ADMS, we define three essential types of data mining components involved in the assisted workflow composition: DM-*elements,*

DM-tasks and DM-*services,* as depicted in Figure 5. In order to design the ADMS, we consider a set of transactions representing its functionality described by DM-tasks. The DM-tasks can be seen as operations of the ADMS realized by concrete operations of involved DM-services using DM-elements as their inputs and outputs.

The following paragraphs introduce the data mining ontology, which is built through the description of the DM-tasks, DM-elements and involved DM-services. The ontology covers all phases of the knowledge discovery process and describes available data mining tasks, methods, algorithms, their inputs and results they produce. All these concepts are not strictly separated but are rather used in conjunction forming a consistent ontology.

Data Mining Elements

The DM-elements are represented by OWL classes together with variations of their representations in XML. It means that a concept described by an OWL class can have one or more related XML schemas that define its concrete representation in XML. The elements are propagated by the ADMS into the KB and can be used in any phase of data mining process. The instances of OWL classes and related XML elements are created and updated by the ADMS service operations as results of concrete services or user inputs. The elements can also determine the behavior of a workflow execution if used in SWRL rules and have an influence on preconditions or effects in the OWL-S processes. In the DMO, we distinguish two types of DM-elements: settings and results. The settings represent inputs for the DM-tasks, and on the other hand, the results represent outputs produced by these tasks. From the workflow execution point of view, there is no difference between inputs and outputs because it is obvious that an output from one process can be used, at the same time, as an input for another process. The main reason why we

Figure 5. Concept overview of the abstract data mining service

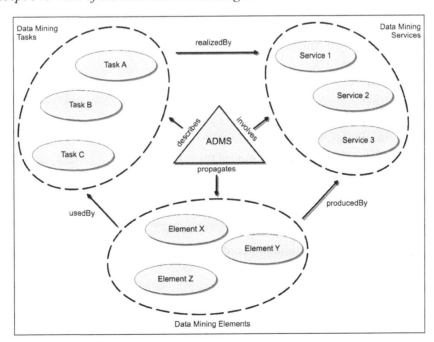

distinguish inputs and outputs as settings and results is to simplify the workflow composition process, to ease searching in the KB, and to exactly identify and select requested classes and their properties.

The **settings** are built through enumeration of properties of the data mining algorithms and characterization of their input parameters. Based on the concrete Java interfaces, as presented in the Weka API and JDM API, we constructed a set of OWL classes and their instances that handle input parameters of the algorithms and their default values (see Figure 6). The settings are also used to define different types of data sets that can be involved in the KDD process. Class *DataSet* and its derived subclasses collect all necessary information about the data set (file location, user name, SQL etc.) that can be represented by different data repositories such as a relational database, CSV, WebRowSet file, and so forth. Properties of the *DataSet* are usually specified by a user at the very beginning of the KDD process composition.

The following example shows a concrete instance of the OWL class *algorithm* keeping input parameters of an Apriory-type algorithm (Agrawal et al., 1994), which produces an association model. The example is presented in OWL abstract syntax (World Wide Web Consortium, 2004).

```
Class (Setting partial Element)
Class (Algorithm partial Element)
Class (Parameter partial Element)

ObjectProperty( hasParameter domain(Setting)
 range(Parameter))

Individual(_algorithm_AprioryType_Setting
 annotation(rdfs:label "Apriori-type algorithm")
 type(Algorithm)
value(hasParameter _number_of_rules)
value(hasParameter _minimum_support)
value(hasParameter _minimun_rule_confidence))

Individual(_number_of_rules
 annotation(rdfs:label "The required number of rules")
 type(Parameter)
value(value "10"))

Individual(_minimum_support
 annotation(rdfs:label "The delta for minimum support")
 type(Parameter)
value(value "0.05"))

Individual(_minimun_rule_confidence
 annotation(rdfs:label "The minimum confidence of a rule")
 type(Parameter)
value(value "0.9"))
```

Figure 6. Basic setting classes used to describe input parameters

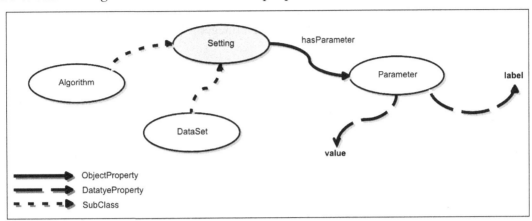

The **results** are built on taxonomy of data mining models and characterization of their main components as presented in the PMML specification, therefore, the terminology used for naming the result elements is tightly linked with the names of the elements in PMML. As a result, it is easy to map its concepts to the concrete XML representations as done in the PMML schema. Figure 7 depicts the basic classes and their relations used to describe the Result DM-elements in the DMO.

From the perspective of a Web service, the DM-elements can be seen as messages exchanged between service and client (XML elements), and from the abstract workflow point of view, as items exchanged between activities of simple or atomic process inside a composite process (instances of OWL classes). The following example shows how the PMML element DataDictionary, having subelements DataField and taxonomy, can be represented as *DataDictionary* class in the OWL.

DataDictionary — XML Schema:

```
<element name="DataDictionary">
  <complexType>
  <sequence>
    <element ref="DataField" maxOccurs="unbounded" />
    <element ref="Taxonomy" minOccurs="0" maxOccurs="unbounded" />
    </sequence>
    <attribute name="numberOfFields" type="nonNegativeInteger" />
  </complexType>
 </element>
```

DataDictionary — OWL Class:

```
<Class rdf:ID="DataDictionary">
  <Restriction>
   <onProperty rdf:resource="#hasDataField"/>
  </Restriction>
```

```
<Restriction>
 <onProperty rdf:resource="#hasTaxonomy"/>
 <minCardinality rdf:datatype="#nonNegativeInteger">0</minCardinality>
</Restriction>
<Restriction>
 <onProperty rdf:resource="#numberOfFields"/>
</Restriction>
</rdfs:subClassOf>
</Class>
```

Data Mining Tasks

The tasks are specialized operations of the ADMS organized in the phases of the KDD process as presented in the CRISP-DM reference model. The GMA composes these tasks into consistent and valid workflows to fulfill selected data mining objectives. The tasks are workflow's building blocks and are realized by concrete operations of involved DM-Services using DM-elements as their settings and results. Furthermore, GMA can automatically select and insert additional tasks into the workflow to assure validity and logical consistency of the data mining processes. We distinguish two types of DM-tasks that are forming the OWL-S *ServiceModel* of the ADMS—*setters* and *getters*.

Setters and getters give a functional description of the ADMS expressed in terms of the transformation produced by the abstract service. Furthermore, the setters are used to specify the input parameters

Figure 7. Basic classes used to describe Results in DMO

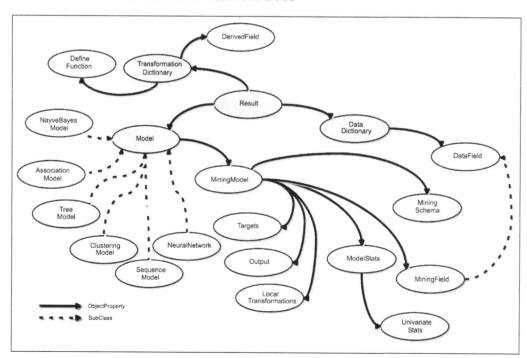

for data mining tasks, and the getters are designed to present results of concrete service operations. The setters interact with a user who specifies values of the input parameters represented as properties of the *settings* class, for example, location of data source, selection of target attributes, the number of clusters, and so forth. The setters do not return any results but usually have an effect on creating and updating the DM-elements. The setters are not realized by concrete operations of involved services but are used to compose compact workflows and assure interaction with the user. The getters are designed to describe actual data mining tasks at different levels of abstraction. Thus a getter can be represented by an instance of the *CompositeProcess* class as, for example, a sequence of several subtasks, or a getter can be directly defined as an instance of the *AtomicProcess* class realized by a concrete operation of a DM-service.

Table 2 presents some of the setters and getters on the highest level of abstraction organized according to the phases of the CRISP-DM reference model and lists their input and output DM-elements.

The setters are designed to interact with the user, therefore, each *setter* has a related HTML input form used by the user to insert or select the input parameters' values of the examined DM-element. The GMA presents the form implemented as a dynamic Web page to the user, and based on his/her inputs, the GMA updates parameters of the DM-elements.

Data Mining Services

Realization of a particular DM-task is done by invoking concrete operations of involved DM-services described in OWL-S as an atomic, simple or composite process related to its *ServiceGrounding* (operators that can be executed) as defined in the appropriate WSDL document. The operations produce DM-elements that can be reused by other operations in further steps of the workflow execution. Within our project, several data mining services were developed including decision tree, clustering, associations, sequences, and neural networks with detailed descriptions of their functionality in OWL-S.

Data Mining Ontology

Based on the concepts and principal classes in the preceding sections, we have constructed the final DMO as depicted in Figure 8. The DMO incorporates the presented OWL-S ontology and its classes describing DM-tasks and DM-services as well as *Result* and *Setting* classes, which describe the DM-elements. The ontology is also supplemented by a set of semantic rules that determine in detail particular relations between involved classes, but its presentation is out of the scope of this chapter.

WORKFLOW CONSTRUCTION

In order to create the final workflow, the GMA follows a combination of the backward and forward chaining approaches. It means that the process begins with a user-based selection of a target task, which produces the desired data exploration output. Additional tasks are automatically inserted into a chain before the target task until a task without any or already satisfied preconditions is encountered (backward phase). Next, by insertion of additional tasks, this chain is automatically extended into a form in which all matching preconditions and inputs parameters are satisfied (forward chain). According to this, our approach to workflow construction is based on two phases as follows.

Table 2. DM-tasks and their DM-elements

	crisp-dm task	dmo dm-task	input	output
data understanding	collect initial data	setdataset	datasetsettings	dataset
	describe data	getdatadictionary	dataset	datadictionary
		settaxonomy	taxonomysettings	taxonomy
	explore data	getmodelstats	dataset	modelstats
	verify data quality			
data preparation	select data	setminingschema	miningschemasettings	miningschema
	clean data	gettransformation	definefunction	dataset
	construct data		derivedfield	dataset
	integrate data		mediationschema	dataset
	format data		miningschema	dataset
modeling	select modeling technique	setminingmodel	miningmodelsettings	miningmodel
	generate test design	settestset	datasetsettings	dataset
	build model	getclassificationmodel getassociationmodel getclusteringmodel getsequentialmodel getneuralnetworksmodel	mininingmodelsettings	model
	assess model	getmodelverification	mininingmodelsettings	model

Tasks Composition

The aim of this phase is to create an abstract workflow consisting of a sequence of DM-tasks. Figure 9 presents an example of the abstract workflow composed of DM-tasks. 'Task D' is the initial task inserted into the workflow in the sense of the previously mentioned backward phase of the workflow composition, and the task's result, represented by a DM-element, is the final goal of the abstract workflow. The DM-element can be, for example, a decision tree model in the data mining phase, a list of all available statistics in the data understanding phase, or the data preparation phase can result in a new transformed data set. Selection of the final result is the only interaction with the user in this phase; the other steps are hidden. The composition then continues with an examination of preconditions and inputs of the target task 'Task D.' If the task has an input which does not exist (KB does not contain an instance of the required DM-element) or condition that has to be satisfied, then the KB is queried for such a task that can supply the required DM-elements or can satisfy these preconditions by its effects; the missing task can be 'Task C' in our case. The design of the ontology ensures that there is only one such task that can be selected and inserted into the workflow prior to the examined task. For example, if we want to obtain a list of statistics (getModelStats task) then there must be an existing DM-element DataSet. It means that a task which creates the DataSet element must anticipate the getModelStats task in the workflow composition (it can be the setDataSet task in our case). The newly added tasks are treated in the same way until a task without any preconditions or already satisfied preconditions is encountered, or a task without any input that is produced as result of another task is reached, which is 'Task A' in our example.

Values Acquisition

Figure 10 presents the same workflow but viewed from another perspective: now 'Task A' is the initial task and 'Task D' is the final one. In this phase of the workflow construction, the task parameters are set up. Their values can be obtained in the following ways: (a) as effects of DM-tasks (getters) or (b) entered directly by a user (setters). In other words, not all values of input parameters can be obtained automatically as results of previous operations and therefore must be supplied by a user. This phase of the values acquisition starts by tracing the abstract workflow from its beginning, 'Task A', and supplying the values by abstract interpretation of the partial workflow or providing them from a user. The user can enter the values directly by filling input fields offered by an appropriate graphical user interface or by selecting them from a list created as a result of a KB query, e.g., a list of data mining algorithms for a specific method is determined by available implementations of services able to perform the task. If the user selects a list item value that has influence on the precondition or effect that has to be satisfied in the next steps, then the KB is searched for such a task that can satisfy this request. The newly discovered tasks are inserted automatically into the workflow. It can be, for example, a case when the user wants to increase the quality of used data adding some transformation tasks, presenting the resulting model in different form, and so forth.

To illustrate the main features of the GMA and explain the phases of the tasks composition and values acquisition, we present a practical scenario addressing step-by-step construction of a simple workflow aiming at discovering of classification model for a given data set. This scenario is taken from a medical application dealing with patients suffering from serious traumatic brain injuries (TBI).

Figure 8. Basic classes and their relations in DMO

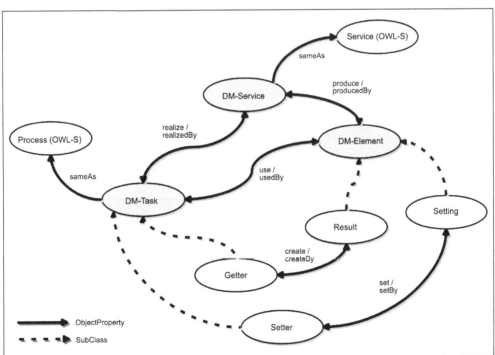

Workflow Construction Example

At the first clinical examination of a TBI patient (Brezany et al., 2003), it is very common to assign the patient into a category, which allows to define his/her next treatment and helps to predict the final outcome of the treatment. There are five categories of the final outcome defined by the Glasgow outcome scale (GOS): dead, vegetative, severely disabled, moderately disabled, and good recovery.

It is obvious that the outcome is influenced by several factors that are usually known and are often monitored and stored in a hospital data warehouse. For TBI patients, these factors are for example: injury severity score (ISS), abbreviated injury scale (AIS), Glasgow coma score (GCS), age, and so forth. It is evident that if we want to categorize the patient, then there must be a prior knowledge based on cases of other patients with the same type of injury. This knowledge can be mined from the historical data and represented as a classification model. The mined model is then used to assign the patient to the one of the outcome categories. In particular, the model can assign one of the values from the GOS to a concrete patient.

As we mentioned in the previous section, in the first phase, the composition of the abstract workflow proceeds by using the backward chaining approach starting with the task and then producing the demanded result. In our case, the classification model is represented by a decision tree. Moreover, in this example, we assume that the data understanding phase of the KDD process was successfully finished, and we have all the necessary information about the data set to be mined. It means that appropriate records corresponding to the *DataSet* and *DataDictionary* DM-elements are already available in the KB, and the workflow can start with the data preprocessing task.

Phase 1: Tasks Composition

As we presented previously, the first step of the task composition is the interactive selection of the final model from a list of all available models. The list can be obtained as a result of the following SPARQL

Figure 9. Example of tasks composing the abstract workflow

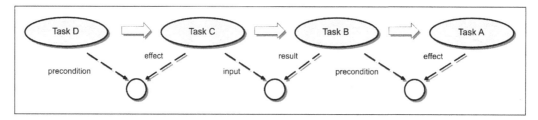

Figure 10. Example of values acquisition phase

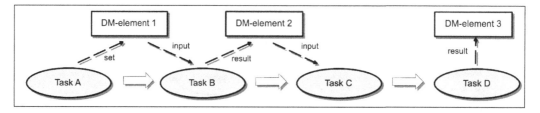

(SPARQL, 2006) query returning a list of DM-tasks and models they produce. This query is issued by the GMA automatically. (See Box 1.)

Selection of the classification model gives us a direct link to the *getClassificationModel* DM-task that can be realized by a concrete service operation. Information about its input DM-elements and the corresponding DM-task producing them can be retrieved from the KB by submitting the following SPARQL query, which is also issued by the GMA automatically (see Box 2).

The discovered DM-task *setMiningModel* is inserted into the workflow prior to the *getClassification-Model* task, and its preconditions and inputs are examined. The only precondition of the *setMiningModel* task is the existence of the *MiningSchema* DM-element. This requirement can be satisfied by inserting the *setMiningSchema* task into the workflow, whose effect is the creation of the *MiningSchema* DM-element. The *setMiningSchema* task has two preconditions: the existence of the *DataSet* and *DataDictionary* DM-elements. Their corresponding records are already available in the KB, so no additional tasks are inserted into the abstract workflow. As the result, an abstract workflow consisting of three DM-tasks (see Figure 11) is created and is instanced as a new composite process of the ADMS in the KB. The figure also presents the DM-elements identified during the composition phase as preconditions of the involved tasks and a fragment of the concrete workflow.

Phase 2: Values Acquisition

The second phase of the workflow construction starts with the examination of the first DM-task in the abstract workflow (*setMiningSchema*). In this phase, the values of the DM-elements' properties, identified in the previous phase, are supplied by the user and additional DM-tasks are inserted as needed. The following paragraphs describe in more detail the steps of setting the DM-elements produced and used by the involved tasks.

Box 1.

```
Query:

        PREFIX dmo: <http://dmo.gridminer.org/v1#>
        PREFIX rdfs: <http://www.w3.org/2000/01/rdf-schema#>
        PREFIX rdf:  <http://www.w3.org/1999/02/22-rdf-syntax-ns#>
        SELECT ?ModelName ?Task
        FROM     <http://www.gridminer.org/dmo/v1/dmo.owl>
        WHERE {
                  ?model rdf:type <#Model> .
                  ?model rdfs:label ?ModelName .
                  ?model dmo:createdBy ?Task
               }
        ORDER BY ?ModelName
```

Result:

ModelName T	ask
Association Model	getAssociationModel
Classification Model	getClassificationModel
Clustering Model	getClusteringModel
…	…

setMiningSchema: This task can be seen as a simple data preprocessing step where data fields (attributes) used in the modeling phase can be selected and their usage types can be specified. The primary effect of this task is a new *MiningSchema* element instanced in the KB, keeping all the schema's parameters specified by the user. Moreover, the user can specify whether some preprocessing methods should be used to treat missing values and outliers of the numerical attributes. Selection of a preprocessing method requires an additional DM-task, which is able to perform the data transformations and produce a new data set that can be used in the next steps. If one of the transformation methods is selected then the KB is queried again for a task able to transform the data set. The *getTransformation* task has the ability to transform the selected data set, therefore, can be inserted into the abstract workflow in the next step.

As we presented in previous paragraphs, the *setters* are designed to interact with the user, therefore, each *setter* has a related HTML input form used by the user to insert or select the values of the examined DM-element input parameters. The GMA presents the form implemented as a dynamic Web page to the user, and based on its inputs, the GMA updates values of the DM-elements' parameters.

Box 2.

```
Query:
        PREFIX dmo: <http://dmo.gridminer.org/v1#>
        SELECT  ?Setting ?Task
        FROM    <http://www.gridminer.org/dmo/v1/dmo.owl>
        WHERE {
                    dmo:getClassificationModel dmo:hasSettings ?Setting .
                    ?Task dmo:create ?Setting
                }

Result:
```

Setting	Task
MiningModel	setMiningModel

Figure 11. Abstract workflow after the phase of tasks composition

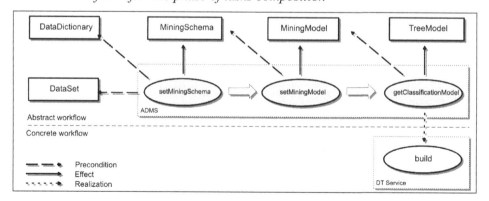

Figure 12 presents the input form used by the GMA to construct the *MiningSchema* DM-element. In this form, there is one mandatory property for the classification task — 'target attribute.' It is one of the categorical *DataFields* from the *DataDictionary* element, which is the GOS in our case. Therefore, the 'target attribute' must be marked as 'predicted' in the *MiningSchema* DM-element. The effect of the *setMiningSchema* task is a newly created DM-element *MiningSchema,* which describes mined fields and their transformations.

getTransformation: This task is inserted into the workflow right after the *setMiningSchema* task. It does not require interaction with the user because its input parameters are already specified in the *MiningSchema* created as the effect of the previous task. The task just examines the *MiningSchema* element and selects a concrete operation from DM-Services available in the KB, which can satisfy the chosen data preprocessing objectives. The task can select operation 'transform' of the specialized *DataPreprocessing* service (DPP service) and insert it into the concrete workflow (see Figure 14).

setMiningModel: Specification of the properties of the selected model is the main purpose of this task. The GMA presents a list of all available data mining algorithms producing classification models and selects its input parameters. Based on the selected parameters, a new DM-element *MiningModel* describing model properties is created as an effect of this task. The following SPARQL query retrieves all parameters for the C4.5 classification algorithm (Quinlan, 1993) that is used to setup the *MiningModel* element in our example. (See Box 3.)

Figure 12. Input HTML form for the MiningSchema

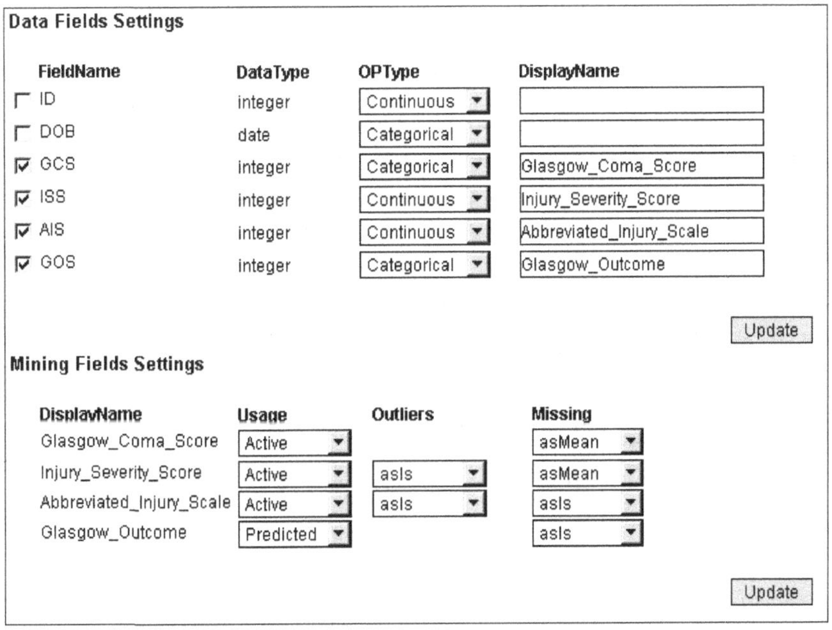
Data Fields Settings

FieldName	DataType	OPType	DisplayName
☐ ID	integer	Continuous	
☐ DOB	date	Categorical	
☑ GCS	integer	Categorical	Glasgow_Coma_Score
☑ ISS	integer	Continuous	Injury_Severity_Score
☑ AIS	integer	Continuous	Abbreviated_Injury_Scale
☑ GOS	integer	Categorical	Glasgow_Outcome

Update

Mining Fields Settings

DisplayName	Usage	Outliers	Missing
Glasgow_Coma_Score	Active		asMean
Injury_Severity_Score	Active	asIs	asMean
Abbreviated_Injury_Scale	Active	asIs	asIs
Glasgow_Outcome	Predicted		asIs

Update

Box 3.

```
Query:

        PREFIX dmo: <http://dmo.gridminer.org/v1#>
        PREFIX rdfs: <http://www.w3.org/2000/01/rdf-schema#>
        SELECT  ?ParameterName ?DefaultValue
        FROM     <http://www.gridminer.org/dmo/v1/dmo.owl>
        WHERE {
                    dmo:_algorithm_c4.5_Settings dmo:hasParameter ?Parameter
                    ?Parameter rdfs:label ?ParameterName .
                    ?Parameter dmo:value ?DefaultValue
                }
        ORDER BY ?ParameterName
```

The GMA presents the results to the user in the HTML form presented in Figure 13, where the user specifies values of the input parameters needed to build the classification model using the C4.5 algorithm.

getClassificationModel: This task examines the *MiningModel* element created in the previous task and identifies the appropriate operation that can build the classification model using *MiningModel* parameters. The task can be the operation 'build' implemented by the DecisionTree Service (DT Service), which returns the classification model represented by the PMML element TreeModel. Moreover, if parameter 'pruned tree' is marked as true (false by default) then the additional operation of the DT Service 'prune' is inserted into to the concrete workflow to assure that the discovered decision tree is modified using a pruning mechanism.

If all required parameters and preconditions of the tasks involved in the abstract workflow are satisfied then the GMA constructs a concrete workflow specification in the BPEL language and presents it to the workflow engine. The concrete workflow is a sequence of the real services and is related to the abstract DM-tasks as presented in Figure 14.

The final output returned from the workflow engine is a PMML document containing a TreeModel element that represents the demanded model that can be used to classify a particular patient into the GOS category.

The following BPEL document created in our scenario contains five variables representing the DM-elements used as inputs and outputs of the invoked operations. The variable DataSet is an XML in We-

Figure 13. Input HTML form for the MiningModel

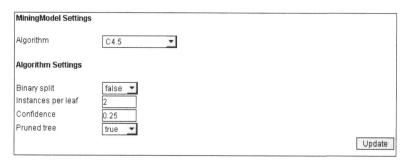

Figure 14. Abstract and concrete workflow after the phase of values acquisition

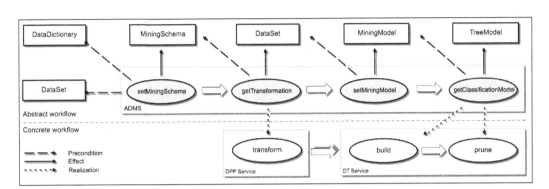

bRowSet format (`RowSet` Java object in XML format) storing all the initial data. TransformedDataset is a new WebRowSet created by the 'transform' operation, and TreeSettings is used as input for the 'build' and 'prune' operations. The variable TreeModel stores the PMML document with the full decision tree, and the PrunedTreeModel stores its pruned version. The BPEL flow reflects the composition as done in the concrete workflow consisting of three operations invoked in sequence. (See Box 4.)

SYSTEM PROTOTYPE

An overview of the first system prototype is shown in Figure 15. We use the OWL editor Protégé (Noy et al., 2001) to create and maintain the DMO, which is stored in the KB. To reason about knowledge in

Box 4.

```
Variables:

<variable name="DataSet" element="wrs:webRowSet"/>
<variable name="TransformedDataset" element="wrs:webRowSet "/>
<variable name="TreeModel" element="pmml:TreeModel"/>
<variable name="PrunedTreeModel" element="pmml:TreeModel"/>
<variable name="TreeSettings" element="dmo:Setting"/>

Sequence:

<sequence>
    < flow>
        <invoke partnerLink="DPPService" operation="transform"    inputVariable="DataSet"
        outputVariable="TransformedDataset" />

        <invoke partnerLink="DTService" operation="build"
        inputVariable="TreeSettings" outputVariable="TreeModel"/>

        <invoke partnerLink="DTService" operation="prune"
        inputVariable="TreeSettings"  outputVariable="PrunedTreeModel"/>
    </ flow>
</ sequence>
```

Figure 15. Overview of the prototype system

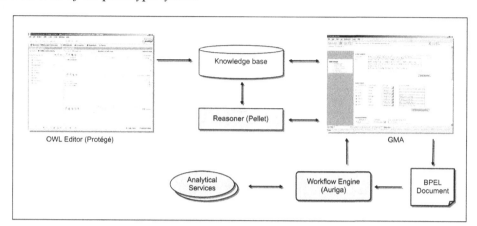

the KB, we use the Pellet reasoner (Sirin & Parsia, 2004), which is an open-source Java based OWL DL reasoner and provides a description logic interface (DIG) (Bechhofer et al., 2003). The GMA is implemented as a standalone Web application supported by the Jena Toolkit (McBride, 2003) and is able to interact with a user to assemble the required information. The GMA communicates over the DIG interface with the reasoner, which is able to answer a subset of RDQL queries (Seaborn, 2004). The GMA queries KB every time it needs to enumerate some parameters or find a data mining task, algorithm, service, and so forth. Moreover, the GMA also updates the KB with instances of DMO classes and values of their properties. The final outcome of the GMA is a workflow document presented to the workflow engine Auriga (Brezany et al., 2006) in the BPEL4WS language. The GMA also acts as a client of the workflow engine, which executes appropriate services as described in the BPEL document and returns their outputs back to the GMA. A more detailed characterization of these major components follows.

- **Auriga** WEEP workflow engine is an easy to execute and manage workflow enactment service for Grid and Web services. The core of the engine is implemented as a standalone application referred to as the Auriga WEEP Core, which orchestrates the services as specified in a BPEL. Auriga WEEP has also a specialized version, which is wrapped by a Grid service implementation focused on using the Globus 4 container as the running environment. The engine has a pluggable architecture, which allows additional Grid specific functionality to be used in the Auriga Core extensions.
- **Jena** is a Java framework for building Semantic Web applications. It provides a programming environment for RDF, RDFS, OWL and SPARQL and includes a rule-based inference engine.
- **Pellet** provides functionalities to see the species validation, check consistency of ontologies, classify the taxonomy, check entailments and answer a subset of RDQL queries. Pellet is based on the tableaux algorithms developed for expressive Description Logics and supports the full expressivity of OWL DL.
- **Protégé** is an ontology editor and knowledge acquisition system. It implements a rich set of knowledge-modeling structures and actions that support the creation, visualization, and manipulation of ontologies in various representation formats including OWL.

FUTURE WORK

We envision the following key directions for future extension of the research presented in this chapter:

- **Active workflow engine:** This approach was already briefly discussed in the background section and sketched in Figure 1. In this case, the interaction mode between the user, workflow composer and the functionality of the composer basically remain the same as in the described passive approach. The functionality of the existing GridMiner workflow engine will be extended to be able to make dynamic decisions about the next workflow execution step based on the actual context of the knowledge base and the results of the reasoning. Moreover, the workflow composer can listen to the changes in the knowledge base and automatically interact with the user when some additional information or hints have to be supplied.
- **Workflow ranking:** The data mining ontology will be extended by estimations of each operation's effects on workflow attributes such as speed, model accuracy, etc. Due to the user's preferences (e.g., speed vs. accuracy) the composer can then better optimize individual selection steps, derive a set of workflows with the corresponding ranking and supply the best option to the workflow engine. In this process, information about the current Grid resource utilization provided by standard Grid information services can also be included into this optimization process.
- **Workflow planning:** We consider upgrading the intelligence of the workflow composer with the development of a supporting planning system which will be able to propose an abstract workflow from the specification of the goals and the initial state. We will exploit and adapt AI planning optimizations.
- **Support by autonomic computing:** We will investigate how the presented framework should be extended to be able to include some functionality of autonomic computing into the workflows composed. This involves investigating workflow patterns, categorizing requirements and objectives, and designing corresponding rule templates.

CONCLUSION

The characteristics of data exploration in scientific environments impose unique requirements for workflow composition and execution systems. In this chapter, we addressed the issues of composing workflows with automated support developed on top of Semantic Web technologies and the workflow management framework elaborated in our Grid data mining project. The kernel part of that support is a tool called the GridMiner workflow assistant (GMA), which helps the user interactively construct workflow description expressed in a standard workflow specification language. The specification is then passed to the workflow engine for execution. The GMA operations are controlled by the data mining ontology based on the concepts of PMML, JDM, WEKA and CRISP-DM. A practical example taken from a medical application addressing management of patients with traumatic brain injuries illustrates the use of the GMA. The results achieved will be extended in our future research whose key issues were outlined in the chapter. Although this research is conducted in the context of the GridMiner project, its results can be used in any system involving workflow construction activities.

FUTURE RESEARCH DIRECTIONS

In this section, we identify three future challenges and research problems in the ontology-based workflow construction and execution.

1. **Extended Data Mining Ontology:** Data mining as a scientific discipline is a huge domain which is still expanding. New approaches to data analyses, visualization techniques, or even new algorithms are continuously being developed. There are also plenty of real applications tailored to the application domain specifically for data mining tasks. Therefore, it is nearly impossible to completely describe this dynamic field of data mining with a static ontology. The ontology proposed in our chapter can only be used for a subset of the high number of data mining tasks. Hence we see new opportunities in extending the proposed data mining ontology with different, application domain specific, tasks that would better express the functionality of the constructed workflows.

2. **Quality of Services and Workflows:** Another issue that is not fully covered in the proposed ontology is the description of the quality of the involved data mining services. Especially in the Grid infrastructures, the properties of the involved resources (e.g., performance, price, bandwidth, etc.) play the crucial role in their discovery and right selection. So we see another opportunity in the detailed description of the data mining services' properties which can be done as a direct extension of the OLW-S language. Moreover, there can also be a detailed description of the composed workflows' quality which can be used for effective ranging of the entire workflows.

3. **Autonomic Behavior of the Workflow Enactment Engine:** Autonomic computing is one of the hottest topics in information technologies. Different areas in computer science, ranging from hardware to software implementation on the application level, try to apply some autonomic features (like, e.g., self-tuning, self-configuration, self-healing, etc.) to assure stability and availability of the system. The autonomic behavior of the Workflow Engine can ensure that the execution of the data mining workflows results in a required goal even in such a dynamic environment as the Grid where the Workflow Engine must react to the changes of the involved resources and adopt its behavior to new conditions and reflect the actual 'State of the Grid'.

REFERENCES

Agrawal, R., & Srikant, R. (1994). Fast algorithms for mining association rules in large databases. In *Proceedings of the International Conference on Very Large Databases* (pp. 478-499). Santiage, Chile: Morgan Kaufmann.

Antonioletti, M., Krause, A., Paton, N. W., Eisenberg, A., Laws, S., Malaika, S., et al. (2006). The WS-DAI family of specifications for web service data access and integration. *ACM SIGMOD Record, 35*(1), 48-55.

Arkin, A. (2002). *Business process modeling language* (BPML). Specification. BPMI.org.

Arkin, A., Askary, S., Bloch, B., Curbera, F., Goland, Y., Kartha, N., et al. (2005). *Web services business process execution language version* 2.0. wsbpel-specificationdraft-01, OASIS.

BEA, IBM, Microsoft, SAP, & Siebel. (2003). *Business process execution language for Web services.* Version 1.1. Specification. Retrieved May 15, 2006, from ftp://www6.software.ibm.com/software/developer/library/ws-bpel.pdf

Bechhofer, S., Moller, R., & Crowther, P. (2003). *The DIG description logic interface.* International Workshop on Description Logics, Rome, Italy.

Beco, S., Cantalupo, B., Matskanis, N., & Surridge M. (2006). *Putting semantics in Grid workflow management: The OWL-WS approach.* GGF16 Semantic Grid Workshop, Athens, Greece.

Bernstein, A., Hill, S., & Provost, F. (2001). An intelligent assistant for the knowledge discovery process. *In Proceedings of the IJCAI-01 Workshop on Wrappers for Performance Enhancement in KDD.* Seattle, WA: Morgan Kaufmann.

Brezany, P., Tjoa, A.M., Rusnak, M., & Janciak, I. (2003). Knowledge Grid support for treatment of traumatic brain injury victims. *International Conference on Computational Science and its Applications.* Montreal, Canada.

Brezany, P., Janciak, I., Woehrer, A., & Tjoa, A.M. (2004). *GridMiner: A Framework for knowledge discovery on the Grid - from a vision to design and implementation.* Cracow Grid Workshop, Cracow, Poland: Springer.

Brezany, P., Janciak, I., Kloner, C., & Petz, G. (2006). *Auriga — workflow engine for WS-I/WS-RF services.* Retrieved September 15, 2006, from http://www.Gridminer.org/auriga/

Bussler ,C., Davies, J., Dieter, F., & Studer , R. (2004). The Semantic Web: Research and applications. In *Proceedings of the 1st European Semantic Web Symposium, ESWS. Lecture Notes in Computer Science, 3053.* Springer.

Chapman, P., Clinton, J., Khabaza, T., Reinartz, T., & Wirth. R. (1999). *The CRISP-DM process model.* Technical report, CRISM-DM consortium. Retrieved May 15, 2006, from http://www.crisp-dm.org/CRISPWP-0800.pdf

Christensen, E., Curbera, F., Meredith, G., & Weerawarana, S. (2001). *Web Services Description Language* (WSDL) 1.1. Retrieved May 10, 2006, from http://www.w3.org/TR/wsdl

Data Mining Group. (2004). *Predictive model markup language.* Retrieved May 10, 2006, from http://www.dmg.org/

Deelman, E., Blythe, J., Gil, Y., & Kesselman, C. (2003). Workflow management in GriPhyN. *The Grid Resource Management.* The Netherlands: Kluwer.

Globus Alliance (2005). *Globus Toolkit 4.* http://www.globus.org

Globus Alliance, IBM, & HP (2004). *The WS-Resource framework.* Retrieved May 10, 2006, from http://www.globus.org/wsrf/

Hornick, F. M., et al. (2005). *Java data mining 2.0.* Retrieved June 20, 2006, from http://jcp.org/about-Java/communityprocess/edr/jsr247/

Horrocks, I., Patel-Schneider, P. F., Boley, H., Tabet, S., Grosof, B., & Dean, M. (2004). *SWRL: A Semantic Web rule language combining OWL and RuleML*. W3C Member Submission. Retrieved May 10, 2006, from http://www.w3.org/Submission/2004/SUBM-SWRL-20040521

Kickinger, G., Hofer, J., Tjoa, A.M., & Brezany, P. (2003). Workflow mManagement in GridMiner. *The 3rd Cracow Grid Workshop*. Cracow, Poland: Springer.

Leymann, F. (2001). *Web services flow language (WSFL 1.0)*. Retrieved September 23, 2002, from www4.ibm.com/software/solutions/webservices/pdf/WSFL.pdf

Majithia, S., Walker, D. W., & Gray, W.A. (2004). *A framework for automated service composition in service-oriented architectures* (pp. 269-283).ESWS.

Martin, D., Paolucci, M., McIlraith, S., Burstein, M., McDermott, D., McGuinness, D., et al.(2004). Bringing semantics to Web services: The OWL-S approach. In *Proceedings of the 1st International Workshop on Semantic Web Services and Web Process Composition*. San Diego, California.

McBride, B. (2002). Jena: A Semantic Web toolkit. *IEEE Internet Computing,* November /December, 55-59.

Oinn, T. M., Addis, M., Ferris, J., Marvin, D., Senger, M., Greenwood, R. M., et al. (2004). Taverna: A tool for the composition and enactment of bioinformatics workflows. *Bioinformatics, 20*(17), 3045-3054.

Noy, N. F. , Sintek, M., Decker, S., Crubezy, M., Fergerson, R. W., & Musen, M.A. (2001). Creating Semantic Web contents with Protege-2000. *IEEE Intelligent Systems, 16*(2), 60-71.

Quinlan, R. (1993). *C4.5: Programs for machine learning*. San Mateo, CA: Morgan Kaufmann Publishers.

Sairafi, S., A., Emmanouil, F. S., Ghanem, M., Giannadakis, N., Guo, Y., Kalaitzopolous, D., et al. (2003). The design of discovery net: Towards open Grid services for knowledge discovery. *International Journal of High Performance Computing Applications, 17*(3).

Seaborne, A. (2004). *RDQL: A query language for RDF*. Retrieved May 10, 2006, from http://www.w3.org/Submission/RDQL/

Sirin, E., & Parsia, B. (2004). *Pellet: An OWL DL Reasoner, 3rd International Semantic Web Conference*, Hiroshima, Japan. Springer.

Sirin, E.B. Parsia, B., & Hendler, J. (2004). Filtering and selecting Semantic Web services with interactive composition techniques. *IEEE Intelligent Systems, 19*(4), 42-49.

SPARQL. Query Language for RDF, W3C Working Draft 4 October 2006. Retrieved October 8, 2006, from http://128.30.52.31/TR/rdf-sparql-query/

Thatte, S. (2001). *XLANG: Web services for business process design*. Microsoft Corporation, Initial Public Draft.

Tsalgatidou, A., & Pilioura, T. (2002). An overview of standards and related technology in web services. *Distributed and Parallel Databases. 12*(3).

Witten, I.H., & Eibe, F. (2005). *Data mining: Practical machine learning tools and techniques.* (2nd ed.). San Francisco: Morgan Kaufmann.

World Wide Web Consortium. (2004). *OWL Web ontology language semantics and abstract syntax.* W3C Recommendation 10 Feb, 2004.

ADDITIONAL READING

For more information on the topics covered in this chapter, see http://www.Gridminer.org and also the following references:

Alesso, P. H., & Smith, F. C. (2005). *Developing Semantic Web services.* A.K. Peterson Ltd.

Antoniou, G., & Harmelen, F. (2004). *A Semantic Web primer.* MIT Press.

Davies, J., Studer, R., & Warren P. (2006). *Semantic Web technologies: Trends and research in ontology-based systems.* John Wiley & Sons.

Davies, N. J., Fensel, D., & Harmelen, F. (2003). *Towards the Semantic Web: Ontology-driven knowledge management.* John Wiley & Sons.

Foster, I., & Kesselman, C. (1999). *The Grid: Blueprint for a new computing infrastructure.* Morgan Kaufmann.

Fox, G.C., Berman, F., & Hey, A.J.G. (2003). *Grid computing: Making the global infrastructure a reality.* John Wiley & Sons.

Han, J., & Kamber, M. (2000) *Data mining: Concepts and techniques.* Morgan Kaufmann.

Lacy, L.W. (2005). *Owl: Representing information using the Web ontology language.* Trafford Publishing.

Li, M., & Baker, M. (2005). *The Grid: Core technologies.* John Wiley & Sons.

Marinescu, D.C. (2002) *Internet-based workflow management: Toward a Semantic Web.* John Wiley & Sons.

Matjaz, B.J., Sarang, P.G., & Mathew, B. (2006). *Business process execution language for Web services* (2nd ed.). Packt Publishing.

Murch, R. (2004). *Autonomic computing.* Published by IBM Press.

Oberle, D. (2005). *The semantic management of middleware.* Springer.

Singh, M.P., & Huhns, M.N. (2006). *Service-oriented computing: Semantics, processes, agents.* John Wiley & Sons.

Sotomayor, B., & Childers, L. (2006). *Globus Toolkit 4: Programming Java services.* Morgan Kaufmann.

Stojanovic, Z., & Dahanayake. A. (2005). *Service oriented software system engineering: Challenges and practices.* Idea Group Inc.

Taylor, I. J., Deelman E., Gannon, D. B., & Shields, M. (2007). *Workflows for e-science.* Springer.

Zhong, N., Liu, J., & Yao, Y.(2003). *Web intelligence.* Springer.

Zhu, X., & Davidson, I. (2007). *Knowledge discovery and data mining: Challenges and realities.* Idea Group Inc.

Zhuge, H. (2004). *The knowledge Grid.* World Scientific.

This work was previously published in Data Mining with Ontologies: Implementations, Findings, and Frameworks, edited by H. Nigro, S. Cisaro & D. Xodo, pp. 182-210, copyright 2008 by Information Science Reference, formerly known as Idea Group Reference (an imprint of IGI Global).

Chapter XXII
Optimization Algorithms for Data Transfer in the Grid Environment

Muzhou Xiong
Huazhong University of Science and Technology, China

Hai Jin
Huazhong University of Science and Technology, China

ABSTRACT

In this chapter, two algorithms have been presented for supporting efficient data transfer in the Grid environment. From a node's perspective, a multiple data transfer channel can be formed by selecting some other nodes as relays in data transfer. One algorithm requires the sender to be aware of the global connection information while another does not. Experimental results indicate that both algorithms can transfer data efficiently under various circumstances.

INTRODUCTION

Distributed data intensive computing, such as gravitational-wave physics (Barish, 1999), high-energy physics (Wulz, 1998) and astronomy (Szalay, 2008), has become an important application of the Grid technology (Foster, 2001; Chervenak, 2001; Rajasekar, 2003). The future of these paradigms is to share a variety of resources within collaboration in pursuit of common goals (Deelman, 2004). All these paradigms are data driven, which means that only when the data is ready will the computing resource work. Hence, "data" are regarded as the most important resources, and they are the bridges via which the activities and people among those paradigms are connected. For the performance issue, it is important to fetch data as fast as possible. In other words, the performance of data transfer is the key factor affecting the efficiency of data intensive distributed computing.

The data transfer between a server and a client over Internet is limited by several bottlenecks (Gkantsidis, 2003). First, the achievable bandwidth by the client is limited by the server's bandwidth to the Internet, which is referred as First-Mile problem. Secondly, the achievable bandwidth is limited by the data transfer speed of the link connecting the server and client. Thirdly, the bottleneck may exist in the client's connection to the Internet, namely the Last-Mile problem. Thus, the data transfer speed may only be as high as the slowest link in the aforementioned setup. The optimization of data transfer is around those three aspects. The typical solutions to the First-Mile and Last-Mile problems are to improve the bandwidth of the client and server using advanced network techniques, such as Gigabyte Ethernet and Fiber channel etc. Usually the bandwidth of the direct connection from a node to Internet is high. However, the data transfer speed is determined by the slowest part of these three aspects. The main reason for low data transfer speed lies in the achievable bandwidth of the path between the server and the client, which is much lower than that of each node connecting to Internet. The bandwidth of the path selected by the routing algorithm, or in other words, the direct bandwidth from the source to the destination, is usually much less than those available to the connections from the source and the destination directly to Internet. Under this circumstance, both the source and the destination have the capabilities of sending/receiving more data given that the larger direct bandwidth those connecting to the Internet can be further utilized.

However, existing common-used routing protocols only support a single path between any pair of nodes on Internet. Aiming at this limitation, the method of multi-path data transfer is proposed to improve the performance of data. The basic idea of multi-path data transfer lies in establishing multiple paths from the node or nodes where data can be stored for delivery to the destination eventually. The multi-path data transfer can be applied either at application level or routing protocol level. At application level, the paths are controlled by the data transfer protocol itself and could be formed according to the two following mechanisms: (1) the client is connected to the sever through multiple channels via some relay nodes (Gkantsidis, 2003), and (2) several clients sending different part of the data to server (Vazhkudai, 2003). The former method requires that the bandwidth between the server and client should be large enough for multiple simultaneous data transfer. The latter method needs several duplicated copies of data to be transferred.

The current routing protocols over Internet naturally form a two-level hierarch: inter-domain and intra-domain. BGP (Border Gateway Protocol) (Stewart, 1998), the *de facto* standard inter-domain routing protocol, often leads to failures and poor performance in end-to-end data transfer. With respect to this, multi-path methods have been developed to tackle the limitation at routing protocol level. Typical examples include Detour (Savage, 1999) and RON (Andersen, 2001), which successfully demonstrate that the multi-path data transfer methods can enable quicker reaction to failures and improve end-to-end performance. When the bandwidth constraints are within a network domain, multi-path data transfer may provide a much higher throughput (Akella, 2003; Akella, 2004).

Most work about multi-path data transfer focus on the *network layer* to improve the single-IP routing of BGP and offer seamless support to the upper applications. However, the feature can only be facilitated at a high price. They demand modification to the current routing protocols over Internet, which means all the routers should be updated. Aiming at this problem, we have proposed two multi-path data transfer algorithms at application level in the Grid environment, namely Specification-Unaware algorithm (*SU-algorithm*) and Specification-Aware algorithm (*SA-algorithm*). Those are both transparent to the lower protocols when improving the end-to-end performance. Moreover, both algorithms are uncoordinated, thus they do not need the global knowledge of the whole Grid network environment. The algorithms perform two major tasks, i.e., path selection and sending rate control. For path selection, the algorithms divide the whole data transfer process into several rounds, and they randomly select relay nodes. Existing work have demonstrated the benefits of randomized path selection (Gummadi, 2004), and it proved that it is an effective mechanism for path selection. Our idea about how to select a relay is inspired by the randomized path selection approach. As for sending rate control, the strategy of best-effort has been adopted to effectively utilize the bandwidth. The main difference between the two algorithms is that: *SU-algorithm* is not aware of the information of clustered nodes by Autonomous System (AS), and *SA-algorithm* fully utilizes such knowledge provided by the Grid environment. This causes the difference of the two algorithms in convergence rate.

We prove that the problem of path selection for multi-path data transfer is NP-hard. In this chapter, we discuss how the two algorithms work in establishing additional path for data transfer at application level. The *SA-algorithm* needs some local information of the network topology and the *SU-algorithm* has to dynamically collect the connection status. The two approaches can converge to a maximized sending rate in different convergence rates. In addition, a method for determining the sending rate through each candidate path has also been proposed.

The rest of the chapter is organized as follows: Section 2 describes the background, and section 3 formulates the problem. The algorithms of path selection and sending rate control are studied in Section 4. The results on performance evaluation are reported in Section 5. With the future trends in section 6, the article is concluded in Section 7.

BACKGROUND

Chen (1998), Zaumen (1998), and Vutunkury (1998) have studied the multipath routing at network layer, an improvement to the single-path routing provided by BGP. Such effort works at routing protocol level and need to rebuild existing network work protocols to support such routing algorithm.

Two examples of multi-path data transfer at application level are presented in Cheng (2003) and Ganguly (2005). Both approaches duplicate data into several copies and distribute them into different site in the network. Cheng's method treats the problem as collecting a large amount of data from several different hosts to a single destination in a wide-area network. Ganguly's method focuses on fast replication or distribution of large data from a single source to multiple sites. Both methods require the global knowledge of the network.

In addition, various improved solutions for data transfer have been proposed in the context of P2P networks, such as BitTorrent (BitTorrent, 2008), Bullet (Kostic, 2003), informed content delivery (Byers, 2004), Slurpie (Sherwood, 2004), ROMA (Kwon, 2004), and SplitStream (Castro, 2003). These methods work at application level. In the context of the above approaches, a client selects a set of peers from where they download a complementary set of blocks that form the original data file. These solutions need the whole copies or parts of the original data file existing in the network.

Some work on multi-homing (Orda, 1998; Wang, 2005; Dhamdhere, 2006; Akella, 2003; Guo, 2004; Glodenberg, 2005) study how to select ISP based on the information of the network's topology. These work are based on the fact that some of the nodes in the network may be connected through multiple ISPs. Correct ISP selection will achieve efficient data transfers.

Significantly different from the above-mentioned work, this study has the following aims: (1) it works at the application level, which need no change to the routing protocols; hence they are easier to be deployed in Internet than those methods working at the routing protocol level; (2) the proposed algorithms need no duplicated copies of data, and the cost on consistency maintenance of the data copies can be avoided; and (3) the number of candidate paths can be much larger than that examined by the existing work of multi-homing, and our approaches deal with a much more complicated path selection process.

PROBLEM STATEMENT

The problem of multi-path data transfer in the Grid environment can be transformed as an optimization problem of the selection of relays. Table 1 lists the definitions to the key notations used in the following discussions.

Castro (1999) and Han (2005) have pointed out that using single relay in multi-path data transfer exhibit a performance close to that using multiple relays. Hence, this study only considers single relay from the source to the destination. Let sent N denote all the storage resources in the Grid system. All the nodes in N may operate as either the source node or a relay node, which form two sets, namely SRC and RLY. Clearly, we have $SRC \subset N$ and $RLY \subset N$. The destination node could be a node in the set N or a client outside the Grid system. Due to the symmetric feature of data transfer, this study only considers the condition of data stored in a node (s) if $s \in N$.

The overall data transfer path from a client to its server can be formed by several smaller paths. Each of these paths contains either only one relay or no relay. A path can be classified into two types:

1. *The default path* selected by the network layer providing by the TCP/IP protocol suite, which contains no relay, and the sending rate is denoted as dsr_i, for $\forall i \in SRC$;
2. In contrast, a *normal* path is referred to as one path that contains exactly one relay $r \in RLY$. The sending rate of this path is denoted as sr_{ir}.

The sending rate of a source $i \in SRC$ can be calculated as:

$$sr_i = \sum_{r \in RLY} sr_{ir} + \alpha * dsr_i,$$

Table 1. Key notations in the problem setting

Notation	Definition
N	Set of Storage Resource in Grid environment
SRC	Set of source containing the requested data
RLY	Set of relays
sr_i	Sending rate of source $i \in SRC$
sr_{ir}	Sending rate of source $i \in SRC$ through the path containing the relay $r \in RLY$
dsr_i	Sending rate of source $i \in SRC$ through default path from the source to the destination
CP_{ir}	Path capacity of the path from the $i \in SRC$ to the destination containing the relay $r \in RLY$
$Utility(sr_i)$	The utility function of source $i \in SRC$

where $\alpha = 0$ means the default path is not selected while $\alpha = 1$ means that the default path is selected in that process. The default path and other paths with relays form multi-path from the client to the server.

Any path in the Grid system has its own capacity determined by the current network condition. A path is composed by several links interconnected by a relay. The path capacity is determined by the link with the lowest capacity. As defined in Table 1, CP_{ir} denotes the path capacity of the path from the $i \in SRC$ to the destination containing the relay $r \in RLY$.

The problem of multi-path data transfer can be treated as how to select relays to construct several paths for sending data concurrently and the control of path rates in order to maximize the utility function (defined in (1)) over all sources. The problem can be formulated as an optimization problem **P**:

$$\textbf{P}: \text{maximize}: \; Utility(SRC) = \sum_{sr \in SRC} sr_i \tag{1}$$

$$\text{Subject to: } sr_i = \sum_{r \in RLY} sr_{ir} + \alpha * dsr_i, \text{ for } \forall i \in SRC, \text{and } r \in RLY \tag{2}$$

$$sr_{ir} \le CP_{ir}, \text{ for } \forall i \in SRC, \text{and } r \in RLY \tag{3}$$

where expression (2) describes the total rate at which a source sends data via all relays, and (3) describes the constraint to the link's capacity. Here the multi-path data transfer problem can be converted to selection of one-hop relay nodes to achieve the maximized throughput and to avoid congestion caused by multiple simultaneous transfer tasks. Theorem 1 indicates that this problem is NP-hard.

Theorem 1: In a single-receiver 2-hop network setting, the problem of choosing relays for every source is NP-hard, when the utility function is maximized and the congestion is avoided.

Proof: The problem of knapsack is NP-hard. If such a problem of relay selection is isomorphic to knapsack, the theorem is proven. The selected paths for a source $sr_i \in SRC$ are indexed from 0 to k-1. Each path has a corresponding relay node, and all of them compose a referred relay set for $sr_i \in SRC$, written as Ri. The sending rate of sr_i is subject to:

$$s_i < \sum_{r \in Ri} CP_{ir}.$$

For all the sources, the total sending rate TS should be subject to the condition,

$$TS < \sum_{s \in SRC} \sum_{r \in Ri} CP_{ir} \tag{4}$$

The condition (3) in problem **P** can be substituted by (4). The problem **P** is isomorphic to the problem of knapsack.

PATH SELECTION AND SENDING RATE CONTROL

This section introduces two alternative algorithms of path selection, namely a Specification-Unaware (SU) algorithm and a Specification-aware (SA) algorithm.

SU-algorithm is absolutely uncoordinated, which needs no global information of network topology and run-time state. The whole data transfer can be divided into a number of rounds for each source, and paths are randomly selected in each round. Congestion will be observed in every round: the sending rate will be largely reduced to release the bandwidth if congestion detected. Each of the sources performs the above operations to ensure that they can use the whole network efficiently. *SA-algorithm* is an extension to *SU-algorithm*. Some additional path selection rules are added into the path selection process, which aim to further improve the convergence rate.

Specification-Unaware (SU) Algorithm

Here we consider multiple source sending data simultaneously in the Grid environment in addition to one source sending rate. Path selection (or relay selection) should avoid the situation in which many sources compete for the same relay node. In the proposed approaches, a data transfer has three tasks: path selection, sending rate control and data transfer. The principle of sending rate control is that each selected path can forward the data from the source to the destination as fast as possible.

The whole process of data transfer is divided into successive rounds between which the interval is the same. In each round, a source randomly selects a path according to the probability of each relay node. The initial probability for every path is the same, with the value of

$$\frac{1}{|RLY|},$$

and this probability may change in the future rounds according to the algorithm depicted in Figure 1.

Every candidate relay has a dynamic probability in which it can be selected. This probability is written as P_{rr}^{n}, where n means it is the *nth* round data transfer, s and r denote that the path is from the source s to the destination node via the relay node of r. In order to have a uniform expression, the probability of the default path is denoted as P_{rr}^{n}. Actually as the default path does not contain any relay node, and the first r in the subscript of P_{rr}^{n} serves as an indication of the path's type. For the *nth* round of data transfer, a source needs to detect whether there was congestion in the selected path in the last round. If congestion is detected, the selection probability decreased to $1/2 * P_{sr}^{n-1}$. If this path is selected for p ($p \geq 1$) rounds successively from the *nth* round, its selection probability is

$$(\frac{1}{2})^{p-1} * P_{sr}^{n-1}.$$

This operation quickly reduces the probability of selecting path in case congestion has been detected for multiple times. On the other hand, the probability of selecting a path will increases, if no congestion has been observed: the new value of the selection probability is $\min(2 * P_{sr}^{n-1}, 1)$. This probability reallocation may result in

Figure 1. The uncoordinated data path selection algorithm

```
begin
    while(transfer task is not complete from ∀s ∈ SRC ?)
        for all the relay node r ∈ RLY
            P_sr^n = P_sr^{n-1}
            if(path through r congested)
                P_sr^n = 1/2 * P_sr^{n-1}
            end if
            else
                P_sr^n = min( 2P_sr^{n-1}, 1)
            end else
        end for
        Normalize P_sr^n for all the r ∈ RLY
        RL_i ← Φ
        while( ∑ sr_ir < min( S_i, D_i) or TSR_v > MSR_v)
            Randomly select relay r ∈ RLY according to P_sr^n
            RL_i ← r
        end while
        Sleep for the next internal start
    end while
end
```

$$\sum_r P_{sr}^n \neq 1.$$

We normalize the new value of the each relay's selection probability to a value between 0 and 1. After that, the source selects the new paths according to each relay node's current selection probability (P_{sr}^n). The number of selected paths is determined by the following condition: (1) the actual sending rate of the source achieving the minimal of *the maximum sending rate* of the source i, D_i, and *the maximum receiving rate* the destination, S_i; or (2) the total sending rate is larger than the relay's maximum sending rate.

Sending Rate Control

The sending rate through each selected path is discussed in this subsection. It adopts best effort as the mechanism of sending rate control which makes the sending rate via each path attains maximum. The data transfer process continues till the next round for path selection.

If some relay is selected only by one source, the source will fully utilize the bandwidth from the source to the destination via the relay. However, when several sources compete for the same node, attempts for fully utilization of bandwidth may cause congestion immediately. Although such congestion can be detected in the next round of path selection, it will have wasted a significantly long time and may lead to chain-reaction propagating to the entire Grid system. In order to avoid this potential problem, an approach of sending rate control is proposed shown as in Formula 5. The basic idea is to let a relay control the sending rate from each source. In our implementation, a node receives the connection request from the source when the source selects it as the relay. Then the relay is aware of which source selects it for forwarding data. The bandwidths from the source to the relay and from the relay to the destination can be detected according to the method proposed in Liu (2003). There exits a maximum value of the bandwidth (labeled as ASR_{ir}) from a source i to the destination via relay r. The value of ASR_{ir} can be affected by the relay's load and the current network condition. Here we use the detected maximum value as the value of ASR_{ir}. R_r denotes a set of sources, and all sources choose r as their relay. When R_r contains only one element (i), for instance, the sending rate from i to the destination via relay r is written as ASR_{ir}. When R_r contains multiple elements, the sending rate of each source via relay r is calculated as: (1) all the p_{ir}^n are normalized to np_{ir}^n, for all $i \in R_r$, such that

$$\sum_{i \in R_r} np_{ir}^n = 1;$$

and (2) the sending rate of each source i via relay r is calculated as $np_{ir}^n * ASR_{ir}$.

$$SR_{ir} = \begin{cases} ASR_{ir}, & |R_r| = 1 \\ np_{ir}^n * ASR_{ir}, & |R_r| > 1 \end{cases} \tag{5}$$

Properties

This subsection presents some properties of the *SU-algorithm*. Theorem 2 and its corollary indicate that the results are convergent and prove that the algorithm can achieve the optimal situation.

Theorem 2: In an ideal situation of congestion detection, the *SU-algorithm* attains at a convergence rate that will maximize a source's sending rate.

Proof: Consider the situation where there exits a source not arriving at the maximized sending rate. There are two possibilities:

1. The source does not reach the maximized sending rate via a set of relays. Then at least one path via a relay does not attain the maximum sending rate. Assume that a source i does not reach the maximized sending rate via a relay r, and the sending rate via relay r is sr_{ir}, which does not reach its maximum. Here sr_{ir}' is the maximum sending rate via the relay r constrained by its capacity. On the other hand, the sending rate control with the principle of best effort implies that the path will be congested if the source attempts to send data at a rate larger than sr_{ir}'. If sr_{ir} is not the threshold to make the path via relay r congested, then sr_{ir} cannot be the maximum sending rate via r.

2. The source does not choose a proper set of relays. We assume that there exists a relay $r1$ which can improve the total sending rate of the source but has not been chosen in the current (nth) round. If the condition of

$$\sum_{r \in RLY} sr_{ir} < \min(S_i, D_i)$$

is not satisfied, the relay can be chosen in the *nth* round with the probability of p_{ir1}^{n}. If this condition is not satisfied, relay *r1* must be chosen in the next *k* round with the probability of p_{ir1}^{n+k}. Without congestion, the possibility of being selected will increase in the next rounds. As this procedure continues, the relay will be chosen eventually. Additionally, any combined condition can be proved by dividing it into the two conditions. The theorem is then tenable.

Theorem 2 denotes that the algorithm converges to a maximal sending rate for a single source. Therefore any sources will converge to a maximal sending rate, as shown in corollary 1.

Corollary 1: If the congestion detection is perfect, the *SU-algorithm* makes all the resources to reach maximized sending rate with a relative large round number.

Specification-Aware Path Selection

In the Grid environment, the network topology can be known to all relays and sources. Typically a pair of nodes in an *Autonomous System* (AS) holds a networking condition (e.g., bandwidth) similar to that between any other two nodes in the same AS. Therefore, in this study nodes in an AS are clustered as a *node set*. Some special nodes may exist in multiple sets. This fact implies that the data transfer rate from node in a set to the destination in another set may be accelerated by selecting such special nodes as relays. The *SU-algorithm* by its nature will not be aware of this information at the beginning, although such configuration can be detected through relay selections in the long run. If we let all nodes in the Grid environment be aware of this configuration, the convergence rate may be shortened. The *SA-algorithm* has been designed based on this assumption.

The relays with the similar connection condition can be considered as in the same set, notated as *SC*. It satisfies the following conditions: (1) $SC = \{CLS_i \mid \text{for all } r \in CLS_i \text{ in the same } AS\}$ and (2)

$$\bigcup_i CLS_i = RLY .$$

The process of path selection in *SA-algorithm* is similar to that in *SU-algorithm*. The source still selects relays randomly as in *SA-algorithm*. However, if the source and the destination belong to different sets, the nodes belonging to these two sets will always be allocated with a high priority. If the source and the destination are in the same set, nodes in this set will be selected with a higher probability than those nodes in other sets. A threshold will be defined in this case. The probabilities assigned to these nodes will not become less than the threshold.

PERFORMANCE EVALUATION

This section presents a performance evaluation of *SA-algorithm* and *SU-algorithm*. The algorithms have been simulated upon Network Simulation 2 (NS2) (Fall, 2008).

In the performance test, we aim to emulate a Grid environment of a medium scale and the network condition is similar to most Grid environments in practice. In the simulation experiments, we assume that there are 200 nodes in the Grid environment and the maximum sending rate of each source is 1 Mbps. Given that all possible connections between any two nodes are the same, the proposed algorithms will introduce additional cost in selecting relay nodes. Hence, the simulations will only consider an asymmetric connection condition. All candidate relays of a source are indexed with an integer (initialized as 1). Here we introduce a skew factor β, where $0 \leq \beta \leq 1$. The bandwidth via the *jth* relay from the source to the destination is proportional to $1/j^{\beta}$. When $\beta = 0$, all the relays have the same bandwidth. As β increases, the bandwidth distribution among the relays becomes more asymmetric. This represents the situation in which although some links have a high bandwidth, the overall networking performance is still poor. We use a *normalized sending rate* as the criteria to evaluate the performance of data transfer under different conditions. The *normalized sending rate* is the normalized average sending rate for all the sources in the environment with the value between 0 and 1. If there is only one source to transfer data, the normalized sending rate is the actual ratio between data sending rate and the maximum capacity of data transfer.

Simulations with a Single Data Source

The first group of simulations compares the normalized source rate of *SA-algorithm* and *SU-algorithm* with a single data source. The main objective of the simulations is to study the convergence rate of the two algorithms. Four simulations have been performed, and each uses four different values of β, i.e., 0.25, 0.5, 0.75 and 1.

The experimental results are presented in Figure 2. The results indicate that when the value of β is 0.25, both of the two algorithms can approach the maximum sending rate in a short time (5 and 8 rounds for SA and AU algorithm respectively). In contrast, when β increases, the convergence rates of both algorithms slow down (27 and 35 rounds for SA and AU algorithm respectively when β is 1). The reason is that when the network becomes more asymmetric, both algorithms need more time to detect the optimal relay nodes. Besides the above, the normalized sending rate of both algorithms decreases when β increases. This is because the number of the relays offering high bandwidths decreases as the network becomes more asymmetric (i.e., the value of β increases), and this indicates that the performance of the algorithms is constrained by the network condition.

Simulation with Multiple Data Sources

The second group of simulations evaluates the performance of the two algorithms in the case that there exist multiple sources sending data simultaneously. β has been set between 0.25 and 1 same as in the previous experiments. Here the number of sources is fixed to 20, which represents the situation that the whole Grid environment is neither too busy nor too idle. With the same values of β adopted, the normalized sending rate of the simulation with multiple concurrent data transfer is less than that with only one sending source (simulation results shown in Figure 3). This is because multiple sending sources may compete for the same relay and cause congestion.

It can also be observed that the difference between the results of the two algorithms decreases when the value of β increases. As the value of β increases, congestion will occur as sources compete for a relay. If the relay happens to be the one with predefined high priority, the relay cannot provide the expected bandwidth. Thus, information of the network configuration will not be properly used as expected.

Figure 2. Normalized sending rate with single sending source and different value of β

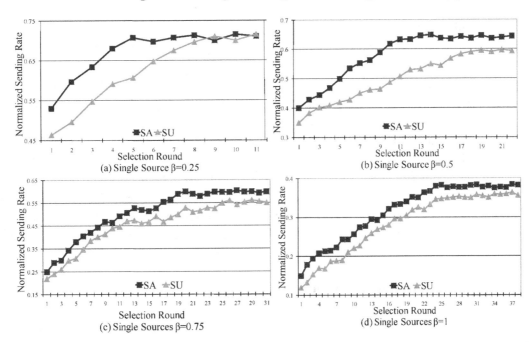

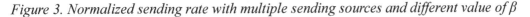

Figure 3. Normalized sending rate with multiple sending sources and different value of β

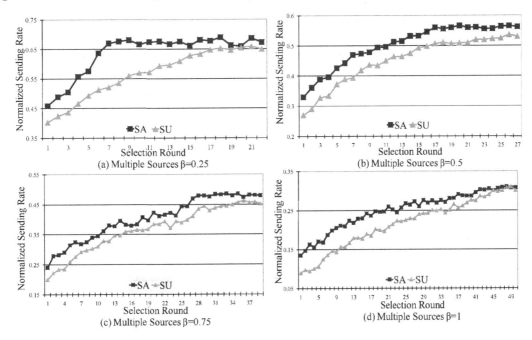

Performance Comparison Between FTP and SU-Algorithm

Another simulation is about the comparison between *SU-algorithm* and FTP. Actually GridFTP is more commonly used in the Grid environment. The comparison was made because FTP is ready for use in NS2 and there is no such a component for GridFTP in NS2. Actually FTP exhibits an even better performance than that GridFTP does. This is not a surprise since GridFTP incurs more overhead with more operations, such as authorization and authentication. The total number of nodes in the Grid environment is still set to 200 and β set to 0.5. We assume that there is only one source in *SU-algorithm* and FTP. Other configurations for the second group of simulations hold the same here.

The simulation results are reported in Figure 4. We can observe that at the initial phrase, the difference of the results from the two protocols is not significant. As long as the *SU-algorithm* discovers the proper relays, the gap between the two sets of results become larger. When the performance of *SU-algorithm* trends to be stabilized (after the 17th selection round), the sending rate achieved by *SU-algorithm* is 61.4% higher than that of FTP. This indicates that the proposed algorithm can effectively improve the performance of data transfer comparing to FTP.

Discussion on Quality of Services

Quality of services (QoS) is an important for a Grid system, and it is also a challenging issue to address. QoS in a Grid system can be evaluated through three metrics: latency, throughput and availability (Menasce, 2004). The process of data transfer in the context of the proposed algorithms can be divided into three stages: selection for the proper nodes as relays, determination of the sending rate for each selected path, and sending data to the destination via selected paths. The first two stages contribute to the latency of the algorithms. The last stage determines the throughput, i.e., how many data can be sent. The availability can be measured by whether the process of data transfer can still continue even if some paths are not available. If it can continue, the availability is secured.

An additional simulation has been performed as an extension those presented in section 5.3 with the same configuration parameters. The simulation aims to evaluate the three aspects of QoS. Both proposed algorithms have been examined in with a single data source and β set to 0.5. We evaluate the two algorithms when they are in three states: initial state, stabilized state, and disrupted state. The initial phrase refers to the period shortly after the simulations start. As shown in Figure 2.b, the initial state

Figure 4. Performance comparison between SU-algorithm and FTP

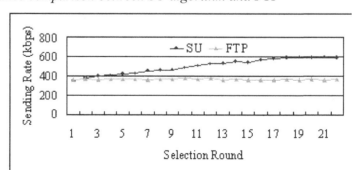

446

Table 2. Simulation result of QoS evaluation

	Initial State		Stabilized State		Disrupted State		FTP	
	SU	SA	SU	SA	SU	SA	Normal	Disrupted State
Latency (ms)	980	670	235	233	450	451	210	N/A
Throughput (bps)	220	250	440	480	160	158	368	0
Availability	100%	100%	100%	100%	100%	100%	100%	0%

covers the first four rounds. The stabilized state represents that the sending rates of the two algorithms converge, and it begins from the 19th round for *SU-algorithm* and the14th round for *SA-algorithm* respectively. After the algorithms reach their stabilized states, we randomly disconnect 50% of the paths to make them enter the disrupted state. FTP is also evaluated in two states: the normal state (the same as the simulation reported in section 5.3) and the disrupted state (randomly losing 50% of the paths). The simulation results are reported in Table 2. The results indicate that the latency of the proposed algorithms is larger than that of FTP especially at the initial stage. Nevertheless, when dealing with huge data, the latency will not be significant to the overall performance. We can also observe that the throughput of the proposed algorithms in the stabilized state is much better than that of FTP (also see Figure 4). When being in the disrupted state, both proposed algorithms achieve 100% availability as showed by the results. In contrast, FTP can only guarantee the availability of 50% (maximum in theory).

FUTURE TRENDS

For future work, we need to address how to apply the proposed algorithms in the real systems. Experimental results indicate that the algorithms can support efficient data transfer. The additional cost incurred by those algorithms can be ignored when dealing with bulky data. Nevertheless, in real applications, the length for each selection round should be studied for different data sizes. Moreover, the tasks of data transfer could be associated with different QoS requirements. A possible direction is the study of adaptive relay selection and priority setting of tasks according to the QoS to be satisfied.

CONCLUSION

In this chapter, two data transfer algorithms aiming at bulky data transfer in the Grid environment have been proposed, namely *SU-algorithm* and *SA-algorithm*. Both algorithms select some nodes as the relays to form multiple paths for data transfer between a source and the destination. *SA-algorithm* requires each node being aware of the status that it connects to other nodes. In contrast, this is not required by *SU-algorithm*, and it can still adapt to dynamic network conditions. Experiments have been carried out to evaluate the performance of the algorithms in a medium scale Grid environment. The results indicate that *SA-algorithm* holds faster convergence rate than that of *SU-algorithm*. The results also show that the proposed algorithms are promising comparing to the traditional data transfer protocols such as FTP. With the improved performance for data transfer, the QoS quality of data transfer can be guaranteed under unstable network conditions.

ACKNOWLEDGMENT

This work is supported by National Science Foundation of China under grant 90412010, and National High-Tech Research and Development Program of China under grant 2006AA01A115.

REFERENCES

Akella, A., Maggs, B., Seshan, S., Shaikn, A., & Sitaraman, R. (2003). A measurement-based analysis of multihoming. In Feldmann, A., Zitterbart, M., Crowcroft, J., & Wetherall, D. (Eds.), *Proceedings of the ACM SIGCOMM 2003 Conference on Applications, Technologies, Architectures, and Protocols for Computer Communication* (pp. 353-364). New York: ACM Press.

Akella, A., Pang, J., Maggs, B., Seshan, S., & Shaikn, A. (2004). A Comparison of Overlay Routing and Multihoming Route Control. In Yavatkar, R., Zegura, E. W., & Rexford, J. (Eds.), *Proceedings of the ACM SIGCOMM 2004 Conference on Applications, Technologies, Architectures, and Protocols for Computer Communication* (pp. 93-106). New York: ACM Press.

Andersen, D., Balakrishnan, H., Kaashoek, M., & Morris, R. (2001). Resilient Overlay Networks. In M. Satyanarayanan (Eds), *Proceedings of the 18th Symposium on Operating System Principles* (pp. 131-145). New York: ACM Press.

Barish, B. C., & Weiss, R. (1999). LIGO and the Detection of Gravitational Waves. *Physics Today*, 52(10), 44-50.

BitTorrent (2008). Retrieved September 27, 2008 from http://bitconjurer.org/BitTorrent.

Byers, J., Considine, J., Mitzenmacher, M., & Rost, S. (2004). Informed content delivery across adaptive overlay networks. *IEEE/ACM Transactions on Networking, 12*(5), 767-780.

Castro, M., Druschel, P., Kermarrec, A-M., Nandi, A., Rowstron, A., & Singh, A. (2003). SplitStream: High-bandwidth multicast in a cooperative environment. In Michael L. Scott, Larry L. Peterson (Eds.), *Symposium on Operating Systems Principles* (pp. 298-313). New York: ACM Press.

Chen, J., Druschel, P., & Subramanian, D. (1998). An efficient multipath forwarding method. In *Proceedings the Seventeenth Annual Joint Conference of the IEEE Computer and Communications Societies* (pp. 1418-1425). Los Alamitos: IEEE Computer Society.

Cheng, B., Chou, C., Golubchik, L., Khuller, S., & Wan, Y.-C. (2003). Large scale data collection: a coordinated approach. In *the 22nd Annual Joint Conference of the IEEE Computer and Communications Societies* (pp. 218-228). New York: IEEE Communications Society.

Chervenak, A., Foster, I., Kesselman, C., Salisbury, C., & Tuecke, S. (2001). The Data Grid: Towards an Architecture for the Distributed Management and Analysis of Large Scientific Data Sets. *Journal of Network and Computer Applications, 23*(3), 187-200.

Deelman, E., Singh, G., Atkinson, M. P., Chervenak, A., Chue Hong, N. P., Kesselman, C., Patil, S., Pearlman, L., & Su, M. (2004). Grid-Based Metadata Services. In Hatzopoulos, M. & Manolopoulos,

Y. (Eds), *16th International Conference on Scientific and Statistical Database Management* (pp. 393-402). Santorini Island: IEEE Computer Society.

Fall, K., & Varadhan, K. (2008). The NS Manual (formerly ns Notes and Documentation), Retrieved September 27, 2008 from http://www.isi.edu/nsnam/ns/ns-documentati

Foster, I., Kesselman, C., & Tuecke, S. (2001). The Anatomy of the Grid: Enabling Scalable Virtual Organizations. *International Journal of High Performance Computing and Applications, 15*(3), 200-222.

Han, J., Watson, D., & Jahanian, F. (2005). Topology aware overlay networks. In *Proceedings of 24th Annual Joint Conference of the IEEE Computer and Communications Societies* (pp. 2554-2565). New York: IEEE Communications Society.

Ganguly, S., Saxena, A., Bhatnagar, S., Banerjee, S., & Izmailov, R. (2005). Fast replication in content distribution overlays. In *the 24th Annual Joint Conference of the IEEE Computer and Communications Societies* (pp. 2246-2256). New York: IEEE Communications Society.

Gkantsidis, C., Ammar, M., & Zegura E (2003). On the Effect of Large-Scale Deployment of Parallel Downloading. *In Proceedings of the third IEEE Workshop on Internet Applications* (pp. 79-89). Los Alamitos: IEEE Computer Society.

Glodenberg, D., Qiu, L., Xie, H., Yang, Y. R., & Zhang, Y. (2005). Optimizing cost and performance for multihoming. In Raj Yavatkar, Ellen W. Zegura, Jennifer Rexford (Eds.), *the ACM SIGCOMM 2004 Conference on Applications, Technologies, Architectures, and Protocols for Computer Communication* (pp. 79-92). New York: ACM Press.

Guo, F., Chen, J., Li, W., & Chiueh, T. (2004). Experiences in building a multihoming load balancing system. In *the 23rd Annual Joint Conference of the IEEE Computer and Communications Societies* (pp. 1241-1251). New York: IEEE Communications Society.

Gummadi, K., Madhyastha, H. V., Steven, D. G., Levy, H. M., & Wetherall, D. (2004). Improving the Reliability of Internet Paths with One-hop Source Routing. In E. Brewer & P. Chen (Eds.), *Proceedings of 6th Symposium on Operating System Design and Implementation* (pp. 183-198). San Francisco, California: USENIX.

Kostic, D., Rodriguez, A., Albrecht, J., & Vahdat, A. (2003). Bullet: High bandwidth data dissemination using an overlay mesh. In M. L. Scott, L. L. Peterson (Eds.), *Symposium on Operating Systems Principles* (pp. 298-313). New York: ACM Press.

Kwon, G., & Byers, J. (2004). ROMA: Reliable overlay multicast using loosely coupled TCP connections. In *the 23rd Annual Joint Conference of the IEEE Computer and Communications Societies* (pp. 385-395), New York: IEEE Communications Society.

Liu, Y., Liu, W., Jia, W.-J., & Jiang, C. (2003). Link bandwidth detection for multimedia streaming in a distributed server environment. *In Proceeding of 2003 Joint Conference of the Fourth International Conference on Information, Communications & Singal Processing And Fourth Pacific-Rim Conference on Multimedia* (pp. 438-442), New York: IEEE Communications Society.

Menasce, D., & Casalicchio, E. (2004). Quality of Service Aspects and Metrics in Grid Computing. In The Proceedings of the 2004 Computer Measurement Group Conference (pp. 521-532).

Rajasekar, A., Wan, M., Moore, R., Kremenek, G., & Guptil, T. (2003). Data Grids, Collections, and Grid Bricks. In F. Titsworth (Eds), *20th IEEE/11th NASA Goddard Conference on Mass Storage Systems and Technologies* (pp. 2-9). San Diego: IEEE Computer Society.

Savage, S., Anderson, T., Aggarwal, A., Becker, D., Cardwell, N., Collins, A., Hoffman, E., Snell, J., Vahdat, A., Voelker, G., & Zahorjan, J. (1999). Detour: A Case for Informed Internet Routing and Transport. *IEEE Micro, 19*(1), 50-59.

Savage, S., Collins, A., Hoffman, E., Snell, J., & Anderson, T. (1999). The End-to-End Effects of Internet Path Selection. In Parulkar, G. & Turner, J. (Eds), *Proceedings of the ACM SIGCOMM '99 Conference on Applications, Technologies, Architectures, and Protocols for Computer Communication* (pp. 263-274). New York: ACM Press.

Sherwood, R., Braud, R., & Bhattacharjee, B. (2004). Slurpie: A cooperative bulk data transfer protocol. In *the 23rd Annual Joint Conference of the IEEE Computer and Communications Societies* (pp. 941-951). New York: IEEE Communications Society.

Stewart, J.W. (1998). *BGP4: Inter-Domain Routing in the Internet.* Boston: Addison-Wesley Professional.

Szalay, A., & Williams, R. (Eds.) (2008). US National Virtual Observatory (NVO). Retrieved August 14, 2008, from http://www.us-vo.org/.

Vazhkudai, S. (2003). Enabling the Co-Allocation of Grid Data Transfers. In *Proceedings of 4th International Workshop on Grid Computing* (pp. 44-51). Los Alamitos: IEEE Computer Society.

Vutunkury, S., & Garcia-Luna-Aceves, J. (1998). MPATH: a loop-free multipath routing algorithm. *Elsevier Journal of Microprocessors and Microsystems, 24*(6), 319-327.

Wulz, C.-E. (1998). CMS – Concept and Physics Potential. In Nieves, Jose F. (Eds.), *the first Tropical Workshop on Particle Physics and Cosmology* (pp. 467-478). San Juan: American Institute of Physics.

Zaumen, W. T., & Garcia-Luna-Aceves, J. (1998). Loop-free multipath routing using generalized diffusing computations. In *Proceedings the Seventeenth Annual Joint Conference of the IEEE Computer and Communications Societies* (pp. 219-327). Los Alamitos: IEEE Computer Society.

Compilation of References

Abdul-Rahman, A., & Hailes, S. (2000). Supporting trust in virtual communities. *International Conference on System Sciences*, Hawaii.

Abowd, G. D., & Dey, A. K. (1999). *Towards a better understanding of context and context-awareness* (No. GIT-GVU-99-22). Atlanta, GA: Georgia Institute of Technology, College of Computing.

Abramson, D., Buyya, R., & Giddy, J. (2002). A computational economy for grid computing and its implementation in the Nimrod-G resource broker. *Future Generation Computer Systems, 18*(8), 1061-1074.

Abramson, D., Sosic, R., Giddy, J., & Hall, B. (1995). Nimrod: A Tool for Performing Parametised Simulations using Distributed Workstations. *In Proceedings of 4th IEEE Symposium on High Performance Distributed Computing*, Virginia, USA.

Aggarwal, R., Verma, K., Miller, J., & Milnor, W. (September 2004). Constraint Driven Web Service Composition in METEOR-S. *In the proceeding of 2004 IEEE International Conference on Services Computing*. Shanghai, China: IEEE computer society.

Agrawal, R., & Srikant, R. (1994). Fast algorithms for mining association rules in large databases. In *Proceedings of the International Conference on Very Large Databases* (pp. 478-499). Santiage, Chile: Morgan Kaufmann.

Agrawal, R., & Srikant, R. (1995). Mining sequential Patterns. *Proceedings of the 11th International Confer-ence on Data Engineering* (pp. 3-14). IEEE Computer Society Press.

Agrawal, R., Imielinski, T., & Swami, A. (1993). Mining association rules between sets of items in large databases. *In Proceedings of the 1993 ACM SIGMOD International Conference on Management of Data* (pp. 207-216). ACM Press.

Akella, A., Maggs, B., Seshan, S., Shaikn, A., & Sitaraman, R. (2003). A measurement-based analysis of multi-homing. In Feldmann, A., Zitterbart, M., Crowcroft, J., & Wetherall, D. (Eds.), *Proceedings of the ACM SIGCOMM 2003 Conference on Applications, Technologies, Archi-tectures, and Protocols for Computer Communication* (pp. 353-364). New York: ACM Press.

Akella, A., Pang, J., Maggs, B., Seshan, S., & Shaikn, A. (2004). A Comparison of Overlay Routing and Multi-homing Route Control. In Yavatkar, R., Zegura, E. W., & Rexford, J. (Eds.), *Proceedings of the ACM SIGCOMM 2004 Conference on Applications, Technologies, Archi-tectures, and Protocols for Computer Communication* (pp. 93-106). New York: ACM Press.

Akyildiz, I. F., Su, W., Sankarasubramaniam, Y., & Cayirci, E. (2002). Wireless sensor networks: A survey. *Computer Networks, 38*(4), 393–422.

Al-Ali, R. J., Amin, K., von Laszewski, G., Rana, O. F., Walker, D. W., Hategan, M., & Zaluzec, N. J. (2004). Analysis and Provision of QoS for Distributed Grid Ap-plication., *Journal of Grid Computing*, (pp. 163-182), .

Alesso, P. H., & Smith, F. C. (2005). *Developing Semantic Web services.* A.K. Peterson Ltd.

Allcock, W., Bester, J., Bresnahan, J., Meder, S., Plaszczak, P., & Tuecke, S. (2003). *GridFTP: Protocol extensions to FTP for the grid.* Lemont, IL: Global Grid Forum.

Allen, G., Daues, G., Foster, I., et al. (2001). The Astrophysics Simulation Collaboratory Portal: A science Portal Enabling Community Software Development. *Proceedings of the 10ᵗʰ IEEE International Symposium on High performance Distributed Computing* 2001.

Allison, C., Cerri, S. A., Ritrovato, P., Gaeta, A., & Gaeta, M. (2005). Services, semantics, and standards: Elements of a learning Grid infrastructure. *Applied Artificial Intelligence, 19*(9-10), 861-879

Allison, C., Ruddle, A., & Michaelson, A. (2002, September 16). Systems support for collaborative learning. In *Proceedings of the 1st LEGE-WG International Workshop on Educational Models for GRID Based Services*, Lausanne, Switzerland.

Alunkal, B., Valjkovic, I., & Laszewski, G. V. (2003). Reputation-Based Grid Resource Selection. *Proceedings of the Workshop on Adaptive Grid Middleware,* New Orleans LA, USA.

Amin, K., G. von Laszewski, and M. Hategan et. al., "GridAnt: A Client-Controllable Grid Workflow System", in *Proc. 37ᵗʰ IEEE Annual Hawaii International Conference on System Sciences*, pp. 3293-3301, 2004.

Amir, Y., Awerbuch, B., Barak, A., Borgstrom, R., & Keren, A. (2000). Opportunity cost approach for job assignment in a scalable computing cluster. *IEEE Transactions on Parallel Distributed System, 11*(7), 760-768.

Anceaume, E., M. Gradinariu, A. Ravoaja, "Incentive for P2P Fair Resource Sharing", *Proceedings of the Fifth IEEE International Conference on Peer-to-Peer Computing*, pp. 253-260, 31 Aug.-2 Sept. 2005.

Andersen, D., Balakrishnan, H., Kaashoek, M., & Morris, R. (2001). Resilient Overlay Networks. In M. Satyana-rayanan (Eds), *Proceedings of the 18ᵗʰ Symposium on Operating System Principles* (pp. 131-145). New York: ACM Press.

Andrews, T., F. Curbera, and H. Dholakia et al, "Business Process Execution Language for Web Services", Version 1.1, 2003.

Antonioletti, M., Krause, A., Paton, N. W., Eisenberg, A., Laws, S., Malaika, S., et al. (2006). The WS-DAI family of specifications for web service data access and integration. *ACM SIGMOD Record, 35*(1), 48-55.

Antoniou, G., & Harmelen, F. (2004). *A Semantic Web primer.* MIT Press.

Apache Software Foundation. (2003). *WSIF: Web services invocation framework, Version 2.0.* Retrieved from http://ws.apache.org/wsif/

Ardagna, D., & Pernici, B. (2007). Adaptive Service Composition in Flexible Processes. *IEEE Transaction on Software Engineering, 33*(6), 369-383.

Argonne, I. F., Gannon, D., Fujitsu, H. K., & Von Reich, J. J. (2004). *Open grid services architecture use cases* (No. GFD-I.029). Lemont, IL: Global Grid Forum.

Arkin, A. (2002). *Business process modeling language (BPML).* Specification. BPMI.org.

Arkin, A., Askary, S., Bloch, B., Curbera, F., Goland, Y., Kartha, N., et al. (2005). *Web services business process execution language version* 2.0. wsbpel-specification-draft-01, OASIS.

Armstrong, R., et al. (1999). Toward a common component architecture for high-performance scientific computing. *HPDC.*

Ashok S., Omiecinski, E., & Shamkant, N. (1998). Mining for Strong Negative Associations in a Large Database of Customer Transactions. *In Proceedings of the 14th International Conference on Data Engineering* (pp. 494-502). IEEE Computer Society Press.

Atkinson, M., Dialani, V., Guy, L., Narang, I., Paton, N. W., Pearson, et al. (2003). *Grid database access and integration: Requirements and functionalities* (No. GFD-I.13). Lemont, IL: GLobal Grid Forum.

Aversa, R., Martino, B., & Mazzoccal, N. (2006). MAG-DA: a mobile agent based Grid architecture, *Journal of Grid Computing, 4(4)*, 395-412.

Axis Development Team. (2002). *Apache Axis, Version 1.0.* Retrieved http://ws.apache.org/axis/

Azzedin, F., & Maheswaran, M. (2002). Evolving and Managing Trust in Grid Computing Systems. *Proceedings of the IEEE Canadian Conference on Electrical and Computer Engineering*, Canada.

Banavar, G., Chandra, T., Mukherjee, B., Nagarajarao, J., Strom, R. E., & Sturman, D. C. (1999). An Efficient Multicast Protocol for Content-based Publish-Subscribe Systems, *International Conference on Distributed Computing Systems* (pp. 262-272). Washington D.C. USA.

Barish, B. C., & Weiss, R. (1999). LIGO and the Detection of Gravitational Waves. *Physics Today, 52(10)*, 44-50.

Barmouta, A., & Buyya, R. (2003). GridBank: A Grid Accounting Services Architecture (GASA) Distributed Systems Sharing and Integration. *Proceedings of the 17th Annual International Parallel and Distributed Processing Symposium, IEEE Computer Society Press* (pp.245-252), USA.

Barsanti, L., and A. C. Sodan, "Adaptive Job Scheduling via Predictive Job Resource Allocation", *Proceedings of the 12th Workshop on Job Scheduling Strategies for Parallel Processing*, 2006.

Barton, J., Thatte, S., & Nielsen, H. F. (2000). SOAP Messages with Attachments, W3C Note. Retrieved November 07, 2007, from http://www.w3.org/TR/2000/NOTE-SOAP-attachments-20001211

Baru, C., Moore, R., Rajasekar, A., & Wan, M. (1998). The SDSC Storage Resource Broker. *IBM Toronto Centre for Advanced Studies Conference (CASCON'98)* (pp.1-12), Toronto, Canada.

Base Object Model. (January). Retrieved November 07, 2007, from http://www.boms.info/

Bausch, W., C. Pautasso, and G. Alonso, "Programming for Dependability in a Service-Based Grid", in *Proc. 3rd IEEE/ACM Int. Symp. on Cluster Computing and the Grid*, Tokyo, Japan, pp. 164-171, 2003.

BEA Systems, IBM Corporation, Microsoft Corporation, SAP AG, & Siebel Systems (2003). Business process execution language for Web services (BPEL 1.1). *Technical Report*.

BEA, IBM, Microsoft, SAP, & Siebel. (2003). *Business process execution language for Web services*. Version 1.1. Specification. Retrieved May 15, 2006, from ftp://www6.software.ibm.com/software/developer/library/ws-bpel.pdf

Bechhofer, S., Moller, R., & Crowther, P. (2003). *The DIG description logic interface*. International Workshop on Description Logics, Rome, Italy.

Beco, S., Cantalupo, B., Matskanis, N., & Surridge M. (2006). *Putting semantics in Grid workflow management: The OWL-WS approach.* GGF16 Semantic Grid Workshop, Athens, Greece.

Begole, J., Rosson, M. B., & Shaffer, C. A. (1999), Flexible Collaboration Transparency: Supporting Worker Independence in Replicated Application-Sharing Systems. *ACM Trans. On Computer-Human Interaction, 6(2)*, 95-132.

Belaid, D., Provenzano, N., & Taconet, C. (1998). Dynamic management of CORBA trader federation. In *Proceedings of the 4th USENIX Conference on Object-Orented Technologies and Systems (COOTS)*.

Bellwood, T., et al. (2002). *UDDI API specification, Version 2.* Retrieved from http://uddi.org/pubs/ProgrammersAPI-V2.04-Published-20020719.htm

Berardi, D., Calvanese, D., De Giacomo, G., Lenzerini, M., & Mecella, M. (December 2003). Automatic Composition of E-services That Export Their Behavior. *In the proceeding of the 1st international conference on service-oriented computing*. Trento,Italy: Springer.

Berger, L. (2003). Generalized Multi-Protocol Label Switching (GMPLS) Signaling Resource ReserVation

Protocol-Traffic Engineering (RSVP-TE) Extensions, *IETF RFC 3473*.

Berman, F., Casanova, H., et al. (2005). New Grid scheduling and rescheduling methods in the GrADS project. *International Journal of Parallel Programming, 33*(2), 209-229.

Berman, F., Chien, A., Cooper, K., Dongarra, J., Foster, I., Gannon, D., Johnsson, L., Kennedy, K., Kesselman, C., Mellor-Crummey, J., Reed, D., Torczon, L., & Wolski, R. (2001). The GrADS Project: Software Support for High-Level Grid Application Development. *International Journal of High Performance Computing Applications, 15*(4), 327-344.

Bernat, G., Colin, A., & Peters, S. (2002). WCET analysis of probabilistic hard real-time systems. *Proceedings of the 23rd IEEE Real-Time Systems Symposium* (pp. 279-288). Austin, TX, U.S.A.

Berners-Lee, T., Hendler, J., & Lassila, O. (2001). The semantic Web: A new form of Web content that is meaningful to computers will unleash a revolution of new possibilities. Retrieved February 10, 2007, from *http://www.scientificamerican.com/*

Bernstein, A., Hill, S., & Provost, F. (2001). An intelligent assistant for the knowledge discovery process. *In Proceedings of the IJCAI-01 Workshop on Wrappers for Performance Enhancement in KDD*. Seattle, WA: Morgan Kaufmann.

Bhatia, R., Kodialam, S., & Lakshman, T. (2006). Fast network re-optimization schemes for mpls and optical networks. *Computer Networks, 50*(3), 317–331.

BitTorrent (2008). Retrieved September 27, 2008 from http://bitconjurer.org/BitTorrent.

Blanquer, I., Hernández, V., Mas, F., & Segrelles, D. (2005). Medical databases and information systems—A framework based on web services and grid technologies for medical image registration. *Lecture Notes in Computer Science 3745*, 22–33.

Bochmann, G., & Hafid, A. (1996). *Some Principles for Quality of Service Management*. Technical report, Universite de Montreal.

Boisseau, J., Mock, S., & Thomas, M. (2000). Development of Web toolkits for computational science portals: The NPACI HotPage. *Porceeding of the 9th IEEE international Symposium on high performance distributed computing.*

Bose, R., & Frew, J. (2004). Composing lineage metadata with XML for custom satellite-derived data products. *SSDBM.*

Bose, R., & Frew, J. (2005). Lineage retrieval for scientific data processing: A survey. *ACM Computing Surveys, 37*, 1–28.

Bose, R., Foster, I., & Moreau. L. (2006). Report on the international provenance and annotation workshop. *SIGMOD Record, 35*(3), 51–53.

Box, D., Curbera, F., et al. (2002). *Web services policy attachment (WS-PolicyAttachment)* (Version 1). Retrieved from http://www.verisign.com/wss/WS-PolicyAttachment.pdf

Box, D., et al. (2000). *Simple object access protocol (SOAP), Version 1.1*. Retrieved from http://www.w3.org/TR/SOAP/

Box, D., et al. (2002). *Web services policy framework (WS-policy), Version 1*. Retrieved from http://www.verisign.com/wss/WS-Policy.pdf

Box, D., et al. (2004). Web services eventing (WS-eventing). *Technical Report.*

Brandes, U., Eiglsperger, M., Herman, I., Himsolt, M., & Marshall, M.S. (2002). GraphML progress report: Structural layer proposal. *LNCS, 2265*, 501–512.

Brandic, I., Benkner, S., et al. (2005). QoS support for time-critical Grid workflow applications. *Proceedings of the 1st IEEE International Conference on e-Science and Grid Computing*, Melbourne, Australia.

Brawer, S. (1989). *Introduction to parallel programming*. San Diego, CA: Academic Press.

Brezany, P., Tjoa, A.M., Rusnak, M., & Janciak, I. (2003). Knowledge Grid support for treatment of traumatic brain injury victims. *International Conference on Computational Science and its Application*s. Montreal, Canada.

Brezany, P., Janciak, I., Kloner, C., & Petz, G. (2006). *Auriga — workflow engine for WS-I/WS-RF services.* Retrieved September 15, 2006, from http://www.Grid-miner.org/auriga/

Brezany, P., Janciak, I., Woehrer, A., & Tjoa, A.M. (2004). *GridMiner: A Framework for knowledge discovery on the Grid - from a vision to design and implementation.* Cracow Grid Workshop, Cracow, Poland: Springer.

Brittenham, P. (2001). *Web services inspection language specification (WSIL).* Retrieved from http://www.ibm.com/developerworks/webservices/library/ws-wsilspec.html

Brown, D. A., P. R. Brady, A. Dietz, J. Cao, B. Johnson, and J. McNabb, "A Case Study on the Use of Workflow Technologies for Scientific Analysis: Gravitational Wave Data Analysis", in I. J. Taylor, D. Gannon, E. Deelman, and M. S. Shields (Eds.), *Workflows for e-Science: Scientific Workflows for Grids*, Springer Verlag, pp. 39-59, 2007.

Bruin, R. et al. (2006). Job submission to Grid computing environment. *UK e-Science All Hands Meeting* (pp. 754-761), Nottingham, UK..

Bubak, M., Gubała, T., Kapałka, M., Malawski, M., & Rycerz, K. (2005, January). Workflow composer and service registry for grid applications. *Future Generation Computer Systems, 21*(1), 79-86.

Bubendorfer, K., & Thomson, W. (2006). Resource Management Using Untrusted Auctioneers in a Grid Economy, *Proceedings of the Second IEEE International Conference on e-Science and Grid Computing* (pp.74-81), Netherlands.

Burchard L.O., Heiss H.U., & De Rose C. (2003). Performance issues of bandwidth reservation for grid computing. In Proceedings of *15th Symposium on Computer Architecture and High Performance Computing.*

Burchard, L. O. (2005). Networks with advance reservations: Applications, architecture, and performance. *Journal of Network and Systems Management, 13*(4).

Burgstahler, S., & Swift, C. (1996). *Enhanced learning through electronic communities: A research review.*

Retrieved February from http://164.116.18.39/research_report.html

Bussler, C., Davies, J., Dieter, F., & Studer, R. (2004). The Semantic Web: Research and applications. In *Proceedings of the 1ˢᵗ European Semantic Web Symposium, ESWS. Lecture Notes in Computer Science, 3053.* Springer.

Buyya, R. (2002). *Economic-based distributed resource management and scheduling for grid computing.* Ph D dissertation, Monash University, Australia.

Buyya, R., Abramson, D., & Giddy, J. (2000). An Economy Driven Resource Management Architecture for Global Computational Power Grids. *Proceedings of the 2000 International Conference on Parallel and Distributed Processing Techniques and Applications* (pp.517-525), Las Vegas, USA.

Buyya, R., Abramson, D., & Venugopal, S. (2005, March). The Grid Economy. *Proceedings of the IEEE, 93*(3), 698-714.

Buyya, R., D. Abramson, J. Giddy, H. Stockinger, "Economic Models for Resource Management and Scheduling in Grid Computing", Special Issue on Grid Computing Environments, *The Journal of Concurrency and Computation: Practice and Experience(CCPE)*, May 2002.

Buyya, R., *High Performance Cluster Computing (Volume I): Architectures and Systems*, Prentice Hall PTR; 1st edition, June 15, 1999.

Buyya, R., J. Giddy, D. Abramson, "An Evaluation of Economy-Based Resource Trading and Scheduling on Computational Power Grids for Parameter Sweep Applications", *Proceedings of the Second Workshop on Active Middleware Services (AMS2000), In conjunction with the Ninth IEEE International Symposium on High Performance Distributed Computing (HPDC 2000),* Pittsburgh, USA, August 2000.

Byers, J., Considine, J., Mitzenmacher, M., & Rost, S (2004). Informed content delivery across adaptive overlay networks. *IEEE/ACM Transactions on Networking, 12*(5), 767-780.

Cabbly, J. (2004). The grid report. Retrieved February 10, 2007, from *http://www.1.ibm.com/grid/pdf/Clabby_Grid_Report_2004_Edition.pdf*

Cabral, L., Domingue, J., Galizia, S., Gugliotta, A., Tanasescu, V., Pedrinaci, C., & Norton, B. (November 2006). IRS-III: A Broker for Semantic Web Services Based Applications. *In the proceeding of the 5th International Semantic Web Conference.* Athens, USA: LNCS.

Cai, W., Yuan, Z., Low, M. Y. H., & Turner, S. J. (2005). Federate migration in HLA based simulation. *Future Generation Computer Systems, 21*(1), 87-95.

Calleja, M., Beckles, M., Keegan, M., Hayes, M., Parker, A., & Dove, M. (2004). CamGrid: Experiences in constructing a university-wide, Condor-based, Grid at the University of Cambridge. *UK e-Science All Hands Meeting.* Nottingham, UK. (pp. 173-178).

Cao, H., & Xiao, N. (2002). A market-based approach to allocate resources for computational grids. *Computer Research and Development (Chinese), 39*(8), 913-916.

Cao, J., Jarvis, S., et al. (2003). GridFlow: workflow management for Grid Computing. *Proceedings of the 3rd CCGrid* (pp.198-205), Tokyo, Japan.

Cao, J., S. A. Jarvis, S. Saini and G. R. Nudd, "GridFlow: Workflow Management for Grid Computing", in *Proc. 3rd IEEE/ACM Int. Symp. on Cluster Computing and the Grid*, Tokyo, Japan, pp. 198-205, 2003.

Cardei, M., & Wu, J. (2004). Coverage in wireless sensor networks. *Handbook of Sensor Networks.*

Cardei, M., & Wu, J. (2006). Energy-efficient coverage problems in wireless ad-hoc sensor networks. *Computer Communications, 29*(4), 413–420.

Cardei, M., MacCallum, D., Cheng, X., Min, M., Jia, X., Li, D., & Du, D. Z. (2002). Wireless sensor networks with energy efficient organization. *Journal of Interconnection Networks, 3*(3-4), 213–229.

Cardei, M., Thai, M., Li, Y., & Wu, W. (2005). Energy-efficient target coverage in wireless sensor networks. *Proc. of the 24th IEEE INFOCOM,* 1976–1984.

Cardoso, J., Miller, J., Sheth, A., & Arnold, J. (2002). *Modeling Quality of Service for Workflows and Web Service Processes.* Technical Report, LSDIS Lab, Department of Computer Science University of Georgia.

Cardoso, J., Sheth, A., & Kochut, K. (2002). *Implementing QoS management for workflow systems.* Retrieved from http://lsdis.cs.uga.edu/lib/download/CSK02-QoS-implementation-TR.pdf

Cardoso, J., Sheth, A., & Miller, J. (2002, April). Workflow Quality of Service. *Proceedings of the International Conference on Enterprise Integration and Modeling Technology and International Enterprise Modeling Conference (ICEIMT/IEMC'02),* Kluwer Publishers.

Cardoso, J., Sheth, A., Miller, J., Arnold, J., & Kochut, K. (2004). Quality of service for workflows and web service processes. *Journal of Web Semantics, 1*(3), 281-308.

Carrington, L., Snavely, A., & Wolter, N. (2006). A performance prediction framework for scientific applications, *Future Generation Computer Systems, 22,* 336–346.

Casanova, H., Bartol, T. M., Stiles, J., & Berman. F. (2001). Distributing MCell simulations on the Grid. *Internal Journal of High Performance Computing Application, 15*(3), 243-257.

Casanova, H., Dongarra, J., Johnson C., & Miller, M. (1998). Application-Specific Tools. In I. Foster & C. Kesselman (Eds.), *The GRID: Blueprint for a New Computing Infrastructure,* (pp. 159–180).

Casanova, H., Legrand, A., Zagorodnov, D., & Berman, F. (2000). Heuristics for scheduling parameter wweep applications in grid environments, in: *IEEE Proceedings of the 9th Heterogeneous Computing Workshop* (pp. 349–363). Cancun, Mexico: IEEE Computer Society.

Casanova, H., Obertelli, G., Berman, F., & Wolski, R. (2000). The AppLeS parameter sweep template: user-level middleware for the grid. *Scientific Programming, 8*(3), 111-126.

Castro, M., Druschel, P., Kermarrec, A-M., Nandi, A., Rowstron, A., & Singh, A. (2003). SplitStream: High-bandwidth multicast in a cooperative environment. In

Michael L. Scott, Larry L. Peterson (Eds.), *Symposium on Operating Systems Principles* (pp. 298-313). New York: ACM Press.

Catlett, C. (2002). The TeraGrid: A primer. Retrieved from www.teragrid.org

Cetintemel, U., Keleher, P. J., Bhattacharjee, B., & Franklin M. J. (2003). Deno: A Decentralized, Peer-to-Peer Object-Replication System for Weakly-Connected Environments. *IEEE Transactions on Computers, 52*(7), 943-959.

Chafle, G., Dasgupta, K., Kumar, A., Mittal, S., & Srivastava, B. (September 2006). Adaptation in Web Service Composition and Execution. *In the proceeding of IEEE 2006 International Conference on Web Services.* Chicago, USA: IEEE Press.

Chaki, S., E. M. Clarke, J. Ouaknine et al, "State / Event-based Software Model Checking", in E. A. Boiten, J. Derrick, G. Smith (Eds.), *Integrated Formal Methods,* LNCS Vol. 2999, Springer Verlag, pp. 128-147, 2004.

Chakrabarty, K., Iyengar, S. S., Qi, H., & Cho, E. (2002). Grid coverage for surveillance and target location in distributed sensor networks. *IEEE Transactions on Computers, 51*(12), 1448–1453.

Chang, T., Popsecu, G., & Codella, C. (2002). Scalable and Efficient Update Dissemination for Interactive Distributed Applications, *International Conference on Distributed Computing Systems* (pp. 143-152). Viena, Austria.

Chapin, S. J., Katramatos, D., Karpovich, J., & Grimshaw, A. (1999). Resource management in Legion. *Future Generation Comput. Syst., 15*(5/6), 583–594.

Chapman, P., Clinton, J., Khabaza, T., Reinartz, T., & Wirth. R. (1999). *The CRISP-DM process model.* Technical report, CRISM-DM consortium. Retrieved May 15, 2006, from http://www.crisp-dm.org/CRISPWP-0800.pdf

Chen, B. B., & Vicat-Blanc Primet, P. (2006). A flexible bandwidth reservation framework for bulk data transfers in grid networks, LIP ENS Lyon, *INRIA RESO Technical Report* - inria-00078069.

Chen, D., Li, B. S., Cai, W., & Turner, S. J. (2003). Design and Development of a Cluster Gateway for Cluster-based HLA Distributed Virtual Simulation Environments. *36th Annual Simulation Symposium (IEEE Computer Society)* (pp. 193-200). USA: The Printing House.

Chen, D., Theodoropoulos, G. K., Turner, S. J., Cai, W., Minson, R., & Zhang, Y. (2008). Large Scale Agent-based Simulation on the Grid. *Future Generation Computer Systems, 24*(7), 658-671.

Chen, D., Turner, S. J., Cai, W., & Xiong, M. (2008). A Decoupled Federate Architecture for High Level Architecture-based Distributed Simulation. *Journal of Parallel and Distributed Computing, 68*(11).

Chen, J., & Yang, Y. (2007). Adaptive Selection of Necessary and Sufficient Checkpoints for Dynamic Verification of Temporal Constraints in Grid Workflow Systems. *ACM Transactions on Autonomous and Adaptive Systems, 2*(2), Article No. 6.

Chen, J., & Yang, Y. (2008). A Taxonomy of Grid Workflow Verification and Validation. *Concurrency and Computation: Practice and Experience, 20*(4), 347-360.

Chen, J., & Yang, Y. (May 2008). Temporal Dependency based Checkpoint Selection for Dynamic Verification of Fixed-time Constraints in Grid Workflow Systems. *In the proceeding of the 30th International Conference on Software Engineering (ICSE2008).* Leipzig, Germany.

Chen, J., and Y. Yang, "Key Research Issues in Grid Workflow Verification and Validation", in *Proc. 4th ACM Australasian Workshop on Grid Computing and e-Research*, Vol. 54, pp. 97-104, 2006.

Chen, J., Druschel, P., & Subramanian, D. (1998). An efficient multipath forwarding method. In *Proceedings the Seventeenth Annual Joint Conference of the IEEE Computer and Communications Societies* (pp. 1418-1425). Los Alamitos: IEEE Computer Society.

Chen, Q., Ferris, M., & Linderoth, J. T. (2001). FATCOP 2.0: Advanced Features in an Opportunistic Mixed Integer Programming Solver. *Annals of Operations Research, 103*(2001), 17-32.

Cheng, B., Chou, C., Golubchik, L., Khuller, S., & Wan, Y.-C. (2003). Large scale data collection: a coordinated approach. In *the 22nd Annual Joint Conference of the IEEE Computer and Communications Societies* (pp. 218-228). New York: IEEE Communications Society.

Cheng, J., & Wellman, M. (1998). The WALRAS algorithm: a convergent distributed implementation of general equilibrium outcomes. *Computational Economics, 12*(1), 1-24.

Chervenak, A., Foster, I., Kesselman, C., Salisbury, C., & Tuecke, S. (2001). The Data Grid: Towards an Architecture for the Distributed Management and Analysis of Large Scientific Data Sets. *Journal of Network and Computer Applications, 23*(3), 187-200.

Chiang, G.-T., Dove, M., Ballard, S., Bostater, C., & Frame, I. (2006). A Grid Enabled Monte Carlo Hyperspectral Synthetic Image Remote Sensing Model (GRID-MCHSIM) for Coastal Water Quality Algorithm. *Remote Sensing of the Ocean, Sea Ice, and Large Water Regions, 6360*, 636009-1. Stockholm, Sweden: SPIE.

Chiang, G.-T., White, T., & Dove, M. (2007). Driving Google Earth from Fortran. *UK e-Science All Hands Meeting* 2007. Nottingham, UK. (pp. 236-243).

Choi, S., Baik, M., et al. (2005). Mobile agent based adaptive scheduling mechanism in peer to peer Grid Computing. *Proceedings of International Conference on Computational Science and its Applications 2005* (pp. 936-947), Singapore.

Christensen, E., Curbera, F., Meredith, G., & Weerawarana, S. (2001). *Web Services Description Language (WSDL) 1.1.* Retrieved May 10, 2006, from http://www.w3.org/TR/wsdl

Chun, B., Ng, J., & Parkes, D. (2004). *Computational resource exchanges for distributed resource allocation.* Technical Report, Harvard University.

Churches, D., et al. (2006). Programming scientific and distributed workflow with Triana Services. *Concurrency and Computation: Practice and Experience, 18*(10), 1021–1037.

Cimatti, A., E. Clarke, and E. Giunchiglia et al., "NuSMV2: an Open Source Tool for Symbolic Model Checking", *Computer Aided Verification*, LNCS Vol. 2404, Springer Verlag, pp. 359-364, 2002.

Cirne, W., F. Berman, "Adaptive Selection of Partition Size for Supercomputer Requests", *the Workshop on Job Scheduling Strategies for Parallel Processing, Lecture Notes In Computer Science*; Vol. 1911, pp. 187-208, 2000.

Cirne, W., F. Berman, "Using Moldability to Improve the Performance of Supercomputer Jobs", *Journal of Parallel and Distributed Computing*, Volume 62, Number 10, pp. 1571-1601, October 2002.

Clarke, Jr., E. M.,. O. Grumberg and D. A. Peled. *Model Checking.* Cambridge, Mass: MIT Press, pp. 1-231, 1999.

Clery, D. (2006). Can Grid Computing Help Us Work Together. *Science, 303*, 433-434.

Cohen-Boulakia, S., Cohen, S., & Davidson, S. (2007). Addressing the provenance challenge using zoom. *Concurrency and Control: Practice and Experience.*

Cohn, E.R., & Hibbitts, B.J. (2004). *Beyond the electronic portfolio: A lifetime personal Web space.* Retrieved December 10, from http://www.educause.edu/apps/eq/eqm04/eqm0441.asp

Collier, N. (2007). RePast: An Extensible Framework for Agent Simulation, Retrieved January 08, 2007, from http://www.econ.iastate.edu/tesfatsi/RepastTutorial.Collier.pdf

Condor Manual (2008). http://www.cs.wisc.edu/condor/manual/v6.8/3_1Introduction.html.

Cooper, R. B. (1981). *Introduction to Queueing Theory.* (2nd edition), (p. 347). Available at: http://www.cse.fau.edu/~bob/publications/IntroToQueueingTheory_Cooper.pdf

Couch, P. et al. (2005). Towards data integration for computational chemistry. *UK e-Science All Hands Meeting*, Nottingham, UK.

Curti, C., Ferrari, T., Gommans, L., Van Oudenaarde, S. et al. (2005). On advance reservation of heterogeneous network paths, *Future Generation Computer Systems, 21*(4), 525-538.

Czajkowski, K. et. al. (2004). From Open Grid Services Infrastructure to WS-Resource Framework: Refactoring and Evolution, Retrieved in 2008 from http://www.globus.org.

Czajkowski, K., A. Dan, J. Rofrano, S. Tuecke, and M. Xu, "Agreement-based Grid Service Management (OGSI-Agreement)", *Global Grid Forum*, GRAAP-WG Author Contribution, 2003.

Czajkowski, K., Foster, I., Karonis, N., Kesselman, C., Martin, S., Smith, W., & Tuecke, S. (1998). A Resource Management Architecture for Metacomputing Systems. *Lecture Notes in Computer Science, 1459*, 62-82.

Czerwinski, S. E., Zhao, B. Y., Hodes, T. D., Joseph, A. D., & Katz, R. H. (1999). An architecture for a secure service discovery service. In *Proceedings of Mobicom '99.*

Daconta, M., Obrst, L., & Smith, K. (2003). *The semantic Web: A guide to the future of XML, Web services and knowledge management.* Indianapolis: Wiley.

DAGMan. http://www.cs.wisc.edu/condor/dagman/.

Dahmann, J. S., Kuhl, F., & Weatherly, R. (1998). Standards for simulation: As simple as possible but not simpler: The High Level Architecture for simulation. *Simulation: Transactions of the Society for Modeling and Simulation International, 71*(6), 378-387.

Dail, H., Casanova, H., & Berman, F. (2002, November). A Decoupled Scheduling Approach for the GrADS Program Development Environment. *Proc. Supercomputing, 55.*

Damiani, D., Vimercati, D., & Paraboschi, S. (2002). A Reputation-Based Approach for Choosing Reliable Resources in Peer-to-Peer Networks. *Proceedings of the 9th ACM Conference on Computer and Communications Security* (pp.207-216), Washington, USA.

Data Mining Group. (2004). *Predictive model markup language.* Retrieved May 10, 2006, from http://www.dmg.org/

Davenport, T. H., & Prusak, L. (1998). *Working knowledge: How organizations manage what they know.* Boston: Harvard Business School Press.

David, L. & Puaut, I. (2004). Static determination of probabilistic execution times. *Proceedings of the 16th Euromicro Conference on Real-Time Systems* (pp. 223-230), Sicily, Italy.

Davies, J., Studer, R., & Warren P. (2006). *Semantic Web technologies: Trends and research in ontology-based systems.* John Wiley & Sons.

Davies, N. J., Fensel, D., & Harmelen, F. (2003). *Towards the Semantic Web: Ontology-driven knowledge management.* John Wiley & Sons.

Davis, J. S., Bisdikian, C., Jerome, W. F., & D. M. Sow. (2001). *Emerging research opportunities in service discovery.* Presented at the New York Metro-Area Networking Workshop.

de Rose, L.A., & Reed, D.A. (1999). SvPablo: A multi-language architecture-independent performance analysis system. *ICPP.*

De Roure D., Jennings, N.R., & Shadbolt, N.R. (2003). The Semantic Grid: A future e-Science infrastructure. In F. Berman, G. Fox, & A.J.G. Hey (Eds.), *Grid computing: Making the global infrastructure reality.* John Wiley & Sons.

De Roure, D., Baker, M., Jennings, N., & Shadbolt, N. (2003). *The evolution of the grid in grid computing: Making the global infrastructure a reality.* West Sussex, UK: Wiley.

De Roure, D., Jennings Nicholas, R., & Shadbolt, N. (2005). The semantic grid: Past, present, and future. *Proceedings of the IEEE, 93*(3).

Deelman, E., Blythe, J., et al. (2004). Pegasus: mapping scientific workflows onto the Grid. *Proceddings of Grid Computing: Second European Across Grids* (pp.11-26), Cyprus.

Deelman, E., Blythe, J., Gil, Y., & Kesselman, C. (2003). Workflow Management in GriPhyN. *The Grid Resource Management.* TheNetherlands:. Kluwer

Deelman, E., Blythe, J., Gil, Y., & Kesselman, C. (2003). Workflow management in GriPhyN. *The Grid Resource Management*. The Netherlands: Kluwer.

Deelman, E., Blythe, J., Gil, Y., Kesselman, C., Mehta, G., Patil, S., Su, M. H., Vahi, K., & Livny, M. (2004). Pegasus: Mapping Scientific Workflow onto the Grid. *Across Grids Conference 2004*, Nicosia, Cyprus.

Deelman, E., C. Kesselman, G. Mehta, L. Meshkat, L. Pearlman, K. Blackburn, P. Ehrens, A. Lazzarini, R. Williams and S. Koranda, "GriPhyN and LIGO, Building a Virtual Data Grid for Gravitational Wave Scientists", in *Proc. 11ᵗʰ IEEE Int. Symp. on High Performance Distributed Computing*, Edinburgh, Scotland, pp. 225-234, 2002.

Deelman, E., Singh, G., Atkinson, M. P., Chervenak, A., Chue Hong, N. P., Kesselman, C., Patil, S., Pearlman, L., & Su, M. (2004). Grid-Based Metadata Services. In Hatzopoulos, M. & Manolopoulos, Y. (Eds), *16th International Conference on Scientific and Statistical Database Management* (pp. 393-402). Santorini Island: IEEE Computer Society.

DeFanti, T., Brown, M., Leigh, J., Yu, O., He, E., Mambretti, J., Lillethun, D., & Weinberger, J. (2003). Optical Switching Middleware for the OptIPuter, *IEICE Tr. on Communications*, E86-B(8), 2263-2272.

Dejan M. S., Kalogeraki, V., & Lukose, R. (2002). *Peer-to-Peer Computing* (Tech. Rep. HPL-2002-57). HP Lab.

Dick, R., Rhodes, D. & Wolf, W. (1998). TGFF: task graphs for free. *Proceedings of the 6th. International Workshop on Hardware/Software Co-design* (pp. 97-101), Seattle, WA, U.S.A.

Dimitrakos, T., & Ritrovato, P. (2004, April 27-28). Progressing with a European learning Grid. In *Proceedings of the 4th International LeGE-WG Workshop — Towards a European Learning Grid Infrastructure*, Stuttgart, Germany.

DIS Steering Committee. (1994). *The DIS Vision, A Map to the Future of Distributed Simulation* (Tech. Rep. No. IST-SP-94-01). Orlando, Florida, USA: Institute for Simulation and Training.

DMSO. (2002). *RTI 1.3 Next generation programmer's guide version 5*. Alexandria, VA, USA: DMSO/DoD.

Dogan, A., & Ozguner, F. (2004). Genetic algorithm based scheduling of meta-tasks with stochastic execution times in heterogeneous computing systems. *Cluster Computing*, 7(2), 177-190.

Dong, F. & Akl, S. (2007 PDCS) A mobile agent based workflow rescheduling approach for the Grid. *Proceedings of the Nineteenth International Conference on Parallel and Distributed Computing and Systems*, Cambridge, MA, U.S.A.

Dong, F. & Akl, S. (2007) PFAS: a resource-performance-fluctuation-aware workflow scheduling algorithm for Grid Computing. *Proceedings of the 16th Heterogeneous Computing Workshop (HCW) in conjunction with IEEE International Parallel and Distributed Computing Symposium (IPDPS) 2007*, Long Beach, CA, U.S.A.

Dong, F. & Akl, S. (2008). A QoS guided workflow scheduling algorithm in the Grid. *Proceedings of the Grid Computing and Applications 2008* (pp.22-27), Las Vegas, NV, U.S.A.

Dou, W., Chen, G., Cheung, S. C., & Cai, S. (2006). Co-operative Cognition and Its Implementation under Web Environment. *Proceedings of the Second International Conference on Semantics, Knowledge and Grid* (pp. 46). Washington, DC: IEEE Computer Society.

Doulamis, N., Doulamis, A., Panagakis, A., Dolkas, K., Varvarigou, T., & Varvarigos, E. (2005). A Combined Fuzzy-Neural Network Model for Non-Linear Prediction of 3D Rendering Workload in Grid Computing. *IEEE Trans. on Systems Man and Cybernetics, Part-B*.

Dove, M. et al. (2007). *Usable Grid infrastructures: practical experiences from the eMinerals project. UK e-Science All Hands Meeting*. Nottingham, UK. (pp. 48-55).

Droegemeier, K.K., et al. (2005). Service-oriented environments for dynamically interacting with mesoscale weather. *Computing in Science and Engineering*, 7(6), 12-29.

Eisenstadt, M., & Komzak, J. (2005). *Peer conversations for e-learning in the Grid.* The Open University, UK: Knowledge Media Institute; and Université Montpellier II, France: Stefano A. Cerri.

England, D., and J. B. Weissman, "Costs and Benefits of Load Sharing in Computational Grid", *10th Workshop on Job Scheduling Strategies for Parallel Processing, Lecture Notes In Computer Science*, Vol. 3277, June 2004.

Enlightened computing project website. (2008). Retrieved in 2008 from http://www.enlightenedcomputing.org.

Ernemann, C., Hamscher, V., Schwiegelshohn, U., Yahyapour, R., & Streit, A. (2000). On advantages of grid computing for parallel job scheduling, in: *Proceedings of the 2nd IEEE International Symposium on Cluster Computing and the Grid* (pp. 39-46). Berlin: IEEE Computer Society.

Ernemann, C., V. Hamscher, A. Streit, R. Yahyapour, ""On Effects of Machine Configurations on Parallel Job Scheduling in Computational Grids", *Proceedings of International Conference on Architecture of Computing Systems, ARCS 2002*, pp. 169-179, 2002.

Ernemann, C., V. Hamscher, R. Yahyapour, "Benefits of Global Grid Computing for Job Scheduling," *Proceedings of the Fifth IEEE/ACM International Workshop on Grid Computing* (GRID'04), pp. 374-379, November 2004.

Ernemann, C., V. Hamscher, R. Yahyapour, "Economic Scheduling in Grid Computing", *the 8th International Workshop on Job Scheduling Strategies for Parallel Processing, Lecture Notes In Computer Science*; Vol. 2537, pp. 128-152, 2002.

Ernemann, C., V. Hamscher, R. Yahyapour, and A. Streit, "Enhanced Algorithms for Multi-Site Scheduling", *Proceedings of 3rd International Workshop Grid 2002, in conjunction with Supercomputing 2002*, pp. 219-231, Baltimore, MD, USA, November 2002.

Ernemann, C., V. Hamscher, U. Schwiegelshohn, A. Streit, R. Yahyapour, "On Advantages of Grid Computing for Parallel Job Scheduling", *Proceedings of 2nd IEEE International Symposium on Cluster Computing and the Grid (CC-GRID 2002)*, pp. 39-46, Berlin, Germany, 2002.

Eugster, P.T., Felber, P.A., Guerraoui, R., & Kermarrec, A.M. (2003). The many faces of publish/subscribe. *ACM Computing Surveys, 35*, 114–131.

Expert Group (2004). *Next Generation Grids 2.* European Commission, Brussels, ftp://ftp.cordis.europa.eu/pub/ist/docs/ngg2_eg_final.pdf

Faerman, M., Figueira, S., Hayes, J., Obertelli, G., Schopf, J., Shao, G., Smallen, S., Spring, N., Su, A., & Zagorodnov, D. (2003). Adaptive Computing on the Grid Using AppLeS. *IEEE Transactions on Parallel and Distributed Systems, 14*(4), 369-382.

Fahringer, T., J. Qin, and S. Hainzer, "Specification of Grid Workflow Applications with AGWL: An Abstract Grid Workflow Language", in *Proc. IEEE Int. Symp. on Cluster Computing and the Grid*, pp. 676-685, 2005.

Fahringer, T., Jugravu, A., Pllana, S., Prodan, R., Seragiotto Jr, C., & Truong, H. L. (2005). ASKALON: A tool set for cluster and Grid computing. Concurrency and Computation: Practice and Experience, *17*(2-4), 143–169.

Fall, K., & Varadhan, K. (2008). The NS Manual (formerly ns Notes and Documentation), Retrieved September 27, 2008 from http://www.isi.edu/nsnam/ns/ns-documentati

Feitelson, D. G., "A Survey of Scheduling in Multiprogrammed Parallel Systems", Research Report RC 19790 (87657), IBM T. J. Watson Research Center, Oct. 1994.

Feitelson, D. G., and M. A. Jette, "Improved Utilization and Responsiveness with Gang Scheduling", *Job Scheduling Strategies for Parallel Processing*, pp. 238-261, Springer-Verlag, 1997.

Feitelson, D. G., L. Rudolph, U. Schwiegelshohn, K. C. Sevcik, and P. Wong, "Theory and Practice in Parallel Job Scheduling", *Job Scheduling Strategies for Parallel Processing*, pp. 1-34, Springer-Verlag, 1997.

Feitelson, D., and L. Rudolph, "Parallel Job Scheduling: Issues and Approaches", *Proceedings of IPPS'95 Work-*

shop: Job Scheduling Strategies for Parallel Processing, pp. 1-18, 1995.

Feldman, M., Lai, K., & Stoica, I. (2004). Robust incentive techniques for peer-to-peer networks. *Proceedings of the 5ᵗʰ ACM Conference on Electronic Commerce*, New York, USA.

Feldman, M., Lai, K., & Zhan, L. (2005). A price-anticipating resource allocation mechanism for distributed shared clusters. *Proceedings of the 6ᵗʰ ACM conference on Electronic Commerce* (pp.127-136), New York.

Ferber, J. (1999). *Multi-agent system: An introduction to distributed artificial intelligence*. Harlow: Addison Wesley Longman.

Ferrari, G. L., S. Gnesi, and U. Montanari et al., "A Model-checking Verification Environment for Mobile Processes", *ACM Transactions on Software Engineering and Methodology*, Vol. 12, No. 4, pp. 440-473, 2003.

Fitzgibbons, J. B., Fujimoto, R., Fellig, D., Kleban, D., & Scholand, A. J. (2004). IDSim: An Extensible Framework for Interoperable Distributed Simulation. In B. Werner (Ed.), *The Proceedings of the IEEE International Conference on Web Services (ICWS2004)*(pp. 532-539). USA: The Printing House.

For more information on the topics covered in this chapter, see http://www.Gridminer.org and also the following references:

Foster, I., & Kesselman, C. (1998). *The GRID: Blueprint for a New Computing Infrastructure*. Morgan Kaufmann Inc., San Francisco.

Foster, I., & Kesselman, C. (1999). The globus project: a status report, *Future Generation Computer Systems*, 15(5-6), 607-621.

Foster, I., & Kesselman, C. (1999). *The Grid: Blueprint for a new computing infrastructure*. Morgan Kaufmann.

Foster, I., & Kesselman, C. (2003). *The Grid 2: Blueprint for a New Computing Infrastructure:* Morgan Kaufmann Published.

Foster, I., & Kesselman, C. (2004). *The GRID2, Blueprint for a New Computing Infrastructure, 2nd Edition,* Elsevier Press.

Foster, I., & Kesselman, C. (Ed.). (1996). *The grid: Blueprint for a new computing infrastructure.* Los Altos, CA: Morgan Kaufmann.

Foster, I., "What is the Grid? A Three Point Checklist", *GRIDToday*, July 2002.

Foster, I., and C. Kesselman, *The Grid: Blueprint for a New Computing Infrastructure*, Morgan Kaufmann Publishers, San Francisco, CA USA, 1998.

Foster, I., C. Kesselman and S. Tuecke, "The Anatomy of the Grid: Enabling Scalable Virtual Organizations", *Int. J. Supercomputer Applications*, Vol. 15, No. 3, pp. 200-222, 2001.

Foster, I., C. Kesselman, J. M. Nick and S. Tuecke, "Grid Services for Distributed System Integration", *IEEE Computer*, Vol. 35, No. 6, pp. 37-46, 2002.

Foster, I., Kesselman, C., & Tuecke, S (2001). The Anatomy of the Grid: Enabling Scalable Virtual Organization. *The International Journal of Supercomputer Applications, 15*(3),200-222.

Foster, I., Kesselman, C., & Tuecke, S. (1998). *The Grid: Blueprint of a New Computing Infrastructure*. Morgan Kaufmann Publishers.

Foster, I., Kesselman, C., & Tuecke, S. (2001). The Anatomy of the Grid: Enabling Scalable Virtual Organizations. *International Journal of High Performance Computing and Applications, 15*(3), 200-222.

Foster, I., Kesselman, C., & Tuecke, S. (2002). *The Physiology of the Grid: An Open Grid Service Architecture for Distributed System Integration, Global Grid Forum.*

Foster, I., Kesselman, C., Lee, C., Lindell, B., Nahrstedt, K., & Roy, A. (1999). A Distributed Resource Management Architecture that Supports Advance Reservation and Co-Allocation. *Proceedings of the International Workshop on QoS*, (pp.27-36).

Foster, I., Kesselman, C., Nick, J., & Tuecke, S. (2002). *The Physiology of the Grid: An Open Grid Services Architecture for Distributed Systems Integration*. Retrieved in 2008 from http://www.globus.org/research/papers/ogsa.pdf.

Foster, I., Kesselman, C., Tuecke, S. (2001). The Anatomy of the Grid: Enabling Scalable Virtual Organizations. *International Journal Supercomputer Applications, 15*(3).

Foster, I., Kesselman, K., & Tuecke, S. (2003). The anatomy of the Grid: Enabling scalable virtual organizations. *CCGRID 2001*, 6-7.

Foster, I., Kishimoto, H., Savva, A., Berry, D., Djaoui, A., Grimshaw, A., et al. (2005). *Open grid services architecture V.1.0* (No. GFD-I.030). Lemont, IL: Global Grid Forum.

Foster, I.T., Vöckler, J., Wilde, M., & Zhao, Y. (2003). The virtual data grid: A new model and architecture for data-intensive collaboration. *CIDR*.

Fox, G.C., Berman, F., & Hey, A.J.G. (2003). *Grid computing: Making the global infrastructure a reality*. John Wiley & Sons.

Fox, R. (2005). Cataloging our information architecture. *International Digital Library Prespectives, 21*(1), 23-29.

Frasson, C., Mengelle, T., Aimeur, E., & Gouardères, G. (1996). An actor-based architecture for intelligent tutoring systems. In *Proceedings of the 3rd International Conference on Intelligent Tutoring Systems (ITS'96), Lecture Notes in Computer Science 1086*, Montreal, Canada (pp. 57-65). Springer.

Fredette, A., & Lang, J. (2005). Link Management Protocol (LMP) for Dense Wavelength Division Multiplexing (DWDM) Optical Line Systems, *IETF RFC 4209*.

Frey, J., Tannenbaum, T., Foster, I., Livny, M., & Tuecke, S. (2002). Condor-G: A computation management agent for multiinstitutional grids. *Cluster Computing, 5*, 237-246.

Friedman, T. L. (2005). *The world is flat: A brief history of the twenty first century*. Farrar, Straus and Giroux.

Fujii, K., & Suda, T. (2005). Semantics-Based Dynamic Service Composition. *IEEE Journal on Selected Areas in Communications, 23*(12), 2361-2372.

Fujimoto, R. (2007). DoD High Level Architecture. Retrieved November 07, 2007, from http://www.cc.gatech.edu/computing/pads/tech-highperf.html

Fukuda, M. & Smith, D. (2006). UWAgents: A Mobile Agent System Optimized for Grid Computing *Proceedings of the Grid Computing and Applications 2006* (pp. 107-113), Las Vegas, NV, U.S.A.

Fukuda, M. Tanaka, Y., et al. (2003). A mobile-agent-based PC Grid. *Proceedings of Autonomic Computing Workshop in conjunction with the International Symposium on High Performance Distributed Computing (HPDC) 2003* (pp. 142-150), Seattle, WA, U.S.A .

Gagne, D., Sabbouh, M., Bennett, S., & Powers, S. (September 2006). Using Data Semantics to Enable Automatic Composition of Web Services. *In the proceeding of 2006 IEEE International Conference on Services Computing*. Chicago,USA: IEEE computer society.

Ganguly, S., Saxena, A., Bhatnagar, S., Banerjee, S., & Izmailov, R. (2005). Fast replication in content distribution overlays. In *the 24th Annual Joint Conference of the IEEE Computer and Communications Societies* (pp. 2246-2256). New York: IEEE Communications Society.

Gannon, D., et al. (2005). Service oriented architectures for science gateways on grid systems. *ICSOC*.

Gao, Y., Rong, H., & Huang, J. Z. (2005). Adaptive grid job scheduling with genetic algorithms. *Future Generation Computer Systems, 21*, 151–161.

Garber, D. (2004). Growing virtual communities. *International Review of Research in Open and Distance Learning, 3*(4).

Gartner, F. C. (1999). Fundamentals of Fault-Tolerant Distributed Computing in Asynchronous Environments. *ACM Computing Surveys, 31*(1).

Gekas, J., & Fasli, M. (October 2005). Automatic Web Service Composition Based on Graph Network Analysis Metrics. *In the proceeding of the 5th International Conference on ontologies,Databases and Applications of Semantics.* Agia Napa,Cyprus: Springer.

Geldof, M. (2004). *The semantic grid: Will semantic Web and grid go hand in hand?* European Commission, DG Information Society.

Ghosh, D. (1997). *Heuristics for Knapsack Problems: Comparative Survey and Sensitivity Analysis.* Fellowship Dissertation, IIM Calcutta, India.

Gkantsidis, C., Ammar, M., & Zegura E (2003). On the Effect of Large-Scale Deployment of Parallel Downloading. *In Proceedings of the third IEEE Workshop on Internet Applications* (pp. 79-89). Los Alamitos: IEEE Computer Society.

G-lambda project website. (2008). Retrieved in 2008 from http://www.g-Lambda.net.

Glatard, T., Montagnat, J., & Pennec, X. (2005). *An optimized workflow enactor for data-intensive Grid applications.* Research Report I3S, number I3S/RR-2005-32-, Sophia Antipolis, France.

Global Grid Forum, RUR-Resource Usage Record Working Group, from http://www.gridforum.org.

Global lambda integrated facility (glif) website. (2008). Retrieved in 2008 from http://www.glif.is.

Globus Alliance (2005). *Globus Toolkit 4.* http://www.globus.org

Globus Alliance, IBM, & HP (2004). *The WS-Resource framework.* Retrieved May 10, 2006, from http://www.globus.org/wsrf/

Globus Project Group. (2004). The Globus Toolkit, Retrieved in 2008 from http://www-unix.globus.org/toolkit/

Globus. (2006). GT 4.0: Security. Retrieved February 10, 2007, from *http://www.globus.org/toolkit/docs/4.0/security/*

Glodenberg, D., Qiu, L., Xie, H., Yang, Y. R., & Zhang, Y. (2005). Optimizing cost and performance for multihoming. In Raj Yavatkar, Ellen W. Zegura, Jennifer Rexford (Eds.), *the ACM SIGCOMM 2004 Conference on Applications, Technologies, Architectures, and Protocols for Computer Communication* (pp. 79-92). New York: ACM Press.

Goble, C. (2002). Position statement: Musings on provenance, workflow and (semantic Web) annotations for bioinformatics. *Workshop on Data Derivation and Provenance.*

Goldin, D., & Wegner, P. (1998). *Persistence as a form of interaction* (Tech Rep: CS-98-07). Brown University.

Goldin, D., & Wegner, P. (1999). *Behavior and expressiveness of persistent Turing machines* (Tech Rep: CS-99-14). Brown University.

Golle, P., Brown, K. L., & Mironov, I. (2001). Incentives for sharing in Peer-to-Peer network, *Proceedings of the 3rd ACM Conference on Electronic Commerce* (pp.264-267), New York.

Gong, L., Sun, X. H., & Waston, E. (2002). Performance Modeling and Prediction of Non-Dedicated Network Computing. *IEEE Trans. on Computer, 51*(9).

Gouardères, G., Mansour., S., Nkambou, R., & Yatchou, R. (2005). The Grid-E-Card: Architecture to share collective intelligence on the Grid. *Applied Artificial Intelligence, 199*(10), 1043-1073.

Gouardères, G., Minko, A., & Richard, L. (2000). Simulation and multi-agent environment for aircraft maintenance learning. In *Actes du Congrès 9th International Conference on Artificial Intelligence: Methodology, Systems, Applications, Lecture Notes in Artificial Intelligence 1904*, Varna, Bulgaria (pp. 152-166). Springer.

Greenwood, M., et al. (2003). Provenance of e-science experiments—experience from Bioinformatics. *UK OST e-Science 2nd AHM.*

Grimshaw, A. S., Ferrari A., & West, E. A. (1996). *Mentat.* In G.V. Wilson & P. Lu (Eds.), *Parallel Programming Using C++* (pp. 382–427).

Groth, P., Luck, M., & Moreau, L. (2004). A protocol for recording provenance in service-oriented grids. *OPODIS*.

Groth, P., Miles, S., Fang, W., Wong, S.C., Zauner, K.-P., & Moreau, L. (2005). Recording and using provenance in a protein compressibility experiment. *HPDC*.

Gu, X., & Nahrstedt, K. (2006). On Composing Stream Applications in Peer-to-Peer Environments. *IEEE Transactions on Parallel and Distributed Systems, 17*(8), 824-837.

Guarino, N. (1998). Formal ontology and information systems. In N. Guarino (Ed.), *Formal Ontology in Information Systems. Proceedings of the 1st International Conference*, Trento, Italy. Retrieved from http://www.ladseb.pd.cnr.it/infor/Ontology/Papers/FOIS98.pdf

Guarise, A. (2003). Data grid accounting system architecture, *(Tech. Rep. No. 1 on Data Grid)*, Italy.

Gui, C., & Mohapatra, P. (2004). Power conservation and quality of surveillance in target tracking sensor networks. *Proc. of the 10th Intl. Conf. on Mobile Computing and Networking, 129–143*.

Gummadi, K., Madhyastha, H. V., Steven, D. G., Levy, H. M., & Wetherall, D. (2004). Improving the Reliability of Internet Paths with One-hop Source Routing. In E. Brewer & P. Chen (Eds.), *Proceedings of 6th Symposium on Operating System Design and Implementation* (pp. 183-198). San Francisco, California: USENIX.

Gunter, D., Tierney, B., Jackson, K., Lee, J., & Stoufer, M. (2002). Dynamic monitoring of high-performance distributed applications. *HPDC*.

Guo, F., Chen, J., Li, W., & Chiueh, T. (2004). Experiences in building a multihoming load balancing system. In *the 23rd Annual Joint Conference of the IEEE Computer and Communications Societies* (pp. 1241-1251). New York: IEEE Communications Society.

Guo, L., McGough, A. S., Akram, A., Colling, D., Martyniak, J., & Krznaric, M. (2007). QoS for Service Based Workflow on Grid. *Proceedings of UK e-Science 2007 All Hands Meeting*, Nottingham, UK.

Guo, W. Shi, X., Cao, L., & Yang, K. (2005). Trust in Knowledge Flow Networks. *Proceedings of International Conference on Semantics, Knowledge and Grid* (pp. 405 -412).

Gupta, M., Judge, P., & Ammar, M. (2003). A Reputation System for Peer-to-Peer Networks. *Proceedings of the 13th International Workshop on Network and Operating Systems Support for Digital Audio and Video* (pp.144-152), USA.

Hamscher, V., U. Schwiegelshohn, A. Streit, and R. Yahyapour, "Evaluation of Job-Scheduling Strategies for Grid Computing", *Proceedings of the 7th International Conference on High Performance Computing, HiPC-2000*, pp. 191-202, Bangalore, India, 2000.

Han, J., & Kamber, M. (2000) *Data mining: Concepts and techniques*. Morgan Kaufmann.

Han, J., Watson, D., & Jahanian, F. (2005). Topology aware overlay networks. In *Proceedings of 24th Annual Joint Conference of the IEEE Computer and Communications Societies* (pp. 2554-2565). New York: IEEE Communications Society.

Harney, J., & Doshi, P. (September 2007). Adaptive Web Processes Using Value of Changed Information. *In the proceeding of the 5th International Conference on Service-Oriented Computing*. Vienna, Austria: LNCS.

Hawkeye. http://www.cs.wisc.edu/condor/hawkeye/

He, E., Wang, X., & Leigh, J. (2006). A flexible advance reservation model for multi-domain WDM optical networks. In Proceedings of *IEEE GRIDNETS 2006*.

He, X., Sun, X., & von Laszewski, G. (2003). QoS Guided Min-Min Heuristic for Grid Task Scheduling. *Journal of Computer Science and Technology, Special Issue on Grid Computing, 18*(4).

Heymann, E., Senar, M. A., Luque, E., & Livny, M. (2000). Adaptive scheduling for master-worker applications on the computational grid, in: *Proceedings of the 1st IEEE/ACM International Workshop on Grid Computing, Bangalore* (pp. 214-227). India: IEEE Computer Society.

Hornick, F. M., et al. (2005). *Java data mining 2.0.* Retrieved June 20, 2006, from http://jcp.org/aboutJava/communityprocess/edr/jsr247/

Horrocks, I., Patel-Schneider, P. F., Boley, H., Tabet, S., Grosof, B., & Dean, M. (2004). *SWRL: A Semantic Web rule language combining OWL and RuleML.* W3C Member Submission. Retrieved May 10, 2006, from http://www.w3.org/Submission/2004/SUBM-SWRL-20040521

HPCVL. http://www.hpcvl.org/

Huang, C. F., & Tseng, Y. C. (2005). A survey of solutions to the coverage problems in wireless sensor networks. *Journal of Internet Technology, 6*(1), 1–8.

Huang, C. F., & Tseng, Y. C. (2005). The coverage problem in a wireless sensor network. *Mobile Networks and Applications, 10*(4), 519–528.

Huang, F., Liu, D. S., Li, G. Q., Zeng, Y., & Yan, Y. X. (2008). Study on Implementation of High-performance GIServices in Spatial Information Grid. ICCS 2008, *LNCS 5102*, 605-613.

Huang, F., Liu, D. S., Li, G. Q., Zeng, Y., Yu, W. Y., Wang, S. G., & Liu, P. (2007a). Discuss on High Performance Grid-Based GIS [in Chinese]. *Geomatics World, 4*(5), 33-39.

Huang, F., Liu, D.S., Liu, P. et al. (2007b). Research on Cluster-Based Parallel GIS with the Example of Parallelization on GRASS GIS. *GCC 2007*, 642-649.

Huang, G. T. (2003). Casting the wireless sensor net. *Technology Review, 106*(6), 50–56.

Huang, H., Richa, A. W., & Segal, M. (2005). Dynamic coverage in ad-hoc sensor networks. *Mobile Networks and Applications, 10*, 9–18.

Huang, K. C., "Minimizing Waiting Ratio for Dynamic Workload on Parallel Computers", *Parallel Processing Letters*, Vol. 16, No. 4, December 2006, pp. 441-453.

Huang, K. C., "Performance Evaluation of Adaptive Processor Allocation Policies for Moldable Parallel Batch Jobs", *Proceedings of the Third Workshop on Grid Technologies and Applications*, December 7-8, 2006, Hsinchu, Taiwan.

Huang, K. C., and H. Y. Chang, "An Integrated Processor Allocation and Job Scheduling Approach to Workload Management on Computing Grid", *Proceedings of the 2006 International Conference on Parallel and Distributed Processing Techniques and Applications (PDPTA'06)*, pp. 703-709, Las Vegas, USA, June 26-29, 2006.

Huang, K. C., P. C. Shih, and Y. C. Chung, "Towards Feasible and Effective Load Sharing in a Heterogeneous Computational Grid", Second International Conference on Grid and Pervasive Computing, GPC 2007, *Lecture Notes in Computer Science*, Editors: Christophe Cerin and Kuan-Ching Li, vol. 4459, pp. 229-240, Springer, Paris, France, May 2-4, 2007.

Huang, Y., Slominski, A., Herath, C., & Gannon, D. (2006). WS-Messenger: A Web services based messaging system for service-oriented grid computing. *CCGrid*.

Huang, Z. C., Li, G. Q., Du, R. et al. (2007). SIGRE — An Autonomic Spatial Information Grid Runtime Environment for Geo-Computation. APPT 2007, *LNCS 4887*, 322-329.

Hull, R., Neaves, P., & Bedford-Roberts, J. T. (1997). *Towards situated computing.* Paper presented at the 1st International Symposium on Wearable Computers, Cambridge, Massachusetts.

Hwang, S., & Kesselman, C. (2003). A Flexible Framework for Fault Tolerance in the Grid. *Journal of Grid Computing, 1*, 251–272.

IBM (2005). Web services data collector. Retrieved from www.alphaworks.ibm.com/tech/wsdatacollector

IEEE 1516. (2000). *IEEE Standard for High Level Architecture.* 3 Park Avenue, New York, NY 10016-5997, USA: The Institute of Electrical and Electronics Engineers, Inc.

IEEE Network, 8(5), 22-32.

IEEE1516.3. (2003). *IEEE Recommended Practice for High Level Architecture (HLA) Federation Development and Execution Process (FEDEP).* 3 Park Avenue, New

York, NY 10016-5997, USA: The Institute of Electrical and Electronics Engineers, Inc.

Iskra, K., Albada, G., & Sloot, P. (2003). Time Warp Cancellations Optimisations on High Latency Networks. In S. J. Turner and S. J. E. Taylor (Ed.), *The Proceedings of the 7th IEEE International Symposium on Distributed Simulation and Real-Time Applications (DS-RT'03)* (pp. 128-137). USA: The Printing House.

Iskra, K., Albada, G., & Sloot, P. (2005). Towards Grid-Aware Time Warp. *Simulation: Transactions of The Society for Modeling and Simulation International, 81*(4), 293-306.

ITU. (1994). *ODP trading function* (ITU/ISO Committee draft standard, ISO 13235/ITU.TS Rec.9tr).

Jackson, L. E., & Rouskas, G. N. (2002). Deterministic Preemptive Scheduling of Real Time Tasks. *IEEE Computer, 35*(5), 72-79.

JADE (Java Agent DEvelopment Framework) version 3.2. (n.d.).

Jaeger, M. C., Rojec-Goldmann, G., & Uhl, G. M. (September 2004). QoS Aggregation for Web Service Composition using Workflow Patterns. *In the proceeding of the 8th IEEE International Enterprise Distributed Object Computing Conference.* California, USA: IEEE computer society.

Jaekel, A. (2006). Lightpath scheduling and allocation under a flexible scheduled traffic model. In Proceedings of IEEE *GLOBECOM 2006.*

Jamoussi, B., et al. (2002). Constraint-Based LSP Setup Using LDP, *IETF RFC 3212.*

Jie, W., Zang, T., Lei, Z., Cai, W., Turner, S. J. & Wang, L. (2002). Constructing an OGSA-Based Grid Computing Platform. In H. P. Lee and K. Kumar (Ed.), *Recent Advances in Computational Science & Engineering: International Conference on Scientific and Engineering Computation (IC-SEC 2002)* (pp. 738-741). UK: Imperial College Press.

Jin, J. J. (2004). *The applications of grids in geosciences* [in Chinese], http://support.iap.ac.cn/bbs/viewthread.php?tid=176&extra=page%3D1.

Jones, J. P., and B. Nitzberg, "Scheduling for Parallel Supercomputing: A Historical Perspective of Achievable Utilization", *Job Scheduling Strategies for Parallel Processing*, pp. 1-16, Springer-Verlag, 1999.

Jun Zheng, Z., & Mouftah, H. T. (2002). Routing and Wavelength Assignment for Advance Reservation in Wavelength-Routed WDM Optical Networks", Proceeding of *IEEE International Conference on Communications (ICC)*

Junsheng, C., Huaimin, W., & Yin, G. (2006). A Dynamic Trust Metric for P2P System. *Proceedings of the 5th International Conference of Grid and Cooperative Computing Workshops*(pp.117-120), Changsha, China.

Kalasapur, S., Kumar, M., & Shirazi, B. A.(2007). Dynamic Service Composition in Pervasive Computing. *IEEE Transaction on Parallel and Distributed Systems, 18*(7), 907-918.

Kamvar, S. D., Schlosser, M. T., & Garcia-Molina, H. (2003). The EigenTrust Algorithm for Reputation Management in Peer-to-Peer Networks. *Proceedings of the 12th International Conference on World Wide Web* (pp.640-651), New York, USA.

Kandaswamy, G., Fang, L., Huang, Y., Shirasuna, S., Marru, S., & Gannon, D. (2006). Building Web services for scientific grid applications. *IBM Journal of Research and Development, 50*(2/3), 249–260.

Kar, S., Kodialam, M., & Lakshman, T. (2000). Minimum interference routing of bandwidth guaranteed tunnels with MPLS traffic engineering applications, *IEEE JSAC, 18*(12), 2566–2579.

Kardaras, D., & Karakostas, B. (2006). E-Service adaptation using fuzzy cognitive maps. *The 3rd International IEEE Conference on Intelligent Systems* (pp. 227-230).

Keahey, K., M. E. Papka, Q. Peng, D. Schissel, G. Abla, T. Araki, J. Burruss, S. Feibush, P. Lane, S. Klasky, T. Leggett, D. McCune, and L. Randerson, "Grids for Experimental Science: the Virtual Control Room", in *Proc. 2nd IEEE Int. Workshop on Challenges of Large Applications in Distributed Environments*, pp. 4-11, 2004.

Keahey, K., T. Araki, and P. Lane, "Agreement-Based Interactions for Experimental Science", in *Proc. Euro-Par 2004 Parallel Processing*, LNCS Vol. 3149, pp. 399-408, 2004.

Kelley, I., Russell,M., Novotny, J. et al. (2005). The Cactus portal. *APAC'05.*

Khanli, L. M., & Analoui, M. (2007). QoS-based Scheduling of Workflow Applications on Grids. *International Conference on Advances in Computer Science and Technology*, Phuket, Thailand.

Kickinger, G., Hofer, J., Tjoa, A.M., & Brezany, P. (2003). Workflow mManagement in GridMiner. *The 3rd Cracow Grid Workshop*. Cracow, Poland: Springer.

Klusch, M., Fries, B., Khalid, M., & Sycara, K. (May 2006). Automated Semantic Web Service Discovery with OWLS-MX. *In the proceeding of the 5th International Joint Conference on Autonomous Agents and Multiagent Systems*. Hakodate, Japan: ACM.

Kompella, K. et al. (2005). OSPF Extensions in Support of Generalized MPLS, *IETF RFC 4203.*

Kona, S., Bansal, A., & Gupta, G. (July 2007). Automatic Composition of Semantic Web Services. *In the proceeding of 2007 IEEE International Conference on Web Services.* Salt Lake City, USA: IEEE computer society.

Kopecky, J., Vitvar, T., Bournez, C., & Farrell, J. (2007). SAWSDL: Semantic Annotations for WSDL and XML Schema. *IEEE Internet Computing, 11*(6), 60-67.

Koperski, K., & Han, J. (1995). Discovery of Spatial Association Rules in Geographic Information Databases. *Proceedings of the 4th International Symposium on Large Spatial Databases* (pp. 47-66), Springer Publisher.

Kostic, D., Rodriguez, A., Albrecht, J., & Vahdat, A. (2003). Bullet: High bandwidth data dissemination using an overlay mesh. In M. L. Scott, L. L. Peterson (Eds.), *Symposium on Operating Systems Principles* (pp. 298-313). New York: ACM Press.

Krueger, P., T. H. Lai, V. A. Radiya, "Job Scheduling is More Important Than Processor Allocation for Hypercube Computers", *IEEE Transactions on Parallel and Distributed Systems*, May 1994, pp. 488-497.

Kuhl, F., Weatherly, R., & Dahmann, J. (1999). *Creating Computer Simulation Systems: An Introduction to HLA.* Upper Saddle River, New Jersey, USA: Prentice Hall.

Kumar, S., Lai, T., & Balogh, J. (2004). On k-coverage in a mostly sleeping sensor network. *Proc. of the 10th Intl. Conf. on Mobile Computing and Networking,* (pp. 144–158).

Kuri, J., Puech, N., Gagnaire, M., Dotaro, E., & Douville, R. (2003). Routing and wavelength assignment of scheduled lightpath demands. *IEEE JSAC, 21*(8), 1231–1240.

Küster, U., Königries, B., Stern, M., & Klein, M. (May 2007). DIANE: An Integrated Approach to Automated Service Discovery, Matchmaking and Composition. *In the proceeding of the 16th International World Wide Web Conference.* Banff, Alberta, Canada: ACM Press.

Kwok, Y., Song, S., & Hwang, K. (2005). Selfish grid computing: Game-Theoretic modeling and NAS performance results. *Proceedings of the Cluster Computing and Grid* (pp.1143-1150), Washington.

Kwon, G., & Byers, J. (2004). ROMA: Reliable overlay multicast using loosely coupled TCP connections. In *the 23rd Annual Joint Conference of the IEEE Computer and Communications Societies* (pp. 385-395), New York: IEEE Communications Society.

Kyriazis, D., Tserpes, K., Menychtas, A., Litke, A., & Varvarigou, T. (2007). An innovative workflow mapping mechanism for Grids in the frame of Quality of Service. *Future Generation Computer Systems, In Press, Corrected Proof, Available online 27 July 2007.*

Lacy, L.W. (2005). *Owl: Representing information using the Web ontology language.* Trafford Publishing.

Lamanna, L. (2004). The LHC computing Grid project at CERN. Nuclear Instruments and Methods in Physics Research Section A: Accelerators, Spectrometers, Detectors and Associated Equipment. In *the IXth International Workshop on Advanced Computing and Analysis Techniques in Physics Research, 534,* 1-6.

Lang, J. C. (2001). Managerial concerns in knowledge management. *Journal of Knowledge Management, 5*(1), 43-59.

Lees, M., Logan, B., & Kings, J. (2007, June). *HLA Simulation of Agent-Based Bacterial Models*. Presented at the European Simulation Interoperability Workshop 2007, Genoa, Italy.

Lees, M., Logan, B., Oguara, T., & Theodoropoulos, G. K. (2003, June). *Simulating Agent-Based Systems with HLA: The case of SIM AGENT - Part II*. Presented at the European Simulation Interoperability Workshop 2003, Stockholm, Sweden.

Leinberger, W., & Kumar, V. (1999, October). Information Power Grid: The new frontier in parallel computing? *IEEE Concur., 7*(4), 75-84.

Lewis, H. R., & Denenberg, L. (1991). *Data Structures and Their Algorithms*. Harper-Collins, New York.

Leymann, F. (2001). *Web services flow language (WSFL 1.0)*. Retrieved September 23, 2002, from www4.ibm.com/software/solutions/webservices/pdf/WSFL.pdf

Li, F., Li, L., & Lau, R. (2004). Supporting Continuous Consistency in Multiplayer Online Games. *ACM Multimedia* (pp. 388-391). New York, New York, USA.

Li, G. Q. (2005). *Report on the SIG*, Beijing, China Remote Sensing Ground Station of Chinese Academic of Science.

Li, H. (2007 CCGrid). Performance evaluation in Grid Computing: a modeling and prediction perspective. *Proceedings of the 1st IEEE TCSC Doctoral Symposium in conjunction with CCGrid 2007* (pp. 869-874), Rio de Janeiro, Brazil.

Li, H., Groep, D., & Wolters, L. (2007). Mining performance data for Metascheduling decision support in the Grid. *Future Generation Computer Systems, 23*(1), 92-99.

Li, M., & Baker, M. (2005). *The Grid: Core technologies*. John Wiley & Sons.

Lim, H. B., Wang, B., Fu, C., Phull, A., & Ma, D. (2008). WISDOM: simulation framework for middleware services in wireless sensor networks. *Proc. the 5th IEEE Consumer Communications and Networking Conference.*

Lin, F. Y. S., & Chiu, P. L. (2005). Energy-efficient sensor network design subject to complete coverage and discrimination constraints. *Proc. of the 2nd IEEE Intl. Conf. on Sensor and Ad Hoc Communications and Networks, 2,* 586–593.

Linewood, J., & Minter, D. (2004). *Building Portals with the Java Portlet API*. Apress, USA.

Linn, J. (1997). Generic Security Service Application Program Interface, Version 2. *IETF RFC 2078.*

Litke, A., Skoutas, D., & Varvarigou, T. (2004). Mobile Grid Computing: Changes and Challenges of Resource Management in a Mobile Grid Environment. *Access to Knowledge through the Grid in a Mobile World Workshop*, held in conjunction with *5th Int. Conf. on Practical Aspects of Knowledge Management*, (PAKM 2004) Vienna, Austria.

Litke, A., Tserpes, K., & Varvarigou, T. (2005). Computational Workload Prediction for Grid oriented Industrial Applications: The case of 3D-image rendering. *In proceedings of Cluster Computing and Grid 2005 (CCGrid2005) 2,* 962- 969.

Litke, A., Tserpes, K., Dolkas, K., & Varvarigou, T. (2005). A Task Replication and Fair Resource Management Scheme for Fault Tolerant Grids. *Lecture Notes in Computer Science,* 3470(Advances in Grid Computing - EGC 2005), 1022–1031.

Litzkow, M., M. Livny, and M. Mutka, "Condor - a Hunter of Idle Workstations", in *Proc. 8th Int. Conf. on Distributed Computing Systems,* pp. 104-111, 1988.

Liu, D.T., Franklin, M.J., Garlick, J., & Abdulla, G.M. (2005). Scaling up data-centric middleware on a cluster computer. *Technical Report, Lawrence Livermore National Laboratory.*

Liu, Y., Liu, W., Jia, W.-J., & Jiang, C. (2003). Link bandwidth detection for multimedia streaming in a distributed server environment. *In Proceeding of 2003 Joint Conference of the Fourth International Conference on Information, Communications & Singal Processing And Fourth Pacific-Rim Conference on Multimedia* (pp. 438-442), New York: IEEE Communications Society.

Low, M., Yoke, H., Cai, W., & Zhou, S. (2007, June). A Federated Agent-Based Crowd Simulation Architecture. In *The Proceedings of the 2007 European Conference on Modelling and Simulation* (pp. 188-194).

Lu, H., Han, J., & Feng, L. (1998). Stock movement prediction and n-dimensional inter-transaction association rules. *Proceedings of the 3rd ACM-SIGMOD Workshop on Research Issues on Data Mining and Knowledge Discovery* (pp. 121-127). ACM Press.

Lu, Y. (2007). Improving Data Consistency Management and Overlay Multicast in Internet-scale Distributed Systems. Ph.D. Dissertation, University of Nebraska-Lincoln.

Lu, Y., Lu, Y. & Jiang, H. (2007). IDEA: An Infrastructure of Detection-based Adaptive Consistency Control. *16th International Symposium on High Performance Distributed Computing* (pp. 223-224). Monterey, CA.

Lu, Y., Lu, Y., & Jiang, H. (2008). Adaptive Consistency Guarantees for Large-Scale Replicated Services. *2008 IEEE International Conference on Networking, Architecture and Storage,* Chongqing, China.

Ludäscher, B., Altintas, I., & Gupta, A. (2003). Compiling Abstract Scientific Workflows into Web Service Workflows. *15th International Conference on Scientific and Statistical Database Management,* Cambridge, Massachusetts, USA., IEEE CS Press, pp. 241-244, Los Alamitos, CA, USA., July 09-11.

Ludäscher, B., et al. (2006). Scientific workflow management and the Kepler system. *Concurrency and Computation: Practice and Experience, 18*(10), 1039–1065.

Ludtke, S., Baldwin, P., & Chiu. W. (1999) EMAN: semiautomated software for high resolution single-particle reconstructions. *Journal of Structural Biology, 128*(*1*), 82-97.

Luethkea, B., Scotta, S., & Naughtona, T. (2003). OSCAR Cluster Administration with C3. *The 17th Annual International Symposium on High Performance Computing Systems and Applications (HPCS2003).* Sherbrooke, Quebec, Canada. (pp. 1-7).

Luo, X., & Fang, N. (2008). Semantic Representation of Scientific Documents for the e-Science Knowledge Grid. *Concurrency and Computation: Practice and Experience, 20*(7), 839-862.

Luo, X., & Hu, Q. (2008). Similar Knowledge Flow based Intelligent Browsing of Topics. *In Proceedings of 3rd International Workshop on Workflow Management and Application in Grid Environments.*

Luo, X., Hu, Q., & Xu, W. (2008). Discovery of Textual Knowledge Flow based on the Management of Knowledge Maps. *Concurrency and Computation: Practice and Experience* (pp. 1791-1806).

Luo, X., Xu, Z., & Yu, J. (2008). Discovery of Associated Topics for the Intelligent Browsing. *The First IEEE International Conference on Ubi-media Computing* (pp. 119-125). Digital Object Identifier: 10.1109/UMEDIA.2008.4570876.

Lyu, M. R. (1995). *Software Fault Tolerance.* Chichester, UK: John Wiley & Sons.

M. P. (1987). *Domain names: Implementation and specification* (STD 13, RFC 1035).

Magowan, J. (2003). Extreme blue grid accounting project (Grid service accounting extensions–GSAX). *GGF Resource Usage Service Working Group.*

Majithia, S., Walker, D. W., & Gray, W.A. (2004). *A framework for automated service composition in service-oriented architectures* (pp. 269-283).ESWS.

Mani, A., & Nagarajan, A.(2002). *Understanding quality of service for Web services.* Retrieved from http://www-106.ibm.com/developerworks/library/ws-quality.html

Mannie, E. (2004). Generalized multi-protocol label switching (GMPLS) architecture. *IETF RFC 3945.*

Mannila, H., Toivonen, H., & Verkamo, A. I. (1997). Discovery of Frequent Episodes in Event Sequences. *Data Mining and Knowledge Discovery, 1*(3), 259-289.

Marinescu, D.C. (2002) *Internet-based workflow management: Toward a Semantic Web.* John Wiley & Sons.

Martello, S., & Toth, P. (1990). *Knapsack Problems: Algorithms and Computer Implementations.* John Wiley & Sons.

Martello, S., Pisinger, D., & Toth, P. (2000). New trends in exact algorithms for the 0-1 knapsack problem. *European Journal of Operational Research, 123,* 325–332.

Martin, D., Burstein, M., & Hobbs, J. (2004). OWL-S: Semantic Markup for Web Services. Retrieved from: http://www.w3.org/Submission/OWL-S/. Accessed on Jul 5, 2008.

Martin, D., Paolucci, M., McIlraith, S., Burstein, M., McDermott, D., McGuinness, D., et al.(2004). Bringing semantics to Web services: The OWL-S approach. In *Proceedings of the 1st International Workshop on Semantic Web Services and Web Process Composition.* San Diego, California.

Massie, M., Chun, B., & Culler, D. (2004). The ganglia distributed monitoring system: design, implementation, and experience. *Parallel Computing, 30*(7), 817-840.

Matjaz, B.J., Sarang, P.G., & Mathew, B. (2006). *Business process execution language for Web services* (2nd ed.). Packt Publishing.

Mayer, A., McGough, S., Furmento, N., Lee, W., Newhouse, S., & Darlington, J. (2003, September). *ICENI Dataflow and Workflow: Composition and Scheduling in Space and Time.* In UK e-Science All Hands Meeting, Nottingham, UK, pages 894–900., Bristol, UK: IOP Publishing Ltd.

MCAT installation guide (2006). http://www.sdsc.edu/srb/index.php/MCAT_Install.

McBride, B. (2002). Jena: A Semantic Web toolkit. *IEEE Internet Computing,* November /December, 55-59.

McCann, C., R. Vaswani and J. Zahorjan, "A Dynamic Processor Allocation Policy for Multiprogrammed Shared-Memory Multiprocessors", *ACM Trans. Computer Systems*, Vol. 11, No. 2, pp. 146-178, May 1993.

McGough, A., Afzal, A., et al. (2005). Making the Grid predictable through reservations and performance modeling. *The Computer Journal, 48*(3), 358–368.

McGough, S., Young, L., Afzal, A., Newhouse, S., & Darlington, J. (2004, September). Performance Architecture within ICENI. In *UK e-Science All Hands Meeting*, Nottingham, UK, pages 906–911. Bristol, UK: IOP Publishing Ltd Sep. 2004.

McGough, S., Young, L., Afzal, A., Newhouse, S., & Darlington, J. (2004, September). Workflow Enactment in ICENI. In UK e-Science All Hands Meeting, Nottingham, UK, pages 894–900. Bristol, UK: IOP Publishing Ltd.

Meder, S., Welch, V., Chicago, V., Tuecke, S., & Engert, D. (2004). *GSS-API extensions* (No. GFD-E.024). Lemont, IL: Global Grid Forum.

Medjahed, B., & Bouguettaya, A. (2005). A Multilevel Composability Model for Semantic Web Services. *IEEE Transactions on Knowledge and Data Engineering, 17(7),* 954-968.

Meguerdichian, S., Koushanfar, F., Potkonjak, M., & Srivastava, M. B. (2001). Coverage problems in wireless ad-hoc sensor networks. *Proc. of the 20th IEEE INFOCOM, 3.*

Menasce, D., & Casalicchio, E. (2004). Quality of Service Aspects and Metrics in Grid Computing. In *The Proceedings of the 2004 Computer Measurement Group Conference* (pp. 521-532).

Menasce, D., & Casalicchio, E. (2004). Quality of Service Aspects and Metrics in Grid Computing. In The Proceedings of the 2004 Computer Measurement Group Conference (pp. 521-532).

Meyer, P. L. (1970). *Introductory Probability and Statistical Applications* (2nd ed.), Chapter 11. Addison-Wesley.

Miles, S., Groth, P., Branco, M., & Moreau, L. (2005). The requirements of recording and using provenance in e-science experiments. *Technical Report, Electronics and Computer Science, University of Southampton.*

Milner, R., *Communicating and Mobile Systems: The Pi Calculus*, Cambridge University Press, 1999.

Minson, R., & Theodoropoulos, G. K., (2004, June). *Distributing RePast Agent-Based Simulations with HLA.* Presented at the European Simulation Interoperability Workshop 2004, Edinburgh, Scotland.

Mohamed, M. (2002). Points of the triangle. *Intelligent Enterprise, 5*(14), 32-37.

Montanari, U., and M. Pistore, "Checking Bisimilarity for Finitary Pi-calculus", *Concurrency Theory*, LNCS Vol. 962, Springer Verlag, pp. 42-56, 1995.

Montgomery, D. C., & Runger, G. C. (2003). *Applied Statistics and Probability for Engineers.* An Interactive e-text, 3rd edition.

Moore, R. W., & Merzky, A. (2003). *Persistent archive concepts* (No. GFD-I.026). Lemont, IL: Global Grid Forum.

Moreau, L., & Foster, I. (2006). *Provenance and annotation of data.* Proceedings of the International Provenance and Annotation Workshop, *LNCS* 4145.

Moreau, L., & Ludascher, B. (2007). The first provenance challenge. *Concurrency and Control: Practice and Experience.*

Morris, P. (1994). *The Management of Projects*, Thomas Telford, p.18.

Morse, K. L., Drake, D., & Brunton, R. P. Z. (2003, June). *Web Enabling an RTI - An XMSF Profile.* Presented at the European Simulation Interoperability Workshop 2003, Stockholm, Sweden.

Morse, K. L., Drake, D., & Brunton, R. P. Z. (2004). Web Enabling HLA Compliant Simulations to Support Network Centric Applications. In *The Proceedings of the 2004 Command and Control Research and Technology Symposium* (no. 172).

Mu'alem, A. W., and D. G. Feitelson, "Utilization, Predictability, Workloads, and User Runtime Estimate in Scheduling the IBM SP2 with Backfilling", *IEEE Transactions on Parallel and Distributed Systems*, Vol. 12, No. 6, June 2001.

Murch, R. (2004). *Autonomic computing.* Published by IBM Press.

Murphy, C., Ram, S., & Manimaran, G. (2001, April). Resource Management in Real-time Systems and Networks. USA: MIT Press.

Nakai, J. (2002). *Pricing computing resources: reading between the lines and beyond* (NAS Technical Report: NAS-01-010), NASA Ames Research Center.

Negri, A., Poggi, A., et al. (2006). Dynamic grid tasks composition and distribution through agents. *Concurrency and Computation: Practice & Experience, 18*(8), 875-885.

Nelson, E. C. (1973). *A statistical basis for software reliability assessment* (TRW systems report).

Németh, Z., and V. Sunderam, "Characterizing Grids Attributes, Definitions, and Formalisms", *J. Grid Computing*, Vol. 1, No. 1, pp. 9-23, 2003.

Neo, H., Lin, Q. & Liew, K. (2005). A Grid-based mobile agent collaborative virtual environment. *Proceedings of International Conference on Cyberworlds 2005* (pp. 335-339), Singapore.

Neteler, M., & Miltasova, H. (2002). *Open Source GIS: A GRASS GIS Approach.* London: Kluwer Academic Publishers.

Neteler, M., & Miltasova, H. (2004). *Open Source GIS: A GRASS GIS Approach* (Section Edition), London: Kluwer Academic Publishers.

Newhouse, S., & Darlington, J. (2001). *Trading Grid Services within the UK E-Science.* London e-Science Center, Imperial College London, London, UK.

Ngan, T. W. J., D. S. Wallach, P. Druschel, "Enforcing Fair Sharing of Peer-to-Peer Resources", *Proceedings of* the 2nd International Workshop on Peer-to-Peer Systems *(IPTPS '03)*, Berkeley, California, February 2003.

Nguyen-Tuong, A. (2000). *Integrating Fault-Tolerance Techniques in Grid Applications.* PhD Dissertation, University of Virginia.

Nguyen-Tuong, A., & Grimshaw, A. S. (1998). *Using Reflection to Incorporate Fault-Tolerance Techniques in Distributed Applications.* Computer Science Technical Report, University of Virginia, CS 98-34.

Nicola, R. D., and F. Vaandrager, "Three Logics for Branching Bisimulation", *J. ACM*, Vol. 42, No. 2, pp. 458-487, 1995,

Nielsen, H. F., Christensen, E., & Farrell, J., (2007) Specification: WS-Attachments. Retrieved November 07, 2007, from http://www-106.ibm.com/developerworks/webservices/library/ws-attach.html

Nissen, M. E. (2002). An Extended Model of Knowledge Flow Dynamics. *Communications of the Association for Information Systems, 8,* 251-266.

Nissen, M. E., & Levitt, R. E. (2004). Agent-Based Modeling of Knowledge Flows: Illustration from the Domain of Information Systems Design. *Proceedings of the 37th Hawaii International Conference on System Sciences.*

Nitais, V. Y., & Schulte, W. R. (2003). Introduction to service-oriented architecture. Gartner:

Nonaka, I. (1994). A Dynamic Theory of Organizational Knowledge Creation. *Organization Science, 5*(1), 14-37.

Nonaka, I., & Takeouchi, H. (1995). *The Knowledge Creating Company.* NY: Oxford University Press.

Novotny, J. (2004). Developing Grid portlets using the GridSphere portal framework. *IBM developerworks..*

Noy, N.F., Sintek, M., Decker, S., Crubezy, M., Fergerson, R. W., & Musen, M.A. (2001). Creating Semantic Web contents with Protege-2000. *IEEE Intelligent Systems, 16*(2), 60-71.

Nurmi, D., Brevik, J., & Wolski R. (2003). *Modeling Machine Availability in Enterprise and Wide-area Distributed Computing Environments.* UCSB Computer Science Technical Report Number CS2003-28.

Oberle, D. (2005). *The semantic management of middleware.* Springer.

Oinn, T. M., Addis, M., Ferris, J., Marvin, D., Senger, M., Greenwood, R. M., et al. (2004). Taverna: A tool for the composition and enactment of bioinformatics workflows. *Bioinformatics, 20*(17), 3045-3054.

Oinn, T., Greenwood, M. et al. (2006). Taverna: Lessons in creating a workflow environment for life sciences. *Concurrency and Computation: Practice and Experience, 18*(20), 1067-1100.

OMG (2006). CORBA component model v4.0. *Technical Report, OMG.*

Overstreet, C. M., Nance, R. E., & Balci, O. (2002). Issues in Enhancing Model Reuse. In *The Proceedings of the First International Conference on Grand Challenges for Modeling and Simulation.*

Ozden, B., & Ramaswamy S., & Silberschatz, A. (1998). Cyclic Association Rules. *In Proceedings of the 14th International Conference on Data Engineering* (pp. 412-421). IEEE Computer Society Press.

Padgett, J., Djemame, K., & Dew, P. (2005). Grid-based SLA Management. *Lecture Notes in Computer Science,* (pp. 1282-1291).

Paik, I., & Maruyama, D. (October 2007). Automatic Web Services Composition Using Combining HTN and CSP. *In the proceeding of the Seventh International Conference on Computer and Information Technology.* Fukushima, Japan: IEEE computer society.

Pallickara, S., Fox, G., Yildiz, B., Pallickara, S.L., Patel, S., & Yemme, D. (2005). On the costs for reliable messaging in Web/grid service environments. *e-Science.*

Paolucci, M., Sycara, K., Nishimura, T., & Srinivasan, N. (2003). Using DAML-S for p2p discovery. In *Proceedings of the International Conference on Web Services (ICWS '03).*

Parallel Workloads Archive, http://www.cs.huji.ac.il/labs/parallel/workload/

Parra-Hernandez, R., Vanderster, D., & Dimopoulos, N.J. (2004). Resource Management and Knapsack Formulations on the Grid. *In Proc. of the 5th IEEE/ACM Int. Workshop on Grid Computing.*

Patil, A., Oundhakar, S., Sheth, A., & Verma, K. (May 2004). METEOR-S Web Service Annotation Framework. *In the proceeding of the 13th International World Wide Web Conference.* New York, USA: ACM Press.

Paurobally, D., Tamma, V., & Wooldrdige, M. (2007). A Framework for Web Service Negotiation. *ACM Transactions on Autonomous and Adaptive Systems, 2(4)*, 14, 1-14:23.

Pearlman, L., C. Kesselman, S. Gullapalli, B. F. Spencer, J. Futrelle, K. Ricker, I. Foster, P. Hubbard, and C. Severance, "Distributed Hybrid Earthquake Engineering Experiments: Experiences with a Ground-Shaking Grid Application", in *Proc. 13th IEEE Int. Symp. on High Performance Distributed Computing*, pp. 14-23, 2004.

Perusich, K., & Mcneese, M. D. (2006). Using Fuzzy Cognitive Maps for Knowledge Management in a Conflict Environment. *IEEE Transactions on Systems, Man and Cybernetics, Part C: Applications and Reviews, 36(6)*, 810-821.

Peterson, L. L., Anderson, T. E., Culler, D. E., & Roscoe, T. (2003). A Blueprint for Introducing Disruptive Technology into the Internet. *Computer Communication Review. Vol. 33(1)*. 59-64.

Petty, M. D., Weisel, E. W., & Mielka, R. R. (2003). A Formal Approach to Composability. In *The Proceedings of the 2003 Interservice Industry Training, Simulation and Education Conference* (pp. 1763-1772).

Phosphorus project website. (2008). Retrieved in 2008 from http://www.ist-phosphorus.eu.

Pisinger, D. (1995). *Algorithms for Knapsack Problems.* Ph.D. Thesis, Dept. of Computer Science, University of Copenhagen.

Plale, B. (2005). Resource requirements study for LEAD storage repository. *Technical Report 001, Linked Environments for Atmospheric Discovery.*

Plank, J. S., Casanova, H., Beck, M., & Dongarra, J. J. (1999). Deploying fault tolerance and task migration with NetSolve. *Future Generation Computer Systems, 15(5)*, 745-755.

Plank, J. S., Casanova, H., Beck, M., & Dongarra, J. J. (1999). Deploying fault tolerance and task migration with NetSolve. *Future Gener. Comput. Syst., 15(5)*, 745–755.

Pollack, M. E., & Ringuette, M. (1990). Introducing the Tileworld: Experimentally Evaluating Agent Architectures. In *The Proceedings of the 8th National Conference on Artificial Intelligence* (pp. 183-189).

Pollack, M. E., Joslin, D., Nunes, A., Ur, S., & Ephrati, E., (1994). *Experimental investigation of an agent commitment strategy* (Tech. Rep. No. TR 94-31). Pittsburgh, PA 15260: University of Pittsburgh.

Prakash, A. & Shim, H. S. (1994). DistView: Support for Building Efficient Collaborative Applications using Replicated Objects. *ACM conference on computer supported cooperative work.* (pp. 153-164). Chapel Hill, NC.

Preiss, B. R. (1999). *Data Structures and Algorithms with Object-Oriented Design Patterns in C++.* John Wiley & Sons.

Prim, R. C. (1957). Shortest connection networks and some generalizations. *Bell Syst. Techno. J., 36.*

Project JXTA, v2.0. (2003). *JavaTMProgrammers guide.* Sun Microsystems. Retrieved from http://www.jxta.org

Puhlmann, F., and M. Weske, "Using the Pi-calculus for Formalizing Workflow Patterns", *Business Process Management*, LNCS Vol. 3649, pp. 153-168, 2005.

Pullen, J. M., Brunton, R., Brutzman, D., Drake, D., Hieb, M., Morse, K., & Tolk, A. (2005). Using Web Services to Integrate Heterogeneous Simulations in a Grid Environment. *Future Generation Computer Systems, 21(1)*, 97-106.

Quan, D., & Altmann, J. (2007). Mapping of SLA-based workflows with light communication onto Grid resources. *Proceedings of the 4th International Conference on Grid Service Engineering and Management* (pp. 135-145), Leipzig, Germany.

Quinlan, R. (1993). *C4.5: Programs for machine learning.* San Mateo, CA: Morgan Kaufmann Publishers.

Racer reasoner. Retrieved on Jun 12, 2008. From: http://www.racer-systems.com/index.phtml.

Ragone A., Di Noia, T., Di Sciascio, E., Donini, F. M., Colucci, S., & Colasuonno, F. (2007). Fully automated Web services discovery and composition through concept covering and concept abduction. *International Journal of Web Services Research, 4*(3), 85-112.

Railsback, S. F., Lytinen, S. L., & Jackson, S. K. (2006). Agent-Based Simulation Platforms: Review and Development Recommendations. *Simulation: Transactions of the Society for Modeling and Simulation International, 82*(9), 609-623.

Rajasekar, A., Wan, M., Moore, R., Kremenek, G., & Guptil, T. (2003). Data Grids, Collections, and Grid Bricks. In F. Titsworth (Eds), *20th IEEE/11th NASA Goddard Conference on Mass Storage Systems and Technologies* (pp. 2-9). San Diego: IEEE Computer Society.

Ramamritham, K., Stankovic, J. A., & Shiah, P. F. (1990). Efficient Scheduling Algorithms for Real-time Multiprocessor Systems. *IEEE Trans. on Parallel and Distributed Systems, 1*(2), 184-194.

Raman, V., Crone, C., Haas, L., Malaika, S., Mukai, T., Wolfson, D., et al. (2003). *Services for data access and data processing on grids* (No. GFD-I.14). Lemont, IL: Global Grid Forum.

Ramaswamy, S., Mahajan, S., & Silberschatz, A. (1998). On the Discovery of Interesting Patterns in Association Rules. *Proceedings of the 24th International Conference on Very Large Databases* (pp. 368-379). Morgan Kaufmann.

Ranganathan, K., Ripeanu, M., & Sarin, A. (2003). To share or not to share: An analysis of incentives to contribute in collaborative file sharing environments. *Proceedings of the Workshop on Economics of Peer-to-Peer Systems*, USA.

Ratnasamy, S., Francis, P., Handley, M., Karp, R., & Shenker, S. (2001). A Content Addressable Network. *ACM SIGCOMM* (161-172). San Diego, CA.

Reed, D. A., Lu, C., & Mendes, C. L. (2006). Reliability challenges in large systems. *Future Generation Computer Systems, 22*, 293–302.

Ren, K., Liu, X., Chen, J., Xiao, N., Song, J., & Zhang, W. (July 2008). A QSQL-based Efficient Planning Algorithm for Fully-automated Service Composition in Dynamic Service Environments. *In the proceeding of 2008 IEEE International Conference on Services Computing(SCC 2008)*. Honolulu, Hawaii, USA: IEEE Press.

Ren, K., Song, J., Chen, J., Xiao, N., & Liu, C. (December 2007). A Pre-reasoning based Method for Service Discovery and Service Instance Selection in Service Grid Environments. *In the proceeding of the 2nd IEEE Asia-Pacific Service Computing Conference.* Tsukuba Science City, Japan: IEEE Press.

Research SPA-19-5971. Retrieved February 10, 2007, from *http://www.gartner.com*

Rheingold, H. (1993). *The virtual community: Homesteading at the electronic frontier.* Addison-Wesley.

Ribler, R.L., Vetter, J.S., Simitci, H., & Reed, D.A. (1998). Autopilot: Adaptive control of distributed applications. *HPDC.*

Richard S. W. (1994). *TCP/IP Illustrated.* Addison Wesley Longman, Inc.

Romberg, M. (1999). The UNICORE architecture: seamless access to distributed resources. *Proceedings of the 8th IEEE International Symposium on High performance Distributed Computing.*

Rowstron, A., & Druschel, P. (2001). Pastry: Scalable, distributed object location and routing for large-scale peer-to-peer systems, *IFIP/ACM International conference on distributed systems platforms (Middleware)* (pp. 329-350). Heidelberg, Germany.

Rycerz, K., Bubak, M. T., Malawski, M., & Sloot, P. (2005). A Framework for HLA-Based Interactive Simulations on the Grid. *Simulation: Transactions of the Society for Modeling and Simulation International, 81*(1), 67-76.

Sabin, G., M. Lang, and P. Sadayappan, "Moldable Parallel Job Scheduling Using Job Efficiency: An Iterative Approach", *Proceedings of the 12th Workshop on Job Scheduling Strategies for Parallel Processing,* 2006.

Sacerdoti, F., Katz, M., et al. (2003). Wide area cluster monitoring with Ganglia. *Proceedings of IEEE International Conference on Cluster Computing 2003* (pp. 289-298), Hong Kong, China.

Sahni, S. (2004). *Data Structures, Algorithms, and Applications in Java.* 2nd Edition, Silicon Press.

Sairafi, S., A., Emmanouil, F. S., Ghanem, M., Giannadakis, N., Guo, Y., Kalaitzopolous, D., et al. (2003). The design of discovery net: Towards open Grid services for knowledge discovery. *International Journal of High Performance Computing Applications, 17*(3).

Sakellariou, R. & Zhao, H. (2004). A low-cost rescheduling policy for efficient mapping of workflows on Grid systems. *Scientific Programming, 12*(4), 253-262.

Sala, G. U., Bordeaux, L., & Schaerf, M. (July 2004). Describing and Reasoning on Web Services using Process Algebra. *In the proceeding of 2004 IEEE International Conference on Web Services.* San Diego, USA: IEEE computer society.

Saleh, A., et al. (2000). Proposed Extensions to the UNI for Interfacing to a Configurable All-Optical Network, *OIF2000.278.*

Sangiorgi, D., and D. Walker, *The Pi-calculus: a Theory of Mobile Processes*, Cambridge University Press, 2001.

Savage, S., Anderson, T., Aggarwal, A., Becker, D., Cardwell, N., Collins, A., Hoffman, E., Snell, J., Vahdat, A., Voelker, G., & Zahorjan, J. (1999). Detour: A Case for Informed Internet Routing and Transport. *IEEE Micro, 19*(1), 50-59.

Savage, S., Collins, A., Hoffman, E., Snell, J., & Anderson, T. (1999). The End-to-End Effects of Internet Path Selection. In Parulkar, G. & Turner, J. (Eds), *Proceedings of the ACM SIGCOMM '99 Conference on Applications, Technologies, Architectures, and Protocols for Computer Communication* (pp. 263-274). New York: ACM Press.

Scheaffer, R. L. (1995). *Introduction to Probability and Its Applications* (2nd ed.), Section 4.9, (Duxbury).

Schilit, B., & Theimer, M. (1994). Disseminating active map information to mobile hosts.

Schollmeier, R. (2001, August). A definition of peer-to-peer networking for the classification of peer-to-peer architectures and applications. In IEEE (Ed.), *2001 International Conference on Peer-to-Peer Computing (P2P2001).* Linko ping Universität: Department of Computer and Information Science.

Schuckmann, C., Kirchner, L., Schummer, J., & Haake, J. M. (1996). Designing Object-oriented Synchronous Groupware with COAST. *ACM conference on computer supported cooperative work .*(pp. 30-38)*.* Cambridge, MA.

Schwiegelshohn, U., and R. Yahyapour, "Fairness in Parallel Job Scheduling", *Journal of Scheduling,* 3(5): pp. 297-320, 2000.

Schwier, R.A. (2004). Virtual learning communities. In G. Anglin (Ed.), *Critical issues in instructional technology.* Portsmouth: Teacher Ideas Press.

Seaborne, A. (2004). *RDQL: A query language for RDF.* Retrieved May 10, 2006, from http://www.w3.org/Submission/RDQL/

Segall, M. D., Lindan, P. J. D., Probert, M. J., et al. (2002). First-principles simulation: ideas, illustrations and the CASTEP code. *J. Phys. Condensed Matter, 14,* 211.

Senge, P. M. (1990). *The fifth discipline: The art and practice of the learning organization.* New York: Doubleday/Currency.

Shaikhali, A., Rana, O. F., Al-Ali, R. J., & Walker, D. W. (2003). UDDIe: An extended registry for Web services.

In *Proceedings of the Symposium on Applications and the Internet Workshops (SAINT '03 Workshops)*.

Sherwood, R., Braud, R., & Bhattacharjee, B. (2004). Slurpie: A cooperative bulk data transfer protocol. In *the 23rd Annual Joint Conference of the IEEE Computer and Communications Societies* (pp. 941-951). New York: IEEE Communications Society.

Shestak, V., Smith, J., Maciejewski, A. & Siegel, H. (2006 ICPP). A stochastic approach to measuring the robustness of resource allocations in distributed systems. *Proceedings of the International Conference on Parallel Processing (ICPP 2006)* (pp. 459-470). Columbus, OH, U.S.A.

Shestak, V., Smith, J., Maciejewski, A. & Siegel, H. (2006). Iterative algorithms for stochastically robust static resource allocation in periodic sensor driven clusters. *Proceedings of the 18th IASTED International Conference on Parallel and Distributed Computing and Systems* (pp. 166-174), Dallas, TX, U.S.A.

Shestak, V., Smith, J., Smith, et al. (2006 PDPTA). Greedy approaches to stochastic robust resource allocation for periodic sensor driven distributed systems. *Proceedings of the 2006 International Conference on Parallel and Distributed Processing Techniques and Applications (PDPTA)*, Las Vegas, NV, U.S.A.

Shirasuna, S., & Gannon, D. (2006). XBaya: A graphical workflow composer for the Web services architecture. *Technical Report 004, Linked Environments for Atmospheric Discovery*.

Siddiqui, M., Villazon, A., & Fahringer, T. (2006). Grid capacity planning with negotiation-based advance reservation for optimized QoS. *Proceedings of the 2006 ACM/IEEE Conference on SuperComputing SC '06*.

Silberschatz, A., J. Peterson, P. Galvin, *Operating System Concepts*, Addison-Wesley Publishing Company, 1991, pp. 106-113.

Simmhan, Y., Plale, B., & Gannon, D. (2005). A survey of data provenance in e-science. *SIGMOD Record, 34*(3), 31–36.

Simmhan, Y.L., Pallickara, S.L., Vijayakumar, N.N., & Plale, B. (2006). *Data management in dynamic environment-driven computational science*. Proceedings of the IFIP Working Conference on Grid-Based Problem Solving Environments (WoCo9).

Simmhan, Y.L., Plale, B., & Gannon, D. (2006). *Towards a quality model for effective data selection in collaboratories*. Proceedings of the IEEE Workflow and Data Flow for Scientific Applications (SciFlow) Workshop.

Simmhan, Y.L., Plale, B., & Gannon, D. (2007). Query capabilities of the Karma provenance framework. *Concurrency and Control: Practice and Experience*.

Simmhan, Y.L., Plale, B., Gannon, D., & Marru, S. (2006c). Performance evaluation of the Karma provenance framework for scientific workflows. *IPAW* and *LNCS* 4145.

Singh, A., & Liu, L. (2003). TrustMe: Anonymous Management of Trust Relationships in Decentralized P2P Systems. *Third International Conference on Peer-to-Peer Computing* (pp.142-149), Sweden.

Singh, G., Kesselman, K., & Deelman, E. (2005). Optimizing of Grid-based workflow execution. In *HPDC'05*.

Singh, M.P., & Huhns, M.N. (2006). *Service-oriented computing: Semantics, processes, agents*. John Wiley & Sons.

Sirin, E., & Parsia, B. (2004). *Pellet: An OWL DL Reasoner, 3rd International Semantic Web Conference*, Hiroshima, Japan. Springer.

Sirin, E., Parsia, B., Wu, D., Hendler, J., & Nau, D. (2004). HTN planning for Web Service composition using SHOP2. *Journal of Web Semantics, 1*(4), 377-396.

Sirin, E.B. Parsia, B., & Hendler, J. (2004). Filtering and selecting Semantic Web services with interactive composition techniques. *IEEE Intelligent Systems, 19*(4), 42-49.

Skyttner, L. (1998). Information theory: A psychological study in old and new concepts. *Kybernetes, 27*(3), 284-311.

Slijepcevic, S., & Potkonjak, M. (2001). Power efficient organization of wireless sensor networks. *Proc. of IEEE Intl. Conf. on Communications, 2.*

Slominski, A. (2006). Adapting BPEL to scientific workflows. *Workflows for e-Science.*

Smallen, S., Cirne, W., Frey, J., Berman, F., Wolski, R., Su, M., Kesselman, C., Young, S., & Ellisman, M. (2000). Combining workstations and supercomputers to support grid applications: The parallel tomography experience. In: *IEEE Proceedings of the 9th Heterogeneous Computing Workshop* (pp. 241-252). Cancun, Mexico: IEEE Computer Society.

Smith, H., "Business Process Management - the Third Wave: Business Process Modeling Language (BPML) and its Pi-calculus Foundations", *Information and Software Technology*, Vol. 45, pp. 1065-1069, 2003.

Snell, Q., Clement, M., Jackson, D., & Gragory, C. (2000). The Performance Impact of Advance Reservation Meta-Scheduling, Proceeding of *IPDPS 2000 Workshop, JSSPP 2000*, Cancun, Mexico.

Sotomayor, B. (2007). The Globus Toolkit 3 Programmer's Tutorial. Retrieved January 08, 2007, from http://gdp.globus.org/gt3-tutorial/singlehtml/progtutorial_0.4.3.html

Sotomayor, B., & Childers, L. (2006). *Globus Toolkit 4: Programming Java services.* Morgan Kaufmann.

SPARQL. Query Language for RDF, W3C Working Draft 4 October 2006. Retrieved October 8, 2006, from http://128.30.52.31/TR/rdf-sparql-query/

Splunter, S., Wijngaards, N. J. E., Brazier, F. M. T., & Richards, D. (2004). Automated Component-Based Configuration: Promises and Fallacies. In *The Proceedings of the Adaptive Agents and Multi-Agent Systems workshop at the AISB 2004 Symposium* (pp. 130-135).

Spooner, D. P., Cao, J., Jarvis, S. A., He, L., & Nudd, G. R. (2004). Performance-aware Workflow Management for Grid Computing. *The Computer Journal.* London, UK: Oxford University Press,

Spooner, D. P., J. Cao, S. A. Jarvis, L. He, and G. R. Nudd, "Performance-aware Workflow Management for Grid Computing", *The Computer J.*, Special Focus - Grid Performability, Vol. 48, No. 3, pp. 347-357, 2005.

Srinivasan, S., S. Krishnamoorthy, P. Sadayappan, "A Robust Scheduling Strategy for Moldable Scheduling of Parallel Jobs", *Proceedings of the Fifth IEEE International Conference on Cluster Computing (CLUSTER'03)*, pp. 92-, December 2003.

Srinivasan, S., V. Subramani, R. Kettimuthu, P. Holenarsipur, P. Sadayappan, "Effective Selection of Partition Sizes for Moldable Scheduling of Parallel Jobs", *the 9th International Conference on High Performance Computing, Lecture Notes In Computer Science*; Vol. 2552, pp. 174 – 183, 2002.

Stemm, M., Katz, R., & Seshan S. (2000). A network measurement architecture for adaptive applications. In *Proceedings of INFOCOM 2000* (pp. 285-294).

Stewart, J. W. (1998). *BGP4: Inter-Domain Routing in the Internet.* Boston: Addison-Wesley Professional.

Stoica, I., Morris, R., Karger, D., Kaashoek, M. F., & Balakrishnan, H. (2001). Chord: A Scalable Peer-to-peer Lookup Service for Internet Applications. *ACM SIGCOMM.* (pp.149-160). San Deigo, CA.

Stojanovic, Z., & Dahanayake. A. (2005). *Service oriented software system engineering: Challenges and practices.* Idea Group Inc.

Subramani, V., Kettimuthu, R., Srinivasan, S., & Sadayappan P. (2002). Distributed job scheduling on computational grids using multiple simultaneous requests, in: *Proceedings of the 11th IEEE International Symposium on High Performance Distributed Computing* (pp. 359-367). Edinburgh, Scotland: IEEE Computer Society.

Subramoniam, K., Maheswaran, M., & Toulouse, M. (2002). Towards a micro-economic model for resource allocation in grid computing systems. In: *Proceedings of the 2002 IEEE Canadian Conference on Electrical & Computer Engineering* (pp.782-785). Canadian: IEEE Computer Society.

Sugavanam, P., Siegel, H., et al. (2007). Robust static allocation of resources for independent tasks under makespan and dollar cost constraints. *Journal of Parallel and Distributed Computing, 67(4)*, 400-416.

Sulakhe, D., Rodriguez, A. et al. (2005). Gnare: an environment for grid-based high-throughput genome analysis. *Proceedings of IEEE International Symposium on Cluster Computing and the Grid (CCGrid)2005* (pp. 455-462), Cardiff, UK.

Sun, Y., He, S., & Leu, J. Y. (2007). Syndicating Web Services: A QoS and user-driven approach. *Decision Support Systems 43 (2007) 243–255, 43(1)*, 243-255.

Sycara, K., Paolucci, M., Ankolekar, A., & Srinivasan, N. (2003). Automated discovery, interaction and composition of Semantic Web services. *Journal of Web Semantics, 1(1)*, 27-46.

Szalay, A., & Williams, R. (Eds.) (2008). US National Virtual Observatory (NVO). Retrieved August 14, 2008, from http://www.us-vo.org/.

Szomszor, M., & Moreau, L. (2003). Recording and reasoning over data provenance in Web and grid services. *ODBASE*.

Takefusa, A., Casanova, H., Matsuoka, S., & Berman, F. (2001). A study of deadline scheduling for client-server systems on the computational grid, in: *Proceedings of the 10th IEEE Symposium on High Performance Distributed Computing* (pp. 406-415). San Francisco: IEEE Computer Society.

Taylor, I. J., Deelman E., Gannon, D. B., & Shields, M. (2007). *Workflows for e-science.* Springer.

Taylor, I., M. Shields, I. Wang, and R. Philp, "Distributed P2P Computing within Triana: A Galaxy Visualization Test Case", in *Proc. 17th IEEE Int. Parallel & Distributed Processing Symp.*, Nice, France, 2003.

Thain, D., Tannenbaum, T., & Livny, M. (2005). Distributed Computing in Practice: The Condor Experience. *Concurrency and Computation: Practice and Experience, 17(2-4)*, 323-356.

Thatte, S. (2001). *XLANG: Web services for business process design.* Microsoft Corporation, Initial Public Draft.

The MadKit project (release 4.1). (2005). Retrieved from http://www.madkit.org/

Theodoropoulos, G. K., Zhang, Y., Chen, D., Minson, R., Turner, S. J., Cai, W., Yong, X., & Logan, B. (2006, May). *Large Scale Distributed Simulation on the Grid.* Paper presented at the Sixth IEEE International Symposium on Cluster Computing and the Grid Workshops, Singapore.

Tian M., Gramm, A., Ritter, H., and Schiller, J. (2004). Efficient selection and monitoring of QoS-aware Web services with the WS-QoS framework. In *Proceedings of the International Conference on Web Intelligence (WI '04).*

Tian, D., & Georganas, N. D. (2002). A coverage-preserving node scheduling scheme for large wireless sensor networks. *Proc. of the 1st ACM Intl. Workshop on Wireless Sensor Networks and Applications,* (pp. 32–41).

Tobias, R., & Hofmann, C. (2004). Evaluation of Free Java Libraries for Social-Scientific Agent-Based Simulation. *Journal of Artificial Societies and Social Simulation, 7(1)*, Retrieved January 08, 2004, from http://jasss.soc.surrey.ac.uk/7/1/6.html .

Topcuouglu, H., Hariri, S. & Wu, M. (2002). Performance effective and low-complexity task scheduling for heterogeneous computing. *IEEE Transactions on Parallel and Distribution Systems, 13(3)*, 260-274.

TORQUE (2008). http://www.clusterresources.com/pages/products/torque-resource-manager.php

TORQUE Quick Start (n.d.). Retrieved 2008 from http://clusterresources.com/torquedocs21/torquequickstart.shtml.

Tsalgatidou, A., & Pilioura, T. (2002). An overview of standards and related technology in web services. *Distributed and Parallel Databases. 12(3)*.

Tuecke, S., Czajkowski, K., Foster, I., Rey, J., Steve, F., & Carl, G. (2007). Grid service specification. Retrieved

January 08, 2007, from http://www.globus.org/research/papers/gsspec.pdf

Turek, J., W. Ludwig, J. L. Wolf, L. Fleischer, P. Tiwari, J. Glasgow, U. Schwiegelshohn, P. S. Yu, "Scheduling Parallelizable Tasks to Minimize Average Response Time", *Proceedings of the Sixth Annual ACM Symposium on Parallel Algorithms and Architectures*, pp. 200-209, 1994.

User Centered Design Approach (n.d.). Retrieved 2008 from http://www.usabilityprofessionals.org/usability_resources/about_usability/what_is_ucd.html

Valdes, R. (2004). New application architectures will impact networks. Gartner: Research TU-21-7470. Retrieved February 10, 2007, from *http://www.gartner.com*

vander Aalst, W. M. P., "Pi Calculus versus Petri Nets: Let us Eat 'humble pie' rather than Further Inflate the 'Pi hype'", *BPTrends*, Vol. 3, No. 5, pp. 1-11, 2005.

Vanides, J. (2002). *A personalized, Web-based learning electronic ePortfolio workspace* (White Paper). Retrieved from http://ldt.stanford.edu/~jvanides/eportfolio/STEP-eportfolio-workspace.pdf

Vanides, J., & Morgret, K. (2002). *STEP ePortfolio workspace: Supporting pre-service teachers with electronic portfolio creation, reflection and online collaboration.* Retrieved from http://ldt.stanford.edu/~keri/project/mySTEPstanford.doc

Varvarigou, T., & Trotter, J. (1998). Module replication for fault-tolerant real-time distributed systems. *IEEE Transactions on Reliability, 47*(1), 8-18.

Vazhkudai, S. (2003). Enabling the Co-Allocation of Grid Data Transfers. In *Proceedings of 4th International Workshop on Grid Computing* (pp. 44-51). Los Alamitos: IEEE Computer Society.

Venugopal, S., Buyya, R., & Winton, L. (2004, October). A Grid Service Broker for Scheduling Distributed Data-Oriented Applications on Global Grids. *Proc. Workshop on Middleware in Grid Computing*, 75-80.

Verma, K., Doshi, P., Gomadam, K., Miller, J., & Sheth, A. (September 2006). Optimal Adaptation in Web Pro-

cesses with Coordination Constraints. *In the proceeding of IEEE 2006 International Conference on Web Services.* Chicago, USA.

Vogel, J. & Mauve, M. (2001). Consistency Control for Distributed Interactive Media. *ACM Multimedia.* (pp. 221-230). Ottawa, Canada.

Vu, L. H., Hauswirth, M., & Aberer, K. (October 2005). QoS-based service selection and ranking with trust and reputation management. *In the proceeding of the International Conference on Cooperative Information Systems.* Agia Napa, Cyprus.

Vutunkury, S., & Garcia-Luna-Aceves, J. (1998). MPATH: a loop-free multipath routing algorithm. *Elsevier Journal of Microprocessors and Microsystems, 24*(6), 319-327.

W3C. (2000). Simple object access protocol (SOAP) 1.1. Retrieved February 10, 2007, from *http://www.w3.org/TR/2000/NOTE-SOAP-20000508/#_Toc478383486*

W3C. (2001a). Web services description language (WSDL) 1.1. Retrieved February 10, 2007, from *http://www.w3.org/TR/wsdl*

W3C. (2001b). XML schema. Retrieved February 10, 2007, from *http://www.w3.org/XML/Schema*

W3C. (2002). Web services description requirements. Retrieved February 10, 2007, from *http://www.w3.org/TR/ws-desc-reqs/#definitions*

Wahl, M., Howes, T., & Kille, S. (1997). *LDAPv3 protocol* (RFC 2251). Retrieved from http://www.ietf.org/rfc/rfc2251.txt

Wang, B., Li, T., Luo, X., Fan, Y., & Chunsheng, X. (2005). On service provisioning under a scheduled traffic model in reconfigurable WDM optical networks. Proceeding of *2nd International Conference on Broadband Networks*, 1:13 – 22.

Wang, F. J. (1992). A Parallel GIS-Remote Sensing System for Environmental Modeling. *IGARSS'92*, 15-17.

Wang, F., Ramamritham, K., & Stankovic, J. A. (1995). Determining redundancy levels for fault tolerant real-time systems. *IEEE Trans. Computers, 44*.

Wegaer, P. (1998). Interactive foundations of computing. *Theoretical Computer Science, 192*(2), 315-351.

Wegner, P. (1997). Why interaction is more powerful than algorithms. *Communications of the ACM, 40*(5), 80-91.

Weishaupl, T., Witzany, C., & Schikuta, E. (2006). gSET: Trust management and secure accounting for business in the Grid. *Proceedings of the Sixth IEEE International Symposium on Cluster Computing and the Grid* (pp.349-356), Singapore.

Weissman, J. B. (1999). *Fault Tolerant Computing on the Grid: What are My Options?* HPDC 1999.

Weng, C. L., & Lu, X. D. (2005). Heuristic scheduling for bag-of-tasks applications in combination with QoS in the computational grid. *Future Generation Computer Systems, 21*(2), 271-280.

Weng, C. L., Li, M. L., & Lu, X. D. (2006). An online scheduling algorithm for assigning jobs in the computational grid. *The IEICE Transactions on Information and Systems, E89-D*(2), 597-604.

Weng, C., & Lu, X. (2005). Heuristic scheduling for bag-of-tasks applications in combination with QoS in the computational grid. *Future Generation Computer Systems, 21*, 271–280.

West, K. (2005). Scoping out the planet. *Scientific American*.

Wieczorek, M., Prodan, R. & Fahringer, T. (2005). Scheduling of scientific workflows in the Askalon Grid environment. *SIGMOD Record, 34*(3):56–62.

Witten, I.H., & Eibe, F. (2005). *Data mining: Practical machine learning tools and techniques*. (2nd ed.). San Francisco: Morgan Kaufmann.

Wolski, R., Plank, J. S., & Brevik, J. (2000). *G-Commerce: Market formulations controlling resource allocation on the computational Grid*, University of Tennessee Technical Report.

Wolski, R., Plank, J., Brevik, J., & Bryan T. (2001). Analyzing market-based resource allocation strategies for the computational grid. *The International Journal of High Performance Computing Applications, 15*(3), 258-281.

Wolski, R., Spring, N., & Hayes, J. (1999). The Network Weather Service: A Distributed Resource Performance Forecasting Service for Metacomputing. *Future Generation Computer Systems, 15*, 757-768.

Wolverton, M. (1997). Exploiting enterprise models for the automatic distribution of corporate information. *In Proceedings of the 6th International Conference on Information and Knowledge Management* (pp. 341-347). New York: ACM Press.

Woods, C. J. et. al. (2005, August). Grid Computing and Biomolecular Simulation. *Philosophical Transactions of the Royal Society A, 363*(1833), 2017-2035.

Workflow Management Coalition (1999, February). *Terminology & Glossary*. Document Number WFMC-TC-1011, Issues 3.0.

World Wide Web Consortium. (2004). *OWL Web ontology language semantics and abstract syntax*. W3C Recommendation 10 Feb, 2004.

Wozniak, J. M., Jiang, Y., & Striegel, A. (2007, March). Effects of Low-Quality Computation Time Estimates in Policed Schedulers. *Proc. Annual Simulation Symposium*, 283-292.

Wu, L., Xing, J., Wu, C., & Cui, J. (2005). An adaptive advance reservation mechanism for grid computing, in PDCAT '05 Proceedings of the *Sixth International Conference on Parallel and Distributed Computing Applications and Technologies*. Washington, DC, USA: IEEE Computer Society, pp. 400–403.

Wu, M., & Sun, X. (2004). *Self-adaptive task allocation and scheduling of meta-tasks in non-dedicated heterogeneous computing. International Journal of High Performance Computing and Networking, 2*(1), 186 197.

Wulz, C.-E. (1998). CMS – Concept and Physics Potential. In Nieves, Jose F. (Eds.), *the first Tropical Workshop on Particle Physics and Cosmology* (pp. 467-478). San Juan: American Institute of Physics.

Wytzisk, A., Simonis, I., & Raape, U. (2003). *Integration of HLA Simulation Models Into a Standized Web Service World*. Presented at the European Simulation Interoperability Workshop 2003, Stockholm, Sweden.

Xiao, J., & Boutaba, R. (2005). QoS-Aware Service Composition and Adaptation in Autonomic Communication. *IEEE Journal on Selected Areas in Communications, 23*(12), 2344-2360.

Xie, Y., Teo, Y. M., Cai, W., & Turner, S. J. (2005). Service Provisioning for HLA based Distributed Simulation on the Grid. In D. M. Nicol and S. J. Turner (Ed.), *The Proceedings of the Nineteenth ACM/IEEE/SCS Workshop on Principles of Advanced and Distributed Simulation (PADS 2005)* (pp. 282-291). USA: The Printing House.

Xin Y., Shayman, M., La, R., & Marcus, S. (2006). Reconfiguration of survivable MPLS/WDM networks, Proceedings of IEEE *GLOBECOM 2006*.

Xu, D., Nahrstedt, K., & Wichadakul, D. (2001). *QoS-aware discovery of wide-area distributed services*. Presented at CCGrid 2001.

Xu, K., Y. Wang and C. Wu, "Ensuring Secure and Robust Grid Applications - From a Formal Method Point of View", *Advances in Grid and Pervasive Computing*, LNCS Vol. 3947, Springer Verlag, pp. 537-546, 2006.

Xu, L., & Peng, X. (2006, May). *SSB: A Grid-based Infrastructure for HLA Systems*. Paper presented at the Sixth IEEE International Symposium on Cluster Computing and the Grid Workshops, Singapore.

Yan, J., Kowalczyk, R., Lin, J., Chhetri, M. B., Goh, S. K., & Zhang, J. Y. (2007). Autonomous service level agreement negotiation for service composition provision. *Future Generation Computer Systems-the International Journal of Grid Computing Theory Methods and Applications, 23*(6), 748-759.

Yan, J., Yang, Y., & Raikundalia, G. K. (2006). SwinDeW-a p2p-based decentralized workflow management system *IEEE Transactions on Systems, Man, and Cybernetics—Part A: Systems and Humans, 36*(5), 922-935.

Yan, T., He, T., & Stankovic, J. A. (2003). Differentiated surveillance for sensor networks. *Proc. of the 1st Intl. Conf. on Embedded Networked Sensor Systems,* (pp. 51–62).

Yang, L., Schopf, J. Foster, I. (2003). Conservative scheduling: using predicted variance to improve scheduling decisions in dynamic environments. *Proceedings of ACM/IEEE Supercomputing 2003* (pp.31-46), Phoenix, AR, U.S.A.

Yang, X., Dove, M., Hayes, M., Calleja, M., He, L., & Murray-Rust, P. (2006). Survey of tools and technologies for Grid-enabled portals. *UK e-Science All Hands on conference*, UK.

Yang, Y., Liu, K., Chen, J., Lignier, J., & Jin, H. (December 2007). Peer-to-Peer Based Grid Workflow Runtime Environment of SwinDeW-G. *In the proceeding of the 3rd International Conference on e-science and Grid Computing*. Bangalore,India: IEEE Computer Society

Yarmolenko, V., & Sakellariou, R. (2006, April). An Evaluation of Heuristics for SLA Based Parallel Job Scheduling. *Proc. High Performance Grid Computing Workshop.*

Ye, F., Zhong, G., Lu, S., & Zhang, L. (2002). PEAS: a robust energy conserving protocol for long-lived sensor networks. *Proc. the 10th IEEE Intl. Conf. on Network Protocols,* (pp. 200–201).

Ygge, F. (1998). *Market-oriented programming and its application to power load management.* Ph D dissertation, Department of Computer Science, Lund University, Sweden.

Yolles, M. (2000). Organisations, complexity, and viable knowledge management. *Kybernetes: The International Journal of Systems & Cybernetics, 29*(9), 1202-1222.

Yu, H., & Vahdat, A. (2000). Design and Evaluation of a Continuous Consistency Model for Replicated Services, *4th conference on Symposium on Operating System Design & Implementation*. San Diego, California.

Yu, H., Marinescu, D., et al. (2006). Plan switching: an approach to plan execution in changing environments.

Proceedings of the 15th HCW in conjunction with IPDPS 2006, Rhodes Island, Greece.

Yu, J., & Buyya, R. (2005). A taxonomy of scientific workflow systems for grid computing. *SIGMOD Record, 34*(3), 44–49.

Yu, J., & Buyya, R. (2005). *A taxonomy of workflow management system for Grid computing*. Tech. rep., Grid and distributed Systems Laboratory, University of Melbourne.

Yu, J., and R. Buyya, "A Novel Architecture for Realizing Grid Workflow using Tuple Spaces", in *Proc. 5th IEEE/ACM Int. Workshop on Grid Computing*, Pittsburgh, USA, pp. 119-128, 2004.

Yu, J., and R. Buyya, "A Taxonomy of Workflow Management Systems for Grid Computing", *J. Grid Computing*, Vol. 3, No. 3-4, pp. 171-200, 2005.

Yu, J., Buyya, R., & Khong Tham, C. (2005). *QoS-based Scheduling of Workflow Applications on Service Grids*. Technical Report, GRIDS-TR-2005-8, Grid Computing and Distributed Systems Laboratory, University of Melbourne, Australia, 2005.

Yu, T., Zhang, Y., & Lin, K. J. (2007). Efficient Algorithms for Web Services Selection with End-to-End QoS Constraints. *ACM Transactions on the Web, 1*(1), 6, Publication date: May 2007., 1(1), 6:1-6:26.

Yu, Z. & Shi, W. (2007). An adaptive rescheduling strategy for Grid workflow applications. *Proceedings of IEEE IPDPS 2007*, Long Beach, CA, U.S.A.

Zaumen, W. T., & Garcia-Luna-Aceves, J. (1998). Loop-free multipath routing using generalized diffusing computations. In *Proceedings the Seventeenth Annual Joint Conference of the IEEE Computer and Communications Societies* (pp. 219-327). Los Alamitos: IEEE Computer Society.

Zeng, L., Benatallah, B., et al. (2004). Chang: QoS-aware middleware for web services composition. *IEEE Transactions on Software Engineering, 30*(5), 311-327.

Zeng, L., Benatallah, B., Ngu, A. H. H., Dumas, M., Kalagnanam, J., & Chang, H. (2004). QoS-Aware Middle-

ware for Web Services Composition. *IEEE Transaction on Software Engineering, 30*(5), 311-327.

Zhang, H. H., & Hou, J. C. (2005) Maintaining sensing coverage and connectivity in large sensor networks. *Wireless Ad Hoc and Sensor Networks, 1*(1-2), 89–123.

Zhang, H., K. Keahey, and W. Allcock, "Providing Data Transfer with QoS as Agreement-based Service", in *Proc. IEEE Int. Conf. on Services Computing*, pp. 344-353, 2004.

Zhang, L., & Ardagna, D. (November 2004). SLA-Based Profit Optimization in Autonomic Computing Systems. *In the proceeding of the 2nd International Conference on Service Oriented Computing*. New York, USA.

Zhang, L.-J. (2002). Next generation Web services discovery. *Web Services Journal*.

Zhang, L.-J., Chang, H., & Chao, T. (2002, June). Web services relationships binding for dynamic e-business integration. In *Proceedings of the International Conference on Internet Computing (IC '02)* (pp. 561-567).

Zhang, L.-J., Chao, T., Chang, H., & Chung, J.-Y. (2003). XML-based advanced UDDI search mechanism for B2B integration. *Electronic Commerce Research Journal, 3*, 25-42.

Zhang, S., N. Gu, and S. Li, "Grid Workflow based on Dynamic Modeling and Scheduling", in *Proc. IEEE Information Technology: Coding and Computing*, Vol. 2, pp. 35-39, 2004.

Zhang, Y., & Tanniru, M. (2005, January 3-6). An agent-based approach to study virtual learning communities. In *Proceedings of the 38th Annual Hawaii International Conference on System Sciences (HICSS'05) — Track 1*, Big Island, Hawaii.

Zhang, Y., Theodoropoulos, G. K., Minson, R., Turner, S. J., Cai, W., Yong, X., & Logan, B. (2005, July). *Grid-aware Large Scale Distributed Simulation of Agent-based Systems*. Presented at the European Simulator Interoperability Workshop 2005, Toulouse, France.

Zhao, J., Kumar, A., & Stohr, E. A. (2001). Workflow-Centric information distribution through email. *Journal of Management Information Systems, 17*(3), 45–72.

Zhao, J., Wroe, C., Goble, C.A., Stevens, R., Quan, D., & Greenwood, R.M. (2004). Using semantic Web technologies for representing e-science provenance. *ISWC*.

Zhong, N., Liu, J., & Yao, Y.(2003). *Web intelligence.* Springer.

Zhou, C., Chia, L. T., Silverajan, B., & Lee, B. S. (2003). UX: An architecture providing QoS-aware and federated support for UDDI. In *Proceedings of the International Conference on Web Services (ICWS '03)*.

Zhovtobryukh, D. (2007). A Petri Net-based Approach for Automated Goal-Driven Web Service Composition. *Simulation, 83*(1), 33-63.

Zhu, S. H., Du, Z. H., Chen, Y. N., Chai, X. D., & Li, B. H. (2007). QoS Enhancement for PDES Grid Based on Time Services Prediction. *GCC 2007*, 423-429.

Zhu, S., Du, Z., & Chai, X. (2006, May). *GDSA: A Grid-based Distributed Simulation Architecture*. Paper presented at the Sixth IEEE International Symposium on Cluster Computing and the Grid Workshops, Singapore.

Zhu, X., & Davidson, I. (2007). *Knowledge discovery and data mining: Challenges and realities.* Idea Group Inc.

Zhu, Y., J. Han, Y. Liu, L. M. Ni, C. Hu, J. Huai, "TruGrid: A Self-sustaining Trustworthy Grid", *Proceedings of the First International Workshop on Mobility in Peer-to-Peer Systems (MPPS) (ICDCSW '05)*, pp. 815-821, June 2005.

Zhuge, H. (2002). A Knowledge flow model for peer-to-peer team knowledge sharing and management. *Expert Systems with Applications, 23*(1), 23-30.

Zhuge, H. (2004). *The knowledge Grid.* World Scientific.

Zhuge, H. (2005). Semantic Grid: Scientific Issues, Infrastructure, and Methodology. *Communications of the ACM, 48*(4), 117-119.

Zhuge, H. (2007). Autonomous semantic link network model for the Knowledge Grid. *Concurrency and Computation: Practice and Experience, 7*(19), 1065-1085.

Zhuge, H., Guo, W., Li, X., & Ding, L. (2005). Knowledge Energy in Knowledge Flow Networks. *Proceedings of the First International Conference on Semantics, Knowledge and Grid* (pp. 3). Washington, DC: IEEE Computer Society.

Zong, W., Wang, Y., Cai, W. & Turner, S. J. (2004). Grid Services and Service Discovery for HLA-based Distributed Simulations. In S. J. Turner, D. J. Roberts, and L. F. Wilson (Ed.), *The Proceedings of the 8th IEEE International Symposium on Distributed Simulation and Real Time Applications (DSRT 2004)* (pp. 116-124). USA: The Printing House.

About the Contributors

Lizhe Wang currently is the assistant director of the Service Oriented Cyberinfrastructure Lab at Rochester Institute of Technology. Dr. Wang received his Bachelor and Master degree from Tsinghua University, China and Doctor degree from University Karlsruhe (German elite University), Germany, in 1998, 2001, and 2007 respectively. Dr. Wang's research interests include parallel & distributed computing, cluster & Grid computing, and distributed information retrieval. Dr. Wang has published 3 books and more than 30 research papers at international conference and scientific journals.

Jinjun Chen received his PhD degree in computer science and software engineering from Swinburne University of Technology, Melbourne, Australia, in 2007. He is currently a lecturer in Centre for Complex Software Systems and Services in the Faculty of Information and Communication Technologies at Swinburne University of Technology, Melbourne, Australia. His research interests include scientific workflow management, service oriented computing (engineering, planning, negotiation, agreement, verification and validation), workflow management and application in cloud computing environments, web services environments and generic service oriented computing environments, reliable workflow software systems, cloud computing.

Wei Jie has been actively involved in the area of parallel and distributed computing for many years, and published about fourty papers in international journals and conferences. His current research interests include grid computing and applications, security in distributed computing, parallel and distributed algorithms and languages, etc. Dr Wei Jie joined the University of Manchester(UK) on February 2007. Prior to this, Dr Wei Jie was a senior research engineer at Singapore's National Institute of High Performance Computing. He received his BEng and MEng in computer science from Beijing University of Aeronautics and Astronautics (China) in 1993 and 1996, respectively. In 2002 he was awarded PhD in computer engineering from Nanyang Technological University (Singapore).

* * *

Selim G. Akl received his PhD degree from McGill University in Montreal in 1978. He is currently a professor and the director of Computing at Queen's University, Kingston, Ontario, Canada. His research interests are in parallel computation. He is author of *Parallel Sorting Algorithms* (Academic Press, 1985), *The Design and Analysis of Parallel Algorithms* (Prentice Hall, 1989), and *Parallel Computation: Models and Methods* (Prentice Hall, 1997), and a co-author of *Parallel Computational Geometry* (Prentice Hall, 1992). Dr. Akl is editor in chief of *Parallel Processing Letters* and presently serves on the editorial boards of *Computational Geometry*, the *International Journal of Parallel, Emergent, and Distributed Systems*, and the *International Journal of High Performance Computing and Networking*.

H. Arafat Ali received the BSc degree in electrical engineering (electronics), M.Sc. and PhD degrees in computer engineering and automatic control from the Faculty of Engineering, Mansoura University, in 1987,1991 and 1997, respectively. He was assistant professor at the University of Mansoura, faculty of computer science in 1997 up to 1999. From Jan 2000 up to September 2001, he has been joined as post doctor to the dept of Computer Science, University of Connecticut, Storrs. From 2002 up to 2004 he was a vice dean for student affair the faculty of computer science and information, University of Mansoura. Since 2004 up now he is associated professor at the Computers Eng. Dept. Faculty of Engineering, University of Mansoura. His interests are in the area of network security, mobile agent, pattern recognition, database, and performance analysis.

Peter Brezany is a professor at the Institute of Scientific Computing, University of Vienna, Austria. He received his PhD in computer science, in 1980, from the Slovak Technical University Bratislava, Slovakia. Since 1990, he has worked at the University of Vienna on automatic parallelization of scientific and engineering applications for distributed-memory systems, parallel input/output support for high-performance computing, and large-scale parallel and distributed data mining. His current research focus is knowledge discovery and data management on computational grids.

Jian Cao is a professor with Department of Computer Science and Technology at Shanghai Jiao Tong University (SJTU), China, and the depute director of the Grid Center of the University. He received his BSc and PhD in automatic control theory and control engineering from Nanjing University of Science and Technology (P.R. China) in 1997 and 2000 respectively. He was a post-doctoral research fellow at Shanghai Jiao Tong University during Jan 2000 to Dec 2001 and then joined SJTU. Dr. Cao was a visiting researcher at Engineering Information Group, Stanford University (Jan-July 2004, Aug-Sep 2008). His research interests include collaborative information system, grid & service computing and software engineering. His main areas of expertise are the developments of software and models to support coordination and cooperation among humans, systems and components. He has authored or co-authored over 80 journal and conference papers in the above areas. His recent research has focused on the development of grid workflow system, grid portal environment and business process simulation environment.

Junwei Cao is a research professor of Research Institute of Information Technology, Tsinghua University and Tsinghua National Laboratory for Information Science and Technology. His research interests are advanced computing technologies and applications.

Dan Chen is a professor with the Institute of Electrical Engineering, Yanshan University (China). He was a postdoctoral research fellow with the School of Computer Science at University of Birmingham (UoB, UK) and the School of Computer Engineering at Nanayang Technological University (NTU, Singapore). He received a BSc in applied physics from Wuhan University (China) and M.Eng. in computer science from Huazhong University of Science and Technology (China). After that, he received MEng and PhD from NTU in year 2002 and 2006 respectively. His research interests include: modeling and simulation of complex systems, distributed computing, multi-agent systems and grid computing. Recently, he has been working in crowd modeling & simulation and neuroinformatics.

Liang-Tien Chia gained a first degree in electronic engineering and a PhD from Loughborough University of Technology (1990 and 1994, respectively). He is currently an associate professor in the division of computer communications, school of computer engineering at Nanyang Technological University. Dr. Chia also holds the position of director of the Centre for Multimedia and Network Technology in NTU. Current research interests are in multimedia storage and retrieval, multimedia processing, error concealment techniques, video communication, bandwidth management, and wireless Internet.

Gen-Tao Chiang is a senior system administrator working with Wellcome Trust Sanger Institute and University of Cambridge. His background is in environmental sciences (training and appointments in Taiwan and the USA). He is now a PhD student of the Department of Earth Sciences, University of Cambridge. His research focuses on using grid computing for environmental science applications. Before he came to Cambridge, he spent two years working for Academia Sinica Grid Computing Centre at Taiwan as a regional operation centre manager. His duty was supporting LCG and EGEE grid systems deployment and operation for Asia Pacific regions.

Yeh-Ching Chung received a BS degree in Information Engineering from Chung Yuan Christian University in 1983, and the MS and PhD degrees in Computer and Information Science from Syracuse University in 1988 and 1992, respectively. He joined the Department of Information Engineering at Feng Chia University as an associate professor in 1992 and became a full professor in 1999. From 1998 to 2001, he was the chairman of the department. In 2002, he joined the Department of Computer Science at National Tsing Hua University as a full professor. His research interests include parallel and distributed processing, cluster systems, grid computing, multi-core tool chain design, and multi-core embedded systems. He is a member of the IEEE computer society and ACM.

Fangpeng Dong received his BSc from the Department of Computer Science and Technology, Peking University, Beijing, China in 2000 and M.E. from the Institute of Computing Technology, Chinese Academy of Sciences, Beijing, China in 2003. He is now a PhD student in the School of Computing, Queen's University at Kingston, Ontario, Canada. His major research interests include Grid computing and other parallel and distributed systems. He is also an IEEE student member.

Cheng Fu received his BEng degree from Xian Jiaotong University, China in 2001, and PhD title from Nanyang Technological University, Singapore in 2005. Dr. Fu currently is with Intelligent Systems Centre (Intellisys), Nanyang Technological University, Singapore, as research fellow. Dr. Fu has both industrial and academic experience in information engineering and communication systems. His current research interests include distributed systems, wireless sensor networks and software engineering. Dr. Fu has published over 40 referred conference papers, journal articles as well as book chapters. Dr. Fu is the member of IEEE since 2002.

Ugo Fiore (Italian physics degree, 1989) has been with Italian National Council for Research at the beginning of his career. He has been working for more than 10 years in the industry, developing software support systems for telco operators. He is currently with the network management/operation centre of the Federico II University, in Napoli, Italy. His research interests focus on optimization techniques and algorithms for improving the performance of high-speed core networks. He is also actively investigating security-related algorithms and protocols.

Dennis Gannon is a professor of computer science and science director of Pervasive Technology Labs at Indiana University. His research interests include programming systems and tools, distributed computing, computer networks, parallel programming, computational science, problem solving environments and performance analysis of Grid and MPP systems. IEEE member.

Fang Huang received the doctor degree from the Institute of Remote Sensing Applications, jointly sponsored by Center for Earth Observation and Digital Earth, Chinese Academy of Science. He received the BS degree of surveying and mapping engineering in Taiyuan University of Technology, Taiyuan, China, the MS in photogrammetry and remote sensing from Beijing Jiaotong University, Beijing, China, in 2002 and 2005, respectively. His current research interests focus on high performance geo-computation fields, mainly including spatial information grid and parallel GIS on cluster.

Kuo-Chan Huang received his BS and PhD degrees in computer science and information engineering from National Chiao-Tung University, Taiwan, in 1993 and 1998, respectively. He is currently an assistant professor in Computer and Information Science Department at National Taichung University, Taiwan. He is a member of ACM and IEEE Computer Society. His research areas include parallel processing, cluster and grid computing, workflow computing.

Yongsheng Hao received a MS degree of engineering from the Qingdao University in 2008. Now, he is a research assistant of Network Center, Nanjing University of Information Science & Technology. His current research interests include distributed &parallel computing and mobile computing, grid computing and Web service.

Ivan Janciak is a PhD candidate at the Vienna University of Technology, Austria and research assistant at the Institute of Scientific Computing, University of Vienna, Austria. He received his MS degree in business informatics, in 2000, from the University of Economics in Bratislava, Slovakia. His research interests include distributed and parallel data and text mining, semantic Web, grid computing, and workflow management.

Hong Jiang received the BSc degree in computer engineering in 1982 from Huazhong University of Science and Technology, Wuhan, China; the MASc degree in computer engineering in 1987 from the University of Toronto, Toronto, Canada; and the PhD degree in computer science in 1991 from the Texas A&M University, College Station, Texas, USA. Since August 1991 he has been at the University of Nebraska-Lincoln, Lincoln, Nebraska, USA, where he is professor in the Department of Computer Science and Engineering. His present research interests are computer architecture, computer storage systems and parallel I/O, parallel/distributed computing, cluster and Grid computing, performance evaluation, real-time systems, middleware, and distributed systems for distance education. He has over 140 publications in major journals and international conferences in these areas and his research has been supported by NSF, DOD and the State of Nebraska. Dr. Jiang is a Member of ACM, the IEEE Computer Society, and the ACM SIGARCH.

Hai Jin is a professor of computer science and engineering at the Huazhong University of Science and Technology (HUST) in China. He is now the dean of the School of Computer Science and Technology at HUST. Jin received his PhD in computer engineering from HUST in 1994. In 1996, he was awarded a German Academic Exchange Service fellowship to visit the Technical University of Chemnitz in Germany. Jin worked at The University of Hong Kong between 1998 and 2000, and as a visiting scholar at the University of Southern California between 1999 and 2000. He was awarded Excellent Youth Award from the National Science Foundation of China in 2001. Dr. Jin is the chief scientist of ChinaGrid, the largest grid computing project in China.

Dimosthenis Kyriazis received the diploma from the Dept. of Electrical and Computer Engineering of the National Technical University of Athens, Athens, Greece in 2001, the MS degree in techno-economic systems (MBA) co-organized by the Electrical and Computer Engineering Dept - NTUA, Economic Sciences Dept - National Kapodistrian University of Athens, Industrial Management Dept - University of Piraeus and his PhD from the Electrical and Computer Engineering Department of the National Technical University of Athens in 2007. He is currently a Researcher in the Telecommunication Laboratory of the Institute of Communication and Computer Systems (ICCS). Before joining the ICCS he has worked in the private sector as Telecom Software Engineer. He has participated in numerous EU / National funded projects (such as IRMOS, NextGRID, Akogrimo, BEinGRID, HPC-Europa, GRIA, Memphis, CHALLENGERS, FIDIS, etc). His research interests include Grid computing, scheduling, Quality of Service provision and workflow management in heterogeneous systems and service oriented architectures.

Bu-Sung Lee received his BS (Hons) and PhD in the electrical and electronics department, Loughborough University of Technology (UK) (1982 and 1987, respectively). Dr. Lee is currently an associate professor at the Nanyang Technological University (Singapore). He is the technology area director of the Asia Pacific Advance Network (APAN) and an associate with Singapore Research & Education Networks (SingAREN). He has been an active member of several national standards organizations such as the National Infrastructure Initiative (Singapore One) Network Working Group, the Singapore ATM Testbed, and the Bio-Medical Grid (BMG) Task Force. His research interests are in network management, broadband networks, distributed networks, and network optimization.

Minglu Li is a professor and vice chair with the Department of Computer Science and Engineering at Shanghai Jiao Tong University, China, and the director of the Grid Center of the University. Prof. Li is subeditor of International Journal of Grid and Utility Computing and on edit board of International Journal of Web Services Research. He is in executive committee of Technical Community for Services Computing of IEEE. His major research interests include grid computing, peer-to-peer computing, service computing, wireless sensor network, and virtualization technology.

Antonios Litke received the diploma from the Dept. of Computer Engineering and Informatics of the University of Patras, Greece in 1999, and the PhD from Electrical and Computer Engineering Department of National Technical University of Athens in 2006. Currently, he is with the Telecommunication Laboratory of Electrical and Computer Engineering Department of National Technical University of Athens as researcher, participating in numerous EC and national funded projects. His research interests include Grid computing, resource management in heterogeneous systems, Web services and information engineering.

Guanfeng Liu received a MS degree of engineering from the Qingdao University in 2008 and a BS degree in engineering from the Qingdao University of Science and Technology in 2005. His research interests include Grid computing, database and embedded system, he is working on combining agent technology to campus data grid for sharing information with different universities and colleges.

Lianchen Liu is an associate professor of National CIMS Research and Engineering Center, Tsinghua University and Tsinghua National Laboratory for Information Science and Technology. His research interests include system integration, grid computing, etc.

Yijun Lu received his PhD in computer science from University of Nebraska-Lincoln in 2007. Before that, he got his MS and BS, both in computer science, from Huazhong University of Science and Technology, China, in 2002, and Chang'an University, China, in 1999, respectively. Research-wise, he is interested in distributed systems in general, with a focus on data management and data delivery in Internet-scale distributed systems. He has published over ten technical papers in areas such as scalable and reliable data consistency management, fair and efficient multimedia delivery—both in the context of Internet-scale distributed systems—and web cluster systems. An avid Linux kernel developer, he joined an Atlanta-based networking startup soon after graduation to do some cool networking stuff in Linux kernel. He is a member of ACM, a member of IEEE, and a member of IEEE Computer Society.

Ying Lu received the BS degree in computer science in 1996 from Southwest Jiaotong University, Chengdu, China; the MCS and PhD degrees in computer science in 2001 and 2005 respectively from the University of Virginia. Since August 2005, she has been at the University of Nebraska-Lincoln, Lincoln, Nebraska, USA, where she is an assistant professor in the Department of Computer Science and Engineering. Her present research interests include real-time systems, autonomic computing, cluster and Grid computing, and Web systems. She has done significant work on feedback control of computing systems. Dr. Lu has over 20 publications in major journals and international conferences and her research is currently supported by NSF. Dr. Lu is a member of the IEEE computer society.

Xiangfeng Luo, leader of Digital Content Computing and Semantic Grid Group. He had been working as a postdoctoral researcher in the Institute of Computing Technology of the Chinese Academy of Sciences from 2003 to 2005. He has been the director of several important projects, including National Natural Science Foundation of China, Innovation of Institute of Computing Technology of the Chinese Academy of Sciences, etc. His current research interests are focusing on semantic Grid, knowledge grid, image processing, data mining, intelligent information processing.

Andreas Menychtas received the diploma from the School of Electrical and Computer Engineering, National Technical University of Athens, Greece in 2004. Currently, he is pursuing his PhD in the Telecommunication Laboratory of Electrical and Computer Engineering School of National Technical University of Athens and works as research associate in the Institute of Communication and Computer Systems. He has been involved in several EU and National funded projects such as GRIA, NextGRID, EGEE, HellasGRID and GRID-APP. His research interests include distributed systems and architectures, Web services, Web portals, security and information engineering.

Mirghani Mohamed is the assistant director for the Data Center at The George Washington University, D.C., he also serves as the director of the Knowledge Management (KM) Technology Center, KM Institute at the same university. He holds MSc and PhD in agronomy/statistics, MSc in computer science and DSc in systems engineering and engineering management with emphasis on knowledge management. In addition, he is an Oracle certified professional. Drs. Mohamed has wealth of operational experience in ICT roadmapping, technology operations, change management, content management, and technology strategic and capacity planning. He supervised many community building, communication and collaboration technologies in the areas of technology operations, financial systems and KM. He worked as a technical lead for deployments of complex ERP and many other enterprise-wide systems. He has worked in many socio-technical projects with the intention to narrow the digital divide and to deliver and share the knowledge with the poor. During his work with INSTORMIL CRSP Drs. Mohamed involved in various regional and national sustainable development and humanitarian efforts in Sudan.

Francesco Palmieri holds two computer science degrees from Salerno University, Italy. Since 1989, he has worked for several international companies on a variety of networking-related projects, concerned with nation-wide communication systems, network management, transport protocols, and IP networking. Since 1997 he leads the network management/operation centre of the Federico II University, in Napoli, Italy. He has been closely involved with the development of the Internet in Italy in the last years, particularly within the academic and research sector, as a member of the Technical Scientific Committee and of the Computer Emergency Response Team of the Italian Academic and Research Network GARR. He is an active researcher in the fields of high performance/evolutionary networking and network security. He has published several papers in leading technical journals and conferences and given invited talks and keynote speeches.

Beth Plale is an associate professor of computer science and director of the Data Search Institute at Indiana University. Her research interest is in the broad area of large-scale data management, specifically stream mining and event processing, distributed metadata and integration, provenance, Grid and service-oriented architectures, and petascale databases. IEEE member.

Kaijun Ren received the BS degree in applied mathematics in 1998 and the MS degree in computer science in 2003 from the National University of Defense Technology. He is currently a joint PHD candidate and visiting Australia at the support of Chinese State Scholarship Fund. He is also a lecturer in the college of Computer Science at the National University of Defense Technology in China. His research and teaching interests include service-oriented architecture(SOA), workflow and applications in service/Grid(cloud) computing environments, service oriented computing (service discovery, service composition, QoS-based composition optimized execution) and Semantic Web.

Vincent Ribière, assistant professor of management of information systems at the New York Institute of Technology (NYIT), received his Doctorate of Science in knowledge management from the George Washington University, and a PhD in management sciences from the Paul Cézanne University, Aix en Provence, France. Vincent teaches, conducts research and consults in the area of knowledge management and information systems. Over the past years, he presented various research papers at different international conferences on knowledge management, organizational culture, information systems and quality as well as publishing in various refereed journals and books. He is a contributing editor and reviewer to journals focused on knowledge management.

Michael Stankosky is professor of systems engineering , lead professor of knowledge management, and co-founder and co-director of the Institute of Knowledge and Innovation at the George Washington University. In those capacities, he oversees the research and education of all academic activites relating to knowledge management and innovation. He collaborates with 12 adjunct faculty, 25 doctoral researchers, as well as with numerous scholars and practitioners from around the world. His latest book, *Creating the Discipline of Knowledge Management*, summarizes some of these efforts.

Aaron Striegel is currently an assistant professor in the Department of Computer Science & Engineering at the University of Notre Dame. He received his PhD in December 2002 in computer engineering at Iowa State University under the direction of Dr. G. Manimaran. His research interests include networking (bandwidth conservation, QoS), computer security, grid computing, and real-time systems. During his tenure as a student at Iowa State, he worked for various companies in research and development that included Sun Microsystems, Architecture Technology Corporation, and Emerson Process. He has received research and equipment funding from NSF, DARPA, Sun Microsystems, Hewlett Packard, Architecture Technology Corporation, and Intel. Dr. Striegel was the recipient of an NSF CAREER award in 2004.

Junqiang Song received the BS degree in applied mechanics in 1983 and the MS degree in applied mechanics in 1986 from the National University of Defense Technology. He is currently a professor with the College of Computer Science, National University of Defense Technology, China. His research interests include Grid, parallel algorithm and high performance computing. He is a vice president of the Specialty Association of Mathematical & Scientific Software, China.

Po-Chi Shih received the BS and MS degrees in computer science and information engineering from Tunghai University in 2003 and 2005, respectively. He is now studying PhD degree at computer science in National Tsing Hua University.

Yogesh L. Simmhan is a doctoral candidate at Indiana University, working on distributed data and metadata management for large scale, data driven applications based on Grid and web-service paradigms. He is particularly interested in issues related to efficient provenance tracking, discovery, quality evaluation, and long term preservation of data generated from scientific workflows, with the overarching goal of building scalable information systems to effectively manage data end-to-end. IEEE member.

A Min Tjoa is a full professor and the head of the Institute of Software Technology and Interactive Systems at the Vienna University of Technology. He received his PhD in engineering from the University Linz in Austria. Since 1999, he has been president of the Austrian Computer Society. His research interests include semantic Web, e-commerce, advanced and scalable data management, and data analysis solutions for management information systems and decision support.

Theodora A. Varvarigou received the BTech degree from the National Technical University of Athens, Athens, Greece in 1988, the MS degrees in electrical engineering (1989) and in computer science (1991) from Stanford University, Stanford, California in 1989 and the PhD degree from Stanford University as well in 1991. She worked at AT&T Bell Labs, Holmdel, New Jersey between 1991 and 1995. Between 1995 and 1997 she worked as an assistant professor at the Technical University of Crete, Chania, Greece. Since 1997 she was elected as an assistant professor while since 2007 she is a professor at the National Technical University of Athens, and director of the postgraduate course "Engineering Economics Systems". Prof. Varvarigou has great experience in the area of semantic web technologies, scheduling over distributed platforms, embedded systems and Grid computing. In this area, she has published more than 150 papers in leading journals and conferences. She has participated and coordinated several EU funded projects such as IRMOS, SCOVIS, POLYMNIA, Akogrimo, NextGRID, BEinGRID, Memphis, MKBEEM, MARIDES, CHALLENGERS, FIDIS, and others.

Bang Wang obtained his Bachelor of engineering and Master of engineering from the Department of Electronics and Information Engineering in Huazhong University of Science and Technology (HUST) Wuhan, China in 1996 and 2000, respectively and his PhD degree in electrical and computer engineering (ECE) Department of National University of Singapore (NUS) Singapore in 2004. He is now working as a research fellow in Intelligent Systems Centre, Nanyang Technological University on wireless sensor networks. His research interests include coverage issues, distributed signal processing, resource allocation and optimization algorithms in wireless networks.

Chuliang Weng received his BS and MS degrees from Southwest Jiao Tong University of China in 1998 and 2001 respectively, and received his PhD degree from Shanghai Jiao Tong University of China in 2004. Now he works in Department of Computer Science and Engineering at Shanghai Jiao Tong University. His research interests include cluster and grid computing, virtualization technology, and high performance computing.

Justin M. Wozniak is currently a postdoctoral appointee in the Mathematics and Computer Science Division of Argonne National Laboratory. His PhD work at the University of Notre Dame was performed as an Arthur J. Schmitt Presidential Fellow under the supervision of Dr. Aaron Striegel. His research interests include the modeling and construction of autonomic schedulers for jobs and data movement on desktop grid infrastructures as well as parallel file system architecture.

Cheng Wu is a professor of National CIMS Research and Engineering Center, Tsinghua University and Tsinghua National Laboratory for Information Science and Technology. He is a member of Chinese Academy of Engineering.

Nong Xiao received the BS degree and PhD degree in computer science respectively in 1990 and in 1996 from the National University of Defense Technology in China. He is currently a professor with the college of Computer Science, National University of Defense Technology, China. His research and teaching interests include Grid computing, ubiquitous computing, P2P computing, parallel computer architecture, distributed computing.

Muzhou Xiong is a PhD candidate in Huazhong University of Science and Technology, P.R. China. Also he currently is a research associate in Nanyang Technological University, Singapore. He obtained his BS degree in computer science from Huazhong University of Science and Technology in 2002. His research interests include grid computing, network storage, automatic storage management, and parallel and distributed simulation. His recent research has focused on modeling of human behavior model for high dense crowds.

Ke Xu is a PhD candidate of National CIMS Research and Engineering Center, Tsinghua University. His research is focused on formal verification of grid workflows.

Xiaoyu Yang is a post-doctorial research associate in Earth Sciences Department of University of Cambridge, and a senior member of Wolfson College, University of Cambridge. He is currently working on a UK government funded eScience *MaterialsGrid* project. The work involves research and development of a service-oriented framework for running quantum mechanical simulation (e.g. CASTEP) of material properties in a Grid environment. Before joining University of Cambridge, Dr. Yang was a research fellow in "Mechatronics Research Centre" at De Montfort University, UK. He undertook research & development work in EU-funded *ELIMA* project and 2 UK government DTI funded projects. He obtained his MSc degree in September 2001 and PhD degree in 2006 in "Faculty of Computing Science and Engineering" at De Montfort University. Dr. Yang has research interests in the area of Grid computing, e-science, SOA, workflow, systems engineering, and product lifecycle information management.

Jie Yu graduated from University of Science and Technology of China and joined Digital Content Computing and Semantic Grid Group in 2007. Over the past five years, she has participated in several important projects, including National Natural Science Foundation of China, Natural Science Foundation of Anhui Province of China and Research Fund for the Doctoral Program of Higher Education of China. Her current research interests are focusing on web knowledge flow, interactive computing, multiple attributes decision making problems.

Fan Zhang is a PhD candidate of National CIMS Research and Engineering Center, Tsinghua University. His research is focused on grid workflow management.

Weimin Zhang received the MS degree in computation mathematics in 1989 and the PhD in computer science in 2006 from the National University of Defense Technology. His research and teaching interests include parallel algorithm, numerical weather forecast, service-oriented architecture (SOA), workflow and applications in service/Grid (cloud) computing environments.

Chen Zhou received his BS degree in computer science and technology from Shanghai Jiao Tong University (China) (2002). After that he has been working towards a PhD degree in the school of computer engineering, Nanyang Technological University (Singapore). His current research interests include: Web services discovery, Semantic Web, service QoS, and middleware distributed systems.

Index

X